xi - x.

79   252-54

134   257-58

173   271-72

183-84   289

          319

190-91   259

191-96   371

202-04   442-95 genus

          96

469-70

481

483-84

528-34

PSYCHOANALYSIS AND PSYCHOSIS

PSYCHOANALYSIS AND PSYCHOSIS

Edited by

Ann-Louise S. Silver, M.D.

DREXEL UNIVERSITY
HEALTH SCIENCES LIBRARIES
HAHNEMANN LIBRARY

INTERNATIONAL UNIVERSITIES PRESS, INC.
Madison   Connecticut

WM
460
P9738
1985

Copyright © 1989, Ann-Louise S. Silver

All rights reserved. No part of this book may be reproduced by any means, nor translated into a machine language, without the written permission of the publisher.

Library of Congress Cataloging-in-Publication Data

Psychoanalysis and psychosis / edited by Ann-Louise S. Silver.
p.   cm.
    Outgrowth of a symposium held at Chestnut Lodge, Rockville, Md. on
Oct. 4, 1985 to commemorate the 50th anniversary of the arrival of
Frieda Fromm-Reichmann.
    Includes bibliographies and index.
    ISBN 0-8236-5183-5
  1. Psychoses—Treatment—Congresses. 2. Psychoanalysis—
Congresses. I. Silver, Ann-Louise S. II. Fromm-Reichmann,
Frieda.
    [DNLM: 1. Psychoanalysis—congresses. 2. Psychotic Disorders—
congresses. WM 460 P9738 1985]
RC512.P736 1989
616.89'14—dc19
DNLM/DLC
for Library of Congress
                                                                    88-13646
                                                                       CIP

Manufactured in the United States of America

To Stu,
And to Jean, Dan and Ted

CONTENTS

Part III
PSYCHOANALYSIS OF NONHOSPITALIZED PATIENTS

Part IV
APPLICATIONS IN HISTORY AND LITERATURE

Part V
FROMM-REICHMANN'S DEVELOPMENT AS A THERAPIST

Part VI
A HISTORY OF THE WASHINGTON PSYCHOANALYTIC INSTITUTE AND SOCIETY

CONTRIBUTORS

Jacob A. Arlow, M.D., is a clinical professor of psychiatry, New York University College of Medicine; visiting professor, Albert Einstein College of Medicine; training and supervising analyst, New York Psychoanalytic Institute. He was formerly president of the American Psychoanalytic Association and editor in chief of *The Psychoanalytic Quarterly.*

L. Bryce Boyer, M.D., is a member of the San Francisco Psychoanalytic Society and Institute, and is in private practice of psychoanalysis. He is co-director of the Seminar for the Advanced Study of the Psychoses, senior co-editor of *The Psychoanalytic Study of Society,* and an honor medalist of the Argentine Psychoanalytic Association. He was formerly associate director of psychiatric training at Herrick Hospital, Berkeley, and was a founding member of the Mexican Psychoanalytic Association.

Henry W. Brosin, M.D., serves as professor of psychiatry at the University of Arizona College of Medicine. He is the former chairman of this department at the universities of Chicago and Pittsburgh, and director of Western Psychiatric Institute. He is past president of the Group for the Advancement of Psychiatry, the American Psychiatric Association, and the American College of Psychiatrists.

Dexter M. Bullard, Jr., M.D., has been the medical director at Chestnut Lodge since 1969. He is a training and supervising analyst with the Washington Psychoanalytic Institute in both the adult and child analytic programs.

Donald L. Burnham, M.D., was a member of the medical staff of Chestnut Lodge from 1950 to 1963, and served as its director of research for six years. He was editor in chief of *Psychiatry,* and is a training and supervising analyst with the Washington Psychoanalytic Institute, and was the president of the Washington Psychoanalytic Society from 1971 to 1973.

Martin Cooperman, M.D., served a residency year at Chestnut Lodge in 1949 while on active duty in the Navy Medical Corps. He then served on the Lodge staff from 1958 to 1968 as senior clinical administrator and clinical director. Since 1968 he has been on the senior staff at the Austen Riggs Center where he is now associate medical director. He is a graduate of the Washington Psychoanalytic Institute.

Jarl E. Dyrud, M.D., was a member of the Chestnut Lodge medical staff from 1953 to 1957 and again in 1967 and 1968 when he served as its director of research. Currently he is professor of psychiatry at the University of Chicago, and a training and supervising analyst with the Chicago Psychoanalytic Institute.

John P. Fort, M.D., has spent his entire psychiatric professional career at Chestnut Lodge, where he serves as the clinical director. He is editor emeritus of *The Psychiatric Hospital.*

Pollianne Curry Freuer has served as a research assistant at Chestnut Lodge and currently is a medical editor with the International Medical News Group.

Frieda Fromm-Reichmann, M.D., served as a training analyst in the Berlin Psychoanalytic Institute prior to her arrival at Chestnut Lodge where she was the first director of psychotherapy. She was a training and supervising analyst with the Washington-Baltimore and then the Washington Psychoanalytic Institute and served as president of the Washington-Baltimore Psychoanalytic Society from 1939 to 1941.

Robert W. Gibson, M.D., was a member of the Chestnut Lodge medical staff from 1952 to 1960. Currently, he is the president and chief executive officer of The Sheppard and Enoch Pratt Hospital and a training and supervising analyst with the Washington Psychoanalytic Institute. He has served as the president of the American Psychiatric Association, Group for the Advancement of Psychiatry, and The National Association of Private Psychiatric Hospitals.

Joanne Greenberg has been "seen" or treated by most of the people on this list between 1948 and 1954. She went to American University and currently writes fiction in Colorado. She has three honorary degrees in letters and teaches anthropology and a fiction course at the Colorado School of Mines. She has retired from the Lookout Mountain Fire Department Highland Rescue. She is a member of AADB and NAD.

Josephine R. Hilgard, M.D., Ph.D., is an emeritus clinical professor of psychiatry in the Stanford University School of Medicine. She served as an associate physician at Chestnut Lodge from 1943 to 1945, while completing her psychoanalytic train- ing. Since then she has engaged in private psychiatric and psychoanalytic practice, along with teaching, supervision, and research.

John S. Kafka, M.D., was a member of the Chestnut Lodge medical staff from 1957 to 1967. He is clinical professor, psychiatry and behavioral sciences, George Washington University School of Medicine, and a training and supervising analyst with the Washington Psychoanalytic Institute. He was president of the Washington Psychoanalytic Society from 1983 to 1985.

Lawrence C. Kolb, M.D., serves as distinguished physician in psychiatry, U.S. Veterans Administration. In this position he has engaged in research on the combat-induced posttraumatic stress disorders. He is professor emeritus, and past chairman of the department of psychiatry, Columbia University, College of Physicians and Surgeons, and formerly director of the New York State Psychiatric Institute. He served as president of the American Psychiatric Association in 1968.

Wendy Leeds-Hurwitz, Ph.D., is associate professor of communication at the University of Wisconsin–Parkside, where she teaches interpersonal and intercultural communication courses. One of her research specialties is the history of the study of communication.

Ruth W. Lidz, M.D., served as clinical professor of psychiatry at the Yale University School of Medicine. She received her psychoanalytic training with the Washington-Baltimore Psychoanalytic Institute in the 1940s, and is a member of the Western New England Psychoanalytic Society and Institute.

Theodore Lidz, M.D., served as Sterling Professor of Psychiatry and former chairman of the department of Psychiatry at the Yale University School of Medicine. He was a former career investigator of the National Institutes of Mental Health, and president of the American Psychosomatic Society. He is a member of the Western New England Psychoanalytic Society and Institute.

Beatrice Liebenberg, M.S.W., is on the faculty of the Washington School of Psychiatry and on the steering committee of the Advanced Psychotherapy Training Program there.

Laurice L. McAfee, M.D., has served on the Chestnut Lodge staff since 1977. Having received her training in adult and child psychiatry at The Johns Hopkins Hospital, she was chief of the Hopkins child psychiatry services at the Baltimore City Hospitals.

Douglas Noble, M.D., had been a training and supervising analyst with the Washington Psychoanalytic Institute, and served as the president of the Washington Psychoanalytic Society from 1955 to 1957. His special interest was the study of creativity, and he chaired the Washington Psychoanalytic Institute's Creativity Seminar until shortly before his death, on September 11, 1986. He was a member of the Lodge medical staff from 1940 to 1946.

John L. Schimel, M.D., is the associate director and training and supervising psychoanalyst at the William Alanson White Institute of Psychiatry, Psychoanalysis and Psychology. He is also clinical professor of psychiatry in the department of child and adolescent psychiatry at the New York University Medical School. He is a past president of both the American Academy of Psychoanalysis and the American Society for Adolescent Psychiatry.

Clarence G. Schulz, M.D., served on the Chestnut Lodge staff from 1952 to 1962. He served as director of residency training at the Sheppard and Enoch Pratt Hospital until 1987 and is currently in private practice of psychoanalysis. A supervising and training analyst with the Washington Psychoanalytic Institute, he served as the society's president from 1979 to 1981.

Harold F. Searles, M.D., was on the staff of Chestnut Lodge from 1949 to 1964. The most recent of his five books is *My Work with Borderline Patients* (1986). A former president of the Washington Psychoanalytic Society, he has been practicing psychoanalysis and psychotherapy in the Washington area for forty years.

Roger L. Shapiro, M.D., was a staff member at Chestnut Lodge from 1954 to 1958. He was subsequently chief of the section on personality development, adult psychiatry branch, National Institute of Mental Health. He is currently clinical professor of psychiatry, George Washington University School of Medicine, and on the faculty of the Washington Psychoanalytic Institute. He is consultant on family treatment at Chestnut Lodge.

Ann-Louise S. Silver, M.D., has been a member of the medical staff at Chestnut Lodge since 1976. She is a member of the Washington Psychoanalytic Society, a clinical associate professor at the Uniformed Services University of the Health Sciences, faculty member of the Washington School of Psychiatry, and a civilian consultant at the Walter Reed Army Medical Center.

Joseph H. Smith, M.D., served on the Lodge staff from 1955 to 1961. He is a training and supervising analyst with the Washington Psychoanalytic Institute.

Samuel V. Thompson, Ph.D., M.D., was a staff psychiatrist at Chestnut Lodge for over twenty-one years and was a member of the Washington Psychoanalytic Society and the American Psychoanalytic Association. Prior to his arrrival at the Lodge, he served as a naval medical officer from 1942 until 1963, when he was chief of the neuropsychiatric service at the U.S. Naval Hospital in Bethesda, Maryland. He died on January 11, 1985.

Benjamin I. Weininger, M.D., served on the Lodge staff from 1936 to 1939 and again in 1946. He served as president of the Washington-Baltimore Psychoanalytic Society and as a training analyst in that institute. He was a co-founder of the Southern California Counseling Center. He died on September 11, 1988.

Otto A. Will, Jr., M.D., served on the Lodge staff from 1947 to 1967, and was Fromm-Reichmann's successor as director of psychotherapy there. He was a training and supervising analyst with the Washington Psychoanalytic Institute. After leaving the Lodge, he became the medical director at the Austen Riggs Center from 1967 to 1978, and is now in private practice of psychoanalysis in Richmond, California.

ACKNOWLEDGMENTS

I would like to take this opportunity to thank Dexter Bullard, Jr., M.D., for his consistent support in the planning of the conference and the preparation of this book. Robert A. Cohen, M.D., has been a source of always wise guidance and collaborative friendship, serving as a behind-the-scenes supervisor of my efforts to chair the conference and to edit this book. Judith Viorst and the members of her class in psychoanalytic writing at the Washington Psychoanalytic Institute have contributed to the improved clarity and cohesiveness of my contributions. Pollianne Curry has been an extraordinarily thorough, patient, and well-organized research assistant. Ellen Boren Rafferty and Patricia Kelly in the Chestnut Lodge word-processing center have helped immeasurably in the research project and in typing manuscripts, revisions, and correspondence to the contributors. Mabel Peterson, former executive secretary at Chestnut Lodge, facilitated the project in innumerable acts of helpfulness. Margaret Emery, Ph.D., editor in chief at International Universities Press, has been courteous and very helpful throughout her involvement in this project. Norman Senior, of Greenfield, Eisenberg, Stein and Senior (380 Madison Avenue, New York, NY 10017) served ably as attorney in our book contract deliberations and inter-author agreement papers. And my husband, Stuart B. Silver, M.D., and my children, Jean, Dan, and Ted, have contributed immeasurably through their dependable support, and their patient listening and editing as I have rehearsed and revised. They have sacrificed much family time to this project, and I am deeply appreciative.

FOREWORD

DEXTER M. BULLARD, JR., M.D.

When Frieda Fromm-Reichmann came to Chestnut Lodge in 1935, change was in the air. Adolf Meyer had demonstrated to a generation of psychiatric residents the value of a detailed life history to the understanding of the symptoms of mental illness. The arrival on our shores of a group of creative and talented psychoanalysts had caught the imagination of America, and Americans embraced this new method of investigating the unconscious. Harry Stack Sullivan had published his studies at Sheppard Pratt that would revolutionize our thinking about schizophrenia. Surely the time was propitious for a new assault on mental illness.

For my father, a rebel and an iconoclast, the arrival of Frieda Fromm-Reichmann was a final step in the transformation of Chestnut Lodge into a psychoanalytic hospital. The director of nursing, after some resistance, had hired new nurses receptive to the fresh ideas of dynamic psychiatry. A young psychiatrist, Marjorie Jarvis, had embarked on psychoanalytic training at the Washington-Baltimore Psychoanalytic Institute and came to Chestnut Lodge to learn about the psychodynamics of the severely ill hospitalized patient. However, the hospital needed an experienced psychoanalyst with knowledge of hospital psychiatry.

Frieda Fromm-Reichmann more than met these requirements. She was a graduate of the Berlin Institute, an experienced psychoanalytic clinician, who had directed her own psychiatric hospital in Heidelberg before emigrating to the United States. Frieda Fromm-Reichmann's reputation had preceded her, and several well-established hospitals offered her positions. My father set out to woo her, determined to succeed. He offered her the position of director of psychotherapy, a house on the grounds of the hospital, and ample time for teaching and research. However, she often reminisced that acceptance of the position was not based on these inducements, but on the immediate rapport she felt with my father and the role she could play in the growth of the hospital. My father often remarked that they "hit it off right from the start," and the collegial relationship that was established became a major source of strength in the development of Chestnut Lodge.

A harmonious working relationship developed between Frieda Fromm-Reichmann and my father which was to continue over the next twenty years. The division of therapeutic and administrative responsibilities introduced by my father several years earlier became a centerpiece of the hospital's treatment program, exemplified by the balance of these two strong personalities: psychotherapeutic issues were ultimately resolved in consultation with Frieda Fromm-Reichmann, administrative questions in consultation with my father. Because of the overlapping nature of most clinical concerns, staff could choose the perspective from which to approach the clinical problem. This encouraged innovation, disagreement, debate, and staff conferences that were always lively and sometimes acrimonious. At this time little was known about the psychodynamics of the major mental disorders and the impact of intensive psychotherapy on these conditions. As with any new treatment, the occasional successes and frequent failures were widely discussed. The freedom of the staff to disagree and hold strongly divergent views rested on their sense of security engendered by the availability of psychotherapeutic or administrative advice, and ultimately on the confidence and mutual respect shared by Frieda Fromm-Reichmann and my father. A variety of psychotherapeutic approaches were attempted, evaluated, and either accepted or discarded. Frieda Fromm-Reichmann's own views and approach to the psychotic patient changed remarkably over time, a tribute to her creativity and ability to continue learning from clinical experience.

The development of Frieda Fromm-Reichmann's own work was greatly affected by her relationship with Harry Stack Sullivan. For several years Sullivan came to Chestnut Lodge to give a series of seminars and to hear case presentations. The application of Sullivan's interpersonal theories in the hospital setting enriched Fromm-Reichmann's understanding of the psychotic process. She, in turn, developed her own concepts of psychotherapy which culminated in her book, *Principles of Intensive Psychotherapy.* Given the strong personalities of both Fromm-Reichmann and Sullivan, it is fortunate that Sullivan did not have a position on the medical staff. This allowed Fromm-Reichmann to develop her psychotherapeutic approach and to embody this approach in the hospital treatment program. This volume examines many aspects of her concept of psychotherapy and its application at Chestnut Lodge.

Frieda Fromm-Reichmann influenced the development of many individual colleagues through her work and teaching, among them Donald Burnham, Robert Cohen, Robert Gibson, David Rioch, Harold Searles, Alfred Stanton, and Otto Will. She saw the psychotherapeutic treatment of the major mental disorders as a new field, and she remained open and receptive to the ideas and formulations of her fellow staff members, giving generously of herself to her work and to the people around her. I remember a cold winter afternoon when she came to my medical school to give a dinner talk to the small Undergraduate Psychiatric Society. Despite considerable inconvenience she changed to a formal dress, lending seriousness and dignity to our group and its deliberations. Her talk was full of the warmth, humor, and dedication of the committed psychoanalyst working with seriously ill patients, and it remains a treasured experience.

Of all her personal qualities I most admired her openness; I found her always approachable, concerned, and responsive. Although I saw her only at intervals, my holidays, she made me feel I was a part of her personal life, and I rediscovered at each visit how special a person she was to me. As I grew older, I observed her impact on those who worked and learned beside her and realized how intensely her personal qualities pervaded the psychotherapeutic program at Chestnut Lodge. Over the years her influence extended far beyond the hospital through her writings and lectures, but at Chestnut Lodge it is Frieda Fromm-Reichmann herself who will be most remembered, much loved and respected, as a remarkable clinician, a charismatic teacher, a deeply caring friend.

INTRODUCTION

ANN-LOUISE S. SILVER, M.D.

Dexter Bullard, Sr., and Frieda Fromm-Reichmann began work together when the world was immersed in a war of massive proportions against an enemy in the grips of a psychotic leader. The rather tall and formidable Dr. Bullard, who could trace his American lineage back to the original settlers along the banks of the Charles River in Massachusetts, combined forces with a German Jewish immigrant four feet ten inches tall, and together this unlikely pair fought their common enemy, psychosis itself. Their teamwork resulted in an atmosphere of intense productivity and high morale at Chestnut Lodge.

The Lodge, a private psychoanalytically oriented hospital located in the "historic" area of Rockville, Maryland, now a suburb of Washington, D.C., has contributed significantly to the dynamic understanding of the hospitalized mentally ill. A review of some of the resulting publications (Fromm-Reichmann, 1950, 1959; Bullard, 1940, 1952; Searles, 1960, 1965; Cameron and Esterson, 1958; Cameron, 1970; Pao, 1969, 1973, 1979; Burnham, 1961a, b; Burnham et al., 1969; Kafka, in press; Will and Cohen, 1953; Will, 1958, 1964, 1965) conveys the intensity with which the staff explored the dynamics of the disorders under treatment and of the patterns of interaction between doctor and patient. A review of the transcripts of the staff conferences transmits a mood of heroic battle. Although false politeness and the avoidance of hurt feelings had no place at these conferences, there was nonetheless a high degree of mutual respect in the way staff members dealt with one another. And although the staff clearly was aware that they were not

1

producing miraculous results, there was a dedication to perseverance and a high degree of realistic hopefulness.

Fromm-Reichmann set forth the tenets of her philosophy in the introduction to her book, *The Principles of Intensive Psychotherapy*, where she stated:

> Emotional difficulties in living are difficulties in interpersonal relationships; and a person is not emotionally hampered, that is, he is mentally healthy to the extent to which he is able to be aware of, and therefore to handle, his interpersonal relationships. In stating this and, by implication, defining psychiatry and psychotherapy as the science and art of interpersonal relationships, I not only wish to say that a person is mentally healthy to the extent to which he is able to be aware of and to handle his overt relationships with other people. But I also wish to refer to a much more far-reaching fact. We can understand human personality only in terms of interpersonal relationships. There is no way to know about human personality other than by means of what one person conveys to another, that is, in terms of his relationship with him. Moreover, the private mental and emotional experiences, his *covert inner* thought and reverie processes   are   *also*   in   terms   of   interpersonal experiences . . . When the experience is a psychotherapeutic one, it is the interpersonal exchange between the patient and the psychiatrist as a participant observer which carries the possiblity of therapeutically valid interpersonal investigation and formulation [p. xiv].

Dexter Bullard, Sr. outlined the history of the Lodge in an unpublished address to the Ontario Psychiatric Association on February 2, 1968. To paraphrase:

His father, Ernest Bullard, was a horse-and-buggy country doctor in Waukesha, Wisconsin, who became interested in politics and was elected to the state legislature. He made the acquaintance of Governor Robert La Follette, Sr., and was subsequently appointed superintendent of the Mendota Hospital for the Insane, across the lake from Madison. He bridled at being a government appointee, had a falling out with the governor after two years, and went into private practice in Milwaukee, later becoming head of the department of neurology and psychiatry at Marquette. He began to look around for a hospital of his own, spending two summers going up and down the East coast with his family in search of a suitable location. He favored the Washington area, reasoning that were there to be a depression, the nation's capital would be more secure than elsewhere.

In 1908, he discovered the Woodlawn Hotel, which had been abandoned for two years, and began refurbishing it, establishing a rest cure asylum typical of the times. He was not analytically oriented, and teased his son Dexter Sr. about his analytic interests. From 1910, when the Lodge opened, until 1917, when Dexter Sr. went to college, Dexter Sr. spent much time with the patients, who first served as his babysitters and later as his companions with whom he played cards and croquet, took walks, etc. This continuing and close contact with hospitalized individuals led to his firm conviction that psychotics could be treated in insight-oriented therapy. Dexter Sr. graduated in 1923 from the University of Pennsylvania Medical School, the only one in his class interested in psychiatry as a career, and after an internship in Hawaii, he did his residency at the Boston Psychopathic Hospital. Meanwhile, Ernest Bullard ran Chestnut Lodge alone, working seven days a week. When he had a coronary, Dexter Sr. returned to Rockville and took over as medical director. In 1927, Dexter Sr. married Anne Wilson. Mrs. Bullard, who still lives at Rose Hill at the Lodge, ran the hotel aspects of the place and planned the now magnificent landscaping.

In 1931, Ernest Bullard died. Dexter gave himself five years to determine which direction the Lodge would take. In 4½ years he knew it would go the psychoanalytic route, applying Freudian theory to the treatment of psychosis. Dexter Sr. saw close parallels between Freud's writings on dreams and the schizophrenics' communications, in particular in catatonic excitement, and he hoped that the careful interpretation of these communications would result in reducing the patients' profoundly disorganizing anxiety.

In 1933, he engaged the first analytically trained psychiatrist, Marjorie Jarvis. They shared the work and soon found that the daily administrative details of patient management intruded on the analytic process. Telling a patient, for instance, that he or she could not go into town because of recent drunkenness might lead to the patient's retaliation by such measures as refusing to talk to the doctor. So they concocted the system of splitting the administrative and analytic functions, with each doing patient management for the other. This system, still in place at the Lodge, was first reported on by Morse and Noble (1942).

In 1935, Fromm-Reichmann was hired, though not without some initial resistance on Dexter Sr.'s part. Dexter was in personal analysis with Dr. Ernest Hadley, and was in a phase of negative transference at the time. Nothing Hadley said seemed right. In February, Hadley, who apparently had been called by Erich Fromm, asked if Dexter would be interested in having a middle-aged German-Jewish refugee come to the Lodge to work. He said absolutely not. Then in May, when both he and Jarvis started planning summer vacations, and there were no other psychiatrists on the staff, he asked Hadley if Fromm-Reichmann was still available. Hired as temporary summer help, Fromm-Reichmann arrived at the Lodge on July 1. Says Dexter Sr., "We fell in love at first sight, and she stayed until her death in 1957."

Fromm-Reichmann, nine years older than Dexter Sr., recorded her autobiography in taped interviews held about a year before her death. The transcript, which forms a chapter of this book, amply conveys her warmth, verve, and sparkling intelligence. It gives clear evidence that Chestnut Lodge became, to Fromm-Reichmann, a superb replacement for the institutions and relationships lost to her because of World War II. It may well have been "love at first sight" for her as well.

After Fromm-Reichmann's arrival, the staff grew gradually to include Bob Morse, Doug Noble, and David Rioch, then Mabel Blake Cohen. Between October 1942 and April 1946, Harry Stack Sullivan began coming out to the Lodge twice a week to conduct seminars in a leisurely question-and-answer format, with many digressions. The transcriptions of some of these meetings form the basis of *Clinical Studies in Psychiatry* (Sullivan, 1956). Fromm-Reichmann attended regularly, and frequently referred to Sullivan's remarks when discussing cases in the Wednesday staff conferences, which at that time were much like traditional rounds. In 1942, Fromm-Reichmann became the first director of psychotherapy, and began recording these meetings. These transcripts document the development of the hospital's gradually evolving perspectives of treatment.

In 1948, Fromm-Reichmann and others initiated the system of "small groups," dividing the medical staff into groups of approximately eight members who met twice a week to discuss whatever clinical matter seemed most pressing. This system is still in place today, with the groups maintaining the same membership for three or four years before reconstituting. This arrangement gives members time to develop trust in each other and to collaborate with each other, after which they move on to work with others on the staff.

Increasingly, Fromm-Reichmann's comments became more instructional and the staff conferences more analytically focused. In 1952, the Lodge began training residents, who would come for their third year of training with the proviso that they would stay at least one additional year. These positions became highly sought after. Many of the residents were supervised by Fromm-Reichmann, usually for just one or two years, sometimes individually and sometimes with another staff member, the two alternating presentations of cases. Among those who joined the staff during those years as residents are some of the contributors to this book: Donald Burnham, Jarl Dyrud, John Fort, Robert Gibson, John Kafka, Clarence Schulz, and Harold Searles. Robert and Mabel Blake Cohen, Samuel Thompson, and Otto Will had completed residency training prior to their arrival.

Fromm-Reichmann had many invitations to speak, and wherever she went, she made a strong impression. Indeed, when she spoke in Topeka at the Menninger Clinic, Karl Menninger, trying to tempt her to join his staff, offered to build her a house. Dexter Sr. notes that "it took us about a week to put our carpenters to work to build the Frieda Fromm-Reichmann Cottage." It became her permanent home for the rest of her life, and it was there that she died. During the 1950s, Fromm-Reichmann traveled regularly, often weekly, to New York City, where she taught and supervised and was a founding member of the William Alanson White Institute. She was also influential in the organization of the American Academy of Psychoanalysis, although she was in California during 1956, the year of its founding. Among her New York supervisees were Rose Speigel and John Schimel.

Both Mabel Peterson, former executive secretary at The Lodge, and Joanne Greenberg, author of *I Never Promised You a Rose Garden* (Green, 1964), a fictionalized account of her treatment by Fromm-Reichmann, commented on Fromm-Reichmann's military style, which persisted from her days as a major in the Prussian Army, when she ran a hospital for brain-injured soldiers. She did not walk but marched briskly, her back always straight and her head high, in soldierly fashion. At the military hospital she insisted that, for their optimal functioning, her medical staff and the brain-injured soldiers be cognizant of army codes. At the Lodge she was also a stickler, insisting that the staff be alert to the nuances of the patients' anxieties and their own countertransference.

From 1955, when she spent the year in Stanford, until her death two years later, Fromm-Reichmann rarely attended conferences, perhaps because of her increasingly incapacitating hearing deficit. When one reads her autobiographical transcript, one is struck by the counterphobic aspect of her choice of psychoanalysis as a career, for both her parents and other family members had suffered from severe deafness in their adult years. She had been gradually recovering from an enervating flu when, on April 28, 1957, she suffered a massive and immediately fatal coronary occlusion. She was sixty-seven years old.

Chestnut Lodge has changed dramatically since the 1940s and '50s. There are three times the number of patients and medical staff. Under the leadership of Dexter Bullard, Jr., who became the medical director of the Lodge in 1969, a separate adolescent division with an independent school has been established. In 1986, E. James Anthony became the adolescent division's first director of psychotherapy. In the adult hospital, Ping-Nie Pao, following Otto Will, served as director of psychotherapy from 1967 until his death in August 1981, just two months before Dexter Sr.'s death on October 6, 1981.

Thomas McGlashan, director of research, has orchestrated an elaborate follow-up study of the patients treated at the Lodge between 1950 and 1975. The initial findings were reported in 1984 and 1986, but the data continue to supply information on many interrelated questions regarding diagnosis and prognosis. Changes in the adult hospital include an intricate outpatient program which is still evolving and which attempts to meet the needs of an ever-increasing outpatient population. New facilities will soon house the adult patients. The doctors will then have their offices in the main building, the former Woodlawn Hotel.

But the most dramatic change has come with the advent of psychotropic medication, whose use has altered the Lodge in both obvious and subtle ways. The place is far quieter. One rarely hears someone screaming reduntantly in hallucinated discourse in a "quiet room." One rarely arrives on a unit to see a group of male psychiatric technicians reviewing their strategy before entering a seclusion room to secure a patient in cold wet-sheet pack—"You take the right leg, you take the left . . . "—or moves aside quickly in the stairwell as psych techs rush to a unit on which the emergency bell has been sounded. It is also rare to learn that a psychiatric technician has been injured during the staff's efforts to place a patient in cold wet-sheet pack so that the patient can meet with his or her therapist for their still-routine four or more full sessions per week. Assaults on therapists are similarly far less frequent. Unpredicted violence, disrobing, incontinence of urine and feces, and prolonged phases of mutism or refusal to eat are now far from commonplace.

With the marked diminution in frequency of these regressive symptoms, the ambience of the place has changed. One can keep potted plants around if they are not to become weapons. As they thrive, they lend a sense of dependability. Similarly, one can develop a library if one is rather confident that the books will not be ripped to shreds. Curtains, pictures, wallpaper, and other furnishings can age gradually, developing a patina of constancy.

For those who return to the Lodge after an absence of many years, these changes are startling. Morris Schwartz, for instance, co-author with Alfred Stanton of *The Mental Hospital* (1954), had last seen the Lodge's Main IV—the unit on which he had gathered sociological data for his book—in 1956. When he attended the 1985 Chestnut Lodge Symposium commemorating the fiftieth anniversary of the arrival of Frieda Fromm-Reichmann, he was eager to see the unit again, and braced himself for an onslaught of waves of nostalgia. He imagined himself thinking, "Yes! That's where such-and-such happened!" or "That still looks the same!" Instead, as he later said, he felt as if he were in an entirely new place. Nothing at all looked familiar. He felt that if a series of photographs of the current Main IV had been mixed in among pictures of places where he had never been, he would have been unable to identify them as the place where he had once had such intense experiences. He felt that the long and interesting conversation he had held during the symposium with one of the patients could just as well have been held with a member of the nursing staff. And when he sought out a patient he had first met in the 1950s, a patient who had required hospitalization continually during the intervening years, he was astounded by her significant improvement in mental functioning and by the intellectual sparkle of her remarks. Schwartz summarized his experience by saying that he felt that the place he encountered in 1985 was more like a college dormitory than like the Chestnut Lodge he remembered.

The increase in use of psychotropic medication was gradually effected during the years that Ping-Nie Pao served as director of psychotherapy, 1967 to 1981. While he did not address the question of medication in his book, *Schizophrenic Disorders* (1979), his theories have been applied to the use and misuse of medication (Feinsilver, 1983). After the introduction of medication, there was an initial, and inevitable, phase of adjustment during which the focus on the therapeutic dyad decreased. When a patient regressed, attention turned first to the medication as the agent of change, and only secondarily to the therapist-patient dyad, the complexities of therapist-administrator splits, and the interpersonal difficulties that were so eloquently explicated in *The Mental Hospital*. Too often, from the therapists' view, members of the treatment team—usually the administrative psychiatrist and the nursing staff—suggested medication. In response, therapists often reacted with adamant rejection of the idea, or with pleas to wait some months longer.

A regular view expressed at staff discussions in the early years of medication was that the therapists were jealous of the power of the medication, and of the intimate and yet nonverbal relatedness of patient and drug. Jealousy aside, the introduction of medication raised issues which continue to be discussed. It is true that some therapists have seen the introduction of psychotropic medication as long overdue, and have often advocated one or another medication. But others feel conflicted about the use of these medications because they sense the drugs' power both to enhance and to detract from the interpersonal exploration.

Although medication is here to stay, Chestnut Lodge continues to adhere to the principles of psychotherapy enunciated by Fromm-Reichmann and Sullivan and many others. Our current director of psychotherapy, Robert A. Cohen, who was an analysand and a colleague of Fromm-Reichmann and a supervisee of Sullivan, has urged us repeatedly to study dispassionately the interplay of psychoanalytic psychotherapy and pharmacotherapy. In the weekly psychotherapy seminars which he chairs, he and others repeatedly demonstrated that analytically based dyadic work proceeds with the *same general pattern* of relatedness modes with or without medication. Thus today we still apply the same rules of treatment which were developed at a time when patients would let a doctor know instantaneously—through assault or mutism or catatonia—that they had lost hold of their fragile thread of trust because of something the doctor had said or done.

Psychotropic medication, it could be argued, has made poorer teachers of our patients. They cannot inform us of the disruptiveness of our mannerisms, styles of interpretation, or errors in understanding, for their greater cohesiveness allows for greater resiliance and impulse control. It is clear, nonetheless, that the dynamic issues or core conflicts are still the same. Defenses such as projection, denial, grandiosity, splitting, and intensification of hallucination must still be analyzed as they develop in the transference, with careful acknowledgment of countertransference phenomena. We need to study the writings of the analysts who worked with psychotic patients during the premedication days, and never lose sight of the underlying conflictual dynamisms in our patients and ourselves. Otherwise, we will be left with little to offer our patients but consolation, behavior modification, and a dependency on external agents.

Without the kind of insight which only develops through interpersonal analytic work, patients cannot gain a sense of mastery over their chaos. But when they are able to resolve the chaos through evolving shared insight and trust, they have something of more personally lasting significance, something which strengthens their sense of autonomy and their pride as a collaborator. Fromm-Reichmann's *Principles of Intensive Psychotherapy* is still available in a paperback edition, is still stocked at medical school bookstores thirty years after its publication, is still standing as an invaluable introduction and guide for those working with the hospitalized mentally ill.

The present book offers new papers by members of the analytic community who have contributed significantly to our understanding of the psychotic process as part of the human condition. We hope that reading their papers and contributions will inspire our younger colleagues to delve into a detailed exploration of these contributors' earlier writings. Trained during a time when hope was exceedingly high that medications would prove curative and when studying the intricacies of intensive psychotherapy had been considered by many to have become obsolete, these younger colleagues may often be unaware of the rich drama occurring in their own and their patients' unconscious as they proceed with their interviews. They are then left with a feeling of uneasiness which can convert readily to boredom and hopelessness. If this trend is not reversed, something very precious may be lost.

The present collection of papers is an outgrowth of the thirty-first annual Chestnut Lodge Symposium, which commemorated the fiftieth anniversary of the arrival of Frieda Fromm-Reichmann. The presenters included Lawrence Kolb, Ruth W. Lidz, Laurice L. McAfee, Harold Searles, Ann-Louise

S. Silver, Alberta Szalita-Pemow, and Otto Will. Robert Cohen who collaborated closely with Silver in the organization of the conference, delivered a posthumous paper by Samuel Thompson.

Because of time restrictions, many distinguished colleagues who had worked with Fromm-Reichmann as patients, supervisees, collaborators, or supporters could not be invited to read papers at this one-day conference. Instead, they were asked to contribute papers to this collection, with the suggestion that they write something which they felt Fromm-Reichmann would have enjoyed reading. Some of the contributors have offered, in addition to their papers, short sections of personal reminiscences and remarks which orient the reader to their connection with Fromm-Reichmann. Taken together, these papers convey a philosophy and ambience of scholarly and dedicated optimism that continues to enrich this extremely challenging work.

References

Bullard, D. M. (1940), Experiences in the psychoanalytic treatment of psychotics. *Psychoanal. Quart.*, 9:493–504.

———— (1952), Problems of clinical administration. *Bull. Menn. Clin.*, 16:193–201.

———— (1968), A history of Chestnut Lodge. Read at the February 2, 1968, meeting of the Ontario Psychiatric Association.

Burnham, D. L. (1961a), Autonomy and activity-passivity in the psychotherapy of a schizophrenic man. In: *Psychotherapy of the Psychoses*. New York: Basic Boks, pp. 208–236.

———— (1961b), Identity definition and role demand in the hospital careers of schizophrenic patients. *Psychiatry*, 24:96–122.

———— Gladstone, A. I., & Gibson, R. W. (1969), *Schizophrenia and the Need-Fear Dilemma*. New York: International Universities Press.

Cameron, J. L. (1970), Symbolism in the treatment of schizophrenia. *Brit. J. Med. Psychol.*, 43:257–263.

———— Esterson, A. (1958), Psychotherapy with a schizophrenic woman. *Psychiat. Quart.*, 32:304–317.

Cohen, M. B., Baker, G., Cohen, R. A., Fromm-Reichmann, F., & Weigert, E. (1954), An intensive study of twelve cases of manic-depressive psychosis. *Psychiatry*, 17:103–137.

Cohen, R. A. (1951), Types of psychotherapy. *Med. Ann. D.C.*, 20:589–595.

———— Cohen, M. B. (1961), Research in psychotherapy. *Psychiatry*, 24:46–61.

Feinsilver, D. (1983), Application of Pao's theories to a case study of the use and misuse of medication. *Psychoanal. Inqu.*, 3:125–144.

———— (1986), *Towards a Comprehensive Model for Schizophrenic Disorders*. Hillside, N.J.: Analytic Press.

———— Yates, B. (1984), Combined use of psychotherapy and drugs in chronic, treatment-resistant schizophrenic patients. *J. Nerv. & Ment. Dis.*, 172:133–139.

Fromm-Reichmann, F. (1950), *Principles of Intensive Psychotherapy*. Chicago: University of Chicago Press.

——— (1959), *Psychoanalysis and Psychotherapy*. Chicago: University of Chicago Press.

Freeman, T., Cameron, J. L., & McGhie, A. (1958), *Chronic Schizophrenia*. New York: International Universities Press.

——— ——— ——— (1966), *Studies in Psychosis*. New York: International Universities Press.

Green, H. (or Greenberg, J.) (1964), *I Never Promised You a Rose Garden*. New York: Holt, Rinehart & Winston.

Kafka, J. (in press), *Perspectives on Psychoanalytic Practice*. New Haven: Yale University Press.

McGlashan, T. H. (1984), The Chestnut Lodge follow-up study: I & II. *Arch. Gen. Psychiat.*, 41:573–601.

——— (1986a), The Chestnut Lodge follow-up study, III & IV. *Arch. Gen. Psychiat.*, 43:20–30, 167–176.

——— (1986b), Predictors of shorter-, medium-, and longer-term outcome in schizophrenia. *Amer. J. Psychiat.*, 143:50–55.

Morse, R., & Noble, D. (1942), Joint endeavors of the administrative physician and psychotherapist. *Psychiat. Quart.*, 16:578–585.

Pao, P.-N. (1969), Pathologic jealousy. *Psychoanal. Quart.*, 38:616–638.

——— (1973), On defensive flight to a new object. *Inter. J. Psychoanal. Psychother.*, 2:320–337.

——— (1979), *Schizophrenic Disorders*. New York: International Universities Press.

Schulz, C. G., & Kilgalen, R. K. (1969). *Case Studies in Schizophrenia*. New York: Basic Books.

Searles, H. F. (1960). *The Nonhuman Environment*. New York: International Universities Press.

——— (1965), *Collected Papers on Schizophrenia and Related Subjects*. New York: International Universities Press.

Stanton, A. H., & Schwartz, M. S. (1954). *The Mental Hospital*. New York: Basic Books.

Sullivan, H. S. (1956), *Clinical Studies in Psychiatry*. New York: Norton.

Szalita-Pemow, A. B. (1952), Further remarks on the pathogenesis and treatment of schizophrenia. *Psychiatry*, 15:143–150.

Will, O. A. (1958), Psychotherapeutics and the schizophrenic reaction. *J. Nerv. & Ment. Dis.*, 126:109–140.

——— (1964), Schizophrenia and the psychotherapeutic field. *Contemp. Psychoanal.*, 1:1–29.

——— (1965), The schizophrenic patient, the psychotherapist and the consultant. *Contemp. Psychoanal.*, 1:110–135.

——— Cohen, R. A. (1953), A report of a recorded interview in the course of psychotherapy. *Psychiatry*, 16:263–282.

Frieda and her sisters—
Anna, Frieda and Greta Reichmann

Frieda as a teenager

Frieda and the obstetrics staff—
medical school years

Frieda in medical school

Fromm-Reichmann's sanitorium
in Heidelberg, Germany

Georg Groddeck

Chestnut Lodge, 1910

Chestnut Lodge staff—summer of 1949 or 1950
Burnham, Dyrud, Stavern, Stanton, Darr, Cohen, Rioch, Eldred
Kvarnes, Bullard, Will, White
Fromm-Reichmann, Block, Searles, Adland, Cooperman

Chestnut Lodge staff—1954
Back row: Hendlich, Baker, Rintz, Coxe, Welsh, Schulz, Fort, Cullander,
Dyrud, Gibson. Front row: Will, Burnham, Adland, Bullard, Fromm-Reich-
mann, Preston, Searles

Fromm-Reichmann and her cocker spaniel,
Muni, a gift from Harry Stack Sullivan

Fromm-Reichmann at her home
at Chestnut Lodge

Joanne Greenberg

Fromm-Reichmann cottage, exterior, 1987

Fromm-Reichmann cottage—her desk,
as it was at the time of her death

Dexter M. Bullard, Sr.

Harry Stack Sullivan

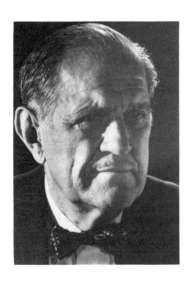

Otto A. Will, Jr.

Harold F. Searles

Robert A. Cohen, Anne Bullard, Dexter Bullard, Sr.
Dr. Bullard's 70th birthday.

Robert A. Cohen

Mabel Blake Cohen

Benjamin Weininger

Josephine Hilgard

Alfred Stanton

John Kafka
Donald Burnham

Robert Gibson

Fromm-Reichmann's summer home—exterior; Santa Fe, New Mexico

Fromm-Reichmann's summer home—interior

Part I
FROMM-REICHMANN AS SUPERVISOR AND RESEARCHER

FROMM-REICHMANN'S CONTRIBUTIONS AT STAFF CONFERENCES

Ann–Louise S. Silver, M.D. and Pollianne Curry Freuer

> I asked what helped towards recovery . . . One thing which she considered very helpful . . . , as she began to get better, I made a remark, and I don't remember in what connection, to the effect that even if she would be well, life would not be a rose garden, but I hoped she would come to the point that she would be strong enough to stand the times when it wouldn't be a rose garden and enjoy the times when it would be. [She said,] . . . "I didn't believe you at the time. I was quite sure that if I really got well, . . . then it would be a rose garden all the way through. But the fact that you said it to me and you obviously believed it gave me the feeling that you really took me seriously and really had confidence in me as a human being. And that's why it meant so much, even though I didn't believe a word."
>
> Frieda Fromm-Reichmann (Staff Conference)

In this chapter, we will report on some of Fromm-Reichmann's contributions to the weekly two-hour-long staff conferences. Her straightforward style of speaking at these conferences was similar to her writing style and evolved with her gradually increasing confidence, stature, and maturity. She was not one to dazzle her listeners with involved theoretical speculation; neither would she paraphrase the writings of others. She simply wanted to see the work done well and carried to a satisfactory completion. She encouraged the staff to stay with the task. If one were to stop midway, one should know the reasons why. Strong feelings such as discouragement, contempt, revulsion, or murderousness could be the very essence of countertransference which, if effectively explored, could provide the insight necessary for effective interpretation. Alternatively, these feelings could provide data necessary for the next therapist's potentially more effective work with that patient. In some way, all her comments related to the exploration of the interrelationship of anxiety, hostility, and loneliness in the patient, the therapist, and other staff members. The more the patient could convey the extent of his or her anguish and confusion, the greater were the chances of recovery.

Fromm-Reichmann *knew* that psychoanalytic therapy was a powerful instrument for profound change. The problems were in how to use it, how to teach using it, and how to improve it. She taught one lecture course per year at the Washington School of Psychiatry, supervised analysts either individually or in pairs or small groups, treated some in training analyses, and led research seminars. In addition, she participated in the two-hour weekly staff conferences which were attended initially only by the medical staff, and later came to include the entire professional staff.

The title of her book, *Principles of Intensive Psychotherapy*, was thoughtfully chosen by her to emphasize the importance of principles, as she herself noted in her autobiographical taped recording. She was intense and intensely dedicated. Many people, both colleagues and patients, have commented on her full use of facial expressions and lively hand gestures to enhance and embellish her comments. She did not try to conceal her emotional reactions to what she heard. With so much nonverbal communication we may sometimes fail to grasp the full flavor of her intent and affect.

Fromm-Reichmann was never falsely polite. This authenticity extended to everyone—patients, staff, and her boss, Dexter Bullard, Sr.—as is illustrated in the following vignette:

> Dr. Bullard: He has told me that everybody tells him he was just born to be a priest. The greatest difficulty I have is of following through from one point to the next and tying it up. I would say we fight just about half of the time. I will say, "I do not believe that is true," and he will say, "Doctor, *you* are a liar." His feeling of resentment and bitterness is genuine and his feeling that I really want to help him is genuine, but where they collide is only confusion.
>
> FFR: You are dealing with an utterly lonely child and

to become a priest meant having lots of people loving you.
And that was the one way he could get love which he wanted.
Now you tell him you do not trust that business, which is
to throw him back to his loneliness.

With such forthrightness, her praise of a therapist's work was
treasured as absolutely sincere.

Although Fromm-Reichmann encouraged therapists to
recognize and acknowledge a patient's unspoken needs, she
became clearly irritated when they offered unwarranted reassurance. She also had little patience when therapists covertly
directed a patient to hide his or her pathological aspects from
them. And she had only slightly more tolerance for a patient
who filled the hours with psychodynamic formulations learned
in previous treatments, or for therapists who regarded these
formulations as anything but resistance to the current work.
While she was often characterized as "gentle," we wondered—as
we read her very tough comments—if this characterization simply meant that she was gentle when compared to the notoriously
temperamental and abruptly caustic Harry Stack Sullivan. But
perhaps her demeanor and mellifluous accent served to soften
her sometimes hard words.

Fromm-Reichmann had a strength of personality which
she seemed to assume everyone else possessed, or could possess.
Thus she did not seem to worry about hurting a fellow colleague's feelings, nor was she condescendingly gentle with her
patients. For both groups, she seemed to work under the principle that "the truth shall make you free." For example, in one
conference, a staff member asked the therapist, in the discussion following his presentation of his work,

> Staff member: Do you really feel you couldn't handle
> her if she jumped you?
> Therapist: If, after a skirmish in which I felt I had to
> get the hell out, I say, I can run pretty fast.
> FFR: What we hear is that you made contact with her
> and that she talks to you, but I have a hard time hearing
> what other directives you have in conducting this treatment,
> other than "Thank God, we talk to each other," not using
> the talking to each other for any *purpose* and it could be that

you haven't been active or positively aggressive there for the reason you just mentioned, that you are afraid.
(and in another conference:)

FFR: Well, you do not only do it inadvertently. I couldn't repeat the examples but while listening, before I knew to what conclusion you would come, I thought at quite a number of places, why do you take the attitude that it could be this or that instead of what is dynamically or genetically behind that?

Therapist: I thought of her, the same thing I said the first time I presented her, that first of all one has to build up a little bit more of what is called the ego or the self before she can make use of insight. It isn't that she doesn't make any use at all, but she doesn't have too much of the ego to assimilate it.

FFR: Then we come to the problem: can somebody use his ego strength by virtue of us telling him how, or by virtue of us helping him to do away with the dynamic and genetic reasons which hinder him? I don't have the feeling that this girl is so weak that she can't follow you if you do it analytically. Try to show her what hinders her from being herself rather than showing her: "This is the way that I, your supporting doctor, think it should be done."

Therapist: Do you have an example about what you are referring to?

FFR: For instance, at the point when she says she wants to go home for Thanksgiving and you say, for this or that reason, you don't think it is good. I would assume that the woman knows it isn't good. And I would ask why she wants to do something which she knows won't work out well. Examples of that kind, I think, happened several times. In a way, I would feel that you give her less credit for what she has, namely, not too bad an intellectual equipment and a not too crushed self, but you don't help her to develop it as long as you believe it has to be developed by supporting it.

Strangers coming to her office in her cottage frequently were said to have mistaken her for a housekeeper. They expected her fame to be accompanied by elegance. But she was four feet ten inches tall, overweight, no longer beautiful or stylish, and she dressed up neither herself nor her ideas and feelings. She

worked, spoke, and lived diligently, with what we came to experience as a *fierce* dedication. It seemed to me as I read these
transcripts that when she spoke, the staff listened with something of the apprehension I would feel when my mother would
check over my ironing or dusting, making me do it over if there
were wrinkles around the buttons or dust on the chair rungs.
Joseph Margolin, a frequent visitor at the Wednesday conferences, sensed that at the end of each presentation the staff
would look toward her to get a sense of her approval or disapproval, and he felt they then often conformed their judg-
ments to what they felt her facial expression conveyed. Margolin's
observations suggest a conformity and deference. However,
Harold Searles, who was very much a participant for years,
when told of this account, adamantly said that he could not
recall anything of that sort occurring.

Historical Chronology

The conferences prior to 1942 were generally inadequately recorded and contained frequent gaps and obvious errors in transcription, but they did convey the character of the hospital as
a much more informal and problem-oriented place. Patients
were mentioned by the small group of doctors within a few days
of their arrival, but not in a detailed or structured way. The
patients who were creating disturbances were the ones most
discussed. Seven or eight doctors would debate whether a particular patient should be allowed an outing with the visiting
family or should be transferred to a more disturbed unit or
allowed to go with another patient on a shopping trip. A commonly discussed matter was that of alcoholic patients sneaking
into town for liquor. A patient of Fromm-Reichmann stole a
bottle of ready-made dry Martinis from her cottage and drank
it on the unit. Fromm-Reichmann commented, "It was especially malicious because she knew that nobody else would have
ready-made Martinis; *anybody* knows well how to mix then, so
that bottle with that label clearly came from me. The hospital
sees she got liquor from her therapist and drank it."
    Sedatives were used surprisingly frequently, including so-
dium thiocyanate, called rhodonate, which, having shown initial

promise in diminishing psychotic agitation, was withdrawn from the market when it was demonstrated to cause neuronal damage.

A vignette from the early 1940s, in which the staff discusses a severely agitated man, illustrates these features:

> FFR: What does Dr. Sullivan suggest?
>
> Therapist: Insulin, but I haven't had enough experience and would not be willing to try.
>
> FFR: But in principle, he thinks we should?
>
> Dr. A: I would like to try sedatives at night and benzedrine in the morning.
>
> Dr. B: You would not want him with a hangover.
>
> Therapist: Not with a hangover but if more relaxed, it wouldn't be so bad.
>
> Dr. C: Some people are actually physically uncomfortable with a hangover but others just dopey.
>
> FFR: Could you change your hour with him, seeing him later in the day?
>
> Therapist: Yes. I am not going to see him until tomorrow afternoon.
>
> Dr. D: Why not small divided doses in the daytime, heavier doses at night, and then if this does not work, we can resort to more drastic doses.
>
> FFR: That doesn't seem to me to be a good idea.
>
> Therapist: He has a reluctance to be dopey. He is pretty well convinced it is a hallucination.
>
> Dr. A: But he is not supposed to accept it as a hallucination?
>
> Therapist: He says he can't believe it is a hallucination because the voice is so much smarter than he ever was.
>
> Dr. B: I would knock him out at night and see what you can do with him in the morning.
>
> FFR: Do you want to knock him out completely or give him enough to relax and then be able to talk to you as he comes out of it, or give him sodium amytol so slowly and in such small doses?
>
> Therapist: I am opposed to that. He has asked for sedatives. What do you think of the idea in general?
>
> Dr. C: It gets right back to what Dr. Fromm-Reichmann said. If given a larger than average dose at night so he would sleep soundly but when you saw him the next morning

maybe he would not be fully awake but still able to see you and then give him another small dose for the day and a larger dose for the night.

FFR: It seems you should give it but not deprive him of his doctor.

In addition, Fromm-Reichmann volunteered to administer sleep therapy. When electroconvulsive therapy seemed to some to be indicated, she wondered about referring patients to other places, and later spoke in adamant opposition to its use at the Lodge.

By 1944, the conference had become more focused, dealing with one patient per conference. Increasingly, Fromm-Reichmann's comments became more instructional, and the conferences became more analytically oriented. In the following vignette from a 1944 conference, Fromm-Reichmann challenged the therapist, as I believe she continually challenged herself.

FFR: Yes, but the way you go on now making her talk about irrelevant things just to keep her talking will *not* do something toward her cure. She gave you quite a number of openings and each time you missed them. If you had asked a question instead of meeting a statement, you would have pushed into the thing considerably. . . . [The patient] said, "If I ask somebody to give me a cigarette and it's not the right thing, I would be too lonely." And you say, "Well, you learn to do it, then you won't be so lonely." In the meantime she burns a hole in her dress in despair, because you give an answer to a statement the validity of which you have no way to understand. You have a chance to find out what she wants to tell you there. See what I mean? You will find out something which is quite understandable, trying to let her see that you go with her. But you respond without knowing what she has told you, and therefore the response is only an expression of your good will, and does that contribute to her understanding, because at that moment, you don't know yet what she is telling you. . . . Consequently there is only one person who can help us to understand what she means, and that is she. If she gets a statement which amounts to reassurance, it closes the discussion, but

we are trying to understand because the patient is schizophrenic and we are not schizophrenic enough to have it
mean the same thing. . . . Perhaps she will tell us what her
mother has done to her, and that is the thing that counts.

This quotation alluded to Fromm-Reichmann's ideas at that
time concerning the schizophrenogenic mother.

Nor were fathers immune from bearing responsibility:

FFR: Would you visualize [the patient] . . . as somebody
who has been told as a child what a wonderful father he
has, told by everybody. And he knew better because in the
relationship with him, he had no wonderful father. . . .
Therapist: Even in the referring doctor's original letter
here, what he said was that he hoped we could take this
fellow because this was such a splendid family.
FFR: This fellow has a terrible secret, "My adorable
father is not adorable, namely, as my father" and that he
can't tell because nobody will believe him.

In later years Fromm-Reichmann came to see the parent-
patient relationship as less one-sided as revealed in a 1954 conference in which we see evidence of the evolution and mellowing
of these ideas.

FFR: I think that . . . now that she is in the strong positive [transference mode]. . . , I think it is terribly discouraging [for her] when she hears you say that the relatives are
a lost cause, and also I don't think it is true. Any patient
who really recovers with insight automatically changes the
entire manner and attitude of the relatives toward her. To
her, if she hears you say that the relatives are a lost cause,
that means she is one. Therefore, I think it is dangerous,
and I think it is not so. It is our experience that whenever
a patient gets well, it has the power to change the relatives.
Now, if she breaks out of all the hostile interplay and resentment by virtue of her insight, the mother and father
will change too. If she learns how to get along with the
parents, the parents will get along with her. You are the
mediary for that.

From late 1949 through mid-1951, Fromm-Reichmann

rarely attended the conferences. The years after 1951 were richest in revealing her style of influence on the Lodge staff. Therapists very frequently acknowledged the helpfulness of her supervisory work with them when they reported in staff conferences. As the following example demonstrates, these therapists were not simply saying "thank you," they were eloquently summarizing essential features discovered in the supervisory process:

> Therapist: I finally saw Frieda on May 26, and I had been trying to do it for a long time. She indicated that I talk too much, and I said, "Oh, no, Frieda, four or five minutes go on and I don't say a word!" She said, "But you use too long sentences, too involved sentences. You should simplify them." And she said that in response to this A–B–C–D–E, she would have immediately said, "F–G–H–I–J." I tried to convince her of the idea that some of my childhood experiences were causing the current anxiety between me and this threatening patient, and she said no, it is a matter of my competitive and critical feelings toward the previous therapist who had worked with this patient. I didn't go along with that and I still don't to some extent, but it is there for what it is worth. I did change. I stopped talking so much and I made a definite point to cut down on the length of my sentences, to make them simple. This was the latter part of May. I went in once and he said, "How are you?" I said, "Here to talk." He said, "You do the talking." Later there was laughter and exchanging of glances, whereas previously I had found it very difficult to look at him. I would usually keep my gaze averted and if we looked at one another, it would be him looking at me and then casting his eyes aside, and then me looking at him and then casting my eyes aside.

Over the years, the conference reports developed a shared focus and organization that very definitely reflected a group responsiveness to Fromm-Reichmann's directives. Much less time was spent reporting past history. In its place came an increasing openness regarding the details of therapeutic exchanges and the therapists' ideas and feelings about the relationships. Evidence of hostility in either the patient or doctor was valued as a potential clue to the underlying anxiety, the ambivalent relationship with a parent, and then (quoting Fromm-Reichmann), the "continual question in the air, 'Where is that true in the relationship with me? [the therapist].' " Very frequently, Fromm-Reichmann would comment that the therapist saw the patient one way, but she had seen the patient in another, and then would give an example. She always added that the question was not which one of them was *correct*, but what could the patient teach them about these different aspects of himself.

Fromm-Reichmann seemed to be more explicit in her praise of therapists' work as well. For example, she said,

> FFR: I could begin with saying that [the therapist] really hasn't done justice to the work that he has done with her. What I have heard in our private conversations was much more extensive regarding this very useful therapeutic exchange than he conveyed to us here. As a matter of fact, I think that he has gotten the woman from a state of being entirely in a defensive escape, trying to escape into sexual relations with him, not talking, and so on, to somebody who is now able to attach realistic labels to some things and who shows some insight about her sickness.

From 1955, when she spent the year in Stanford, California, at the Center for Advanced Study in the Behavioral Sciences, until her death in 1957, Fromm-Reichmann rarely attended conferences, perhaps due to her increasingly incapacitating hearing deficit. During those years the Lodge held some fascinating conferences and seminars on the initial impact of the psychotropic medications, but so far we have found no record of any comment made by her on this subject.

Although Fromm-Reichmann's conference comments were quite explicit, she was never verbose. Indeed, her contributions over the years reveal her to be the master of the one-liner, our favorite of which is, "We may be as wise as they come, but we don't like outpatients who have relapses."

Fromm-Reichmann's Presentations

As we read Fromm-Reichmann's presentations of her own work, we found that the legend of her godlike immunity to fear is only slightly exaggerated. Her work with a thirty-year-old chronically paranoid, hallucinating, assaultive man, when she was in her sixties, attests to that.

> FFR: Well, when he first came in, pretty soon without any challenge as far as I know, he looked around and seemed kind of surprised that I would see him in my office which, since I live in it, did not seem sufficiently officelike to him, and he said after we closed both doors, "But you know, I could knock you down in no time. You are an older person and I am a strong young man." I said, "Yes, I know." "Did you hear me? I could knock you down in no time? Do you want it?" I said, "No, I definitely don't want it, first because I don't want to be hurt, but second, and you may be surprised about that, I don't want it because I know you will feel so God-awful lousy if you do such a thing that I would like you to be spared from that." This seemed to impress him and he promised that he would never hurt me, a man wouldn't fight with a woman. This was half amorous and half in a despising way.

Later in the work, the patient was clearly attached to Fromm-Reichmann and had raged at her that she wouldn't be able to go on an announced vacation, because he would kill her rather than let her go away for four days. Since he previously had barged into her office in her home, when he did so again, Fromm-Reichmann latched the door. She described in her case presentation,

> FFR: He shouted, "So you really think you need protection from me!" He kicked the screen door in with his heel. I closed the wooden door and told the girls to close the other wooden doors which he heard. He took the chair from the front porch and tried to get through the wooden door. In the meantime, we called for some attendants to help. As he saw them coming, he went down the porch and took the chair and battered it against the house, not against the windows.

Fromm-Reichmann and the patient continued to work together. After a phase in which he was regularly in cold wet–sheet pack for the sessions, the man gradually became calmer and more social. As he came to trust Fromm-Reichmann enough to reveal the secret that he hallucinated—and then to work on analyzing the meaning of these hallucinations—he developed increasing insight into, and partial resolution of, his paranoid psychosis.

The next two clinical examples illustrate the very rapid and profound changes in therapeutic technique that occurred between 1945 and 1955, changes which are still evolving but not as easily evaluated when one is in the midst of them. In the mid-1940s, she presented her work with a woman who had been chronically psychotic and then profoundly apathetic; she had made a very impressive partial recovery during her two years of work with Fromm-Reichmann. At that point, the patient guided Fromm-Reichmann through a shared reading of Emily Dickinson's poetry, after which she was able to share past efforts of her own and then resume writing poetry. Fromm-Reichmann sent the patient's poetry, with the patient's permission, to Conrad Aiken, who said, "I think the girl has undoubted ability." He had carefully annotated her poetry as to quality and poetic rationality.

When it seemed to Fromm-Reichmann that the patient experienced all this as a straying too far from a doctor-patient relationship, she purposefully told the patient she had been keeping process notes on their work together and would review these with her whenever the patient felt ready. The patient declined, but the two of them did a careful and lucid outlining of the pivotal features of the patient's history and of their work together. Fromm-Reichmann summarized the lively staff discussion by saying,

> I remember when, maybe one year and a half ago, Sullivan and I weren't much acquainted and he did not know much about my work, I told him about this patient and he felt called upon to say something like, "But your life should not depend on whether your patients get well or not." And I laughed and said, "Well, what do you think? I try what I can and if she doesn't get well, she doesn't get well." And he said with a great sigh of relief, "Oh, then it is all right what you are doing."

Ten years later, in the closing remarks concerning a re-covered schizophrenic, Fromm-Reichmann had been asked how she coped with a patient who seemed so awesome in her potential. She said,

> FFR: As I told some of you when she first came, this girl reminded me of myself as a young child. She was ov-ergrown, I was always too short. She was too fat, I was too fat. And as a little girl, I used to wear my hair the way she did. I think somehow that helped me to develop a very warm countertransference. Then too, I had a mother who was very proud if her daughters would develop as best they could all the talents which mother didn't have, but she didn't do it well. She got competitive. So, as long as I can think, I have done better along those lines. About ten years ago, I treated a young boy who knew the whole American and English literature and I caught myself being terrifically in-hibited in working with him because at times he looked down on me. I didn't know what books he was referring to. . . . I discussed that with Dr. Sullivan and I think getting this kind of thing very clearly into focus with that boy helped me with this girl. . . . Now here is the first one in my 40 years of doing therapy who I think was not obsessional but schizophrenic and I think it is wise to work more intensely on *how* we know, who is *not* schizophrenic now. That means so much to me to have a brand-new professional experience at my present stage of life.
>
> [In another conference on this same patient, she said,] It is an intense satisfaction to help that girl grow up to be better endowed than I am. Then I think I have done well in the way I would have liked to teach my mother to do, in fact, I have tried to, in her way of handling my younger sisters. Then the problem would come now after all, be it competitive? Sure, that girl is incredibly well endowed. If you ask me, I am pleased about every new accomplishment that I see in her and I believe it is true maybe for both reasons which I give. It is a little like a noncompetitive mother figure. And also it is very exciting to me.

It was interesting that with this patient she very scrupulously avoided any involvement in nonanalytic reading of the patient's poetry and acknowledged the change in her own technique, contrasting it herself with the case I mentioned previously. Her style of work changed over the two decades here, and, as with Freud, she demonstrated an extraordinary ability to remain flexible and not locked into a loyalty to a formerly cherished approach. Over the years she gradually involved herself less in the events of her patients' lives, and was less actively interpretive in the sessions. The analytic directives had become increasingly internalized, and her supervisory comments in the conferences indicated that she had succeeded in conveying this approach to the staff as well.

Areas of special interest

Fromm-Reichmann was a researcher and she continually suggested areas for further study, noting, for instance, our lack of data on who should work with whom and our inability to predict outcome. She observed:

> FFR: I can only repeat time and again as we discuss these things, that . . . many times, the patients we think have the very bad prognosis make it sometimes, and those about whom we think it will go quickly don't make it. That is, we do not yet know, first, what therapy can do, and we do not yet know what all the other therapeutic elements are doing which work in the hospital. Of course, gradually, we have to learn to have some prognostic ideas.

Fromm-Reichmann thought this issue could be approached by studying therapists' discouragements with particular patients. She urged the therapist, when the work began to get into trouble, immediately to begin making detailed process notes and to obtain supervision, whose helpfulness she repeatedly emphasized. In one conference, she stated,

> FFR: One thing that came very clearly out in our work together is the significance of supervision—not because of what the supervisor may have to offer, but for the very fact that the privacy of two is changed into a relationship of three. There is the danger we have in entire privacy with a psychotic patient even more than with a neurotic; this is

broken through because we put in front whatever has gone on.

She repeatedly observed that when a therapist sought supervision on a case, his or her anxiety diminished as understanding increased. This was *then* followed by diminution of anxiety and hostility in the patient.

Fromm-Reichmann embarked on her own research project in group therapy with caution, meeting with six female patients who had not responded to individual therapy. Two talked; the others were mute, initially "expressing themselves, if things went well, exclusively with gestures, [otherwise] with urinating on the floor or laughing to themselves." Morris Schwartz, author, with Al Stanton, of *The Mental Hospital* (1954), was the group's observer and kept process notes. All six patients showed evidence of improvement, and there were many gratifying examples of group relatedness.

In 1950, Fromm-Reichmann's pivotal contributions to the staff discussions resulted in the formation of the small groups, an idea which had originally been introduced by Robert Cohen. These groups consisted of seven doctors who met twice weekly, with no set agenda, to discuss whatever clinical matter seemed most urgent or interesting, the groups keeping the same membership for about four years. This system still continues at the Lodge and is a cherished feature of the work week. Fromm-Reichmann had also been among those instrumental in the organization, in 1948, of study groups which focused on particular topics. One of these groups, headed by Robert Cohen, reported in 1949 on their study of countertransference. In the discussion that followed, Fromm-Reichmann commented:

> FFR: Freud originally took as countertransference the reaction of the therapist to the patient which was not rationally called for by what the patient said or did, in or outside of his "transference reaction" with the analyst. Then he called countertransference *repetitional* reactions with the patient of the doctor . . . [of his] difficulties with his parental figures. . . . What you add here is what I think what Freud meant too, but it wasn't mentioned in so many words, that the *security operation* (Sullivan, 1954, p. 102) following

from these irrational "countertransference" reactions should be included in the concept. When we call it countertransference, it means it has its irrational factors stemming from other experiences of the doctor in early life or later. . . . leading up to *parataxic distortions* (Sullivan, 1940, p. 92).

There are some interesting data about that, incidentally. If it's true that each symptom is an expression of an innerness of which the patient wants to get rid, but also the symptom is a means of warding off more serious things, namely, anxiety, then by virtue of the therapeutic process, we are simultaneously the friend and the enemy of the patient. We are the friend of that part in the patient which wants to get rid of [that] innerness and we are the enemy of that part which needs symptoms to defend itself. I believe that in our great effort to see the single experience in terms of transference and countertransference reactions, we are a little in danger to forget that it is due to the dynamic bipolarity of symptomatology, an equally inevitable bipolarity in the reaction of the patient to the doctor and in the reaction of the doctor to the patient.

She was constantly alert to evidence of *unconscious* anxiety in the therapist, as is illustrated in the following vignette in which she deals firmly with the therapist, and conveys a sense of how she might have been similarly firm with the patient:

FFR: I feel there is something in her making you uncomfortable because . . . you didn't mention the word "anxiety." That is, you must have been somehow preoccupied and therefore at least not alert to conveying to us that behind all of this is a terrific anxiety. I would be very interested to know what other females were in her childhood. I have the feeling that she not so much wants to be a man and identify with father as she would like to be a female if she would know how, but she doesn't know how, has never learned how, and would therefore be afraid of it. I have a feeling that when she expresses all of her dependent needs on you, one might say, "What makes her so afraid of this dependency and why can't she fully express it, and why does she need it? Where is her anxiety there?" And where is her anxiety, if this woman with her very good intellectual equipment, can't listen? Is it also because she is being preoccupied with being threatened to death about that which you may tell her?

So, I think there are the two problems: the terrific uncertainty first about what is male and female because father fulfilled the motherly needs on the one hand, and a longing for being female which she doesn't know how. I hear her all the time driven by anxiety and I would think if one would take that fully into account, the difficulty Mary was talking about would also not be quite so terrific.

If you know that you are dealing with somebody who, as Margaret [Rioch, psychologist, who had reported on psychological testing of the patient] told us is pretty near the border of panic, I believe I would forget my own anxiety and discomfort, because I would get thoroughly preoccupied with "How can I relieve the anxiety of the other?" Therefore, from there I find it easier to deal with all the defenses you have told us about. For instance, "I would like to be friendly the way Father was, but I can't because I am not a man. I would like to be a female, but so help us, I would not like to be incapable as Mother was. I would like to listen to you, but I can't because you are telling me something which makes me more frightened, or that I am so preoccupied with warding off panic that I can't listen to you."

I would like to offer one more suggestion. Could it be that a patient who asks for so much, for such a tremendous amount of what she should get and what she has to get, what she didn't get, is really talking about her great distress about her sense of inability to ever give? I think she is. I think this woman is alert to knowing that here she runs around and is not ever to give anything to anybody. I think it is part of her complaint. . . . Would you say that we can say something like, "No matter what you didn't get as a baby, it cannot be made up at the present time, and that we can only get it if we give. Baby time is the only time that we get without giving, and unfortunately it is over and it can't be made up."

The following vignette illustrates that Fromm-Reichmann's supervisory commentary was not limited to the therapist then presenting his or her work.

Staff doctor: I was wondering about Frieda's remark which I've heard many times that a schizophrenic is confused not about his sex, but rather, confused as to how to play it, what position to take; because I never saw one that was confused about his sex.

FFR: I can't remember any schizophrenic where I couldn't see that.

Dr: I was wondering how they express it. How do you know that they're confused about their sex, or whether it is confusion about the role to play in various situations.

FFR: It is expressed very differently, of course, depending on the patient and the type of exchange you have with them and how articulate or not articulate he is. With many of them it is expressed, "Am I lovable or am I not lovable? And if I were a girl or a boy, would I be more acceptable?" And then in terms of the childhood history. That is one thing, and of course, we need to find out what is behind that terrible concern about being acceptable or not, or being able to perform or not. Problems of ability to accomplish or perform have sexual elements in it.

Dr: I took your statement to mean though that they didn't know what sex they were. Now, what you said then was the same thing I did.

FFR: Well, I think you could say that you find it in all degrees, not knowing, being very doubtful as to whether or not they are acceptable, having the fantasy then if they are doubtful, "Maybe I could try to be the other way around," and then being mixed up about the difference between fantasy and reality, which gets lost.

She focused on the patient's anxiety when listening to *administrative* decision-making as well as in listening to therapists' work. For example,

FFR: Does the patient, when he gets encouragement and permission to do something like going to the library, go into a panic because he can't stand the library, or is it sometimes because he gets terribly frightened because [he feels] we don't know how sick he is? I've had the feeling with [a patient of mine], when she made her first attempt to go on the outside, that she would become severely sick because it meant [to her that] I might have lost sight of how sick she was, and that her panic states were not the response to what she did, but the response to the actual or alleged error in judgment on the part of her doctor.

Fromm-Reichmann demonstrated her skill in working with dreams in another conference, stressing the danger that the analyst can see himself or herself in these dreams to too great an extent. The therapist had lost sight of the dreams as conveying unresolved difficulties from the past, or with others in the patient's current life. Fromm-Reichmann stressed that this danger related closely to guilt feeling in the therapist, which put the work in jeopardy, as the therapist would then feel a need to atone for previous errors.

There were examples of her impressively focusing on the central transference dynamic, which had been overlooked by the therapist and administrator. In one such instance, the therapist had endured a prolonged, silent, withholding regression of an obsessional schizophrenic who had, early in their work, seemed to show great promise. He had seen the patient's facial expression as continually hostile, while another therapist had seen it as grief-stricken. Fromm-Reichmann joined in the discussion with the question:

> FFR: Has he brothers?
> Therapist: He has one brother. The patient has two older sisters, and had a younger brother who died of peritonitis when he was nine and the patient thirteen. This brother had been by far the most outgoing, spontaneous, gifted and attractive of the children. The patient had told me he felt very much glossed over by the family.
> FFR: Do you think that much that has gone on with you may be, especially where there is anger or jealousy, is a transfer from that brother who it seems first was a menace because he did away with his being the only son after four years, then because he was more alive, and then because he became glorified as a dead brother? I would think it might, all the more because I think there is one funny factor regarding your relationship. He faintly resembles you, and I would wonder what that means in his relationship with you. He could very well be your brother.

This came through as a stunning insight elucidating the therapeutic impasse, and was done in a way that would free the therapist to make maximal use of his then potentially liberated empathy.

While we have emphasized Fromm-Reichmann's remarks concerning the treatment of patients suffering from schizophrenia, we want to add that she spoke often about manic-depressive psychosis. She organized a long-term study and research group. It is especially important to keep its findings in mind in an era when we too readily imagine that lithium has somehow eradicated the illness.

> FFR: Well, the manic-depressive, when you ask him about incidents in his personal life, will either evade it or will say that he doesn't know anything about it, whereas the schizophrenic *will*, if he can communicate, even though very mute and very symbolic about it. He will give you information about it because he is accustomed to thinking about it and has grown up in an environment toward which he is very hostile or ambivalent or which was very hostile or ambivalent [toward him], but which was very concerned about the child and themselves. Whereas with the manic-depressives, they are so concerned that everybody lives up to the Joneses and that the environment accepts them, they have much less real acquaintance with, and therefore very little ability to communicate about, their own problems. . . . I think that it is quite interesting that we have the feeling that we do not have enough information from and about the family. It's a feeling that we will always have about the manic-depressive because the information is so superficial and stereotyped that even if we talked with all of them, we still have the feeling that we have so little information about the background.

Vignette Categories

The twenty categories into which we organized Fromm-Reichmann's remarks included statements regarding the evolution of a philosophy of treatment; specific hospital techniques and research projects; remarks regarding signs, symptoms, and diagnoses; therapists' styles, aspects of which have already been covered. Finally, what became the fullest categories were those under the headings of Fromm-Reichmann's style of supervision in conferences. A particular quotation would often be indexed in two or more categories.

We listed fourteen rather loose and somewhat overlapping types of supervisory comments, which could be consolidated to the following, listed in decreasing order of frequency. By far the most frequent were Fromm-Reichmann's suggestions, which were usually very practical and based on her personal knowledge of the patient. She also frequently theorized and interpreted, or clarified areas of confusion in a presentation. On many occasions, she taught by example, sometimes drawing on her own experiences either with the particular patient being presented or with one of her own patients, and sometimes drawing on the work of her colleagues, especially Harry Stack Sullivan. Less frequently, Fromm-Reichmann played detective, asking increasingly specific questions of the presenting therapist. In other types of interactions, she sometimes linked remarks of the therapist with another staff member's contribution; she was sometimes confrontative; she was sometimes simply supportive. The smallest category of supervisory comments was "humorous."

Conclusion

Fromm-Reichmann was profoundly dedicated to a belief in the ability of analytic insight to transform a person's life through the resolution of anxiety. She assumed a similar fortitude in her colleagues and dignified them through that assumption, interrogating them while implicitly believing that they too wanted their own defensive patterns to be revealed and then resolved. Fromm-Reichmann felt strongly that schizophrenic patients respond well to, and even require, clear administrative statements. While she did not say so, it seemed to us that she felt that therapists and administrators needed such clearly stated directives as well, and she *treated* them accordingly. She was absolutely even-handed in her statements to the male or female staff members, but seemed to bristle at defensiveness and to attack vehemently masochism and self-blaming.

She aggressively and positively searched for the unconsciously hidden truth, sometimes patiently waiting, at other times actively seeking. While remembered for her tact and politeness, she still maintained that false gentleness and reassurance are really despicable and destructive. Her alertness to the vicissitudes of manifestations of anxiety informed perhaps every comment she made, and formed the core of her helpfulness, a helpfulness that has been so powerful that we are still expressing our gratitude over thirty years after her death. Reading these charts, we found Fromm-Reichmann's comments impressing upon us yet again that while we may prescribe medications, we, as therapists, administrators, or other hospital personnel, are psychoactive agents. Whether things are going wrong, or, more challengingly, when they seem to be going along well enough, we must always be working, whether in a listening or an interpreting mode, with a psychoanalytic *directedness*, defining the patient's patterns of defenses, formulating what they seem to be defending against, and being continually alert to that which is being stirred in *us*.

> The general psychodynamic conception that anxiety plays a central role in all mental illnesses and that mental symptoms in general may be understood simultaneously as an expression of and as a defense against anxiety and its underlying conflicts holds, regardless of the severity of the picture of illness and regardless of its more or less dramatic character. Hence we make the exploration of the dynamic roots of the schizophrenic's anxieties our potential goal through all phases of illness [Fromm-Reichmann, 1959, p. 195].

References

Fromm-Reichmann, F. (1950), *Principles of Intensive Psychotherapy*. Chicago: University of Chicago Press.
——— (1959), *Psychoanalysis and Psychotherapy*. Chicago: University of Chicago Press.
Stanton, A., & Schwartz, M. (1954), *The Mental Hospital*. New York: Basic Books.

Sullivan, H. S. (1940), *Conceptions of Modern Psychiatry*. New York: Norton.
———— (1954), *The Psychiatric Interview*. New York: Norton.

2

RECOLLECTIONS OF SUPERVISION WITH FRIEDA FROMM-REICHMANN

CLARENCE G. SCHULZ, M.D.

This case is selected as an overall report of treatment from its beginning to its termination.

This patient was a chronically disturbed schizophrenic in his mid-twenties when he was admitted for treatment as a transfer from another hospital. His illness had begun twenty months previously with a sudden catatonic excitement marked by assaultiveness and destructiveness. He was a single man, who lived at home and worked as a chemist for a large firm. About three months prior to the onset of his illness, the patient had become engaged. His mother voiced some objection, because the girl's religion was different from that of his family. The evening of the day that the patient had become engaged, he wet his bed. He seemed upset, but his parents assured him that the religious difference was of no consequence. Two weeks prior to his initial hospitalization, the engagement was made official, and the patient began to voice uncertainties about marriage. He implied that he felt unequal to it. Suddenly one Sunday morning, he became quite disturbed. He wrapped a bookend in newspaper and threw it up against the wall, broke some windowpanes, and became so upset that the police were called.

He was admitted to a state hospital where he received a total of 23 electroshock treatments, 85 insulin treatments, and 22 combined treatments. He also had some group psychotherapy. Any improvement noted was only of brief duration.

The case for this supervision was fully described in *Case Studies in Schizophrenia*. Permission to reproduce portions of it was granted by Basic Books, Inc.

In the description given of him at the state hospital, "his affect continued hostile, angry and explosive, boisterous and assaultive. His conversation was arrogant, profane, defiant, and obscene, with bizarre nonsensicalities." It was at this point that the state hospital psychiatrist recommended transorbital lobotomy. The family obtained a consultant who recommended transfer to another hospital with a psychotherapy program. At that hospital, the patient experienced continued prolonged disturbed periods and was placed in a seclusion room. Attempts were made at individual therapy and electroshock treatment was used. It was during this second hospitalization that his fiancée broke their engagement upon the suggestion of the medical staff. The staff believed that she was maintaining her relationship with him only out of a sense of guilt. His disturbance made him unmanageable. It required eight male attendants to move the patient from the seclusion room to the bathroom. After a period of twenty months of assaultiveness, destructiveness, and psychotic disorganization, his continued disturbance finally led to his transfer to the treatment program about to be described. In order to enable the transfer to be carried out, he received shock treatment on the two days prior to his transfer.

BACKGROUND AND EARLY TREATMENT

The patient was the only surviving one of three children. His father was a hard-working, quiet man who had very little to do with his son when he was growing up. His mother, however, was very interested in him throughout his life. She emerged in the historical account as a much more emotional, guilt-ridden, and terribly involved parent than the patient's father. Prior to the patient's birth, an older sister, aged four, was killed. As she alighted from a bus with her mother, a car struck her and killed her instantly. This had a lasting effect on the mother, who dealt with the accident by declaring it to be unmentionable within the family. The patient was born two years after this accident. It was his mother's stated intention that he was to be perfect in order to make up for what she thought was her fault in the death of her firstborn child. When the patient was two-and-a-half years old, a younger brother was born. The brother, like the patient, was very precocious but tended to be much more friendly and popular with people. When the patient was in his third year of college, his brother was killed in a skiing accident. Again, his mother was very shaken, but the patient showed little reaction. He felt that since it was so upsetting to his mother, he had to protect her by retaining his own composure. When the patient was small, he fulfilled the mother's expectations in many ways. He developed quite early. Although his mother thought that he was inclined to be a rather placid child, she considered him to be quite independent. To illustrate this, she described an incident that occurred when he was left alone with a baby-sitter. When the parents returned, they found that the sitter was asleep and that the young child was amusing himself. She gave the following description of him: "We never thought that he was emotional. We thought, on the other hand, that he was phlegmatic. He went along all the time. I never saw him lose his temper. He was never depressed. He seemed to be the same all the time. I never saw him express anger—never in his life. Never in all his life did he give any evidence of having a bad disposition. He was conciliatory. He greeted me every morning with 'I have the best little mother in the world.' "

The two boys were guided in the direction of nonhazardous play and games because of the mother's feeling of responsibility for the death of the sister. While the patient did play with other children in the neighborhood, he did not develop any close relationship with any particular boy. He did very well scholastically. In high school, when he found that he could not excel in athletics, he turned to chess, at which he became extremely proficient. Even though the patient enjoyed frequent dating, his brother seemed to be more naturally popular with girls. His father felt that he dated mainly to impress other people with his popularity rather than from any genuine interest in the girl herself.

He went away to college and telephoned his mother almost daily at her request. He was at the top of his class in college and was active in fraternity life. The middle of his college period was interrupted by two years of compulsory military service, which was uneventful. He had one passive participation in a homosexual experience while in service and no heterosexual genital experience at all, although opportunities were available. His brother was killed after the patient's return from the service. Because his brother's death left him as the only remaining child, he turned down two postgraduate fellowships that would have taken him away from home. Instead, he remained at home, worked at his job during the day, and attended graduate school in the evenings. About a year before the onset of his illness, he had his first serious romance. While his parents were away on vacation, he broke off his relationship with his first fiancée without, as far as they knew, any apparent reaction.

At the time of his admission to the hospital, partly because of his psychotic disorganization but also as a result of the shock treatment, he showed considerable confusion and retardation. His responses were quite fragmentary. He was careless about his dress and appearance. Physically, he was tall, thin, and rather gaunt-looking.

The treatment program, which lasted for a period of four years, was divided into an acutely disturbed period lasting five months followed by a postpsychotic period. During the latter, he reorganized along the lines of obsessive-compulsive defenses. At first, these defenses largely excluded feelings, but with subsequent psychotherapy, the feelings became much more accessible to him.

In spite of this patient's degree of disturbance, fragmentation, and threatening assaultiveness, he showed flashes of a sense of humor and seemed to be rather well-liked by the female nursing personnel. From the beginning, when he came to talk with me, he was extremely suspicious. He felt that the hospital was wired for television and that everything was being recorded. He questioned me and I gave information about myself in brief answers. Somewhere toward the end of our first appointment, he said, "I've told you enough. I've told you more than I've told anybody." I felt rather encouraged. In the second interview, when I was trying to set up a treatment arrangement with him, he protested, saying that I was not friendly enough. Then, a few sentences later, he asked what the schedule would be. I wrote one out on a piece of paper and handed it to him.

During the initial phase, we had many battles in which he

would slam the door in my face or throw a chair at me. Sometimes, he would barricade his door. I approached him from the standpoint that there must be reasons for his behavior, and I thought we could talk it over. At one time during this early period, I had him placed in a wet sheet pack. He fought this procedure. The only thing he said when he was in the pack was to ask, "Is this your king of clubs?" For the next few days, about the best I could do was to sit outside his door while he remained aloof. At other times, I would sit at the end of the hall in an area adjacent to where he was sitting. If there were other people around, we both seemed comfortable enough to exchange a few words. He was fairly persistent in offering me cigarettes, even though I do not smoke. I answered some of his questions, each time trying to find out why he wanted to have the information. When the questions became too personal, I declined to answer.

In a session three weeks after beginning treatment, I came to his room and found him nude except for a piece of cloth wrapped around his thigh. He was sitting on the bed. He was pushing the edge of a post card against the base of his penis and smoking vigorously. I asked him what this was about. He said very little but did say something about being a "devil worshiper." I asked if he felt that his penis got him into trouble, and he said it did. A few minutes later, he threw his cigarette at me. I jumped up, stamped it out, and told him how much this annoyed me and that we would have to do something about his violence. I said that I thought that if he couldn't control himself, he should ask for a wet sheet pack. His reply was, "Alright, give me a pack now." Aides were called in, and he cooperated with the pack. In my attempt to continue the discussion about his being a devil worshiper, I asked why he wanted to castrate himself, and he said, "because of bastards like you." Following that, it was necessary to pack him on only one occasion for a treatment hour. At that time, he requested it himself. Usually when I saw him and felt somewhat frightened of him, I would ask him if he felt that he should ask for a pack. He would often quiet down after that and cause me very little difficulty. At one of the sessions, he initially refused to see me. Then he said, "Give me a half hour to think it over." I read a newspaper for a half hour and then reapproached him. As he came out of his room with his food tray, he gestured as if he were going to throw it at me. Instead, he handed it over to the aide and met with me for the remaining time.

After the first month of these verbal and sometimes physical attacks on me, he complained that the treatment would never work and that it was impossible. I replied by saying that I thought it was rather early to come to any conclusive opinons about it. He then surprised me by asking me what my opinion was of him. I replied, "Well, you impress me as a person who must be terribly burdened by all this resentment and hostility that you're carrying around; that you're suspicious of anyone if they take an interest in you; but I think you're a pretty bright person, and you seem to have a capacity for relating to somebody. This is all pretty general, but it is about as much as I can say now. What do you think?" He said, "Well, that's all true. Another thing I found that if you're ever happy, then people can take advantage of you." I felt very good about this interchange. In the subsequent period, he began to tell me how he felt depressed and suicidal. After an instance when he threw some fruit juice on me and I took this up with him, he said, "Well, did you ever think that I might be as frightened of you as you are of me?" Actually, I had not realized this, and with this having been stated, there was much less fear on both sides. The fighting decreased noticeably.

Seven weeks after we started, the patient had been complaining quite a bit about having no privacy and about people barging in on him. He would be masturbating, and the aides would come in with a tray. There would be fights around this in which he would kick people and complain about living in a goldfish bowl.

At that time, the parents visited. At the end of the visit, his father was urging his mother to begin their drive home. She said, "I would like to stay with him forever." She wept and pleaded, "Oh, if he would only get better, if he'd only get better I would take cancer if he would only get well." She had a sheaf of papers that she had removed from his desk. These contained some writings that he had made just prior to the onset of his psychosis. There was something about the way she offered these to me that led me not to accept the papers from her. I felt this would be an intrusion upon some of his private possessions. I declined, saying that if in the future I thought it could be of use, I would ask her for them. In the next appointment with him, I told him that I had met his parents. He asked me what I thought of his mother. I replied, "Well, you know, I think she has a tremendous interest in you and that you might have felt that as a lack of privacy. I wonder if that doesn't carry over here at the hospital when you feel that everybody is barging in on you." At the end of that hour, he shook my hand, and I felt that we were on the right track.

More and more, we began to hear about his feelings of depression. At the same time, his sense of humor began to shine through. On one occasion, I arrived and noticed him holding his ear to the wall and making movements with his face. I asked what the voices were saying. He said, "Oh, I'm not listening to voices, I am watching my two flies, 'Amos' and 'Andy.'" We laughed about this. Then as I pursued the topic, he went ahead to describe his feelings of loneliness and how he felt very suicidal when he was put in seclusion. He then compared his education to mine. He also noticed the kind of car I drove and said that he had a car at home. More and more, he began to relate facts about himself and some of his problems. When I asked him about his brother and sister, he said that he did have a brother who died and quickly added, "I didn't kill him." Some of this information came out in a way that made it difficult to decide whether it was fact or fantasy. He spoke of his mother waking him up every morning and bathing him. According to him, if he started to curse, she would threaten to wash his mouth out with soap. He felt terribly frightened. He thought that she was going to try to drown him. He would say, "Don't, Mother, do you want to kill me, too?" He alleged this would jolt her out of it, and she would cease pressuring him.

He seemed most resentful of the male aides and was much more accepting of female personnel. Even while he was quite upset, one of the nurses was able to take him from the ward to the hospital canteen. He showed steady improvement, became quieter, began dressing, and would go out to activities. He seemed particularly drawn to the student nurses. In the early phases when he was being spoon fed, he in turn would feed the nurse a cracker. He also began helping the student nurse make his bed. When he started going to occupational therapy, he requested instructions in knitting. He would bring his knitting back to the ward and tell the nurse that his mother wanted him to knit. I also noticed that he would imitate some of the behavior, speech, and accents of other patients. On one occasion, he was playing "Chopsticks" as a piano duet with a student nurse. Quite spontaneously, she said that they should be on television. Much to her surprise, he stopped, picked her up, and sat her on top of the television set.

As his behavior began to improve, his psychotic thinking decreased, and he began to report dreams. These dreams contained the identical content that was present in the psychotic period. The delusions were now no longer available during his waking life.

An incident from the treatment that occurred five-and-a-half months after its beginning was especially moving. The patient was still being seen in his room. In this session, he complained that the head nurse from that ward was leaving. This was the nurse who first took him out to the canteen. I had not heard she was leaving and expressed my surprise. I asked where she was going. He said that she was moving to Kansas. He then began to make all kinds of paranoid accusations about the possibility of her spreading information from the nurses' notes to the people out there. Because of her, they would find out about him and so forth. He went on in this manner for a long time, and I listened to him. I remembered how important that nurse was to him. Actually, she felt quite fond of him, and they had had a very good relationship. When his outpouring subsided somewhat, there was a pause, and I said, "You really will miss her, won't you?" With that, the whole paranoid outpouring stopped, and he choked up with tears. He then handed me a *Time* magazine he was holding with the back cover turned toward me. On this cover was a Coca Cola advertisement and a picture of a nurse carrying some charts with the caption, "Always dependable, always reliable." After he stopped crying, he was able to tell me that he wondered whether he had driven her away and how he felt quite responsible for this. He said that once he had playfully rolled up a newspaper and patted her on the head with it as they were going down in the elevator. He wondered whether any of this had caused her to leave to go to Kansas.

Psychological Examination

The first of three psychological examinations was accomplished when the patient had calmed down sufficiently. He was seen in my office about six months following his admission to this hospital. At the time of admission, he had been too disturbed to permit testing. His manner during the tests was very quiet. He did everything he was asked to do with no objections and few questions.

Wechsler-Bellevue Intelligence Scale

The patient's earned I.Q. places him in the bright normal group, but this is obviously not a valid estimate of his capacities. His performance on the subtests varies from far below average (Comprehension and Picture Arrangement) to very superior (Digit Span, Arithmetic, and Block Design).

The patient probably has superior or very superior general intelligence, but his present functioning is impaired by grossly psychotic ways of thinking. His attention and concentration, however, are good, and his ability to solve problems that do not involve human relationships or verbal concept formation is excellent. But his judgment in these latter areas is grossly impaired, and his ability to synthesize or integrate material involving social situations is at present very poor.

	I.Q.		Weighted Scores
Full Scale	112	Arithmetic	16
Verbal Scale	113	Similarities	7
Performance Scale	109	(Vocabulary)	(13)
		P. Arrangement	7
	Weighted Scores	P. Completion	14
Information	13	Block Design	16
Comprehension	5	Object Assembly	10
Digit Span	16	Digit Symbol	8

Rorschach Test and Other Projective Techniques
(Drawing and Four Pictures)

The tests indicate clearly that the patient is grossly psychotic. The schizophrenic process seems to pervade almost all of his experience.

His thinking is confused and highly autistic. His perceptions are distorted. His ability to respond to complex social situations is limited, and his behavior is rather rigidly set.

He is probably constantly preoccupied with defending himself in one form or another against attacks of all kinds. He must experience authority, particularly masculine authority figures, as unreasonable and tyrannical. He has to react either as a slave or as a violent desperate rebel. A third alternative is withdrawal into a private world in which he can secretly make fun of all the nonsense that goes on in the "real" world.

He probably has suffered a great deal from feeling pushed to be manly when he felt quite helpless.

Prognosis

Time before patient can engage in normal life: very long.
Active interest in therapy: weak.
Rigidity of defensive structure: strong.

Middle Phase of Therapy

During this postdisturbed period, he scheduled his life completely. He would go to the library and read fifty pages of the encyclopedia every day. He obtained a college mathematics book and began working on the problems from the beginning of the book all the way through to the end. He had a large number of correspondence chess games going simultaneously, and he drew cartoons for the hospital newspaper. He felt comfortable during this time and had a considerable amount of freedom in the hospital. During his therapy appointments, he would recite his activities in a mechanical fashion without any willingness to explore them. For example, although his cartoons were really quite revealing of his psychopathology, he would say that they were funny—they were just cartoons. I would agree with what he said, but felt that we could also use them to understand him. One cartoon depicted a patient about to step out of an eight-story window. As the patient looked back into the doctor's office, he said, "Thanks very much, you have helped me a lot, doc." In another one, the patient in the doctor's office looks out the window at a policeman approaching the patient's car parked in a no-parking area. The patient in the cartoon comments, "Yes, you're right, doctor, I am worried about something." His dreams were filled with content about gladiators, men hitting each other, and pointing guns at each other. His waking life was largely free of this content except for occasional vague fears of airplanes crashing into the hospital ward or someone shooting him or killing him with an automobile. On the whole, he thought that he had greatly improved and was ready to go back to work. He saw no reason to continue his therapy. There was a strong denial of any need for me, and he resented the cost of treatment. He thought talking into a tape recorder or writing down his thoughts, then tearing up what he had written, would be equally effective. He was glad whenever I took a vacation, because then he didn't have to think up things to say to me. His sessions had the quality of being thoroughly prepared and thought out ahead of time. It was more difficult for him when the appointments were bunched together for several days, because fewer events occurred between our sessions. He might then be caught with a spontaneous thought that he would have to report. He was surprised that after about two weeks when I was away on a vacation, he felt a little upset and wished that he had his appointments. He indicated that he had thoughts that maybe Al Capone would have benefited from having spent time in therapy. "He wouldn't go out and do a job until he had first talked this over with his psychiatrist."

Denial was a prominent feature of our sessions at this time. The patient wondered why, on his admission to the hospital, he had been placed in a ward where he might be injured by those other disturbed patients. I learned that he did not want to tell some of his thoughts, because they were "indecent" or "incoherent." By consistently focusing on instances where he was concealing his thoughts and feelings, dents were made in this move toward a generalized denial. He presented himself as a model patient, one who brought in his dreams and reported the events of the previous twenty-four hours. Such efforts to please me were interpreted as being similar to his attempt to be a model boy for his mother. While he made vigorous efforts at keeping silent about his resentment toward others, I gradually began to hear how he was discovering instances of his rudeness toward some of the hospital personnel. Approaching a markedly obese employee, he commented, "Travel is broadening," and he referred to a stout nurse as "blimpo." Recognizing this in himself, he seemed genuinely astonished, saying, "This isn't like me."

Two general categories of reasons for concealing parts of himself during the hour sessions were: (1) he believed that he could get out of the hospital if he could convince me he was all right; and (2) he was afraid that he might have a harmful effect on me. As a result of our discussions, he made excursions into being more open with me. This openness was at first primarily in the direction of disclosing dreams. One particular dream was concerned with his sexual participation with a mermaid who has helpless, because she had no arms. This theme of the female sexual partner being made helpless became a prominent feature of his later fantasy life, but at this time, it was manifest only in dreams. In the same hour, he was able to tell me that prior to my vacation two months earlier, he had been all set to enjoy not having his hours, but after a week of my vacation, he had felt a longing for the hours. In the next hour, he spoke of another patient whom he considered to be homosexual. He wondered if I thought he was homosexual, because he played chess almost exclusively with men. He described an actual previous homosexual experience of his own and went on to develop the idea that much of his dating was to prove to his fellows that he was not homosexual. He also voiced some of his uncertainty about his ability to perform heterosexually, conveying his feelings of being threatened by heterosexual participation together with his concern that attachment to me would be considered homosexual and therefore unacceptable.

As the time for his move to outpatient living was approaching, we began to see further manifestations of his separation anxiety. He had a dream in which I had asked that he come to his hour twenty minutes early and had said we would have the hour in the hospital building where he was living. He came for the appointment; however, I wasn't there but in the next room.

He left, and I was very angry. Later in the dream, people started throwing stones at him, and he awakened very frightened. During this period of therapy, he made complaints about the high cost of treatment. After returning from a search for a room in town, he remarked how nice and warm his room was in the hospital. In an hour three days before moving out, he appeared to be rather guarded. Upon inquiring, I learned that he was thinking that if he had plans to run away, it would be sabotage to tell me about them. I replied that it would be the wisest thing he could do so that we could understand more about it. He said that I wouldn't care anyway. I would just get another patient. "You didn't know me before a year and a half ago, so you wouldn't care."

He had a dream in which he had to move a huge pile of weights on a cart with ball bearings. In our discussion about the dream, he felt weighted down by responsibility. He had a razor now and must tell himself not to cut his wrist. This led him to tell me about his auditory hallucinations that had occurred a year previously in which women's voices told him to jump out of the window, put his head under water and drown himself, or to castrate himself.

In the next hour, his conflict about therapy was highlighted when he felt no need to be in treatment, but he also had thoughts that it might be a good idea if he could see a doctor for the rest of his life. He questioned his right to continue to see me forever, thereby preventing someone else from seeing me. This brought up a discussion about his brother's appearance on the family scene. He was thus reliving the situation with his mother in which his exclusive relationship with his mother had been shattered by the appearance of his younger brother. The act of moving out of the hospital was a concrete indication to him that our relationship would some day come to an end.

Many of his plans were efforts to achieve independence from other people. His father had always filed the patient's income tax return. The patient became afraid that his father would make a mistake; therefore, he began to make out his own tax return. One feature of chess that appealed to him most of all was that it did not involve a partner. Responsibility for a win or a loss was strictly an individual one. Another example of his attempt to be independent was his plan for dating several girls concurrently so that he did not feel rebuffed if one of them turned him down. When his hospital roommate made him a present of a book, the patient arranged through one of the nurses to reimburse the roommate.

In a discussion of his wish to obtain a job in order to be independent, we discovered that for him independence was in part equated with being masculine, a sign of being more like other people, and a way of not needing his therapist. A warning that we should not be taken in by this came in the form of a dream in which he was acting in a play, "trying to impress some other guy what a good actor I was."

Comparison of Rorschach Tests

The second psychological testing was performed twenty months after the patient's admission. He was retested primarily because his clinical improvement had been very marked, and we were interested to see whether this would be shown on the projective techniques.

On the second test, the diagnostic impression is still clearly that of a manifest schizophrenic psychosis.

The most obvious difference between the two tests is the great increase in number of responses on test no. 2 (36 compared to 15 on test 1). Since the total time has scarcely increased at all (test 1: 22 minutes; test 2: 24 minutes), the larger production on test no. 2 suggests that the patient is freer both to allow associations to arise in his mind and to express them in words.

The second most striking difference is the increased liveliness of the record (Pure F percent on test 1: 87 percent; test 2: 65 percent). The patient seems to be more flexible in his ability to respond to various aspects of the environment. He can let himself go more and put more of himself into his communication with others.

In this process of increased communicativeness, one gets a clearer picture on the second test of the paranoid quality of the patient's thinking. This is shown particularly as a need to fit every aspect of a situation into an arbitrarily chosen "meaning" with a strongly autistic flavor. Whereas on the first test the patient's mental process might be called "blocked" and "disintegrated," putting things together, but the organizing principle is inadequate. This shows up in several ways: (1) he forces things together without developing a significant relationship; (2) he seems to think he has formed an integrated structure when all he has actually done is a series of isolated entities loosely strung together; (3) if it suits his emotional needs to form a causal or logical connection between two entities, he does not exercise any objective critique about forming such a connection but simply does it arbitrarily. This last point may be obscured by a tendency toward expressions of self-doubt and self-criticism, but these are often badly misplaced.

The prognosis was fair. It was made solely on the basis of his test, disregarding, insofar as possible, knowledge of the patient's actual progress.

Therapy Completed

Two years after beginning treatment, the patient enrolled in a postgraduate course at a local university. This enabled him to continue keeping himself busy in an effort to avoid feelings. However, sexual feeling and feelings of depression would intrude into his awareness. In therapy, the emphasis continued to be on pointing out his defenses, such as his first effort to prevent the experience of rebuff by first rejecting the other person. For example, he told a student nurse he had been seeing that he would not miss her when she completed her affiliation and had to return to her home school.

At this time, there was evidence of his identification with me. The patient began to interpret some dreams of a student nurse and commented on how easy it was to be a therapist. He offered to see my patients for me if I became ill.

As a result of consistently focusing on his defenses against feelings together with his more active dating experiences, the patient began to be more aware of sexual feelings. Concurrently, he had a series of dreams involving violence. As he reported his associations, I noticed the sequence of topics involving sexual feelings and violence as illustrated in the following examples. On one occasion, he was commenting on how satisfying his life was at the present time. He had everything—an apartment, a car, a television set, school, cats, girlfriends, chess, and "even my hours." The only thing missing that he would have in marriage was sexual intercourse at regular intervals. From there, he began to wonder if anyone would care for his cats in the event that something would happen to him. "Supposing I should be killed in a car wreck? Would the police go to my apartment and feed the cats?" In another hour, he had been referring to an episode of necking with a girl. Immediately following this, he mentioned that he heard an airline advertisement on the radio. A plane belonging to this airline was bombed by a youth whose mother was a passenger.

I summarize a session in detail in order to illustrate the patient's growing awareness of feelings toward me. This session occurred two-and-one-half years after the onset of the treatment. In the first part of the hour, he described a number of his recent activities. He had purchased a rug with money he had received as his veteran's disability compensation. He allowed himself to buy the rug, because it was the government's money, not his. He had had some difficulty in cashing the check, because he did not have an account with a bank. He had also been busy working on his chess game. He described a letter he had written to his girlfriend in which he had been careful not to mention people so that she would be likely to do the same, and he would thereby avoid hearing about the other boyfriends. They had planned not to see each other for six months, and he wanted to tell her not to go with other boys. There then followed a description of how he had consistently used a certain chess opening in order to become proficient with its use. The only problem about this was that the opponents study your opening, prepare their defense, and "lay in wait for you." After this, he mentioned a number of disappointing experiences: a correspondence chess opponent had taken back a move; his television aerial was broken, and he had a makeshift solution by leading a wire to a screen; he burned his hand grasping a hot pot while absentmindedly clasping a potholder in the other hand; and he had broken a bottle while trying to dissolve powdered milk on the stove using inadequate utensils.

After hearing this report of self-destructive behavior, I asked whether he was mad about something, but there was no answer. I added, "Possibly your girlfriend?" No reply. I asked why he made it so difficult for himself. He then compared his apartment with my office, pointing out that it was just as well-equipped. I said that I didn't attempt to prepare meals here. This seemed to get nowhere, so I switched abruptly and said, "If you are content, that is the important thing." He then enumerated many of the discontents he felt about his present life.

After this, he recited his version of a "Fight Song," which he had planned to enter in his college's song contest. This song made reference to scratching out somebody's eyes and similar expressions of anger; he was not aware of the implications of this at the time.

He then told of a dream in which the usher in a theater had shot him in the right hip while the usher was in a gun battle with another man. A girl was also shot. When the patient came out of the theater, he saw Hitler and Mussolini in a car. The patient then hailed a German taxi, which would not wait for him.

In his association to this dream, he told of his father's warning that he might be shot by mistake if he came home late at night. This was apropos their discussions about a prominent family in which the wife accidentally shot her husband. I pointed out that he had felt threatened in the dream. He said that automobiles threatened him; they may run him down. I wondered aloud about a previous discussion of gun-equals-penis. He thought that sounded homosexual but said nothing further about it. He pointed out that my name was German and that the taxi that would not wait for him was equivalent to my ignoring a packet of letters he had given me to read. These were letters he had written to his parents while he was in service.

He spoke of my plans to cut down my case load of patients in order to take on more administrative work and added, "You may take over all the administration, and I will not be seeing you at all any more." I said, "I guess that does threaten you." There was a pause, and he asked, "Would you like a Life Saver?" I accepted it from him. He said that the idea that he was homosexual was farfetched.

He continued by saying he didn't like losing in chess to T. As he pointed out, this person had the same last name as his fiancée (at the time of his breakdown), and he added, "I lost to her." I questioned what he meant by losing to her. Hadn't he lost her? He explained that maybe he said "lost to her" out of his feeling that she left him, because he was something terrible and that she had won by not being married to him but to someone else.

I suggested that being emotionally close to a man may be something he thought of as "homosexual" or "bad." He said that he had lived in fraternities and had male friends, but he liked to "size up a guy" before being friends with him or before becoming closely related to him. "He may take a poke at me." That was the end of the hour.

It is my impression that in this hour he became aware of feeling threatened by a positive attachment to me, which he felt might bring harm to me (as indicated by his offer of a Life Saver) or harm to him (as indicated by his need to "size up a guy"). His labeling the attachment "homosexual" was giving it a culturally disapproved stamp, which would account for his feeling of being threatened.

Toward the latter part of the third year of treatment and on into the fourth and final year, the themes of dependency and castration anxiety became especially vivid.

In the beginning of an hour during the end of the third year of his treatment, he asked why I had become interested in psychiatry. I did not answer his question; rather, I asked for his thoughts in connection with the question. He spoke of having read in the *Wall Street Journal* that engineering and business administration were two of the top three professions in demand. When he did not receive an answer from me, he complained that another patient's analyst talked about himself. I replied that he must feel left out of my life. The patient then said, "You cannot like somebody unless you get to know him." I asked what he wanted to know. His next associations had to do with money, and his impression that I went into psychiatry because it "pays well." After some comments that psychiatry was "inefficient," because it could not be adapted to assembly-line methods, he focused on his concern about his own career. He had forgotten much of his chemistry and had doubts about his business course. As he put it, he felt he was "inbetween—like a dog who chases two rabbits and doesn't catch either one." I then said that maybe his question was whether or not he wanted to be in business. The patient then described how he had selected accounting as his major when his advisor, in listing a series of possibilities, remarked that he probably wouldn't want accounting. The patient's impulsive choice was based on a negative reaction to his advisor's suggestion. Such a negative choice was also evident in the transference.

An example of negativism in the transference occurred when he avoided eating meat altogether for two weeks after I suggested a more balanced diet to correct a digestive disturbance he was having at the time. In this hour, he related a dream during which he was threatened by a steak knife. In his associations, he described the movie *Carousel*, in which a man fell on his own knife. After this, he revealed his own concern that he might cut himself with his butcher knife. Here, the elements of self-destruction, or more accurately, destruction of an introjected mother, continued to be present in a dissociated way. Subsequent examples will show the extent to which such impulses were acted out and then integrated.

In the next hour the following day, the conflict of his doing something for what he wanted out of it as opposed to his need to oblige others was prominent. He had wanted to purchase a mechanical rabbit for his cats to play with and thought that this was "silly." He then thought that if he wanted it, he ought to get it, remarking, "That is what mother would say." He described a television program about parents who expected their children to do well in school and how this was parallel to his own situation. He spoke of his talking this way as "junk." After this, he told of writing letters to keep on good terms with the people to whom he was writing and that the contents of this letters was a waste of time. There were additional examples of his conflict about wanting something and having to pay the price for it. To him, the dreams he was reporting and the things he had to say seemed without value. The implication was clear that in these hours, he felt he was not getting anything out of it for himself.

I summarized the instances in which money and paying a price were a concern: (1) in his dream in which he had to pay to see a girl; (2) in his concern about how much it will cost to go on a date; (3) in how he paid to see me; and (4) in his concern about the cost of the things he wanted. I went on to point out the way in which he thought in terms of money as a way of avoiding any personal feelings about another person. By "paying," he freed himself from any obligation. I reminded him of the example where he had paid his roommate for the gift of a book. This was part of the way in which feelings of dependency could be avoided. Money became an insulation from emotional attachment to people.

The third hour in this series occurred just before the patient was to leave for a weekend visit with his parents. He had been speaking about his girlfriends and his thought that maybe he was looking for something impossible—an ideal woman. While talking about his engagement and his first admission to the hospital, he remarked, "I don't see any reason for going to the hospital, frankly." I asked if he was now ready to get some information about how he got into the hospital. He seemed reluctant about asking his parents, thinking that this might lead to a discouraging talk, and he didn't want to go through it now. Then after a pause, "Maybe it's best." I asked, "Is there some feeling that as long as you don't find out how you got into the hospital, it will not matter?" He replied, "I don't think I can stand it." I asked, "What do you envisage?" He answered, "Suppose they said that a week before you threatened to kill yourself. It would be very degrading and humiliating. They wouldn't want to tell me, and I wouldn't want to hear it." The discussion then centered around how, in the past, his mother would break down at the mention of his brother's death and how the family could not talk about his sister's death. Thus, he was identifying with his mother's apparent fragility when he thought of himself as being unable to face a discussion about a tragic event in his own life.

In the hour following his weekend visit home, he described his conversation with his mother. Instead of learning that they wanted to break up his approaching marriage, he heard about his own doubts concerning marriage. His mother tearfully related the events leading up to his hospitalization. On one occasion, he had said he would wash the dishes, but when she volunteered to help, he became angry and said he didn't want any help and threatened to throw a chair.

From this and other information, he concluded that he must have felt "pretty lonesome" when he proposed, and he thought that in marrying a Catholic, he would be forced to have his children become Catholic, and he didn't want this.

He expressed considerable objection to my urging him to ask his mother about this, since she had already given most of the information to the hospital upon his admission. He felt "betrayed" by me and spoke of it as a "low blow to have me find out something you already knew" but then added, "Maybe you were right to have me find out for myself."

From the time of that weekend visit and thereafter, he never again used projection and denial in discussing the events preceding his hospitalization.

In the next hour, he mentioned his feeling of relief on not having hours over the weekends. He felt burdened with the task of thinking up "light and airy things" for his hours. I then made a connection between this and his not wanting his mother to get upset by what he told her. He said that he hardly ever told her anything significant and that everything they talked about seemed so inconsequential. He then described his "re-bellion" over the weekend visit when he refused to eat eggs and ate only his cereal, whereas formerly he would try to please her by eating everything that she cooked for him.

In the subsequent months, the patient showed a recurrent activity that was considerably under the influence of primary process, i.e., primitive, prelogical, unrealistic thinking. This activity consisted of cutting his own hair with the clearly self-destructive result of giving his hair the appearance of a plowed field. Each haircutting occasion was preceded by some kind of disappointment, frustration, or other depressive experience.

Just prior to the first occasion of cutting his own hair, he had been rejected by several girls he was dating. Instead of feeling rebuffed or depressed, he experienced compulsions. At that time, he expressed fears of leaping from a theater balcony. He made sure that he kept the cap on his fountain pen, so he would not absentmindedly stab himself in the arm. The difficulties with girlfriends, loss of several chess games, and similar disappointments in his life culminated in the haircut. When he discussed his thoughts about it, he emphasized his effort to be able to do everything for himself. He didn't want to pay a barber, and he thought he could complete college on his own without instruction. During crises, he often practiced talking to his cats instead of talking to me. He considered it a weakness to patronize barbers and analysts. These attitudes were illustrative of his strivings to avoid dependency.

A similar series of disappointments resulted in the second episode of cutting his hair. Our earlier analysis of his defenses of the denial of his needs and desires made many of these disappointments prominent at that time. As his pathological defenses were rendered less effective, his needs became more apparent. He was less distant from people and became more assertive with girls while on dates and consequently was more often frustrated when they refused him. With this freeing of his sexual impulses, there were increasing castration elements in his dreams. In one dream, for example, he was on his way to a fraternity house where he wanted to go to bed with a "loose" girlfriend of another man. He looked for her and then went over to another fraternity house where they thought he was the guest lecturer. He attended the lecture. He dipped his hand into carbon tetrachloride and was told it was poisonous and that he had better take his fingers out. This was one of a series of dreams occuring in this period where he never quite reached the sexual object.

Just before his second self-administered haircut, he had told me that his cat had been killed, one of his girlfriends was cool toward him, and a second girlfriend announced her engagement to someone else. He attempted to take the sting out of these events by saying that he was thinking of getting rid of the cat anyway and that he no longer had to worry about his children being brought up Catholic, since these two girlfriends were both Catholic and were now out of the picture.

We saw an additional example of how he insulated himself from feelings when he described the way he spent money and paid his bills. He said that doing these things was "like a game, like Monopoly. I used to like that game." When I took up this way of dealing with so many of his experiences and said that

I thought he must be concerned about having his feelings break loose, he was reminded of a dream of his car breaking loose and careening down the mountain. All he could do was close his eyes. Since this dream came to him as an association to my comment, it had much more meaning for him than if the comment had followed his report of such a dream.

The above developments were followed by a change from remoteness to greater assertiveness with a new girlfriend. Fortunately, she was able to respond to him, and although there was no attempt at genital intercourse as yet, there was greater physical intimacy. She was also more open about telling him of some of her objections to his behavior. For example, she pointed out his contemptuous attitude toward girls and also observed that he would crack a joke whenever the discussion became serious. Coming from her, these confrontations had more validity than when he and I had discussed them.

At this time, he told of a dream in which his female cat was beaten up by her lover. He was erotically excited by the dream. He thought the dream pointed out his concerns linking sex with danger. These concerns included both the harm that might come to him as a result of sexual activities and the injurious results to his sexual partner.

Then in an hour just before the third episode of cutting his hair, he told a joke which one of his current professors had told in class. The joke was a definition of "African Roulette." A man goes into a hut where there are six Negro women. All are "cocksuckers," but one is a cannibal. This joke reminded him of how his girl had put her head near his penis, and he had the wish that she would take it into her mouth. He then thought that if she bit it, the only thing he could do was to hit her. We discussed examples of his repeated concern about danger to his penis. He then told of a dream in which he was going to Africa, and his parents warned him about infectious diseases and the natives. Continuing on in the dream, he was trying out his screwdriver several times. Then he was on a familiar road and saw his brother in a bus and realized he wasn't dead after all.

In his associations to this dream, he said that his parents deterred him from doing many things he would have liked to do. The screwdriver reminded him of his mailbox, which fell down. I asked him how he spelled "mail." He thought a minute, laughed, and said it was my dirty mind. Of the reference to his brother's death, he thought he might look up a *New York Times* of that date to see if there was any article about his brother. This was his way of obtaining more information about another family tragedy that had been shrouded in secrecy.

In the above example, we see how his ambivalent feelings toward this girl became prominent as he became more intimate. Following an evening when she was quite cool toward him, he returned home and gave himself another haircut.

After this latest girl broke off with him, he found himself passing two cars on a narrow road, and he had to pull back quickly when another car came out from a side road. He didn't know why he was taking such chances, since he really was in no rush. He talked about passing the car as not giving a damn, after discussing a dream from which he concluded that it showed how lonely and frustrated he was.

Rorschach Test

The patient was retested primarily to discover whether or how the Rorschach would reflect changes that were observable in his behavior. The test, if taken by itself, would be considered by most, if not all, Rorschach workers to be that of a schizophrenic patient. Whether or not a psychosis is grossly manifest could be an open question, but that schizophrenic thinking still takes place in this patient seems clear. There is no evidence, however, of serious distress at the present time. The patient seems to be in good humor. The test shows that he is an intelligent person, imaginative, and original. But his perceptions are so distorted and they take account of so little of the complex, real elements of the blot that a very strong trend toward autistic thinking is suggested.

In comparing this test with the two administered to him on previous occasions, it is clear that the first one represents a much more serious degree of disorganization than either the second or the third. It is also clear that the patient's productions on the first test are much more impoverished than on the last two, both in quantity and in quality. At the time of the first test, the patient was markedly blocked—either quite unable to think of *anything* that the blots reminded him of or very efficient and grossly hampered. This was borne out of the impairment shown on the intelligence test. The earned I.Q. of 112 was clearly not representative of the patient's superior capacities.

On tests no. 2 and 3, the patient functioned much more efficiently. His speed of production doubled on no. 2 and remained at this level on no. 3. He produced the most quantitatively on no. 2 (R 36). In no. 3, he seemed less willing to spend time looking at the blot (T24 to 14) so that the quantity drops (R21), although the speed remains the same. I am not sure of the meaning of this increase followed by decrease in quantity, but my impression is that it is associated with a change in the patient's attitude toward test and tester, which can be described as follows. On no. 1, the patient felt and was relatively impotent and incompetent. In no. 2, he was much more competent and was making a rather conscientious, serious effort to put forth his best. On no. 3, he was feeling still more competent, even a little cocky, and did not bother so much about putting forth his best. In a test full of so much pathology, this attitude suggests a rather brittle defense.

In considering the quality of the patient's productions, there is a steady increase in liveliness from no. 1 to no. 3. This is particularly true in the increased perception of human movement (0 to 1 to 3). With regard to the other elements of liveliness in the test (other types of movement, color, shading), the big change came between no. 1 and no. 2.

On all the tests, the patient has given a few responses that have a humorous quality. They are clearly schizophrenic, but unlike the autistic responses of many schizophrenics, they strike the listener as communicative of conscious whimsy. This quality is clearer on no. 2 and no. 3 than on no. 1.

On test no. 3, oral themes (food, open jaws, teeth) emerge in significant quantity, which has not been true on either of the other tests.

On test no. 2, the patient showed a strong tendency to "organize" the blot in an autistic fashion, that is, to force every aspect of it into an arbitrarily chosen meaning. On test no. 1, there was less ability to organize in any form. On no. 3, the need to "organize" and find "meanings" seems less compulsive.

On no. 1, the patient perceives only one of the ordinarily seen "popular" responses. This is characteristic of severe psychosis. On no. 2, he sees nine, which is a good normal amount. On no. 3, he sees only four. This is a quite low number and fits with his slightly cocky and less earnest approach to the test. It is a little bit like a declaration of independence from doing what is expected of him. It must be hoped that this is a phase of his development toward real independence rather than a largely defensive manner.

Conclusion

In the months that followed, there were many examples of his growing awareness of his derogatory approach toward women. This occurred when he felt inferior in a social situation or when he had some feelings of jealousy. For example, he looked at his girlfriend and thought of her as "dumpy" just when she had turned away from him to talk with someone else.

In another session, he told about how he had come to an hour more than a year previously and had carried a banana in his pocket as if he had an erection. He thought at that time that I was curt with him and disapproving toward him. From his thoughts about this, I made a transference interpretation of how he thought his father might disapprove of such a bold display of sexual assertiveness. This was followed by his decision to enclose a letter to his father and not just send the financial statement that his father had requested. As he gained greater freedom of expression with me, he became more collaborative with his parents—having neither to avoid them completely nor to conform to what he thought were their expectations.

There were many occasions where he could see himself repeatedly expressing hostility when his own narcissism was threatened by failure, criticism, and frustration. Along with this, there were successful attempts at working through his castration fears and loss of independence in relation to women. As a result, his pathological need to dominate women, render them helpless, or humiliate them decreased. As he mastered his hostility, he was able to be more considerate and tender. Along with this, he was able to participate successfully in intercourse. His relationship to his parents became one in which he was independent of and respectful toward them without feeling rebelliously tied to them. He enjoyed visits with his family and once commented to them, "You are not half as bad as I tell Dr. Schulz you are."

In going over his plans about marriage and discontinuing treatment, he brought up a dream of running away. He was able to interpret this and talk about whether or not he was running away from me with his feelings of needing me.

He eventually married a nurse whom he had dated for a year and a half during the latter part of the treatment. By mutual agreement, we decided to discontinue therapy four years after we had begun. He subsequently obtained a job and set up a home with his bride.

POSTSCRIPT. At the time of this writing, twelve years have elapsed since this man terminated treatment. During that time, he completed his work toward an advanced degree. He has done well in his work and has required no further psychiatric treatment. His marriage has continued satisfactorily. His wife describes him as a devoted father to their two children—a long, long way from lobotomy.

Supervision

Here we will be concerned with some of the personal qualities of Frieda in conducting the supervision on this patient.

The setting and arrangements of the supervisory process were in themselves unique. In 1953, four of us on the staff of Chestnut Lodge gathered with her in the living room of Frieda's cottage for tea and cookies following the regular Wednesday afternoon clinical conference. Two hours were devoted to two cases. Dr. Norman Rintz presented his work with a female hysteric patient, and I, by contrast, reported on a disturbed male schizophrenic patient. Other regularly attending members of our seminar were Milton Hendlich, who had done the extensive admission workup on my patient, and Robert Gibson, who was the clinical administrator on the third floor where my patient resided. The successful outcome of my patient's treatment was due in no small part to the resulting close communicative link involving the clinical administrator's orchestration of the patient's nursing/occupational therapy milieu with the four-times-a-week psychoanalytically oriented psychotherapy seminars. This was before the days of the generalized use of antipsychotic tranquilizing medications. This patient received no medications during the four-year course of treatment. Frieda designed our educational experience to best compare and contrast issues of technique and psychopathology of two quite different patients and almost equally different therapist personalities.

By then, she was already having deficits in her hearing acuity. Since we were presenting via tape recordings of sessions with the patient, it became necessary to have a sample session transcribed and typed up in advance of the supervisory session. She made the very helpful suggestion that I simply record all sessions from the week and select one at random to be transcribed. In this way, I would be spared trying to select my best—or worst—example of treatment that week. It worked to lessen my anxiety and served as an example of her attentiveness to the possibility of diminishing anxiety to increase performance whether with staff or with patients. Similarly, my main impression from these sessions was her forthrightness in recommending confronting the patient in a matter-of-fact manner about his deepest conflicts. Paradoxically, the assumption that he could stand to hear these anxiety-provoking topics conveyed a respect for him which served to allay his anxiety. "He knows it, and you know it, so why not talk about it" was her attitude.

At that same time, one of the items on her agenda was to demonstrate that the same therapist could treat the patient both during the acute psychotic disturbance as well as during the quiescent clinical period. Shortly after my arrival at Chestnut Lodge from St. Elizabeths Hospital, Frieda had me over to her cottage for lunch. The two memories I have of that occasion were the lamb chops tastefully prepared by her maid and our discussion of Frieda's challenge to Kurt Eissler's opinion (1952) that a therapist who was able to bring the psychotic patient out of the disturbed phase of his illness would be involved in too many parameters from the classical analytic approach to be able to conduct the analysis in the later phase.

In those days, it was her custom to interview each recently admitted patient. The following excerpt comes from her participation in the staff conference (April 7, 1954) on my patient.

> I was warned that it would be better for me not to go and see him when he first came without being first sure that he wanted to see me. So the first time, he said, "She had better not come, I'll knock her head off." The second time, he said, "No." The third time, I said, "Well, if he were uncomfortable, we could have him packed, but I would want to see him." As I came—he is a very tall fellow—and he looked at me, put his hand on my head, and said, "Oh, you're such a little thing. Come in." And then after a few minutes, I felt quite comfortable, and he seemed comfortable. We discussed his treatment and how things went on the ward, etc. The other contact was just last week. He usually comes up from his hour to the ward when I leave the ward after having seen my patient, and I am a little reluctant to be shutting the door, and here are the two of us, and especially now when he is looking banged up after his fight. But I did it. I opened the door, and he said, "Do you think it is right for me to be here now on the ward with you?" As though he had to tell me, "Look, I am entirely not a dangerous fellow." So from these contacts, it makes me feel that the main thing is really his own fear of his own hostile side.

During the initial disturbed period, the patient requested that I examine his groin. At that time, it was not unusual for us to have his sessions in a seclusion room with him being in various stages of undress. He was unable to give any coherent responses about his complaint, and Frieda speculated that it might represent an overture for physical contact on the part of the patient who would at the same time be frightened by the homosexual implications of the contact. Her suggested technique was to respond by placing my hand on his shoulder, which would be a partial gratification and at the same time inform the patient that we would have a surgeon examine him. This did reassure the patient who was later on discovered to have an inguinal hernia requiring surgical repair.

While all of us learned a great deal from these Wednesday afternoon sessions, they did not always run smoothly. There were several features in my interaction with her that put me under tremendous pressure. Eventually, the air was cleared after discussing my feelings with her. One problem for me was a reflection of her tremendous intuitive clinical understanding of patients. She was often far ahead of the patient and myself. During supervision, after what I reported what I thought to be a particularly productive and illuminating section of a session, she would inquire, "What kept you from asking about so and so?" I had the feeling she was never satisfied, even though the therapy was moving along remarkably well.

Periodic psychological testing was employed to monitor the progress of the treatment. An example of her clinical mastery of the case was revealed when we asked her to predict what the psychologist's next report would reveal, and she spelled it out with uncanny accuracy. Another source of pressure resulted from her frequent reporting of clinical examples of a key turning point occurring with one of her patients. This left me in constant search of the elusive response or gesture that would unlock the case. When I took this up with her, she admitted that things were not that simple, but she did consider it valuable to inquire of patients as to what they attributed their improvement. Her most quoted example was the time she showed sufficient trust to remove a patient from wet sheet pack herself rather than call in other staff to unpack the patient. Later on, her patient cited this act of trust on the part of her therapist as allowing her to proceed on to recovery.

I think these examples of the resolution of personal pressures I had been experiencing with Frieda serve to illustrate her receptivity to the clarification of sources of tension between us. This receptivity in turn served as a model for me, as therapist to my patient, to be alert to instances of tension between us. Having located the tension, we could then openly explore it and arrive at a mutual understanding with consequent resolution. This process was a continuous one in supervision and in therapy. It reflected the assumption of confidence in a developing trust based on growing mutual respect.

One of the most important lessons I learned from her was

to be respectful of the potential sense that could be made out of the fractured, pathological interactions with my patient. One last illustration will reflect the change that Frieda experienced in her giving greater expectation to the potential to improve. As I had been walking up the path to her cottage, I passed a patient leaving her session with Frieda and returning to the main building. The patient was carrying a painting and looking thoughtful and dejected—a condition not in itself unusual for someone emerging from her psychotherapy session. Frieda welcomed me at the door and pointing to the patient explained that the latter had offered her a gift of a partially completed by-the-numbers oil painting. Frieda explained that in the past, she would have simply accepted what was proffered as an overture on the part of the patient in order not to aggravate the schizophrenic patient's already endangered self-esteem. Now, she thought it more respectful toward the patient to thank her but decline the gift with the expectation that she could finish the painting, at which time she would be very pleased to receive it. This was the parallel type of expectation she had of the two supervisors and their auditors every Wednesday afternoon.

References

Eissler, K. R., (1952), Remarks on the psychoanalysis of schizophrenia. In: *Psychotherapy with Schizophrenics*, ed. E. B. Brody & F. C. Redlich. New York: International Universities Press, p. 148.

Fromm-Reichmann, F. Staff conference, April 7, 1954.

Schulz, C. G., & Kilgalen, R. K. (1969), *Case Studies in Schizophrenia*. New York: Basic Books.

ہے

3

TRANSFERENCE AND AUTHORITY

Joseph H. Smith, M.D.

It would be difficult for me to write of Frieda Fromm-Reich-mann's work and of my brief work with her without at least touching on the issue of authority invested in the physician by virtue of transference. "Transference" carries a dual meaning. In the broader sense it is the capacity to love, hate, and otherwise be engaged with old and new objects. In the narrower sense it is both the tendency to interpret new objects and situations in terms of previous ones and also the means of reexperiencing old objects in the light of one's experience of new objects. A new object or situation or a new view of an old object or situation presents the opportunity and challenge of confronting the extent to which the prior presuppositions, bases, and ways of engaging were unknown.

Since transference is universal, the question of transference and authority could as well be pursued in connection with non-physician therapists or, in fact, with any authority figure, e.g., parents, teachers, employers, etc. However, I mention physicians because, at least in the past, a particularly strong transference authority has been invested in them, an authority that derives from the special quality and intensity of transference that occurs in those seeking help for illness. The question is open as to whether the diminishment of this traditional authority is consequent to a more enlightened clientele, together with the modern resistance to regression and dependency even when ill, or the extent to which it is less because of an increased anxiety in physicians about the assumption and therapeutic uses of this authority. Obviously the issue appears in sharpest relief in the case of the psychiatrist and especially the physician or

79

nonphysician psychoanalyst where the experience and study of transference and countertransference phenomena are the cental therapeutic task. I choose this occasion to think about the issue because I see the way in which Frieda Fromm-Reichmann talked to patients and about patients, and also her style of supervision, as manifesting an undaunted courage to accept the authority that work with severely ill patients requires. More than any other, it was she who saw that schizophrenic and manic-depressive patients, rather than not forming a transference as Freud believed, developed a more intense and more primitive transference—a transference psychosis rather than a transference neurosis. Finally, Fromm-Reichmann was an active participant in the conference to be discussed.

Perhaps the clearest way of approaching comprehension of Fromm-Reichmann's stance is to note that good enough parents do not anxiously avoid the dependency of children nor lightly dispel important idealizations. Their natural concern is directed toward that which is important to the child at a particular phase of development. This willingness and the capacity to be the parent are particularly intensified and specially shaped in the therapist through his or her work with severely ill patients. The therapist listens to the patient with the conviction that what the patient is saying is of importance, even though its meaning may not yet be clear. The conscious and preconscious weighing and timing of what is to be interpreted are selected as that which is centrally pertinent and is thus said with conviction. There is a passionate involvement, not proximally so much with the patient, but with the importance of discovering what the need for symptoms has been and is, and an urgent faith that such meanings can come to light—an urgency born of a clear view of the continuing tragedy should recovery not be achieved. Attunement to this tragic dimension is an essential aspect of accepting authority. It probably hinges on an underlying catastrophic view of development—a view of mental illness wherein the accent is not so much on illness as distortion of reality, but as an undefended experience on the part of the patient of the catastrophic dimension of reality. The acknowledgment of this does not so much fall to verbal interpretations as to their nonverbal accompaniments, including the conviction and sobriety of the analyst's speech and silence. Whether one is ill or not, life is not a bed or roses.

I did not know Fromm-Reichmann long enough or well enough to feel confident that these elements describe sufficiently her way of assuming and deploying authority. It is, however, a reliable account of the picture I developed of her in reading her work and hearing one lecture prior to joining the Chestnut Lodge staff in 1955, together with what I then observed in contacts with her there. The latter included a brief period of supervision of a manic-depressive woman (not the patient discussed here) during the few months preceding Fromm-Reichmann's death. In the main, the elements listed are also what I regard as essential to all therapeutic authority. However, they are not items that can be simply taken as precepts to consciously model oneself toward. The working through is a matter of each analyst finding his or her own voice. The way in which these elements are integrated into the style of each can vastly differ. Humor, for instance, need not involve a lack of sobriety. While it can be defensive and destructive, for some analysts it is at times a crucial mode of acknowledging the seriousness of the situation which, at the same time, allows for at least momentary release from pain plus a glimpse of a more hopeful perspective. I would guess that it is not often written about because the caring conveyed in its rightful use in the therapeutic situation would seldom come through in the printed word. Besides, to advocate or adopt its use as a therapeutic "technique" would be clearly wrong.

For the reasons just mentioned I shall not attempt to give examples of what I regard to have been therapeutic uses of humor. I shall instead give a retrospective account of a conference in which Fromm-Reichmann responded to a puzzling and mainly defensive manifestation of humor. Perhaps—but only perhaps—her response was conditioned because even nondefensive uses of humor were, to the best of my knowledge, not a prominent part of her own therapeutic style.

On February 20, 1957, I presented my work of one year's duration with Rebecca, a childless forty-three-year-old widow. She had entered Chestnut Lodge following two hospitalizations elsewhere that included insulin therapy, ECT, and trials of whatever was available at that time in the way of pharmacological treatment. Her condition was refractory to all of these. At the time of admission and for a considerable period thereafter she was in a severely agitated psychotic depression. For the typed transcript of a conference on such a patient to show eight entries of "Laughter" is noteworthy. Fromm-Reichmann, who attended the conference with a guest, was, I believe, particularly puzzled because she had been on leave of absence the prior year, so had not directly experienced the impact of the patient on the hospital community. While her interpretive responses in the conference were, nevertheless, mainly correct, they were affected by this lack of knowledge, i.e., had she been present, she would have been less astonished, though no less inclined to interpret the defensive humor.

The patient was initially markedly narrowed in her capacity to think or communicate anything other than angry demands that something be done about her tension. Were I seeing her now, I would immediately prescribe medication. However, I could not do that without at least a shadow of doubt that the modest recovery she did achieve might have been more impeded than facilitated by such medication. In any event, this was before the days of antidepressants and, at the Lodge, before the time that antipsychotic medications of any kind were used. Her severe bouts of agitation came in the form of "spells" of partially disowned feelings that would overwhelm her. These would often persist for hours during which she would be pacing, wringing her hands, and yelling loud enough to be heard over much of the hospital grounds, in sounds that many heard as a kind of animal utterance. The sound was actually "Ike" continuously and exasperatingly repeated—I suppose a childlike contraction of "I sick."

Prior to the husband's rather sudden death the patient had been treated for depression. She had apparently withdrawn from virtually all contact with anyone other than her husband or else the couple had maintained an isolated position all along. Her acutely psychotic depression commenced shortly after her husband's death. From what I could gather of her prior treatment, there had been urgent efforts to respond to her demands and as these efforts repeatedly failed, personnel would withdraw from her in despair and anger. For various reasons, I was able to spend time with her without feeling unduly pressured and without, most of the time, feeling the need to withdraw. During periods when she was not having a spell, verbal interchanges between us were still very conventional. It was as if "I sick" had become a statement of her identity. The constriction of thought and affect and the narrowed identity claim seemed to reflect the extreme caution necessitated by her vulnerability to being overwhelmed. It was not just a matter of a near zero frustration tolerance in the usual sense. She was also disconcerted by the mildest of positive feelings and not only by reason of their possible sexual overtones. It did evolve that overwhelmingly intense sexual feelings, experienced as strange by reason of efforts to disown them, were a part of her spells. However, any change was disconcerting. The fact that she felt more pleasure and excitement on a first trip into town than she thought appropriate was also reason for self-criticism.

The first steps in clarifying precipitating factors in her spells took the form of denials. "That couldn't be the reason because I've been having these all along." She offered that, for instance, in revealing that one spell had occurred on her wedding anniversary. I began to accept these "negative" explanations as good enough, especially since their elaboration was accompanied by a diminished intensity and frequency of the spells.

There were several ways in which the component of envy in her anger became manifest. I don't know whether I hit upon a way of ducking her envy or facilitating its acknowledgment or both, but it was interesting. One day, for reasons not consciously known to me, I responded (truthfully) to her usual rather grim and hostile "How are you feeling" by responding "Not so hot." She immediately, in radically uncharacteristic fashion, brightened up, and there ensued a virtual torrent of cheerful, though slightly teasing solicitation. Anything other than angry depression and constriction of thought and affect was so welcome that I did not thereafter attempt to hide depression in me.

But I am getting ahead of the story. Before the spells subsided, she had alienated everyone part of the time (including me) and the majority of patients and personnel most of the time. One interchange I reported in the conference was of an hour in which she was angrily yelling at me. The yelling was loud, her face was red, blood vessels engorged, and her eyes seemingly exophthalmic. In my silence I found myself becoming aware of the fact that I did not have the wish to choke her. Then I began to wonder why I did not want to choke her. As best I could tell, it was because I did not want to get close to her physically, although if thoughts could kill, that would be okay. In the conference this evoked a couple of outbursts of laughter, but in the actual hour reported I was rather shocked by my thoughts, just as I am now in writing this. I was chilled by my own distancing and had the further thought that it would be better if I could have wanted to choke her. What I actually did was to say, "Rebecca, sometimes when you are like this, you are terrible." She responded with a big smile and said, "What's the matter, Dr. Smith? Don't you feel well?" I said, "I feel miserable."

Not long before Thanksgiving she had met my wife and children on the hospital grounds. In the last session before the holiday she had genuinely wished me and my family a happy Thanksgiving. However, in the hour the day following she was yelling and angry and either was then or reported having the day prior episodes of gagging. As a shot in the dark, I asked what it was that she could not swallow. She ignored that and went on to tell me what a terrible day she had had on Thanksgiving. After listening for about a half hour, I said, "Well, you did the very best you could under the circumstances. As I hear you, you were telling yourself that you should just be thankful. It's no matter that you are at Chestnut Lodge on the most disturbed floor in the hospital and that you have been sick for two years and that other people are at home with their turkey and families. You're not supposed to mind all of that and you're just supposed to be thankful. I couldn't swallow that either." Immediately, she began hollering "Stop!" in affirmation and obvious relief.

By the time of the conference, the spells had ceased. She was still often tense, but regularly the tension subsided upon beginning a session and she would characteristically remain free of tension for a considerable period afterward. She was able to talk more about events precipitating her tension and the content of her thoughts and feelings while tense. She also described the tension as different. "I still have it, but it's not the same. It's not so bad." In one session while describing a period of tension she said, with the most relaxed sort of smile on her face, "I say, 'no,' and I say 'no,' but these feelings just come on me anyway." I replied that maybe the no-saying had led to a build-up of tension to a point of being overwhelmed and that it sounded like she was now close to being able to say "yes" to some of her feelings. Even though what I said was true, it didn't add anything to what she had said and strikes me now, thirty years later, as a defensive and intellectualized response to her clear statement of acceptance of her sexual feelings with all that that implied regarding our transference/countertransference involvement at the time. My anxiety about the matter was probably one factor in my giving the emphasis in the conference to aggressive interchanges.

Diagnostic testing on admission was interpreted as indicating that the patient suffered "from a psychosis of very severe proportions. Either she is one of the schizophrenic patients whose test performance resembles in some respects those of patients with organic brain damage or there is some actual organic component in her illness." Fromm-Reichmann's initial statement in the conference was to question the diagnosis in favor of manic-depressive illness based on the stereotypy, emptiness, and conventionality, but also, as it evolved later in the discussion, on the reaction of laughing and "seeming cheerfulness of the total staff." She saw this "desperate gaiety" as a measure of the patient's despair and of the impotent rage she could call forth in others, all of which she saw as more associated with manic-depressive than with schizophrenic disorders.

I had taken the patient to be manic-depressive from the beginning. However, I did question (as did several other conference participants) the interpretation of the "gaiety." It was my position in the conference that while there had been a great deal of joking about the patient and fun made of her, possibly that had, in part, allowed us to stick with her. Fromm-Reichmann agreed but insisted it was an expression of despair. She

then went on to say in reasonably diplomatic fashion that even
though a number of aspects of my way of relating and intervening were helpful to the patient, the therapy was not guided
and directed by a plan, even though it was going well.

> Now, I think that getting her to behave and cheering her
> along are, symptomatically speaking, good, but I also think
> that it gets her to repress a terrific anxiety which I think this
> woman is suffering from. At least what I would try with her
> would be to get her more depressed so that one can really
> get at that anxiety which is underneath the whole attempt
> at dramatizing and of pleading which steers the whole
> staff—medical, nursing, social worker—away from her real
> central problem which has to do with her anxiety regarding
> her own hostility and resentment against what life has done
> to her. I think it has to do with her feeling that she is a
> fraud and in a way trying to convince herself and her ther-
> apist that she is. Finally, feeling that the therapist believes
> this of her and the nurses, too, "because they keep away
> from me" and then hating everybody because everyone
> seems to be saying, "Yes, you are a fraud," and so having
> a painful vicious circle. Then because [of rationalized and
> refuted] hostility . . . she becomes even more anxious. I be-
> lieve that while it is a terribly difficult job with this kind of
> a person, her best bet would be to go back to being really
> depressed and then when she tries . . . either demands for
> help or any of the dramatizations, to give her the feeling
> that all you are waiting for is that you hear at last what
> makes her so God-awful frightened that she needs all of
> these crutches even to handle life in a mental hospital. I
> don't mean that this can be put in so many words, but that
> is the atmosphere out of which I would approach her.

I quote these remarks at some length because I take them to
be vintage Fromm-Reichmann. Attunement to the heart of the
matter is the proper assumption of authority. It is, as portrayed
in her writings, what had drawn me in the first place to Chestnut
Lodge. (One should read her advice to get the patient more
depressed as meaning more soberly in touch with the serious
issues of her existence. That state more resembles mourning
than depression. Getting depressed is not a good basis for ac-

complishing anything. Depression is sobriety and mourning denied.)

Naturally I was stung by her thinking that I was interested in mere symptomatic improvement. My response was that I expected the patient's anger and depression (using Fromm-Reichmann's word) to return at a time when the patient could experience them as her feelings and that would be the proper basis for her coming to terms with them. All in all, I thought myself to be more in agreement with Fromm-Reichmann than I believed she thought me to be.

In retrospect, my opinion is divided. Her astonishment at the laughter in the conference I believe I understood better than she. It was not just a manifestation of despair (although, ultimately, that probably was the heart of the matter) but also a manifestation of the rage and the guilt about the rage in an entire hospital community, an issue that my presentation had in no way covered. Nevertheless, also in retrospect, I think my claimed agreement with the statement of what she saw as crucial in the treatment was still an intellectualized one—a goal toward which I was striving rather than a position I had achieved. My anxiety about allowing a woman almost old enough to be my mother to really level with me about her sexual desire and her sexual desire for me would be a case in point. The capacity to allow for that directness would have been a way station toward the level of interchange about whatever else was also crucial. No doubt my fantasy of not wanting to choke her was both a denial and an acknowledgment of my sexual response to her floridly masochistic seductiveness. One bit of evidence for that would be her vividly pleasurable response to my telling her, "When you are like this, you are terrible." This brings me back to the issue of authority. Authority is not achieved simply by taking, for example, the precepts and stance of Fromm-Reichmann as one's ego ideal. The working through is arduous and often lengthy. I remember early in my own training being chagrined by Erikson's mention of the first ten years of an analyst's experience as the formative period.

I should here mention some of the things going on that were not reported at the conference. Although I participated in and partially evoked the humor of the conference, I did not have a joking relationship with Rebecca. I was, in fact, very much identified with her and very angry about her being the butt of jokes and the object of rather massive hostility and contempt by virtually all personnel. Though I was angry at her myself a few times, I was never contemptuous and I never made fun of her. Some of this I would have talked about in supervision and in the biweekly small group meetings with several Lodge colleagues. Mostly it was reserved for my own analysis. I had arrived as a third year resident only about eight months prior to Rebecca's being admitted. I was involved in finding a role and a way to exist in this mecca for understanding the severely ill, just as was Rebecca. My not yet feeling at home there, together with real and transferentially distorted reasons for being angry at the institution, were such that I felt not only ashamed but also considerable vicarious satisfaction in her yelling from the porch of the fourth floor loud enough to disturb the whole neighborhood. I suppose it is not so infrequent that we thus exploit our patient's symptomatology. That is something to think about, but so also is the fact that such points of pathology in common are often the occasion for a needed contact with a difficult patient that a more experienced and healthy analyst might miss.

For many months Rebecca overtly protested the anger and contempt, thus evoking even more of what she was protesting. While I was trying to help her out of this vicious cycle, I mostly swallowed my sense of protest or depended on her to express it. I swallowed my protest because I did not want to actualize my being caught in the same position of painfully angry isolation she was in. But that was not the only reason. Her gradually finding a way out also depended on my achieving and maintaining a reasonable working relationship with personnel on the fourth floor. If the nurses and aides initially felt a high degree of anger and scorn for Rebecca, one had to accept that as a starting point. If Fromm-Reichmann had been on the scene during the intense period of Rebecca's spells, I have no doubt that her conference responses would have essentially carried the same message. However, there would have been the chance that her 'authority' (in single quotes because here I use it in a different sense than elsewhere in this paper) might have elicited compliance such that the anger, contempt, and joking at and about Rebecca would have gone underground and been even more difficult to overcome.

I still have not forgiven some of my colleagues for their treatment of Rebecca. (One of them persisted in holding a large mirror in front of her during an intense spell, I suppose facing her with what he had to endure.) However, I did achieve acceptance of the anger of the nurses and aides on the fourth floor, partly because their constant involvement and frustrated wish to be helpful were more palpable. I think that also became clear to Rebecca. In any event, a nonvicious cycle got going. The intensity of her anger and the quality of her tension changed, and those changes were further enhanced by the pride we all took in her and in our work with her.

However, what Fromm-Reichmann spotted on her return from a year in California was something in me and something still in the response of the total staff that promised less than full recovery for Rebecca. And, sure enough, not many months after Rebecca had achieved freedom from her symptoms and just as I was thinking we could now talk more deeply about her past life and our relationship, Rebecca opted to leave treatment. By then Fromm-Reichmann had died. I was not reassured by the comments of my supervisor and others that I should consider it a good outcome. I was, in fact, bitterly disappointed.

What else might be said about my failure to assume authority in the work with Rebecca? I have already outlined some indications of lack in this regard—my inhibition about hearing fully her desire, my somewhat paranoid identification with her, the narcissistic aspect of needing to prove myself combined with some general need to maintain distance, notwithstanding the intensity of my involvement with her. I would now take the fact that I in no way shared with her the intensity of my disappointment about her decision to leave treatment as an indicator of unhelpful and perhaps spiteful reserve on my part.

To find one's own voice it is with some such cluster of issues—one's own issues—from which every therapist's development must begin. It is no use trying to slip into the shoes of and be Frieda Fromm-Reichmann, Otto Will, or Harold Searles, impressive as they might be on various scores.

I am pretty sure that I could do better were I starting with Rebecca now. That is not to claim that I have fully solved all the issues that hampered my work with her thirty years ago. I have made headway, but the nature of the work is such that encountering and working through such countertransference issues is of the essence. No doubt in beginning from a different point, I would begin with a different cluster of issues. But there is a sense in which starting with a new patient is starting over again, reworking what one has worked through before, in addition to encountering issues unique to the particular patient. It is both the repetition and the novelty that make the work interesting. Patients finally come to understand that, but often only after years of believing that since we have heard it all before we must be bored, and that the authority with which we speak or remain silent was all previously established rather than reachieved with each patient.

4

FROMM-REICHMANN AT THE
WASHINGTON SCHOOL OF PSYCHIATRY

BEATRICE LIEBENBERG, A.C.S.W.

I have a kaleidoscope of memories of Frieda Fromm-Reichmann. I see a short bird-shaped woman, bosomy and thin-legged with a plain everyday face. I recall the demure respect and modesty with which she introduced visiting lecturers, including Erich Fromm. Yet on the podium when she lectured she was exuberant and lively and displayed what Bullard called "superb showmanship."

I was not immune to the inspiration and enchantment of her lectures, yet in two individual encounters I experienced her as fearsome. She was a woman of force. Charles Rycroft said of Anna Freud that when she walked into a room, she gave the impression that one was meant to notice she was self-effacing, that she was "retreating into the limelight." This might be said of Frieda Fromm-Reichmann as well.

I came to the Washington School of Psychiatry because of Harold Lasswell's affiliation. My training had been in political psychology, but I was already committed to a clinical route. My orientation had been in libido theory, and now I was learning to focus on the relationship between therapist and patient.

Fromm-Reichmann taught and encouraged an attitude of respect and acceptance of the patient participant. It was implicit in all her teaching that the therapist cannot respect the patient unless she recognizes that the patient's difficulties in living are not too different from her own. The difference between the person who suffers a severe mental disorder and the so-called healthy person is one of degree and not of kind.

In her class, Assets of the Mentally Handicapped, we
learned to trace the roots of artists and philosophers, including
Schumann and Nijinsky, Van Gogh, Strindberg, Oscar Wilde,
Schopenhauer. She stressed that the difficulties they encountered in living and which constituted their emotional handicaps
were also a source for the development of their assets. So that
aloofness might enable one to express himself in music, and
muteness would be no deterrent in the dance.

I was struck by her tremendous interest in writers. One
class was devoted to the writing of several of her patients, their
poetry and short stories. They were interesting in their expression of feeling. They were not in league with Oscar Wilde or
Strindberg, but she had affirmed her own positive judgment
of their worth by consulting several editors. She read several
of her own short stories as well. I have never seen them published.

The brief biographies provided by Edith Weigert and Dexter Bullard in their prefaces to her books are extremely interesting. This past summer I learned more about what may have
motivated Fromm-Reichmann to study these artists and to be
drawn to patients who struggled with artistic expression.

I arranged an interview with Berti Gideon, who lived with
the Reichmann family in Berlin weekends for several years in
the early 1930s. Gideon was studying for her doctorate in economics at that time. Relatives of the Reichmanns lived in Stutt-
gart, Gideon's home, and insisted that the Reichmann home
would be hers during her years of study.

Fromm-Reichmann was in Heidelberg during this period,
having completed her psychoanalytic studies. The father was
already dead. He had been a businessman and banker. There
was almost no mention of him. It was a household of women,
extremely close to each other, guided and directed by the
mother, Clara Reichmann, a strong and dominating woman.
She was a woman of culture.

An unmarried aunt, Helene Simon, was also a member of
the household. She was one of the first women in Germany to
seek permission to attend classes at the University. Later she
studied in England and wrote a voluminous work on Owen, the

father of Fabian socialism. A building in Düsseldorf still carries her name.

Another aunt who spent much time with the family published two volumes of poetry. A pervasive theme in her poetry was the conflict of being both German and Jewish. A housekeeper who had lived with the family since Frieda's birth was yet another member of the household. Despite the intimacy she enjoyed with the family, the housekeeper always addressed the mother as *gnädige Frau*.

Frieda Fromm-Reichmann was the oldest of three daughters. Greta was about four years younger and Anna was the youngest. The sisters were very attached to Frieda. Greta was the more dependent. She would visit her older sister frequently and would vacation with her. She was a music teacher, physically unattractive and depressed. The youngest sister was beautiful and vivacious and married a psychiatrist, Hans Jacobson, introduced by Fromm-Reichmann. The mother had difficulty tolerating his leftist political views, but he nevertheless held fund raisers in her house.

The mother's family came from the Rhineland and were all very talented. Frequent mention was made of the maternal grandmother who had been adopted by a man who was an intimate friend of Heinrich Heine.

The apartment was quite luxurious with a large library that included all of Freud's work. The family enjoyed concerts and opera. Despite their complete absorption in German life and culture, this was a very traditional orthodox Jewish family. They maintained a kosher house. They did not travel or work on the Sabbath. Various members of the extended family were Zionists and emigrated to Israel in the 1920s. With the onset of the Hitler regime, Greta left for Israel, Anna and her husband moved to Paris and then to Israel. The mother and aunt went to England. Frieda Fromm-Reichmann arrived in America in 1935.

Clara Reichmann was deaf, as was her sister, Helene Simon. Frieda Fromm-Reichmann also suffered deafness in the later years of her life.

Gideon, when she arrived in this country, worked with the Jewish council in New York, which aided refugees. Many of their clients had severe emotional problems and were sent to various psychiatrists for evaluation. One man, who had attempted suicide, was referred to Frieda Fromm-Reichmann. Her report to the agency stated that he did not have a mental illness, but that he suffered from the enormous pressure he had borne. She added that she was not billing for the interview because she had no wish to add to his heavy burden.

Although she was viewed primarily as a clinician, Frieda Fromm-Reichmann understood theory and I understood many of Sullivan's more abstruse concepts because of her translation. She was lucid in her discussion of other theorists, including Melanie Klein. She saw Klein's work as close to her own, thinking that there was a similarity between the infantile and psychotic state of mind.

I have often compared the two women. Their similarity and differences are characterized by their study of loneliness. Both women published papers in 1959. Klein talked about grief and depression, the sense of being alone regardless of external circumstances, feeling lonely even among friends, which she traced to yearning for that ideal situation, the close contact between the unconscious of the mother and the unconscious of the baby, the understanding without words.

Fromm-Reichmann in her notes (later compiled into a paper) dealt with desolation and despair and how that desolation raises anxiety in the listener. She would say that the therapist must recognize aspects of his own loneliness in order to be able to listen to the patient. She wrote, "One forgets that there were people in one's past life and there is no hope that there will be interpersonal relationships in the future."

Edith Weigert says of Fromm-Reichmann that in her later years she felt lonely and distressed, but she could not let other people know about her discouragement. She felt too many people depended on her.

I have had countless teachers during my life, many of them now nameless and faceless except when a transcript jogs my memory. Not so with Frieda Fromm-Reichmann. I remember her. I remember what she taught me. I try to practice what she taught me. And I am grateful to her always.

5

FRIEDA FROMM-REICHMANN AND THE NATURAL HISTORY OF AN INTERVIEW

WENDY LEEDS-HURWITZ, PH.D.

Introduction

My first personal recollection of Frieda Fromm-Reichmann was on a cold, blustery, rainy night in Chicago in 1939 when I attended a dinner meeting arranged by J. S. Kasanin, then at the Michael Reese Hospital. The dinner was followed by the presentation of papers which were eventually published with Kasanin as editor under the title *Language and Thought in Schizophrenia,* by the University of California Press at Berkeley in 1944. It was a memorable group, for besides Kasanin and Fromm-Reichmann, there were Kurt Goldstein, Norman Cameron, S. J. Beck, E. Von Domarus, and Andras Angyal. The published volume includes a chapter by H. S. Sullivan, but I honestly do not specifically remember him that night. John D. Benjamin (Denver) sent in a paper, but could not attend because of illness, and I was delegated to read it in a shortened version because time was running out. I was thrilled to sit at the same table with Frieda, who brought great warmth and clinical insight to the proceedings, even though her paper was not published in the 1944 Kasanin collection.

I saw her periodically at professional meetings. She was immensely popular, and the hall was usually crowded to hear her straightforward, direct recitals of her transactions with patients. Sometime after World War II when I was on a committee of the University of Chicago Press, I became aware of her lectures to residents and students at Chestnut Lodge on the psychotherapies and thus was an intermediary in arranging the

publication of her popular text, *Principles of Intensive Psychotherapy*, by the University of Chicago Press in 1950. Psychiatrists
and members of other disciplines were acutely aware of her
frontier explorations in the psychotherapy of acute and chronic
schizophrenics along with her colleague, Harry S. Sullivan, at
the Washington School of Psychiatry. There was a great hunger
for detailed information about inpatient and outpatient care of
the chronically ill, and Frieda, Dexter Bullard, and the staff of
Chestnut Lodge were among the foremost proponents of psychological care. Their students are our leaders now. Even the
advent of Thorazine after 1955 and the second and third generation antipsychotics has not diminished the need for sensitive,
trained, insightful management of the chronic psychotic. Frieda's
name is secure in history as a leader in this movement.

My next encounter with Frieda resulted from her desire
to study linguistic, and later the kinesic (body-motion) concom-
itants to verbal productions. She arranged, probably with the
help of Franz Alexander, to have two outstanding linguists who
would be willing to do interdisciplinary work at the Center for
Advanced Study in the Behavioral Sciences at Stanford, California. The director, Ralph Tyler, was most sympathetic to this
project and selected two highly talented and productive an-
thropologist-linguists, Professors Norman A. McQuown of the
University of Chicago and Charles F. Hockett of Cornell University, to be in residence at the same time, namely, the fall of
1955 and winter-spring of 1956. Because Alexander left the
center in December 1955, I was selected to work with the team,
arriving in late December 1955, and remaining eleven months.
It was a thrilling time with an abundance of ideas in constant
flow. Ray Birdwhistell came for about a week in January 1956,
and again for three weeks during the summer of 1956. Gregory
Bateson was the ethnologist-in-residence at the Palo Alto Veteran's Administration Hospital and was available for conferences, especially about the concept of the "double-bind" which
was new at that time. Gregory furnished us with the "Doris"
films which were the basis for *The Natural History of an Interview*
(N. A. McQuown, ed. Microfilm Collection of MSS on Cultural
Anthropology. Fifteenth Series. University of Chicago, Joseph

Regenstein Library, Department of Photoduplications, 1971. Also at the University of Michigan Film Collection).

The enormously tedious work requiring hundreds of hours to do a microanalysis of even 120 seconds of film with twenty-four frames per second was beyond all of us except Norman McQuown for the linguistics, and Ray Birdwhistell during the summer of 1956 for the kinesics.

Frieda's popularity as a therapist occupied much of her time at the center, but she was the originator and motivator and deserves full credit. Her untimely death in the spring of 1957 prevented her contributing a chapter to the monograph, but it is her book in a very real sense.

I am most grateful for having had the privilege of knowing Frieda as a colleague who brought warmth, goodwill, and good cheer to our relations. She was a rare person who could retain her radiance in a troubled world.

Henry W. Brosin

The Natural History of an Interview

During 1955–1956, at Stanford University's Center for Advanced Study in the Behavioral Sciences (CASBS), a diverse group of scholars began a multidisciplinary project later titled *The Natural History of an Interview (NHI)*.[1] Frieda Fromm-Reichmann was one of the scholars involved in this seminal project, so critical to our current understanding of what occurs during interaction. Although NHI was not ready until 1971, and she was involved for little more than the first year, her presence was of great importance to the group. Fromm-Reichmann established the goal of the work: it was to be an objective and detailed analysis of interview materials, originally designed to be immediately applicable to psychiatric interviews. In addition to setting the direction of the project, Fromm-Reichmann helped establish and maintain group cohesion; she played the

[1] I would like to thank Ray L. Birdwhistell, Henry W. Brosin, Norman A. McQuown, and Charles F. Hockett for their comments at various stages in my research. The paper has benefited extensively from the comments of four of the early participants in the NHI, and they have been very patient with my questions. A more complete version of the history of the NHI project may be found in Leeds-Hurwitz (1987a).

role of group therapist, albeit informally. She did not contribute to the major portion of the analysis, since she died shortly after the analytic work began (in 1957), and she did not write any of the chapters included in NHI; yet the project was hers as much as anyone's.

Although many writers refer to NHI as a single unified research project, it divides rather neatly into four distinct parts. Two of these took place at CASBS: seminars comprised primarily of Center fellows in residence during 1955–1956. Fromm-Reichmann actively participated in both of these. The first seminar, broadly exploratory, resulted in a brief analysis of a tape-recorded psychiatric interview prepared by Norman A. McQuown and published almost immediately. It was a general investigation into an area that appeared promising, fueled by Fromm-Reichmann's interest. The second seminar extended the initial exploration, more clearly focusing on a specific problem. Work continued through 1961 in a series of brief but productive meetings between the available members of the original team, plus a few others, added as their expertise seemed appropriate. These periodic meetings constitute phase three, and they resulted in much of the analysis of the material, as well as a large number of presentations to academic associations. Fromm-Reichmann participated in the first group meeting, but died before the completion of phase three. The last phase, work at the home institutions of three original seminar members, continued until they completed the final document in 1968. This involved a final spurt of effort devoted to writing up the analysis of the data in a form to be made available to others, so that the project could have greater impact. Even so, in its final form, NHI is a positively unwieldy document, essentially unpublishable due to a combination of its length and the complexity of the transcription which forms the body of the material. In 1971 McQuown submitted it to the University of Chicago for inclusion in its microfilm series, which thus made it at least somewhat available beyond those involved in its creation.

In the fall of 1955 a CASBS seminar began to study the ways in which language was related to aspects of behavior. Two psychiatrists (Frieda Fromm-Reichmann and Henry W. Brosin), together with two linguists (Charles F. Hockett and Norman A. McQuown) and three cultural anthropologists (Alfred L. Kroeber, David M. Schneider, David Aberle), held CASBS appointments during that year. All except Aberle participated in the seminar. It is quite likely that the CASBS deliberately brought together people from these disciplines to see what they could produce (see Leeds-Hurwitz, 1987b).

Once those invited as Center fellows were present, it was Fromm-Reichmann who served the crucial role of defining the particular research project. According to Bateson (1958), Fromm-Reichmann

> came with the definite intention of adding to the tools of her insight. She hoped to synthesize into her psychoanalytic background whatever skills and insights she might be able to glean from semantics, linguistics, and the theories of communication. . . . She already had extraordinary sensitivity to the overtones and nuances of human behavior, but she said that she felt insufficiently conscious of the actual non-verbal cues from which she arrived at her conclusions. It was her hope to achieve a greater consciousness in this sphere for herself. She was also concerned for psychiatrists in general, and especially for psychiatric students. She hoped that if it were possible to transcribe and point to the nonverbal transactions, this would provide an enormously valuable tool for the teaching of psychiatry [pp. 96–97].

Fromm-Reichmann was known for her insightful analysis of schizophrenic patients. She was interested in finding tangible evidence of psychiatric intuitions, and hoped that either linguistics or anthropology could provide the key to that evidence. It was becoming increasingly clear that the key was to be found in systematic analysis of nonverbal interactions occurring during psychiatric interviews. Interest in nonverbal behavior from the viewpoint of psychiatry was not limited to Fromm-Reichmann but was shared by others at this time (Brosin, 1971c). Fromm-Reichmann hoped to learn what it was that she did right so she could pass it on to her students before she died, and she hoped this information could be retrieved through the study of nonverbal communication. In addition, Fromm-Reichmann "was losing her hearing and knew she needed to *see* with more control" (Ray Birdwhistell, personal correspondence).

Fromm-Reichmann's 1955 paper provides an example of her interest in what she was then calling the "intuitive processes"; she suggested that nonverbal behavior was a part of that intuitive process. The article demonstrates her concern with "the factors which inhibit and promote intuitive processes in psychoanalytic psychotherapy with schizophrenics" and her awareness of the need for further research into the matter (p. 88). In that piece she concludes

> first, that intuitive processes are essentially the same as other thinking processes, and that there is nothing magical or mysterious about them; second, that the working of the intuitive processes in the analyst who treats schizophrenics may be looked upon as a function of the analyst's countertransference and his clear awareness of the realistic and transferred elements in the doctor-patient relationship; third, that severe anxiety in the analyst and his defenses against it constitute a serious source of interference, mild anxiety a potential source of stimulation of the successful operation of the analyst's intuitive processes and their therapeutic validity [p. 88].

At the request of Fromm-Reichmann, McQuown set aside his own project at the center in order to prepare a linguistic analysis of psychiatric interview materials. For convenience, he used a tape supplied by Otto Will, a colleague of Fromm-Reichmann's at Chestnut Lodge. He presented his findings to the group in January 1956, and published them in *Psychiatry* in 1957. He reports that the seminar group decided they needed tangible evidence for the reality of a psychiatrist's intuitions, and that research on language could supply such evidence (p. 79). His work involved creating a detailed phonetic transcription of the speech of the participants in the psychiatric interview, although the published article consists primarily of an analysis of that transcription. This analysis is really an early paralinguistic analysis, although it is not so labeled. (*Paralanguage* is generally defined as the study of vocal but not verbal phenomena, that is, sounds which are not words. This is usually taken to include such aspects of speech as near-words like "um hmm," sounds that clearly are not words, like a laugh, as well as intonation or pitch.) McQuown cites Edward Sapir (1927) for the initial insight that language provides the "largely out-of-awareness manifestation of the personality," and argues that no one had previously taken the time to follow up Sapir's idea. He implies, but does not quite state, that Sapir is to be credited with the initial insight that paralanguage is one of the means used to convey personality. The article concludes that researchers in the field of psychiatry might eventually be able to call on linguists and other social scientists to provide tools useful in four areas: (1) the initial diagnosis; (2) for checking the progress of therapy; (3) for prescribing appropriate personal and social contacts; and (4) as a teaching tool (p. 86).

Henry W. Brosin arrived at CASBS later than the others to find the project already under way. As a psychiatric educator, Brosin took particular interest in improving the training of students of psychiatry, much as Fromm-Reichmann did. Of all the psychiatrists who might have been selected for this project, Fromm-Reichmann and Brosin proved excellent choices, Fromm-Reichmann having published on nonverbal behavior as a part of the psychiatric interview, and Brosin having prior experience in multidisciplinary collaboration through the Macy Conferences on Cybernetics. In addition, they already knew each other from Chestnut Lodge, which may have proved useful during the early stages of the project.

The first seminar revealed that the study of paralinguistic phenomena was integral not only to the analysis of communicative behavior but also to the study of kinesic phenomena. *Kinesics* is the technical term for what is popularly labeled "body language." It involves the study of all communicative body motion, everything from raising an eyebrow to shifting posture. And so the participants began a second project to deal more explicitly with paralanguage and kinesics. Early in 1956, Fromm-Reichmann had Ray L. Birdwhistell, an anthropologist even then known for his work on kinesics, invited to the center for three days in order to judge the extent to which kinesics could contribute to the project. As a result of that visit, it was agreed that kinesics was a necessary part of the study, and so Birdwhistell joined the seminar in the summer of 1956.

Gregory Bateson was the last member of the group brought into the project. At the time he was nearby, at the Veteran's Administration Hospital in Palo Alto. As Bateson (1958) tells it:

> The team needed films of psychiatric material upon which they could immediately start work. I was present at their planning session on the first day of Birdwhistell's time at the Center, and found them dismayed at the prospect of losing precious weeks while appropriate film was prepared. I was able to say that I had such film ready for their examination [p. 97].

Bateson was then exploring family interaction in households where psychiatric problems were known to exist. However, it is important to note that the film Bateson supplied was not actually of a psychiatric interview, but a series of filmed interactions in a home, most of which consisted of Bateson interviewing various members of the family.

The initial film provided by Bateson, a part of which came to be known as the "Doris" film, became the primary source of data for the detailed analysis performed by the group. This actually was a series of settings filmed on the same day: the most important of these was the interview of "Doris" by Bateson, with her son, "Billy," playing nearby, which formed the basis of the detailed analysis in NHI. There were several other parts to the original film, however, and these were taken into account by the researchers: a conversation between Bateson and Doris's husband, "Larry," which took place while Doris made supper; and the supper itself. In addition, several subsequent films were made: Billy playing in the garden, Billy being bathed by his father, and an informal party at the house.

In June one additional film was made of Doris and her therapist specifically for the seminar's use. Also, Fromm-Reichmann and Brosin made four visits to Doris's therapist, one visit to Doris and Billy at home, and had several conferences with Bateson about the family during the summer of 1956 in order to obtain further information (Bateson, 1958, 1971b; Brosin,

1971b). Bateson (1958) suggests that the visits Fromm-Reich-mann and Brosin made to the real people, as opposed to the viewing of the same people on film, made a significant differ-ence in the analysis of the interaction.

> I had the feeling from the films and from the experience of participating in the making of the film that one of the families upon which we were working showed signs of grave distortion of communication but, while it was possible to discuss these signs, they did not seem so serious to the two psychiatrists. Later, they went together and visited the fam-ily and saw its members not flattened on the movie screen, but in the flesh. They then very quickly perceived that there was something seriously wrong, and both agreed about this [p. 98].

Bateson concludes from this that diagnosis must be based on more than purely objective data: it must have the additional data of personal experience (pp. 98–99).

It must be emphasized that only a few scenes from Bate-son's original interview of Doris were ever analyzed in detail; everything else was viewed as being necessary context to reach-ing a correct interpretation of those scenes. Furthermore, while the group's initial interest was the analysis of psychiatric inter-views, the interview chosen for detailed analysis was not a psy-chiatric interview. This is rarely mentioned, and so may be unintentionally misleading.

Setting the problem, locating the data to be analyzed, and gathering together the group members to do the analysis oc-cupied the spring and early summer of 1956. The problem set was a microanalysis of several short segments of the filmed interview. This involved the transcription (that is, creating a written record) and interpretation of the linguistic, paralin-guistic, and kinesic communication during the interview, with the addition of a psychiatric interpretation as well. It was to be comparable to the transcription and analysis prepared earlier by McQuown for the tape recording, but extending the focus from speech alone to movements as well. The data would be the films provided by Bateson, especially the segment labeled the "Doris" film. The group members were to be Fromm-Reichmann, Brosin, McQuown, Hockett, Birdwhistell, and Bateson, although even at this point Bateson's role was a tenuous one: unlike the others, he was still working full-time and so was only an infrequent participant in the analysis.

During the months of June, July, and August, the major portion of the analysis took place. At this point it consisted of the following stages:

1. "Soaking" (multiple viewing-listening): the film, with sound, was played fourteen times in joint sessions. This is a necessary preliminary stage to microanalysis, since a single viewing of a film is relatively uninformative. Each time the material is reviewed, more is noticed; so the more often it is viewed, the more likely it is that something significant will not be overlooked.

2. Scene selection: the group collectively decided which scenes should be given special attention. Microanalysis is extremely time-consuming, and it would not have been possible to prepare a transcription and analysis of everything. Therefore it was necessary to choose several short scenes which seemed to be particularly noteworthy. They chose the "cigarette" scene, the "sofa" scene, the "pillow" scene, and the "airplane" scene. The cigarette scene was chosen because it seems to mark a critical point in the interviewer-interviewee relationship. In it, Gregory lights Doris's cigarette. The sofa scene was chosen in order to observe all three persons present interacting together, where Doris and Gregory talk while Billy listens. The pillow scene was chosen in order further to observe the interaction between Doris and Billy. In it Billy gives Doris a pillow, and they struggle as to where it will be placed. The analysis of that scene was ambiguous, so the airplane scene was the next chosen, in order further to study the interaction between mother and son.

3. Intensive study: the initial study of each of the chosen scenes took place that summer. The initial transcript and analysis could be prepared, but there was no time during those few months to prepare a full transcription and analysis (McQuown, 1971b).

Steps 1 and 2 were joint efforts; step 3, the actual analysis, could not be performed by everyone together. Most of the initial analysis was performed by McQuown, Birdwhistell, and Brosin, with the others participating as necessary and possible (Brosin, personal correspondence). It was not Fromm-Reichmann's role to do the actual analysis; she had neither the appropriate training nor the interest in that aspect of the work. While the others were engaged in "soaking," Fromm-Reichmann and Brosin participated, but also spent time gaining further information on Doris, her family, therapist, and neighbors.

Bateson (1958) provides several comments describing Fromm-Reichmann's role at this stage of the research. First, he suggests that since the group was not trained in psychiatry, they found it difficult to observe family interaction in detail, and she served informally as group therapist during the sessions, making it easier for all of them to cope with the material. Second, Bateson notes,

> one of her great contributions to this team was that we fought very little about matters which were not worth fighting about. One did not in Frieda's presence say things which one could recognize as second-rate. Perhaps even one's power to recognize the second-rate was in some way enhanced when she was around. It was not that she behaved didactically, but rather that her very presence insisted upon simplicity [p. 98].

In other words, her very presence influenced the quality of the work, more than anything specific she might have said to the group. Third, and most important for Bateson himself, she served as an ever-present therapist for Bateson as the group analyzed his actions on screen, since

> there were for me moments of considerable pain when the others were interpreting my actions, and I was forced to see those actions on the screen. At such times, Frieda extended a basic wide friendliness which made it easier for me to evaluate what was being said without those feelings of rejection which would otherwise make the comments unacceptable. It was not that she reassured by diminishing the force of the critical comment. What she did was to lend that strength which enabled one to receive the comment [p. 99].

This is essentially the same role she played for the rest of the group members, helping them to cope with the material they were analyzing, but it was much more critical for Bateson, since he was at one and the same time participant in the interaction, and analyst of it, whereas the others were solely analysts.

Ray Birdwhistell (1959b) has also supplied a picture of Fromm-Reichmann's role in the NHI team:

> My memory of Fromm-Reichmann can best be expressed by relating the events of a single day in Stanford. Clear in my memory is the afternoon when she scolded the linguist who did not believe that he could be concerned with applied research and be a good linguist. Then she lectured a psychiatrist who, for the moment, was, to her way of thinking, being overconcerned in a research situation with being a physician. She then soothed the two younger members of the group, and summarized the interdisciplinary research issue in such a way that we all knew we were going back to work instead of giving up on the research.
>
> That night a cocktail party was given at the center, and a great number of very attractive young wives attended. Frieda arrived late, looked at the situation, took a rose out of the centerpiece, tucked it under her wristband, looked at it, looked around, and gradually most of the males in the placed drifted over next to her [n.p.].

Birdwhistell supplies several brief comments actually made by Fromm-Reichmann during the analysis of the data that summer in his published revision of appendix 6 (1970b). This is a detailed examination of one brief section of the film, the cigarette scene. The scene is eighteen seconds long, and had by then been subjected to the most intense microanalysis, but he was still able to say in 1970 that the scene "has remained a rich, only partially analyzed corpus" (p. 228). The focus of his analysis is one particular sentence in which Doris says to Gregory: "I suppose all mothers think their kids are smart, but I have no worries about that child's intellectual ability." In describing the tone of voice used by Doris here, Birdwhistell mentioned that she uses what Fromm-Reichmann "once described in conference as the 'voice of despair'" (p. 234). He goes on to mention that both Brosin and Fromm-Reichmann saw the word "but" as "the central lexical signal of the sentence" (p. 236). Since Birdwhistell includes a complete linguistic, paralinguistic, and kinesic transcription, this article provides a good example of what microanalytic transcriptions look like (see especially the final three charts, 3A, 3B and 3C, pp. 247–248).

Once the stays of the various fellows at the center came to an end, there was to be no further opportunity for the same sort of concentrated effort. That did not mean that no work could be done, just that it would take a longer period of time to accomplish the same amount of work. The project continued through a series of brief meetings of team members held sporadically from 1956 to 1961.

The analysis at this point consisted of the following steps:

1. Matching (and tagging with a frame number) particular points in the kinesic record with their counterparts in the linguistic record. In this way the linguistic and kinesic analyses could be coordinated. Since different people were preparing the analysis of speech and movements, it was critical that their transcriptions be carefully matched.

2. Identification of symptomatic features: those parts of interaction which served to punctuate activity in the scene were identified. *Punctuation* refers to division of the continuous stream of behavior into segments. An example would be Billy's interruptions of the conversation between Doris and Gregory. McQuown makes the point that everyone agreed on the identification of the critical points.

3. Specification of clusters of symptomatic features: the items labeled symptomatic were located in a variety of contexts throughout the film. The film was then reviewed, and all further examples of these same behaviors were noted.

4. Uncovering the interaction profile: the entire film was studied to establish the major shifts. There are frequent shifts in interaction, generally every few seconds, but there are also a small number of major shifts which needed to be located (McQuown, 1971b).

McQuown (1971c) provides some general comments which can be taken as applying to all of the meetings held during this period:

The course of our team work was not always smooth, there
was occasional distress, and rare but nonetheless real anger.
That four out of the original six members had had previous
extensive interdisciplinary contact, in fair part at the Josiah
Macy Foundation symposia, certainly contributed to the remarkable fact that the essential disciplinary components of
the original team are still represented on it [p. 3].

The Macy Conferences on Group Process served the function
of establishing a basis of common ideas and patterns of interaction between some of the participants (specifically, Bateson,
Birdwhistell, and Fromm-Reichmann), although the topic of
discussion was no longer the same. That the group members
had prior experience with multidisciplinary efforts (even if with
one another) could only minimize conflicts, not eliminate them
entirely.

The meetings can be divided into two parts: those held in
Buffalo (at Birdwhistell's home institution) from 1956 to 1958,
and those held in Pittsburgh (at Brosin's home institution) from
1958 to 1961. The meetings in Buffalo focused on refining the
methods of coding behavior and on preparing presentations
for a series of academic conferences: these included the American Orthopsychiatric Association, the American Psychiatric
Association, and the American Psychological Association (all
with Birdwhistell, McQuown, and Brosin participating), as well
as a special five- or six-day post-American Psychiatric Association meeting (with Birdwhistell, Brosin, and Bateson). In addition, there were many individual lectures and presentations,
specifically discussing the NHI analysis, especially by Birdwhistell and Brosin. The meetings in Pittsburgh focused on
turning the various papers into a single coherent draft of a
manuscript (Brosin, personal correspondence).

At the first Buffalo meeting, linguists Henry Lee Smith,
Jr. and George L. Trager were brought in as consultants. Trager and Smith were well known as descriptive linguists, spe-
cializing in the analysis of American speech patterns. They
participated in the meetings held in Buffalo but did not stay
with the group when it moved to Pittsburgh. Fromm-Reichmann was able to participate in only the first of the meetings

in Buffalo, and died on April 28, 1957, so her contributions to the group essentially ended with phase 2. Bateson (1958) says of Fromm-Reichmann's role at this stage:

> I don't think she said very much at all. She was enthusiastic, she was critical, and she was a touchstone. We would offer her our interpretation of this or that group of data, and she would comment, usually adding her interpretation to ours rather than pushing ours aside [p. 98].

Hockett originally had planned to spend the summer of 1957 working with Fromm-Reichmann, as an extension of the work at CASBS, and had obtained a grant to do so, but upon her death had to revise plans. At that point he began the work in Syracuse with Robert E. Pittenger and John J. Danehy that led to *The First Five Minutes* (1960), also a microanalysis of psychiatric interview materials. Hockett participated only infrequently in the Buffalo meetings, and withdrew formally when the meetings shifted to Pittsburgh, leaving his linguistic materials with McQuown.

Although the group had lost Fromm-Reichmann, Hockett, Smith, and Trager by the time it moved to Pittsburgh, Erik Erikson was added as a consultant briefly. Bateson attended both sets of meetings only sporadically, and ceased active participation by 1960, as he was becoming increasingly involved in studies of animal communication at that point. Thus the Pittsburgh meetings were regularly attended by only three members of the original group: McQuown, Birdwhistell, and Brosin.

The primary results of this period were the series of conference presentations made by group members, and the early draft of NHI. Although many of the conference papers have remained unpublished, they did serve to bring attention to NHI through the 1950s. The meetings were all within either psychiatric or psychological organizations, as shown by the examples mentioned above, which reveals the audience to which NHI was directed. Fromm-Reichmann had established the orientation of the project as the illumination of psychiatric intuition, and this continued to determine the audience more than the method of analysis did. If, on the other hand, the group had taken a greater interest in demonstrating the method for its own sake, it might have found a greater audience among those studying social communication in general. During the late 1950s, such people would have been found mainly within linguistic and anthropological associations.

Work continued through the 1960s at the home institutions of the three remaining members of the original team: Birdwhistell at the Eastern Pennsylvania Psychiatric Institute, Brosin at the Western Psychiatric Institute and Center, and McQuown at the University of Chicago. Each man worked with a team of associates and students, training them in methods of microanalysis through analyzing the "Doris" film. By September of 1968, *The Natural History of an Interview* was ready for publication. It was cited repeatedly by members of the group as being "in press," and there was every expectation that it would, in fact, be published by Grune and Stratton. Hope of publication, however, had to be abandoned due to the prohibitive cost of reproducing the transcription of the data. Finally the decision was made to include NHI in the microfilm series of the University of Chicago in 1971 so that it would at least be generally accessible at various libraries: in this version, the entire document is five large volumes, the transcription taking up three.

Since a large number of people were involved in each of the various stages, and since those involved at one point were not necessarily the same as those involved later, it may clarify the presentation to summarize who was involved when.

Phase 1: First CASBS Seminar (11/55–1/56)

    Frieda Fromm-Reichmann
    Norman A. McQuown
    Henry W. Brosin
    Charles F. Hockett
    Alfred L. Kroeber
    David M. Schneider

Phase 2: Second CASBS Seminar (2/56–8/56)

    Frieda Fromm-Reichmann
    Norman A. McQuown
    Henry W. Brosin
    Charles F. Hockett
    Ray L. Birdwhistell

Gregory Bateson
Phase 3: Infrequent Meetings (9/56–2/61)
    Norman A. McQuown (Buffalo, Pittsburgh)
    Henry W. Brosin (Buffalo, Pittsburgh)
    Charles F. Hockett (Buffalo)
    Ray L. Birdwhistell (Buffalo, Pittsburgh)
    Gregory Bateson (Buffalo, Pittsburgh)
    George L. Trager (Buffalo)
    Henry Lee Smith, Jr. (Buffalo)
    Erik Erikson (Pittsburgh)
Phase 4: Final Analysis (1961–1968)
    Norman A. McQuown at UC
        Starkey Duncan, Jr.
        William M. Austin
        William Offenkrantz
        Raven McDavid, Jr.
    Henry W. Brosin at WPIC
        William S. Condon
        Felix Loeb
        E. Joseph Charny
        Harvey Sarles
        Adam Kendon
        Kai Erikson
    Ray L. Birdwhistell at EPPI
        Albert Scheflen
        Margaret R. Zabor
        William M. Austin
        Raven McDavid, Jr.

Such a list leads to an overly simplistic view of NHI, and does not encourage consideration of the interaction among researchers and the role each played in the project. Such things are perhaps the most difficult to reconstruct after the fact, but also perhaps the most significant to know. What follows is a reconstruction of the role of each of the major participants aside from Fromm-Reichmann, whose role has already been described in detail.

Henry W. Brosin, as the other psychiatrist in the group, suggests that he and Fromm-Reichmann were the "clinicians and support-troops [used] to help the others see that it was all worth while to us" (Brosin, personal correspondence). But, un-like Fromm-Reichmann, Brosin was deeply involved in the ac-tual effort of transcription and analysis. He was one of the core group of three who were part of the project for the majority of the time it was in process. Not only did he participate while at CASBS, but he continued to participate in the group meetings at Buffalo and Pittsburgh, and trained a new generation of researchers using NHI while at WPIC. He wrote several of the chapters which make up the final volume (two alone, one jointly, and two appendices), and included explicitly related material in presentations at professional meetings and in his publica-tions.

Norman A. McQuown took over the leadership role from Fromm-Reichmann shortly before her death. He wrote the majority of the linguistic transcriptions and coordinated the efforts of the other three linguists (Hockett, Trager, and Smith). He was part of the group from the very beginning until the very end. He participated in virtually all of the meetings at every stage, and is still the acknowledged memory of the group (both Birdwhistell and Brosin suggested he should be trusted to know the details everyone else has forgotten). He participated in conferences, wrote the foreword, a chapter, three append-ices, and three joint chapters. He not only used the final product to train his students at the University of Chicago, but has made Spanish translations of much of the material to use in training students in Mexico today (published in McQuown, 1983).

Ray L. Birdwhistell joined the group well into phase 2, but remained one of the core members to the end. His was the primary responsibility for the kinesic transcription. He partic-ipated in the group meetings and not only read papers at professional meetings but incorporated conclusions from NHI into numerous presentations on kinesics to the public, thus broadening the audience. He wrote two chapters, three ap-pendices, and three joint chapters. He used NHI to train col-leagues at EPPI, just as Brosin did at WPIC.

Gregory Bateson supplied the initial data source in the films he made available to the group. He participated sporad-ically, in phases 2 and 3 only. He did write two chapters: one, the introduction, sets the frame for the remaining volume. Bateson was not known for his interest in the sort of meticulous detail work necessary for microanalysis, in fact, quite the contrary: he was known for his investigations of large overarching patterns. Yet the project was similar to much of his own work, both in its natural history method and application to psychiatric materials. He did participate in some of the early analysis of the data, and was a part of one of the group conferences.

Charles F. Hockett, part of the group in the beginning, dropped out in the middle of phase 3 in order to join a new research team at work on a similar problem. He is acknowledged for his genius in linguistics, but that did not necessarily fit him to this particular group. He did, however, write one chapter and one appendix of NHI and was one of the three authors of the transcription that makes up the bulk of the manuscript. Although a direct citation rarely appears in his work, he "regularly drew on the broadening of orientation the NHI work had given all of us" in later teaching and writing (Hockett, personal correspondence).

The advantage of a multidisciplinary team was that it provided different perspectives on the data. In the end, all of the participants contributed to the final project. Of the entire group, Brosin says: "We were all there, and each added something to the ongoing process. It was beautiful to have six opinions on one exchange between Doris and Gregory" (Brosin, personal correspondence).

Some discussion of the phrase "natural history" may be useful, since it plays such a significant role in the project. In the interview itself, while explaining the rationale for the filming session to Doris, Bateson (Birdwhistell et al., 1971a) described his original interest in gathering films as being part of a natural history:

> We're studying the disruption of communication between parents and children, trying to get some idea of the various gambits that the two sides use, in trying to get together, or the degree to which the gambits separate them or bring them together. There's very little been done, actually, on the natural history of what does happen between parents and children. . . . It's very obvious, it's very accessible, ready to do. And most of what is said about parents and children

is on somebody's report of what happens. So we're trying
to get in and do the natural history of it a little [pp.
60L–60O].

Bateson (1971a) expands on this:

We start from a particular interview on a particular day
between two identified persons in the presence of a child,
a camera and a cameraman. Our primary data are the mul-
titudinous details of vocal and bodily action recorded on
this film. We call our treatment of such data a "natural
history" because a minimum of theory guided the collection
of the data [p. 6].

The reasons for choosing a natural history approach are con-
cisely put in a statement published by Birdwhistell (1970a) but
attributed to Bateson: "Our new recognition of the complexity
and patterning of human behavior has forced us to go back
and go through the natural history phase of the study of man
which earlier scholars skipped in their haste to get to laboratory
experimentation" (p. 39). This comment is undeservedly buried, for it provides an important explanation of their choice of
method.

The most extensive discussion of the natural history
method contained in NHI, however, comes not from Bateson
but Brosin, in chapter 4. In this he examines the differences
between a natural history and an experimental approach in
detail. Brosin (1971b) argues that although both have their
place, "It appears to us that naturalistic methods are essential
in the early phase of the development of a science" (p. 48). The
division between naturalistic and experimental approaches has
been a significant issue over the years: the experimental approach has been traditionally highly valued as the appropriate
way to do legitimate scientific research, while the naturalistic
approach has been devalued, since (among other arguments)
it is neither easy to replicate nor to generalize from the results.

It is important to remember that NHI was not viewed by
its authors as an ending but as a beginning. It was an exploratory
project, designed to discover what could be learned about communication through microanalysis. The group came to recog-

nize that communication involves much more than words alone, and Bateson (1971a) suggests they wanted "to see every detail of word, vocalization, and bodily movement as playing its part in determining the ongoing stream of words and bodily movements which is the interchange between the persons" (p. 9). The result was that they needed to begin by developing adequate methods of transcribing vocalizations and body movements (a good system for the transcription of language was already available). Initial work on both paralanguage and kinesics had been started in the 1940s at the Foreign Service Institute, but the notation systems were not yet complete (Leeds-Hurwitz, 1987b).

The completed work was envisioned as a training manual for those beginning to study social interaction, and has been used as such by McQuown, Birdwhistell, and Brosin (during phase 4 of the project itself, primarily, although to a lesser extent after). McQuown is the team member who has been most committed to actually using the completed document as a training manual with new students, and he is the only one still actively using it for that purpose today. Presumably, it was intended to be a self-sufficient manual, although it is difficult to use without the addition of the "Doris" film (available only to severely restricted audiences, due to the need for confidentiality) and, preferably, one of the participants of NHI as a guide to the materials presented.

Chapter 1, "Communication," is an introduction to the whole by Bateson (1971a). It begins by describing the various strands of research which led to the project, ending with the presentation of one of Bateson's own contributions, the significance of learning to learn. He explicitly states one of the important assumptions of the project: "that the microscopic will reflect the macroscopic" (p. 39). This is a critical point which is rarely discussed elsewhere in the manuscript. Bateson (1971a) explains further that

> we are concerned in this book to present the techniques for the microscopic examination of personal interaction. While, of course, the words that people say to each other have importance, the question with which we are concerned, the

problem of describing the relationship between persons, is not a question which can be answered by any summary of the dictionary meaning of their messages. . . . The ultimate goal of the procedures outlined in this book is a statement of the mechanism of relationships [pp. 39–40].

The analysis of interaction had to be preceded by a detailed description of that interaction. Description, in turn, required good notation systems.

Chapter 2, "Vocal Activity," is a summary of research in descriptive linguistics and paralanguage by Hockett. Although it is appropriate to treat paralanguage as an extension of the study of language, that is, to assume that an adequate study of language will include paralanguage, this approach, as followed here by Hockett, has rarely been followed by later researchers. This chapter assumes no knowledge on the part of the reader, and is a good, clear introduction. As Bateson did earlier, Hockett (1971) explicitly states one of the assumptions of the research of importance to his chapter: "All habits of vocal activity, and of responses thereto, are part of human *culture*, and, as such, are *patterned, systematic*, and therefore *susceptible to analysis and description*" (p. 4).

Chapter 3, "Body Motion," is a parallel introduction to kinesics by Birdwhistell (1971). The main point made is that "while body motion behavior is based in the physiological structure, the communicative aspects of this behavior are patterned by social and cultural experiences," so specific meanings cannot be associated with specific movements but "can be derived only from the examination of the patterned structure of the system of body motion as a whole as this manifests itself in the particular social situation" (p. 1). In other words, the common assumption that individual movements always convey particular meanings is completely incorrect: movements can only be correctly interpreted if the context in which they occur is taken into account. The majority of the chapter is devoted to acquainting an untrained reader with the basics of kinesic analysis.

Chapter 4, "Implications for Psychiatry" by Brosin, is perhaps the most relevant chapter for an audience of psychiatrists. In addition to an extensive literature review of prior efforts on the part of psychiatric researchers to deal with speech as well as movements, he supplies a detailed description of what he considered the most useful positive and negative implications of the NHI research for psychiatrists. On the positive side of the balance, Brosin (1971a) suggests: (1) intensive repeated viewing and listening to a short but carefully selected segment of filmed interaction provides new perspectives and insights; (2) it also provides increased awareness of minimal cues; (3) it provides the possibility to analyze and substantiate clinical insights on the part of one person through the observation of data available to several therapists; (4) it provides evidence that all events in human interaction are interrelated, especially in family interaction; (5) the techniques of analysis can help a clinician to ask highly specific questions of the data; (6) very small samples of interaction can provide considerable information if carefully chosen; (7) filmed interaction can be used as training devices; (8) in the future, analysis of filmed interaction may lead to dynamic diagnostic formulation of an illness from a relatively small sample of behavior; (9) they can be used to help compare and evaluate different therapeutic procedures by studying "control" patients; and (10) they can lead to easy presentation of specific cases to other clinicians at professional meetings.

And on the negative side of the balance: (1) it is unlikely that film can ever replace contact with real people in clinical research; (2) film destroys the privacy of the therapeutic transaction; (3) analysis of filmed interaction requires specialized training, and is not immediately possible for everyone; (4) the mechanics of recording interaction may introduce distortions and omissions which could lead to misinterpretations; (5) there is a danger of seeing only that which we have been trained to see; (6) it requires much time and effort to analyze even a short filmed interaction and many researchers feel that this may not be warranted given the amount of material requiring analysis; however, he concludes more positively that microanalysis has the potential of producing new data and hypotheses inaccessible otherwise; (7) comparative data are urgently needed; (8) more comprehensive psychological theories of personality to test are needed; and (9) microanalysis leads to the accumulation of a large body of data very quickly.

In chapter 5 Bateson (1971b) provides an accounting of "The Actors and the Setting." He supplies details of how he made the acquaintance of Doris, and a descripton of the filming itself, as well as information about the camera, film, size of the living room, etc. His one criticism of his own data is that too little interaction between Doris and her husband, Larry, was documented. This would have added considerably to the filmed record.

Chapter 6, "Transcript, Transcription, and Commentary," is the heart of the document. It is a detailed transcription of selected portions of the filmed interview, prepared by Birdwhistell, Hockett, and McQuown (1971a). Its creation required the majority of the time devoted to the project, and it makes up the majority of the report. It represents the transcription of approximately ten minutes of interaction, that is, selected scenes, not ten continuous minutes of interaction. Physically this chapter consists of a small number of enormously complex charts. Every movement, every sound made by any of the participants has been graphed onto paper. The result is, of course, unreadable to anyone not trained in linguistic, paralinguistic, and kinesic notation systems (although guides to these are provided in the appendices). It is at one and the same time the reason for existence of NHI and the reason NHI was never published. There was no easy way to print the charts, and so the whole has remained unpublished.

Chapter 7, "Communicative Baselines and Symptomatic Features," provides verbal summaries of what was learned from the detailed microanalysis provided in chapter 6. It also has sections by Birdwhistell, Hockett, and McQuown (1971b). Baselines are described as being generalizations about an actor's idiosyncratic variation from the cultural norm, that is, descriptions of "normal" behavior to be expected from a particular individual. Symptomatic features are those events which help access idiosyncratic contributions to the interaction.

Chapter 8 is "The Psychiatric Overview of the Family Setting," presented by Brosin (1971c). He provides summaries of each individual (father, mother, and son) and then of the family as a whole. He concludes with an analysis of Bateson's role as interviewer in the film, and his interactions with the family members. A sample of the description of Bateson's role when interviewing Doris with Billy playing nearby will make clear the type of analysis presented.

> At times he is able to carry on the interplay in harmony with Doris and Billy at several different levels simultaneously in a manner which is reassuring to both. As various narcissistic, erotic or aggressive components emerge in the interaction system, the observer can detect the interviewer's skill either at encouraging or at dampening the steady flow of messages by his use of the matchbox or the beer stein. If one accepts the challenge that no human interaction can be absolutely neutral, and that "intellectual" and "emotional" levels of communication are merely abstractions, the observer can follow the interaction from beginning to end as an intelligible continuum like a chess game or a drama in which the opening exploratory movements can be clearly distinguished from the middle and the end of the game [p. 18].

Chapter 9, entitled "Collation," is a summary prepared by McQuown (1971b) of what was learned from the transcription and analysis previously presented. It provides some details on the separate stages of the project, but the bulk of the chapter is taken up by a list of twenty-two hypotheses (created by Brosin as the psychiatrist on the team at the time) that would be of interest to therapists and which could be checked by the methods used in NHI. Discussion of what was learned about each through the project, with details of the transcription used to provide evidence, is also provided. The original discussion cannot be reproduced or even summarized easily here, since it involves the presentation of extensive amounts of data, but one of the twenty-two will be discussed briefly as an example.

In a series of hypotheses about the problems of organization of the interchange between patient and therapist, McQuown (1971b) quotes Brosin as suggesting, "*Props* are important to the regulation of therapist-patient interaction and their precise function may be specified by focusing on the speech and body-motion activity which involves such regulators" (p. 15). Six pages detailing the use of props during the film are provided, after which McQuown draws the conclusions that props are extensions of speech and body motion activity, that they are always potentially multivalent, and that the contextual data are necessary to decide how to interpret their use (p. 51).

Chapter 9 concludes with a comparison of what was learned from the linguistic, kinesic, and psychiatric analyses of the material. The focus here is on the division markers between units of interaction, and the different forms of analysis. There is no one-to-one correspondence between the units as analyzed in the three topic areas in the stream of discourse. Instead, McQuown (1971b) quotes Birdwhistell's summary that "the body-motion behavior tended to break into two-second sequences, the linguistic into three-second intervals, and the complexes evaluated by the psychiatrists [at this time Erik Erikson was working with Brosin] into four-second stretches" (p. 67).

Chapter 10, "Summary, Conclusions, and Outlook," is also written by McQuown (1971c). It provides a brief overview of the entire project, a listing of the conclusions of the various team members after the project had been completed, and a variety of contexts to which the conclusions gained from NHI could be applied. These included doctor-patient relationships, classroom interaction, courts of law, international conferences, relationships between anthropological field workers and informants, and a host of others. The comments provided by the participants make clear what they felt was learned from NHI. This is not available elsewhere in such explicit form, and so will be quoted at length. Additional comments from these participants are provided from other sources where available.

From Bateson's point of view: (1) We have learned more about *interaction* as punctuated into *contexts of learning* and we have accumulated empirical data on the continuity and cyclicity of the double-bind. (2) We have discovered *empirical markers* for shifting logical types and have found that such markers tend to be metacommunicative. (3) We have seen that both the *digital* analysis of "pip" and "bit" phenomena and the *analogic* analysis of total pattern or system phenomena are appropriate on every level. (4) We have experienced both the value of *microanalysis* of the structure of short sequences and the usefulness of *macroanalysis* of the structure of total scenes. (5) We have both new information and new kinds of information on the *resistance of systems* to parametric change (pp. 4–5).

From Birdwhistell's point of view: (1) *Kinesics* as a research area has been revived and a new macrokinesic recording system has been worked out and tried out. (2) We have been forced both into *technological innovation* (better film focus, better sound track) and into a recognition of the need for it (good color film, a fool-proof calibration system for coordinating sight and sound). (3) We have been obliged to explore the area of *parakinesics* and to devise a frame within which to describe parakinesic phenomena. (4) We have learned that the amount of the body involved in *simultaneous language and gesture* is large and we have begun to explore the extent to which they supplement or reinforce each other. (5) We have been forced to recognize that no single channel and no single unit within any type of channel by itself means any particular thing: *what* is conveyed must be *discovered anew in each context*, and whatever it is, though it may involve ambiguity, it never gives rise to contradiction (pp. 5–6). During the course of his data analysis, Birdwhistell further suggested that the researchers had not forgotten their original concern with psychiatric intuition. He mentions that "it may very well be possible to equip psychiatrists with sufficient insight into the nature of the communicational process to make their own intuitions explicit and thus more available to their colleagues" (1959a, p. 103). This is, of course, just what Fromm-Reichmann had originally hoped would be possible.

Returning to McQuown (1971b), from Brosin's point of view: (1) Our work has strengthened the assumption of *psychic determinism*: we have discovered system within system within system in multilevel homeostasis. (2) We have been provided with new tools for the study of *group dynamics*, and their use has forced us to recognize new dimensions of complexity in group organization. (3) Our investigations have provided new support for *social matrix theories* of personality (character?) (temperament?) development and have reinforced the conviction that items of behavior as such are never abnormal—only constellations are. (4) We have been forced to suspect the artificiality of recognized *physiological limens* and to expand tremendously the area of subrecall learning (of things which happen in as little as 1/24 of a second). (5) We have an entirely new conception of *psychological time* and a new appreciation of how much interaction takes place in a second of chronological time. (6) With Fromm-Reichmann we now recognize the possibility of still further restricting the working area of unspecifiable intuition: describable and communicable bases for *psychiatric intuitions* are now at hand. (7) We can now detect specifiable speech and body-motion behavior that confirms for us the adage that *repression is the price of civilization* and shows us the details of this mechanism for learning not to learn (pp. 6–7).

Brosin (1959) also mentions that the original goal of making a psychoanalyst's intuitions explicit was felt to be near: "We have reason to believe that 'intuition' can be recorded, studied, and compared with various kinds of clinical and social science data which will make the bases for such insights intelligible" (p. 120). He also said: "I believe that, at bottom, I have only one major conclusion, namely, that human communication can be studied systematically, rigorously, and objectively" (personal correspondence).

From McQuown's (1971b) point of view: (1) We have seen that although the *general principles of behavioral analysis* are the same for both speech and body-motion behavior, there are no two cultural systems with entirely analogous structures. (2) We have come to realize that we have no established baselines for speech and body-motion behavior in any of our sociocultural groups (none for children, none for suburbia, none for geographical areas), against which we might find it possible to measure individual behavior. (3) We have been forced to recognize that without *comparative studies* of speech and body-motion behavior in families which would give us some idea of the norms for such behavior and its range of variation, we cannot place the behavior of any one family along that range. (4) We have been obliged to develop the area of *paralinguistics* devoted to a systematic study of all those vocal phenomena which are separate from language, but in which language is embedded. (5) We have been brought to a realization of the need for new linguistic research into larger-than-sentence-size units, into spontaneous conversational materials, and into the variability manifest in the speech of members of a much wider variety of social groups (pp. 7–8).

Hockett was not included in McQuown's summary statement since he was no longer part of the NHI team when that overview was prepared, but he suggests, "Actually, perhaps the most significant consequences of NHI were important reorientations for the participants in their own work" (personal correspondence).

One way of summarizing the extensive comments given above, without implying that any less was gained from the project, is to say that NHI provided the basis for a view of communication which suggests that it is patterned (nonrandom, rule-governed, predictable, and therefore analyzable); learned (not inborn, and therefore different for each culture); context-bound (behavior has meaning only in a specific context); multichannel (more than just words, communication is a complex combination of words, movements, use of space, etc.); and continuous (it never stops).

The manuscript concludes with ten projected appendices, only eight of which are actually included. These consist primarily of details of the notational systems used in the transcription, as well as extensive bibliographic citations.

Conclusion

Frieda Fromm-Reichmann was interested in obtaining tangible evidence for her intuitive reactions to her psychiatric patients. She hoped that linguistics and anthropology would be able to provide such evidence, and that detailed study of psychiatric interviews would lead to concrete findings that could be relayed to her students. In this way she hoped to be able to pass on some of the knowledge she had but could not verbalize to her students before her death. She used the time at CASBS in 1955–56 to first check out the possibility of applying techniques of linguistic analysis to other aspects of communication, and when that proved appropriate, she helped to launch a more detailed research project designed to study interaction in detail, and discover what parts were the basis for intuition.

Fromm-Reichmann was interested only in psychiatric interviews, and the data used in the first brief seminar were taken from such an interview. Due to time constraints, the data used for the longer research project were from an interview of a patient by someone accustomed to working with psychiatric patients. The results of the project certainly can be applied to psychiatric interviews, but the distinction is important.

Fromm-Reichmann set the direction of the project: she was not interested in research for its own sake, but wanted results specifically applicable to the training of psychiatric residents. In part due to this initial impetus, related articles written by the project members were generally published in psychiatric journals, such as *Psychiatry* and *Psychiatric Research Reports*, and conference presentations on the data were generally made to organizations such as the American Psychological Association, the American Psychiatric Association, and the American Orthopsychiatric Association. This kept discussion of the research before psychiatrists, but meant that those who would further the research did not have an easy time locating the publications. In addition, the fact that NHI was essentially unpublishable in its final form did not help convince anyone, either in psychiatry or the behavioral sciences, that the research was significant.

Throughout the entire project there was a dual focus: (1) on the specific problem of creating an adequate transcription of interaction; and (2) on generalizations that could be learned about communication from this detailed study of a single interaction. Both of these aspects of the project have had an impact on later work, but the specifics of creating a transcription have perhaps unjustly been considered by others to be the more important contribution of NHI to the study of behavior. Only a few researchers will ever spend the time and effort necessary to learn the techniques of microanalysis of interaction, yet a large number of researchers can benefit from the broader conclusions of the project.

Specifically, in terms of creating methods of transcribing interaction, NHI led to the creation and development of methods of transcribing paralanguage, and all current research in that area can be traced to the initial work on NHI; methods of transcribing kinesic behavior were developed, and all current research in that area can be traced to the initial work by one of the participants of NHI, Birdwhistell, who used NHI as his largest project in developing that area. In addition, film is generally accepted as an essential tool for the study of interaction today, and NHI was the first project to study social communication in detail through the use of film. And in terms of generalizations learned from the project about the nature of communication (in any context, not just interviews, psychiatric or otherwise), the project led to the current understanding of communication as patterned, learned, context-bound, multichannel, and continuous behavior.

The initial hypothesis that Fromm-Reichmann brought to the group was proven correct: it is possible to use analytic techniques developed by linguists and anthropologists to investigate intuition, and to demonstrate that nonverbal behavior is the source of intuitive decisions made by therapists. This finding has had an impact on research into other communicative contexts than interviews: all communication is patterned, and therefore can be analyzed in detail by researchers.

At the same time that the project was successful in the above ways, it failed to achieve initial goals. That is, it did not lead to new methods of training for psychiatric residents beyond the small group influenced directly by members of the team (Brosin, Scheflen, and others involved directly in psychiatric research and training). This can be attributed to several factors: (1) NHI was never published, so has influenced a smaller number of people than it otherwise might have; (2) the methods developed require extensive training before they can be applied, and so do not appeal to a wide audience; and (3) the traditional bias toward quantitative data in clinical studies leads to skepticism of qualitative methods, such as those used in NHI, and to questions of replicability.

In a sense the project lies between two territories, not fully a part of either because it was part of both. In method, NHI clearly fits in the behavioral sciences: closely linked to linguistics and anthropology initially, some of the material covered (paralanguage, kinesics) is now more often found in the discipline of communication. In content, the project was specifically intended as an investigation of psychiatric interviews, which would lead to immediate training applications, a very narrow focus of interest primarily to psychiatric educators. This is the danger of all multidisciplinary research: it may not be fully accepted by any of the contributory disciplines as appropriate because it is different from the usual research in all.

References

Bateson, G. (1958), Language and psychotherapy. *Psychiatry, 21:96–100.*
——— *(1971a)*, Chapter 1: Communication. In: *The Natural History of an Interview*, ed. N. A. McQuown. Microfilm Collection of Manuscripts on Cultural Anthropology, Fifteenth Series. Chicago: University of Chicago, Joseph Regenstein Library, Department of Photoduplication, pp. 1–40.
——— (1971b), Chapter 5: The actors and the setting. In: *The Natural History of an Interview*, ed. N. A. McQuown. Microfilm Collection of Manuscripts on Cultural Anthropology, Fifteenth Series. Chicago: University of Chicago, Joseph Regenstein Library, Department of Photoduplication, pp. 1–5.
Birdwhistell, R. L. (1952), *Introduction to Kinesics.* Washington, DC: Department of State, Foreign Service Institute.
——— (1959a), Contribution of linguistic-kinesic studies for the understanding of schizophrenia. In: *Schizophrenia*, ed. A. Auerback. New York: Ronald Press, pp. 99–123.
——— (1959b), Memorial to Dr. Fromm-Reichmann. In: *Group Process*, ed. B. Schaffner. New York: Josiah Macy Foundation.
——— (1970a), There are smiles. In: *Kinesics and Context: Essays on Body Motion Communications.* Philadelphia: University of Pennsylvania Press, pp. 29–39.
——— (1970b), A kinesic-linguistic exercise: The cigarette scene, In: *Kinesics and Context: Essays on Body Motion Communication.* Philadelphia: University of Pennsylvania Press, pp. 227–250.
——— (1971), Chapter 3: Body motion. In: *The Natural History of an Interview*, ed. N. A. McQuown. Microfilm Collection of Manuscripts on Cultural Anthropology, Fifteenth Series. Chicago: University of Chicago, Joseph Regenstein Library, Department of Photoduplication, pp. 1–93.
——— Hockett, C. F., & McQuown, N. A., (1971a). Chapter 6: Transcript, transcription and commentary. In: *The Natural History of an Interview*, ed. N. A. McQuown. Microfilm Collection of Manuscripts on Cultural Anthropology, Fifteenth Series. Chicago: University of Chicago, Joseph Regenstein Library, Department of Photoduplication, n.p.
——— ——— ——— (1971b), Chapter 7: Communicative baselines and symptomatic features. In: *The Natural History of an Interview*, ed. N. A. McQuown. Microfilm Collection of Manuscripts on Cultural Anthropology, Fifteenth Series. Chicago: University of Chicago, Joseph Regenstein Library, Department of Photoduplication, pp. 1–15.
Brosin, H. W. (1959), Discussion of Ray Birdwhistell's contribution of linguistic-kinesic studies for the understanding of schizophrenia. In: *Schizophrenia*, ed. A. Auerback. New York: Ronald Press, pp. 118–122.

——— (1971a), Chapter 4: Implications for psychiatry. In: *The Natural History of an Interview*, ed. N. A. McQuown. Microfilm Collection of Manuscripts on Cultural Anthropology, Fifteenth Series. Chicago: University of Chicago, Joseph Regenstein Library, Department of Photoduplication, pp. 1–26.

——— (1971b), Chapter 8: The psychiatric overview of the family setting. In: *The Natural History of an Interview*, ed. N. A. McQuown. Microfilm Collection of Manuscripts on Cultural Anthropology, Fifteenth Series. Chicago: University of Chicago, Joseph Regenstein Library, Department of Photoduplication, pp. 1–82.

——— (1971c), Appendix 9: Bibliographic citations of clinical examples of nonverbal behavior. In: *The Natural History of an Interview*, ed. N. A. McQuown. Microfilm Collection of Manuscripts on Cultural Anthropology, Fifteenth Series. Chicago: University of Chicago, Joseph Regenstein Library, Department of Photoduplication, pp. 1–26.

Fromm-Reichmann, F. (1955), Clinical significance of intuitive processes of the psychoanalyst. *J. Amer. Psychoanal. Assn.*, 3:82–88.

Hockett, C. F. (1971), Vocal activity. In: *The Natural History of an Interview*, ed. N. A. McQuown. Microfilm Collection of Manuscripts on Cultural Anthropology, Fifteenth Series. Chicago: University of Chicago, Joseph Regenstein Library, Department of Photoduplication, pp. 1–7.

Leeds-Hurwitz, W. (1987a), The social history of *The Natural History of an Interview*. *Research on Language and Social Interaction*, 20:1–51.

——— (1987b), Intercultural communication and anthropology: Understanding their common history. *Practicing Anthropology*, 9:4, 11.

McQuown, N. A. (1957), Linguistic transcription and specification of psychiatric interview materials. *Psychiatry*, 20:79–86.

——— (1971a), Foreword. In: *The Natural History of an Interview*, ed. N. A. McQuown. Microfilm Collection of Manuscrips on Cultural Anthropology. Chicago: University of Chicago, Joseph Regenstein Library, Department of Photoduplication, pp. 1–5.

——— (1971b), Chapter 9: Collation. In: *The Natural History of an Interview*, ed. N. A. McQuown. Microfilm Collection of Manuscripts on Cultural Anthropology. Chicago: University of Chicago, Joseph Regenstein Library, Department of Photoduplication, pp. 1–69.

——— (1971c), Chapter 10: Summary, conclusions, and outlook. In: *The Natural History of an Interview*, ed. N. A. McQuown. Microfilm Collection of Manuscripts on Cultural Anthropology. Chicago: University of Chicago, Joseph Regenstein Library, Department of Photoduplication, pp. 1–10.

——— (1983), *El microanalisis de estrevistas. Los Metodos de la Historia Natural Aplicados a la Investigacion de la Sociedad, de la Cultura y de la Personalidad* [*The Microanalysis of Interviews: The Methods of Natural History Applied to the Investigation of Society, Culture and Personality*]. Mexico City: Universidad Nacional Autonoma de Mexico.

Pittenger, R. E., Hockett, C. F., and Danehy, J. J. (1960), *The First Five Minutes: A Sample of Microscopic Interview Analysis*. Ithaca, NY: Paul Martineau.

Sapir, E. (1927), Speech as a personality trait. *Amer. J. Sociol.*, 32:892–905.

PART II
PSYCHOANALYTICALLY ORIENTED TREATMENT OF SCHIZOPHRENIA

6

IN MEMORY OF FRIEDA

Otto Allen Will, Jr., M.D.

As do all of us, I remember Frieda Fromm-Reichmann, whose impact on me was profound. She touched my life, both personal and professional, in many ways, and it is about the part she played in influencing my thinking that I want to talk today.

My first encounter with Frieda was when I attended a lecture she gave on "Assets of the Mentally Handicapped." I came to it puzzled, discouraged, and often repelled by the welter of psychotic performances in which I felt entrapped by my job at the time. What she said made sense to me, giving me both relief and encouragement to look at my work in a different way.

Up until that time, my attitudes toward psychiatry were negative. In medical school I had planned to be a psychiatrist, having known in my home a strange and puzzling mixture of attachment, fear, hatred, dependency, prejudice, poorly founded ideas and beliefs, and a caring that was not far from love. However, after seeing the psychiatric practices of the day and the contempt often expressed for "mental" patients, I turned to the seemingly more concrete and tangible world of internal medicine. Just before the war, I had been appointed as fellow in internal medicine at the Mayo Clinic, but then came military service, followed by a severe surgical illness. As a result, I ended up as a navy psychiatrist in charge of the service at St. Elizabeths Hospital in Washington.

For some time, necessity forced me to forgo involvement in my administrative duties at the hospital. By 1945 I had interviewed and written reports on over 4,000 patients, variously classified and labeled in accordance with the current customs, but I had not spent more than a few minutes with any of them.

I could no longer shield myself from the distress in my surroundings by concerning myself with the ever-present needs for provision of food, clothing, shelter, the restriction of violence, and the giving of physical medical care.

That lecture by Frieda was a spur to taking a second look at what could be done with severely disturbed patients. The glass was turned and I began to see through it another view of what was included under the rubric *psychiatry*. I met Dexter Bullard, David and Margaret Rioch, Robert and Mabel Cohen, Alfred Stanton, and Anne Bullard who, with her hope, faith, and courage, helped guide and promote the growth of the Lodge. There I personally found new meaning for what we call mental illness, and for life itself.

Influenced by some of my reading and colleagues, I began to stay still—to listen to and observe some of the people called "crazy" in contrast to treating them with procedures designed to reduce or eliminate their troubling behavior at almost any cost. For me this task was not easy. Reluctant to confront facts of uncertainty and ignorance, I wanted understanding, clarity, and explanations. I had spent much time in authoritarian situations—home, school, the military—and although I might in all humility have denied the goal, I wanted to be an authority in charge of events in the professional and personal fields in which I lived. It took me some time to learn that the field into which I had now stumbled was the wrong one for someone with these ambitions. Even to this day I have not always been able to avoid them and learn the acceptance of ambiguity presented to me by Frieda and her kind. For the good of us all, I am glad she is not so unique that she stands alone in promoting the confrontation of uncertainty.

Personal Memories of Frieda

After the death of Sullivan in 1949, I became a patient of Frieda's and continued as such until her death in 1957. I was also a member of the staff at the Lodge. The purity of transference was therefore not unsullied, but about this I have no regrets. Transference of past to present—and to expectations of the future—exists in all circumstances. In its recognition acceptance, and study lies the source of much learning. I learned a great deal, and I am most grateful for the fact that processes were set in motion that enabled further and necessary learning to occur. Of greatest importance to me was the demonstration of kindness and compassion in a situation marked by both closeness and distance, whereby I was encouraged to seek the freedom to be myself and to accept the loneliness that may accompany that search.

I have many remembrances of the "little lady on the hill," and I shall mention very briefly a few that have stayed with me most prominently.

Fromm-Reichmann, unlike some other physicians I have known, made house calls. On one occasion I was ill at home with the flu. I was alone, as my wife, Gwen, was in Europe with World Health. Frieda came to visit, simply saying that she wanted to check on my state of health. There was no fanfare. Nothing could have been more simple. She was good medicine, and despite my feeling a bit awkward at this appearance of such a personage, now briefly detached from the more familiar surroundings of office and conference room, I pulled myself together and rapidly improved.

Of course during therapy I spoke frequently of my mother and of what to me were the many mysteries of her being. Frieda said that she would like to meet her, and on one of her visits to the West she loved, visited my parents' home in Colorado. At first I resented the realistic intrusion on my life, but I could not avoid thinking about her comments on my mother and about the part I myself had played in the disturbances at home. That Frieda cared enough to make that visit was extremely important in the therapeutic relationship between us.

Frieda served as godmother to our son. At often unexpected hours my wife would receive a telephone call: "Gwen, I have a vacancy in my schedule and I'd like to see Patrick." Gwen would immediately bring the baby to the cottage and sit aside while Frieda and Patrick enjoyed each other. The request was not exactly a command, but I don't think it was ever refused! Inconvenient as they sometimes were, those were good visits, giving pleasure to infant, mother, doctor—and to me.

I recall an occasion when I was fatigued, anxious, and discouraged to the extent that I told Frieda I could not meet my scheduled appointments for the day. There was a slight chill in her response. "You are a doctor. This is your work. You are needed." I felt ashamed, much as I had a few years before when, aboard ship and tired of what I had seen of the war, I said to the pharmacist's mate that I'd like to turn my back on all of it and get out on some nonexistent idyllic island. I shall never forget his sharp response and call to responsibility. "Lieutenant, we are officers. We are navy men." For such remarks I am thankful.

There were many accounts of Frieda's perceptiveness and ability to get to the center of things with deeply disturbed and psychotic people. By comparison with some of these tales, my own revelations as a patient seemed to me to be unendingly repetitious, dull, boring, colorless, and at times actually tawdry. I rather envied the boldness of action of some patients and their apparent ability to incite interest and useful response on Frieda's part. One day I said, "I suppose if I were lodged on the disturbed floor, had strange visions, cut myself, and made a mess, you would be really interested in me and pay more attention to what is going on." Her reply was useful to me. "You are probably right," she said, "but in the end I don't think it would be worth all the effort." I agree.

On the evening of April 27, 1957, Frieda visited our home, ate supper, talked with us, and played with our son who was by then nearly 14 months old. At one point he turned from her and, briefly, she seemed hurt and rejected by his action. On the drive to her home at the Lodge I spoke of my current work with a patient and heard her say. "Don't get too involved." I felt both warning and rebuke, and was caught up in a sense of loneliness I did not then understand. At the door of her house I heard her small but firm good night, and waited outside until the lights went on, reassuring me by their glow that everything inside was all right.

I saw her the next afternoon in that house. She was dead of a coronary occlusion. I wish I could have told her things not for the telling, and asked questions not for the asking. But it was too late.

Looking Under the Lid

As I have said, my way of thinking about patients, and about my own attitudes toward people and life, was profoundly influenced by association with my personal therapists, both within and outside the actual therapeutic hours. I speak of certain attitudes and concepts of myself that enter into my work as a therapist which I came to recognize and comprehend more fully after my formal treatment was terminated.

After Frieda's death I no longer sought personal therapy but continued to learn about myself and my behavior from friends who cared enough to tell me what they observed and from patients who often "laid it on the line." I studied in the analytic training programs, benefited from good teachers and supervisors, and learned many things. There was a quality of excitement and competition in the classes, at conferences, and in supervisory sessions as we sought a better comprehension of behavior in terms of past events, current happenings, and anticipation of the future. I learned techniques, engaged in teaching, and in a conventional sense became in a small way what is called "successful." It seemed to me that I did the "right things" and that by pursuing a "proper course" things should work out. I wanted a well-ordered life and its just rewards. Such ideas, however, did not fit well with many events I could not entirely escape noticing. There was still a lot about myself that I did not know.

I recall now an episode in the book *The Maltese Falcon* by Dashiell Hammet. In this book the detective, Sam Spade, has been employed to seek out a man who had disappeared, leaving his successful business, his wife and children, his friends, and the various appurtenances of having "made it." Years after his disappearance, Spade finds the man who has made a new life for himself and who is once again successful much as he had been before.

Spade speaks of the man who is named Flitcraft: "Here is what happened to him. Going to lunch, he passed an office building that was being put up—just the skeleton. A beam or something fell." The beam hit the ground close by the man but did not injure him. Spade continues,

He was scared stiff, of course, he said, but he was more
shocked than really frightened. He felt like somebody had
taken the lid off life and let him look at the works.

Flitcraft had been a good citizen and a good husband
and father, not by any outer compulsion, but simply because
he was a man who was most comfortable in step with his
surroundings. He had been raised that way. The people he
knew were like that. The life he knew was a clean, orderly,
sane, responsible affair. Now a falling beam had shown him
that life was fundamentally none of those things. He, the
good citizen—husband—father could be wiped out between
office and restaurant by the accident of a falling beam. He
knew then that men died as haphazard like that, and lived
only when blind chance spared them [pp. 77–78].

I thought of the navy line officer that I helped pull out of
the water after his ship was sunk. He was dead. I could, at first,
find no wound but then discovered a tiny puncture in the blood
vessel of the inner part of his elbow where a bit of shrapnel had
found a way to bleed him out. "There is no sense to it," I said.
"To hell with it."

Through the years I have had to take a look at a number
of things "under the lid." Many of these were things I should
have known more about but that I kept under cover because
they did not fit with what I wanted to see or be. I shall mention
a few of these which seem relevant to the way I think about my
work with my patients.

In lifting the lid I have come to recognize that I see life
from a narrow point of view. I have led a sheltered existence.
In the main, all has gone smoothly. I have not been treated
badly, and my bodily sicknesses have been dealt with by medical
experts. In a certain sense I have been a witness, not fully a
participant. I saw a bit of warfare—people killed and hurt—but
I came out unscathed through no virtue of my own. The pharmacist's mate referred to previously said, after we watched the
sinking of a ship, "Doctor, I believe somebody gave us a ringside
seat to watch some of the action. We're lucky." We were.

The point of all this is that recognizing the narrowness of
my view and my fortunate position as observer, I realized that
I should attempt to show my respect for my good fortune by

at least trying to understand what comes my way rather than denying its existence and possible importance to others in my professional and personal life.

I realized to some extent in my own therapy—and more importantly, in other contexts—that I really did not wish to know a great deal about myself or anyone else. It was often more convenient for me to preserve a stereotyped view of another person or group. The smiling child should be seen as happy, the attractive woman as lovely and understanding; the courageous hero as without ugly fear, and the poltroon as without virtue.

Sullivan said, "We are more simply human than otherwise." I found this to be a comforting idea until I grasped the unconcious and deeper meaning that there is no escape from our humanity—no way out by thinking of others as angels, devils, "animals," or members of some species other than our own; that the good, the evil, the hope, the creativity, and the destructiveness lie, in the more practical sense, in ourselves.

As to the beginnings and the endings of what now exists, I don't know, and I quarrel only with those ideas about past and future that would appear to evade responsibility for what is—here and now. So in my work I try to say, "Let's look at each other and see what we can make of it all." However, I continue to shy away when I should not do so. I have become more aware of this tendency.

I have come to some peace in that I don't expect to know "everything"—or perhaps very much—of myself or of anyone else. To those who are my patients I say quite simply that not only am I unable to read minds, I'm not even very clever at piecing together accurately the possible meanings of subtle behaviors. I ask the other fellow to spell it out for me, and very often he or she does it well enough for our purposes. I also say that the other fellow can keep secrets, but I ask him or her to note the purpose of doing so. The patient has a right to privacy even in my office.

I did not know how prejudiced I could be; this knowledge was often concealed by my prejudice against prejudice. "Under the lid" I took a peep at my concept of women. About this I shall speak in a limited way, not wishing to prejudice unduly any ideas that you may hold about me.

It took me a long time to recognize that I shared certain attitudes with my tyrannical father whose family background had instilled in him a contemptuous view of women in common with that of others in a society which in many ways permits, encourages, or ignores "soul murder" of many of its components. I had to recognize that although thinking I admired, respected, and loved women, I actually held many of these same derogatory views and to a certain extent shared responsibility with my father for the hurt and near-destruction of a mother for whom I cared deeply. I can console myself only by the knowledge that I made it possible for her to get help from a therapist who drank tea with her, listened to her, and pulled her out of the morass into which she had plunged. Seeing her improve was a big encouragement to me in my work, and the whole experience taught me much.

I work with many women in my practice and they too have taught me much. They have been rather tolerant of me, and I have come to be more truly accepting of them.

I have had to take a look at hatred and cruelty in myself. In my growing up there was little physical violence in the family, but there was much talk of brutality and apparent admiration for it, even as it was decried. Violence and cruelty were often the subject of jokes, as if their association with pain, death, destruction, and humiliation were unreal or to be ignored. I had to face the fact that at least to some extent I participated.

I have been hurt, and I have hurt others. I know that all creatures who have life in their own way suffer pain and distress, but I no longer want to have any part in producing it. I no longer think that my hurtfulness has been to anyone's "good." I have grave doubts about purification of the soul through suffering. I know quite a lot about the hatred that comes in response to torture. I think cruelty and some forms of violence are a form of plague.

Even as I speak, the words seem to express a weakness, and I am tempted to assert that I can indeed be tough when the occasion demands. I shall, if necessary, forcibly stand between another and his hurt to himself or others, including me.

I am not expressing guilt, although I see no reason not to experience that sentiment wisely, but I do inveigh against the perpetuation of ignorance. I just do not wish to exert dominion over others, or to cause them pain.

I am concerned with how much a person values his or her own life. Despite many pronouncements to the contrary, it seems that life is more often than not held in low repute. I refer here to the killings of the past and to those in this century—the time of the greatest mass killings of people by people in the history of the world so far. I speak of triage, i.e., the labeling of some groups as less worthy than others and thus more "suitable" for elimination through direct destruction or the withdrawal of help. (As an aside, I do think there are circumstances in which people should enjoy the right to die, but that is not the topic of the moment.) With my patients I cling to the idea that life is worth the living partly because that is what we are built to do. At times I have my doubts, but there is no belief that is not enriched by doubt and question.

The people who come to consult with me have trouble in their dealings with people. Certainly that observation is not news to anyone. These patients seek to become more comfortable in their human relationships, and speak of such matters as affection, closeness, relatedness, love, etc. They speak of the rarity of such in their lives, and the need to do something that will be of help. I am no expert in dealing with these phenomena, so we set ourselves to the task of defining their meaning as best we can. In the course of such investigations we usually discover that I am somehow lacking in the full possession of these virtues. If we continue our meetings, this leads us to some idea about acceptance of imperfection and the need for trust. As trust develops, a good beginning is made for discovering some semblance of the other sentiments.

Loneliness is a factor in the lives of all of us. This may be too broad a statement if we consider the many devices set up to obscure its possible appearance. Loneliness is a painful experience, as is so well expressed by both Fromm-Reichmann and Sullivan. There is the loneliness of being isolated from people, the loneliness of being in a crowd, the loneliness of holding a secret, the loneliness of being with friends who must be kept friendly, the loneliness sometimes experienced with the person to whom we feel most closely attached, and the loneliness with one's self. And then, unless one holds to a concept of comprehensible purpose in the universe, extending even to the individual (human, animal, plant, or whatever), there is the loneliness of the unknown.

With such uncertainty comes the wish to know, to comprehend, to guide, to control, and to govern. I have learned some things in my life that give me some reasonable confidence in what I can do. We have learned a great deal about human—and other animal—behavior, and such knowledge has been put to good use (at least in some quarters) in improving the practice of psychotherapy in its many forms. But it is useful to recognize and acknowledge, without despair or surrender, our ignorance of so much in our lives.

Often I feel futile as a therapist when I hear, again and again, "You don't help. You don't understand. You are cold and indifferent. You are of no use. You have no idea of a good relationship or of love. Nothing changes." I do take the best look I can at such charges, knowing that the patient may have a valid point and that his or her observations may be in some ways correct. Often all I can say is, "I wish I could give you a helping hand. But since I'm not being very good at that—at least for now—let's go on together, and see what we can find."

This leads to hope, so often denied by some and made extravagant by others. Patients may deride hope as foolish wishing and useless attempts to make reassuring gestures, but hope must be present for any therapeutic enterprise to thrive. Some patients (there are others who are not patients who act in similar ways) seek to seduce me into accepting a stance of hopelessness, finally leading me to face up to the foolishness that may seem to exist in any belief in the usefulness or goodness of the human being.

To some of these I sometimes quote (or misquote) the following, which I think comes from some writings of Aldous Huxley:

> The leeches kiss, the squids embrace,
> the prurient ape's defiling touch.
> And do I love the human race?

No—not much.

And then I think, and say, that I see much that would seem to justify a feeling of despair about the human being. Perhaps in his or her reckless despoliation, destruction, and increase he or she is a form of cancer on the earth to be dealt with finally by radiation with the hope that the body earth will not be done away with at the same time. But here I pause, as in the service of possible despair I may attribute to myself far more knowledge than I can possibly possess. We human and other forms of life may be capable of even greater things than what we have accomplished—perhaps even some toleration of differences (human and otherwise) and of self-governance. "Bull," says my respondent. "Perhaps you're right," I say. "But that's too easy. Come along." And the process of attempts at mutual seduction continues—one of the ways of preserving life.

I hear a great deal about love. I like the idea of love. But when I look under the lid, I find that in our profession it is a word to be used cautiously, if at all. It is a word to be feared, being used in association with sex, seduction, sin, sickness, transference and its counterpart, pleasure, and so on. There is object love, which I guess I have for a small statue in my office that I care about and attempt to protect from harm. Can I, as a therapist, in my work feel love? I think so, if I refer to Sullivan's definition (1947) of love which had meaning for me: "When the satisfaction or the security of another person becomes as significant to one as are one's own satisfactions or security, then the true state of love exists. So far as I know, under no other circumstances is a state of love present regardless of the popular usage of the word" (pp. 42–43).

With this idea in mind, I think of parent, teacher, and therapist having much in common. Each promotes attachment, furthers interest in learning, encourages growth, offers protection, and helps to enable the child, student, or patient to separate with affection and confidence. From one point of view, love and good-bye go properly hand in hand.

Under the lid I also found the idea that I was truly, in some hidden or secret fashion, not as empathic, insightful, understanding, gifted, creative, and intellectually greatly endowed as some of my associates have been and are—no fooling! So I found envy, and some sorrow, that somehow my virtues were not fully recognized. I am very glad to say that Sullivan helped me with such maunderings some years ago. He said something like the following.

> I don't see you as particularly empathic, whatever that may be. I'm sure that some of these people, schizophrenic or whatever, are going to look upon you as rather stupid in terms of comprehending their difficulties and ways of thinking. But some may note that at times you are curious about them, and even might want to learn something. And some of them may attempt to teach you, and as you learn, there is some likelihood that they'll improve in their ways of living.

That was the most encouraging news I ever received about my being a therapist. It gave me hope. As a therapist I work to get what data the patient and I can dig up, and he or she instructs me about how to view the world. Patience is required to teach me. As the one becomes a good teacher, at the same time learning his subject well, and the other becomes a good student, their need for each other decreases and they may separate with respect and even a semblance of love.

Beneath the lid there is also death, a topic that is frequently avoided. With me, death is talked about more frequently now. It is obvious that I am not young and there is, so I hear, the possibility that I may die sometime. Last week a patient said that I shouldn't die because I was needed. I replied that being needed was an important stimulus to the force of life. As she had been suicidal, I pointed out that in order to get the job done, it was required that we both stay alive. She agreed, and we settled on that.

After all this rambling, I say again that this strange, puzzling world is not what I once took it to be. I often feel far out of date amid the mysteries (to me) of this scientific, still ignorant world. "What do I do to earn my keep?" I ask myself. And I reply that I sit down and discuss things with peole in an effort to make some sense of things. "Final sense?" I ask. "No," I answer, "just a semblance of current sense related to the past and possibly to the future. "Is that good enough?" I ask. "I don't know," I reply, "but it's the best we have."

A few years ago one of my colleagues at a meeting in which psychiatric ideas and treatment methods were discussed asked me: "How does it feel to be a horse-and-buggy doctor in this modern world?" "Not bad," I replied. "I don't like or understand all—or much—of what I see. But I like the ride, even at this slow pace."

And now to conclude with a quotation which means much to me. With it in mind I can lift the lid and not be so discomfited by some of the things that I see. The speaker-writer is Montaigne, and Frieda Fromm-Reichamnn along with him helped in viewing, accepting, and changing to some degree what we observe in the lives of ourselves and others.

> We are all patchwork, so shapeless and diverse in composition that each bit, each moment, plays its own game. . . . And there is as much difference between us and ourselves as between us and others. . . . Not only does the wind of accident move me at will, but, besides, I am moved and disturbed as a result merely of my own unstable posture, and anyone who observes carefully can hardly find himself twice in the same state. I give my soul now one face, now another, according to which direction I turn it. If I speak of myself in different ways, that is because I look at myself in different ways. All contradictions may be found in me by some twist and in some fashion. Bashful, insolent; chaste, lascivious; talkative, taciturn; tough, delicate; clever, stupid; surly, affable; lying, truthful; learned, ignorant; liberal, miserly and prodigal: all this I see in myself in some extent according to how I turn; and whoever studies himself very attentively finds in himself, yes, even in his judgment, this gyration and discord. I have nothing to say about myself, simply and solidly, without confusion and without mixture, or in one word. . . .
>
> In view of this, a sound intellect will refuse to judge men simply by their ourward actions; we must probe the inside and discover what springs set men in motion. But since this is an arduous and hazardous undertaking, I wish fewer people would meddle with it [pp. 242–244].

References

Hammet, D. (1984), *The Maltese Falcon.* San Francisco: North Point Press.
Montaigne, M. E. (1967), *The Complete Works,* trans. D. H. Frame. Stanford, CA: Stanford University Press.

Sullivan, H. S. (1947), *Conceptions of Modern Psychiatry*. New York: Norton.

7

PSYCHOANALYSIS WITH FEW PARAMETERS IN THE TREATMENT OF REGRESSED PATIENTS, RECONSIDERED

L. BRYCE BOYER, M.D.

Although I never had the privilege of studying under Frieda Fromm-Reichmann personally, she and her work inspired me and contributed substantially to my decision to work psychoanalytically with so-called primitive patients. I have two special memories of her that periodically delight me, pertaining to her presentation of a paper in a panel devoted to the difference between psychoanalysis and psychotherapy at a meeting of the American. Her contribution was, as it seemed to me, treated with smug contempt by two leading figures in the Association; she was imperturbable in her quiet rebuttal that made them both look somewhat foolish. That evening, at a social gathering, someone asked her what she did when psychotic male patients wanted to have sexual relations with her. With a quiet smile, she replied, "The last time that happened, I told the man I would have no objection to making love with him, but I did not believe it would be in the best interests of his treatment."

In this communication I shall review briefly my experience in working with regressed patients, present some rough statistics pertaining to the efficacy of treatment, and give clinical material demonstrating the utility of the therapist's making

This chapter is an expanded version of a paper presented at the Porto Alegre Psychoanalytic Society, October 2, 1985; the symposium "Intensive Psychotherapy with Disturbed People: Fact and Fiction," Children's Hospital, San Francisco, October 11, 1985; and the 16th Latin American Psychoanalytic Congress, Mexico City, July 23, 1986.

interpretations on the basis of his reactions to material presented by the patient.

For more than thirty-seven years my practice has consisted largely of patients who have suffered from disorders now included under the broadly defined category borderline syndrome, frequently a primitive and psychosis-prone variety. During the past thirty years, all patients have been seen privately in my consultation room.

After having spent some years in treating such patients in traditionally recommended manners and studying the writings of therapists who, like Frieda Fromm-Reichmann (1950), were gifted in understanding and working with primitive patients, I concluded that Freud's belief that such patients were incapable of developing therapeutically useful transference relationships was incorrect. I knew that soon following the introduction of the structural theory with its profound influence on goals and technique, a few therapists had suggested that relatively unmodified psychoanalysis might be applicable to the treatment of patients who had "narcissistic neuroses" (Brunswick, 1928; Garma, 1931; LaForgue, 1935; Landauer, 1924; Waelder, 1924) and that many case histories written by respected mid-century analysts showed that they maintained an orthodox analytic stance when their patients underwent serious regressions (Balint, 1959; Jacobson, 1954; Lewin, 1946, 1950; H.A. Rosenfeld, 1952). Accordingly, I attempted psychoanalysis with few parameters as the experimental treatment mode for regressed patients. In 1961 I suggested that such therapy might be the treatment of choice for some primitive patients and ventured the then highly unpopular opinion that a principal impediment to the successful outcome of their therapy was to be found in unresolved countertransference problems. That position now receives considerable support (Ekstein, 1966; Giovacchini, 1979; Grinberg, 1962; Kernberg, 1975a, b; Maltsberger and Buie, 1974; McDougall, 1979; Milner, 1969; Racker, 1968; Volkan, 1982; Wilson, 1983; Winnicott, 1960). Later, with many others, I became aware that the therapist's reactions to the patient can be used to the great enhancement of therapy (Cohen, 1952; Gill, 1982; Hann-Kende, 1933; Little, 1981; Searles, 1979; Szalita-Pemow, 1955; Volkan, 1984).

My subsequent experience affirms my conjecture that psychoanalysis is the treatment of choice for many of such patients and is based on the following statistics.

I have treated 106 such patients; fifty patients were seen in face-to-face psychotherapy, once or twice weekly; the remainder received psychoanalysis, four or five, rarely three, times weekly. The choice of treatment was determined almost exclusively by finances and geography. Of the fifty patients seen in psychotherapy, thirteen improved and one was much improved. These individuals were principally from lower economical strata and had a long record of social irresponsibility; the vast majority terminated their therapy after only a few interviews. Of the psychoanalytic patients nine stopped during the first year; one was improved; eighteen left in less than two years; fifteen were somewhat and one was much improved; twenty-nine continued to planned termination; three were improved and twenty-six were much improved. Treatment lasted seven to twelve years with patients whose pathologies included severe narcissistic disorders, long-term, fixed fetishism and/or antisocial trends, as contrasted with four to seven years spent with other patients.

Marked impulsivity was a common trait but no patient was addicted to hard drugs. No immoderate user of marijuana or alcohol did well in treatment until the practice was renounced. The patients ranged in age from seventeen to sixty when treatment began (17-20, 1%; 21-30, 38%; 31-40, 32%; 41-50, 16%; 51-63, 13%). A few patients had not received previous treatment, but the great remainder had undergone therapy of various kinds for from three to twenty years.

All of the figures cited concerning the incidence of improvement result from the patients' and my subjective assessments. Even if they are roseate, they are far more encouraging than the figures given by others for treatment by other means than psychoanalysis (Carpenter et al., 1975; Stanton et al., 1984). Most writers provide no figures. Recent studies indicate that psychoanalysis is being used more frequently than formerly for the treatment of the so-called high-level patient and that others who function less well receive classical analysis following earlier psychotherapy with modifications (Adler, 1985).

Those who have reviewed my work have been impressed with two primary qualities that emerge from my approach (Meissner, 1985). The first pertains to my "capacity to tolerate the patient's regressive manifestations and to maintain the therapeutic contact with such patients through the course of the regression, thus maintaining the basic structure of the therapeutic situation and keeping the therapeutic alliance within reach" (p. 90). From boyhood I had an unusual capacity to understand primary process dominated thinking and early in my psychiatric training it became clear that patients' regressive manifestations provoked less anxiety in me than in most of my peers (Boyer, 1983, preface). In working with patients during periods of psychotic regression, I am ordinarily able to hold the analytic position calmly, both tolerating and dealing with the patient's behavior.

The second quality pertains to the structuring of the therapeutic context. I believe the most important element of the successful outcome of such treatment to be the provision and maintenance of a consistent, optimistic, empathic environment in which indirect ego and superego support is given. In structuring the setting, the prospective analysand is given details having to do with the specifics of running the therapy, such as appointment times, fees, arrangements for payments, being charged for missed appointments and other details to be mentioned later, many having to do with the patient's responsibility within the therapy. The therapist's role and function are similarly carefully delineated. Treatment is carried out in a manner that constantly reinforces and never undermines the supposition that the patient carries much responsibility for his own growth and development of self-knowledge.

Social relationships of any degree are discouraged and telephone contacts are exceedingly rare. Searles has commented that I am more abstemious and employ fewer parameters in my treatment of primitive patients than he does with neurotics. Obviously this stance gives the patient the correct idea that I deem him to be less helpless and more capable of growth than he had thought himself to be.

On empirical grounds, some thirty years ago I discovered that the appearance early in the treatment of regressed patients of strongly cathected triadic relationship material regularly served to defend against the patient's dealing with dyadic conflicts (see also Rosenfeld, 1966; Volkan, 1976). When such material was interpreted from its aggressive and defensive aspects, early serious impasses were avoided. Today, with our advanced understanding of the development of object relations, it is commonplace knowledge that the development of dyadic conflicts in the transference and their mutative interpretation usually must precede the analysis of oedipal data.

Fully cognizant of the regressed patient's preoccupation with separation and abandonment and also of the fact that I frequently absent myself from my practice for varying periods, I let my patients know from the outset that I shall be away four or five times yearly for from one to four or more weeks and I shall inform them of the dates of my proposed absences as soon as I know them myself. I have found that the patient's continuing background awareness of coming separations has kept active issues pertaining to abandonment and its causes, and facilitated their analysis. Patients who are being reanalyzed after treatment by others have often opined that their previous analysts' anxiety about separations had frightened them and made them more dependent. My attitude that patients can tolerate separations is quickly internalized by them.

The use of intellectualization as a stubborn defense is often troublesome, particularly with some patients who are schizoid, highly narcissistic, or have anal characters. Its resolution depends in large part on the patient's developing the capacity to cathect his thoughts affectually. Traditionally, analysts instruct their patients to try to disclose their thoughts during the session. I ask them to make a sincere effort to disclose also whatever emotion, physical sensation, or urge of which they become aware. It is my impression that this maneuver, with the patient's being reminded of it from time to time, may shorten the period taken before he begins to look for an emotional accompaniment to his thinking and to get to the genetic material that led to separation of affect and thought.

It is clear that the nature of the transference of the regressed patient differs significantly from that of the person who suffers from a transference neurosis. The type of material projected by primitive patients is determined by the immature nature of their mental operations, including the selectively deficient modulation of their drives. Many therapists have noted the central position of conflicts related to the presence of untamed aggression (Fromm-Reichmann, 1958; Hartmann, 1953; Lidz and Lidz, 1952). When the infantile nature of the transference is in full flower, the analyst is reacted to tenaciously as though he were representative of the infantile mother. Although Giovacchini (Boyer and Giovacchini, 1980, chapter 9) believes that the psychopathology of borderline patients may be rooted in earlier periods of development, most observers think that it lies in patients' failure to traverse successfully the rapprochement subphase (Mahler, 1972; Masterson, 1972).

My belief in the importance of the unfolding transference-countertransference situation has led me to view automatically each session as if it were a dream, the most likely day residue determinant of which is to be found in an unresolved transference conflict of the last interview or series of interviews. That day residue will energize and be energized by a relevant unconscious infantile conflict or combination of conflicts. I regard the content of the interview as though it were the product of the dream work and, of course, attempt to influence that work. As do Greenacre (1975) and others, I keep copious process notes that make review dependable when I remain confused following a session or series of sessions, review that reduces the number of analytic impasses. This viewpoint has enabled me to be more objective while simultaneously empathetic. Its assumption has been particularly helpful to those of my supervisees who have overestimated the degree to which the patient responds realistically to the therapist. I think most analysts in essence treat interviews as though they were dreams, probably without labeling their behavior as such, but perhaps without focusing so specifically on the unresolved transference issue as the day residue of the "dream."

Previous communications have delineated technical changes over time (Boyer, 1971, 1977) and this chapter, too, will focus on alterations in technique. Partly they have resulted from my growing conviction that a too-passive stance on the part of the therapist at best lengthens and at worst stultifies analytic progress with primitive patients. Partly, they have come about because of my increasing understanding of the contributions of British object relations theorists, particularly Winnicott, and synthesis of their views with those of ego psychological theorists, especially Jacobson and Mahler. In what follows, I present background data and then clinical examples.

Background Data

During the sixty-five-odd years since the advent of the structural theory, we have come to understand better the interaction between the individual's environment and the formation, development, and integrity of the psychic apparatus. Attention has been focused more and more on the nature of ever-earlier aspects of the interactions of mother and child and of the importance of a "facilitating" (Winnicott, 1965) or "holding environment" (Modell, 1976) for healthy psychological growth. At first, the most influential element of that surround will be the mothering figure whose capacities will determine her ability to enhance or retard the baby's psychic differentiation. The *Anlagen* of psychic structure that are established then materially influence all subsequent relationships (Loewald, 1979) and the ability to handle optimally the potential traumas of later family interactions (Boven, 1921).

The goal of therapy has come to be to establish structural changes in the patient's personality, that is, to resume ego development (Loewald, 1960), and to progressively recapture self-alienated personal experience, that he may become more fully alive as a subjective, historical being (Ogden, 1985). This resumption and recapturing depend on his relationship with a new object, the analyst. Probably the more the patient is regressed, the greater is the importance of environmental facilitation in his treatment and of the capacities of the analyst to interact comfortably with the individual whose drives are urgent and untamed, whose superego is archaically sadistic and whose communication techniques are confusing and determined, as is much of his perception and behavior, by his use of primitive psychical mechanisms.

The Working Alliance

It is generally conceded that the development of a cooperative relationship with such patients may be difficult to achieve. Fenichel (1941) named that relationship the "rational transference" and Stone (1961) wrote of the "mature transference." Today the relationship is commonly called the "therapeutic" (Zetzel, 1956) or "working alliance" (Greenson, 1965). Its accomplishment depends on the patient's developing the capacity to form a special variety of object relationship in which he can simultaneously experience and observe with adequate neutrality. Its presence will enable the borderline patient to listen and effectively use the analyst's or his own interventions to recover from primitive reactions and reestablish the secondary process, to split off a relatively reasonable object relationship to the analyst (Greenson, 1965), and devote himself to work. In my experience, the regressed patient in analysis is much more likely to achieve such an alliance than he who is in psychotherapy. The establishment of the cooperative alliance depends on the interactions of the various factors discussed below. Perhaps the most important of these factors is the establishment of the holding or facilitating environment.

The Holding or Facilitating Environment

If there is a premature rupture of the facilitating environment in infancy, the baby soon becomes a reactive creature, developing hypertrophied, rigid defensive structures (Ogden, 1985; Winnicott, 1965). The latter characterizes structurally defective patients. On the other hand, if the environment is too permissive for too long, the infant is prevented from experiencing dosed frustration, tolerable anxiety, desire and conflict, and will not develop internal differentiation and the capacity to traverse dyadic relationships satisfactorily.

The mutual influences of transference and changing object relationships in analysis have been discussed masterfully (Loewald, 1960) and will not be dealt with here. Suffice it to say that internalization is not, of course, with reality, but of an interpersonal experience. The child identifies first with his mother's and later with others' experiences of reality. In Winnicott's terms (1971), "the behavior of the environment is part of the individual's own personal development" (p. 53). Primitive patients retain a fundamental disturbance in the early development of object relationships (Blatt et al., 1975). In analysis, especially the regressed patient internalizes his analyst's experience of reality. Among the qualities any analyst possesses is that of giving emotionally tamed, sublimated, and appropriately delayed responses. My consistent, indirectly supportive, and investigative stance and therapeutic optimism are readily available to the patient and are generally internalized. A most unusual, but demonstrative case fragment comes to mind.

A brilliant research scientist, a woman of forty-five, had suffered for twenty years from depression during which she was unable to work for about six months of the year. During the other semester, she was hypomanic, often requiring brief hospitalization, but worked so effectively that she was world renowned for her contributions. Her four years of treatment were occupied principally with analysis of her oral aggression and fears of its magical effects. Although she improved steadily from the outset, each interpretation I made during the first three-odd years was greeted with scorn and conscious rejection, often remarkably vitriolic and obscene. During the fourth year, she had brief periods of mild elation and scant depression; to my surprise, no regression preceded her planned termination date. To the end of her work with me, she never wholeheartedly agreed with any interpretation I made. Bemused, I asked her why she had improved so obviously, since she had disagreed with everything I had said. She looked surprised and scornfully said, "I fell in love with you and you wanted me to get well."

Analytic Tolerance and Regressive Behavior

Oscillation between regression and progression are necessary aspects of psychological development (A. Freud, 1965; Khan, 1960). Regression and ego disorganization are crucial steps in the progressive consolidation of the personality (Loewald, 1960). In analysis, through interpretation within the holding environment, the primitive parts of the psyche that emerge through regressive experiences acquire structure and meaning (Loewald, 1982). As noted earlier, I have given examples previously of my handling of dramatic regressive episodes of acting-out (or acting-in) patients during treatment (Boyer, 1971, 1977, 1982); I shall not repeat them here.

Borderline and other regressed patients regularly use two primitive defensive mechanisms, splitting and projective identification, as do some other analytic patients when undergoing regressive episodes (Grotstein, 1981; Ogden, 1982; Shapiro, 1978). The use of splitting involves reversion to an omnipotent fantasy that unwanted parts of the personality or internal objects can be split, projected into an external object, and controlled. (For dissenting views see Gunderson and Singer, 1975; Mack, 1975; Pruyser, 1975; Robbins, 1976.) In their transference, these patients split the love and hate associated with internalized relationships to avoid the anxiety that would result if they were experienced simultaneously (Kernberg, 1975a, 1976; Volkan, 1976). During treatment, the patient's use of splitting is generally fairly obvious and causes the experienced analyst who works with regressed patients little anxiety and thus results in few countertransference-caused impasses. Projective identification is quite another matter.

An ever growing number of analysts turn to the concept of projective identification to understand their responses to primitive patients (Bion, 1962; Flarsheim, 1972; Garma, 1962; Grinberg, 1962; Kernberg, 1975a, 1976; Paz et al., 1975–76; Racker, 1968; D. Rosenfeld and Mordo, 1973; H.A. Rosenfeld, 1952, 1965; Searles, 1963). The patient unconsciously fantasizes that he has gotten rid of an unwanted part of his own personality by projecting it into the therapist. Such unwanted parts usually have to do with aggression and its potential magical aspects, but regressed patients sometimes project love they deem to be destructive (Fairbairn, 1941; Giovacchini, 1975; Klein, 1946; Searles, 1958) and even sanity (Bion, 1962). The patient retains an unconscious connection with the analyst by means of the projection he believes to have become a trait of the therapist.

The therapist is used as a "container" (Bion, 1956) that will help process the projection (Grotstein, 1981; Ogden, 1982).

One of my patients said that her projection had been "detoxified." Speaking of it late in her analysis, she said that until she had been in treatment for two or three years, she had been aware only of anxiety, fears, and obsessions, and believed she had never had an angry thought or feeling. Now she knew that she had treasured her anger as a child, believing it gave her power. However, she had kept it secret from herself and others because she feared that her thoughts and feelings had realized in deaths and abandonment. Speaking of her relationship with me, she said that the first time I had gone away for longer than a weekend, she had spent her days and nights kneeling on street corners, praying that God would keep me alive. She went on, "I know now that for years I've tried to hurt you with my thoughts, words, and actions, although I thought for a long time that it was you who were trying to hurt me with yours. Now I know that my anger is not dangerous like I thought before."

Sometimes the patient's behavior induces the analyst to believe that the ascribed trait is in fact his own (Racker, 1968). It has long been known that countertransferences are determined largely by the analyst's introjection of qualities of the patient that come into contact with the therapist's unresolved infantile conflicts (Federn, 1952; Fenichel, 1945; Fliess, 1953). The therapist's unconscious assumption of the patient's projection may lead to serious impasses and even termination of treatment (Giovacchini, 1979). I have written previously of therapeutic fiascos of my own, due to this phenomenon (Boyer, 1977, 1982).

In primitive patients, traumatic infantile relationships have been split off from the main psychic current and continue to exert their pathological effects on both the patient's mental equilibrium and external adaptations. Such early "islands" of trauma pathologically influence emotional and structural development, resulting in constriction, arrest, and distortion of the innate drive toward maturation. The split-off infantile relationships regularly cause such patients to develop psychotic transference reactions (Hoedemaker, 1967; Little, 1958; H.A. Rosenfeld, 1965; Searles, 1963). If the holding environment and the working alliance have been well-established, such psychotic reactions will be confined almost exclusively to the consultation room. The analyst and patient must be able to tolerate them, learn from them, and use them for therapeutic ends. The analyst's comprehension of the extent to which projection and projective identification are involved will help him preserve his objectivity.

Technical Modifications

Earlier I noted that I expect my patient to pay especial attention to his emotional and physical experiences during the interview, in addition to his thoughts. The first of my relatively recent technical modifications consists of my turning more of my attention to my own emotional and physical reactions to the patient's productions. To my awareness, this approach has not been specifically recommended by others, although many analysts, past and present, especially some Latin American followers of the British object relations theorists infer similar activity. The second modification is that I am now selectively more aggressive in the pursuit of information.

Jaffe (1986) recently wrote, "The psychological perceptiveness of psychoanalysts depends on their ability to regress and thereby to utilize their own unconscious processes. This provides an effective base upon which a cognitive elaboration can then build a more comprehensive understanding than is otherwise possible of the emotional life of patients as well as of one's own" (p. 239).

Although much of my thinking during analytic sessions with regressed patients continues to be directed and secondary process dominated, I have become progressively more able to let my attention wander simultaneously, to permit the development of a split-off, slightly altered ego state, and then to become aware of more of the nuances and symbolism implied by the patient's manifest productions, to "listen with the third ear" (Reik, 1949). To achieve such free-floating attention is easier with neurotic patients with their slower orientational shifts. Obviously, we are all attentive not only to the content of the patient's utterances but to the qualities of their deliverance, and attempt to remain aware simultaneously of gestures, however slight, and signs of physiological changes. I have come, however, to pay increasing attention to my own emotional shifts and physical sensations and consistently to analyze privately the fantasies I have during my altered ego states and the rare related dream that subsequently occurs when I am still confused about the meaning of the patient's productions or behavior. I assume that my emotional, physical or mental experience reflects the patient's hidden message, perhaps on the basis of my transitory concordant and complementary identifications (Kernberg, 1984), and subsequently interpret on the basis of my extrapolation from my experience. I am able to relax and achieve free-floating attention almost solely while patients are reclining. As is clear from the above, my apperception is influenced varyingly by different combinations of primary and secondary process thinking during the session, as will be illustrated by the clinical material.

Clinical Material

First I shall speak of a use of my personal experience in the treatment of these patients. Analysts respond differently to even ordinary behavior. Patients' silence, having been discussed from the standpoint of resistance, transference, and countertransference, is a case in point (Atkins, 1968; Bergler, 1938; Flarsheim, 1972; Levy, 1958; Loomie, 1961; Waldhorn, 1959). The patient's words have been viewed as nutriment for the therapist (Racker, 1957) who, feeling deprived or frustrated by his inability to comprehend the meanings of the patient's inability or refusal to talk, and to influence the analysand to change his behavior, may be retributively hostile (Zeligs, 1960). Some analysts are incapable of tolerating the intimacy of silence (Searles, 1976) and some refuse to treat silent patients (Erikson, personal communication).

In what follows, I discuss my reactions to and interventions during a patient's being silent for long periods, while her body was rigid and immobile. Her analysis was begun immediately following a hospitalization for an acute psychotic reaction characterized by confusion, terror associated with persecutory delusions, and a conviction that during her sleep or while driving her car she had murdered a mother surrogate and forgotten the act. Highly successful in the business world although in her mid-twenties, she had had to stop working to spend her days checking gas jets and door locks and seeking to find corpses in areas where she might have walked in her sleep or driven her car.

She had docilely conformed to the demands of her perfectionist, manipulative, aggressive mother, achieving excellent grades, advancing rapidly professionally, and being an active organizer in activities supporting Zionism. She conformed also to her sexually inhibited mother's covert demand that she be promiscuous with men of lower social strata and regale her mother with disguised recountings of her thrilling activities. Her seduction and discarding of men was apparently ego-syntonic and met with maternal approval. It reflected symbolically the mother's historical behavior with her passive, easygoing husband.

When the patient reached high school, she had begun to be somewhat aware that she resented her mother's different behavioral requirements for two younger siblings, a boy and a girl, whose irresponsibility and peccadillos received overt approval. Unaware of the involvement of the vengeful aspect of her action, she fell madly in love with an antisocial, promiscuous gentile athlete who was totally uninterested in education or being successful in any practical way. She unconsciously identified him with her father. Although her lover continued his sexual relations with a number of other women, the patient successfully excluded the obvious evidence from her awareness. She felt no anxiety while she focused her attention on perfectionist self-starvation and her torrid affair and continued to feed her mother with recountings of her conformation to the two sets of approved activities. Finally, when she had become almost skeletal, her lover abandoned her. Then she became anxious, ridden with the obsessions and fears mentioned previously, and sought psychotherapy.

Thus far in her analysis, three unconscious motivations for her development of anorexia have been uncovered. In addition to the achieved resolution of the incestuous conflict posed by her affair, she imagined she could make her mother feel guilty for having nursed the two younger siblings while symbolically starving her with bottle feedings performed by hired help, and also conquer a dangerous oral impulse to cannibalize her mother.

In her supportive, noninterpretational psychotherapy, she made of her male therapist a mother surrogate. While she believed herself to be his favorite patient, she regained her weight. Her therapist, obviously alarmed by her deepening emotional involvement with him and apparently unaware of its transference aspects, eventually defended himself by telling her of his adulterous affairs and emotional involvement with other patients. Then she became terrified that she had unwittingly murdered him, and was hospitalized.

During that psychotherapy, she had become increasingly angry with her mother and sought vengeance through frustrating that woman's need to be fed words. From the beginning of her analysis, she was predominantly silent. Knowing something of the functions both of her talking and muteness with her mother, I felt I understood some of the reasons for her silence and did not feel frustrated. For a few weeks I limited my remarks about her preferring not to talk to its obvious defensive functions. Her response to my mentioning her fear that if she spoke she might become emotionally involved once again, was a scornful sniff. She was sarcastic when I suggested that she feared that saying words aloud would make her fears more believable and lead to rehospitalization. She told me that she had no need for me to tell her what she already knew, and resumed her customary silence and watchful rigidity. She responded similarly when I told her that she sought to protect me as a mother surrogate from her fear that she would harm me if she verbalized her anger and disappointment in me, saying that unreported dreams had given her *that* knowledge.

Eventually during a silent period, I become somewhat drowsy, although I had had ample sleep and her session came very early in the morning. During the altered ego state I saw myself as a small child, playing of my own choice in a room adjoining one in which my mother was reading. Then I recalled themes from Winnicott's *Playing and Reality* (1971) and said that perhaps during her silence she was permitting herself to be alone in my presence and to play with her own thoughts. Her response was dramatic. Obviously grateful, she physically relaxed for the first time and tentatively and briefly touched the blanket that lay alongside her. Also for the first time, she cried aloud and the next few hours were flooded with spoken memories of her rapturous daydreams and imagined games, which clearly involved themes from favorite fairy tales during silent periods when she was with her lover.

Then, following a recounted dream that obviously indicated, along with her associations to it, the development of erotic conflicts pertaining to me as a mixed father and mother surrogate and her fear that she would hurt me by ridiculing my obesity as mother derided father's lack of competitive elan, silence ensued for several interviews. My rare queries and statements, related to defensive functions of her silence, were just ignored.

Finally, I became aware of a pattern, namely, that she appeared to be willing or able to speak a few words only after I had made some noise, commented, or asked a question. While musing about this phenomenon, I became aware that I felt hungry, although I had just eaten. Then I thought of Racker's (1968) work and that I had empathized with a need of hers. I suggested that she could not talk until she had felt fed by my words. Again, she was highly gratified that I had finally understood something and released much affectively charged related material for a couple of weeks.

Earlier, I spoke of another patient having talked of her handling aggression in her therapy by means of projective identification. I shall now speak of how she became aware during analysis of the existence of anger and hatred within her.

This physically attractive virgin in her late thirties had graduated from a prestigious university with high honors in a scientific field and had been encouraged by her faculty to become an academician. Unconsciously fearing that her comparative success would devastate her three older sisters and kill her father, a medical school professor whose skills and reputation had declined following a brain injury, she had become instead a skilled technician. She had been relatively schizoid during much of her life and had undergone minimally helpful lengthy psychotherapy during her latency and teens for a very severe obsessive-compulsive disorder. She had begun to date occasionally two years earlier and was being pressured to have intercourse. Her fears of pregnancy and that her father, actually happily married, would be devastated if he learned that she had had intercourse, conflicted with her wish to get married and have children, and caused her great anxiety to which she reacted by spending many hours daily checking the safety of her home. At work she rechecked chemicals endlessly lest an error result in the deaths of experimental animals.

So far as she could recall, she had never had an angry thought or impulse. Her intense unconscious hostility was manifested in fears, obsessions, and compulsive behavior. She had always been concerned about her health, dieting carefully and exercising extensively. She claimed her athletic activities—running, hiking, and swimming—had always been solitary. During the first years of her analysis, she remained unaware of anger. She lay motionless, usually rigid on the couch, with her arms at her sides, and either spoke monotonously or cried as she endlessly recounted her fears and worries. My careful interpretations directed toward helping her become aware of her anger were without effect. Eventually, I noted that she occasionally slightly pronated her left arm, but I discerned no connection with spoken subject matter. She was unaware of her arm movement and when I called it to her attention, was indifferent. The activity became more frequent over a period of some months, remaining ununderstood. Finally I found myself imitating her movement, but to no avail. Then I recalled that while she was left-handed, I was not, and imitated it with my right arm. As I did so, I remembered having similarly pronated my arm while serving at tennis as a youth. I asked my patient whether she had ever played tennis; her answer was a flat no.

She soon began to have dreams in which she was watching competitive athletics and two weeks later dreamed that she herself was engaged in a tennis game. This led to her amazed recollection that when she was eight or nine, she had been playing tennis with her next oldest sister with whom she had been highly rivalrous for parental favoritism. On one occasion, she had intentionally smashed a ball into her sister's face and had been both delighted and terrified. As she recalled the incident, she became aware of rage. This event proved to be the most significant turning point of her lengthy and highly successful analysis.

I turn now to instances of my having become selectively more aggressive in the pursuit of information.

Thinking about that which has been repressed follows regressed patterns. Preverbal thinking often employs visual imagery (Arieti, 1948; Freud, 1900). When a patient becomes silent even for a short time and then shifts the subject matter in such a manner that I cannot follow the latent linking idea, I may ask him to return to the silent period and recall the omitted thought. If the patient states he had none, I inquire whether he had become aware of a sensory experience then, or become aware while remembering the intermediary silence. If the analysand recalls such an experience, the sensory mode will usually entail vision and the recollected visual perception may stimulate the recovery of a significant memory or provide analyzable symbology. The same will be true of other sensory experiences, but I shall recount here only an instance of the recovery of a visual image during a silence.

A physician who was sincerely dedicated to doing the very best for his patients had been involved in a series of malpractice suits resulting from his having forgotten to perform obviously necessary medical and surgical procedures while treating patients. He was depressed and bewildered. Early in his analysis it became quite clear to me that he had identified with his mother, a woman devoted to taking care of children but so insecure that if she felt unappreciated, she cried, took to her bed and slept for many hours, sometimes failing to prepare dinner or perform other necessary routine tasks. My patient was unaware of anger and vengeful impulses when he considered his efforts to have been unappreciated, knowing only of his feeling hurt.

Several months into analysis he opened a session wondering in passing whether I knew how hard it was for him to arrange his schedule to permit his treatment. That was the first time he had hinted that he felt himself to be unappreciated by me. Then he found himself anxious while talking of a patient's having complained about his bill. He became silent for a few seconds and then talked of something totally unrelated in emotional or topical theme. When I interrupted him to inquire, he denied recalling a thought during the interim but remembered a fleeting vision of a child in a forest. This led during the same session to memories of childhood involvement with fairy tales and especially with Hansel and Gretel, a story that has been interpreted to deal with conflicts pertaining to oral sadism and wishes for reunion with the mother (Lorenz, 1931; Róheim, 1953). At the end of the hour he recalled the "absurd" thought that he might want to bite me. During following hours he began to get into contact with the oral-sadistic urges that had been hidden by his feeling hurt and being forgetful.

Eventually, his forgetfulness with his patients was understood as a repetition of his mother's withdrawals into sleep. It kept unconscious his urges to devour them as maternal surrogates to attain fantasized fusion with her. Simultaneously it resulted in their being deprived and damaged as he had considered himself to be by his mother's actions.

In play therapy for children, the therapist may choose to suggest games or other make-believe situations as a means of access to threatening material. At times, I use a similar device, one in which I ask the patient to imagine a situation.

A patient who suffered a primitive borderline personality disorder had been severely traumatized as a child in various ways, one of which was her having been frequently subjected to the observation of sadomasochistic primal scene activities (Boyer, 1977). She became an alcoholic and a promiscuous masochistic victim who repressed her sexual experiences. During her analysis, when she finally could remember having engaged in sex with men whom she had picked up in bars, and her occasional masturbation, it became clear that her attention during any sexual activity was focused exclusively on physical sensations and the achievement of orgasm. After some months during which her sexual fantasies continued to remain hidden, following a reported episode of masturbation, I asked her to visualize what she might have fantasized if she could shift her attention from the physical experience and her fear that either she would not have orgasm or, if she did, it might damage her. She closed her eyes and saw angular geometric forms about which she became curious (Tustin, 1980). During subsequent interviews the forms became rounded and eventually unified into a hand and an arm, tearing at her perineum as she now revealed she did in fact during her sleep. She was sure she continued to have pinworms from childhood. When stool examinations were negative, she could enter into an examination of her fusion of clitoral, vaginal, urethral, and anal sensations and the meanings of her having failed to differentiate them. Parental sexual activities had frightened and excited her. She had sought to interrupt them by noisy bathroom activities, while simultaneously discharging her perineal excitement through urination and/or defecation.

I limit myself to two further examples of my heightened clinical activity in an effort to speed the return of the repressed.

Christmastime stimulates much emotional arousal in the United States and particularly revives problems surrounding unresolved sibling rivalry (Boyer, 1955). In an attempt to make it easier for patients to focus on their reactions to the Yuletide, I have come to place some reminder of Christmas in my consultation room early in December. One year Channukah and Christmas came very close together. A paranoid, hypomanic Jewish woman had not referred for three weeks to either holiday despite the presence of a lighted candle and a hanging ornament (Boyer, 1985, Mrs. E). Finally I said she had avoided speaking of the holidays and that I wondered why. She could then tell me that she was furious because I had imposed my personal life on her, reminding her through the decorations that I was a patriarch who reveled in my grandchildren's adoration at Christmastime while I consigned the women in my "tribe" to "inferior, scut-work roles." She could not elaborate until I inquired whether she had seen a mental picture. She was surprised to become aware that she then saw me in biblical garb, on a throne, with a chained woman washing my feet. For the first time she recalled that her mother had been incapable of permitting happiness on any holiday and often complained about the debased role of women, although she had ostensibly been solely proud to have supported her rabbinical husband.

Eventually, my patient recalled her childhood belief that a brother had stolen from her a prized Christmas present, a "magical" pen that could write in three colors, one of which matched that of the candle. Like the candle, the pen was viewed as erect in her mind, and this observation led in another way to fantasies that she had been born with a penis that had been stolen from her, this time within the framework of sibling rivalry.

Finally, I have learned that when a patient is dealing actively with a conflict and suddenly stops doing so, he may have undertaken unreported acting out of the transference. After a long period of sexual abstinence, a woman became aware of wishes and fantasies that I enter into sexual activities with her; she adamantly rejected the idea that transference was involved (Boyer, 1971). The subject preoccupied and frustrated her for some weeks and was abruptly discontinued, being replaced by old and little-cathected conflicts. Finally I said I did not understand why the subject had been discontinued in the absence of any resolution and asked whether she was engaged in some unreported activity. She could then tell me that she had begun a torrid affair with a man of my age. When to her surprise she became cognizant that he looked like and resembled her father in other ways, she became aware to some degree of her viewing me as a father surrogate and stopped the affair.

Discussion

It is commonly held that the effectiveness of psychoanalysis as a therapeutic mode depends on properly timed interpretation as the effective mutative agent. In my view, this principle holds as well in the treatment of regressed patients and those who suffer from the transference neuroses. In working with either group of patients, the provision of a setting within which a working alliance can be established is mandatory, since without such an alliance interpretations are usually ineffective in achieving structural change, our true therapeutic goal. In a sense, every analysand must be trained to be a patient, and this is more true of the disturbed person, whose drive-derivative urges are less controlled, and whose infantile transference projections often make him perceive the analyst as a grossly distorted early maternal surrogate, an actual caretaker, one who will gratify his wishes promptly. Obviously, not all regressed patients are so transparently clamorous and many are simultaneously closer to their need to have the therapist help them learn to view reality as do others around them, and also to be able to communicate in manners that will be understood and not be provocative. But beyond our need to train the analysand to be a patient, ultimately our goal is to help him to become a constructive person who can use his innate capacities to his fullest and enjoy doing so, while at the same time being empathic to the needs of others, a potential caretaker. Loewald (1960) has brilliantly discussed the manners in which transference and real object relationship changes are interactive in the analytic setting, the analysand learns to be a patient and, hopefully, ultimately an empathic adult, through a complex process that includes identification with attributes of the analyst and the setting, using the word setting in its broadest sense.

I have found that the traditional analytic environment and the exclusion of the use of parameters achieves these goals in a high percentage of patients who continue to planned termination. During the past twenty years or so, this has been particularly true. This change coincides with my growing awareness of the nature of the development of early object relationships and the degree to which the primitively functioning patient distortedly perceives the therapist. While the ego psychologists contributed much to my comprehension, especially Mahler, Jacobson, and Erikson, I was made more consciously aware of the facilitating nature of the therapeutic environment for these patients through increased understanding of the British object relations therapists, especially Winnicott. Study of their views also gave me more understanding of primitive defenses. I have spoken here particularly of projective identification. It is easier for me to comprehend the all-important transference-countertransference interactions in the treatment of regressed patients when I use this concept, although I am aware that others find it unnecessary.

This contribution has delineated recent changes in my ever-progressing technique in working with primitive patients.

What I have stressed is my having become selectively more aggressive in treatment, in addition to my having come to pay especial attention to my own reactions to the patient and his productions, verbal or nonverbal. As illustrated, I have found that sometimes reactions that occur when I am in a slightly altered ego state while listening prove to be especially illuminating and helpful. I have concluded that two reasons contribute to my preference to treat disturbed patients while they are on the couch. I am more comfortable and less inappropriately and defensively active when the patient is not scrutinizing me and automatically changing what he might have produced, on the basis of hints resulting from observations of my reactions or spontaneous physical contributions to the interchange. Secondly, it is evident to me that the patient's remaining on the couch helps him to establish distance between urge and action and to learn that delay is possible and even an accomplishment.

It will have become clear from my presentation that I believe the active pursual of fantasies, whether they are expressed verbally or perceived nonverbally by the patient, assists in making the unconscious conscious in manners that permit analysis of defenses and resistances. I refer here to my asking the patient to give information he consciously or unconsciously prefers to conceal, rather than waiting for its subsequent emergence, either spontaneous or as the result of interpretation.

Conclusion

The provision of a facilitating environment is all-important in the treatment of the regressed patient. A significant aspect of that environment is a clear understanding of the degree to which the disturbed patient perceives the therapist to be a distorted version of his infantile caretaker(s). The comprehension of the nature of the transference-countertransference interaction is mandatory.

In this contribution, I have described how I have come to include a study of my own reactions to the patient's behavior and verbal productions, be those reactions mental, emotional, or physical, and to make interpretations at times on the basis of my eventual understanding of those reactions. In addition,

I have spoken of manners of more aggressively pursuing suppressed or repressed information.

References

Adler, G. (1985), *Borderline Psychopathology and Its Treatment.* New York: Aronson.

Arieti, S. (1948), Special logic of schizophrenia and other types of autistic thought. *Psychiatry*, 11:325–338.

Atkins, N. B. (1968), Acting out and psychosomatic illness as related to regressive trends. *Int. J. Psycho-Anal.*, 49:221–223.

Balint, M. (1959), *Thrills and Regressions.* New York: International Universities Press.

Bergler, E. (1938), On a resistance situation: The patient is silent. *Psychoanal. Rev.*, 25:170–176.

Bion, W. R. (1956), Development of schizophrenic thought. *Int. J. Psycho-Anal.*, 37:344–346.

——— (1962), *Learning from Experience.* London: Heinemann.

Blatt, S. J., Wild, C. M., & Ritzler, B. A. (1975), Disturbances of object relations in schizophrenia. *Psychoanal. & Contemp. Sci.*, 4:235–288.

Boven, W. (1921), Études sur les conditions du developpement au sein des familles, de la schizophrenie et de la folie maniaque. *Arch. Suisses de Neurol. & Psychol.*, 8:89–116.

Boyer, L. B. (1955), Christmas "neurosis." In: *The Regressed Patient.* New York: Aronson, 1983, p. 239–258.

——— (1971), Psychoanalytic technique in the treatment of certain characterological and schizophrenic disorders. In: *The Regressed Patient.* New York: Aronson, 1983, pp. 89–120.

——— (1977), Working with a borderline patient. In: *The Regressed Patient.* New York: Aronson, 1983, pp. 137–166.

——— (1982), On analytic experiences in working with regressed patients. In: *Technical Factors in the Treatment of Severely Disturbed Patients*, ed. P. L. Giovacchini & L. B. Boyer. New York: Aronson, pp. 65–106.

——— (1983), *The Regressed Patient.* New York: Aronson.

——— (1985), Christmas "neurosis" reconsidered. In: *Depressive States and Their Treatment*, ed. V. D. Volkan. New York: Aronson, pp. 297–316.

——— and Giovacchini, P. L. (1980). *Psychoanalytic Treatment of Schizophrenic, Borderline and Characterological Disorders*, 2nd ed. New York: Aronson.

Brunswick, R. M. (1928), A supplement to Freud's "A History of an Infantile Neurosis." *Int. J. Psycho-Anal.*, 9:439–476.

Carpenter, W. T., Gunderson, J. T., & Strauss, J. S. (1975). Considerations of the borderline syndrome: A longitudinal comparative study of borderline and schizophrenic patients. In: *Borderline Personality Disorders*, ed. P. Hartocollis. New York: International Universities Press, pp. 231–253.

Cohen, M. B. (1952), Countertransference and anxiety. *Psychiatry*, 15:231–243.

Ekstein, R. (1966), *Children of Time and Space, of Action and Impulse. Treatment of Severely Disturbed Children.* New York: Appleton-Century Crofts.

Fairbairn, W. R. D. (1941), A revised psychopathology of the psychoses and psychoneuroses. *Int. J. Psycho-Anal.*, 22:250–279.

Federn, P. (1952), *Ego Psychology and the Psychoses.* New York: Basic Books.

Fenichel, O. (1941), *Problems of Psychoanalytic Technique.* New York: Psychoanalytic Quarterly.

—— (1945), *The Psychoanalytic Theory of Neurosis.* New York: Norton.

Flarsheim, A. (1972), Treatability. In: *Tactics and Techniques in Psychoanalytic Therapy,* ed. P. L. Giovacchini. New York: Aronson, pp. 113–134.

Fliess, R. (1953), Counter-transference and counter-identification. *J. Amer. Psychoanal. Assn.,* 1:268–284.

Freud, A. (1965), *Normality and Pathology in Childhood.* New York: International Universities Press.

Freud, S. (1900), The Interpretation of Dreams. *Standard Edition,* 4 & 5. London: Hogarth Press, 1953.

Fromm-Reichmann, F. (1950), *Principles of Intensive Psychotherapy.* Chicago: University of Chicago Press.

—— (1958), Basic problems in the psychotherapy of schizophrenia. *Psychiatry,* 21:1–6.

Garma, Á. (1931), La realidad exterior y los instinctos en la esquizofrenia. *Rev. Psicoanál.,* 2:56–82.

—— (1962), *El Psicoanálisis.* Buenos Aires: Paidos, 3rd ed., 1978.

Gill, M. M. (1982), *Analysis of Transference,* I. *Psychol. Issues,* Monog. 53. New York: International Universities Press.

Giovacchini, P. L. (1975), *Psychoanalysis of Character Disorders.* New York: Aronson.

—— (1979), *Treatment of Primitive Mental States.* New York: Aronson.

Greenacre, P. (1975), On reconstruction. *J. Amer. Psychoanal. Assn.,* 23:693–712.

Greenson, R. R. (1965), The working alliance and the transference neurosis. *Psychoanal. Quart.,* 34:155–181.

Grinberg, L. (1962), On a specific aspect of countertransference due to the patient's projective identification. *Int. J. Psycho-Anal.,* 43:436–440.

Grotstein, J. S. (1981), *Splitting and Projective Identification.* New York: Aronson.

Gunderson, J. T., & Singer, M. T. (1975), Defining borderline patients. *Amer. J. Psychiat.,* 132:1–10.

Hann-Kende, F. (1933), On the role of transference and countertransference in psychoanalysis. In: *Psychoanalysis and the Occult,* ed. G. Devereux. New York: International Universities Press, 1953, pp. 158–167.

Hartmann, H. (1953), Contribution to the metapsychology of schizophrenia. *Psychoanal. Study Child,* 8:177–198. New York: International Universities Press.

Hoedemaker, E. D. (1967), The psychotic identifications in schizophrenia. The technical problem. In: *Psychoanalytic Treatment of Schizophrenic and Characterological Disorders,* ed. L. B. Boyer & P. L. Giovacchini. New York: Science House, pp. 189–207.

Jacobson, E. (1954), Contribution to the metapsychology of psychotic identifications. *J. Amer. Psychoanal. Assn.,* 2:239–262.

Jaffe, D. (1986), Empathy, counteridentification, countertransference. *Psychoanal. Quart.,* 55:215–243.

Kernberg, O. F. (1975a), *Borderline Conditions and Pathological Narcissism.* New York: Aronson.

—— (1975b), Transference and countertransference in the treatment of borderline patients. *Strecker Monograph Series*, No. XII. Philadelphia: Institute of Pennsylvania Hospital.

———— (1976), *Object Relations Theory and Clinical Psychoanalysis.*New York: Aronson.

———— (1984), Projection and projective identification. Presentation at the First Conference of the Sigmund Freud Center of the Hebrew University of Jerusalem, May 27–29.

Khan, M. M. R. (1960), Regression and integration in the analytic setting. *Int. J. Psycho–Anal.*, 41:130–146.

Klein, M. (1946), Notes on some schizoid mechanisms. *Int. J. Psycho-Anal.*, 27:99–110.

LaForgue, R. (1935), Contribution a l'étude de la schizophrenie. *Évolution Psychiat.*, 3:81–96.

Landauer, K. (1924), "Passive" Technik. *Int. Z. Ärtz. Psychoanal.*, 10:415–422.

Levy, K. (1958), Silence in the analytic session. *Int. J. Psycho-Anal.*, 39:50–58.

Lewin, B. D. (1946), Sleep, the mouth, and the dream screen. *Psychoanal. Quart.*, 15:419–434.

———— (1950), *The Psychoanalysis of Elation*. New York: Norton.

Lidz, R. W. & Lidz, T. (1952), Therapeutic considerations arising from the intense symbiotic needs of schizophrenic patients. In: *Psychotherapy with Schizophrenics*, ed. E. B. Brody & F. C. Redlich. New York: International Universities Press, pp. 168–178.

Little, M. (1958), On delusional transference (transference psychosis). In: *Transference Neurosis and Transference Psychosis*. New York: Aronson, 1981, pp. 81–92.

———— (1981), *Transference Neurosis and Transference Psychosis*. New York: Aronson.

Loewald, H. W. (1960), On the therapeutic action of psychoanalysis. *Int. J. Psycho–Anal.*, 41:16–33.

———— (1979), The waning of the Oedipus Complex. *J. Amer. Psychoanal. Assn.*, 27:751–776.

———— (1982), Regression. Some general considerations. In: *Technical Factors in the Treatment of the Severely Disturbed Patient*, ed. P. L. Giovacchini & L. B. Boyer. New York: Aronson, pp. 107–130.

Loomie, L. S. (1961), Some ego considerations in the silent patient. *J. Amer. Psychoanal. Assn.*, 9:56–78.

Lorenz, E. F. (1931), Hänsel und Gretel. *Imago*, 17:119–125.

Mack, J. E., ed. (1975), *Borderline States in Psychiatry*. New York: Grune & Stratton.

Mahler, M. S. (1972), A study of the separation-individuation phase and its possible application to borderline phenomena in the psychoanalytic situation. *Psychoanal. Study Child*, 26:403–424. New Haven, CT: Yale University Press.

Maltsberger, J. T., & Buie, D. H. (1974), Countertransference hate in the treatment of suicidal patients. *Arch. Gen. Psychiat.*, 30:645–653.

Masterson, J. F. (1972), *Treatment of the Borderline Adolescent. A Developmental Approach*. New York: Wiley.

McDougall, J. (1979), Primitive communication and the use of countertransference. In: *Countertransference: The Therapist's Contribution to the Thera-*

peutic Situation, ed. L. Epstein & A. H. Feiner. New York: Aronson, pp. 267–304.

Meissner, W. M. (1985), Review of L. Bryce Boyer, *The Regressed Patient. Psychoanal. Quart.,* 54:89–91.

Milner, M. (1969), *The Hands of the Living God—An Account of a Psychoanalytic Treatment.* New York: International Universities Press.

Modell, A. H. (1976), "The holding environment" and the therapeutic action of psychoanalysis. *J. Amer. Psychoanal. Assn.,* 24:285–308.

Ogden, T. H. (1982), *Projective Identification and Psychotherapeutic Technique.* New York: Aronson.

———— (1985), *The Matrix of the Mind. Aspects of Object Relations Theory.* New York: Aronson.

Paz, C. A., Pelento, M. L., & Olmos de Paz, T. (1975–1976), *Estructuras y Estados Fronterizos en Niños, Adolescentes y Adultos,* 3 vols. Buenos Aires: Ediciones Nueva Visión.

Pruyser, P. W. (1975). What splits in "splitting"? *Bull. Menn. Clin.,* 39:1–46.

Racker, E. (1957), The meanings and uses of countertransference. *Psychoanal. Quart.,* 26:303–357.

———— (1968), *Transference and Countertransference.* New York: International Universities Press.

Reik, T. (1949), *Listening with the Third Ear: The Inner Experiences of a Psychoanalyst.* New York: Farrar, Straus.

Robbins, M. D. (1976), Borderline personality organization: The need for a new theory. *J. Amer. Psychoanal. Assn.,* 24:831–853.

Róheim, G. (1953), Hansel and Gretel. *Bull. Menn. Clin.,* 17:90–92.

Rosenfeld, D., & Mordo, E. (1973), Fusión, confusión, simbiosis e identificación proyectiva. *Rev. Psicoanál.,* 30:413–422.

Rosenfeld, H. A. (1952), Transference-phenomena and transference-analysis in an acute catatonic schizophrenic patient. *Int. J. Psycho-Anal.,* 33:457–464.

———— (1965), *Psychotic States. A Psycho-Analytical Approach.* London: Hogarth Press.

———— (1966), Discussion of *Office Treatment of Schizophrenia,* by L. Bryce Boyer. *Psychoanal. Forum,* 1:351–353.

———— (1975), Negative therapeutic reaction. In: *Tactics and Techniques in Psychoanalytic Therapy,* II, ed. P. L. Giovacchini, A. Flarsheim, & L. B. Boyer. New York: Aronson, pp. 217–228.

Searles, H. F. (1958), Positive feelings in the relationships between the schizophrenic and his mother. In: *Collected Papers on Schizophrenia and Related Subjects.* New York: International Universities Press, 1965, pp. 216–253.

———— (1963), Transference psychosis in the treatment of chronic schizophrenia. In: *Collected Papers on Schizophrenia and Related Subjects.* New York: International Universities Press, pp. 626–653.

———— (1976), Transitional phenomena and therapeutic symbiosis. In: *Countertransference and Related Subjects.* New York: International Universities Press, 1979, pp. 503–576.

———— (1979), *Countertransference and Related Subjects.* New York: International Universities Press.

Shapiro, E. R. (1978), The psychodynamics and developmental psychology of the borderline patient. A review of the literature. *Amer. J. Psychiat.,* 135:1305–1315.

Stanton, A. H., Gunderson, J. G., Knapp, P. H., Frank, A. F., Vannicelli, M. L., Schnitzer, R., & Rosenthal, R. (1984), Effects of psychotherapy in schizophrenia: I. *Schizophren. Bull.*, 10:520–563.

Stone, L. (1961), *The Psychoanalytic Situation.* New York: International Universities Press.

Szalita-Pemow, A. B. (1955), The "intuitive process" and its relation to work with schizophrenics. *J. Amer. Psychoanal. Assn.*, 3:7–18.

Tustin, F. (1980), Autistic objects. *Int. Rev. Psychoanal.*, 7:27–39.

Volkan, V. D. (1976), *Primitive Internalized Object Relations: A Clinical Study of Schizophrenic, Borderline and Narcissistic Patients.* New York: International Universities Press.

—— (1982), A young woman's inability to say no to needy people and her identification with the frustrator in the analytic situation. In: *Technical Factors in the Treatment of the Severely Disturbed Patient*, ed. P. L. Giovacchini & L. B. Boyer. New York: Aronson, pp. 439–466.

—— (1984), *What Do You Get When You Cross a Dandelion with a Rose? The True Story of a Psychoanalysis.* New York: Aronson.

Waelder, R. (1924), The psychoses: Their mechanisms and acessibility to treatment. *Int. J. Psycho-Anal.*, 6:259–281.

Waldhorn, H. F., reporter (1959), The silent patient. Panel discussion. *J. Amer. Psychoanal. Assn.*, 7:548–560.

Wilson, C. P. (1983), Contrasts in the analysis of bulimic and abstaining anorexics. In: *Fear of Being Fat, The Treatment of Anorexia Nervosa and Bulimia*, ed. C. P. Wilson, C. C. Hogan, & I. L. Mintz. New York: Aronson, pp. 169–193.

Winnicott, D. W. (1960), Counter-transference. In: *The Maturational Processes and the Facilitating Environment.* New York: International Universities Press, 1965, pp. 158–165.

—— (1965), *The Maturational Processes and the Facilitating Environment.* New York: International Universities Press.

—— (1971), *Playing and Reality.* London: Tavistock.

Zeligs, M. A. (1960), The role of silence in transference, countertransference and the psychoanalytic process. *Int. J. Psycho–Anal.*, 41:407–412.

Zetzel, E. R. (1956), The concept of transference. In: *The Capacity for Emotional Growth.* New York: International Universities Press, 1970, pp. 168–181.

8

DELUSION AND METAPHOR

JACOB A. ARLOW, M.D.

According to psychoanalytic theory, human thought, particularly perception and cognition, is, from its very inception, essentially metaphoric in nature. This is a natural consequence of what Freud (1900) called the primitive, primary process tendency of the human mind. In the face of somatic need, there is a tendency to bring about diminution of feelings of unpleasure by attempting to reexperience a set of perceptions identical with those connected with a memory of previous gratification. The fundamental modes for processing experience in the earliest phases of life conform to the criteria of familiar or unfamiliar, pleasurable or unpleasurable. Since no new experience can, in fact, achieve a complete perceptual identity with a memory of previous gratification, it may safely be assumed that the grouping of mental presentations according to pleasure and familiarity involves a set of approximations rather than identity. Accordingly, the various memory systems or schemata are established, in which experiences are associatively linked according to the criterion of similarity. Experiences associatively linked easily transfer elements of signification from one to the other.

The transfer, or carrying over, of meaning is the essence of metaphor. The term itself is derived from two Greek words meaning "to carry over," and it is defined as a set of linguistic processes whereby aspects of one object are carried over or transferred to another object, so that the second object is spoken of as if it were the first. Substitution is not arbitrary but is based on a point of resemblance between the substituted word or phrase and its referent, which is stated or implied by the sentence as a whole or by the context of the communication.

173

Since language is the vehicle of our thought, considerations of metaphor are fundamental in any analysis of normal and pathological thought processes. Metaphor is considered to be the most fundamental form of figurative language (Hawkes, 1972). Figurative language is language which does not mean what it says, or, to put it more precisely, it says one thing while meaning another. Figurative language deliberately interferes with a system of literal usage by the assumption that terms literally connected with one object can be transferred to another object. It does so with the aim of achieving new, wider, special, or precise meaning. Figurative language usually results in images, but not always. Of the various figures of speech, metaphor is generally considered to manifest the basic pattern of transference involved. The other figures of speech tend to be versions of the prototype supplied by metaphor.

Metaphor supplies language with flexibility, expressibility, and a method by which to expand. "It is the power whereby language, even with a small vocabulary, manages to embrace a multimillion things" (Langer, 1948). Most current authorities are of the opinion that, philogenetically and ontogenetically, metaphor originates at that point of development where the stock of words is insufficient to express the complexity (and, psychoanalysis would add, the overdetermination) of thought.

Translated into terms of clinical experience, metaphor may come to serve as a vehicle to express what is ordinarily unexpressible. This brings to mind one of Freud's early formulations of the relationship between the repressed and the preconscious. In 1915, Freud spoke of the difficulty the psychotic patient has in investing preconscious verbal representations with the cathexes of unconscious thoughts. Expressed in terms of modern structural theory, in the face of conflict over forbidden or inexpressible wishes inherent in certain unconscious fantasies from childhood, compromise formations eventuate. In analysis, when one traces these compromise formations back to their unconscious sources, one can see that they express the same idea or wish, only using different words and images. In effect, the familiar compromise formations we engage in analysis, e.g., symptoms or character traits, are verbal and/or motor metaphors of some unconscious fantasy, and transference represents a metaphoric acting out of such unconscious fantasies (Arlow, 1979a). As we shall see from this presentation, the difference between the normal and neurotic, on the one hand, and the psychotic, on the other, is that the latter tends to deal with the metaphor as reality. He takes it seriously.

The difficulty that the psychotic has with metaphor is inherent in the relationship between metaphor and reality. Ordinary words convey only what we already know. It is through metaphor that we are able to get hold of new ideas, with which we expand our growing knowledge of the world about us. Metaphor is part of the learning process and, through its use, we try to grasp the nature of reality. According to Hawkes (1972), there are two fundamental views of metaphor.

> There is what might be called the classical view, which sees metaphor as 'detachable' from language, a device that may be imported into language in order to achieve specific prejudged effects. These aid language to achieve what is seen as its major goal, the revelation of the 'reality' of a world that lies unchanged beyond it: and there is what might be called the view which sees metaphor as inseparable from language which is 'vitally metaphorical' and the 'reality' which is ultimately the end product of an essentially 'metaphorical interaction' between words and the sensory impressions of daily encounter [p. 90].

This latter view, which is closer to modern philosophical concepts of the relationship between language, thought, and reality, is best articulated by Richards (1965). He states,

> Words do not mean, we mean by words. The total fabric of our meanings, which constitute the world as we know it, consists not of actual or inherited experience, each attached to an appropriate word or set of words, but linguistic and psychological laws regarding recurrent likenesses of behavior in our mind and in the world to which words are variously adapted by us [p. 12].

In keeping with this point of view, speech, with its inherently ambiguous nature, is taken as language's primary and defining form and reflects man's unique status as a talking animal.

> His language is an organic, self-contained, autonomous system, which divides and classifies experience in its own terms and along its own lines. In the course of the process, it imposes its own particular shape on the world of those who speak it . . . a language creates reality in its own image. To use language thus essentially involves getting at one kind of reality through another. This process is fundamentally one of transference, i.e., a metaphorical apprehension of the world and its realities. From this point of view, all language, by the nature of its transferring 'relation to reality,' is fundamentally metaphorical" [Hawkes, 1972, p. 59].

Understood in these terms, we can say that each individual integrates his early experiences, his wishes and disappointments, his hopes and his fears, into a set of metaphorical statements that constitute his stock of persistent unconscious fantasies. As I stated previously (Arlow, 1969a, b), it is in terms of these unconscious fantasies, i.e., the guiding metaphors, that the patient perceives, interprets, and responds to subsequent experiences in life. The process, as we know, is primarily unconscious, and the derivative metaphoric expressions are dealt with in their own terms and not treated literally as if they were direct expressions of unconscious fantasies. From every level of psychosexual development, different character traits may evolve, each expressing a metaphoric interpretation of experience in terms of the guiding unconscious fantasy. Thus, the pessimistic, orally frustrated, depressed and angry patient experiences object relations as a metaphor of the dry, ungiving breast (Arlow, 1969b). What we recognize as the so-called anal personality, in effect, categorizes his experiences in terms of a metaphor relating to feces. Things are either clean or dirty, valuable or useless, to be retained or expelled, in the proper place or not, at the proper time or not, glorious or disgusting, admirable or contemptible.

Clinical experience demonstrates that it is not a very long step for the disappointing world, as a metaphor of the dry breast, to be transformed into the delusion of being poisoned.

Similarly, by a process of projection, the unpleasant effects of the fecal mass in the body of the paranoid patient can be transformed into delusions of persecution (Arlow, 1949; Ophuijsen, 1920; Staercke, 1920). The metaphor is taken as reality. The tendency for schizophrenic patients to interpret language and experience literally has long been recognized, and it is exemplified in the usual methods of testing mental status by asking such patients to interpret proverbs.

I now propose to present what seems to be a particularly illuminating example of the principles described up to this point. Only the elements essential to illustrate the points will be presented. The patient is a middle-aged man, unhappy, and constantly brooding. He is obsessed with thoughts of death and murder. He could kill people who make dirt, who frustrate him, and who, in one way or another, seem to stand in his way. The most striking feature of his history, which for a long time remained unrevealed, was the fact that he had a congenital stenosis of the anus, which made the passage of any stool a painful experience. The passage became infected, so that secondary stricture developed. For reasons which do not pertain to our present discussion, this condition remained uncorrected surgically until the patient was an adult. Throughout his younger years, he thought that this was the natural course of events, that bowel movements had to be painful. For him the usual experiences in life all seemed to be fraught with pain. He complained about all the work that he had to do in connection with paying his income tax, and it became for him a restatement of his conviction that this was a painful matter and nothing could be done about it.

The patient presented an elaborate fantasy in the form of a hypothetical scenario for a movie. In this fantasy, the hero struggles against the forces of evil, as epitomized by the members of the board of a large corporation. The hero is introduced to the board at a meeting, and he notices that all the men are wearing big aluminum cups over their genitals. The size of the cup becomes larger as one goes up the line of authority in management. The chairman of the board has the largest one of all. In addition, there are stars on each one of the cups, just as, during wartime, markers are placed on airplanes to note the

number of enemy planes shot down. The hero is disgusted with
this brand of macho competitiveness. He also notices that each
one of the members of the board has a large pair of nutcrackers,
the idea being that one advances in standing by cracking the
balls of the other members of the board.

When asked what he thought about the scenario, the patient said he felt it described his own life and what had happened to him, how he had withdrawn in disgust from the macho
world. It was pointed out to him that, according to the scenario,
everything is measured in terms of the size of the penis,
strength, position in the hierarchy, etc. The patient insisted that
this was exactly how it was in real life. If this were the case, it
was pointed out, then he was interpreting his relationship to
men in reality in terms of a fantasied fear of castrating or being
castrated. The patient, however, insisted that this was not fantasy. This was how it was in the real world. He could not accept
the idea that victories in real life, or humiliations, were metaphoric representations of unconscious fantasies, or even of conscious fantasies of castrating or being castrated. The patient
refused to deal with the idea as a metaphoric expression. If a
person is defeated in a tennis match, he feels bad and humiliated. To the patient it was the same as being castrated. "It
makes no difference. It's just the same if you defeat somebody
in a game or an election or a business deal, as if you had actually
castrated him. Maybe it's even worse." To the patient a derivative metaphoric expression and the actual primitive impulse
were identical. "There is no difference between winning a tennis
match and shooting your opponent's balls off." I said to him,
"In reality, there is quite a difference. The police would certainly intervene if you shot at his genitals." To this, the patient
responded, "That's just the legal point of view."

The quasi-delusional nature of his anal metaphors became
clear in the following experiences. The exterior of the building
in which the patient lived was being sandblasted. Dirt came into
his apartment and some of his windows were damaged. The
management refused to do anything about it, and the patient
began harboring extreme fantasies of revenge. He was also
annoyed with a neighbor whose shower leaked into his apartment. His fantasies of revenge were murderous in content.

Subsequently, there was an additional complaint. A man who lived in the building kept leaving his bicycle in the lobby. The patient felt this defaced the lobby. When discussion with the management and the young man proved unavailing, the patient was determined to destroy the bicycle. When it was pointed out to the patient that he took the affront personally, as if he himself were being defiled, he replied that there was not any "as if" quality about the experience. It was being done to him. He felt the same rage when someone permitted his dog to urinate on the building. "It's just as if they were pissing in my face. I wish I had a water pistol that I could fill up with urine or excrement and shoot it back at these people." He had fantasies of strangling people who permitted their dogs to defecate on the street.

Ideas of intrusion into his space and of injustice done to him translated into terms of being dirtied. It was in this context that I pointed out to him that he had earlier made some vague reference to some anal discomfort. It was then that I learned of the longstanding history of suffering and pain from his anal condition. It had not been possible for him to pass his stool comfortably until a few years ago when he had the condition somewhat corrected surgically. The stool was so tiny that it resembled a string, not a ribbon. There were repeated episodes of wetness, dirtiness, bleeding, and pain. He could understand that the stool, as a constant source of pain and discomfort, could be experienced by him as his enemy.

At the following session, the patient connected the irritability of his anus with his fighting with his wife. She was "a pain in the ass." He had discussed some of these connections with his previous analyst, and had been made aware of a certain pleasurable component and a gratifying erotic quality that suffused the relief that came after a buildup of painful tension. He could appreciate the similarity of this feeling to the buildup of painful tension as a result of the accumulation of feces and the pleasurable relief when he was able to discharge them. This idea was extended to the concept of unconsciously identifying people who annoyed him with his inner enemy, the stool. The patient's response was that, while he was helpless to do anything about the pain caused by the stool, he could do something about the people who annoyed him.

In one of his dreams, the identification of the enemy with the contents of the bowel was clearly expressed. The dream occurred on the patient's return from a trip to Paris. On the trip he had been concerned about terrorists blowing up the plane. In his dream, there are terrorists who attempt to blow up the plane. The police come. The terrorists flee. They take refuge in the sewers of Paris, where the police pursue them.

This patient had a paranoid attitude toward the world in general and, in particular, toward people whom he experienced as dirtying him or obstructing his way. At times this attitude took on a delusional nature. His attitude toward the world represented a metaphoric variation of his relationship to the stool. He projected the internal suffering caused by the passage of the stool onto external objects, viewing them as harmful, dangerous, and potentially murderous. This was his attitude, in fact, toward practically all objects. He looked upon life as basically painful, essentially a series of quiet periods in between pain—corresponding to the experiences of passing the stool. He felt the same way about his marriage—basically painful, with interludes of quiet and peace. When the intrusive effects of the unconscious fantasy are so great as to lead an individual to interpret derivative expressions literally and not metaphorically, delusion appears. The patient misinterprets metaphor for reality.

During treatment, the therapist endeavors to make the patient understand that his symptoms, in particular, and his difficulties, in general, result from a subjective, metaphoric misapprehension of interpersonal relationships. In order to do this, the therapist has to be sensitive to the nuances and patterning of the patient's speech. In a large measure, this is inherently an aesthetic process. Beres (1957) has described the analytic situation as a counterpart of a creative process, in which therapist and patient affectively influence each other and, in the tranquility of the psychoanalytic situation, master the powerful drives—"tame the chaos"—by bringing order and reason to the patient's productions. In order to do this, the analyst has to be able to establish an effective empathic relationship with his patient. He must have the ability to identify with the patient (and with the language that he uses), and to break off the identification and observe that his own reaction is a commentary on the patient's productions (Beres and Arlow, 1974; Arlow, 1979b). In particular, the therapist must appreciate how any use of figurative language may represent a derivative expression of a basic, unconscious, conflictual fantasy, defensively distorted by means of metaphor. What the therapist does in the treatment situation is to apprehend the significance of the metaphoric idioms the patient uses and translate them into everyday, realistic language and concepts.

The interpretation of transference is based on a simile, that is to say, unconsciously the patient treats the analyst as if he were the important object of his childhood. There is an unreal, "as if" quality to the relationship. It is a simile that the patient can readily apprehend as an intrusion of an unconscious fantasy. As a result of the interpretive work, what had been a metaphoric experience is now understood as a simile.

The situation in the case of delusion is more complicated. In a simile, A is said to be like B. In a metaphor, A is described in terms of B. In symbolism, B is mentioned and A does not appear. While, at times, the structure of a delusion may resemble that of a symbol, the content of the delusional ideation identifies it with metaphor. Delusion represents the metaphor taken literally. The neurotic can appreciate the simile implicit in his object relationships. The psychotic cannot conceptualize his delusional object relations in terms of simile. He persists in seeing them as metaphors. Through a process of projection, the subject of the psychotic's delusions is endowed with the characteristics of the primary object of the patient's drives and is treated as if he were actually that object.

The diffuse and extensive use of metaphoric transformation of object relations renders the task of understanding the meaning of the psychotic's productions very difficult. To appreciate what lies behind the ubiquitous metaphoric transformation of reality which the psychotic effects requires skill, experience, and perhaps a special gift for empathic identification and intuition. These were the qualities which Frieda Fromm-Reichmann exemplified to the greatest degree. Hers was a special ability to understand a patient's metaphoric language but, more than that, she had the ability to communicate the understanding in a way that helped to create for her patients a bridge that led from metaphor to simile to objective communication. It was her special gift not only to understand the nature of the unconscious conflicts hidden behind the patient's delusions and metaphors, but also to use language that indicated to the patient that he was being understood. This perhaps was the first step on the road to recovery.

References

Arlow, J. A. (1949), Anal sensations and feelings of persecution. *Psychoanal. Quart.*, 18:79–84.
——— (1969a), Fantasy, memory and reality testing. *Psychoanal. Quart.*, 38:28–51.
——— (1969b), Unconscious fantasy and disturbances of conscious experience. *Psychoanal. Quart.*, 38:1–27.
——— (1979a), Metaphor and the psychoanalytic situation. *Psychoanal. Quart.*, 48:363–385.
——— (1979b), The genesis of interpretation. *The Amer. Psychoanal. Assn.*, 27:193–206.
Beres, D. (1957), Communication in psychoanalysis and in the creative process. *J. Amer. Psychoanal. Assn.*, 5:408–423.
——— Arlow, J. A. (1974), Fantasy and identification in empathy. *Psychoanal. Quart.*, 43:26–50.
Freud, S. (1900), The Interpretation of Dreams. *Standard Edition*, 4 & 5. London: Hogarth Press, 1953.
——— (1915), The unconscious. *Standard Edition*, 14:166–204. London: Hogarth Press, 1961.
Hawkes, T. (1972), *Metaphor*. London: Methuen.
Langer, S. (1948), *Philosophy in a New Key*. New York: Mentor.
Ophuijsen, J. H. W. (1920), On the origin of feelings of persecution. *Int. J. Psycho–Anal.*, 1:235–239.
Richards, I. A. (1955), *Speculative Instruments*. Chicago: University of Chicago Press.
——— (1965), *The Philosophy of Rhetoric*. New York: Oxford University Press.
Staercke, A. (1920), The reversal of the libido-sign in delusions of persecution. *Int. J. Psycho-Anal.*, 1:231–234.

9

THE APPLICATION OF
PSYCHOANALYTIC PRINCIPLES TO THE
HOSPITALIZED PATIENT

ROBERT W. GIBSON, M.D.

Please Call Me Frieda

I first met Frieda Fromm-Reichmann in October 1952 when, fresh out of residency training in psychiatry, I joined the staff at Chestnut Lodge. In that first meeting she introduced herself by saying, "Please call me Frieda." Although many years my senior and light years ahead in professional experience and maturity, Frieda's request that I call her by her first name seemed perfectly natural. From this very first meeting, Frieda always treated me as a colleague. Inexperienced as I was, Frieda had a sincere interest in and respect for my opinion.

Just a few years later, Frieda was treating a male patient on the third floor where I was that unit's administrative psychiatrist. For several months, Frieda conducted her psychotherapy sessions with this patient in her house a short distance from the main hospital building. Based on my observations of the patient's behavior, I became concerned that there was some increase in the intensity of the patient's paranoid thinking. I shared my concern with Frieda and suggested that she see the patient in my office in the main building where assistance was readily available if needed.

Although Frieda had not discerned any obvious change in the patient's behavior during psychotherapy, she acknowledged the significance of my observations and those made by the nursing staff who had been with the patient twenty-four hours a day for many months. She began seeing the patient in my office. Within a few weeks, the patient was able to express his anger more openly. In a brief outburst, he displayed his underlying rage—the only damage was an ashtray broken when he slammed his fist on the table.

A few days later, I received a new ashtray with a note: "Dear Bob, Here is an ashtray to replace the one that R. broke. Thank you for letting us use your office. Frieda." I can recall dozens of similar experiences illustrating Frieda's respect for the opinion of all staff members, her receptivity to suggestions, and the respectful relationship she maintained with her patients.

Frieda often referred to Harry Stack Sullivan. As time progressed, I began to hear more about Sullivan from Dexter Bullard, Otto Will, Robert Cohen, and the many others who had known him personally. Although I had never met Sullivan, I began to develop a picture of the man and what his treatment approach to patients might have been. It finally dawned on me that I pictured Sullivan to be a most detestable person whom I would have thoroughly disliked. In my fantasy of Sullivan as a therapist, he seemed arrogant, callous, even cruel.

It puzzled me that many of my Chestnut Lodge colleagues, including Frieda, not only respected Sullivan's ability as a psychiatrist, but recalled him with warmth and affection. I asked several senior staff if they could explain this paradox. The best they could suggest was that despite his caustic, vicious, intimidating manner, Sullivan, on occasion, had related to them with sensitivity, concern, and compassion. In fact, they had found his hostile barbs often to be incisive and on the mark.

Harry Stack Sullivan at Sheppard Pratt

Harry Stack Sullivan did not actually treat patients at Chestnut Lodge. The bulk of his direct clinical work with hospitalized patients was at The Sheppard and Enoch Pratt Hospital in Towson. Ross McClure Chapman, M.D., then superintendent of Sheppard Pratt, brought Sullivan to that hospital as an assistant physician in 1923 after only one year of experience in psychiatry at St. Elizabeths Hospital in 1922–1923. In 1925,

Sullivan was appointed director of clinical research and was allowed to have his own six-bed unit for the treatment of young male schizophrenics. He continued on the staff of Sheppard Pratt until 1930.

Soon after I joined the staff at Sheppard Pratt in 1960, I began to hear a new set of war stories about Sullivan's seven years at the hospital some thirty-five years earlier. When I sought to learn about Sullivan through the medical records of the patients on his special unit, I discovered that beyond bare-bones demographic information about the patients, no records existed. As far as I can ascertain, Sullivan never wrote a single note in the hospital records of any of the patients, although it is said that he kept voluminous personal notes.

In the mid-sixties, in an effort to overcome the lack of written records, I brought together a group of individuals who had all known and worked directly with Sullivan. The group that had worked with Sullivan in varying capacities included Leo Bartemeier, M.D., analysand and later colleague; Harry M. Murdock, M.D., third medical director of Sheppard Pratt; William W. Elgin, student and colleague; G. Wilson Shaffer, Ph.D., colleague from 1927 to 1930 at Sheppard Pratt; Elizabeth Winstead, R.N., and Ralph Linton, R.N., both of whom were at Sheppard Pratt during Sullivan's tenure; and Ruthwin Evans, hydrotherapist at Sheppard Pratt. Not a part of this group meeting but rich sources of information were Alex Martin, M.D., and his wife, Nancy, who lived in the same residence with Sullivan at Sheppard Pratt for many years and knew him not only professionally but personally. The reminiscences of this group provided a fascinating picture of Harry Stack Sullivan and his seminal work at Sheppard Pratt.

Sullivan terrified almost everyone. He could be sarcastic, caustic, disdainful—an absolute terror. Will Elgin recalled his reputation as unpredictable, irritable, demanding, aloof, and isolated. As evidence, he cited a passage from the *Proceedings, Second Colloquium on Personality Investigation* (1930) in which Sullivan refers to certain of his attitudes regarding training.

> There come to me physicians seeking insight into problems
> of the mind. They come to me as well-trained physicians

and therefore with an acquired inability to understand anything that I say to them. I don't believe that if they stayed with me from now on until Gabriel blows his hornpipes, they will acquire much notion of what I am talking about—or privately give a damn. They are already educated, they have a degree of Doctor of Medicine, and they have a whole system of ideas that takes its origin from certain misunderstandings about physical chemistry—on things which they probably don't realize are physico-chemical subjects—and they are pretty well organized [p. 138].

Speaking of nurses, Sullivan (1930–1931) had this to say about his unit at Sheppard Pratt,

The administration supervision and patient-doctor contacts were segregated and entirely supervised. Specifically, by eliminating supervision of the Nursing Service of those never-enough-to-be-admired miracles whose life is so glaringly illuminated by the professional ideal, often shining the more brilliantly—and casting the more perfect and Stygian shadows—because it is without any competing ideal, I was able to grow in the sub-professional personnel a lush crop of self-respect from good accomplished with the patient. The modern nurse is usually so well-trained in: (a) The Ethics of Nursing—including a tacit "my Profession, right or wrong, but always my Profession"—and (b) all sorts of valuable word phrases, conceptions of diseases and treatments—especially for distributing blame—, techniques and crafts, that her aptitude for integration into the complex uncertainties of the mental hospital milieu is vestigial, and only by a personal personality upheaval is she apt to come again to that intuitive grasp of personal totalities that was once her property in common with all preadolescents.

The graduate of our medical schools, for somewhat different reasons, is so detached from a "natural" grasp on personality that it usually takes him from 12 to 18 months residence on the staff of an active mental hospital to crack crust to such effect that he begins to learn "what it is all about." The graduate nurse, however, harassed as she is by upstart interns, inefficient physicians, utterly unmoral male personnel, etc., etc., seems usually too preoccupied ever to make this beginning [p. 984].

In sharp contrast to these caustic statements are Will Elgin's memories of Sullivan's warm interest in his patients and his extremely gentle, tolerant, and understanding attitude both toward them and the people working through them. Elgin recalled a specific situation in which Sullivan went out of his way to be kind, helpful, and supportive to the mother of a schizophrenic patient:

> In those days, we did not have a residing internist; the low man on a totem pole did the medical work of the hospital. I was at the bottom of the pole in those years, so Sullivan asked me to go with him to visit the mother of one of his patients about whom he was much concerned. Instead of being the cranky, disagreeable, sarcastic rascal that he was alleged to be, he was a sensitive, supportive friend and a good doctor to this woman who was a widow and had a schizophrenic son who happened to be his patient. I truly believe that under his façade of disagreeableness, Sullivan was basically a very understanding person when he dealt with the things with which he was concerned. All the same, he could be very callous and far from understanding in other areas.

Sullivan had a great respect for Adolf Meyer, even though the patient population and treatment approach at Hopkins differed drastically from Sheppard Pratt. Will Elgin recalled that at Phipps the students saw very little of psychotics. Adolf Meyer acknowledged that because of restrictions on taking patients into the Phipps Clinic, acutely psychotic patients were not available for teaching purposes. For that reason, Elgin spent four months in a state hospital in Massachusetts before coming to Sheppard Pratt. When Elgin arrived at Sheppard Pratt, he was impressed by the different atmosphere that prevailed. Although the patients were the same as in the state hospital, there was an attempt to do something; the whole atmosphere and attitude of the staff were helpful. He felt that in the state hospital similar patients were never given decent care. Elgin considered Harry Stack Sullivan to have been a major force in creating the therapeutic climate of Sheppard Pratt, particularly as it related to the severely ill hospitalized patient.

Summarizing his contact as a third-year medical student

with Sullivan, Elgin (1964, personal communication) said, "I find it difficult; after these years, to summarize just what I carried from my contact with Dr. Sullivan as seen through the eyes of a third-year medical student. Probably the most important thing was to learn that patients are human beings and can be treated as such and that all who deal with them share some responsibility for their care and treatment. It is certainly almost impossible to put in words what one observed in Dr. Sullivan's actual dealing with very sick, young, male, schizophrenic patients, but I do remember him as a warm friend, and perhaps one of his major contributions is summarized in Helen Swick Perry's introduction to Sullivan's book, *Schizophrenia As a Human Process* (1962)."

Evans, who first met Sullivan in 1927 when he came to work at Sheppard Pratt, recalled that Sullivan had just bought a new automobile—a Franklin—but still kept his old Studebaker out in front of the building. Evans did not have $125, which was Sullivan's asking price. When Evans asked about buying the car, Sullivan said, "You take the car and you pay me what you think you can. But if you ever decide you cannot pay me, please do not quit your job here to get away from paying me because I would rather give you the car and you stay here." Evans recalled how Sullivan later on made arrangements for him to get specialized training in hydrotherapy. This was the beginning of a lasting friendship.

Evans recalled that he accompanied a husky young patient to Sullivan's office for treatment and stayed during the interviews. During one therapeutic interview, the patient became angry and slapped Sullivan. Sullivan just sat there and motioned Evans away when he started to intervene. He then went on to ask the patient if he was satisfied or if he wanted to slap him again. The patient, dumbfounded, simply stood there and never assaulted him again. Over the years he knew him, Evans could recall no instance in which Sullivan displayed overt anger toward any of his patients.

Wilson Shaffer recalled his first meeting with Sullivan in 1928: "I had just gotten my degree and was settling into my office. I had a telephone and books around me, and I thought I was a big shot when Sullivan walked in. Although we had not met, I knew him by sight. Without saying anything to me, Sullivan walked in, took a chair alongside my desk, pulled out the desk drawer, and propped his feet on it."

Sullivan said, "Tell me, doctor, what is your theory of dreams?" Shaffer protested that because he was just out of school, he really had no theories. Sullivan pushed the issue. Shaffer recalled, "I felt I had to say something. I can't remember what I said—it couldn't have been very important. Sullivan puffed on his cigarette and said, 'Hmmm.' I was getting more and more annoyed; then he said, 'Tell me, doctor—what is your theory of schizophrenia?' I protested again and said I was just out of school. Finally, Sullivan backed off."

A few weeks later, Sullivan stopped Shaffer in the hall and said, "Say, Shaffer, why don't you get out of this business? You're quite comfortable for an extrovert, and you're never going to understand people." And Shaffer stopped and thought for a minute, and finally said, "Well, I guess maybe you're right, but since I am a relatively comfortable extrovert, I don't think I'm going to quit, because it appears to me that it's just possible that there may be some people who haven't got problems and might be able to deal with people who do have them. This really irked him."

Shaffer recalled, "Not terribly long after that, I published a book in which I said this, and the book was barely on the street before he telephoned me and said, 'What's the idea of writing about me in your book?' And I said, 'I really wasn't talking about you but a group of persons of whom you happened to be one.' You would have thought from this he would have continued to regard me with anger. But, in spite of it all, whenever he went away, he never failed to send me a postcard. I think in some way he was kind of fascinated by someone who could talk back to him because he wasn't used to having anybody talk back to him."

Leo Bartemeier first met Sullivan in 1924 when he was a first-year resident at Phipps. Bartemeier recalls that first contact as follows: Sullivan said, "Are you Bartemeier?" And Bartemeier said, "Yes, I am." Sullivan said, "Well—I'm Sullivan, and I want you to know that I'll tear you limb from limb if you don't leave that poor schizophrenic boy on West 1 alone." It really blew him up when Bartemeier said, "I didn't know he was related to you." Two minutes later he said, "Let's have lunch together." On the way to lunch, he said, "By the way, how have you regarded your personality?" Bartemeier said, "Oh, I think I am a manic-depressive." Sullivan disagreed and gave Bartemeier a lecture on his inadequate ability to understand human nature and challenged him as to why he was in psychiatry.

Bartemeier recalled that many years later he was urged to have an analysis with Sullivan, who then was with the White Foundation in New York. Bartemeier was then practicing psychiatry in Michigan and had a wife and three children, while Sullivan was in New York. "I begged him to take me into analysis. He refused until I told him I wouldn't go to anybody else; then he agreed. Then came the question of how could I get the hours in the shortest possible time? So, I was on the couch eight hours a day on Friday and Saturday. Sunday, we had only four hours because I had to catch the train to Detroit. Yes—eight analytic hours in a day. During each weekend, I had two days and one-half. That was intensive treatment!"

When asked his opinion of this unorthodox approach, Bartemeier said, "It was the most valuable experience of my whole life. For all those hours, he was most attentive. He was most careful. He was diabolical, as he could be at times, when he felt the need to be so. But when I became acutely ill with an acute infection during one of those first weekends, I called him up and told him I was sick in bed. He said, 'I'll be over shortly.' And he dropped in to see how I was feeling; and, 'I'll get a doctor for you right away, stay right there in bed.' He got a doctor for me, and he got a nurse."

Bartemeier, too, was struck by the paradox that Sullivan could be the most cruel of human beings and at the same time could be kind and deeply concerned. Bartemeier recalled: "Although I seemed to have a knack of infuriating him, I always understood that this was perfectly all right. This was Sullivan, and he was still very friendly towards me and very fond of me. So that when he would fly off his collar, I still knew he cared for me."

Leo Bartemeier was convinced that Harry Stack Sullivan was really the first person in the history of American psychiatry to provide hope for the treatment of schizophrenics, "Think it through. Who else could have been so influential? Sullivan was known across the country for his understanding and his ability to help schizophrenics recover. Whether he did or did not is another question. I think he probably did."

In 1926 Sullivan participated in the design of what was called the Reception Building at Sheppard Pratt to house approximately ninety patients. Many of the architectural idiosyncrasies of the building are attributed to him. I have found little hard data to support these stories and suspect that, for the most part, they are apochryphal.

It is a fact, however, that a small six-bed unit on the second floor, center front and known as R-I, was placed under Sullivan's sole direction by Ross Chapman. The patients were all relatively young male schizophrenics. The staff were all male—what Sullivan referred to as subprofessionals. With only one exception, no women were permitted on the ward; the one exception was Betty Winstead, R.N., who participated in our discussion of Sullivan at Sheppard Pratt. She recalled that he did not have any regularly scheduled appointments with patients and saw them at irregular times, often at night. Typically, he included other staff members in the interview and would draw them into the conversation by asking their opinions. He often instructed staff members as to how they should respond to the various facets of the patients' behavior. It was clear to everyone at Sheppard Pratt that these were Sullivan's patients, and, indeed, he was described as reacting like a tiger if he had the slightest suspicion that anyone was interfering with the treatment of one of his patients. There is no evidence that Sullivan at the time articulated an organized treatment approach. Based on the recollections of those who were there, it seems safe to assume that he encouraged staff to approach patients in much the same way he did. In any event, it appears clear that Sullivan's work from 1927 to 1930 with the six patients on R-I constitutes the bulk of his direct clinical experience with hospitalized schizophrenics.

Although Sullivan made no notes in the charts, it was the custom during the 1920s when Sullivan was at Sheppard Pratt to hold formal staff conferences on each patient. Verbatim notes of these conferences were recorded, including an interview with the patient. Sullivan frequently conducted these interviews as the designated *interrogator* (an interesting choice of terms). Although these were interrogations (interviews, if you will), there is much to suggest that they reflect the approach Sullivan used in his therapeutic sessions. These interviews provide abundant insight into Sullivan's approach to patients as well as into his thinking about schizophrenia. For that reason, I have chosen to present in some detail an example of one of Sullivan's "interrogations" to give a picture of his approach to patients.

Sullivan as Interrogator

SULLIVAN: The Conference is considering what should now be done in regard to you. What is your sentiment about it?

PATIENT: You mean in a business way or discharge from the hospital or what? I don't understand.

S: All those things must be considered. We are thinking of the immediate future for you.

PT: What have you in mind? I thought I would go to college in the fall.

S: And what in the meanwhile?

PT: I don't know, unless go to my father's place and work for a month or so.

S: What else is interesting you?

PT: Nothing else that I know of. I like time enough for recreation—don't like to work six days a week with no time off on Saturday.

S: You are not one of those who would get up at 4 A.M. in order to play golf?

PT: I have done that, years ago, but playing at that time in the morning, not many people want to play then; furthermore, I think it would be dark then.

S: I wouldn't argue over fifteen minutes—and isn't it necessary to get out early because of the large number of people, if one plays on the public links?

PT: Yes, on Saturdays and Sundays.

S: You can get up and get in two hours before time to go to work if you are that anxious, can't you?

PT: Oh, yes, easy enough. But I want Saturday afternoons off.

S: Then, you'd perhaps seek employment in which you could work every other day?

PT: Oh, no, five-and-a-half days a week. I like the half-day off. I worked six days a week, and it had a bad effect on me.

S: Now, you are bearing on the question of your illness?

PT: I don't know. They say. . . .

S: May I ask who "they" are? You say, "They say." Who?

PT: The people who say—doctor says, that the hours don't suit.

S: The trouble you had then resulted because the hours didn't suit?

PT: I don't know whether it is the work or my personality or what.

S: Well, that really doesn't sound favorable for your future. I had no idea you were really so ignorant as to what it is all about.

PT: I understand my father's place had. . . .

S: Well, we seem to be becoming more and more concrete. Now what were the factors, the effective factors, in your father's place that brought on your mental illness?

PT: I don't know. Not getting along down at the place, and arguing all the time. At least that is what Dr. H. said.

S: And Dr. H. impressed you as a fairly intelligent person, I gather?

PT: Fairly, yes.

S: Having expressed these weighty opinions of his

	intelligence, do you find any answering feeling of belief in you regarding what *he* "told" you?
PT:	I realized there were weeks and weeks I had arguments.
S:	Can you explain to us how these things brought about your trouble?
PT:	Well, I can't find anybody to blame.
S:	Really, I am amazed at your present mental condition. Everything is very uncertain.
PT:	I don't know very much about that, whether it is my mental condition or what it is.
S:	Well, do you feel you are involved in any cosmic network that takes dominance over your mind?
PT:	I don't believe there is. I don't know very much about it—who is to blame for it.
S:	In your work with Dr. H., did you get the idea that everything must be explained on the basis of blaming somebody?
PT:	I don't know whose fault. . . .
S:	You will pardon me if I insist that the use of the word "fault" implies blame.
PT:	I don't know whether it was lack of ability or what.
S:	Do you think that your mental illness has led to a very serious dilapidation of your mental ability?
PT:	I don't think so.
S:	Have you cultivated this manner of extreme doubt with the notion of annoying your environment?
PT:	I don't know how to explain that.
S:	Well, do you think you are anywhere near able to meet the world on an even footing, or do you feel that you are very badly handicapped as compared to most people?
PT:	I don't think I am handicapped at all.
S:	In your dealing with other people, I suppose that you sometimes observed that they had an opinion about something. I don't discover that

you have an opinion about anything of importance to yourself.

PT: Maybe.

S: You feel that is an advantage to you?

PT: No, I don't think that is an advantage at all, but
I wasn't helped by those arguments.

S: I thought history recorded that you broke down
under circumstances quite different.

PT: Yes, I know, but doctor said that that wasn't
important; that anything else could have come
along and caused a breakdown.

S: In other words, you might have gone for a swim,
and found the water cold, and experienced a
breakdown?

PT: I don't know anything about that.

S: Well, you said anything might come along.

PT: Yes, but Dr. H. . . .

S: He was a great help to you in justifying your
own opinions about things, wasn't he?

PT: I don't know how you'd prove that.

S: If you had to choose exactly the environment
in which to pass the next ten years of your life,
how would you describe it?

PT: I don't know.

S: Oh, we admit that. We can take that for granted
on all questions from now on. But I asked you
for information.

PT: I suppose living at home, the same as I was
doing. But I'd like recreation.

S: Well, go beyond that. Surely, you can find somewhere better than home, couldn't you?

PT: Well, maybe, but. . . .

S: Well, just draft a preliminary sketch that would
be better than home.

PT: Well, I expect I could go to college, if not too
old; I am twenty-two years of age.

S: People have been known to learn after that age.

PT: I know that; that is probably what I'll do.

S: Do you think self-consciousness had anything to

	do with your getting ill?
PT:	Yes.
S:	Well, good lord, how?
PT:	But lots of people have that. I used to be much more self-conscious.
S:	I don't suppose it has ever occurred to you, has it, that there might be something about yourself that caused your self-consciousness?
PT:	I suppose that has something to do with it.
S:	Well, are you filled with any burning desire to find out what it is?
PT:	I don't know.
P:	When do you suggest you are to leave the hospital?
PT:	Well, I understand I was leaving next week. I was told by my people.
S:	Be yourself for a moment. What do *you* think about it?
PT:	Well, I think that would be very fine.

Patient excused.

Staff psychiatrist: I suppose we can't do anything more for the boy. I haven't any faith in him and in his ability to get along. I suppose we must let him go and perhaps break hard later on.

S: I think that is about the situation. He has made a social recovery from a very serious illness without any marked reorganization of his personality. I object to his going home; but, on the other hand, it doesn't seem as if the parents' influence could warp him very much more than he is warped. It will perhaps sensitize him dangerously to other influences again. I think that he should perhaps go from here to some purely recreational community—the sea shore or whatever—and then enter a school, for example, the Wharton School, in the fall. I believe that he does not have to work for a living.

Disposition: To be discharged.

In an effort tto delineate Sullivan's approach, Clarence

Schulz (1978) conducted an extensive review of Sullivan's interviews recorded in Sheppard Pratt medical records. From the study of the interviews he was able to identify ten aspects of Sullivan's technique: (1) confronting of denial and negation; (2) integrating and understanding of conflictual experiences rather than forgetting about the past; (3) pressing the patient to delineate conflict areas; (4) avoiding agreement with delusional content, yet giving credence to the patient's viewpoint; (5) confronting reality, even to ridiculing the patient's unrealistic point of view; (6) resorting to humor and sarcasm to provoke the patient; (7) setting limits on the patient's tendency to waste Sullivan's time; (8) proposing hypotheses and inviting the patient to comment on them; (9) providing examples from his own life in an effort to engage the patient; (10) placing emphasis on the history of the onset of the difficulty through repeated questioning, even when this leads to frustration for both the patient and Sullivan.

Sullivan utilized virtually all these techniques in the interview reported: confronting denial, delineating conflict areas; confronting reality to the point of ridicule; resorting to sarcasm proposing hypotheses; emphasizing the history of onset; and so forth. Sullivan's almost simplistic summation stands in sharp contrast to his active engagement with the patient during the interview.

From Sheppard Pratt to Chestnut Lodge

In the years after he left Sheppard Pratt, Sullivan was a major influence at Chestnut Lodge as a teacher, analyst of some of the staff, supervisor, and advisor. His earlier work and continued presence undoubtedly served as an inspiration. During the 1950s when I was a member of the Chestnut Lodge staff, many of Sullivan's principles were apparent—the consistent effort to establish bridges of communication with the patient; the attempt to understand the patient's experience, even when psychotic; placing emphasis on the onset of the difficulty; and most of all, conceptualizing schizophrenia as a human process.

In my judgment, Frieda Fromm-Reichmann's work at Chestnut Lodge provided the major impetus to the organized and systematic application of psychoanalytic principles to the hospitalized patient. And remember that Frieda's work predated the discovery of neuroleptics. She treated a few individual patients and saw each patient admitted, which wasn't too difficult because there were only about thirty admissions a year. Then, after about a month, she met with the therapist. She also did training analyses and conducted seminars. I had the privilege of participating over a two-year period in such seminars on a case that Clarence Schulz was treating and for whom I was the clinical administrator. She was a role model, counselor, a source of strength and stability.

The core of Fromm-Reichmann's approach was the establishment of a relationship to the patient on whatever basis was possible; she had great respect for the functioning part of the patient's ego and looked for this in even the most psychotic patient. She stressed that psychoanalysis could be used with the psychotic patient, which stirred much controversy and caused many people to think her a fool. She certainly was no fool. She spent her life in personal work with severely ill patients and had no illusions that they would respond to the classic analytic technique, and she certainly did not apply it. I believe that the controversy at that time really centered around her belief that the boundaries of psychoanalytic thinking were too narrow and that the concepts should be expanded. Indeed, the boundaries have been greatly expanded in part by her pioneering work.

Traditional Psychoanalysis and Psychoanalytically Oriented Psychotherapy

Although there are similarities, there are distinct differences between the technique of traditional psychoanalysis as practiced with the neurotic outpatient and psychoanalytically oriented psychotherapy with the hospital inpatient who is suffering from a postpsychotic or borderline personality disorder.

The neurotic outpatient is usually seen four to five times a week for sessions of forty-five to fifty minutes. The patient generally uses the couch. The analyst is neutral, gives minimal feedback, and presents a blank screen. Free association is encouraged.

The postpsychotic or borderline inpatient is more often seen three times a week, with a more flexible approach. Frequency, and even length, of sessions may be varied during different phases of treatment, and particularly during times of crisis. The patient is seen face to face. At times when behavior is unpredictable or possibly suicidal, therapy sessions may be held on the inpatient unit. The psychotherapist is more of a participant, gives more feedback, and, if necessary, reaches out to the patient. The therapist seeks to establish a relationship of trust through a consistent, accepting approach and by demonstrating his desire to understand the patient.

With the neurotic patient, interventions by the analyst are kept at a minimum to permit the transference to evolve with a minimum of distortion. The analyst, through questioning, may seek clarification. Through confrontation, areas of avoidance and contradiction are identified. The ultimate goal is to establish genetic linkages between earlier life experiences and present behavior, including that which is symptomatic.

The psychotherapist for a hospitalized patient reaches out to the patient by asking questions that elicit more information and, at the same time, shows a willingness to share the patient's experiences. During the early phases of treatment, when the therapist has little grasp of the dynamics, challenges by the patient in the therapeutic session or behavior on the patient unit may force the therapist to respond. Failure by the therapist to respond is not neutral; it may be the most dramatic communication. During this phase of therapy, the therapist can be most effective by asking questions that convey acceptance and an interest in understanding the patient.

I recall an intellectually brilliant but highly schizoid man in his mid-twenties whom I treated at Chestnut Lodge. For several months, he gave a detailed history interspersed with his idiosyncratic views, not only of his family, but of the world in general. Much of his thinking could have been labeled bizarre, but I found it creative, original—unusual to be sure—but fascinating. It was clear that the treatment relationship had progressed to a new phase when he said, in effect, "I have always felt strange, weird; people couldn't understand me, didn't seem to want to; you seem to be interested in trying to understand and that makes me feel like I am part of the human race."

The transference neurosis is the crucible through which psychoanalysis uncovers and ultimately works through early life experiences. The initial goal of traditional psychoanalytic treatment is to allow the transference to unfold against the analytic blank screen. By abstaining from interaction with the patient, the analyst deepens and intensifies the transference relationship to the point that it can be described as a transference neurosis. Or, as Dexter Bullard, Sr., once described it, "The patient is hooked." The transference neurosis is only an instrumental goal, not an end in itself. It becomes the focal point around which the patient can gain further insight into the dynamic linkages between past and present.

Sigmund Freud believed that what he termed the *narcissistic neuroses* (which would include schizophrenia) made the patient inaccessible because of an inability to develop a transference neurosis. Freud was certainly correct in his observations about the difficulty in achieving and utilizing the transference relationship in the treatment of the schizophrenic patient. In my judgment, however, the problem is not the inability to form a transference relationship. Rather, it is the threatening, even overwhelming quality of the transference as experienced by the schizophrenic patient. This quality of the schizophrenic's relatedness leads to what Burnham et al. (1969) called the need-fear dilemma.

This need-fear dilemma arises out of a defect in ego function which has as its origin disturbances in the processes of differentiation and integration. The ego functioning is characterized by (1) a vulnerability to disorganization; (2) a relative lack of autonomy from internal drives and external stimuli; and (3) a disturbance in reality testing. Three major patterns of response are available to the schizophrenic as he attempts to solve the dilemma of his object relations: (1) he may avoid objects; (2) he may cling to objects; and (3) he may try to redefine objects to achieve the illusion that a benevolent protector is always available.

Dreams are a critical part of psychoanalytic treatment—what Freud so aptly described as the royal road to the unconscious.

The latent content of the patient's dreams provides a bridge connecting earlier experiences, current life experiences, the transference, and the dynamic interplay of all of these elements. The sophisticated patient entering analysis is aware that dreams are viewed as significant, but even without that knowledge, there is something about the analytic process that leads patients to remember and report their dreams.

Dreams have a less prominent role in the treatment of the hospitalized patient. The patient recovering from psychosis is more intent upon shoring up his defenses against unconscious processes than on opening a link with the shattering psychotic experience. Nevertheless, dreams can be of value in the treatment of the hospitalized patient. Rather than focusing on the latent content, we can accept the dream simply as an effort by the patient to communicate. I recall Frieda saying that whenever a patient reported a dream, she asked herself, and by implication the patient, "What is it that you want to tell me through this dream that you cannot tell me directly? And what prevents you from telling me about it directly?"

I recall a Chestnut Lodge patient who, for the first six weeks, was resistant to the point of assaultiveness. Our therapy sessions on the unit were dominated by her tirades against all psychiatrists, and me in particular. Understandably, it came as a surprise when the head nurse called saying that the patient wanted to see me—and the head nurse stressed that, in her judgment, I should see the patient. When I saw the patient an hour or so later, she told me that she had fallen asleep, had a long dream, felt a need to tell me about it, and wrote it down in great detail—some five pages.

We spent the next four therapeutic sessions going over the manifest content of the dream and the patient's associations. I made no effort to interpret, although there were scores of opportunities. Rather, my questions and responses were aimed at acknowledging that she had broken through her hostile resistance and was attempting to relate to me in the only way that she could. The patient's dream—her reaching out—and my acceptance signaled the beginning of a therapeutic alliance.

In psychoanalytic treatment, conflicts are seldom resolved by the illumination of a single insightful experience. Conflictual experiences are experienced and reexperienced many times. Insights are interspersed with resistance. Transference distortions are clarified and reclarified. Analysis is successful as the recapitulation of these experiences leads to a process of working through.

A process analogous to working through occurs in the treatment of the psychotic or borderline patient. There are, however, qualitative differences. The therapist becomes a participant, not just a detached observer. As a participant, the therapist cannot avoid countertransference. To do so would require lack of involvement, and little or nothing can happen in psychotherapeutic work with the hospitalized patient without meaningful exchange. I believe it would be more accurate to describe therapeutic work with the hospitalized patient as *living through* rather than *working through*.

The participant involvement—living through—can be illustrated by a clinical vignette. A twenty-two-year-old college student, who had had brief periods of psychotic disorganization, characteristically appeared lifeless, drab, and asexual. At the end of a therapeutic session, I automatically helped her with her coat. She became apprehensive and perplexed as she left my office. Suddenly, I felt uncomfortable and awkward and was concerned that my action might have been seductive.

I recalled that in the previous hour, the patient had been more communicative—livelier, even vivacious. For the first time, I had perceived her as feminine. Only when I recognized that she was a woman did it occur to me that helping her with her coat might have been perceived as seductive.

In the next hour, the patient was hostile, angry, hurt. She spoke of a child inside her that was angry. She described how she had felt. Something had happened as she left my office that was upsetting; somehow I was different: cold, harsh, uncaring. She could not identify what it was that made her feel that way, but it was very real.

I acknowledged that I had felt concerned as I helped her on with her coat and that I had probably shown my discomfort. I recalled that in that session she had been more communicative, livelier, even vivacious. I had perceived her as more feminine and was concerned that my helping her with her coat might have been seductive.

She was relieved that her anxiety had some basis in our interaction and was not simply a distortion on her part. She recalled how as a child, she had loved to sit in her father's lap. She sensed the pleasure she got from his warmth and affection. At about age eight, something happened—he became more reserved, stiff; their closeness and intimacy was no longer acceptable. She speculated that her father must have thought it wrong to be physically close as she began to mature physically. She recognized a linkage both at an intellectual and a feeling level to what she had experienced with me in the preceding hour and her early experiences with her father.

Psychotherapy of the schizophrenic patient inevitably activates the dilemma—the need for a relationship and the fear of it. The activation of this conflict in itself may open the way to new object relations and offer an opportunity for a different resolution of the dilemma. Within the context of the transference relationship, the therapist opens himself to the patient and lets him experience the therapist as both a threatening and a need-fulfilling object. This willingness of the therapist to open himself provides a model that gives the patient the courage to expose himself to the hazards of object relations. The therapist helps the patient to identify and become thoroughly familiar with both poles of the need-fear dilemma. He helps the patient to discover the origins of early conflictual object relations. Perhaps most of all, the psychotherapist shares in the need-fear dilemma and in so doing establishes a new kind of relationship for the patient, a relationship that nurtures ego growth (Gibson, 1967).

The Future

The introduction of psychoanalytic principles into hospital treatment spans some sixty years. The application of these principles has been influenced by what has happened in the field over this period of time: (1) psychoanalysis has expanded its boundaries; (2) hospital psychiatry has moved to develop and refine the concept of the therapeutic milieu; (3) psychopharmacologic agents have made patients more accessible; (4) socioeconomic forces have shifted the emphasis toward sicker patients.

Much of what we do at hospitals such as Chestnut Lodge and Sheppard Pratt has become such an integral part of the fabric of our treatment that we are no longer aware of its linkage to psychoanalytic principles. I hope, perhaps, that I have highlighted some of those links. I am concerned that external pressures are making it more difficult to apply the psychoanalytic principles, that we are being pressed toward stabilization and the rapid relief of symptoms.

I believe that the advances in psychopharmacology are enormously valuable, but I cannot conceive of a drug as doing the total job. I am concerned when I hear that some highly respected academic centers are making psychotherapy an elective in their residency program. Psychoanalysis has provided basic knowledge that will continue to be of initial importance in the treatment of hospitalized patients regardless of the advances in biological psychiatry. For example: (1) relationships are important, be they interpersonal or transferential; (2) there is a dynamic interaction among people, feelings, and ideas; (3) communication—both verbal and nonverbal—is a critical element in the treatment of all patients; (4) ego growth and maturation should be part of the goals of treatment; (5) working through or, as I have called it, *living through*, associated with a conflict resolution and insight are fundamental principles of psychoanalysis and are applicable to all patients.

Nothing will make these principles obsolete. Given the dramatic changes in the mental health care delivery system, I wonder, will we be able and *will we be willing* to continue to apply what we have learned over the past sixty years about the application of psychoanalytic principles to hospitalized patients?

I hope so!

References

American Psychiatric Association and the Social Science Research Council (1930), *Proceedings: Second Colloquium on Personality Investigation.* Baltimore, MD: Johns Hopkins University Press.

Burnham, D. L., Gladstone, A. I., & Gibson, R. W. (1969), *Schizophrenia and the Need-Fear Dilemma*. New York: International Universities Press.

Gibson, R. W. (1966), The ego defect in schizophrenia. In: *Psychoneurosis and Schizophrenia*, ed. G. Usdin. Philadelphia: J. B. Lippincott, pp. 88–97.

—— (1967), On the therapeutic handling of aggression in schizophrenia. *Amer. J. Orthopsychiat.*, 37:926–931.

Schulz, C. S. (1978), Harry Stack Sullivan colloquium. *Psychiatry*, 41:117–128.

Sullivan, H. S. (1939–1931), Socio-psychiatric research. *Amer. J. Psychiat.*, 10:977–991.

—— (1962), *Schizophrenia as a Human Process*. New York: Norton.

10

THE USE OF ANXIETY AND HOSTILITY IN THE TREATMENT OF SCHIZOPHRENIC PATIENTS

Ruth W. Lidz, M.D.

I first met Frieda in 1922 and so may have known her longer than anyone—at least in the United States. I say "have known" because she was a very important person to me and has continued to be with me. The occasion of our first meeting was when I was accompanying my father who was then chairman of the Department of Psychiatry at the University of Heidelberg to the Botanical Gardens to obtain some orchids for my mother. We passed by Frieda's institute and she was in her garden cutting flowers and we stopped to greet her.

My father's major interest, like Frieda's, was in schizophrenic patients. Although at that time academic psychiatrists in Germany had little interest or respect for psychoanalysis, he admired Frieda's knowledge and therapeutic efforts. He told me that she was not only a psychoanalyst but a good psychiatrist, and he permitted her to use the seminar room in his clinic for meetings with her students—an action that puzzled his assistants.

I had no personal contact with Frieda thereafter until I emigrated to Baltimore in 1937 and my father wrote that she lived "near Baltimore" and sent her address at Chestnut Lodge. I got in touch with her and visited her several times and later she supervised me when I was in training at the Washington-Baltimore Institute. I recall how grateful I was to her when she permitted me to bring my two- or three-year-old son with me who would play in the waiting room during the supervision.

This was during World War II when my husband was in the South Pacific.

Then, some years later I was in psychotherapy with her for a short time concerning a problem my analysis had failed to resolve. I was nursing my youngest child at the time and feared I would have to wean him; but to my surprise and pleasure, Frieda had made arrangements for me to see her in the evening, stay overnight in a local motel, and have another hour the first thing the next morning after her maid had given me some orange juice. I was then able to return home to nurse my child. Actually, I later found such evening–next morning arrangements very helpful with a patient who had moved from New Haven to New York. She came to see me in the same way which enabled her to return to New York in time to teach. She found it very helpful to be able to concentrate free of distracting influences on her feelings and dreams during the night and work with them the first thing in the morning.

I learned many things from Frieda but to my mind the outstanding thing was her openness about what she had learned from a particular patient, her willingness to teach so frankly from her own experiences or even mistakes. It has helped me to consider each patient a new personal experience and to keep an open mind in trying to understand the feelings of the patients about their experiences and the different meanings events can have.

One famous story about Frieda's learning from her experience with a patient: She went to meet a new woman patient whom she found sitting on the floor. Frieda, standing up next to the patient, didn't feel comfortable "talking down" to the patient who did not move, so she sat down next to her to talk to her. When the patient had recovered and was gaining distance from Frieda and her therapy, she told Frieda, "You know, that was my worst day when I felt you didn't know how to take care of yourself either." The lesson Frieda learned was never to lower herself to the patient's level—here in a literal sense—but it applies to more complicated situations like acting as if you understood when a patient talks irrationally.

My interest in schizophrenic patients started actually in

childhood since it was inherent in my family background. When I was six years old, my father was director of a psychiatric hospital in southern Germany. I had many opportunities to watch and learn to know patients as we lived on the grounds of the hospital. Our schizophrenic gardener was a friend, though often very puzzling to me. On many days he would do his work neatly and talk with me in a friendly way, but on the next day, while I watched him from behind a bush, I saw him throw his hoe away and yell at the Russians in St. Petersburg—as this was during World War I, the Russians were "the enemy." I knew this was not to be my day with him, but then on the following day we would chat and he might lift me up to get a pear from our tree. Thus, at a very early age I learned that a schizophrenic's irrationality need not be continuous.

When I was a teen-ager, my father, then professor of psychiatry in Heidelberg, asked me on several occasions to take young women who were recovering from psychosis to a cafe for coffee and cake in the afternoon. He taught me that I had to keep them talking and be with them at all times. He warned me that they were impulsive and might want to leave or even interrupt eating their cake to go to the bathroom, but I was to go with them; and be certain they returned to the hospital at the proper time. The patients and I would talk about our parents, about school, perhaps about a dress we had seen together in a shop window, but sometimes they would talk about what had happened before they became ill.

My first experience treating a schizophrenic patient dates to 1935 when I worked for a short time in an excellent, small, private psychiatric hospital near Geneva, Switzerland. On the disturbed patients ward there were always several patients who had been in a hospital for a year or longer, totally cared for by the nurses, and sometimes kept in isolation or in a camisole for protection. The analytically trained doctors were not interested in these mute patients. In making rounds, I had become interested in a young woman who constantly stood in a corner of her room, with her arms carefully held behind her, eyes closed and head drooping. In her early to mid-twenties, she had been a promising young concert pianist before becoming schizophrenic.

After seeing her in this position every day, I began to have the impression that she was saying, "Okay, I will not hit anybody with my arms and I will not scratch myself. I will just stand here and let you take care of me." All aggressive, hostile feelings were suppressed in an effort to control or deny her anger or in an overadjustment to what she felt the staff expected of her. Of course, she had the satisfaction of being fed like a baby and perhaps in having a passive-aggressive outlet by soiling herself and getting the nurse to change her clothes. After obtaining permission to work with the patient, I approached her one morning after rounds, introduced myself, touched one of her arms, and said to her that it seemed to me her arms were becoming extremely weak from never being used. I said I would like to do some exercises with her to strengthen her arms again. (This seemed quite natural to me then, for I had recently studied gymnastics, massage, and surgical aftercare in Sweden.) I proceeded to do arm and chest exercises for about ten minutes without eliciting any visible response from the patient. I told her I would return the next day and that perhaps she would join me in doing the exercises. But there was no reaction from the patient for several days. However, just as I began to feel frustrated, when I walked into her room on the fifth or sixth day, she immediately started to do the exercises correctly (so she must have watched me doing them!) but with such violence that I was afraid she might hurt herself. With the violent moves, words came pouring out of her, mostly French curses and obscenities. I finally stopped her and asked if we could sit down and talk together. She said, "Yes, and I want to get out of this place" (her first words in some months!). I chose to answer by saying, "Yes, perhaps we can go for a walk on the grounds." She said, "I need clothes. I can't go out like this." I agreed and remarked that her clothes were stored and the nurse would bring them. Then she said, "I need a lipstick." I answered that we could buy one. What color would she like? She said, "One like yours." In the next few months we fell into the routine of after rounds taking a walk on the beautiful grounds of the hospital, or rowing on the lake, or taking a swim in the lake. The patient began to talk freely about many things, past and present. Gradually her remarks helped me to understand the deeper meaning of the defiant inactivity of her arms and hands. Her mother had herself sought to become a famous pianist but was unsuccessful. She transferred her ambition to her daughter in a very controlling way, so that the patient felt she was being forced to become a famous pianist "for her." I began to understand why she had not wanted to use her hands in silent defiance against her mother's intrusiveness and as a first step in differentiating from her mother.

The patient eventually chose a therapist she called "the gray-haired man"—a father figure—and with the patient's permission, he (an analyst) and I cooperated during my last month at the hospital in that I was to tell him things she had told me—things she found easier to tell me but that he "should know." This mother-father-child relationship seemed to work well for her.

I focus on the fostering of the expression of aggression, hostility, and anxiety by schizophrenic patients as a necessary aspect of enabling them to release strongly repressed feelings and then explore the reasons they have such untenable emotions, because currently neuroleptic medications are all too often utilized to quiet and calm patients, and in so doing narrow or close off a highly useful opening in the patient's protective armor.

Another patient with whom the theme of aggression led directly into his anxieties and the center of his problems was a surgeon from a southern state whom I treated some ten years later. Then in his early thirties, he had functioned reasonably well on the surgical staff of a hospital. His colleagues considered him reliable in the care of patients but recognized that he was paranoid. He repeatedly complained of how he was unfairly treated; that his colleagues were against him, talked behind his back, etc. He hid his auditory hallucinations from everyone except his mother. He had never married. Eventually, he was dismissed from his hospital, which proved to him that his suspicions were correct. He was referred to me by an analyst in Baltimore to whom he had been sent. After three appointments of an hour and a half for three days in a row, we decided to work together. He was very slow and vague in his talk and I found it difficult to obtain a history from him. He told me that

his father had left his mother but would not amplify. Toward
the end of one session, I suggested he try to tell me about his
mother. During the next hour the patient sat in his chair across
from me, spoke little, and played with his large pocketknife,
opening and closing it. I again tried to get him to talk about his
mother. He seemed more anxious and complained about the
woman who cleaned his apartment. The following session he
was agitated; he kept getting up from his chair, walking between
his chair and mine, while he pulled the knife from his pocket
and kept snapping it open and shut. Somehow I began to feel
threatened and decided I needed to take care of myself first
before I could help him. I told him he was making me anxious
by standing near me with an open knife and that when I was
preoccupied with *my* feelings, I could not properly think of his.
He uttered an "oh," returned to his chair, closed and pocketed
the knife. Silence followed. The end of the hour was approaching and I could not let it end this way. I told him that it seemed
to me that he had gotten very anxious when I had suggested
he talk about his mother, and perhaps he had felt he needed
the knife to protect himself against my intrusion as he had
against his mother's. He started to cry and went on talking
about her domination and his dependency on her so urgently
that we went well over time before I ended the session. So began
his movement toward independence, security, and self-assur-
ance.

The third patient I wish to describe was a young woman
in her early twenties who had been a patient at the Yale Psychiatric Institute and was considered sufficiently recovered
from her psychosis to be living outside of a hospital. However,
she was difficult, since for years she had been getting herself
into some trouble in order to make her parents anxious, which
she had learned was the only way to gain their attention. This
pattern was difficult to overcome and other therapists had
found it unacceptable and stopped treating her. Through the
time we worked together, there were occasional late night
phone calls with anxious complaints like "I think I broke my
leg" and twice her car caught fire in the driveway of our home!
The patient was the daughter of a professor who spent little
time at home and his wife who had several physical complaints,

was lonely, and spent much time in bed. The patient wanted to talk about "practical problems" with me and it was difficult to keep her on a subject of personal meaning or to talk about her older brother or her parents. She talked freely about the maid who ordered the groceries and cooked. She wanted to learn to cook herself and asked me for recipes. When I tried to get her to talk about her mother, she insisted she was unimportant. Yet, she appeared more anxious and—to my surprise and shock—when she hurriedly left the office and passed by me she rubbed her hand against my breasts, ran out, and slammed the door. Ten minutes later she phoned. She anxiously apologized, saying, "I know I should not have done this, don't throw me out. I won't do it again." I answered, "We will have to try to understand what happened." The next time she was quiet, reluctant to talk, brought up "practical problems" like trouble with her car, etc. I did not push her (perhaps I was afraid to!) and she managed to avoid the subject. The next hour, I brought up the question of her feelings about her mother at the beginning of the hour and she insisted that all she had to do was to learn to take care of herself, be a good mother to herself—an expression I had once used. At the end of the hour, she rushed by me again, quickly touching both breasts. Again she phoned a few minutes later. I felt like having her come back right then but did not have the time. The next day I suggested at the beginning of the session to "take more time today," one-and-a-half hours, to try to understand better the complicated feelings she had and what had brought them on. Gradually, throughout the session and a number of subsequent sessions, she described scenes with her "sickly" mother—how she had never gotten anything from her, not even food. She had received only criticism. Eventually she discussed her belief that her mother might have gotten pleasure from examining her bodily "faults." She then came to tell that when she had come home from school, the maid would tell her that her mother wanted to see her. When she went to the bedroom, her mother would tell her to take off her clothes. She then "commanded" her to turn "front" and "back" and would then tell her that her breasts were flabby and her buttocks were hanging down. She should do exercises to improve her shape, and her mother gave her a book that would teach her the proper exercises. She eventually brought up the reason she suspected that her mother had enjoyed examining her body; she believed that her mother masturbated when criticizing her body because her mother held "her hand between her legs" when examining her.

I have chosen these three cases because the attention to an aggressive act led to a dramatic change in chronic patients and therefore can be described quickly; but with many schizophrenic patients only long, patient work will lead to comfortable, cooperative work and the resolution of problems. The reported episodes were, of course, focusing on the aggression and anger which had to be acknowledged and gradually accepted before the patients could begin to overcome the conflict between their symbiotic or anaclitic needs and their hated dependency. I have come to feel that the therapist needs to recognize the positive aspects of the patient's expressions of anger and even of aggression and help the patient express these feelings in attempts to define themselves rather than continue to repress such feelings. These patients have profound fears of displaying negative feelings and even more of defining what they are about. Often the patient's aggression or hostility helps the therapist make the first contact with the patient. I try to help patients feel proud of discovering their angry feelings and to use them appropriately, to learn to express them in words, and to understand what provoked such feelings rather than to hurt others, which would get them into trouble and might lead the therapist to increase their medication and put the patient back in a dependent situation. Some patients are aware of the power of their anger: I heard of a patient whose doctor wanted to increase his medication after the patient had attacked someone. When the doctor told him, "This will quiet you down so you won't attack and hurt people," the patient replied, "You want me to give up my anger? That's all I've got, Doc." The key to helping the aggressive patient is obviously to enable him to express his feelings in words rather than action. One of my patients had to "learn to control his hands and feet." He did so by gripping the sides of his chair fiercely while trying to say what it was that upset him.

Actually, when I worked in Swiss hospitals in the 1930s and later at the Phipps Clinic in Baltimore, the doctor had his office on the ward and was available at all times during the day (and sometimes in the evening as well) and if a patient suddenly became excited or aggressive, he would be put in a wet pack and the doctor sat beside him. As the patient sweated and relaxed, he might be able to explain to his therapist just what had upset him. Both the patient and doctor would learn from the experience and gain new insights into the patient's sensitivities and their origins.

If aggressive outbursts are seen as expressions of anxiety and anger and not looked upon negatively simply as psychotic hostility, the therapist can relate to the patient in a positive way, which helps the patient realize that the therapist is trying to work with him to examine why he gets aggressive and what had transpired that provoked his rage. The goal is to enable the patient to work together with his therapist to learn what had aroused the patient's feelings. Direct interpretations of the meanings of psychotic behavior are not likely to help, as the patient often feels blamed. Moreover, the therapist conveys by such interpretations that he is omniscient and knows without being told, repeating the patient's experiences with a parent who interpreted the patient's behavior in terms of the parent's own needs or preconceptions. This may increase the patient's insecurities and foster further anger over his inability to defend his boundaries or to think for himself.

The intense conflict between the patients' neediness and their dependency on needed but resented, if not hated, parents is to be gradually clarified and understood. Since the studies of the families of schizophrenic patients carried out in the 1950s, we have increasingly come to understand that at the root of their projections, hallucinations, and withdrawal into fantasy are very real distorting and tragic family experiences which often started at an age when the patient was not able to understand, much less control, what was happening; but also that such disorganizing intrafamilial experiences usually continued throughout the patient's childhood and adolescence.

When patients come to recognize what they have to work through, what effort and anxiety and misery it will take to overcome their past experiences, they naturally feel depressed and often regress, and may even try to commit suicide and will need special support from the therapist who may also feel dismayed as the patient's true circumstances become apparent. The fact that the patient gets depressed at this point does not mean that he is not schizophrenic. The idea that schizophrenic patients have no emotions is incorrect; rather they must keep themselves from being overwhelmed by feelings of hate, worthlessness, and guilt—the deep conflicts of hate and love for the needed person from whom they had not differentiated.

This brings me to the great concern that psychiatrists are forgetting what we learned from Frieda Fromm-Reichmann and Sullivan in the 1930s and 1940s. Their knowledge of schizophrenic patients together with what we learned in the 1950s about the reality of the patients' families and our increased knowledge about what the therapist's actions mean to the patient have put us into a situation where we can treat most schizophrenic patients with some success provided we get to see them early in their psychoses. Treating schizophrenics is difficult and not everyone can or should try it; but the experience fascinates some of us who find it a high road to the understanding of human development and not only of the unconscious but the deeply hidden roots of human behavior. However, what has happened is that—at least in most hospitals that I hear about—the therapist has become more distant, comes to see the patient at set times but may not be there at the most important time. Often there are several people aside from the psychotherapist in charge of the patient who may give different messages that can confuse the patient. Then, all too often, the patient is judged in terms of his behavior that is being controlled with antipsychotic medication. The patient who gets upset, noisy, and aggressive in a certain situation is given more medication to quiet him down and is no longer in touch with his feelings by the time he sees his therapist. Are we forcing a patient to adjust to what we think is "right" for him before he knows his own feelings and who *he* is? These patients who have frequently grown up in an intensely symbiotic relationship with their mothers or fathers are often more tuned into the parent's feelings and needs than into their own—are we to try to teach them to take care of *our* feelings rather than explore their frustrations, to re-create the circumstances that contributed to their disorder?

We have to help these patients to express their feelings and their anger, and to understand that underneath this anger at the staff or the therapist lies the more fundamental hostility concerning the way they had been treated in their families. Not only have many been kept as extensions of a parent and never been allowed to become independent persons, but many have been caught up as pawns in the conflict between parents, and it has become apparent that incestuous seduction is not uncommon in their families. One can be quite certain that if a person is schizophrenic, he or she has grown up in a very disturbed, distorted, or even bizarre family setting. For example, among the last few schizophrenic patients whose treatment Theodore Lidz and I have supervised, there is a woman whose schizophrenic father made her practice a variety of sexual perversions with him, and who has been enraged that her mother knew about it but did not stop it; a young man whose father actually handed him over as a homosexual partner to the father's best friend and the mother let the boy know that she was having a lesbian relationship with the man's wife; a woman whose mother's boyfriend tried to seduce her and routinely exposed himself to her—just to cite a few isolated instances in very complex and confusing family settings. Unless one is ready to hear, one does not hear.

Some years ago I had a patient whose father had masturbated her frequently and she was much relieved to express her anger about this and toward her mother who had not interfered, but it was not until after she had come to remember and accept that she had enjoyed it sexually and had appreciated that she was so important to her father that she began to feel in control of her own sexuality and could enjoy her sexual relationship with her husband and then eventually could come to terms with her father. In his old age after her mother had died and he needed care, she solved her conflicts by placing him in a nursing home near her house where she could visit him daily and see to his care, but she would not take him into her home in order to protect her two daughters.

As therapists with schizophrenic patients, we need to be very aware of our own feelings and countertransference reactions at all times, particularly because these patients are very sensitive to any pretense or cover-up, even the slightest change of voice or expression. Directness and honesty are vital. We have to be aware and willing to admit a mistake and never give patients reasons to believe we are omniscient. In the case of the young woman who rubbed my breasts, I seriously considered my own feelings and actions. I knew I was annoyed by her actions as well as angered by her unnecessary emergency phone calls but thought to utilize these incidents as openings to investigate why such maneuvers were necessary and how they arose from her relationship with her parents. She could then talk of the negative attention she received from her mother, her wish to be fed, and eventually of her way of trying to make care-giving people anxious—the only way she had ever been able to get attention from her parents. I was reassured later about my own reaction to her in that she had frequently made her therapists quite upset while in the hospital.

I also believe that we need to start working with these patients with current situations and gradually work toward the past experiences and feelings. Psychoanalysis has focused on the early deprivations of these patients, but we now know that the difficult and abnormal experiences in their lives continue into adolescence and sometimes adult life and are conscious but defended against by withdrawal and paranoid displacements onto persons other than the parents.

Over the many years of observing and treating schizophrenic patients and supervising their psychotherapy, it has often struck me that my first contact with "the person" in the schizophrenic patient came through watching and learning to understand their angry outbursts as a way of defining themselves, to gain distance from what or whom they hated. I have stressed here the usefulness of hostility and aggression in the treatment of schizophrenic patients, but I want to accentuate that the expression of such emotions alone will not be helpful unless the patient is being helped to get at the sources of his anxiety and to uncover earlier critical experiences. Aggressive behavior in the hospital has to be understood like anger at the

therapist as a transference problem, and we need to work toward and into the anxiety and not cover it up. Once patients
have come to deal with their past and have accepted their own
feelings, they can sometimes begin to understand their parents'
problems and develop a new and responsible relationship with
them.

11

THE ANNIVERSARY SYNDROME AS RELATED TO LATE-APPEARING MENTAL ILLNESSES IN HOSPITALIZED PATIENTS

JOSEPHINE R. HILGARD, M.D., Ph.D.

The background for my interest in the understanding and treatment of hospitalized psychiatric patients began during the two years that I spent at Chestnut Lodge between late 1942 and early 1945. I was privileged to work closely under the influence of Frieda Fromm-Reichmann.

The Chestnut Lodge Experience with
Hospitalized Psychotic Patients

When I arrived at Chestnut Lodge, I was thirty-six and had completed medical training at Stanford. Just prior to coming, I had been in Chicago on the staff of the Institute of Juvenile Research and the Neuropsychiatric Institute of the University of Illinois. In addition, I had studied at the Chicago Psychoanalytic Institute where I also completed an orthodox personal analysis with Dr. Margaret Gerard. There the less orthodox views of Franz Alexander, to a certain extent, had prepared me to be open to the dynamically oriented therapy of schizophrenic patients at Chestnut Lodge. My husband's work with the Office of War Information during World War II moved us temporarily to Washington and I was eager to continue my training. Chestnut Lodge provided the opportunity, where I was welcomed as an associate psychiatrist. I shall return later to indicate how I built upon my Chestnut Lodge training and a number of other experiences before I became interested in the anniversary syndrome.

Let me first indicate some recollections of Chestnut Lodge, particularly as they relate to Frieda Fromm-Reichmann, who became my teacher, supervising therapist, and friend. In 1942 she was fifty-two and had been in this country for seven years.

Frieda Fromm-Reichmann

Dr. Fromm-Reichmann, called Frieda by all of us, had a rich background in psychiatry before she became a psychoanalyst. She was well prepared for psychiatric service in a mental hospital by the time of World War I and had worked closely with Kurt Goldstein. His studies of the perceptual consequences of gunshot wounds, in collaboration with Gelb, were among the more important neuropsychological findings from that war. As I learned from her, there was a shortage of psychiatrists in Germany, and she was put in actual charge of a military psychiatric hospital, although because of her youth, her diminutive size, and her sex, there was always a burly officer nominally in charge. She told some amusing stories about going through the ward when an inspection was about to be made, telling the patients who had come to respect her, that now, for her sake, they must sit upright on their beds with their arms folded in an official position as the inspectors came by. She knew that that was no way to ask patients to behave, but their hospital would receive a higher ranking if, just for the inspection, they did this silly thing. They did it so well that her commander was decorated for the discipline that he was able to maintain in a mental hospital. I could just see her trotting along behind the military men in her white service outfit, calling the shots inconspicuously for the front man. Her neuropsychiatric experience stood her in good stead when, after going into psychoanalytic practice, she determined to work with hospitalized schizophrenics. That was the phase of her work in which I knew her.

She had some readjustments to make as she conducted therapy in English and in a culture that differed from that of her own native Germany, but she adapted readily. She told of having been very much puzzled by one of her first patients after coming to this country. The patient, a woman, had been in tears most of the hour, and was still emoting deeply when the hour drew to a close. Having had the end of the hour called to her attention, the patient sat up, wiped her eyes, got out her comb and mirror and lipstick, and proceeded to make herself presentable for leaving the consultation room and confronting the outside world. Frieda felt baffled lest the patient may have deceived her by role playing, for in Europe the same patient would have slipped down the back alleys, weeping all the way home. She quickly found out how social norms could account for differences as great as this.

Frieda As My Supervisor

With no experience in the psychotherapy of schizophrenic patients I was apprehensive about my ability to communicate with them and was not reassured when I discovered that the two young female patients assigned to me were so disturbed that they were confined to "quiet rooms." Perhaps I should explain for the benefit of younger colleagues who have grown up in the era of tranquilizing drugs that we possessed no tranquilizers in the early 1940s. Instead, in this progressive hospital we depended upon individual, locked, "quiet" rooms. At the moment each of my prospective patients was confined in one, bare of furniture due to their propensities for destructive action, soiling, and the like. Each patient often also preferred to be partially or completely unclothed.

The other staff members felt that I, as a new member, would wish to gain the greatest range of experience, so they had thoughtfully postponed the therapy of these patients until I could get there. Of course, they also realized that I could hardly say no!

I found that attempting to treat these very disturbed, young patients was baffling and threatening to my self-esteem. At the start of therapy Amy and Mary were potentially assaultive.

Frieda's supervision began with simple suggestions about my own attitudes. "Never, ever, turn your back to a patient." This bit of advice came after Amy had seized a heavy gold chain at the back of my neck and the chain had broken. It led to further discussion of why I had let myself be careless, even for a moment. Apropos of therapy with both patients who were prone to smearing feces, she asked, "Would it make you more comfortable to wear a cotton washable dress instead of one that will need dry cleaning?" These incidents led to opportunities for analysis of my addiction to cleanliness. This was sorely tested in another context when Amy offered a gift of food that had clearly been exposed to unsanitary handling. Frieda called my attention to the fact that my defense against messiness was blinding me to the significance of the gesture that Amy was making toward me. When I could separate the distasteful aspect of the object offered from the act of sharing something that was valued, I had gained understanding of the two people who were sharing this experience, both Amy and me. A gift from a schizophrenic patient was always to be cherished.

One more example from this early period: I learned that to communicate with Mary, it was necessary to wrap her in a cold pack because she could be so out of control that otherwise she could not be reached. Even in the pack Mary would continue to shout until her shouting wore itself out. Then her attention would focus partially on my voice. What did I talk about? At a loss as to how to proceed I recall that I told stories. One was about a child who was alone on a mountain trail where she met different small animals and befriended them. I tried to think of calming stories about animal friends because Frieda had suggested that they would be more acceptable to some disturbed patients than people.

In retrospect I believe that an important part of these initial experiences for me lay in the fact that I never felt belittled by Frieda, even when I was quite insecure about what I was doing. I often thought I should have been more aware of my shortcomings, but Frieda invariably treated me with respect and support, which in turn enabled me to face my feelings.

During the initial phases of supervision, the two teen-agers' symptoms were those of acting out their hostility and regressive tendencies. I began to see how acting out could prove an immeasurable aid to therapy. Because I was initially an intruder, the patient had to deal with my intrusion by making an active response and this permitted an interactive relationship and an attachment to develop. The patients made progress so that after three or four months the isolation rooms were no longer needed. Each established a positive emotional tie with me, though negative feelings sometimes predominated. Frequently we were able to understand the angry outbursts, particularly those associated with separations when I had been absent due to illness or vacations. When I left Chestnut Lodge for California, Amy wanted to come too. Mary was ambivalent and was transferred to another therapist.

Amy resided first in a small private psychiatric hospital, then moved to a private home. I saw her three times a week in therapy. From the beginning of this move she continued the high school studies that had been interrupted by her illness years before. After two years she graduated credibly from high school, returned East to be with or near her family, and taught in a nursery school.

By incredible chance I happened to run into Mary on the street in Washington about fifteen years after I had left Chestnut Lodge. She kept a certain distance but was cordial and friendly. From her therapist I understood that the course of her life had been difficult, but she was living outside the hospital.

Frieda as a Person

In addition to my professional relations with Frieda, I knew her socially at Chestnut Lodge and saw her frequently thereafter, especially during her year at Stanford as a fellow at the Center for Advanced Study in the Behavioral Sciences, 1955–1956.

It was always a joy to be with Frieda because, no matter what the occasion, she was enthusiastic, vivacious, an eager listener, and willing to give of herself. To have her as a friend and companion made me feel good about myself.

Although she was a successful therapist and a fine teacher, I believe it is fair to say that she was not primarily a theoretician. Rather, she had derived meaningful and communicable practices from her long clinical experience. Hence she had a clear set of orienting principles rather than a structural, logical system.

Foremost among these principles was a deeply felt respect for each individual. As a part of this respect she tried to understand what the patients were trying to communicate, no matter how disturbed they might be. When, for example, a patient talked in words that seemed meaningless, she would say that she knew the patient was trying to tell her something that she was not now understanding but hoped to understand sometime. Frieda would do a great deal to get into communication with a patient; if necessary, climbing on the furniture or sitting on the floor next to a patient who refused to talk sitting in a chair. She was not always able to explain why she acted in a particular way, but when pressed she was apt to reply, "It just occurred to me that it was the right thing to do." Such spontaneity and naturalness were expressions of an intuitive understanding and empathy.

One of Frieda's central principles was *answering* a patient's communication rather than *interpreting* it. In her own writing, Frieda gave many illustrations of this. One of the incidents she told me appeared in her book.

> Translating a cryptic schizophrenic communication was done, for example, with at least temporary success in the case of a formerly meticulously well-dressed woman who was seen on the disturbed ward with her clothes reduced to rags, her hair hanging untidily over her face. This patient suddenly shouted at the psychiatrist "Best, best, best! Why do you always have the best?" etc. The doctor noticed the patient's quick glance at Best's label on the coat which she had put down. Since Best's was a good woman's apparel store, the psychiatrist grasped the meaning of the patient's envious hostile outburst. She therefore expressed the hope that the time was not too remote when the patient could go into Garfinckel's again, to buy attractive clothes for herself. (Garfinckel's was a department store in town considered to be superior to Best's.) Immediately after that, the patient quieted down. During the following few weeks, the patient was freer from manifestations of acute hostility and anxiety than she had been for a long time [Fromm-Reichmann, 1950].

The same orientation of answering, rather than attempting

to interpret, a communication can be of value in treating withdrawn adolescents, schizoid individuals, and those who are suffering from extreme anxiety. For Frieda, the distinction between the answer and the interpretation might not be sharp. What she did and said depended upon the opportunity that presented itself. For example, when she was walking on the lawn of the hospital with a patient, the patient leaned over to pet a dog that came by and Frieda remarked, in essence, "Isn't it too bad that people have treated you more unkindly than animals, so that you find it harder to reach out to people than to a dog?" This remark led to opening a small channel of communication between them, which soon widened.

Frieda emphasized yet another principle. Her quiet insistence on searching out and building upon the strengths of each patient meant that she was always treating a whole person. Among schizophrenic patients, positive achievements represented residual strengths in otherwise shattered personalities. I believe that she was successful in this because she was herself a person of strength, resourcefulness, and compassion.

These principles are vivid to me because I experienced them personally in Frieda's supervision. I found them echoing in my ears through the decades that I treated patients.

Harry Stack Sullivan

Although I have been reviewing primarily my recollections of the influence of Frieda Fromm-Reichmann upon my work with schizophrenics, the experiences at Chestnut Lodge provided a well-rounded experience with hospitalized patients bearing other diagnoses: obsessive-compulsive, alcoholic, and depressive syndromes. Nevertheless, the psychotherapy of schizophrenia remained a dominant theme because of the presence of Harry Stack Sullivan. One of the patients I treated under his supervision was a man whose reactions alternated between paranoid schizophrenia and stomach ulcers as a psychosomatic alternative. The patient was a college professor, the successful author of a textbook in political science. He was in his late forties, married, and with two children in their twenties.

J. G. did not take well to being treated by a female psychiatrist who was younger than he, and his competitiveness with me soon became a major issue. He noticed my slightly bowed knees and spoke of my legs as being "pleasure-bowed." His repeated message was intended to show that he knew more than I did. I might be the psychiatrist, but he was a successful professor. Had I written a textbook? He had. One day when questioning my credentials, he suddenly reached into his coat pocket, took a golf ball from it, and forcefully threw it at my head. I ducked just in time.

What was happening in the transference during psychotherapy mirrored J. G.'s behavior on the ward toward staff members and other patients. Aggressive and competitive feelings, when fully vented, were often of psychotic intensity. When the overtly psychotic symptoms were successfully handled, the patient's long-standing stomach ulcer symptoms, recently characterized by a life-threatening degree of bleeding, would start. Intensive medical treatment was then imperative. Cared-for in bed during this passive phase, J. G. was no longer psychotic but accepting of his dependent status. The same was true during his convalescence when diet and hours of rest were carefully monitored by special nursing attention.

Throughout this alternation of symptomatology, psychotherapeutic sessions continued. In a supervisory session with Sullivan, one day I reported not only the interreactions within the hour, but, as usual, the broad outlines of J. G.'s adjustment on the ward. He was now recovering from a particularly severe bout of his stomach ulcers and was quite rational. Sullivan was forthright and confident as he offered advice about a vital step that must be taken. I have never forgotten what he said. "You need to tell the patient that your reputation is not at stake, even if he dies from a bleeding ulcer while he is in treatment with you. You would regret this development. However, your reputation would not be harmed and you would continue to treat other patients." I didn't find it easy to convince myself that I could convey this message because such a direct assertion about my degree of control was stronger medicine than I was accustomed to using. With Sullivan's help, however, I recognized that the present tyrannical behavior, as though J. G. were all powerful, was actually a regression to the omnipotence of childhood. It was unsuitable for adult adjustment and had to be met with the firmness that Sullivan recommended. It marked a turning point in therapy. Subsequently the working through of this issue took time, but the patient was on his way to rehabilitation. He could combine rationality and freedom from somatic symptoms. Gradually his visits home lengthened and he resumed some of his professional activities.

I was particularly interested in the change the interaction between Sullivan, the patient, and me had on me. It brought to the forefront another dimension of my therapeutic resources. I became more confident and able to take charge. As a consequence I felt less conflict between my empathy for the suffering patient and the hard realities I had to help him face.

Frieda Fromm-Reichmann and Harry Stack Sullivan

The relationship between Frieda Fromm-Reichmann and Harry Stack Sullivan at Chestnut Lodge was a significant part of my experience. The administrative arrangements were as follows. Dexter Bullard, Sr., was director of the Lodge and, in addition to his administrative responsibilities, he treated patients and supervised young staff members. He conducted weekly staff conferences which all of his staff attended. Sullivan was a part-time consultant who, though he did supervision, did not himself treat patients there and so was not a part of these meetings. However, he conducted teaching seminars for the staff.

In following the progress of cases during the staff conferences, discussions were apt to be lively. Senior as well as junior staff members reported details of what had happened during treatment sessions with their patients, and in this setting everyone was free to comment. Frieda was outstanding in the way she listened and offered gentle critical comments on the cases. Equally outstanding was the way this experienced and most senior of therapists listened to, and learned from, criticisms which the rest of the staff directed toward her as they heard her report on the patients she was treating.

In Sullivan's twice weekly seminars held in the recreation room of the Bullard residence, what he presented was informative, but the atmosphere was very different from that of the staff conference. Although called a seminar, it was primarily a lecture, with discussion at the end. These talks were recorded, later transcribed, and became the basis of books edited after his death. Frieda always deferred to him. Even when announcing views that were just as much her own, she would preface her remarks by saying, "As Dr. Sullivan has taught us. . . ." This deference contributed to Sullivan's need to feel secure enough to develop his own theoretical position freely.

There were some amusing moments in the interchange between Frieda and Sullivan. Frieda once told me of the following experience. Sullivan decided to express his admiration and affection for her by presenting her with a cocker spaniel that he had trained from puppyhood. Because he was so sure that the dog's attachment to him would be hard to break, after having made the gift he took it upon himself to spend one period of time each day at Frieda's house, transferring the dog's affection from himself to her. She was quite capable of getting along with the dog, but this ceremony occurred day after day until Sullivan was satisfied that the separation anxiety (on the part of the dog) had been overcome.

Sullivan was not always as gentle as Frieda. He supervised my work with a young, male, schizophrenic patient. Fred was disoriented, irrational, but rarely assaultive. His room was on the locked ward when I saw him in therapy. On one occasion when he was in the midst of disjointed communications, he suddenly remarked that as a boy he had put together an engine that worked, and gave a brief description of it, then just as suddenly switched back to irrationalities. I had not interrupted to comment on this successful experience, which was the first time Fred had said something good, something positive, about himself. When I reported this sequence to Sullivan he was furious and told me that my failure to take advantage of such a moment was unbelievable. In a cold and aloof manner he expanded this point and dismissed me. I felt crushed and defensive. I called Frieda who arranged to see me the next day. She helped me see that momentarily Sullivan had identified completely with the patient. He had spoken to me as the patient might have spoken to people who, many times, had failed to recognize his accomplishments.

On one occasion the same patient said he was seventy-six years old. Sullivan quickly interpreted Fred's age as either nineteen or thirty-eight. "He is telling you that he feels twice as old or four times as old as he is because so many problems have weighed heavily upon him." Fred was nineteen. This episode brings to mind Sullivan's gifts for understanding the veiled language of the schizophrenic patient.

Prior to the Chestnut Lodge years so much of my psychoanalytic background in San Francisco and Chicago had emphasized intrapsychic conflicts that it was illuminating to work with those who had learned from psychoanalysis but had supplemented it with an emphasis upon interpersonal relationships as well. With this enriched background from Chestnut Lodge, I was prepared for new opportunities that would arise when I returned to California.

PART II
THE ANNIVERSARY SYNDROME

After my return to Stanford following the war, I pursued a second strand of my psychiatric background that would lead me into studies of the anniversary syndrome. The history of this phase antedated that at Chestnut Lodge. Experience at the Institute for Juvenile Research in Chicago had brought me directly into contact with children as well as parents in treatment—useful because both generations are often involved in the anniversary reaction. While still at the Lodge I had been recruited for a half-time position as director of the child guidance clinic at Children's Hospital in San Francisco, where in the tradition of child guidance clinics diagnosis and treatment always involved three disciplines: psychiatry, clinical psychology, and social work, with both parent and child involved in diagnosis and treatment.

When I began to accept some patients in private practice, the training at Chestnut Lodge proved useful. Local psychiatrists who knew of my training began referring a few already hospitalized patients to find out whether they might be suitable for psychotherapy. One of these patients was a mother whose symptoms upon hospitalization resembled those her father had shown at the time of his death. A second patient whom I saw, this time in my capacity as a consultant at the VA Hospital in Palo Alto, referred to the loss of his father and linked his symptoms to his son's present age. This second case had been in treatment with a resident who continued to treat him under my supervision. These two cases are described in detail as revealing the essence of anniversary reactions precipitated by children.

Anniversary Reactions Precipitated by Children

The two cases to be presented show that symptoms in a parent may be precipitated when the parent's child reaches the age at which the parent had a traumatic episode in childhood. The anniversary reactions are related to, though different from, symptoms aggravated recurrently on a birthday, death day, or other fixed dates.[1]

Case 1. Mary Bancroft, the mother of a six-year-old, Jenny, developed pneumonia, pleurisy, and a psychosis. When she was a child of six, her own father had died of pneumonia and pleurisy, with a terminal meningitis. The possible anniversary nature of Mrs. Bancroft's illness was indicated by the fact that the acute symptoms appeared when her daughter reached the age she had been at the time of her father's death, and by the fact that her pneumonia and pleurisy mirrored her father's symptoms in his final illness. The psychotic symptoms appeared while she was still in the hospital for the pneumonia. The patient announced one morning that she had had a talk with God, and that she was divine and could not be harmed by mortals. She became combative and disorderly and assumed bizarre postures. She showed a flight of ideas, sang, whistled, and shouted.

The patient's psychosis had continued for a year before I saw her. During this time she had been hospitalized with three courses of electric shock treatment. These resulted twice in temporary mild improvement; on one of these occasions she left the hospital for a trial visit with her husband, but again became agitated and psychotic. The time I first saw her, she

[1]Much of the material in this section appeared in Hilgard (1953). A paper on the topic was read before the American Psychoanalytic Association in Atlantic City, May 1952.

had been on a long course of subcoma insulin, and had made some improvement but was on a plateau.[2]

Mrs. Bancroft commonly related her daughter's experiences to her own experiences as a child: how Jenny saw her taken away on a stretcher, and how she herself had seen her father taken away on a stretcher; how her mother had rejected her, and how she was now rejecting Jenny through her absence. Mrs. Bancroft found that she was doing many things that her own mother had done, things that were unlike her usual self. When her present illness was treated as a reenactment of something she was unable to handle as a child, there were noticeable therapeutic gains. She became friendly and more decisive.

Case 2. The second case is that of James Carson, thirty-four years old, who was hospitalized on the basis of his complaint that he had had headaches for four years. At the time of admission his headaches were described as practically continuous, agonizing, and unbearable. Immediately before entry he had attempted suicide by taking fifty phenobarbital tablets. The acute symptoms had begun when his son was four years old, the age he had been when his own father died suddenly of influenza.

In searching the history for prodromal signs, one finds a startling change of employment for the patient the same year that the son was born. The patient shifted from department store work, in which he had been employed for more than ten years, to become a "criminologist" on a private policing job. When one evaluates subsequent events, this shift in interest, occurring simultaneously with the birth of his son, appears to have been the beginning of an unconscious directional trend. Did the patient need to uncover wrongdoing and to police himself for certain unconscious wishes which he sensed were arising? When his son was four years old, at the time his severe headaches began on the anniversary date, he obtained employment as a special policeman with the railroad for which his father had worked, though he had said earlier that he would never work for that railroad. At this possible anniversary, do

---

[2]The patient was at first treated by another psychiatrist who consulted with me about the case; later, upon his invitation, I saw the patient in treatment over a period of several months.

we see an unconscious identification with the father? During the next three years the patient presented a picture of a man who was going downhill in his work until he was about to be demoted or discharged. It was a picture of a man fighting a severe battle inside himself. His symptoms included increasingly frequent and severe headaches, roughness toward suspects and finally mistreatment of them, and suicidal thoughts which were climaxed by an almost successful suicidal attempt.

At the time that I first reviewed him, the patient had already been hospitalized for several months and the situation was considered hopeless. He was subject to delusions and hallucinations, and was on the maximum security ward as both homicidal and suicidal. However, once the working hypothesis of the anniversary nature of the illness was adopted, there were gradual therapeutic gains.[3]

Statements similar to the following were brought out spontaneously and with much feeling as he continued to improve: "If my father had lived, I wouldn't be in this spot. Damn it, if my father hadn't died I wouldn't be in this mess. Doctor, I know what you were thinking yesterday, you were thinking that I was acting like a four-year-old child. Father got promoted and got knocked off for being promoted. You know it just came to me he had a boy and a girl and I have a boy and a girl." After making leather gifts in occupational therapy for his wife and daughter, with difficulty he began to make a belt and holster for his son. One day he told the therapist, "I never had a belt like that. I've resented every punch I put into that leather holster for the boy. Somehow I had the feeling that he was me and I was my father."

Why do I refer to these cases as illustrating "anniversary reactions?" Mary Bancroft's psychosis began when her daughter was six, her own age when her father died. She also showed her father's symptoms. James Carson's illness began when his son reached the age of four, his age when his father died. His father's death, as he unconsciously interpreted it, was mirrored in his own symptoms. These losses by death in childhood are

[3]Dr. Edward L. Simmons, in residency training, was the therapist, and I was the consultant on the case. I am greatly indebted to Dr. Simmons for his permission to use some of the material obtained in the course of intensive psychotherapy.

the focal episodes that led to a possible explanation of the illness, and, when understood, to some therapeutic gains. Before the central theme was discovered, these were among the most baffling of cases. The symptoms seemed to appear with no discernible precipitating cause. After the focal episodes were understood, the rest of the material began to fit into place. One reason that cases such as these often go unrecognized is that the central figure—a young child, with relatively few signs of involvement—provides the clue to the parent's disturbance.

Hospitalized Adolescent Schizophrenia and Adult Schizophrenia in Anniversary Cases

My experience in the intensive therapy of adolescent schizophrenic patients at Chestnut Lodge sensitized me to the fragmentation of their thought and affect. Communication was difficult because of the flight of the ideas and the incoherence of all the material. What the therapist confronted can be described as the return of the repressed in the form of primary process thinking. Contact in therapy was built slowly.

In the cases of Mary Bancroft and James Carson, contact could be established with relative ease. To explain this, we need to remind ourselves that we are dealing with a very restricted subsample of schizophrenic patients who were hospitalized after marriage and parenthood. In other words, although the ego was fractured, more consistency had already been achieved in the component parts.

It turned out that the components of the fractioned self were usually represented by identifications with significant persons, rather like those found in the defined forms of a multiple personality. The three identifications that entered into the conflictual responses in the schizophrenic reactions were (1) the identification with the dead parent whose loss produced the original trauma and set in motion the anniversary syndrome; (2) there was an identification with the surviving parent who had suffered the loss of a spouse; (3) there existed an identification with the patient's own childhood self. The consequence was a reliving of events, emotions, and fantasies at the time of the parental death.

The interaction with the patients' own child—the one whose age triggered the anniversary reaction—was related to the identification of the patient with the self at that age in childhood. This showed in jealousy, fear, and hostility toward the child, which was revealed in treatment as the patient emerged from the psychosis. A good illustration was James Carson's description of how he resented making a belt for his son when he never had such a belt as a child.

The parent often had not recognized the involvement of the child in the unfolding drama until this became clear in therapy. Some of these observations will be amplified as we review additional evidence for anniversary reactions beyond those of the two cases presented as an introduction to the kinds of anniversaries under study.

Establishing the Reality of the Anniversary Syndrome

Individual cases led to a possible rational explanation of symptom formation in the Anniversary Syndrome, but there was danger of generalizing too widely from accounts of individual cases. This appeared to be the time for a statistical study to establish the reality and prevalence of the observed relationships. A desire for hypothesis-testing based on quantitative data arose because of my statistical training in the course of acquiring my Ph.D. in psychology prior to the medical education. An application to the National Institute of Mental Health for a five-year grant which would fund systematic clinical research was successful.

The Hospitalized Group Study. Our team initiated a study of hospitalized patients at a nearby state hospital and screened all admissions during selected months of the years 1954–1957. It is fortunate that we undertook the study when we did, for since then the large mental hospitals have been emptied and such a study could not be done today.

After screening all admissions to the hospital during selected months of the years 1954–1957, we eliminated those over age fifty or with diagnoses of alcoholism, organic disease, and psychopathic personality. A pool of 2,402 patients remained, of which approximately three-fifths were diagnosed schizophrenic, one-fifth manic-depressive, and one-fifth psychoneurotic. These were the diagnoses entered upon the official hospital records and they suffer the limitations of any such recorded diagnoses.

For inclusions into the experimental group of patients designed to test the anniversary hypothesis, we imposed the following essential qualifications: the selected patients must have had their first admission after marriage and parenthood, loss of a parent by death between the ages of two and sixteen, and a date of parent loss that could be firmly established through interviews with the patient, relatives, letters from relatives, and a thorough check of hospital records.

Only 184 patients or 8 percent of the total met these criteria; 37 were male and 147 were female. This smaller group followed the same proportion of diagnoses as that found in the larger group. The median level of education was high school graduation; 50 percent were Protestant, 35 percent Catholic, 1 percent Jewish.

Among the female patients, age coincidences appeared in 14 of 65 women whose mothers had died, but in only 9 of 82 women whose fathers had died. Both groups were large enough to permit statistical study. We asked the help of two professors of statistics, Lincoln Moses, of the mathematical statistics department, and Quinn McNemar, of the psychology department. For each patient two ages were recorded. The first one was the age at first admission to the hospital and the second one was a hypothetical anniversary age, i.e., the age the patient had to have been at admission *if* her oldest child was to be her age at parent loss. The problem for the statisticians was to determine whether the correspondence between these two ages occurred beyond the frequency expected by chance. They used two different methods of estimation and obtained the same results, indicating that the correspondences they obtained were most *unlikely* to have arisen by chance. In statistical terms, the significance was at the .03 level for women with mother loss. Ordinarily a significance of .05 is acceptable, so the anniversary data for women, with a figure below .05, demonstrated the fact that women who had lost mothers in childhood were more apt to be the ones who developed an anniversary illness when they had children who reached their own age at childhood loss. For the 82 women whose fathers had died, the significance was at the level of chance; there were 9 actual age coincidences, while the numbers of coincidences that would be expected by chance were 11. Among women who showed the .03 significance, fewer than 8 would be expected by chance, but there were 14.

It is unfortunate that the number of men who conformed to the criteria for inclusion in the experimental sample remained too small for statistical analysis. However, in terms of our finding that women were more apt to have anniversaries when a parent of the same sex had been lost, the data for men do show a similar trend. Four of the 18 men with father loss showed coincidences with childhood age at loss, while none of the 17 men with mother loss had such coincidences. Thus a tendency toward identification with a parent of the same sex emerged.

This differential effect by sex calls for an explanation. In the standard patriarchal family, the culture assigns certain gender roles to men, and other roles to women. With the advent of motherhood, an identification with a woman's role becomes more fixed. A man's role presents alternatives that permit him more flexibility in meeting conflictual feelings brought out by a new baby in the home. Alcoholism is one of these.

The design, sample, and quantitative data of this statistical test of the anniversary hypothesis, so briefly summarized here, was published by Hilgard and Newman (1961).

Varied Manifestations of the Anniversary Syndrome in the Hospitalized Sample

The statistical study seeks for such uniformities as may be found in the course of the development of the anniversary syndrome. These similarities among cases lead to useful generalizations. There is a richness, however, that goes beyond the bare bones of statistics. The flavor can only be communicated by the study of individual cases.

Additional Typical Cases. The anniversary syndrome, triggered by the age the patient had been when a parent died, was described in two early patients: Mary Bancroft who had lost her father by death and James Carson who had lost his father by death (Hilgard, 1953). Because systematic study revealed that women whose mothers had died were much more frequent, several typical cases of this nature were reported by Hilgard and Newman (1959, 1961).

Double Anniversaries. In some instances, anniversary reactions arose on two occasions. Martha Newell was an only child, whose mother died when she was thirteen years old. When Martha's oldest child Mark became thirteen, she was admitted to the state hospital and released after a few months. Three years later when her daughter Mary became thirteen, she was again admitted to the hospital. She had deliberately given both children names similar to her own and both children were said to resemble her in personality. In another instance, a patient's parents were lost through murder and suicide when she was ten. Her first hospitalization had occurred when her first child was ten years old; we saw her at the time of her second hospitalization a number of years later when her second child was ten (Hilgard and Newman, 1961).

Parental Loss by Psychosis Instead of Loss by Death. With data as extensive as ours, we were able to make other analyses concerned with permanent loss of a parent. One of the most informative concerned women who had lost their mothers because the mothers had been permanently hospitalized for psychosis. In all respects these patients conformed to the same criteria as those who had lost mothers by death. We found a total population of fourteen cases. These fourteen cases, though rare, were of great theoretical interest because of the high percentage that conformed to the anniversary hypothesis. *Nine of the fourteen had entered the hospital when she had a child who was within a year of the age she had been at the time of her mother's permanent hospitalization.* (This compares with fourteen anniversary cases in the total population pool of sixty-five women I have already discussed when loss of the mother was by death.) Since our team treated the anniversary cases psychotherapeutically, there is considerable dynamic material to supplement the fact of age coincidences. Priscilla was hospitalized within one week of her thirty-second birthday when her older child was seven. These ages reflected the age her own mother had been at hospitalization and her age at childhood loss when the event occurred. A detailed account of treatment illustrated clearly the persistence into adult life of a core of confused and unintegrated identifications in a person who at the same time had managed to achieve a sufficiently intact ego to graduate from college, marry, bear two children, and raise them through their early years. It was only when circumstances of the early trauma were repeated—now she was the mother instead of the child—that the trauma, encapsulated since childhood, was triggered (Hilgard and Fisk, 1960).

Each of these anniversary patients had had a special position in the family. She was always the first daughter. She might be an only child or she might be a first daughter if not a firstborn child. Birth order was important. The mother had established a symbiotic relationship with this chosen child.

One of the most persuasive factors in the life history of some of these patients was the "saga of psychosis." One patient whose mother was permanently hospitalized when she was five, commented, "Mental illness was pushed into my head." She meant that relatives with whom she subsequently lived were convinced that she was not only like her mother but that she would become ill as her mother had. The message could be communicated subtly or openly.

One can speculate as to whether there was a hereditary factor of ego weakness in these cases. If such cases of mother and child, each diagnosed schizophrenic, had not been studied carefully, the causal factors might have been assumed to be innate. The presence of a psychogenic factor, however, never denies some potential due to heredity. What we could see and trace was the immense contribution of certain environmental factors that began in the childhood years of these patients. We sensed how much a particular position in the family, a special symbiotic relationship with a sick mother or with a disturbed substitute mother, a traumatic separation, an inability to mourn in this type of loss, guilt, and a subsequent saga could exert an inexorable effect on the course of human development.

Alcoholism in Men as a Possible Alternative to Psychosis in Women. In this report, I have omitted the large segment of alcoholic patients who entered the hospital during our period of sampling. They were studied separately. The number of men admitted for alcoholism exceeded women admitted for alcoholism, and women admitted for psychosis exceeded men admitted for psychosis, although the totals for men and women in both categories were approximately equal. What this suggests is that for some men, at least, the alcoholism was protecting them from psychosis.

There were a few anniversary cases among alcoholic men.

One case is cited as Mr. X in Hilgard and Newman (1959). The patient experienced two anniversaries, the first when the son he had named for himself reached the age of six, the age he was when his parents separated and the second when this same son reached the age of twelve, his age when his father had died. At both dates he was hospitalized for alcoholism. Another male patient became alocholic when his son reached the age he had been at his father's death. The cases are convincing when discovered, even though they are rare (Newman and Hilgard, 1967). That alcoholism may be an alternative for men to psychosis in women derived from the far greater number of men hospitalized for alcoholism than of women hospitalized for alcoholism. The sum of those admitted for alcoholism and psychosis were remarkably similar for both sexes.

The Metropolitan Community Study

Because many persons have lost parents in childhood and do not become disturbed, it was important to determine, next, what circumstances allowed the death of a parent to be taken in stride. With the help of Wilbur Schramm, professor of communications and journalism at Stanford, it was possible to sample an area of a nearby metropolitan community that was similar in demographic characteristics to that from which the state hospital patients had come.

The sampling method used was probability sampling. His interviewers, trained like census enumerators, gathered the statistical information.

To select an appropriate sample, four census tracts were chosen in this metropolitan area. Within the tracts they devised a probability sample of residence units resulting in over 2,000 residences visited in the search for those who belonged to the age group 19 to 49 (the same age range as in the hospitalized group). They found 1,136 persons to be interviewed for the data on parent loss in childhood, 493 men and 643 women. Those who lost parents represented 21 percent of this group, as compared with 27 percent in the hospital sample, remarkably similar under the circumstances.

For the purpose of our study, this group had to be reduced further to those who had not only lost a parent in childhood but now were married and had children. This reduced the number to ninety-eight for whom the attempt was made to arrange more intensive interviews. We completed sixty-five interviews designed to determine answers to the question: What protective factors did this parent-loss group possess so that the parent did not end up in the hospital and the presence of a child did not evoke a reliving experience of the emotions connected with the loss (Hilgard and Newman, 1963a, 1963b; Hilgard et al., 1960)?

Circumstances Faced by the Family Following the Loss of the Mother or Father

The death of a parent is itself a tragic event for the spouse and the children. The consequences for the family rest, first of all, on the emotional loss of a loved one. Accompanying the loss, there are necessarily changes in the structure of the home. The members of the family would not have faced the problems of a broken home had not this event occurred. The deprivation of a parent makes inevitable painful reorientations in the life of the family.

A child whose parent remarried after loss of a spouse faced hazards contingent upon the success of that marriage. The marriage might prove unsuccessful or be unable to supply much gratification for the child of the deceased parent. In any event, after remarriage a child has to adapt to a substitute for the lost parent. If a mother's or father's remarriage ends in separation or divorce, the single-parent family is again reinstated.

Boys whose mothers had not remarried after the father's death might be singled out by the mother as individuals toward whom she could devote special attention. In time this led to the son's continued dependency upon her. When sons reached the adult years, they tended not to marry or they entered upon rather unsuccessful marriages and might return to the mother. This same motif existed among women whose fathers had died but was less common.

When we compared the gratification of dependency needs in the metropolitan sample with that in the hospitalized sample, we noted that in the hospital population almost all of the patients had known a checkered career of unreliable fulfillment from the earliest years and were continuing to face frustration in their current situations.

Factors that Protected Those in the Community Sample from Serious Psychological Damage. A stable marrige of the parents prior to a death of one of them augured well for the next generation. Many of the surviving parents under these circumstances were strong enough to keep the family together after the loss. It was surprising in this generation of the 1950s, how well some of the widowed mothers played the dual role of breadwinner and homemaker to the benefit of their children.

Within a home feelings of grief and mourning had been acknowledged, shared, and adaptive steps to compensate for the loss had been taken. If networks of family and/or community resources were available, these had provided additional support for the bereaved parent as needed. Nearby family members, members of the church, personnel from social agencies proved useful.

In a comparison of the community group and the hospitalized one, a striking difference became evident in the way these resources were used. In the hospitalized sample, the bereaved parents' capacity for utilization was minimal, with the result that not only was the parent relatively isolated after the death of the spouse but so was the child. The child who was in danger of suffering mental illness as an adult was less apt to find satisfying friendships at school, church, or in the neighborhood.

The Presence of Mild Anniversaries. Although we did not run across major anniversary reactions in the community sample, we recognized the presence of milder types of anniversary reactions. Many people become anxious as they approach certain milestones of age because their expectations, based on earlier stressful experiences, are deeply meaningful, while at the same time they seldom led to incapacitating problems. These milestones or time markers have been known and written about for centuries. There are occasional reports of them in the current psychiatric and psychological literature.

One of our respondents expected to die at age twenty-five, the age of her mother at death. She was surprised, and relieved, to live out her twenty-fifth year. Now she felt destined to live out her mother's life, and this sense of destiny had continued. She did not marry until she reached age twenty-five, and, as though to carry out the magical continuity, she set her marriage date for her mother's marriage day. The first daughter was named for the dead mother, as though the magical reincarnation must continue. Her marriage had been satisfactory for twenty years.

Another of our respondents expected to die at fourteen, the age at which an older brother had died, a few months after her mother's death. When she had successfully passed this landmark, she reported that she had relaxed. Of course, if we scrutinize the situation carefully, we see that this time marker actually included two coincidental deaths.

Lifetime Development of the Anniversary Syndrome and Implications for Therapy

The presenting symptoms of a patient later found to have been affected by an anniversary syndrome are initially puzzling because they often seem too exaggerated to be explained by present circumstances in the life of the patient. When other efforts at explanation fail, an alert therapist may seek to review the life history of the patient anew, alert to any age coincidences between present and past that may possibly be anniversary related. It is only then that the sequential steps of the anniversary reaction come to light. Such knowledge can prove useful in therapy.

The syndrome develops, often over a time span of many years, in three stages:

1. The target date is implanted at the first stage. The affected person experiences a trauma such as the loss of a parent by death. These circumstances are emotionally distressing and leave residues, often unconscious, which lead to a later reliving of the experiences. At the same time the events have implanted the target date for reliving, based, for example, on the age of the parent who was lost by death or the childhood age of the affected person when the parent died.

2. The second stage is a quiescent one. With parent death in childhood, the home has been disrupted but some supportive features of the environment remain. The affected person gets along, although with difficulties that may not be readily recognized.

3. When the target age or date is reached, this serves as a trigger for reliving the experience. The affected person shows symptoms, called anniversary reactions. These represent a reliving of the implanted trauma. The form that this takes for the affected person varies but carries a demonstrable, dynamic relationship to the original trauma.

Implications for therapy. The aim of the therapy is to recognize the continuity between the present and the past. Within treatment each patient can be helped to understand and integrate, to the extent that is possible, the consecutive events of his or her personal history that bear on the anniversary syndrome. The trauma, in the form that it lives today, is placed in the perspective of the trauma that antedated it.

The relationship which the therapist is able to establish with the patient is fundamental to progress. It provides trusted support which is a basic need for each patient. The therapist helps the patient build upon past successes and strengths. In the midst of the more severe reliving experiences characteristic of the syndrome, the "negative self image" may predominate to such an extent that it obscures the positives. An essential corrective is to call attention to past strengths.

The therapist remains alert to the meaning of even short separations during therapy. A traumatic separation in childhood underlies the syndrome, and separation anxiety needs to be worked through, step by step.

The task of individualized therapy is to seek the integration of present and past. Ego-alien memories that have been sealed off need to be integrated. To achieve this goal, ideas and emotions such as anxiety and guilt, anger, grief and mourning need to be more freely expressed, understood, revised, and put into perspective. As a consequence the patient can order his or her experiences according to a new narrative, one that includes the formerly dissociated material. Present and past are reconnected.

Growth in personal-social relationships in family and community can be encouraged. In establishing this growth, significant family members may be included in the treatment program because the patient needs a supporting network that will remain in place after individual therapy is terminated or becomes less frequent. Inclusion of family members may assist in therapeutic gains for all those involved.

Additional types of therapy may supplement individual dynamic psychotherapy. The armamentarium of the psychotherapist should include knowledge of other therapeutic approaches which may be needed as adjuvants to the type of therapy described above. Sharing experiences with others in therapeutic groups in which the members have had similar experiences may prove desirable and helpful.

As another alternative, desensitization may assist in overcoming the parental patient's mixed feelings about the target child. If, in the course of improvement, the hospitalized patient makes brief visits to the home at first, the parent-child interactions can be observed and the visits gradually lengthened. Although the advantages of drug therapy were not known in the 1950s when this investigatory work was performed, today drug therapy would have a place in the midst of psychotherapy. Furthermore, community resources may be activated, such as church groups and community social service agencies.

Summary

The approaches taken in this chapter rely in many ways upon my experiences at Chestnut Lodge under the guidance of Frieda Fromm-Reichmann and the related supervision of Harry Stack Sullivan. Both were deeply concerned with interpersonal relationships of the patient in the outside world as well as within the patient-therapist interactions.

By focusing upon the unusual coincidences between the loss of a parent by death (or psychosis) when the patient was a child, and now had a child as a reminder, our group extended the Chestnut Lodge teachings. What was new was the recognition of the specific syndrome created when contextual coincidences resulted in the reinstatement and reliving of early traumas which could lead to severe mental illness.

The psychotherapeutic treatment of the illustrative cases was very much in the spirit of Chestnut Lodge. It is appropriate to end this chapter by the recognition that this is another anniversary—fifty years since Frieda came to this country—and that the date itself evokes memories of what many of us, long ago, learned from her.

References

Fromm-Reichmann, F. (1950), *Principles of Intensive Psychotherapy.* Chicago: University of Chicago Press.

Hilgard, J. R. (1953), Anniversary reactions in parents precipitated by children. *Psychiatry,* 16:73–80.

—— and Newman, M. F. (1959), Anniversaries in mental illness. *Psychiatry,* 22:113–121.

—— (1961), Evidence for functional genesis in mental illness. *J. Nerv. & Ment. Dis.,* 132:3–16.

—— (1963a), Early parental deprivation in schizophrenia and alcoholism. *Amer. J. Orthopsychiat.,* 33:409–420.

—— (1963b), Parental loss by death in childhood as an etiological factor among schizophrenic and alcoholic patients compared with a non-patient community sample. *J. Nerv. & Ment. Dis.,* 137:14–28.

—— and Fisk, F. (1960), Strength of adult ego following childhood bereavement. *Amer. J. Orthopsychiat.,* 30:788–798.

Newman, M. F., & Hilgard, J. R. (1967). Is alcoholism in men sometimes an alternative to schizophrenia in women? *Psychiat. Digest,* 28:33–37.

12

PRESENT-DAY TREATMENT OF SCHIZOPHRENIA

John P. Fort, M.D.

I. Thoughts about Frieda

I grew up in an era of male-dominated professional people. In all of high school, college, medical school, and residency I had only one woman teacher, a research internist, before I arrived at Chestnut Lodge and met Frieda, Mabel Cohen, and Alberta Szalita. It was a change indeed.

For a person of such small physical stature, Frieda Fromm-Reichmann fairly glowed with toughness, strength, and power. To me, this came across more than love, for in my naïve conception, love was a given—so I didn't need to notice it. She was a consummate actress without in any way being false or posing. She gestured with her hands more than any woman I have known, certainly any American or Northern European woman. This dramatic flair simply added a quality of projection of the self which is useful though not absolutely required of a therapist, but which is necessary to be a really good teacher. It has something to do with the capacity to inspire others. She was clever and articulate. Some people actually hated this in her. When a paranoid man waved a cigar in her face and said, "How would you like this, Dr. Fromm-Reichmann?" she reached in a drawer, pulled out an entire box of cigars, and said in a kindly but artful way, "Oh, put it in here with the others." When I told her in supervision that a male character-disordered patient was wearing dark glasses because, he said, the sun hurt his eyes, she told me, "You should say, 'Eyes? Eye-balls? Balls? Is it your balls you are worried about?' " I told her that she might be able to make such a statement, but the very idea of doing so appalled me. Now I'm quite sure Frieda partly enjoyed showing off and shocking the neophyte resident and partly wanted to loosen me up because, God knows, I needed to—but then again some of the older analysts were quite free with what we'd think of today as preposterous sexual interpretations. It was part of the game and mythology of psychoanalysis.

Frieda had quite an interesting and varied life—in many ways a hard life (she knew there were few rose gardens)—but one with a lot of success. She had grown up as an attractive, petite, definitely Jewish girl in Prussia. She had worked for the Prussian army in World War I; they were only too happy to have her on the one hand, and on the other were ashamed to have a woman, and a Jewish woman at that, on their staff. She had worked for Dr. Schulz—later a Nazi—in the famed Wiesser Hirsch sanitarium where the younger staff were required to be social partners with the patients at dinners and dances. She had married Erich Fromm who later became the avatar of the value of work but found him a "lazy German boy" unwilling to work with his hands when the two of them started a private sanitarium. She tried to get me to work harder with my somewhat chronic schizophrenic patient. She said, "You must make each hour with this woman a memorable experience." I felt awed and utterly inadequate, but I did work harder. Most of the time, though, Frieda was very supportive and complimentary. One tends, as Hans Strupp has said, to remember most clearly those occasions when one's analyst or one's supervisor seemed a bit out of character.

Chestnut Lodge used to require its new doctors who were on call to sleep there overnight once a week for two years in a rather depressing room in the Charles Adamsy Main Building. Out of the window one could see the lights in Fromm-Reichmann's cheerful cottage. One night I had a dream that Frieda's house was on fire and I rushed over to try and put the fire out, but when I arrived Frieda and Dexter Bullard, Sr., were sitting on the front porch together in a swing and there was no fire to be seen. I felt quite stupid and ridiculous and climbed a nearby tree as if that was why I had come over in the first place. As the expression has it, "Yes, Virginia," there is something called an Oedipus complex—at least in some of us. Fromm-Reichmann, however, did not believe in the universality of the Oedipus complex—one of many points on which she opposed the doctrinaire views of the establishment analysts.

Frieda had a very open mind about therapy. She was quite ready to try medication and tried electroshock on a patient once, but thought after this rather traumatic attempt, "Never again at Chestnut Lodge." She and Edith Weigert both were delighted with Harry Stack Sullivan and felt how wonderful it was to find a really gifted teacher when one was middle-aged. They also never considered themselves really disciples of his. Edith Weigert once revealed to me that she had had considerable anger at Dexter Bullard at the time of Frieda's death—feeling that perhaps he had worked Frieda too hard which contributed to her rather early death. Somehow I doubt that Dexter or any other male could have intimidated Frieda. The Prussian army couldn't when she was barely out of medical school, and it always seemed to me that she was the one person who consistently got her own way with Dexter Bullard. Lest it sound as if this was some sort of manipulation, let me say that Dexter obviously loved and admired her.

As I said, Frieda was not really a revolutionary as much as she was a clear thinker. She was distressed by the many dogmatic, rigid people in the psychoanalytic world with whom she came in contact. She said in a lecture around 1952, "If Marx were alive today, he would not be a Marxist; and if Freud were alive, he would not be a Freudian." Those could be called fighting words. Yet Frieda never abandoned the basic tenets of the Freudian discoveries. Those were, as Fromm-Reichmann understood Freud, "a genetic, dynamic concept of child development; an understanding of transference phenomena; and an assumption that at least part of the psychic life is unconscious." I suppose what I got from her most of all, in really only a couple of years acquaintanceship, was her enthusiasm for all kinds of people and especially all sorts of patients. Optimism was her hallmark. I suppose she was well-acquainted with loneliness and wrote about it beautifully. Accordingly, she also was familiar with depression but never allowed that to show to her students or patients. She felt they had problems enough and they should not be burdened with her own struggles, a point which Sullivan also made.

I think Frieda's greatest contribution was, of course, the finding that psychoanalytic concepts and psychoanalysis itself could be applied to the treatment of the seriously mentally ill, especially to schizophrenia. She added conceptualizations to these views which others had begun to accept. She showed that such people who had what Freud called "narcissistic neuroses" were capable of developing transference—indeed often intensely so. In many ways she legitimized the idea of "psychoanalytically oriented psychotherapy," now the most widely used form of treatment in the Western world. In some ways she may have set some of her disciples on a course which overvalued psychotherapy alone. Sullivan had felt that he had "wasted his time" with the most severely schizophrenic patients. Frieda felt that everyone could be helped. I think today we have proven Fromm-Reichmann correct, but we now know that psychotherapy must be augmented by a whole host of auxiliary methods if it is going to prove reasonably effective. It is too bad that in this day and age people are so intent on finding either that something works or does not work, cures or fails, there is a tendency either to overvalue or to undervalue psychotherapy with the psychoses.

I want to mention some other Fromm-Reichmann ideas which I have found especially helpful. One is the awareness that schizophrenic people greatly exaggerate in their inner concepts their capacity for accomplishment and at the same time undervalue their actual performance. I suppose this is true of all disordered people but qualitatively different with schizophrenic patients. This grandiosity is accomplished by exaggerated ideas concerning their powers of destructiveness.

It is not fashionable these days to refer to the schizophrenogenic mother. In fact the general movement in the American *Zeitgeist* is away from dynamic concepts. People do not want to feel guilty or responsible for the life courses of their offspring. Certainly some adjustment of the pendulum was in order. There are more inborn traits in the infant, we now believe, and the chance fit with the mother plays a bigger part than once thought. It is also true that the parent of a schizophrenic child may have his own personality distorted by interactions with the child. Nevertheless, the concept is still a true one. The efforts by Stanley Greenspan and others may ultimately explain just how it works, at least in vulnerable children.

Another most important idea is the constant principle of never forgetting that the regressed patient is still an adult person. Respect for both the child and the adult in a person is a hallmark of successful therapy, even in the sickest patients.

The May 1982 issue of *Psychiatry* was devoted largely to excellent accounts of Fromm-Reichmann by some of her students. Along with the 1958 article in the same journal by Edith Weigert, I heartily recommend it. Here are articles by Robert A. Cohen, Hilde Bruch, Ralph Crowley, Virginia Gunst, Sylvia Hoff, and Alfred Stanton, and a commentary by Fromm-Reichmann herself on the "rose garden" case. In these articles the overwhelming impression of Fromm-Reichmann, which I share, is one of enthusiasm and hope—along with an acceptance of the real difficulties of life.

Frieda told Joanne Greenberg (Hannah Green), "Getting well doesn't mean that your life thereafter will be a garden of roses. Enjoy your rose garden when it is in bloom and take it in stride when it is not in bloom."

II. Present-Day Treatment

This paper provides an overview of the current treatment of schizophrenia and examines more specifically the place of psychotherapy in that treatment. My comments are largely personal conclusions and are highly condensed. Almost every statement would deserve a separate page or even a chapter, but in a short commentary the ideas must be taken as representing some broad conclusions based on a good deal of thought and practice. In no way do I presume to survey all aspects of the subject or even credit my own major sources or teachers. I can, however, write nothing on this subject without mentioning Fromm-Reichmann and her successor at Chestnut Lodge, Otto A. Will, who together gave me a more compelling orientation than any others.

Schizophrenia remains an enormous, worldwide, serious

disorder—a major public health problem, a catastrophic illness, a chronic source of misery for many millions. Adolf Meyer called it a "living death." In this country alone there may be two million people disabled by the disorder with 100,000 to 200,000 new cases occurring each year. The economic costs of treatment or custody and loss of productivity have been estimated to be twenty to forty billion dollars annually.

Treatment ideally follows from a clear understanding of pathogenic agents and processes. In the case of schizophrenia, treatment efforts are confounded at the outset by, as yet, unanswered etiological questions. The cause or causes of this disorder remain basically quite unclear. The heterogeneity of symptoms has led many to call the disorder not one disease but several—a spectrum. I view it as one disorder, not many, and as a peculiarly human disorder, but with many gradations of severity. Animals do not become psychotic. More recent genetic studies cast doubt on any actual specific inheritance, but clearly both nature and nurture are involved. The cause of schizophrenia may turn out to be intimately related to the "cause" of being human. Thus, the origin of the disorder is no doubt concerned with the evolution of human thinking processes. It seems that the chromosomal genetic changes which led to *homo sapiens* may have teetered on the edge of being totally self-destructive of the species by virtue of overextending the reflective process. The ability to contemplate the future, including individual death, might have little to do with species viability and, indeed, threaten it. Paradoxically, the schizophrenic capacity for survival may once have played an important part in the continuation of the species (Fort, 1965).

At present we must accept the idea that the illness is interactive—probably both environmental and genetic. It is usually chronic to a degree and, as with most chronic diseases, one must aim, in the majority of cases, toward amelioration of the symptoms and change in its course. The specific treatment which will be meaningful in all individual cases cannot be standardized because the range of severity is so wide.

Severity of illness is then the critical factor determining the kind of treatment. Many people suffer acute, psychotic decompensation, at times under unusual amounts of inner or outer stress. There is good evidence that the potentiality for the psychotic state exists in all humans, although it may never be manifested in more than the briefest of waking experience. A person who has experienced for even a matter of hours the full eruption of a psychotic episode will never be quite the same again. The individual will still harbor a lingering fear and may avoid certain aspects of human experience which would push in that direction. One cannot assert that all such individuals should receive psychotherapy or psychoanalysis, but it is clear that many do and are successfully treated. They go on about their lives with only a minor disorder and are never listed as "schizophrenic patients" who have been successfully treated. A prototypical example of this type of case is a twenty-eight-year-old man I saw a few years ago. He was a successful chemist-researcher who came to my office complaining of people following him. He had been having a difficult time with his wife who had left him briefly. He had been under extreme work pressure and had felt he was failing. Friends had seemed to leave him. Once or twice he had heard a voice calling him, which frightened him. He was sleepless and anxious. He had a similar episode in college at which time he was hospitalized and treated with neuroleptic medication and psychotherapy (which he did not continue). With only a few night-time doses of a neuroleptic, a vacation from work, and several hours of psychotherapy, his psychotic symptoms vanished almost entirely. He remained in psychotherapy for some months and although showing evidence of some difficult personality problems, he has continued to function quite well, but continued to show some personality defects.

The framers of the Diagnostic and Statistical Manual III of the American Psychiatric Association were so impressed with the number of people who had relatively brief psychoses and recovered—even without medication or at least without long-term medication—that they instituted a new term, "schizophreniform," to describe any apparent schizophrenic psychosis of less than six months duration. The six-month period was, of course, purely arbitrary. One could just as well have used three months, thereby excluding more severe cases or, conversely, used nine months as the criterion, thereby including more severe cases. Many of these acute cases never find their way into psychiatric units and are not part of the official statistics of schizophrenia. Others do get hospitalized and become part of the successfully treated, by whatever method used. The point I wish to make is that there is a steady linear progression from least severe to most severe. These are not two different groups—the reactive and the process. For practical purposes, however, the "six months" rule of DSM-III and the reactive versus process distinctions are useful, for the difference in degree of severity between the modal points of the two groups is enormous and the respective treatment approaches highly divergent. This should be no surprise. The same situation exists in most chronic diseases—hypertension, for instance. An individual with a diastolic blood pressure of ninety-five can be treated with weight reduction, low salt diet, and life-style changes. The person with a diastolic pressure of 130 may require not only the above measures but also several potent medications and even hospitalization. Thus determining the degree of illness is critical in deciding what kind of treatment is needed.

In the treatment of "established" or chronic schizophrenia it has proved to be useful to divide the chronic disorder into four grades of severity as originally described by myself (1973) and elaborated by Ping-Nie Pao (1979). Those with type I become overtly ill in a more acute way. Often, their developmental years seem relatively normal, and they become ill in later adolescence. Their problem lies more toward the conflict side in the conflict-deficiency axis. They are usually amenable to psychotherapy. Patients with type II have had a more disturbed infancy and tend to first show overt illness in middle adolescence. Family problems are usually obvious. Treatment may be prolonged and require family intervention and medication. Type III patients show clear evidence of psychopathology in childhood and often an insidious psychotic process in early adolescence. Treatment will be long and often require multiple forms of therapy and rehabilitation. Patients with type IV may begin as any of the previous, but after years of illness the patients have lost almost all hope. The pace of therapy will be slow and the outcome uncertain. All four types are seriously ill, and for these patients treatment of any kind remains difficult and uncertain. Almost all subchronic and chronic schizophrenic patients, we now feel, require a combination of individual psychotherapy, pharmacotherapy, social and vocational rehabilitation, and sometimes family counseling.

Recent authoritative studies by McGlashan (1984), Gunderson et al. (1984), and Stone (1986) make it clear that the use of psychotherapy is largely ineffective as a *cure* for chronic schizophrenia. All authors, however, report some cures and a good deal of improvement. We are dealing with a generally chronic illness for which total cure is bound to be the exception. The one-third rule enunciated by Black (1810) still holds more or less for schizophrenics without specific treatment. That is, one third recover, one third remain about the same, and one third get worse over the years. Psychotherapy modifies this; so does drug therapy—but neither cures the disorder. The use of major neuroleptic medications is an enormous advance, but these medications are not curative. Recent findings of an incidence of tardive dyskinesia as high as 40 percent with prolonged use make their long-term employment as the sole treatment a matter of much doubt. Clearly, treatment must involve the care of both mind and body. Neither alone has proved satisfactory. The emphasis in this paper is on psychotherapy.

Psychotherapy of Schizophrenia

In 1896 Freud reported an attempt at psychoanalysis or psychotherapy, then called hypnotic therapy, with a woman suffering from paranoid schizophrenia. This treatment lasted about six months; the patient participated and gained some insight, but she suddenly became much worse (today we would say regressed) and was hospitalized. In what was then considered a surprise, she recovered after a few months and returned home, had another child, and functioned well as a housewife for twelve years. Again she suffered a relapse and was returned to a state hospital where she remained for the rest of her life. Today we might consider this twelve-year remission a fairly good result, but the final outcome may have deterred Freud from working with what he called the narcissistic neuroses (psy-

choses). However, he encouraged Carl Jung and Eugen Bleuler
among others to continue this work. In the 1930s further psychotherapy with the psychoses was carried on in Germany and
Switzerland and later in the United States by many pioneers,
including Frieda Fromm-Reichmann, the Menningers, Harry
Stack Sullivan, John Rosen, and many others.

Although by now the psychotherapy of schizophrenia has
a long and distinguished history and much experience of success, its place in the future as a generally accepted treatment
for this disorder is not clear. What is clear is the time and
sustained effort required to treat schizophrenia. No one except
the psychotherapist is likely to bring to the treatment the force
and the continuity of his or her person and sustained interest.
One finds the "clinical relationship" referred to by many (Carpenter, 1986) as vital but there is a wariness in identifying the
clinician in this relationship as the "psychotherapist." Much of
this hestitation stems from some disappointment in the results
of psychotherapy when used alone or even in combination with
pharmacotherapy. While Carpenter and others acknowledge
that ongoing talking and relating to the patient are still required, they avoid calling this process "psychotherapy."

Manfred Bleuler (1979) has said that "what the schizophrenic needs is long continued contact with the same supportive people over a long period of time with just the right amount
of frustration." Only an overall plan which envisions three to
ten years of consistent treatment and the continuation of at
least some of the same team throughout that period of time can
hope to show a reasonable degree of progress. This does not
mean that the patient must be hospitalized for ten years or
necessarily even in intensive psychotherapy all that time. The
protracted length of treatment is difficult for patients and families to face.

The protracted time is equally difficult for the treating
people to contemplate. Patients tend to move from one hospital
to another, from one clinic to another, or nowadays from one
rehabilitation facility to another. Personnel of these treatment
settings also tend to move. Motility is a particularly American
response to difficulty. A therapist moving from one private
hospital to another or from one outpatient clinic to another

may encounter a number of the chronic schizophrenic patients he or she knew in a previous setting. In spite of at least a good deal of knowledge of the difficulties at hand, it has taken the staff of Chestnut Lodge and other similar places many years to realize that a long, continuing program including outpatient rehabilitation is the expected form of treatment, not the exception.

It is necessary to emphasize the importance of the psychotherapist. He or she most of all gets to know the patient in an intimate way and gradually develops an understanding of the patient's symptoms, character structure, and defenses. At best, the therapist often is able to relate to the severely ill patient on a purely secondary process level in which the schizophrenic person seems little different from the neurotic patient. This is often interspersed with hours or weeks of time when the person is psychotic and unrelated. The patient may be aggressive or withdrawn or apathetic or overwhelmingly depressed. One is able to fit all these experiences into a pattern and to help the patient recognize the cause and even the meaning of these episodes. The response to exacerbated psychotic episodes may involve mainly action-oriented interventions such as increasing the medication, hospitalizing the patient, counseling the family, decreasing work or community involvement, or making a change in the psychotherapeutic interventions. It may, of course, involve all these aspects or only one.

The psychotherapist is usually the person concerned most vitally. He or she may, for example, find that the patient has detected the therapist's discouragement or ambivalence. Schizophrenic patients are exquisitely sensitive to such feelings. For example, the patient says that he thinks he will miss the hour "next Wednesday." The therapist asks why, and the patient answers that he has thought of going shopping that day. Unfortunately some therapists argue half-heartedly and in a convoluted way that the patient "should not miss hours" while apparently investigating the reasons for the statement. Perhaps in this example the therapist greatly needs an extra hour next Wednesday for whatever purpose, and his or her own ambivalence will be apparent to the patient. Here it seems clear that the proper response is either an unequivocal "No, you are not going to miss your hour" or a rather straightforward statement of the facts, "Joe, as it happens, I terribly need to take the Wednesday hour off also. I have to attend a special meeting that day" or whatever the true reason is. The type of response one does not want to make is the "interpretive" sort which asks, "Joe, does that mean you are discouraged with your psychotherapy?" Such a question is often flat-footed and naïve. Only the psychotherapist in all likelihood knows the patient well enough to detect the hinted-at meanings behind the various assertions and has at least a reasonable chance of giving the appropriate response.

The therapist has the knowledge and investment to keep hope alive. The *Vedanta* states, "Hope is the sheet-anchor of every man." Hope is the most severely threatened aspect of the schizophrenic's self, and its loss is the hallmark of the most severe schizophrenia. Only the psychotherapist can be in sufficiently close touch with the despair of the schizophrenic person to be able to understand the rise and fall of hope. Only he or she can be sufficiently trusted by the patient to be made aware of the true nature of the psychological injury. For a beautiful description of despair and hope see Leslie Farber's paper "The Therapeutic Despair" (1976).

There is another aspect of the treatment of schizophrenia which must be considered—regression. In 1976 I wrote cautiously of the possible value of a period of regression in the treatment of newly admitted patients who had had many years of treatment with antipsychotic medications with poor results. A period off medication seemed to promote a "clearing" of the system and a realignment of forces in the patient's inner psychological structure and an all-out mobilization of (primarily) psychiatrist and nurses to demonstrate their ability to deal with the raw forces of psychosis which greatly reassured the patient. This theoretical position still has its appeal, but so much was lost and the journey back to reality was so fraught with peril that we are less inclined today to allow this to happen with most patients. There are some, however, who cry out for an approach in which, at least for a prescribed period of time, medication is not used. In my view, this is especially true of those schizophrenics who are more or less committed to paranoid defenses and are less fragmented at the time of admission. For the great majority, however, it seems better to initiate a trial off medication only when the patient has formed a reasonably solid attachment to the people who care for him. Most hospitalized chronic schizophrenics will require neuroleptic medication, but description of this usage is outside the scope of this paper. We often slowly reduce the antipsychotic medication but do not eliminate it. What we would hope for is the ephemeral state known formerly as the "benign regression." This phrase was largely a contradiction in terms and yet to a degree it sometimes happens. The patient becomes receptive to gratification of primitive, oral-dependent needs without eruption of violent aggressive impulses. William A. White once said, "What is a mental hospital if it is not a place where patients can be crazy?" In making the decision about when and how to use medication one must listen to the voice of the patient as well as to one's own therapeutic voice. Some patients will simply refuse to take medication for a time, often months. Others will ask for medication, either in so many words or in a nonverbal way will indicate a feeling of profound fear and desolation which shows no signs of health or change. The therapist is not always the best judge of the severity and prognosis of this state as he can often read into small variations a greater sense of hope than the situation actually warrants. Psychotic regression or the "psychotic regressive adaptive state," as Joseph Sandler has termed it, is not in itself a state which anyone with good sense would want to induce. What one does want, however, is to encourage a state of empathy and intimacy. As with the ordinary person, this inevitably involves some regressive processes. Judging how much is felicitous requires much experience and profound sensitivity on the part of the psychotherapist.

In the remaining portion of this paper I would like to discuss some particular issues regarding the psychotherapy of schizophrenia. As I have indicated earlier, psychotherapy with schizophrenic patients is performed on a much wider basis than is generally acknowledged. There are great numbers of less severely ill patients treated in varying degrees of intensity in private and clinic practice everywhere. Many of these are also receiving medication, but a sizable number have either never been placed on medication or received it at one time in a hospital or have stopped taking it regularly. Many of these are surprisingly amenable to an expressive investigative type of therapy. For hospitalized patients, organized, intensive psychotherapy has become more the exception than the rule except in a few institutions. The length of the required work, the difficulty, and the uncertain outcome have tended to discourage most therapists. Many people make a small attempt without getting deeply committed, which saves both them and the patient from the dangers of disappointment. If more professional therapists would regard the work as primarily intended to alleviate and modify the disorder—not cure it—the ranks of therapists might swell considerably. One must never abandon the possibility of a significant improvement, even a cure, but one simply cannot afford to be constantly centered on that goal without the danger of disillusionment and grief.

We can consider the analogy of the arch to describe the treatment of the schizophrenic. The force vectors are known—what the patient's team will have to sustain. The foundation is first put in place—equivalent to the patient's own ego and the milieu in which he finds himself. Piers are then erected which in this analogy would be the use of drugs on the one side and the steady relationships on the other (milieu therapy). The side stones or voussoirs are carefully chiseled and may represent family therapy, vocational therapy, social-skills training or other more deciphered efforts. Still the arch would collapse and be useless if one did not sculpt the keystone—a large but variably sized block which must be fitted in and which locks all the other parts into place. The precise shape is difficult to describe, but as an entree I want to describe some of the hoped-for characteristics of the psychotherapist.

One might list a long series of ideal attributes for the psychotherapist, but I want to emphasize a few particularly needed for work with schizophrenic patients (see Farber, 1976). I do not list these in any order of importance, and the list is far from exhaustive.

First, the therapist must have an interest in the *disease*, including etiology, pathology, dynamic diagnosis, treatment, and also be at least working within a theoretical framework. By this I mean an overall concept of what the disorder is about. One's conception of the illness can no longer be purely psychodynamic but must encompass as well a broad understanding of the fledgling neurophysiological theories of the disorder. The above interest usually requires a second attribute—professional training and intellectual development. Otherwise, quite generally the therapist will drop out of the work, often sooner but at least before many years; or, equally sadly, he or she may become a cult leader. I have seen these two things happen over and over. The work alone is too difficult and not sufficiently successful to sustain any of us without some secondary rewards. The latter are best realized in the research and theoretical areas or at least in the attempt to fit these somewhat strange people into a philosophical concept of human life.

The second criterion I would postulate might seem to contradict the point just made—namely, therapeutic zeal. This cannot be taught. We hope that all therapists would have it—a drive to help people, a view of death and disease as our enemies. Christian Muller (1984) has written: "The therapist of the schizophrenic must conclude an unwritten contract with the patient involving a long time obligation and binding his own destiny to that of the patient." That's a monumental demand, perhaps. Few of us would consciously enter such a contract. It sounds like marriage at least; yet it captures the kind of spirit which must prevail at times during treatment. To my mind, this does not have to contradict intellectual interest. There can be an interplay between the two.

Third, I would list persistence and patience. Psychotherapy, like psychoanalysis, takes a long time. No one seems to think it so strange that the psychoanalytic treatment of a neurotic patient takes several years. Why is it any surprise that the schizophrenic does not come around quickly? Yet one hears over and over that the treatment takes too long. Not only does the schizophrenic have a devastating psychological and possibly physiological problem with massive deprivation and shattering conflict; he usually also has serious character problems which continually interact with the basic disorder to pull him back toward psychosis. Even the fine follow-up studies alluded to earlier make inadequate distinction between those treated for a few months and those for many years.

Fourth, a capacity for drama and projection of the self is almost a requirement. As exemplars of this, I think of the fiery John Rosen of the old days in Philadelphia and the consummate actress Frieda Fromm-Reichmann. At least there is little room for the quiet, passive, blank-screen therapist in this work, but I do not mean to imply that the flamboyant therapist is best for schizophrenics either. Expressed emotion must be well-modulated and generally noncritical.

Fifth, some capacity for sadism is necessary. Otherwise one cannot stand the vicious sadism which characterizes certain aspects of the schizophrenic patient. One of the pleasures in doing long-term psychotherapy with schizophrenic patients is that a degree of openness emerges which allows one to interact in a way which social conventions do not allow one in ordinary life—or even usually in the course of psychoanalysis. Surprisingly, in one sense, one gets into "deeper" relatedness with schizophrenics.

A schizophrenic woman patient once said to me, in the intensity of the therapeutic interaction, that if I would spend every moment with her for twenty-four hours, she would be well. Although I thought about doing just that, I decided instead to engage in a fantasy about what this would be like. I pictured ourselves together on a desert island. At first I felt she was getting well, but I began to feel devoured by her and in the final scene of the episode I killed her. I was able at a later point on another occasion to quite pointedly but comfortably describe to her my occasional thoughts of killing her, to which she responded in a thoroughly accepting way. Of course, it matched her thoughts of killing me.

Sixth, another quality is a lack of arbitrary dogmatism, of a single-minded secular belief. There must be a mixture of treatment for the body and the mind and for the practical as well as the spiritual. I speak here of a broad-based humanism tempered by a streak of quite practical willingness to compromise. At the same time there can be no limp eclecticism in which one does not really mind what is done for the patient. There must be respect for the individual in spite of his pathology.

One's thinking must embody the words of Shakespeare that "One touch of nature makes all men kin," or of H. S. Sullivan, "We are all more simply human than otherwise." One must have a complex belief in life, not in a way of life. Orthodoxy is anathema to most schizophrenic patients. One of my patients wished to paint his apartment black and use purple curtains. One member of the team was appalled and virtually forbade him to purchase the paint. When the patient and others persisted, it turned out to be a rather delightful decorative scheme, at least for this particular person.

As the seventh point I list empathy and imagination. They seem so obvious as qualities needed in any sort of therapist that I hesitate to mention them at all. Let me give an example. At a recent case presentation, I heard about a newly admitted male patient who had as a prominent delusion the idea that he was "the daughter of God." This delusion was so preposterous that the entire professional staff taking care of the patient tended to smile or even laugh about it. Even the therapist, normally an imaginative person, tended to dismiss it (at least as having any reality in it). Since I was not treating the patient, it was easy for me to let my thoughts roam. I asked the therapist if he could prove to me that the patient was not the daughter of God. Now it seemed obvious in the first place, he said, that God had endowed the young man with the anatomical attributes of a son, not a daughter. That was not so compelling an argument to me, as God in his omniscience might have had good reason to disguise the identity of his daughter. It was also true that the patient had said that he had the *soul* of a woman. Historically many people feel that since there has been a son of God on earth, a daughter would be the logical next choice. As the boy struggled in his psychotic world to find an identity, it might have struck him in a flash that this explained it all. No doubt, also, if he were a woman, he would escape in a curious way from any conflict over homosexuality, which might otherwise exist. I mention all this as the exercise of a peculiar imagination with which one can see how the patient's conclusion makes sense if one accepts his premises, which again are understandable in light of the conflicts and so on. Thus, empathy and imagination are wide-ranging in their importance.

Further comments that I wish to make on attributes of therapy and therapists could be subsumed under the general category of technique. It is so easy here to list all the things one should not do and so difficult to find the affirmatives.

First of all, one must not do a lot of interpretation or preaching to the schizophrenic patient. Unfortunately interpretations, unless very carefully worked up to, usually carry a negative valence, as do exhortations to do better. To the schizophrenic the "usual" interpretation is a veiled criticism. It may well be that one or even two generations of psychotherapists of schizophrenics have been contaminated by rigid applications of psychoanalytic technique. Bellak (1979), among others, believes this to be true. By this I do not mean to oppose psychoanalytic training. It is most valuable for treating all kinds of patients. There has been a tendency, however, blindly to apply ideas of neutrality, lack of gratification, and interpretation as if there were something magical about these to all patients. I feel that the absence of a proper theory of therapy has hampered psychoanalysis as there has been too much emphasis on the understanding of pathology and too little on the process of treatment and nowhere is this more true than in work with schizophrenic patients.

Likewise, there tends today to be a mounting division between so-called insight psychotherapy or, as Gunderson has called it, expressive insight-oriented therapy and supportive psychotherapy. This division goes along with the belief that schizophrenia is either a conflict disorder or a deficiency disorder. This dichotomy to me is a false one. Can one imagine a kind of *therapy* which would be *nonsupportive* (as literally meant)—the two words are contradictory in terms. It is all a matter of timing and sensitivity to the issues at hand. To withhold from a schizophrenic patient an important piece of understanding and insight is as much an error as to withhold regularly any pleasant comments from a high-level neurotic because they might be supportive. In a sense, the schizophrenic patient already has "too much" insight of a limited sort. He may well be more aware than the obsessional neurotic, for instance, of murderous thoughts or incestuous wishes. His overall judgment of the implications of these ideas is simply exaggerated, often wildly so.

Another thing to keep in mind is the value of simplicity. A few well-understood ideas are worth a thousand half-understood ones. I almost never use the word "why" in treating schizophrenics. As a matter of fact, I ask few questions except about factual events. "Why" to the schizophrenic is frequently seen as a dagger—"*Why* did you do that?" The reverberations of what is heard is the thunderous voice of the parent, as it is internally represented in the mind of the schizophrenic (Thompson, 1981).

The imaginative use of words is important, even at times the clever use. It comes naturally to some people but can also be learned. What probably comes across to the schizophrenic from this is a deep appreciation that he is worth the effort of creativity on the part of the therapist; indeed, such mental work also makes the therapist feel good. It builds the therapeutic alliance. It can also serve to detoxify dangerous impulsive feelings and hopelessness. I would seldom say (at least early on) to the paranoid patient, "Your problem is that you mistrust people." I might say, "Your problem is an excess of pride. You hate to let anyone claim to offer anything of use to you as you want to know it all yourself." This kind of statement has less of a pejorative ring. Pride, although one of the seven deadly sins, is far less noxious than distrust. The resistant patient says, "Why should I spend my life doing what others want me to do? So far it's been a terrible mistake." I say, "You've never really felt your life was your own—not even in kindergarten—except at moments. Is it possible that your own interests might just happen to coincide with what other people want?" It is always a surprise when the schizophrenic says, "Quite possibly you're right." This patient and others like her feel a terrible dilemma about separation and individuation, but a very ill patient such as this can get into a relatedness where defensiveness and resistance are diminished. The difficulty is that after a thoughtful exchange like the above, the patient my come back the next day and say, "You've never done anything for me. I hate psychiatrists and I always have. You are only out after my money, etc." Now that's not so worrisome in itself, but the cycle can go on week after week, month after month, and sadly, even year after year, but with some advance each time.

In the past what has kept many therapists going is the intense pleasure exemplified in the story of Pygmalion—the sense of being able to create a human being out of an ill-defined chaotic mess. I don't mean to derogate this motivation. It's one of the things that makes this work almost fun. But at its worst it is too narcissistic, too seductive, too all-encompassing, and basically too much an attempt at a literal repetition of infancy and childhood without the eager drive toward health and outside experimentation which the normal child has. There has to be real outside improvement. The patient has to move out, has to get a job, has to have other meaningful relationships besides the one with the psychotherapist.

Some day, off drugs perhaps, or on only low doses of medication, the patient's grandiose goals have been reduced and pleasure in small things expanded. I don't think one can successfully graft this rehabilitation onto chronic schizophrenic patients without the personal inner growth resulting from psychotherapy. Otherwise, what one gets is a grotesque-trained monkey appearance.

Let me cite a few lines from a brief communication entitled "Can We Talk" (1986). It is written by an anonymous schizophrenic patient who is undergoing psychotherapy. The author, a patient, says:

> With the struggles back and forth it almost seems questionable whether all this is really worth it. There are days when I wonder if it might not be more humane to leave the schizophrenic patient to his own world of unreality, not to go through the pain it takes to become a part of humanity. . . . But it seems that only through psychotherapy can the world of unreality truly be dispelled. . . . The question of whether the fragile ego of the schizophrenic patient can withstand the rigors of intensive therapy to me is an unfortunate hindrance. A fragile ego left alone remains fragile. . . . It seems there must be some balance that can be achieved so that schizophrenic patients can receive the benefit of psychotherapy with therapists who are sensitive to their special needs and can help their ego emerge little by little. Medi-

cation or superficial support alone is not a substitute for the feeling that one is understood by another human being.

Where is the treatment of schizophrenia headed in the decades to come? Have we really made any great strides from the days of "moral treatment?" Barring catastrophe we will never return to the inhuman warehousing of patients that characterized so much of the approach in the recent past—up until the second half of this century. There seems little likelihood that either the exact cause or treatment of schizophrenia will be identified. In a truly humanistic and affluent society much can be done to alleviate the terrible impact of the disorder. Many will always veer away from close and sustained contact with the schizophrenic, but enough will be willing to devote their lives to make a great difference.

References

Anonymous Recovering Patient (1986), Can we talk? *Amer. J. Psychiat.*, 143:68.

Bellak, L. (1979), *Specialized Techniques in Individual Psychotherapy*. New York: Brunner/Mazel.

Black, W. (1810), A dissertation on insanity. In: *Three Hundred Years of Psychiatry*, ed. R. Hunter. London: Oxford University Press, 1963, pp. 644–647.

Bleuler, M. (1978), *The Schizophrenic Disorders*. New Haven, CT: Yale University Press.

———— (1979), On schizophrenic psychoses. *Amer. J. Psychiat.*, 136:493–499.

Carpenter, W. T., Jr. (1986), Thoughts on the treatment of schizophrenia. *Schizophrenia Bull.*, 12:527–539.

Farber, L. (1966), *In Ways of the Will*. New York: Basic Books.

———— (1976), *Lying, Despair, Envy, Sex, Suicide, Drugs and the Good Life*. New York: Basic Books, pp. 84–105.

Fort, J. P. (1965), Schizophrenia and human evolution. Chestnut Lodge Symposium.

———— (1973), The importance of being diagnostic. Read at the 19th Annual Chestnut Lodge Symposium.

———— (1976), Regression. *J. Nat. Assn. Priv. Psychiat. Hosp.*, 8:15–19.

———— (1979), Milieu therapy. *J. Nat. Assn. Priv. Psychiat. Hosp.*, 10:12–16.

Freud, S. (1896), Further remarks on the neuro-psychoses of defense. *Standard Edition*, 3:174–188. London: Hogarth Press, 1953.

Fromm-Reichmann, F. (1959), *Psychoanalysis and Psychotherapy*. Chicago: University of Chicago Press.

Green, H. (or Greenberg, J.) (1964), *I Never Promised You a Rose Garden*. New York: Holt, Rinehart & Winston.

Gunderson, J. G., Will, O., & Mosher, L. (1983), *Principles and Practices of Milieu Therapy*. New York: Aronson.

———— ———— ———— (1984), Effects of psychotherapy in schizophrenia. *Schizophrenia Bull.*, 10:564–598.

Harding, C. M., Brooks, G. W., Ashikaga, T., Strauss, J. S., & Breier, A. (1987), The Vermont longitudinal study of persons with severe mental illness, II. *Amer. J. Psychiat.*, 144:727–735.

Kernberg, O. F. (1981), The therapeutic community. *Nat. Assn. Priv. Psychiat. Hosp.*, 12:46–55.

McGlashan, T. H. (1984), The Chestnut Lodge follow-up study: II. *Arch. Gen. Psychiat.*, 41:586–601.

Muller, C. (1984), The psychotherapy in schizophrenia. *Schizophrenia Bull.*, 10:618–621.

Pao, P.-N. (1979), *Schizophrenic Disorders.* New York: International Universities Press.

Stern, D. (1985), *The Interpersonal World of the Infant.* New York: Basic Books.

Stone, M. (1986), Exploratory psychotherapy in schizophrenia-spectrum patients. *Bull. Menn. Clin.*, 50:287–306.

Thompson, S. V. (1981), Some considerations regarding psychoanalytically oriented psychotherapy. *J. Nat. Assn. Priv. Psychiat. Hosp.*, 12:34–39.

13

PROGNOSIS: HOPELESS (1966); A SEQUEL (1977)

Samuel V. Thompson, M.D., Ph.D.

Frieda Fromm-Reichmann:
The Gentle Giant

The psychoanalyst we honor here today was one of the giants in our field.

The psychoanalyst we honor here today was a petite woman, under five feet tall, who was often mistaken for the housekeeper when she opened the door of her cottage to greet a new patient.

Allow these two images to meld in your thoughts and the real essence, the true spirit of Frieda Fromm-Reichmann will emerge. The warm, gentle, feisty, petite, dynamic, brilliant giant.

That essence of Fromm-Reichmann permeates every corner of Chestnut Lodge: in her cottage, where she worked and lived and died, throughout the grounds where she walked and talked, challenging all those she came in contact with, both patients and staff alike, to reach their ultimate goals, to expand their horizons and mental capabilities to the fullest. She gently urged and prodded; soothed the enraged and then raged herself against injustice, and against the illness within us all. She reminded us of our humanity *and* she did it all in English, a

This paper excerpts from a posthumous paper read by Robert A. Cohen, M.D., Ph.D., at the 31st annual Chestnut Lodge symposium, October 4, 1985.

[Dr. Thompson wrote this manuscript during a holiday trip to the Caribbean. He died on January 11, 1985, in his sleep during the airplane trip back to the Lodge. He spent less time away than did his wife, since he felt that a longer interval would disrupt work with his patients.—Ed.]

little accented it's true, but in English, not psychoanalytic jar-
gonese.

But we here at Chestnut Lodge cannot lay claim to the
spirit of Fromm-Reichmann. Her teachings, her writing, her
training òf so many analysts has given this claim to the world
and raised the understanding of the treatment of schizophrenia
to new and greater heights.

She once had the audacity to put forth the idea, before an
august body of her peers, that the therapist should conduct the
therapy hour with a patient wherever and however it would be
most productive for the patient—even if it meant forgoing the
hallowed couch to go walking with the patient, or, if need be,
to go swing through the trees with the patient. I haven't yet
seen anyone swing through the trees here at Chestnut Lodge,
at least, not any of the patients, but it is certainly not an uncommon sight to see patient and therapist strolling the grounds,
sharing a Coke in front of the Kiosk, or walking into town
during the patient's therapy hour.

Another important legacy Fromm-Reichmann left us is the
awareness of the value of allowing the patient to move forward
at his or her own pace. This is not always the pace that we
therapists would like to feel we have motivated or have the
power to produce. She was always mindful and sensitive to the
fact that the patient, too, has his own timetable and cannot, and
in most cases should not, try to conform to the therapist's need
for a more rapid recovery.

Most important of all, Fromm-Reichmann never treated
a sick person—she treated the sickness within a person.

As a much younger doctor stationed at Bethesda Naval
Hospital, I was privileged to attend Fromm-Reichmann's discussion groups and lectures here at her cottage and at the Institute. Needless to say, she, and that other gentle giant, Dexter
Bullard, Sr., left a deep mark on my identity as a psychotherapist.

In an earlier paper of mine, "Some Considerations Regarding Psychoanalytically Oriented Psychotherapy," I laid out
my observations regarding the general techniques of therapy
at Chestnut Lodge. At that time I had been retired from the
navy and on the staff of Chestnut Lodge for seventeen years.

Now, five years later, I still hold those observations to be both valid and viable.

I feel it appropriate now to reiterate just a few of those observations—and, at my age, I feel it perfectly acceptable to be repetitious, at a time like this!

1. I always insist on obtaining a detailed history of the patient *from* the patient with both of us understanding from the start that this history, or the memory of it, will be modified and sometimes radically changed as the work we do together progresses and we *both* learn more about the situation as viewed by the patient.

2. I feel that seeing the type of patients we have here at Chestnut Lodge four times a week is simply not enough and I therefore schedule at least five appointments, and more often than not, six or seven appointments each week. Too often much of the patient's difficulties stem from experiencing, or feelings of experiencing, abandonment or desertion early in life. For the therapist to disappear three out of seven days of the week is simply too much of a rerun of the patient's early, disruptive memories.

3. I make it a point always to speak plain English with the patient. By the time a patient reaches Chestnut Lodge, he has learned all the technical jargon there is to spout from previous therapists and his own readings. It is simply too easy for both patient and therapist to get caught in the subtle trap of "out-jargoning" each other, thus losing the humanity involved only to be left with a cold, dry case history of an ongoing illness.

4. I believe we must always try to find some area, however small, of health within the patient and begin our work from that point, helping it to nurture and grow, like a healthy garden choking out the weeds and undergrowth. In that way, with careful nourishment and encouragement, that small nucleus of health will grow and finally take over for a much stronger, healthier emotional state.

5. I am always mindful of the other twenty-three hours in the patient's day—all grist for the mill, as we so often say. A case in point is the fact of the tremendous role other members of the Chestnut Lodge staff play in the well-being or sometimes,

sad to say, the ill-being of the patients during those twenty-three hours.

6. The last observation I shall present again touches on the pace with which we must learn to approach each individual patient. Their escape into psychosis takes many separate forms. Some descend into a hell of pain and uncontrollable fear and panic. Another flees into a world of escapism and reality distortion, and so on.

To return to the reason we are gathered here today, I would like to mention the work of Elaine Morgan, *The Descent of Woman*, published in 1972. In this thesis she puts forth her theory as to why the human female is the only mammillary species to have a menopause. She hypothesizes that the reason for this fact is that, before the written word, women were the fountains from which knowledge and lore poured. Mother Nature, therefore, protected her from bearing children later in life in order to preserve this fount of knowledge upon which the tribe or clan depended for its survival. What leaves helped heal a wound? What herbs helped lower an elevated temperature? She had learned all this from her predecessors and then passed it on to the next generation.

To me the essence of Frieda Fromm-Reichmann epitomizes the theory of Morgan. Although she never had a child of her own, her love of mankind, her love and excitement of exploring and learning, her all-encompassing drive to help us all live life to our fullest potential certainly could be interpreted as her inspiration as the mother figure of our tribe.

For Frieda was *indeed* a fount of knowledge: a refiner of past, present, and future exploration into that mystical thing we call the human mind. To her we owe much. She has brought our "tribe" and our work out of the misty shadows and shed light.

As I deliver this paper I will have just passed my seventy-seventh birthday, a venerable age indeed. An age when a little cynicism, weariness, and lack of enthusiasm should be perfectly acceptable—even welcome. However, before leaving on my vacation, during which I compiled this paper (whenever the blackjack tables were closed), I reread many of Frieda Fromm-Reichmann's papers—and they renewed me—excited me!

There is still so much to learn, still so much to explore and discover! Still so much excitement ahead!

To again quote myself from an earlier paper, "Prognosis Hopeless" (1966), A Sequel (1977), I first quoted Socrates who said, "It's time to go, the slow runners are catching up." I then revised the quote to say, "Welcome, all ye slow runners. It is not time to go. We are holding out in all directions with loving arms, and inviting—come on in. The water is fine."

Here and now I shall have the audacity to put forth my idea of what Frieda Fromm-Reichmann must now be exclaiming to her friend and mentor Dexter Bullard, Sr., "Mein Gott im Himmel! Why all this lollygagging? Let us all get on with our work, there are still mountains to be climbed, still so much to do!"

Prognosis: Hopeless (1966); A Sequel (1977)

This article is a brief capsule presentation and an attempt to present a situation in which a person was admitted to Chestnut Lodge in horrible, terminal, physical and mental condition.[1] Her diagnosis indicated chronicity, with death to follow permanent institutionalization for custodial care. The prognosis was hopeless. After two years, however, this person was well on the road to recovery.

At the October 1966 Chestnut Lodge Symposium, I presented a brief paper entitled "Prognosis: Hopeless." This presentation in a way is a follow-up report—the same patient, and the same conclusions that I reached then. Those conclusions in 1966 were mentioned briefly in some eight ideas why hopelessness in a particular patient changed to hope. I repeated the question "Why did this particular patient improve?" at the end of the presentation; and, my answer then, and now, is: I do not know. Today, twelve years later, same patient, same question, and same final answer. She is now seventy-seven years old. This is a person who defied our objective criteria. The question is: Why?

[1]Permission to reprint this article has been obtained from *The Journal of the National Association of Private Psychiatric Hospitals*, where it first appeared in 10:22–27, 1978.

Brief Case History

At the age of sixty, this woman was hospitalized in a general hospital elsewhere in "horrible" physical and mental condition. She was terribly emaciated. For about two to four years, she had been hopelessly addicted to morphine, barbiturates, and other drugs; she was consuming on many days, a quart of sherry, plus a fifth of scotch. For days, weeks, she had been semicomatose, incontinent, constantly belligerent, agitated, abusive, suicidal, and confused. Large gangrenous, decubitus ulcers developed over the sacrum and ankles. Her ninety-plus-year-old husband was dying.

During that hospitalization, attempts were made to improve her nutritional condition and to clear up the decubitus ulcers. These attempts included three major surgical skin grafting procedures. Her husband died. She remained addicted, uncooperative, suicidal, and hopeless. Institutionalization was recommended for permanent custodial care until her death. The treatment suggested was prefrontal lobotomy; she might then be a more cooperative and more comfortable vegetable.

Her major past medical and surgical history included a cerebral vascular accident (embolus in a branch of the left middle cerebral artery), bilateral mastoidectomies, a total thyroidectomy, and the recent major skin grafting procedures.

On admission to Chestnut Lodge, she appeared to belong to a medical, surgical, emergency unit. This opinion was openly expressed by many of us, including her unit administrator, her social worker, and myself as her therapist. An outstanding example of our feelings was the opinion expressed by one esteemed colleague: "The only reason she is admitted here is because her family has enough money to pay the bills here. Our facilities, our abilities should be reserved for those who are not obviously so hopeless." Her chief nurse said, "God damn it, what is she doing here. She should be in a general hospital. She will be dead before we get back to work tomorrow."

The patient herself shared this hopeless feeling. For weeks, she had desperately attempted to join her dead husband. For weeks after arrival here, she pleaded to be permitted to die among friends, "Not in a nut house being stared at by a stone-faced beady-eyed head-shrinker." Her family also shared her hopelessness; they refused, however, to transfer her despite her threats and pleas.

"It Can't Be. It's Too Good To Be True"

Six months after admission, this patient's physical condition was excellent. All ulcers were healed, her weight was normal. No drugs, except replacement hormones and a digitalis preparation, were administered. No alcohol was consumed. Therapy was moving along. She eventually became an outpatient. In 1966, she was about to become a private patient. The best summary comes from her social worker, "It can't be. It's too good to be true."

Why this improvement? A partial answer perhaps can be found in the ever-present dilemma of the diagnosis-prognosis complex. An illustrative example comes from Harry Stack Sullivan (1955), "It is well known among physicians that all persons suffering from tuberculous menningitis die. A patient at a hospital, so diagnosed by three outstanding internists and confirmed by the laboratory, recovered. The internists became unhappy about their diagnosis." Another example derives from my own experience when I was considerably younger and was able under oath to testify in courtmartial with certain and objective authority that a person with a certain diagnosis had a hopeless prognosis. "What," asked the opposing counsel, "if the patient recovers?" "Then," said I, "the diagnosis was wrong."

"It can't be." Objectively that is, it can't be.

But it is.

I do not propose in this article to attempt to describe any details of our work together, of our early interactions together, nor to discuss in any detail further personal clinical data concerning the patient. She was seen five to seven times weekly. There were many staff discussions and conferences concerning her care and treatment programs, but all of this is not an unusual procedure at Chestnut Lodge.

Why the Improvement?

The following are a number of ideas and thoughts that have occurred to me and which may have played a part in this patient's improvement; many of them are related to each other and are not mentioned in order of their obvious importance:

1. What about the challenge to us? Everyone else had given up, had turned down admission, except for custodial and/or a prefrontal lobotomy. This may have played some role, at least it certainly enhanced our feelings of omnipotence and polished our image. However, this could not be unique to this particular patient. In a sense, this challenge is a factor surrounding almost every patient admitted or transferred to Chestnut Lodge. For example, another patient admitted here was assigned to me with a history of repeated hospitalization, seven courses of electroshock therapy, intensive therapy elsewhere, repeated courses of drug therapy including practically all known drugs, many then known only by an experimental number. This type of challenge is about us here all the time.

2. The burden of expectation. This was not present in the usual sense with this person, particularly in comparison to other patient situations. I feel that goals or expectations are a burden to the patient, to the therapist, to everyone. In this patient, this burden did not seem to be present. She was expected to die.

3. This hopeless patient did something to our therapeutic roles. I speak only for myself in this regard, but for me, a psychiatrist, a psychoanalyst, it gave me a chance once again to be a "real" M.D. I found it surprisingly easy to recover certain neuroanatomical details that would tell me the lesion-producing bilateral homonymous hemianopsia or the diagnostic symptoms and findings of auricular fibrillation, both of which this patient had; and, I reviewed the use of digitalis and diuretic medications. Furthermore, during the withdrawal period from her morphine, the use of a synthetic preparation called Dolophine stimulated some reading that I have not done seriously for a considerable period of time.

4. Hope in a hopeless situation. It has occurred to me that in a situation that is objectively, completely, and totally hopeless, subjectively there is hope. An example: John Nardini (1952) has written several papers regarding his own experiences as a prisoner of war of the Japanese during World War II. I quote from his papers, plus some personal communication from him:

For three and one half years, there was wearisome sameness of deficiency of food; there was physical misery and disease; squalid living conditions; constant fear and despair; horrible monotomy completely unrelieved by pleasurable interludes; inadequate clothing and cleansing facilities; temperature extremes; and physical abuse. Disease was abundant, treatment was totally inadequate. To treat in a bamboo shack, a ward of 100 critically ill men, sick with malaria, dysentery, beriberi, pellagra, scurvy, wounds, and so forth—the drug armamentarium to treat these 100 critically ill men consisted of several quinine pills, six aspirin pills, and general amounts of Lydia Pinkham's vegetable compound, and Dr. Carter's pink pills for pale people. Occasionally, an individual would develop a depressive reaction under these circumstances in which he would lose interest in himself and his future, which was reflected in a quiet or sullen withdrawal from the group, filth of the body and clothes, trading of food for cigarettes, behavior inviting abuse from the Japanese guards, and an attitude of not giving a damn, or what's the use. If this attitude was not met with firm resistance, death inevitably and quickly resulted.

Objectively, therefore there was no hope; the situation was hopeless. Subjectively—question. The work of Engel et al. (1967) suggests that when a person perceives his life's situation as hopeless, and that he is hopeless, this is of prime etiological significance, not only in the so-called psychosomatic diseases, but also in development of all organic disease. "It Can't Be"—objectively, that is, it can't be.

5. Diagnostic and prognostic data are based on history obtained as objectively as possible, plus other relevant objective information. From all these, we arrive at an objective diagnosis and prognosis, and hopefully an objective treatment program. As scientists we must be objective, we must deal with reality, not the unreal; with facts, not fantasies.

The Scientific Approach

If we could somehow measure speed, dosage, number of trial events necessary for extinction of a conditioned reflex; if we could collect enough history, then we could come up with a scientific law like the one that governs the fall of an apple à la Newton—S = 1/2 G/T² Except that the "objective scientists" did not stop there; the "scientists" we attempt to emulate have gone beyond this. Consider the laws of behavior of light, which may be considered waves, or particles, or both. And, consider the laws of thermodynamics and Einstein's most famous equation: E = MC²; that is, energy, E, and the mass, M, are related, and that the relationship between the two is, of all things, the speed of light squared. We seem to have gotten ourselves stuck with a philosophy that if you can't measure, codify, computerize, or make a scientific law out of it, then forget it.

Objective scientific laws are based on repeated histories. The results are averages. They are merely statistical. All of them have elements or probability of unpredictability. It was a physicist who "discovered" that laws apply to masses and not to the individual molecule or atom, or what have you. Greater detail regarding these concepts may be found in Joseph Wood Krutch's *The Measure of Man* (1954).

Hopelessness Becomes Hope

With the individual—be it atom, molecule, horse race, or person—and with this patient, subjectivity becomes the reality. And this I cannot measure. What cannot be true—the untrue—becomes the true; the unreal, the real; the fantasy, the fact. Hopelessness becomes hope. Or did it? It seems to me that the items I viewed as untrue, unreal, as fantasy and hopelessness, were links in my own chain to the scientific approach. All of these concepts involve reality-unreality, the objective-subjective dichotomy; the hope-hopelessness split; the psyche-soma separation.

What is this scientific approach? This primary task? To discover laws? What is such a law? To attempt to make some sort of order out of things is an understandable goal or primary task. This leads me to arrive at some diagnosis, and this leads me to writing a prognosis. A prognosis? In our profession, prognosis is a future biography for the patient and the future autobiography for each of us. When these future biographies and future autobiographies are hopeless, what happens? With prisoners of war (Nardini's papers), they frequently died and often without sufficient physical reason. In the hopeless concentration camp situation add what Menninger speaks of as hope, with a capital "H," and one sees the kind of hope that led prisoners to make a workable X-ray machine.

In the case of this patient, someone, apparently, did not get the word. Some had other future biographies and future autobiographies different from hers, from her family's, and from most of us.

And heaven help us when a set of biographies with hope collides with a set of hopeless future biographies.

For example, about six months after admission, the patient's prognosis had changed from hopeless to an extremely favorable one. In other words, we had rewritten her future biography. She had a future autobiography. All of us had changed our own future autobiographies, that is, to include her in our lives for some time to come.

At this point, her son visited for the first time. This visit was a disaster. The situation was similar to a man, erroneously reported dead for five years, who arrives home much alive to find his wife remarried, with new babies, his business and his family in other hands. The situation requires some kind of updating and revamping of all the future biographies and autobiographies of the persons concerned. In our patient, there were her son and his wife and their children, her daughter, her daughter's husband, and their children. Even today, we still encounter a strong and strikingly rejecting emotional reaction to this changed biographical and autobiographical tale with a future, that is, with her alive.

In 1966, I ended the paper as follows: At the beginning, I asked the question "Why did this patient improve?" and I answered objectively "I don't know." Subjectively, I've tried to put into words that which probably cannot be verbalized.

In December 1966, the patient became a private patient, and in June 1968, she was discharged from treatment. Since that time, for approximately nine years, she has returned to this area twice a year for a week at a time. The purpose of these visits, usually held in November and May and lasting from six to nine days, is to have daily sessions with me. She and I meet at regularly scheduled appointments, seven times a week, and during these periods she is checked physically by an internist and a cardiologist in this area. She spends the greater part of her time in her former winter home in Florida on the mid-gulf coast, works as a volunteer with patients on a small emergency care psychiatric unit in a general hospital, and is active in other community affairs. She travels extensively, has made several trips to Africa on tenting safaris, has traveled to most of the European countries, and has traveled in the South Pacific, Indonesia, and Australia.

Every Thanksgiving I receive a personal note from her. The following will give some flavor:

> Dear Dr. Thompson:
> You have, I suspect, gathered that I'm not addicted to fan letters—that after hearing a commentator speak of counting our blessings and being thankful, I just couldn't let this Thanksgiving go by without letting you know how truly grateful and thankful I am to and for you, and the job you are doing. Having someone I can talk to and who I feel is really interested in me—all I have been and all I hope to be is an entirely new and very wonderful experience. In short, I have so much to be thankful for and you and your listening ear are at the top of my long list. With very real affection, [signed by the patient].

Why, what, how is this patient, now seventy-seven years, living a remarkably active, and in many ways very constructive, life despite her auricular fibrillation, the residuals of a stroke, her bilateral progressive deafness, for which she has a hearing aid—why, how?

Acceptance of Aging and the Aged

I am not going to belittle the fact that she has financial security, but I do not consider her financial security to be the entire answer. Consider Howard Hughes.

I would emphasize her and my acceptance of aging and the aged, with loss of relatives, peers, and friends through deaths and disease. It seems to be that with the aging patient, the consideration of the separation anxieties is even more important than our usual considerations with patients much younger. This is so obvious to me, that I shall simply mention it as being even more important than in the younger age group.

Handling and coping with losses not only of friends and relatives but also losses of bodily functioning, such as hearing, the ability to accomplish locomotion as easily and skillfully as previously, the ability to handle one's self in airports, on airplanes, in buses, on highways—all these require adjustments equally as difficult as graduating from high school, graduating from college, or being promoted. Yet there are tremendous rewards in working with these elderly individuals, even though many of us tend to assign them to nonroles and consider that they should be put on the shelf to make room for the younger aged group.

Unfortunately, the greatest hazard of the elderly is inactivity and isolation. The disengagement from activity, the disengagement from others was prevented in this patient by an insistence by all of the possible activities that she was capable of.

I would like to quote from Elaine Morgan's *The Descent of Woman* (1972) on the functions of the aging and aged individual:

> After Homo became Sapiens, age itself brought honor. One of the most vital factors in the human evolutionary success was the power to accumulate knowledge, to profit not only from personal experience, but from the experience of others, even of others long dead. Before the invention of writing, this was made possible only by the long life and memory of older members of the tribe. When something unprecedented happened—a flood, an epidemic, a plague of locusts—old men and women who had seen it all before could look back 50 or 60 years and "prophesy." "The water will rise no further than that rock" or "many will sicken, but few will die" or "if you do this, it will be of no avail."

Today, things do change so fast that the experience of the last generation is increasingly irrelevant, and the bottom has dropped out of the market for venerable sages of either sex in a certain way.

Menopause is yet another of those biological phenomena, unique to our species, that seem perfectly easy to explain until you start thinking about them. The obvious explanation of the menopause is that after a certain age it became more dangerous and harmful to a woman to conceive, bear, and raise children; therefore the benevolent forces of evolution protect her against this danger by making conception impossible. But this is not the way things work. The forces of evolution have no interest in benevolence toward the individual. Gestation and nurturance may become equally harmful and debilitating for an aging chimpanzee or an aging gorilla, or, for that matter, an aging cow; but in no other species is a female biologically compelled to retire from these duties in order to prolong a serene and untrammeled old age.

The only way of accounting for the evolution and the emergence of the menopause in women is by the assumption that the tribe as a whole, not merely the individual, derives some benefit from the presence of those females who although sterile live to a ripe and healthy old age. In some way or other, and in a way that applies to no other species that we know of, grannies were good for them.

An explanation of this can only be found in their function as repositories of wisdom, and especially as it relates to their particular craft—the care of the young. The best way of treating, for example, a child with a broken leg could only be discovered by trial and error. And, in the case of such infrequent hazards, only someone of a long memory would be likely to recall a time when it was handled rightly and another time when it was handled wrongly, compare the results, and draw the inference. True, there were men around, not driven to an early grave by childbearing, but their attention tended to be concentrated on other concerns. Old women were repositories of child lore, as old men were repositories of hunting lore; so it was adaptive for the species that females should not continue childbearing to the point where it would have drastically shortened their lives. Any group in which a menopausal mutation occurred and became established would be more fitted to survive than in groups in which this had not occurred.

It is nonsense to pretend that the aged should be ostracized and neglected. It is true that at present things are in a state of flux: they are confused and the aged are as confused about their role in the present as are the adolescents. If we, who are in the geriatric group, feel trapped or disenchanted by the status quo, we might remember James Thurber's answer: "We are all disenchanted."

Conclusion

It seems to be that as far as the so-called geriatric population is concerned, *homo sapiens* has the ability to utilize the abilities, the qualities, the ingeniousness that need not be hidden simply because of passing years. We may feel a little odd for a few generations because we are not accustomed to living with so many over sixty-five alive humans, but the human race has passed more violent vicissitudes than this and has survived. The human is still the most miraculous of the creatures ever made, or the earth ever sprawned.

Regarding the role of the aging and the aged, the words of Bertram Russell, "To love is wise—to hate is foolish," seem appropriate. Any damage it might do to the hated is nothing to compare to the corrosive effect it has on the hater; so, hating aging, and hating the aged, is of no useful purpose.

Socrates, in preparing to drink the hemlock and refusing all possible assistance to prolong his life, said, "It's time to go—the slow runners are catching up." Today, 2376 years later, I revise that remark with the following: Welcome, all ye slow runners. It is not time to go. We are holding out in all directions with loving arms, and inviting—come on in. The water is fine.

References

Engel, G. L., Wolff, H., & Hinkle, J. (1967), A psychological setting of somatic disease. *Proc. Roy. Soc. Med.*, 60:553–555.

Krutch, J. W. (1954), *The Measure of Man.* New York: Grosset & Dunlop.

Morgan, E. (1972), *The Descent of Woman.* New York: Stein & Day.

Nardini, J. N. (1952), Survival factors in American prisoners of war of the Japanese. *J. Amer. Med. Assn.*, 109:241–248.

Sullivan, H. S. (1955); *The Collected Works of Harry Stack Sullivan*. ed. H. Perry & M. Gawel. New York: Norton.
Thompson, S. V. (1966), Prognosis: hopeless. Chestnut Lodge Symposium, Rockville, MD.

PART III
PSYCHOANALYSIS OF NONHOSPITALIZED PATIENTS

14

BORDERLINE PSYCHOPATHOLOGY AS REVEALED BY THE PATIENT'S (A) PAUSES AND (B) UNGRAMMATICAL WORD ORDER

HAROLD F. SEARLES, M.D.

In 1949, when I was in prospect of going to Chestnut Lodge as a psychiatric resident, Frieda Fromm-Reichmann had a legendary, international reputation as possessing a kind of awesomely superhuman, inborn intuition in treating schizophrenic patients, although I am sure she would have scoffed at such a view of herself. Parenthetically, my years of work on the staff while she was still here—including participation in her research project concerning intuitive processes in the psychotherapy of schizophrenic patients (Fromm-Reichmann, 1955)—only deepened my own respect for her intuitiveness.

But to go back again to when I was in prospect of coming here, my two years of experience as an army psychiatrist (including three months of training at Pilgrim State Hospital on Long Island, probably one of the largest mental hospitals in the world), followed by two years of experience as a psychiatrist in the V.A. Mental Hygiene Clinic in Washington, D.C., had given me some appreciation of the overwhelming challenge to psychotherapy which was constituted by the enormous numbers of schizophrenic patients who needed such treatment. I had become convinced, before coming here, that no matter how priceless were a handful of intuitively gifted teachers scattered about the world, if psychotherapy were to have any real chance of coping with the enormous social problem facing it, intuition would have to become translatable into sufficiently prosaic terms to be teachable to very large numbers of quite human-sized therapists. In the subsequent years, I wrote my papers concerning schizophrenic patients, and my more recent papers concerning borderline ones, in the spirit of this same conviction that psychotherapy with either of these two varieties of our fellow human beings is not beyond the reach of any reasonably intelligent and well-analyzed, human-sized therapist.

Both sets of data included in this paper—the patient's pauses and his use of ungrammatical word order—can be regarded as types of parapraxes. Moore and Fine (1968) define parapraxes as "Faulty acts or blunders, as in slips of the tongue or pen, or lapses in memory. Freud demonstrated in 1901 that these seemingly meaningless errors are, in fact, symptomatic acts determined by *unconscious* motives." Freud (1901) did not mention the two kinds of parapraxes—pauses and ungrammatical word order—upon which I am focusing here.

I have made a fairly diligent search of the relevant literature and have found that any other references to these two kinds of data are so scanty as not to warrant mention here. I have wondered if there is a large-scale lack of existing literature about these for the reason that these are so humdrum and ordinary a part of the daily work of any psychoanalyst or psychoanalytic therapist; but I do not believe so. I believe that the importance of these two kinds of data, of which I have been collecting clinical examples for about fifteen years, has not become widely recognized.

I shall interlard the two kinds of clinical vignettes in discussing each of the following categories of borderline psychopathology: (1) unconscious aspects of the patient's identity; (2) his unconscious time distortions, including subjectively omnipotent functioning in past and future as well as present; (3) his unconscious emotions; (4) his dissociated perceptions of other persons; and (5) his unconscious transference reactions.

Except in those infrequent instances wherein I describe my calling the patient's attention to the data in question, it can be assumed that I made no attempt at this time to interpret the material to him or her. In the final section of the paper I shall discuss briefly the matter of interpreting these parapraxes.

Unconscious Aspects of the Patient's Identity

An obese woman, speaking of a recent conversation with an office partner, evidently consciously meant to convey to me,

"I was telling her that people like me who eat a big noonday meal have to eat very little in the evening." But her actual word order was, "I was telling her that *people who eat a big noonday meal like me*[1] have to eat very little in the evening." This was my first glimpse of her unconscious identity as being, not a human being, but a big noonday meal.

Another woman, remembering a childhood incident, evidently consciously wanted to convey, "My Aunt Ethel got an Alice in Wonderland costume from a toy store for me." But the order of her actual words was, "*My Aunt Ethel got me from a toy store* an Alice in Wonderland costume." This revealed to me for the first time her unconscious identity component as not having been born as a human baby into her own parental family, but rather as being essentially a toy which had first been brought upon the family scene by Aunt Ethel.

A man who had grown up in New York City was remembering, "When I was a kid I usta be a baseball [PAUSE]—a New York Yankees baseball fan." It is typical of these "pause" vignettes that the portion of the sentence prior to the pause is said with a subtle intonation which helps to convey the unconscious meaning that it is a sentence in itself, as, in this instance, "When I was a kid I usta be a baseball."

A woman who had had two previous therapists, both female, clearly wanted to convey the idea, "I think I probably don't trust you because you are a man." But her ungrammatical word order was, "I think probably as a man I don't trust you," revealing her unconscious self image as being, herself, a man.

A man, remembering his difficulties with individuating from his mother, going off to school, and so on, said, "I walked at 21 [PAUSE] months." It sounded for all the world as though he meant 21 years, so that I surmised that, at an unconscious level, that had been the case. My 1977 paper is relevant here.

A supervisee reports, concerning a hospitalized man who

---

[1]Unless otherwise indicated, italicized words or phrases represent my emphasis. The patient's own emphasis will be indicated by [*].

recurrently is a serious suicide risk, "He said that he wants to kill himself again." To me, this had a different meaning than if the supervisee had said, "He said again that he wants to kill himself," or "He said that he again wants to kill himself." The way the supervisee actually put it, "He said that he wants to *kill himself again*," suggested to me the idea that, in the patient's unconscious experience, he does indeed kill himself again and again—a concept which I find not foreign to my own work with severely depressed borderline patients.

A woman was remembering "my fear of *getting caught as a child*." She evidently intended to express the idea of "my fear, as a child, of getting caught." But her ungrammatical word order, "My fear of getting caught as a child," provided a glimpse into her unconscious conviction, in her childhood, that to reveal oneself to be a child was a bad thing. It was apparent that even in her early childhood, she had had to try to appear to be grown up—to be an adult—in order to gain at least quasi-acceptance.

A woman who had been fired, essentially in disgrace, from an important job, was saying, "I was talking to my brother on the phone last night. I was describing *what had happened to him*, and I got very depressed." It is notable that she did not say in grammatical word order what she clearly intended consciously to convey, "I was describing to him what had happened," but instead put it, "I was describing what had happened to him." This ungrammatical word order revealed her unconsciously having gotten her introjected brother fired in disgrace. That is, in her unconscious, this had not befallen her, but was instead something which she had managed to inflict upon her brother, the object of her unconscious, jealous hatred. In a recent paper (Searles, 1985) I described that the acting out which the borderline patient does consists in his inflicting loss, deprivation, and other forms of injury upon his introjects derived in part from part-aspects of the therapist in the transference.

A woman, concerned about the—as she sees it—disturbing effect her sister's analysis is having upon the sister, says, "She's headed for a nervous breakdown, is the way I feel." This word order revealed to me her unconscious identity component as one who was herself heading for a nervous breakdown—an identity component which she was struggling to keep projected into her sister.

This is an example which was reported to me about two years ago by a supervisee whom I had helped to become aware of the significance of the two parapraxes in question. The patient, a psychiatric nurse, says after a brief pause about twenty minutes along in her session, *"I'm thinking of this schizophrenic girl that I've decided I am* [PAUSE] not helping at all on the ward, and I've decided to let someone else make the major effort with her." The part before the pause, "I'm thinking of this schizophrenic girl that I've decided I am," was said as a startlingly complete statement.

Several borderline patients have utilized, unconsciously, pauses to reveal their underlying sense of a pervasive inability to *feel*, or their nagging doubt as to whether they have any ability to really experience any *feelings*; I shall give a few examples. A man says, "I usta think I felt very guilty about not really feeling [PAUSE] very close to my eldest brother." Another man is saying, about a woman with whom he has been living for some weeks, "I don't know whether I feel [PAUSE] more of fondness or contempt for her." A married woman says, concerning a man whom she used to date before her marriage, "Bill *always** made me feel [PAUSE] in a turmoil about where I stood with him." This was said in a context of unconscious uncertainty as to whether she was *able to feel*.

During a session with a woman, I suggested to her that she has "a deep-seated impression that a girl is more attractive to the opposite sex if she is mindless, or mentally at sixes and sevens." She replied, "That's probably true. I *do** think that a *part** of me feels [PAUSE] that the ideal homemaker, to the opposite sex, is . . ." I heard in this the unconscious meaning, "I *do* think that *part* of me feels."

Several patients have utilized unconsciously, similarly, pauses to reveal their unconscious identity as not *being*—not *existing*. A man says, "I could eat ten meals a day and not be [PAUSE]—and not be full." I felt that this revealed both his unconscious sense of not being, and his eating as an unconscious attempt to *be*. Another man says, "I *would** like to be [PAUSE]—I

would like to be respected for having the courage of my convictions."

A woman is saying, "I just realized something: *I've got a
false impression of myself as being* [PAUSE]—I was going to say,
'competitive'; I *am* competitive." My relatively brief work with
this woman did not reach sufficient depth for her to become
conscious of this unconsciously expressed sense of not *being* as
a self. But later in the same session this unconscious identity
component was revealed again when she said, "This feeling I
get in the morning when I wake up, of sadness and loneliness
and depreciation, *it's because there's nobody there* [unconscious
meaning: no *self* there] to tell me what to do—and when I talk
to my older sister on the telephone, that makes me feel good,
because she tells me what to do." She reminded me of other
borderline patients who, on the way to developing a more tangible sense of existing as a self, report experiences of waking
up at night, "afraid that there's someone there," or who hear
noises in the house and are "afraid there's someone in the
house."

A man whose as-if dynamics (Deutsch, 1942; Greenson,
1958) had been explored on many occasions for many months
was saying, "I see Joanne [his new girlfriend] as hungry, and
at the moment *I'm feeling too hungry to be* [PAUSE] trying to fill
her hunger."

In completing this category of clinical examples, I shall
present vignettes which reveal a variety of other kinds of unconscious identity components.

A man who lives in a small, outlying community is reporting
that a friend was discussing with him, last evening, the friend's
plan to move to Baltimore. *"I said I couldn't imagine living*
[PAUSE] in such a large city; I'm a small-town guy." Another
man says, concerning his younger sister, *"She's one of a few people
I've ever known* [PAUSE] who seem to really enjoy being alive."

An attorney is speaking bitterly of his wife's endless recri-
minations against him. "Marie is in a class by herself. *I haven't
ever met anybody* [PAUSE]—even one of my most dissatisfied
clients, who can make you feel so worthless." I felt that his
schizoid, unconscious identity component was revealed in his
saying, unintentionally, "I haven't ever met anybody." It is ad-

ditionally significant that this was said in the closing one minute of the hour, an hour in which relatively early I had declined a request from him about a matter very important to him, such that he undoubtedly had been left feeling rejected and let down by me, and had found reason to feel that I—like all the others before me—had proved disloyal to him.

A man had learned from someone else that I had grown up in the Catskill mountains. He commented, "*I don't think I've ever known anybody* [PAUSE] who had grown up in the Catskills."

A woman is speaking of the youngest of her three daughters, a girl whom she regards as essentially mentally retarded. The patient has been, consciously, very devoted to the girl, all through the sixteen years of the girl's life, and only after a number of years of this mother's analysis has she herself started making even distant contact with her own hostile-depreciatory feelings toward this daughter. She is saying, in reference to this girl, "*I've never heard Edna* [PAUSE] speak of liking any of her teachers." On hearing the part before the pause, "I've never heard Edna," I immediately felt there to be much truth in it, as an unconscious statement complete in itself. Much later in the session, she was remembering her own having felt depreciated and largely shut out by her own mother. Similarly in the transference, it was becoming clear that her long-unconscious doubt was emerging, as to whether, in the years of our work together thus far, I had ever really heard her.

A man is saying, "I think my problem is that *I wanta live in a world* [PAUSE] where there are lots of beautiful women who are genuinely interested in my legal career." His having unconsciously expressed his desire to live in a world, and his feeling that he does not live in a world, reminds me of the innumerable instances, in our sessions, when he has tried, often by being defiant and unruly, to provoke me into imposing a reliably consistent structure upon his behavior in the sessions—as well as between sessions—to enable him, as I now see it, to "live in a world."

A woman is saying, in regard to her lover, "When I had Jim there in the apartment, *we looked like an adult* [PAUSE] couple." In her unconscious experience, she and her lover appeared to comprise one adult. This reminded me of a woman whose predominant problem was one of multiple identity. This woman, in one of her sessions, was going into detail about the striking differences between her two young sons, and said, in a philosophical tone reminding herself, "They really are two different children." I sensed this as meaning something deeper than simply a highlighting of the striking contrasts between the two boys, and I said, "You have to remind yourself that they are not one child?" to which she readily agreed, saying, "I think of them as just one—or as parts—I probably see them as parts of me."

The Patient's Unconscious Time Distortions

A man who does fiction writing was saying, "This links up with the novel I was thinking of *writing yesterday*," conveying the unconscious meaning that he could have written the whole novel yesterday, a meaning quite different from his evidently consciously intended one, which in grammatical word order would have been expressed as, "This links up with the novel I was thinking, yesterday, of writing." Another man, who makes fine furniture as a hobby, spoke of "the table I thought of *making this morning*." He had described, earlier in the session, a complex furniture project he had thought of doing, and now goes on to describe another.

A woman who paints as a major hobby has been speaking, for more than half a session, of many details of her painting activities, and says, "*Tomorrow there's a painting in Baltimore* I'd like to do" (namely, a particular scene which has intrigued her). The "Tomorrow there's a painting in Baltimore" was said as though the painting already existed. That is, I sensed that there was in her (1) a lack of differentiation between present and future time; and (2) a lack of differentiation between the image in her mind of the painting she is intending to do tomorrow, and the yet-to-be made painting in outer reality.

Another woman says, regarding a man with whom she had a sexual relationship years ago, "I'm thinking about *having an affair in the past* with Bill." This ordinary-seeming sentence is said with an intonation conveying an unconscious meaning of *being able in the present to have an affair in the past*; i.e., it is a glimpse of her yet-unresolved, unconsciously fantasied omnipotence. Had she said, "I'm thinking about having *had* an affair in the past with Bill," that meaning would not have emerged.

Another woman says, regarding her current lover with whom she has been involved for several years, "Some of my feelings about *having sex with him in the past* is feeling spent. I'm worn out, trying to please him." I sense in this the unconscious meaning that when she is having sex with him in the *present* in actuality, she is doing so, psychologically, in the *past*, and I surmise that the maintenance of this unconscious splitting helps to account for her feeling so worn out by such experiences.

A man, speaking of his hating to apologize to anyone, said, "That's why I never said, 'I'm sorry' to Mr. Perez after *I knocked him out for ten months*." His ungrammatical word order expressed his unconscious wish to injure, or conviction of having injured, Mr. Perez far more than would have been portrayed in a more grammatically correct statement, "That's why I never—for ten months—said, 'I'm sorry' to Mr. Perez after I knocked him out."

A man who was chronically preoccupied with food, and whose sessions often felt interminable to me, was saying that on the previous day, at a picnic given by his son and daughter-in-law, "They had hamburgers, and hamburgers are a treat for me—I probably haven't had a *hamburger cooked on a grill for five years*." In the transference, I had been cooking on the grill of his largely unconscious sadism for a number of years.

A woman says, at a time when she is clearly defending unconsciously against sexual feelings toward me as a mother in the transference, and is consciously preoccupied with heterosexual interests, "I've been thinking about *having sex with my husband for more than ten days*." This conveyed something far more prodigious than her conscious meaning, which in grammatical word order would have been, "I've been thinking, for more than ten days about having sex with my husband."

A man is feeling abandoned by his wife, who has been living in Mexico for several months. He fears that she doesn't want to live any longer with him, but prefers to live by herself instead, in Mexico, "because *it's where she has wanted to live in the past*." I pointed out to him that his saying, "it's where she has wanted to live in the past" means something different from "she has wanted, in the past, to live." He saw readily enough the question of whether she wants to live in the past; but he did not explore this any further. I knew that he himself had a powerful, unconscious longing to live in the past; but he was still highly resistant to recognizing this in himself.

A woman had had to undergo, in her childhood, a painful hip operation. In a session in which she was describing the previous night spent with a new man friend, she said, "I told him that *I had this operation on my hip last night.*" Her ungrammatical word order revealed that the experience with him, last night, had involved for her, unconsciously, a reliving of the painful hip operation in her childhood.

A woman who recently had returned from Buenos Aires was saying, "That reminds me of my dream in *Buenos Aires, which I still carry around in my purse.*" The ungrammatical word order in this statement revealed that unconsciously she was still carrying Buenos Aires around in her purse. The unconscious grandiosity in this reminded me of that of another borderline patient who referred to her long-standing inner conflict as to whether to settle in Washington or Chicago as being "the Washington-Chicago conflict"—said, each time, as though those two large cities (upon which so much of her conflictual feelings were projected) were at war with one another.

A woman, presently in her second marriage, says, "*I'm furious at my husband's* [PAUSE] trying to *dominate* me all the time." She was consciously referring only to her present husband; but the significantly placed pause revealed that she was furious, unconsciously, at both her husbands and that, more significantly, she was still as much married to the first one as to the current one. As regards the distortion of time, her past marriage was unconsciously not in the past, but fully in the present.

The Patient's Unconscious Emotions

In my discussion of the first category of borderline psychopathology, unconscious aspects of the patient's identity, I presented examples of various patients' unconscious experience of themselves as pervasively unable to feel anything, or as doubtful whether they had any ability to feel any emotions whatsoever.

In this category, I shall give examples of patients' dissociating one or another kind of emotion or segment of their emotional life.

A man who consciously is very devoted to his two young sons says, "I'm determined that my *sons** aren't gonna grow up [PAUSE] the way *I** grew up." A woman who consciously feels very devoted to her teen-aged daughter says, "*I don't like her*—spending so much time doing her hair; but I have to get used to that."

A middle-aged man who has never married has been dating, for some months, a woman whom he is more inclined to marry than has been the case with any others among the women he has known in many years. He is largely unaware that his pervasive rejectingness, toward all his fellow human beings, also is intensely at work in his relationship with this woman. I, too, was not aware of the intensity of this until I heard him say, concerning an experience with this woman, Martha, at a recent party, "*I didn't want her* [PAUSE] to act the way she was acting, I guess; I wanted her to be the Martha *I'm** used to."

Another man was trying to emerge from decades-long reclusiveness by having become seriously involved with a woman whom he was thinking of marrying. This was stirring up various of his borderline conflicts. Early in a session he reported a dream of nuclear warfare. Then, later in the same session, he described that, on the previous day, he had gone with his girlfriend to look at some jewelry for her. Of one ring she had liked, he had told her, "No; that looks too much like a wedding ring." He next said to me, "I know that's because *I don't want people* [PAUSE] to think that she and I are married."

A woman, speaking of an interview she had had with her employer that morning, said, "*I felt a great deal of hostility* [PAUSE] emanating from him." Her significantly placed pause gave a glimpse of the unconscious hostility which she was projecting into him.

A woman has had a succession of male friends who have tended to be alcoholic. When her current boyfriend started to have, in her opinion, one drink too many, "I told him to quit; that *I've had a gutful of people I like* [PAUSE] getting involved in drinking themselves to death." Her unconscious statement,

"I've had a gutful of people I like," revealed pervasively mis-
anthropic feelings quite beyond any which she had been exploring in the years of her analysis thus far.

A man says of his two daughters by a previous marriage,
"*They sensed that I didn't want them* [PAUSE] to have anything to
do with their mother."

A man has managed to obtain, in the course of a divorce,
custody of his three daughters. This custody is something
which, at a conscious level, he unambivalently sought, and currently cherishes. But after describing some special care he is
taking in regard to his daughters currently, he explains, "*I don't
want the custody* [PAUSE] endangered in any way."

A woman who had never married and who dated men
infrequently, having intercourse no more than a few times a
year, spent much of a session in detailing the complexities which
she found in attempts at sexual intimacy, then added, "And *sex
is really the only thing in life* [PAUSE] that is so complicated." Her
unconscious statement, that sex is really the only thing in life,
provided a glimpse into still-unexplored depths of the bleak-
ness, the depression-ridden, nature of her life, its near mean-
inglessness.

A female law school graduate had been studying, for some
months, for her bar examination, consciously wanting very
much to be successful, but unconsciously defending against
wishes to fail. She said, "I want to pass the bar very badly." I
must acknowledge, here, that it would have been only somewhat
less suspicious if she had used the grammatical word order,
"I want very badly to pass the bar."

A middle-aged man who has an administrative post in the
government was unconsciously defended against both his ruth-
less feelings toward aging subordinates and his anxiety lest his
own aging render him unable to carry on. But these matters
had not yet come upon the analytic scene, and were first hinted
at when he said, "I was thinking about *government workers on the
way out*." He had meant consciously to convey, "I was thinking,
on my way out here to the session, about government workers."

An attorney has long been involved in an unresolved, neg-
ative-oedipal relationship with his younger son, who is now
thirty years of age. The patient is still unaware both of his

fantasies of having given birth to the children, and of his wishes to be the wife of his second son. But it is significant that, in speaking of another attorney whom he had known years ago, he said, "He was married and *he had a child* and *they* weren't happily married and they eventually got divorced." The "they" seems unconsciously to refer to the man and his child (a son). This fit precisely with the patient's detailed description of a telephone conversation he had had with his younger son the previous evening, a conversation which sounded to have a strong element (as often before) of passionate homosexual love, of which the patient was still massively unaware.

A woman says, of her boyfriend whom she has been dating for several months, "He has avoided talking about *sex all the time*." There seemed an unconscious meaning, in this ungrammatical word order, of "sex all the time"—a glimpse of her having or wanting, unconsciously, sex all the time.

A man is speaking about a female colleague whose self-destructive ways of relating, in their office group, are of much conscious distress and concern to the patient. He consciously likes and admires her, and long has been trying to get her to mend her ways. He says, *"She's a woman whom I hated* [PAUSE] to see this happening to." When he said, "She's a woman whom I hated," his unconscious hatred of this woman was startlingly clear to me.

Another man says, "My wife's mother is dying and Edna, my wife's eldest sister who lives with their mother, *is too ill herself to look after* [PAUSE] their mother." His pause had revealed his unconscious urge to abandon the ill and infirm as being unworthy of being looked after—cared for—by their fellow human beings.

A woman's largely unconscious disinclination to live was expressed, unwittingly, in a context of her talking about the fact that a move which she and her husband had been planning was no longer financially feasible. She said that she was not disappointed that the purchase of the new house did not go through, for she always found various things wrong with that prospective new house. "On the other hand, it would have meant a change of area, and *I'm tired of living* [PAUSE] over there where we are, with all that traffic noise." A couple of minutes later, she was saying, "Now again it's hard to adjust to this development, that *we're going to live* [PAUSE] in this smaller house for, probably, the next five years."

Another woman, although consciously concerned about leaving a university post which she has held for some years, and unsure of her ability to succeed as a teacher in a private school, is unaware, as was I, until I heard the following statements, of her underlying fear lest her death be imminent: "*Today may be my last day* [PAUSE], I have a feeling *it may be my last day* [PAUSE] at the University. I'm somewhat uneasy about that, because I'm not sure I'll be able to survive, teaching in a private school."

The Patient's Dissociated Perceptions of Other Persons

A man was remembering that "my family was not a talkative one, in general. *Maybe as a baby my mother talked* to me a great deal; but I don't remember it." The ungrammatical word order revealed his unconscious perception of his mother as a baby. A woman, whose father had died during her teens, expressed some thought about having competed with him as regards who could be the more infuriating. A few minutes later, she was saying, "That makes me think of going to Macy's with *my father as a youngster*." Her ungrammatical word order revealed her unconscious image of her father as having been, not an adult, but a youngster.

A woman, after describing her current and long-time arguments with her mother, arguments in which both would get to shouting, then said of her father, "When I rejected *my parents as a teen-ager*, I would get into the same arguments with him." She clearly meant, "When, as a teen-ager, I rejected my parents. . . ." But her actual word order, "When I rejected my parents as a teen-ager," revealed her unconscious perception of both her parents having been a single teen-ager. I was able to hear this unconscious meaning partly because I had been sensing repeatedly, earlier in the session, that her mother had come to react, relatively early in the patient's upbringing, to the daughter as being the mother's *parent*. Also, the analysis had yielded abundant evidence that the patient's father had never matured much beyond the emotional level of a very little boy.

A woman is speaking of something which, she has come to realize, she has been hoping for from me: to make her life more soothing and comfortable for her, "in the way that I looked to *my mother as a child* to do for me." She clearly meant, grammatically phrased, "in the way that I as a child looked to my mother to do for me." But the actual word order revealed her unconscious image of her mother as having been, during the patient's own childhood, a child herself. I said nothing to the patient about this; but about twenty minutes later in the session, she was describing a recent visit to her parents, and emphasized that she now could see how like a child her mother was, and had been all along.

A man speaks of "the feeling of adoration I had for *my grandmother as a little boy*." He clearly meant, consciously, "the feeling of adoration I had, as a little boy, for my grandmother." But the ungrammatical word order revealed his unconscious image of her as a little boy. Over the years of this man's analysis, the little boy in his grandmother played a significant role in his transference perceptions of me, and in the exploration of his own confusion about his own sexual identity.

A woman was remembering that "*As a child my parents* would take me to visit my uncle." Her ungrammatical word order revealed her unconscious image of her two parents as being a single child. This was a concept new to me at the time, and I did not interpret it to her. Later in the same session, however, some corroborative data emerged: she herself noticed how she kept referring to her parents as "they"; it was becoming increasingly clear that she had been reacting to them unconsciously, all along, as being a single "they," rather than two separate individuals.

Another woman was remembering that she had felt, during her adolescence, that her parents were unaware of how much she had changed and was changing. She said, "I felt that way toward *my parents in high school*." She clearly meant, consciously, that when she had been in high school, she had felt that way toward her parents. But her ungrammatical word order, which included the phrase, "my parents in high school," revealed her unconscious attitude that it had been her parents, not she, who had been having her "own" high school experience. Introjection was prominent among this woman's unconscious defenses.

A woman was realizing how prematurely she had had, during her upbringing, to start acting as though she were an adult. She said, "I've been acting like an adult version of my father. I mean, I've learned how to be an adult by watching *my father as a child*." This word order, "by watching my father as a child," conveyed her unconscious image of her father as being a child—a child presumably himself *acting* adult; and it was partly, indeed, through her identification with her pseudo-adult father that she herself had become a pseudo-adult. Her initial, unintendedly revealing, quickly amended phrase, "an adult version of my father," had disclosed her unconscious image of him as being less than truly adult, and the ungrammatical word order of her revised statement only further confirmed the same perception of him.

Another woman speaks of not having had a relationship with her mother—and she is referring to her own whole life thus far, and is trying to understand why she feels guilty about this. "Why the hell should *I** feel so guilty? Just because *she's my mother, I guess.* She clearly meant to convey, "I guess just because she's my mother." But the actual word order, which included, "she's my mother, I guess," revealed the unconscious meaning that she is unsure whether her mother really is her mother.

A young Jewish woman says, "I had been told about *the pogroms by my parents*," which revealed a quite different unconscious meaning from the consciously intended one, "I had been told by my parents about the pogroms." The analysis was coming to plumb the depths of her paranoid grandiosity, and of her subjectively omnipotent malevolence, which involved unconscious identifications with her parents perceived as being innumerable Nazi-like mass murderers.

A middle-aged woman says, "I tend to forget *I have a brother very frequently*." She was referring to her only brother, ten years younger than herself. She clearly meant, "I tend very frequently to forget I have a brother." But the actual order of her words revealed her unconscious experience that she very frequently has a brother, but in the interims has no brother. The unconscious experience of the borderline individual typically involves much of discontinuousness of existence of himself and of other persons.

A man whose mother had died not long before he had started in therapy said, "Lately I've been wanting to know *what my mother died of again.*" It was clear that he consciously meant that lately he's been wanting again to know the cause of his mother's death, about which he had never been fully informed. But the unconscious meaning, "what my mother died of again," was conveyed to me also, and this immediately opened up a valuable realm of meaning, which I did not attempt to interpret at this time. I immediately heard this unconscious meaning as related to a dream he had reported a week previously, in which his mother was sitting at a table appearing alive, but was actually dead. I was finding data, time and again, which indicated that, in his experience during his growing up, his mother had died over and over again and had been, at such times, although physically present, psychologically dead. In the transference, there emerged much data, many times over some years of the work, which indicated that, at an unconscious level, he was experiencing me as physically present but dead.

A man's elderly father had just been hospitalized with kidney disease, and the patient feared that his father would die, and was highly aware that his own much older sister had died a few years previously. He had depended much upon his sister as being a mother figure to him. He remembered that a fire had occurred at the parental home some years before, and he had had to take care of various matters having to do with that. *"My sister was not alive at the time,"* he commented in the process of his narrative about the fire. This seemingly mundane statement conveyed the unconscious image of his sister as having been someone who was at times alive, and at other times not alive—an unconscious image consonant with his unconscious transference perceptions of me as being at times alive, and at times dead.

A woman reported that "Joe [her husband] was telling me where *he wanted to be buried last night.*" She clearly meant that "Joe was telling me, last night, where he wanted to be buried." But her ungrammatical word order, which included, "he wanted to be buried last night," revealed the unconscious image of her husband's burial as occurring not in the distant future, but last night. Both she and her husband were chronically depressed, and it is probable that both of them had unconscious longings to be buried that very night, as well as unconscious murderous wishes for this to happen to his or her partner.

A woman with prominent voyeurism and exhibitionism came to report, after much analysis, that "instead of staring at *all the men I see in the fly* [of their trousers], there's the feeling that what I have in my pubic area, these men want. . . ." The unconscious communication, "all the men I see in the fly," revealed something of both her multiple-ego functioning and her contempt toward men: she unconsciously sees many men in one fly.

Another woman remembers, of her childhood, that "sometimes when I was playing in the garage, I could *hear my mother come home through the open windows.*" She consciously meant that she could hear, through the open windows, her mother come home. But her ungrammatical word order revealed her unconscious image of her mother as coming home through the open windows. This unconscious perception of her mother reminded me of a chronically schizophrenic woman's saying of herself, after many years of psychotherapy, "I used to be an element; now I'm a person."

A woman's long-unconscious yearning to marry her father was first revealed to me when she was describing a paternal aunt's forthcoming marriage: "My Aunt Marie presented the idea of *getting married to my father.* They've always confided a great deal in one another." She clearly meant to convey, "My Aunt Marie presented to my father the idea of her getting married." But the patient's ungrammatical word order revealed her own unconscious wish, projected into her aunt, to marry the father.

A man says, "I had a dream last night about the economist *that* lives in *my building, Irwin.*" This was reminiscent to me of Winnicott's (1941) concept of the holding environment, and of my first book's (1960) discussion of every human being's struggle to differentiate between human and nonhuman.

Another man was remembering that in his childhood his

mother, in the company of her friends, used to discuss in his presence how much cuter and brighter his younger brother was than he. He said, feelingly, "*I usta hate those people my mother* [PAUSE] made friends with." Later in the session he was describing two very different behaviors on his mother's part, as though his mother had been at *least* two different persons.

A man was recalling "My father was a short man, only two or three inches [PAUSE] taller than I am." The pause revealed his unconscious scorn toward his father.

A woman was remembering, "When I was 14 I was having a heavy flow with my periods *and my mother took me* [PAUSE] to a gynecologist." I heard in this the unconscious meaning, "and my mother took me sexually." There was much corollary data from this session, and from many other sessions, to substantiate my impression.

A woman reported a dream which was indicative of sexual feelings on her part toward the eldest of her three daughters—a prominent theme for some years in her analysis. Later in the same session, she mentioned that a neighbor had been working in his yard over the weekend, "*and then he had his daughter Edith* [PAUSE] take care of the flower beds." The "and then he had his daughter Edith" was said in a tone of ending a complete statement, and conveyed the unconscious meaning that he had had his daughter Edith sexually.

A man whose negative oedipal conflicts were, for years, a major theme in his analysis was remembering, "My father used to sit at the kitchen table and say, '*Never marry a woman* [PAUSE] who has more money than you!' " The patient added, "He was very dogmatic."

A woman described her parents' having "tried to make me more perfect. *They just didn't want their girl* [PAUSE] to cause them any trouble." Through my work with various patients such as she, I have come to regard it as a general principle that such a patient unconsciously feels unwanted, feels chronically on the verge of being abandoned—a patient, that is, whose parents press him or her toward perfection. Such a patient has to manifest pseudo-adulthood very early. One chronically schizophrenic woman said, "I grew up at the age of eight."

Another woman said, while ruminating about the nature

of her relationships with people including me, "*I may be convinced that I'm the only person* [PAUSE] concerned with taking care of me." She reminded me of a borderline man whose treatment I supervised some years ago. This man revealed his previously unconscious view that, in his parental family, he himself was the only *person*, and in consequence all his later interpersonal relationships had not eroded his unconscious conviction that, in his whole experienced world, he himself had what we would call the only developed and functioning ego. Such a person is typically oriented, as a child, toward being the therapist for the family as a whole.

The Patient's Unconscious Transference Reactions

A woman says, toward the end of a morning session, "*I almost came in here this morning* planning to tell you that I'm finally going to stop this analysis." Her ungrammatical word order revealed her unconscious experience of having not actually come in here but, rather, having *almost* done so.

A man, after speaking about having read a newspaper column on popular psychology, says, "Sometimes I think it must be irritating to you that I talk about what *I'm reading all the time.*" This word order suggested that, at an unconscious level, he is reading all the time during the sessions.

Another man, who had not had a session scheduled for the previous day, said, "I was dreading *coming here yesterday,*" and then noticed the word order of his statement and corrected it himself, saying, "Yesterday I was dreading coming here today," but did not go on to explore this—to see, that is, what associations he might have to the statement in its previous word order. It is typical of borderline patients (as well as other highly resistive patients) simply to "correct" such things as this, or the more common slips of the tongue, without reacting to these as valuable opportunities for self-discovery. I heard the way he first expressed it as revealing his unconscious conviction that time places no barriers upon his omnipotence, that he can do things in the past and the future as well as in the present.

A man who had been in analysis, four times a week, for several years, had been here on the previous day when he now began today's session with, "It seems like ages since *I've been here, for no good reason at all.*" He clearly meant, consciously, to convey the experience, "It seems, for no good reason at all, like ages since I was here yesterday." But his actual word order gave expression to his unconscious conviction that he has been here, in these sessions all through the years, for no good reason at all.

A man says, slowly and thoughtfully, in reference to his previous analysis with a male analyst, whom I shall call Bennett, "I was able to talk about *sex with Bennett.*" This clearly gave expression to his unconscious fantasy that he had actually had sex with Bennett, a meaning quite different from what he evidently intended to convey: "I was able to talk with Bennett about sex." A sexually repressed, unmarried young woman ways, "I still don't feel able to talk about *sex in here.*" She clearly meant, consciously, "I still don't feel able to talk, in here, about sex." But her word order revealed her unconscious fantasy that sex is going on in here. I found other evidence, from other sessions, to indicate also that, at an unconscious level, *talking about* sex in here was not differentiated from the idea of *actually having* sex.

Another woman protests, when her female therapist tries to explore the former's resistance to speaking about sexual matters, "To talk about *sex here* would be crude and rude." The patient clearly meant, consciously, to express the view, "To talk here about sex would be crude and rude." But the word order of her statement invoked the reality of "sex here."

Still another woman said, "My sister never used to be able to talk about *sex with her analyst,*" revealing an unconscious meaning quite different from the consciously intended one, "My sister never used to be able to talk with her analyst about sex."

A man says, "I just had a thought of *my sucking your penis again.*" This was said with the impact of his unconscious conviction that he actually had sucked my penis in the past. His conscious thought, grammatically expressed, "I just had a thought, again, of my sucking your penis," would have had a far milder effect upon me.

Another man says, "I feel guilty about complaining so much about *my wife here.*" He clearly meant, consciously, "I feel guilty about complaining so much, here, about my wife." But the word order of his statement, containing the phrase, "my wife here," gave a glimpse of the extent to which his conscious complaints about his wife contained displacements of his unconscious dissatisfaction with me as his wife, in the transference.

A man who has been sexually dissatisfied in his second marriage, as he had been in his first one, says, "I was looking forward to *coming more* today than I had been in months." He consciously meant, evidently, to express the thought, "I was looking forward more to coming to the session today than I had in months." But his ungrammatical word order expressed the unconscious meaning that he had been looking forward to *coming more*—having in the session today more full and prolonged orgasm than, at an unconscious level, the orgasms he experienced in the usual sessions.

A woman says, "I know you're teaching at Georgetown Hospital through my Uncle Ed, who's on the staff there." She consciously meant, "I know, through word from my Uncle Ed, who's on the staff at Georgetown Hospital, that you're teaching there." But she unconsciously fantasied my teaching through her Uncle Ed; this was a glimpse of her unconscious view of me as able omnipotently to control other people as being essentially robots.

A man says, "I read the article you wrote about transitional phenomena this morning." This ungrammatical word order suggested to me two unconscious fantasies on his part: (1) that I had written the article that very morning; and (2) that transitional phenomena were occurring that morning.

A woman is ruminating about "whether I should read *the books you've written during my analysis*." Her analysis had begun less than a year previously. Had she put it, "whether I should read, during my analysis, the books you've written," this would have been unremarkable. But her word order gave a glimpse into her unconscious conviction that my books had been written during the year, thus far, of our work, and had exclusively to do with her.

A man says, "I was thinking about talking with you about it on the way over." He clearly meant, "I was thinking, on the way over here, about talking with you about it." But the word order revealed that, while on the way over here, he had been talking with me about it. As is typical of many borderline patients, at this stage in his therapy he had a much more fond, intimate, and comfortable relationship with his internalized therapist than he did with me in outer reality, giving me to feel, at times, appreciably jealous of the Dr. Searles in his mind.

Another man says, midway through a session, "When I told you *I dreamed the last time I was here* about my three sisters." He clearly meant, "When I told you, the last time I was here, that I had dreamed about my three sisters. . . ." But the word order in which he actually said it, "I dreamed the last time I was here" revealed his unconscious lack of full reality feeling—his at times not knowing, when he is here, whether he is dreaming or awake.

A man whose fiancée is in analysis with another analyst says, "I think I must be angry with Marie because she has not discussed *a problem we're having with her analyst*, and that makes me feel I'm only tangential to Marie's life." He clearly meant to say, of Marie, that "she has not discussed with her analyst a problem we're having." But the actual word order, including the phrase, "a problem we're having with her analyst," gave unconscious expression to his determination to dominate every aspect of his fiancée's life, including her choice of analyst. I had long known him to be domineering.

An attorney who has, as one of his clients, a psychoanalyst's son, said, "Then yesterday when I was involved in a discussion with the man who is *the son of the analyst that I see*." He clearly meant to convey, "Then yesterday when I was involved in a discussion with the man whom I see, who is the son of an analyst." But his actual word order gave expression to his unconscious fantasy that his client is my son—that is, "the son of the analyst that I see."

A man, upon return from a rare visit to his parents in California, reported many details of this visit which, at a conscious level, had gone largely unsatisfactorily, and concluded this account by saying, "I was kinda glad to *leave in some ways*." He clearly meant that "I was kinda glad, in some ways, to leave." But his actual word order gave expression to his unconscious feeling that he had *left* there only in some ways—that, in other ways, having to do with the more cherished, unreported aspects of the visit, he was still there in California. Two of my previous papers (1982, 1985) have had to do with borderline patients' difficulties with integrating losses.

A woman says that she is realizing how many things she refrains, in daily life, from doing "because I don't wanta talk about having done it *here**; for example, last night I masturbated, with a fantasy of sucking Al's penis; Al is that man whom I met two days ago." She clearly meant, "I don't wanta talk *here** about having done it." But her actual word order included the phrase, "I don't wanta talk about *having done it here*," which revealed her unconscious fantasy of having done it, in actuality, here.

Another woman, who had become deeply involved in negative oedipal conflicts in the transference, said, "As I was driving over from Virginia to this session, I was having a *passionate desire for my mother* to die." She clearly meant, consciously, a passionate desire for her mother's death—her mother as personified, of course, by me in the transference. But although she had become relatively well able, rather long ago, to find access to her death wishes toward her mother, she was still having to maintain largely dissociated her sexual desire for her mother.

Another woman says, "I doubt that you've ever had a patient [PAUSE] before who was as talented in music as I am." Typically, the part before the pause was said fully as though she were making a complete statement, "I doubt that you've ever had a patient."

A man who had been in analysis for several years was speaking of his wife's trying to get him to promise her that he would not reveal, in his analysis, anything about a recent, violent argument they had had. He said, *"Really it's absurd for her to think that I would be in analysis* [PAUSE] and make no mention of that argument." This patient manifested typical "as-if" dynamics, and I sensed his unconscious conviction that although he might behave, for years, *as if* he were in analysis, it was absurd for his wife to think that he would *really* be in it.

A woman who had been in analysis for several years said, "This morning while I was playing golf I was trying to imagine what it would have been like to be in analysis [PAUSE] with a much younger analyst." In this regard similar to the just-mentioned man, she was revealing her unconscious conviction that she had just been making the motions, over the years, of being in analysis—that she had been it only to outward appearances. I found notable the unconscious contempt which would have it that I am totally incapable of fostering a genuinely analytic situation.

A man is describing a recent experience of attending a rock concert at the Washington monument. He says, "I doubt that *you've** ever *seen** people [PAUSE] like the people who go to rock concerts," and he went on to give many details concerning the appearance and behavior of those people, toward whom he had found himself having feelings of intense contempt throughout the concert. His unconscious statement, "I doubt that *you've* ever *seen** people," shed new light upon an aspect of his transference to me, as being a mother *so* filled with contempt toward people as to give one reason to doubt that I had ever actually *seen* people.

Another man says, "If you're in [meaning, "If one is in"] contact with people [PAUSE] a great deal of the day, you get many more chances to despise people than to admire them, don't you?" This was the first indication that he, who had been in analysis with me for several years, had unconscious doubt that I was in contact with people—a doubt which was part of his yet-unresolved transference to me as being his reclusive and fantasy-ridden father.

A woman who had driven by my house said, in the next session, "I wouldn't mind living in a house like you [PAUSE] do." Her unconscious image of me as being a house emerged from this statement. In the work with borderline patients at such a phase of the transference evolution, I usually find it antitherapeutic to endeavor to do much of verbalized sharing, with the patient, of my own feelings and fantasies. At a moment when the patient is reacting unconsciously to the therapist as being an essentially nonhuman holding environment, any sign of aliveness on the therapist's own part is reacted to negatively by the patient.

A man had been in analysis for a number of years when, in the opening minutes of a session, he spoke of having felt jealous, in my waiting room that day, when he had seen my previous patient, a woman, looking back at me with a friendly smile as she came out of my office. He said, "I don't think I've *ever** left this office [PAUSE] with that sort of expression on my face." As is typical of these clinical vignettes involving pauses, he said the part before the pause, "I don't think I've *ever** left this office," emphatically, as though making a complete statement. This unconscious communication from him was a revelation to me, for I now realized that his seemingly incessant, recurrent threats, year after year, to leave treatment, were determined in part by his deeper-lying doubt that he had *ever* succeeded in leaving this office.

Another man says, "I've looked *enough** into *myself** now [PAUSE] to see that I'm always trying to please whomever is making any demand upon me." I felt momentarily startled, and even a bit shaken, at the hammer-of-Thor, confrontational decisiveness in his tone in saying, "I've looked *enough** into *myself** now." I sensed an unconscious meaning, on the part of this man who typically projected, year after year, most of his own demandingness: "I've looked *enough* into *myself* now. From *now* on, I'm going to look into *you!*"

A man is telling me of his irritation at my having dozed briefly during the previous day's session (something which has occurred in my work with many patients during the past several years). He comments that, in his telling me of his irritation and dissatisfaction with me in that regard, he is not afraid that I will be angry. "*I don't think you have any reason to be* [PAUSE] angry." I had been familiar for years with his severe demands upon me, and with knowing that I fell far short of his expectations; but his angry scorn for me had unconscious depths I had not seen before: "I don't think you have any reason to be."

Discussion

While I cannot claim originality in the portrayals of these various realms of the borderline patient's unconscious life, I do hope and believe that these many clinical vignettes convey an unusually rich picture of the multiplicity of his identity-bearing introjects; his nondifferentiation between human and nonhuman, and between animate and inanimate, in his internal and/or external worlds; the myriad distortions in his unconscious perceptions of himself and others; his unconscious use of projective and/or introjective identification; the impoverishment of his interpersonal relations and of his emotional life; his unconscious perception of himself as not existing; his nondifferentiation between himself and other persons; his nondifferentiation between fantasies, on the one hand, and perceptions of external reality on the other hand; the distortions in his experience of time; and his myriad difficulties in integrating loss experiences.

As I have indicated, I do regard as an original contribution the highlighting of the significance of the two parapraxes which I have described. The most extensive reference system available to me, namely, the Chicago Institute for Psychoanalysis' computer-indexed file of psychoanalytic publications, reported that nothing was found in their indexing system under the rubrics of pauses, word order, or syntax. In an earlier paper (Searles, 1980), concerning the development, in the borderline patient, of an internalized image of the therapist, one of my clinical examples showed a patient's unconscious use of a pause in the fashion which the present paper details.

While I hope that the reader has found these clinical vignettes to highlight vividly many points about borderline psychodynamics, I am aware that he may have found them less gripping than some of my previously published accounts of intense patient-therapist interaction. In the latter regard, I want to emphasize that one tends not to notice the significance of these parapraxes if one is too close to the data, so to speak, and one does tend to be too much immersed in the data if one is compulsively caught up in feelings of responsibility for the patient's illness, in feelings of compulsive need to cure him of the illness, and in a guilt-based need to remain blind to the true depths—the full ramifications—of that illness. In my work with one man, similarly, who manifested a narcissistic personality disorder, I found myself having the rueful thought from time to time, after several difficult years had passed with relatively little change in him, that he needed an analyst who inclined more toward the remoteness and isolation of the astronomer than toward the study of the intense interpersonal involvements of therapeutic symbiosis of which I have written time and again.

Some few of the clinical examples which I have presented here came from my work with this man, and I would not have acquired these clinical vignettes—nor those from any of the other patients whom I have cited—if I had remained too closely involved, too much intertwined, with the patient, too prone to guilt at seeing previously unsuspected depths of illness in him or her.

As to the matter of whether to interpret, upon sensing the unconscious significances of a pause or a statement made in revealingly ungrammatical word order, I want to emphasize that, in *many* of the vignettes which I have presented, this was the first time I had discovered the dynamic in question; hence this was a major reason why it would have been premature for me to interpret on that occasion. Secondly, one of the disadvantages in a therapist's doing much of interpreting of these parapraxes is that this makes for an undue and inhibiting self-consciousness on the patient's part as regards his vocalizations—and I write, here, as a therapist who has had this experience with an occasional patient.

Presumably the two parapraxes which I have been discussing may reveal other kinds of psychopathology than merely borderline processes; but I have not attempted to explore other varieties of illness in this connection.

The reader may have protested, early in the reading of this paper, "But aren't these speech idiosyncrasies part of the everyday speech of all of us? Surely it does not mean that anybody is borderline if he fails, for instance, to use consistently Oxonian word order." It is my impression, on the contrary, that the presumable prevalence of these parapraxes among the population as a whole is testimony to our all having some grounding, however subtle, in borderline psychodynamics. As in my earlier work with schizophrenic patients, my work with borderline individuals has helped me to see, ever more deeply, the truth in Sullivan's (1947) oft-quoted observation, "We are all much more simply human than otherwise." I have had on occasion the experience of finding that a patient whom I have helped to become attuned to the significance of these two parapraxes will help me to notice how revealing are some of my own pauses and ungrammatical word orders, how revealing—and the patient has no need to be explicit and detailed about this—of borderline processes at work in myself. I feel sure that any other therapist who becomes accustomed to exploring these parapraxes will start to notice his own heretofore-unconscious utilization of them, in disguised expression of the borderline realm of his own ego functioning. The realm of the counter-transference has come to be generally acknowledged as crucially important in psychoanalytic therapy with borderline patients, and the two kinds of parapraxes which this paper has described provide two useful keys to the countertransference.

Summary

I have described the patient's unconscious use of pauses and ungrammatical word order as revealing of his borderline psychopathology. I have discussed this topic mainly by presenting clinical examples which highlight the following categories of borderline psychodynamics: (1) unconscious aspects of the patient's identity; (2) his unconscious time distortions, including subjectively omnipotent functioning in past and future as well as present; (3) his unconscious emotions; (4) his dissociated perceptions of other persons; and (5) his unconscious transference reactions. I have made a few comments, in closing, concerning the matter of interpreting these kinds of data and concerning the ubiquitousness of a stratum of borderline psychodynamics among people generally.

References

Deutsch, H. (1942), Some forms of emotional disturbance and their relationship to schizophrenia. *Psychoanal. Quart.*, 11:301–321.
Freud, S. (1901), The psychopathology of everyday life. *Standard Edition*, 6:1–310. London: Hogarth Press, 1960.
Fromm-Reichmann, F. (1955), Intuitive processes in the psychotherapy of schizophrenics. *J. Amer. Psychoanal. Assn.*, 3:5–6.
Greenson, R. R. (1958), On screen defenses, screen hunger, and screen identity. In: *Explorations in Psychoanalysis*. New York: International Universities Press, 1978, pp. 111–132.
Moore, B. E., & Fine, B. D., eds. (1968), *A Glossary of Psychoanalytic Terms and Concepts*. New York: American Psychoanalytic Association.
Searles, H. F. (1960), *The Nonhuman Environment in Normal Development and in Schizophrenia*. New York: International Universities Press.

———— (1977), Dual- and multiple-identity processes in borderline ego functioning. In: *Borderline Personality Disorders—The Concept, the Syndrome, the Patient*, ed. P. Hartocollis. New York: International Universities Press, pp. 441–455.

———— (1980), Psychoanalytic therapy with borderline patients—the development, in the patient, of an internalized image of the therapist. Presented as the Fifth O. Spurgeon English Honor Lecture at Temple University School of Medicine, Philadelphia.

———— (1982), Some aspects of separation and loss in psychoanalytic therapy with borderline patients. In: *Technical Factors in the Treatment of the Severely Disturbed Patient*, ed. P. L. Giovacchini & L. B. Boyer. New York: Aronson, pp. 136–160.

———— (1985), Separation and loss in psychoanalytic therapy with borderline patients: further remarks. *Amer. J. Psychoanal.*, 45:9–27.

Sullivan, H. S. (1947), *Conceptions of Modern Psychiatry*. Washington, DC: William Alanson White Psychiatric Foundation, p. 7.

Winnicott, D. W. (1941), The observation of infants in a set situation. *Inter. J. Psycho-Anal.*, 22:52—69.

15

HOW DO WE CHANGE?

JOHN S. KAFKA, M.D.

It is appropriate that a memorial lecture deal with the topic of change, since we wish to preserve the memory of powerful agents of valued change. Robert Cohen (1982) and Sylvia Hoff (1982) have recently written about Frieda Fromm-Reichmann and the lasting effects of the changing perspectives we owe her. First and foremost, she thought that psychoanalytic understanding is pertinent for treatment of severe psychopathology.

I think I should add a personal note. I am among those who really came to this area because of Frieda Fromm-Reichmann and her influence. She died just a few months before I actually started working at Chestnut Lodge, but she still interviewed me and essentially hired me. She interviewed me twice. Once, when I was thinking of coming here, and once when I formally applied. I think the total interview time was around seven hours and there was very little about me that she did not know. I do not know what it means that after all this time she thought I should also talk to Dr. Weigert before I actually got the job.

Of all the things she said about change and resistance against change, her description of a patient who had emerged from psychosis, became essentially symptom-free, but held on to one symptom comes particularly to my mind. Efforts to understand the persistence of this one symptom, the peeling of skin from her heel, failed until the patient explained the importance of the maintenance of the symptom as a bridge to her former self. Fromm-Reichmann touches here on one aspect of

Presented as the Annual Frieda Fromm-Reichmann Lecture of the Washington School of Psychiatry, April 4, 1983, Bethesda, Maryland.

the topic: change as trauma because it involves loss, a theme forming a backdrop to all psychoanalytically informed discussion of change in life and treatment.

Every clinician is always a student of repetition and a student of change. The hope *not* only to repeat what others have said prompts my immediate introduction of clinical material, of necessity greatly disguised and more than usually condensed, but perhaps solid enough to serve us as an anchor. My title sounds more ambitious than what I will do. I simply tried to free myself temporarily from theoretical preconceptions and see what central themes might emerge for me now when I look retrospectively at some cases in which significant change had occurred in the course of treatment. I will be long on clinical material and somewhat sketchy on some aspects of theory.

Mrs. A, around forty, married since her early twenties and mother of four boys, has been greatly concerned about her husband's health in recent years. Her anxiety seems to have been somewhat contagious to both Mr. A and some physicians, and Mr. A was hospitalized twice for diagnostic work-ups which, however, resulted in a clean bill of health. Marital dissatisfaction of recent origin—she apparently found him much more aggressive and sarcastic than previously and he found her more anxious, provocative, and critical—had led to their seeking couples' therapy at her initiative. Marital tension continued to increase, however, a mutual accusatory pattern could apparently not be broken, and the couple's therapist in this instance recommended some form of individual treatment to both. According to Mrs. A, her husband had become vehemently opposed to any treatment for anybody by the time her increasing depression and difficulties—now also in her relationship with her sons and many of her friends—led her to seek some consultations and the eventual decision to enter psychoanalysis. In and through this analysis the following story emerged. As you hear the story, you can probably imagine where the areas of major resistance were and reconstruct for yourself the approximate sequence of its unfolding.

Mrs. A was the youngest of a large number of children, all girls. When she was between four and five years old, a brother was born who died at the age of two. Mrs. A became an attractive adolescent and young woman; she had many dates whom she usually brought home to meet her family. Her future husband was studying the same narrow subspecialty of the technical field in which her father worked. Of all the young men she brought home, he was the only one with whom her father had lengthy conversations, the only one with whom her father developed a genuine relationship, which continued and prospered after Mrs. A's marriage. Mr. A's career was successful. The A's, as I have already mentioned, had four sons who grew and developed well. Mrs. A apparently experienced no *signs* of dissatisfaction with her life. Her concern for her husband's health, the complaints and symptoms which led to couples' therapy and eventually to her entering analysis, followed by a few months her father's death. This information, I might add, was somewhat slow in emerging because of a sequence of "errors" made by Mrs. A in giving and elaborating on her history. Eventually, however, she described how one morning, not long after her father's death, she had awakened and had looked critically at her sleeping husband, had experienced him briefly as a stranger, and then had the thought: "What am I doing being married to *that*?" You can imagine, on the basis of this story, that an understanding emerged from psychoanalytic work that Mrs. A had death wishes for her younger male sibling who was so much desired—especially by her father. You can anticipate a formulation involving her guilt feelings connected to her brother's death, the replacement or restitution motive in her marital choice, the central place in her emotional life of her relationship to her father, for whom she also produced and raised her four sons, and finally the collapse of the essential meaning of her life with the death of her father. You can also imagine the degree of resistance and the complexity of the maneuvers employed to avoid facing an emotional bankruptcy when her father died since her husband, when not serving a bridging function to her father, was considered by her an inappropriate mate, a genuinely poor choice. Eventually she divorced her husband, and relatively late in life continued her education, prepared herself for and entered a professional career. The points I wish to develop could, however, also be made if the patient had discovered that the marriage was more meaningful than ever to her, that she was married to a man with whom she could have a loving relationship now that he had no longer to serve such a concrete bridging function.

Schematically presented, the transference-related *action* in the analysis began to surface around a remark indicating that the patient was hiding the time of her analytic session from her husband. Why? He is a violent man who does not want her to be in analysis. But he knows she is, she has told him, she continues to tell him. What would be the effect of his knowing the days and the time of day? Well, he might just kill her, or (and variations on the theme were rapidly played out over several sessions) he might kill the analyst. It became clear, in any case, that by informing him of the analysis and making a point of being secretive about the days and hours, she was very provocative. Exploration of the theme of provocation of violence (she might also have to kill him in self-defense or in defending the analyst—of course, from an attack on him that she would have provoked) led through dreams and associations to her death wishes directed among others against her husband and the analyst (in various transferentially determined roles), then to corrections and amplification of the previously given history, to affectively charged memories of her brother's death and finally to the formulation given above.

How do we change? Affectively charged recall in a treatment in which a transference neurosis had developed, insight—in this case led to specific action. We do have with these concepts at least a framework for a psychoanalytic description of change.

Has there been "structural" change? I believe that a link between "structure" in the psychoanalytic sense (superego, ego, and id) and concepts of "structure" which have emerged in other fields can and should be attempted. For the present, however, let us return to the clinical situation.

A great part of Mrs. A's life had been organized around her guilt connected to her brother's death. One could say that her psychic reality was that she *had* killed him, a psychic reality reactivated in the heat of the transference. One could also say that in a sense life had played a cruel joke on Mrs. A, that she had unconsciously organized a good portion of her life as if she had killed her brother, and that psychoanalysis had helped her to change—escape from the role of victim of a cruel joke in part by illuminating the "adult" reality that she had *not* killed her brother. Perhaps one could say that she learned in analysis just *how much* she had wanted to kill her brother in the context of her repressing various aspects of her wishes, including sexual ones, for her father. Perhaps, her learning in analysis something about the intensity of her death wish on different developmental levels (i.e., Greenspan's schema built on Piaget's foundation involving somatic learning, consequence learning, and representational-structural learning). In any case, this learning was more important for change, possibly for "structural change," than her learning that she had not actually killed her brother—nor anybody else. It is accurate, but insufficient and too simple, to speak of her discovering in a situation laden with transference affect that wish and deed are not identical, a differentiation which was not solidly established at the time of her brother's death. I wish briefly to remind you of her admission, i.e., admitting to consciousness the thought: "What am I doing—being married to *that*?" I have gradually learned to pay attention to the literal meaning here: *that* was not human; *that* was not animate; *that* was a thing. The frenetic activity which followed, the hypochondriasis for her husband, were efforts to breathe some life onto the scene.

I am moving toward the exposition of my thesis that a crucial factor in "structural" change is some contact during the course of treatment with life and death issues in a form which may hark back to the dawning of awareness in the infant of the differentiation of the inanimate and animate worlds. (In one sense "dead" can only be applied to that which was once "alive," but anyone who has seen children's encounters with death will appreciate how formidable is the task eventually to perceive the dead as inanimate.) This is the area of the uncanny—only briefly touched more or less explicitly in treatment by some, like Mrs. A—and an area of recurrent or prolonged immersion during the treatment for other patients. These others include, but are *not* limited to, patients who are generally considered to have more severe psychopathology. While my *central* thesis connects change in treatment, i.e., also changed insight to the reexperience during psychoanalytic regression of early contact with the animate-inanimate bvorder, developmental variations in coming to terms with this border could explain differences in the readiness to take *action*.

The change in Mrs. A's life is easily visible even in a brief presentation of the case because she *acted*—after acquiring insight—to alter her situation. Rangell (1981) has tried to understand psychoanalytically the difference between patients whose response to insight is "So what" and "I see this, but what shall I do now" from those who move autonomously from insight to the initiation of change. Rangell refers to Waelder's statement that analysis offers patients a possibility of working out a viable, nonneurotic, solution, but the limits of current formulations of the difference between those who also act from those who only understand are illustrated by Rangell's need to include unspecified constitutional factors in the formation of more or less action-prone "executive egos." It is my hypothesis that vicissitudes in the development of the individual's ability to differentiate the animate from the inanimate contribute through the formation of self representations as animate—implying action-initiating—to this behavioral dimension. Despite its importance in the background and possible emergence at nodal points of change, material related to the animate-inanimate differentiation may either not be noticed at all, or will not usually demand focused attention in the analysis of a patient with a *relatively* uncomplicated developmental history of this differentiation. I believe that this was the case for Mrs. A and is characteristic for many patients with so-called good "executive ego" function. I believe, however, that Mrs. A, as is the case with many patients without major "ego deficits," was spurred into action in treatment, and then in life, not only through a transferentially activated confrontation with destructive wishes, but also by a regressive brief encounter with the uncanny breakdown of the inanimate-animate boundary—when her husband had been transformed into "that." Inasmuch as he had, in a deep sense, been a quasi-inert instrument of contact with her father who was the real object of her live cathexis, the experience of her husband as "that" was of course accurate.

The following example also illustrated what I have come

to consider a significant encounter with the animate-inanimate boundary in treatment. In one session, a brilliant and highly creative young scientist was discussing his doubts about whether or not to marry his girlfriend, the possibility that she may be pregnant, and related issues which could justify a considerable degree of emotional turmoil. Yet his agitation and, at times, bewilderment in the session seemed somehow disconnected from the content. The analyst commented on that impression and inquired about other areas in the patient's life. In response, the patient was flooded with tears and suddenly recalled a dream. He was flying over a beautiful city which he described in exquisite detail. It was, however, as he discovered when he flew lower and lower over the city and searched for signs of life an absolutely dead city—no bustling activities downtown, no children in the schoolyards, no life in the residential areas. His associations led to his work. In a creative storm—working night and day—he had just solved a very fundamental problem, a problem which had been recognized for over a hundred years, about which many books had been written and about which there had been many lively controversies. He had found a simple and elegant solution to the old problem, he could fly over the city now, but the intense life around a basic scientific question, an area of research and agitation in which he had been a major participant, had come to an abrupt end. The problem was dead. The significance of the patient's achievement (and "achieving," incidentally, also means killing), was soon widely recognized and led to a meteoric rise in his career. It was also noted by his colleagues that his writing style at this point changed radically. Although working in a rigorous and highly abstract scientific field, he was often complimented thereafter about a change from a dry style, similar to the one usual in his field, to a remarkably readable animated style which conveyed with simple elegance the growth and unfolding of his thought.

This patient had been raised by his father on fierce chess battles which were closely connected to his subsequent scientific interest. Rich analytic material illustrated how his scientific breakthrough was related to oedipal issues and his ability to deal with an oedipal victory. This information does not, however, detract, I believe, from the significance—at the moment of profound change—of his contact with the uncanny boundary of the lifeless, perhaps with the *structural* difference of animate and inanimate.

Freud discusses this encounter primarily in his cultural and anthropological works, although these interests are, of course, not segregated for him from clinical concerns. The topic is a central one in his paper on "The Uncanny" (1919), but in *Totem and Taboo* (1912) he already touches on the connection between the uncanny experience and the animate-inanimate boundary: "We appear to attribute an 'uncanny' quality to impressions that seek to confirm the omnipotence of thoughts and the animistic mode of thinking in general, after we have reached a stage at which, in our *judgement*, we have abandoned such beliefs" (p. 86).

In the two clinical examples given so far, the intrusion, the shock, was the appearance of the inanimate in an animate world. I also have an example of a patient referred to analysis because of fugue states during which she experienced inanimate objects as strangely alive. Searles (1959) has collected rich clinical material in his work on the nonhuman environment. For my patient, this pseudoanimism, reexperienced in mini-fugues during analytic sessions, proved to be defensive against the reliving of a particularly unexpected encounter with death in a situation when she had made light of potential danger.

Until recently I have thought that I was simply using Winnicott's transitional object theory when I was dealing with the animate-inanimate border. The transitional object, however, is for Winnicott precisely that object which is at the same time treated as animate and inanimate. Its ambiguity—and Winnicott emphasizes that point—is *unchallenged*. The child, who ferociously dismembers a mama or a papa doll in play therapy, senses some anxiety in the therapist and turns around to say, "Don't worry, I know it's a doll." He has at that moment integrated the transitional object in its nonchallenged territory. The fugue state of my patient is the mark of the *lack* of integration. Schematically, animism is a defense against the encounter with the inanimate; and when this defense fails in the face of violent death wishes and death fears, when the truly inanimate threatens, the defense of dissociation may be activated.

Under the title "The Body as Transitional Object: A Psychoanalytic Study of a Self-Mutilating Patient," I have previously described the work with a patient who had a severe skin disorder during the language-learning period and whose later symptomatology included repeated cutting of her skin when she experienced herself as inanimate (Kafka, 1969). She stopped each cutting episode when she felt it—and she felt it—and that was unfortunately not as soon as the incision began. Today I would modify my discussion of this case somewhat. I would focus more on the encounter with deadness, would emphasize more the failure of the transitional object and her compulsive search for a functioning transitional object, a search which also manifested itself in her decorating practically every inch of her room with fur. The failure of a transitional sphere to protect against absolute destruction might account for this patient's recurrent dream, a falling dream which was unusual in that she did not, as is generally the case, wake up just before reaching bottom. This patient in the dream experienced the impact of her being smashed.

The question of the essential structural differences between the animate and the inanimate has received the attention of philosophers and scientists for a long time, but before sketching in briefly some pertinent theoretical vistas, I would like once more to return to a situation in which the animate-inanimate problem presents itself perhaps *most* frequently and typically in psychoanalysis and psychotherapy.

A young divorcee starts her Monday morning hour with a barrage of complaints centering on her inability to cope with a baby who cries all hours of the night, a boyfriend in whom she is more interested than he in her, and without any differentiation in her tone between the things which *happen* to her and things which she *does*. She continues to complain about her own bad driving, her overeating, oversmoking, and her wish to kill her baby. The whole thing is presented as an attack on the analyst, who has not helped her with any of these problems. She continues: "It is not safe for me to drive. I have had some vague thoughts of killing myself and the car seems to agree with me. Wouldn't start."

You will recognize in this brief sketch features which some

clinicians would refer to as "entitlement," a label which is frequently applied when what is the result of action, consciously or unconsciously volitional, is not differentiated from events which are external, events not related to anyone's intentionality. The therapist's problem in such situations has to do with the ego syntonicity for the patient of this lack of differentiation, the fact that it does seem so natural to the patient not to differentiate between her complaint that she smokes too much, that the car wouldn't start, or that there was a thunderstorm. Sartre (1960a,b) whose later work has largely been ignored by psychoanalysts has emphasized the distinction between *praxis* (actions resulting from intentionality) and the processes related to inert matter. An important axis on which change occurs, if the therapeutic efforts with the patient I described are successful, deals with the formation in the patient of a differentiation between the results of "praxis" on the one hand, and the inert processes or the haphazard on the other hand.

A close look at the process in the analytic session may illustrate a direct technical application of some ideas developed here. Because her car wouldn't start, the patient took a taxi. This woman, whose friend had recently been mugged, experienced acute anxiety in the taxi when the driver took her over an unfamiliar route and through a part of the city where there were few people on the street. At the time of this session, several years into an analysis, the analyst had learned that any confrontation with the fact that she treated events which she had *caused* in the same manner as events with which she had apparently nothing to do was unproductive. So, having learned a lesson, the analyst asked if she had thought about the mugging while in the cab. The patient replied that she had indeed and that she had also thought about some murders she had read about in the newspaper. The analyst's next intervention was based on the idea that the danger in the atmosphere, so to speak, should be addressed rather than the location of the source of the danger since the patient's difficulties were seen by the analyst as having their roots in an uncompleted differentiation of who or what can initiate action, that is, ultimately what is animate from that which is acted upon, i.e., the inanimate. Very carefully choosing his words, the analyst said: "You have been in touch with a lot of murderous feelings since our last session. You had murderous feelings against your baby, and you had thoughts about murderous feelings directed against you." Again, what was important, I believe, is the analyst's *not* confronting the patient with the analyst's differentiation of praxis and process, of not differentiating for the patient the actor from the acted upon, but rather to watch carefully over the development of this differentiation in the patient. (Note, however, the analyst's differentiation of "feelings" on the one hand and "thoughts about feelings" on the other.) It does not advance the work if the analyst, feeling unfairly accused and held responsible for everything that goes wrong in the patient's life, might be tempted to respond, or, more realistically to retaliate with confrontation, in effect saying that the patient *should* be big enough to differentiate between what she is doing and what happens to her.

How then does such a change occur? A few months after the session described above, the patient again spoke of a series of unfortunate developments in her life. She had had a bad night. For various reasons the analyst believed that the patient was not reporting a dream. He asked: "In this terrible night, did you have any dream?" The patient becomes restless and says: "Yes, but I can't remember." Restlessness continues and the patient says after a fairly long pause: "Well, there were people, and I was literally coming apart. The buttons on my blouse wouldn't stay closed." "Too many demands pulling you apart," the analyst says. "But it is not exactly like that," the patient continues, "there was something sloppy about it, self-demeaning. I'm getting fat." Note that the patient is not attacking, does not blame the analyst for her overeating. There are some indications of embarrassment. She uses the neutral way of phrasing which had been characteristic of the analyst's way of doing it: "There was something sloppy about it." She moves to "self-demeaning" which is followed by "I am getting fat." She is en route to the autonomous experience that she eats too much and that she can initiate eating less. The patient proved to be en route to more autonomous experience generally. I will not go into how this can be reconciled with some definitions of Strachey's (1969) about change. He talks about it in terms of identifying with the analyst: how she is taking in small doses of reality about the analyst.

In any case, becoming conscious changes process to praxis. Let me elaborate: she says she "wanted" to come to her analytic session and thought that the stalling engine was a process phenomenon, the fault of inert matter. Suppose, however, that in analysis it becomes clear that her neglect of her car is related to the ambivalence which she harbors vis-à-vis her treatment. Then the process has been changed to praxis. The unconscious transforms much that is "accidental" into meaningful sequence. Slips are no longer haphazard (a cornerstone of psychoanalytic thinking). Our discovery of the uncertainty of the boundary between the meaningful and the haphazard has its consequences, however. We do not trust the border anymore. Is there meaning everywhere or is there meaning nowhere?

The transformation of process into praxis also has obvious clinical consequences. If nothing is haphazard, there is either omnipotence or paranoia.

The connections between the animate-inanimate dichotomy and the usually more visible issues of boundary between inner and outer are often most clearly visible in nonschizophrenic patients with many different diagnoses. Still, the animate-inanimate problem seems to be near the psychotic—the autistic—core. A young man who had been hospitalized for years with flagrant schizophrenic pathology has apparently made a remarkable recovery. The degree of his insight and his descriptive abilities are considerable. He described his emergence from psychosis. He characterized his first transitory moment of feeling normal again as "feeling that he was feeling." "Feeling that he was *not* feeling" was his characterization of his abnormal state. His surroundings at that time—the walls, cars, rugs, etc.—were not real, were placed there perhaps to fool him he thought, to make him believe that there was *something*. At times, he seemed to succeed, however, in a kind of "cogito ergo sum." Then he existed, but there was no possibility of having any kind of effect on what was around him. There is, he said, no possibility that what exists can have any impact on what does not exist. I interpreted this as an absence of an *integrated* feeling of oneself as animate. His descriptions brought to my mind science fiction stories about isolated heads or perhaps brains existing in nutrient solutions. The patient said, "What saved my life [I translate, "What made me feel alive"] was a psychiatric aide, saying, 'You are somebody, you can do what you want.' " I do not know what factors were responsible for the patient's ability to *hear* at that particular moment, to experience himself as an autonomous center of action which can "connect," which can have an impact on what surrounds him. When only he existed and the other existences around him were pretend, he was not truly animate. Anima means breath, animate means movement, or the potential of a movement that connects and that in connecting establishes if the other is inert matter or is another animate *center of autonomous action*.

I now come to the theoretical part of my presentation. I would like to deal more specifically with the question of structural change and considerations of the concept of structure. I quote from Loewald (1960, p. 16), "If structural change in the patient's personality means anything, it must mean that we assume that ego-development is resumed in the therapeutic process in psycho-analysis." For Loewald the analyst is a *new* object in the patient's life. Loewald thinks of the analyst as a sculptor, but we must specify a sculptor whose vision of the finished statue is influenced by the characteristics of the marble. He frees the form which is kept captive by the stone. There are several problems with this analogy, which I will not discuss here. Loewald's conception, however, offers me a convenient platform for my own speculative ideas because of his emphasis on a cooperative venture and the formation of a *new* structure. I prefer a temporal analogy to the spatial one. Longuet-Higgins (1968) has developed the conceptual model of a phonogram, using the mathematical formula of the hologram, but substituting the time values for the space values used in the formula.

Many of you, I am sure, are familiar with holography. If you have a picture of a man and you cut it in two, you do not get an upper and a lower picture of the man, but rather two pictures of the whole man that are a little bit less distinct. Every point in space has some information about other points in space. In Longuet-Higgin's model, temporal concepts are substituted for spatial concepts, so we have a model where each point in

time has some information about all other points in time: a
psychologically useful model because in our psychological present we indeed have some information about our past and some
information about the future, at least the planned future. In
this model, the memory access bank is based on rhythmic, i.e.,
temporal structure rather than on spatial one. The structure,
the new structure which is being created in the psychoanalytic
work, resembles a symphony more than it does a sculpture.

Although I prefer the concept of a temporal structure to
that of a spatial one, Loewald's (1960) formulation of structural
change remains applicable: "The interpretation takes with the
patient the step towards true regression, as against the neurotic
compromise formation, thus clarifying for the patient his true
regression-level which has been . . . made unrecognizable by
defensive . . . structures . . . by this very step it mediates to the
patient the higher integrative level to be reached . . . the possibility for freer interplay between the unconscious and preconscious systems" is thus created by the interpretation. "The
analytic process then consists in certain integrative experiences
between patient and analyst as the foundation for the internalized version of such experiences: reorganization of ego,
'structural change' " (p. 25).

Elsewhere I have developed in considerable detail the notion that our subjective realities depend on object constancies,
which are in turn dependent on the speed with which we scan
the environment to select patterns of stimuli, patterns which
are "judged" to be subjectively equivalent. For such subjective
realities of analyst and analysand to match, to overlap to a
certain extent, for a certain agreement about an "objective"
reality to exist, there also may have to be some shifts in the
reality organizations of the analyst. As Loewald puts it, "The
analyst in his interpretations reorganizes, reintegrates unconscious material for himself as well as for the patient" (p. 25).
To arrive at a common wave length, the rhythms organizing
reality may have to shift for both analyst and analysand in the
analytic or therapeutic dyad.

At this point in the development of my ideas I would like
briefly to describe an experiment by Bavelas (1970), an experiment which I believe to be of considerable interest for our

understanding of the process of change. The experimental subject is confronted with a board on which there is an array of buttons. The subject is to discover the correct pattern of pushing the buttons, and success is to be rewarded with the sound of a bell. After a while a bell sounds indeed and the subject is told to punch the correct pattern again. This time the bell sounds after a briefer interval. The process is repeated several times until the subject is interrupted and asked to describe the correct pattern. Usually the subject will describe an intricate pattern and when the experimenter tells him that there was no correct pattern, that the intervals between bell soundings were based on a theoretical learning curve, the subject simply will not believe the experimenter. The only way to convince the subject is to have him discover that another naïve subject will discover a completely different pattern and will be equally convinced of its correctness and distrustful of the former subject, now experimentor, when he informs him of the coupling of the bell intervals to a theoretical learning curve. The experimental subject is, of course, correct when he says he has been lied to. The only error is the timing of when he was lied to. The lie was when he was told there was a correct pattern of pushing the buttons. I think it is an experiment of some interest to all therapists. Although we could profitably discuss this experiment in terms of its implications that role changes are necessary for alteration in belief systems and how such role changes may be related to the flow of transference and countertransference, trial identifications, etc., there may be a more profound way of looking at the experiment of Bavelas. A perhaps somewhat oversimplified statement of the views of Jacques Monod (1972) is that the universe is chaotic and that our perceptions of order, or our hopes of discovering ever greater, more encompassing and fundamental laws of nature, are vain. If this is so, if there is no ordered structure, then the establishment of any shared views of reality, any possibility of communication, any common wave length between analyst and analysand is truly remarkable. We really do create our own structures, and to some extent structures which we can share with each other, in a universe, which, if Monod is correct, is unstructured.

Whether or not, however, the universe is ultimately chaotic, a shared structure is formed between the mothering figure and the infant, an area of shared realities without which communication would be impossible. It is Loewald's—and also my—view that shared realities, which again make communication possible where it had previously been crippled, are constructed in the interaction process between analyst and analysand. This is the structural change, which can be expressed in such conventional psychoanalytic terminology, for instance, as "a change from an archaic, severe superego to a more benign one."

A few more words about the nature of *structure* in our field. David Rapaport (1960), recognizing that the term "structure" could lead to a reification which is counterproductive to our theory building, developed the notion that structure differs from function only in their respective rates of change. Structure is not static. The order of magnitude of the rate of change of a psychological structure compared to the rate of change of what we commonly call psychic *function* corresponds to the differences between the rate of change of geological epochs compared to the rates of change, for instance, of a fast runner.

The de-reification, the de-materialization of structure also receives support from Ann Hayman's study (1969) of how psychoanalysts actually use a structural concept such as id. In her paper "What Do We Mean by Id?" she describes her finding a practically exclusive adjectival use of the concept. Patients talk more or less "iddish."

A brief mention should also be made here of a recent development in the understanding of structural change in physics, a development which several psychiatrists believe to be relevant to our field. Prigogine's (1976) dissipative structures deal with such matters as heat diffusion in liquids and the fact that under certain circumstances there is a sudden switch from conduction to convection, the emergence of a structure, the formation of regular, mostly hexagonal convection cells, a kind of streaming molecular cooperation replacing the speeded-up, random molecular activity. The possible direct applicability of the physical findings to groups of nerve cells—a semiliquid mass—is being studied by some, while others are exploring the possible behavioral and psychiatric analogies, mood switches, and switches into psychosis, using the mathematical tools developed in connection with Prigogine's work. It is not surprising that psychiatrists are interested in work dealing with the formation of new structures. Could the formal description of a system permitting the formation of new structures (apparently a system in which the second level of thermodynamics does not hold) be pertinent to the formal description of *animate* structures?

Bipolar fluctuations are involved in Prigogine's physics, and our thinking about psychic structures seems always to involve polarities, even when we return to clinical ground from such abstract speculations.

The distinction between self and other, between inside and outside, is closely linked to the differentiation between animate and inanimate, yet, I believe, it is not the same.

At this point, my working hypothesis remains that the animate and the inanimate are "representational structures" which serve as anchors in our organization of ourselves, and thus as anchors in the interpersonal network which makes communication possible. The structural differences between the animate and inanimate are, I believe, fundamental. This difference must be learned on all levels, and the learning on all levels must be integrated to avoid the danger of *action* contamination of our ideational contact with and use of the inanimate. When there has been a wrong hook-up, so to speak, when a human is experienced as inanimate, a true regression in the analysis occurs and a restructuring is not only essential but may be precipitated by the encounter.

Research on infancy is a particularly active field at present—Joseph Lichtenberg (1983) has surveyed much of it recently—and in such work the development of the differentiation of the animate and inanimate is bound to receive considerable attention. Much of Piaget's work (1969)—especially on decentering—being increasingly integrated with analytic thinking, is pertinent and I believe that clarification of the development of the animate-inanimate differentiation will contribute to our understanding of the process of change in treatment. Margaret Mahler (1974, personal communication) has told me of some research by Sterneman in 1947 on infants' different grasping reactions to a proferred finger, a gloved finger, a glove without a finger, and a stick. These stimuli could be differentiated in the first hours of life. As usual, a fairy tale has already dealt with our topic. The "raw-cooked," the fundamental cannabilistic anxiety of the animate-inanimate boundary, is dealt with in the story of Hansel and Gretel. The witch in Hansel and Gretel obviously cannot make the distinction between the animate and the inanimate, and it is this characteristic which permits Hansel and Gretel to survive, since the witch, mistaking stick for finger, believes the children are not yet fat enough to eat. If we were to psychoanalyze the witch and the distinction integrated on all levels of learning between animate and inanimate were again possible for her, her cannibalistic tendencies would undoubtedly become confined to the ideational or fantasy level and she would be much less prone to *act* like a witch.

References

Bavelas, A. (1970), Description of experiment on persistence of erroneous convictions regarding "causality." in: *Problem-Solving and Search Behavior Under Noncontingent Rewards*, ed. J. C. Wright. Ann Arbor, MI: University Microfilms.

Cohen, R. (1982), Notes on the life and work of Frieda Fromm-Reichmann. *Psychiatry*, 45:90–98.

Freud, S. (1912), Totem and taboo. *Standard Edition*, 13:1–162. London: Hogarth Press, 1955.

——— (1919), The uncanny. *Standard Edition*, 17:217–252. London: Hogarth Press, 1955.

Greenspan, S. I. (1982), Three levels of learning. *Psychoanal. Inqu.*, 1:659–695.

Hayman, A. (1969), What do we mean by "id"? *J. Amer. Psychoanal. Assn.*, 17:353–380.

Hoff, S. (1982), Frieda Fromm-Reichmann. *Psychiatry*, 45:115–121.

Kafka, J. (1969), The body as transitional object: A study of a self-mutilating patient. *Brit. J. Med. Psychol.*, 42:207–212.

Lichtenberg, J. D. (1983), *Psychoanalysis and Infant Research*. Hillside, NJ: Analytic Press.

Loewald, H. W. (1960), On the therapeutic action of psychoanalysis. *Internat. J. Psycho-Anal.*, 41:16–33.

Longuet-Higgins, H. C. (1968), The non-local storage of temporal information. *Proc. Roy. Soc. London*, 171:327–334.

Monod, J. (1972), *Chance and Necessity*. New York: Random House.

Piaget, J. (1969), *The Psychology of the Child*. New York: Basic Books.

Prigogine, I. (1976), Order through fluctuation: Self-organization and social system. In: *Evolution and Consciousness: Human Systems in Transitions*, ed. E. Jantsch & C. H. Waddington. Reading, MA: Addison-Wesley, pp. 93–133.

Rangell, L. (1981), From insight to change. *J. Amer. Psychoanal., Assn.,* 29:119–141.

Rapaport, D. (1960), *The Structure of Psychoanalytic Theory.* New York: International Universities Press.

Sartre, J. P. (1960a), *Critique of Dialectical Reason.* London: Verso.

——— (1960b), *Search for a Method.* New York: Vintage Books.

Searles, H. F.)1959), The effort to drive the other person crazy. In: *Collected Papers on Schizophrenia and Related Studies.* New York: International Universities Press, 1965, pp. 254–283.

Strachey, J. (1969), The nature of the therapeutic action of psychoanalysis. *Internat. J. Psycho-Anal.,* 50:275–296.

Winnicott, D. W. (1953), Transitional objects and transitional phenomena: Hate in the Countertransference. In: *Collected Papers.* New York: Basic Books, 1957, pp. 229–242.

16

DEFEATING PROCESSES IN PSYCHOTHERAPY

Martin Cooperman, M.D.

This presentation will be primarily a clinical one, that is, it will depend upon clinical vignettes, which, with one exception, come from my own experiences and observations. I shall deal primarily at the working level of intensive psychotherapy, and I will be addressing a process that regularly appears in such work and that, if not properly dealt with, can lead to an impasse and too often to an unfavorable outcome, including chronicity.

A good example is in the literature having been put there by Freud (1905) in his "Fragment of an Analysis of a Case of Hysteria." Dora came to Freud for treatment of hysterical symptoms. Freud was enthusiastically involved in working out the structure of her neurosis and the unraveling of her dreams. These were his then major concerns, activities in which he had an intense personal and professional stake. He felt great progress was being made and success was imminent. Then disaster struck. Dora left precipitously: calmly, even friendly, but unexpectedly and decisively. His anguish was great, his success frustrated. In my thesis, he was defeated.

Let me quote Freud:

> Dora had listened to me without any of her usual contradictions. She seemed to be moved; she said good-bye to me very warmly, with the heartiest wishes for the New Year, and—came no more. Her father, who called on me two or

This paper, somewhat modified, was originally presented to the Topeka Psychoanalytic Society in 1969. Portions appeared in "Some observations regarding Psychotherapy in a Hospital Setting. *Psychiat. Hosp.*, 14:21–28, 1983. Reprinted by permission.

three times afterwards, assured me that she would come back again, and said it was easy to see that she was eager for the treatment to continue [pp. 108-109].

I knew Dora would not come back again. Her breaking off so unexpectedly, just when my hopes of a successful termination of the treatment were at their highest, and her thus bringing those hopes to nothing—this was an unmistakable act of vengeance on her part. Her purpose of self-injury also profited by this action. No one who, like me, conjures up the most evil of those half-tamed demons that inhabit the human breast, and seeks to wrestle with them, can expect to come through the struggle unscathed. Might I perhaps have kept the girl under my treatment if I myself had acted a part, if I had exaggerated the importance to me of her staying on, and had shown a warm personal interest in her—a course which, even after allowing for my position as her physician, would have been tantamount to providing her with a substitute for the affection she longed for? I do not know. Since in every case a portion of the factors that are encountered under the form of resistance remains unknown, I have always avoided acting a part, and have contented myself with practising the humbler arts of psychology. In spite of every theoretical interest and of every endeavour to be of assistance as a physician, I keep the fact in mind that there must be some limits set to the extent to which psychological influence may be used, and I respect as one of these limits the patient's own will and understanding [p. 109].

Freud's frustrated hopes followed by the remark that, in effect, Dora *too* was injured bespeak his own intense injury, his being scathed. He goes on to wonder about his enterprise, justifying it, questioning it, torturingly doubting himself. Restitution or reorganization seemed to come with the realization that he ran into Dora's "will and understanding." I would agree. She opposed his will with her will; she understood full well where he was most vulnerable and she struck. It seems as though it was not until he lost that he became aware that he had been in this struggle.

I should like now to reflect a bit on the venture of intensive psychoanalytic psychotherapy. In that venture, the two participants are human. There are injunctions to remind us that patients are human, and injunctions and reminders that therapists should be beyond their humanness. I want to note simply that it is human to feel good when one's ventures prosper. This is usually such an integral part of human functioning that one is often not aware of it except when an undertaking is frustrated or when the good feeling is complicated by one or another of the it's-not-supposed-to-be-that-way feelings. This good feeling is an important impetus for difficult tasks. Therapists feel good when their psychotherapeutic work is prospering.[1] Their training has been long and arduous, and they have put tremendous effort, energy, and time into the preparation and into the treatment. Their stake is a very meaningful one. As such it is a forceful impetus. It can also become an area of great vulnerability—especially if not appreciated or acknowledged. Patients know this about us and use this knowledge regularly. Dora's timing—when Freud felt his venture was on the verge of success—is indicative.

A middle-aged woman, diagnosed a schizoaffective reaction, expressed it explicitly. We had been working together for several years and I was shortly to discontinue treatment because of changes in my life course. I was uncertain whether or not to suggest that she continue with another therapist. I tried to bring the question up with her only to have it brushed aside. In the next to the last hour, I again raised the issue in the context of some of her reports of difficulty in functioning alone. She erupted with "Oh, come off it, Dr. Cooperman, you don't really want me to go to another therapist. You want me to fly right." This was accurate but quite oversimplified. She had demonstrated markedly increasing ability in functioning in and out of therapy and we both knew this. She then added that it was in her power—by "flying right"—to make me feel good and to be thought of by others as a good therapist or by not "flying right" to make me feel bad and look bad.

---

[1]I am reminded of a personal discussion with Frieda Fromm-Reichmann in the living room of her house during which she humorously commented on how optimistic, even elated, we as therapists can get when a severely disturbed patient is allowed off a closed unit to come to his or her session in the therapist's office, albeit with an escort who is required to wait outside the office door.

I have said the psychotherapeutic venture is a human one, one between human participants. That may sound commonplace but some elaboration: by definition, these two human beings (patient and therapist) are met with the more or less avowed purpose of altering the living of one, living which has taken forms that are disturbed and disturbing to self and others.[2] Fundamental to human realization—fundamental to the realization of one's social and personal potentialities—is the development of the ability for mature one-to-one human relationships. Included in the characteristics of a mature one-to-one relationship are the following: it is increasingly intimate in the sense of permitting increasing self-revelation of both participants; it is internally and externally consistent in its goal directness; it is appropriately sustained; and it permits participants to form simultaneously other mature one-to-one relationships. It promotes or is associated with increasing recognition, acknowledgment, and acceptance of each as such and in relation to the other. That is, the individuals involved deal with each other as unique total human beings with recognized differences from others, including from each other rather than as things, part persons, appendages, other persons, and do not feel the need to present themselves as things, part persons, appendages, or other persons. Just as in the meeting of two parallel lines, I suspect such a relationship occurs at infinity. Nevertheless, as a concept or model, I find it useful. Fortunately, too, for many of us, this degree of maturity is not required—at least not all the time—to function reasonably well.

A patient, by definition and in fact, does not function maturely, as defined. One way of affecting this is to make possible the development of this ability. How? *By developing such a relationship with him.* That is the psychotherapeutic venture. Its methodology is the exploration of the vicissitudes of the venture. A person handicapped in the forming of mature relationships meets with a person more capable of forming such relationships, with the goal of developing a mature relationship. One will present symptoms, the other will present technique.

---

[2]This issue was discussed widely at Chestnut Lodge during and in continuity with the Fromm-Reichmann era.

As the venture prospers, both of these stereotypical presentations will diminish to be replaced by mature functioning. Such
a prospering venture will be a steady progression toward that
goal—albeit the course will be irregular and uncertain. Patients
may at times engage in behavior and deal with the therapist in
such fashions as to interfere with or halt, temporarily or permanently, this progression. When such behavior is used to
thwart the therapist and his human stake in the prospering
venture, I have come to think of it as a defeating process—*a
process to defeat the therapist by defeating the therapy.* I believe it is
a witting process and am impressed by the high price such a
patient is willing to pay to succeed, to "win."

Let me repeat the two clinical characteristics of defeating
processes. First, the progressive development of a mature relationship between patient and therapist is interrupted by the
patient's performance. Second, the therapist experiences a loss
of good feeling; in its place he feels thwarted, often anguished,
helpless, frustrated, lost, angry, hurt, and even, when the in-
terference is precipitously introduced, as though physically
struck.

I will be more concrete. A thirty-seven-year-old male came
to treatment because of severe depression with intense suicidal
thoughts. He had been an active homosexual since early adolescence and had engaged in prolonged psychotherapy with
three previous therapists. During the work with his last therapist—for about three years in another city—the patient gave
up his homosexuality, married, and was making progress with
his living. Shortly after the death of his father, marital difficulties developed and he became partially impotent, a development which frustrated and infuriated his wife. Again he
sought out homosexual companions and he and his wife gradually drifted toward legal separation. He withdrew in his therapy, became contemptuous of the therapist, finally broke
treatment, came to his home city, and obtained a good job. He
felt isolated, avoided old friends and relatives, engaged in
promiscuous homosexual "cruising," and became increasingly
depressed.

He sought treatment, was referred to me, and our venture
began and was progressing satisfactorily. Some eighteen months

after our work began, I was standing outside the door to my office talking softly to a colleague about a hospital problem. My patient entered the corridor to approach my office for our scheduled meeting as was his wont. I gestured to him to stop approaching and briefly continued the discussion with the colleague. When our session began shortly thereafter, he entered the room, strode to a chair (I left the use of couch or chair to him), slumped into its farthest corner and glared at me silently. Although glaring at me, he seemed in hard thought. I began to experience a tense, foreboding feeling, as though I was about to be struck. I noted this to him. He responded with intense anger, stating that I had treated him like an intruder, when he was operating as always, by my rules. He insisted that I give him a satisfactory explanation, stating adamantly that he was entitled to know why I had treated him with such disregard, even contempt.

Since I had experienced some annoyance when he appeared on the scene, mostly related to my wanting to complete the conversation with the colleague, his perception was essentially accurate, although exaggerated. I explained my situation simply and also apologized. He remained angry but continued to say that I was right about feeling about to be struck, he had been debating whether to strike back at me by continuing to come to the sessions, going through the motions, not making any progress, and leaving after several months.

He then went on to note that he had done this to his previous therapist. On the night of his father's death, he called the therapist. He felt the therapist's responses, then and subsequently, to be cold, unsympathetic, and clinical. There had been no expressions of sympathy or concern. His reversal of progress in the therapy and his attitude in the therapy sessions were now related by him to attacking the therapy and its accomplishments in order to defeat the therapist.

Following this externalization and feeling satisfied although not pleased by my simply factual explanation, change occurred. He began viewing his then homosexual marital partner more realistically, and made tentative advances toward females, his ex-wife included, beginning to see them more as people than as either dangerous or safe, better or worse sexual objects. In our sessions, the shift was to a more total view of his mother. He recognized the limitations of her mothering that her long-standing depression imposed as well as the concerned and effective mothering he had experienced from her. Both his depressed, helplessly driven, and destruction-inviting homosexual cruising and the destructive vengeful withdrawal in therapy could be seen as mimicking his mother's depressed behavior with her apparent inviting of death by failure to seek care for herself in what became a terminal "grippe." Her apparent helplessness had left him bitterly helpless. Had the threatening impasse not been broken, the genetic and transference aspects could not have been developed as had happened with the previous therapist.

Another vignette: I had been seeing for about a year a forty-year-old woman who had been diagnosed at two hospitals and by several previous therapists as a chronic, undifferentiated schizophrenic. Although progress, if any, had been slight, I did think, when asked, that some was being made. She attended the sessions regularly, some collaborative effort seemed to go on at times, and both she and the nurses reported some improvement in their relationships, in her relationships with other patients, and some greater participation in activities. I had even received a telephone call from her mother stating that she thought there was improvement and that she was content with the therapy even if she continued to have doubts about the hospital. Because of some illness in my family, there was a period when I missed some sessions and rescheduled others. The family illness had come suddenly, I had had to bolt the hospital, and the patient was informed of my first absence by my secretary when she appeared for her session. For various reasons, my secretary had been unable to locate her sooner.

When I next met with her I explained the situation. Further sudden cancellations were necessary and communicated via my secretary. To me, the patient expressed sympathy rather warmly. The family illness subsided and I was again meeting with her on our regular schedule. Shortly after my return to regular meetings, and with an approaching holiday season, she asked about making a trip home for the holiday period. She expressed herself as wanting the change; her mother and old friends were eager to see her and she them. Her performance had been improving and was socially adequate. She had seemed to weather my sporadic attendance period well. I agreed to the trip simply and quickly, adding that I did not plan to be away from the hospital during this period, and, if she got too anxious, she could call me or return ahead of schedule. During the next several sessions, she began describing difficulties arranging the practical aspects of the trip: arranging flights and connections, buying tickets, getting to the airport, etc. She described feeling confused and impatient with schedules and facilities. She also began exploring how the visit might not go well. Friends might be away, her mother would have other activities, she'd be a tag-a-long, she might get into fights with her mother, etc. At first, all this seemed like good work. I too dislike making the arrangements for a trip; I couldn't fault her too much, and the anticipation of where difficulties might arise sounded like useful foresight.

I began, however, to realize that practical arrangements continued not to be made, and the repeated explorations of possible difficulty were beginning to sound more like a prediction of failure. I began to feel tense in the sessions with a sense of foreboding. This became quite intense in one session and I noted to her that I felt she was threatening me with the failure of her visit. With that, she let me have it. She had been furious at my absences and shifting hours. Not only that, it was inconsiderate and disrespectful of me to get the information to her via a secretary. She didn't care one bit about the welfare of my family. She had thought of the visit home to show me she too had other meaningful people in her life; it was an attack on me. When I readily agreed to the visit, it was humiliating and infuriating: I had not even opposed her leaving me. Paradoxically I had not offered to help her with her travel arrangement difficulties or to accompany her on the visit. She planned to go home, and make the visit a fiasco. This would upset her mother who would then realize that I was a poor therapist and, since she already had doubts about the hospital, would stop paying for treatment and take her out. She would then stay home with her mother, even though neither of them could stand it. My status as a therapist would be damaged with the staff and with the medical director. Her plan was complete, the purpose precise. In fact, she added, she had not really come to the hospital for therapy; she came to have me and the medical director find her a husband. I told her that I could understand her feeling somewhat neglected; I had not been as available. I explained the necessity for her being informed by way of the secretary, but agreed that personal contact would have been better. I said that I agreed to the visit because I thought she could enjoy it and because I should be at the hospital and easily available if necessary. By the next session she had completed all the practical arrangements for the trip. The visit was a success.

I want mostly to note in this vignette the feeling of foreboding and threat that was my clue, the planned destruction of treatment to defeat me, and the price she was willing to pay to accomplish this end.

Another vignette concerns a married male patient who was clearly cyclothymic, with recurrent episodes of hypomania. Treatment with me began with him hospitalized in a hypomanic episode. The episode subsided fairly rapidly, and we continued in outpatient treatment. Although he lived and performed at a moderately inhibited level, he and his family were delighted with his improvement. He functioned with them and others much better than in the past. Some months later we weathered a short, milder hypomanic episode. This was the first reversal of a sequence of hypomanic episodes of increasing duration and severity; the previous one had necessitated the hospitalization. Despite my stated misgivings that he had to make it in therapy before he could make it at home, he nevertheless discontinued treatment shortly before summer vacation time. I heard from him about a year later. Things had gone well, but he was beginning to get anxious and frightened. We arranged to meet regularly. He was again in a hypomanic episode. Somehow it was aborted before he could do significant damage—personally, maritally, financially and socially—a change in the pattern of the past. He was pleased, and with the encouragement of his family he decided to continue meeting with me. We did a great deal of work on his living, but in the sessions I continued to feel a certain constraint, and he remained essentially polite and considerate, gratefully thanking me at the end of each session. Our relationship could be touched on and alluded to, but we remained essentially like close business partners, utilizing and showing our respective skills. It was now some eighteen months since his last "high."

As part of the general economics of the times, I decided to increase his fees sometime in about the fourth year of treatment. For practical reasons, we had developed the format of meeting for two hours at a time on two successive days. I told him of the raise on the first of two such days. He responded by appreciating that this was the first raise since we started treatment and that the cost of living had been going up. A raise therefore was in order, but a $5.00 per hour raise was a 20 percent one and the cost of living had not gone up that much. However, he felt they were my rates and he had no choice: I was the doctor and he needed me. It was clear that he felt badly used and helpless simultaneously. The very next day he reported having had fantasies during the previous evening of building a financial empire. This was the evening after my announcement of raising the fees. Since such as fantasy had preceded his previous "high," I experienced his disclosure of the expansive fantasies with the sure knowledge that a hypomanic episode was begun. Simultaneously I felt a personal impact of threat, dread, and dismay. Overriding, however, was a sense of fascination with the apparent clarity of the onset of this episode and the repeated initiating fantasy; I felt I was in a unique and privileged position to work out the dynamics.[3] I knew from the time he had become a private patient and we had first discussed payment of fees directly to me (rather than to the hospital) that this was a difficult area for him. Actually he experienced himself as entitled to love and care just because he existed and this feeling was at odds with his having to pay for treatment.

I became interested in his reactions to the precipitating event and in "analyzing" them. I overlooked the precipitating event as also a real issue between us, requiring a direct response to him. I responded to the feeling of fascination instead of to the feeling of assault. Note the similarity to Freud's feelings

[3]Such dynamics were of special interest to several colleagues and myself.

about the work with Dora. We entered a therapeutic impasse and I was not aware of it. This hypomanic episode lasted longer than any previous one, although it was less destructive to his family, business, and social relationships than most. With the persistence of the episode, I began getting first questioning, then doubting, and finally angry calls from his family and friends. The patient, too, on advice of a friend, arranged some consultations to investigate the use of Lithium. Parenthetically, Lithium at that time was not yet widely accepted; in fact was frowned upon by most psychiatrists. A telephone call one evening from his wife left me feeling frustrated, helpless, and angry. At the "therapy" session the next morning, I finally noted to him that I was experiencing his behavior and its fallouts on others as an attack on me. In a loud, raucous voice that I experienced as a slap—a type of tone he found intolerable and frightening when used by his mother—he told me that I was exactly right. With glee he noted to me an odd twist: by his wife and family he was now viewed as the sick person to be cared for and I as an incompetent and uncaring doctor. For the first time he agreed that his "high" might have been related to the raise in fee, but would not elaborate, almost like taunting me. That afternoon he defiantly accepted his first Lithium tablet. The next day he told me this, was polite and friendly, stated that he really did not believe Lithium was the answer, that he did believe psychotherapy was, but he would go with the Lithium. It was the last session of the month; he paid his bill then and there—he had never done this before—and left. I knew, I think, how Freud felt when he had to write about a "Fragment of a Case."

The clinical vignettes represent interactions with patients with different symptom complexes and character structures. I have so chosen because it seems to me that *defeating processes* are ubiquitous. This has led me to speculate some about their patterning. Defeating processes seem to be composed of three interrelated elements: *vengeance, power struggle, and mimicking identifications*. Each patient presented above described feeling hurt, humiliated, or badly used (narcissistically wounded), and rendered helpless by a considered and *concrete act of mine* which directly affected the arrangement of therapy: the male depressed patient by my waving back his approach; the female schizophrenic person first by my changing the regularity and timing of the sessions and then agreeing to a separation; the male hypomanic patient by my declaring a change in the fees. With each, I believe I had precipitously and arbitrarily forced into focus our separateness. Feeling cast adrift, detached, treated more like a thing than a sensitive human, each experienced intense hurt and struck back, retaliated. Simply put, feeling hurt, each hurt back. The means was to destroy the therapy, each in a manner personally distinctive.

In this connection it is worth emphasizing that each, including Dora, seemed willing to pay a high price in disturbed and disturbing living to hurt back. I do not see this as serving the "purpose of self-injury," rather I see it as the price of triumph.

Obviously, the outcome of defeating processes is not always propitious; I was defeated in one of the three examples I have provided. Nor does the working through of one with a patient preclude its recurrence. Over the years I have participated in this process with patients of my own—again, not always successfully—and watched it many times as supervisor and as observer with patients of colleagues. I have composed a composite scenario of what may follow if quick diagnosis and resolution do not take place. Note the development—inevitably, I think—of the power struggle. The patient has halted the therapeutic progression by attacking therapy. He creates an impasse. Florid syptomatology may recur. He may run away. If the patient comes to sessions, he presents as helpless and hopeless, as if without skills or talent, or as viciously vituperative. He may ask for a new therapist, stating only such generalities as the therapist was cold or talked too much or not enough or was too old or too young or whatever.

Feeling the situation slipping away, the therapist tries harder. (The power struggle now becomes joined.) Interpretations and questions increase in numbers, often manifesting in a certain belittling quality more the desperation than the insight of the therapist. With no change or even further patient withdrawal, the therapist often experiences impotent frustration and rage. He exhorts, predicts an unsavory future for the patient, and begins engaging in passive-aggressive maneuvers himself. He meets patient withdrawal with angry withdrawal, silence with retributive silence. He contemplates and then orders medications. He begins to dread the sessions, and comes late or is guiltily pleased when the patient misses. Or he overreacts and prepares carefully for the patient's arrival, only to be furious if the patient is late or misses the session. In the hospital setting he then searches out the patient or blames staff for dereliction, even sabotage in not getting the patient to his office—as if the patient had nothing to do with it. Ultimata may be delivered. By this time the therapist is often in a crisis of doubt: he is not cut out to be a therapist, he is not the right therapist for this patient, or psychotherapy is not the answer, the patient is untreatable, the hospital is antitherapeutic, etc. These doubts are not raised to be examined for elements of validity; they are declaimed as explanations and justifications. The power struggle spreads. Family and staff become aware of the impasse and the struggle. They get involved by taking sides. Some see the patient as evil, poorly motivated or untreatable, others as poorly treated and the therapist as incompetent or even malevolent. The therapist sees the nursing as sabotaging, the family as interfering, and so it goes. Again, these happenings are not examined for validity, but viewed as causes. Interdisciplinary and family conferences are held, to communicate better, to heal "splits." This is helpful provided the focus is on the patient and not in the service of the implicit power struggles. Externalizing the latent power struggles may make it possible to focus on the patient, but they are not the same. A consultant, from the staff or a distinguished professor, may now see the patient. Often the conclusion is a "transference hassle" or a "countertransference hassle" or a semantic variant thereof, and an authoritative statement that the patient should or should not continue. Usually it is that he should and the patient is exhorted to cooperate. Everything is treated except the motive for the impasse. No change occurs, the patient slips out of therapy by transfer or chronicity, a wry and costly triumph. Some years ago, I watched what I retrospectively realized was such a diversionary power struggle carried to—as seen by the proverbial observer from Mars—ludicrous extents. A patient had been in an angry impasse with her therapist. She eloped and turned up at another hospital, one from which she had been transferred to our hospital on the strong recommendations of a consultant because the therapy was foundering there. The family, not the other hospital, notified our hospital of the arrival of the eloped patient. There then ensued an exchange of letters between the hierarchies of the two hospitals, pejorative, self-righteous, each sanctimoniously accusing the other of mistreating the patient. The patient and her motivation were lost; shortly thereafter a request for a clinical abstract came from still a third hospital.

The third element in the defeating process relates to its manner, its how. My patients acted in fashions which seemed to mimic behavior they had experienced as dysjunctive and intolerable with their mothers. The first of my patients destroyed his previous therapy and threatened to do that to our relationship by becoming physically present but functionally nonparticipant so as to leave me helpless and defeated. This mirrored his view of his mother's death, and of her as physically present but unavailable to him as a child because she tended a store with her husband, turning his care over to a cleaning woman and to an elder sister. His defeating process mimicked this. His homosexual cruising, which had the feel of helpless inevitability and irresistibility to him, invited destruction physically and professionally. His destructive plan for me was to be present in the sessions in body but to keep himself out and then slip away. This behavior of his mother, chronic in their relationship and epitomized in her death, regularly left him frustrated and helpless—the effect he wanted to have on me, and the feelings he experienced as most intolerable with his mother and since.

The chronic schizophrenic patient similarly mimicked her mother. Her tirade at me took the form of finding everything I did unsatisfactory. Her anticipated behavior with her mother was to find everything mother did or did not do unsatisfactory and unsatisfying. This would upset the mother and she would be taken out of treatment. This unsatisfactory and unsatisfying behavior was the way she experienced her mother, whom she had never felt able to satisfy. Her way of being most devastating was to present herself as unsatisfiable. Thus, earlier in life she was spurned by a prospective suitor. She managed to seduce him and then for several years maintained a liaison with him that consisted of periodic visits dedicated to her insatiable demanding of sex in any and all forms. He never could satisfy her completely; he would be left spent, impotent, and sexually defeated. Some years after he had married another woman, he died of a heart attack. She remained triumphantly sure that it was she that had spent him and thereby destroyed him.

The cyclothymic man in his defeating behavior also mimicked his mother. One of the things that characterized his behavior when "high" was a loud, raucous, harsh voice. As he grew more agitated, it would rise in speed, decibels, and raucousness, with the result that the listener felt assaulted by it. At such times his mother and his wife separately described feeling frightened of an actual physical assault. His wife described herself as being more frightened of his voice than of a bodily attack, although on one occasion he did in fact hurt her with a blow. This behavior was essentially that which he had described receiving from his mother. Once in his late teens, she had become enraged and yelled at him in a voice that became so loud and harsh that he felt hit bodily. He described stepping back and leaving in order to avoid slapping her in return. Again in his early twenties, under somewhat similar circumstances, she finally did slap him. He also described that at about age four, his newborn baby brother was brought home from the hospital and developed a diffuse skin infection. This became progressively worse and a specialist was brought to see the infant. The patient stood at the open door to the nursery with his parents and doctor within. His mother shut the door in his face. He described feeling as if he had been slapped—shut out and slapped. This was the way his mother had made him feel; this was to him the most intolerable of all feelings. In addition, during his early adult years, when he was thought of more as evil and bad than as sick, his mother tried to control him and punish him by turning family, friends, trustees of his estate against him—again, slapped and shut out. And this was the way I felt when he left as he did.

The mimicking of mother in the defeating process is quite interesting. When I noted this to each of the patients, somewhere in the course of treatment, each found the thought horrifying and at first disclaimed it. The schizophrenic woman said she would rather die than be seen as like her mother. I mentioned that one hypomanic episode of my manic-depressive patient had seemed to be aborted. This came about when, during a session, he became agitated and spoke in the "slapping voice." I noted that his behavior was similar to the way he had described his mother. He stopped, sat down, pondered disbelievingly, and within a few days the episode subsided. At the end of many subsequent sessions he spoke of getting back to that, but he never did.

This mimicking identification as used in the defeating process is not then an integrated aspect of the patient's functioning. Rather it represents the presenting of oneself as someone else. As such, it is a return to less mature functioning as defined and thereby a halt or reversal in the therapeutic progression.

Now, to the precipitating event. I see this as the arbitrary insertion into the treatment of my separateness, abruptly, unrelated to factors or people that my patients could know I was even involved with, and which they were helpless to deal with. They were told in effect this is the way I will have it. Earlier in their work, each had indicated some envy and competitiveness with other of my relationships (patients or staff) or obligations (conferences, work) that they knew of; they could assert themselves in these situations. To expect them to operate maturely as defined, to function in a one-to-one relationship with me that would also allow me other such one-to-one relationships, was not to see them as they were. Of the three vignettes presented, one patient emphasized the disregard, experiencing it even as contempt, another the separation, and the third the arbitrariness.

The mimicking methodology of the defeating process interestingly seems also to serve the function of undoing or providing self-restitution or healing the forced intrusion of separateness. The mimicking—that is, behaving similarly to mother—serves as an alliance with mother: we behave alike, therefore we are together feeling. In this way, the associated dysjunctive feelings of abandonment, loss, isolation, not being wanted, etc., are counteracted. Unfortunately, the price of that

maneuver is high, namely, interrupting the therapeutic progression.

I want next to note some implications for therapy. The
validity of my thesis rests with its clinical utility. The major
significance of defeating processes is that they may and do work.
Of the three cases of mine that I presented, in one the defeating
process was successful, in another it had been successful with
another therapist but could be undone with me, in the third it
was undone before much mischief was accomplished. From a
review of these, as well as other personal experiences and the
experiences of other therapists reported during supervision
and in conferences, certain principles would seem to follow.

First, is to bear the concept in mind. In medical terms to
be aware that the diagnosis exists: a patient may destroy the
therapy in order to defeat the therapist, regardless of the price
he pays for doing so.

To me, the distinctive clue that this process is about to or
has begun is my subjective sensation. In an ongoing venture,
there is a relatively sudden onset of a disturbance in my feeling
of well-being, experienced as a feeling of tension, foreboding,
and threat. This has an inexplicable quality, unaccounted for
by the actual physical state of the patient. Instead it is associated
with an equally relatively sudden shift toward lesser maturity
in the therapeutic venture.

A collateral process is the diminution of the therapist's well-
being as the result of comments, behavior, etc., of staff and/or
family. When staff or family begin directly or indirectly blaming
the therapist for the patient's behavior, and thereby setting the
stage for extrusion or removal of the patient, it is important to
consider that this may be the patient's way of attacking the
therapist by defeating the treatment.

It is noteworthy that the patient whose defeating process
was successful was one where I experienced the clue but failed
to heed it. "Fascination" intervened. Again and again, it seems
to me, two states interfere with the heeding of the affective
clues. These are described as "fascination with the patient" and
"liking the patient." Although I have no statistical supportive
data, it is with remarkable frequency that I hear of patients who
defeat the therapy and the therapist described by their thera-

pists as liked by them or fascinated by them. This applied to
the successful defeater I described above. It is not that other
patients are not liked or not fascinating, it is just that they are
not thought of or described in those terms or frames of reference. In actuality, what is there that is likable or fascinating
about these patients? At the time, they are not making progress,
they are making the therapist feel quite uncomfortable, get him
at odds with other staff, bring him to crisis of doubt and of
conscience, etc. What is likable or fascinating about such a person? One usually hears there are other aspects to him. There
is his healthy side, his potential, his appeal. True. But that is
not in the relationship at the time. The vicious, nasty, defeating
behavior is. Thus, "fascination" or "liking" might represent the
therapist's withdrawal or recoil, his attempt to feel what he does
not feel or to not feel what he does feel. I can sum up this
aspect by noting that I have come to look at liking a patient or
fascination with a patient under these circumstances as an ob-
verse clue, and of poor prognostic import if maintained.

When the diagnosis of a defeating process in or about to
be set in motion is made, it is important not to fall into the trap
or the power struggle. This is not only diversionary but tends
to develop a life of its own. Besides, the therapist cannot win.
The patient is willing to pay a higher price; each of the vignettes
presented demonstrates this.

The most useful approach has been to externalize the therapeutic impasse. For me this starts by externalizing my feelings
of threat, bordering on assault. Sometimes when the process
has developed momentum and the scenario I noted above is
being enacted, it may be necessary to note the process to the
patient and attempt to engage the patient in looking back to its
origin and the circumstances of the origin. The patient's behavior can then be seen as in response to behavior by the therapist, something by omission or commission that is experienced
as hurtful by the patient. Often, I then feel I owe the patient
an explanation and at times an apology. Put another way, when
therapy begins to stumble or fail, the therapist should look first
to his participation, what he did and how he did it. Looking at
the patient's reponse as transference or disease is not enough.
In fact, that looking may obscure the reparative work that is

necessary first. Without a functioning therapeutic alliance no useful psychotherapeutic work can be expected.

Reference

Freud, S. (1905), Fragment of an analysis of a case of hysteria. *Standard Edition*, 7:7–122. London: Hogarth Press, 1953.

17

SOME NOTES ON NUANCE AND
SUBTLETY IN PSYCHOANALYSIS: HUMOR

JOHN L. SCHIMEL, M.D.

I attended a course entitled "Principles of Intensive Psychotherapy" in 1947. The instructor was Frieda Fromm-Reichmann.
The place was the William Alanson White Psychoanalytic Institute in New York City, in which I had enrolled as a psychoanalytic candidate the previous year. Frieda's lectures were
also given at the Washington School of Psychiatry in the District
of Columbia. The lectures were published under the same title
in 1950. The book became an instant classic in the field. Recently I was pleased to note that my copy had been autographed
by Frieda, although I do not recall the circumstances under
which this occurred. I can tell you that her signature is larger
than life. It bespeaks vitality and confidence and the openness
that characterized her. It is legible.

Her signature conjures up Frieda. Small, maybe four feet
ten inches or so, she had a largeness of spirit that is amply
demonstrated in her book and her numerous published articles.
In browsing through her book recently, I became more aware
of how much of her patience and wisdom flows through the
work of my generation of psychoanalysts.

I believe that I began supervision with Frieda in 1948 and
continued until 1953, although I was graduated from the White
Institute in 1951. It was common in those years for many of us
to continue supervision after graduation, feeling there was still
a lot to learn. In the early years, Frieda (along with Harry Stack
Sullivan and David Rioch) traveled to New York City every
other week to teach and supervise psychoanalytic candidates at

the White Institute. In turn, Clara Thompson, Janet Rioch Bard, and Erich Fromm traveled to Washington to teach and supervise candidates at the Washington School of Psychiatry. Frieda gave up the commuting in 1951 or thereabouts, and some of our New York candidates commuted to Washington for supervision with Frieda. I was one of them. This continued until one day Frieda observed that I was "doing good work and it was time to start thinking on your own." I have been trying to do so ever since.

I used to spend a lot of time in Baltimore; that was before they built the tunnel. I would be driving, on my way from New York to Washington, for supervisory hours with Frieda. I'd walk my dachshund while waiting for the traffic to move again and think of what I would say to Frieda. Frieda had a dog, too, and the two dogs became fast friends. Frieda and I compared notes on dog rearing. She felt I was a bit too rigid in my handling and suggested a looser rein. I learned that it had to do with the countertransference, and it provided useful material for my personal analysis. Two of my other supervisors, Margaret Mahler and Clara Thompson, on the other hand, kept cats in their offices and I did not establish as close a relationship with them as I did with Frieda, even though I did pretend to admire their cats. Freud is reported to have kept an irritable chow in his office and some of his analysands have reported being bitten—probably in a state of resistance. Clara offered me a kitten. Mahler never did, but she gave me coffee. But Frieda showed more empathy. One day, while we were discussing our dogs, I interrupted and told her that I had just become engaged. She looked at me intently, quietly, and responded, "Has the girl been analyzed?" I was touched. It seemed so much more penetrating than the questions my mother had asked, mostly having to do with the girl's family and what did she do and how old was she and was I sure and was she Jewish and was I sure. Well, I *wasn't* sure, but it was evidence, at least, of good enough mothering. And so I became fond of Baltimore.

I felt fortunate to be her supervisee, from our very first session. Frieda was reported to focus on the countertransference manifestations of the therapist in the psychoanalytic encounter and a number of my colleagues had felt crushed when

Frieda exposed countertransference phenomena in their work. Sure enough, a countertransferential problem was exposed in my very first session with her. My response was sheer delight. I recall leaving her office and literally hugging myself as I realized I'd gotten a countertransference interpretation. No doubt, a large part of the delight was that I hadn't felt crushed. If anything, I felt loved. And perhaps this essay, in part at least, is an exploration of the intricacies of human communication and how, in the psychotherapeutic encounter, they can be used by the psychoanalyst to convey not only information to but also respect for the patient.

Frieda defined "psychiatry and psychotherapy as the science and art of interpersonal relationships." She stressed the art of "helpful reformulation," of "stating plainly" important matters, of conveying to the patient that she had heard, rather than by a verbalized interpretation. It was important for a therapist "not to know" when, in fact, he does not know. She believed that there are marked assets relating to, or engendered by, the liabilities of mental patients and that these should be uncovered and acknowledged rather than be referred to "in a devaluating way, as we psychiatrists are easily apt to do." The patient is to be regarded as a "psychotherapeutic co-worker, as it were, and so, by implication, he invites further interpretive collaboration." Formulations should be short, simply and plainly meaningful, and in the vein of matter-of-fact leads offered by one person, the therapist, to another human being, the patient, who needs guidance. The psychotherapist, she believed, "must call upon those devices which are available to him in accordance with his skill and experience and which are contingent upon his own and his patient's personalities."

The foregoing lays the groundwork, I believe, for the psychotherapist "to do more than just soberly give pertinent information." Frieda cites the example of a female adolescent patient filled with fearful misinformation about menstruation and pregnancy. Following a discussion, Frieda reports, "I leaned toward her, cupped my hands around my mouth and whispered, 'I'll tell you a secret—delivery is not only painful but can also be both lustful and enjoyable.' " The patient spread the exciting news to a friend. Subsequently, the two ceased having painful menstrual cramps.

In discussing the foregoing incident with her patient, Frieda did not elaborate on some aspects of the encounter. She was clearly comfortable with the use of play and playfulness on the part of the therapist, as well as the use of humor as part of the art of interpretation. With the appropriate use of play, playfulness, and humor, a facilitating element may enter the process of psychotherapy. The communication may be subtle and depend on nuance. This may enable the patient to respond on a level that bypasses the censor and to assimilate information that may be useful to him.

Generally speaking the word "humor" refers to an overall attitude toward the human condition in which a perspective broader than the immediate circumstances is brought to bear, along with a genuinely compassionate attitude. It can be contrasted with wit, which is more intellectual and primarily verbal. Wit utilizes pungent, sharp, incisive speech and may be unkind, in contrast to humor. It points to unexpected congruities or incongruities in the matter at hand. Grotjahn (1957) explicated that on another level wit can be seen as a more or less socially acceptable way of communicating sexual or aggressive thoughts or impulses.

I start with a small example reported by Schimel (1978):
Pt. (complaining): You always point out the positive aspects of everything.
Psa.: That isn't true.
Pt.: Then what is true?
Psa.: I simply point out the areas you habitually neglect.
Pt.: (laughter).

This is wit. It is sharp, intellectual, clever, subtle, not particularly kindly, though not unkind. There is an unconscious (or unspelled-out) linkage of ideas which gets through to the listener and results in laughter. It unexpectedly, or in an unexpected manner, highlights congruity, i.e., the patient's consistent complaining and his depressive and obsessional preoccupation with the negative aspects of his living. It links the patient's present complaint about the analyst, "You always point out the positive aspects of everything," with his consistently complaining attitude in general. The consequence is laughter and an accompanying reduction in anxiety. The working through, consensual validation, and the repetition necessary for the acquisition of functional insight are still required.

A young male patient reported despondently that his girl-friend had complained that he "came" too fast, although she felt that on the second round he could be terrific. The therapist noted that the prolonged foreplay they engaged in would incline him to rapid ejaculation on penetration and that the notion of premature ejaculation seemed to depend on who defined it and who timed it! The therapist added that many young men and women subscribed to the identical belief that sex required prolonged foreplay, prolonged and vigorous thrusting, and prolonged afterplay. The patient began to chuckle. He had grasped the implication that he and his girlfriend had gotten caught up in a current cliché. He realized the comic aspects of their frantic efforts to be terrific lovers. He was amused and relieved.

Kubie (1971) warned against the use of all forms of humor in psychotherapy, and believed that the use of humor was invariably destructive. My supervisors were all serious men and women. True, we occasionally smiled or shared an amusing anecdote after a supervisory session, but the work was something else. Frieda, during a supervisory session, once timidly asked me if I was Jewish. I thought, "I'm about to get one of her famous countertransference interpretations," and I readily confessed, wondering what was going to come next. "Well," she said, "I noticed in your remarks to your patient a certain wry and ironic attitude that I associate with Jewishness." I thought about that for a long time. I wondered first about the effect of this on her and eventually about the effect on patients, which I believe was her goal in the first place. I decided *not* to give up being Jewish. I also decided to pay close attention to the responses of patients to my style. I believe that all the productions of a patient should be studied as possible artifacts fashioned in response to the therapist, his regional accent, his humor or lack of it, his office decor, fees, and other amenities.

The psychotherapist faces a dilemma. If he is to earn his keep, he must sooner or later say something of significance to the patient and hence risk an augmentation of anxiety which will make it difficult or impossible for the patient to reflect on the matter at hand. I am aware that this situation fosters the manifestation of defenses which can be profitably analyzed. Alas, we do not always have the opportunity or leisure to follow the fascinating unraveling of defenses. Indeed, in some such · situations, the most basic conflict in psychotherapy is triggered—the conflict between the couch and the door. I expect that all therapists have experienced this kind of denouement: the correct interpretation, followed by the disappearance of the patient.

I believe the foregoing has something to do with the tortured language used in interpretations by therapists who report themselves saying such things as, "I suppose it is possible that in such situations as you describe as now occurring with your wife or husband, there may be some elements that resemble those early experiences you may possibly have had with certain earlier figures in your life, possibly your early mother imago and perhaps also certain later mother or father surrogate figures." Willy-nilly, the therapist learns this kind of double talk if he wishes to eat regularly. Clara Thompson once suggested that the best way to become a successful and prospering psychoanalyst is to leave your patients' neuroses undisturbed.

I would suggest that humor (1) can be utilized in the service of candor, i.e., telling it like it is; (2) in such a way that anxiety may, in fact, be diminished rather than augmented; (3) thus permitting reflection and introspection; and (4) the continuance of a true dialogue between patient and therapist.

There are, in fact, a number of related qualities to be considered, qualities that bring together the fields of child and adolescent psychiatry, and living in general. As Fromm once put it, the richness and vitality of the person and his relationships depend on the *childlike* qualities that the person manages to retain through the stages of development and into adult life. Here Fromm was referring to the capacities for excitement, enthusiasm, zest, and joy. Ernest Jones (1956) offered a study of the qualities of genius, with Freud as his subject. Jones stressed *gullibility* as a necessary element of genius. Gullibility means the ability to take in ideas wholeheartedly, and even enthusiastically, without the cynic's or critic's eye sounding the alarm at every point and thus interrupting the creative process. One might suggest that the defenses that appear in psychotherapy can be viewed as failures of gullibility. Jones gave an account of Freud's excitement and belief on hearing his early patients' accounts of sexual seduction as children. When he learned that some of these were actually fantasies, unchastened, he went on to his important discovery that fantasy can be a potent factor in the psychic life of the person.

The child psychiatrist realizes the importance of play and playfulness in his patients, although I have little evidence that they value these qualities in parents or themselves. Play and playfulness are natural modes of behavior with a large capacity for the communication of care, concern, affection, understanding, and the communication of problem areas in symbolic form. Play and playfulness can be considered to be modalities in which a perspective broader than the specific matter at hand is invoked. Play and playfulness can, in fact, be seen as forms of humor. I am making a case for the utility of playfulness and humor on the part of the therapist. They are not a panacea. Ideally, sound clinical judgment informs the choice of humor no less than that of other psychotherapeutic interventions.

In my early practice I was assigned a child living in a home for children. Saul was seven. Undersized and wizened, he looked like an unhappy gnome. He was selectively mute and did not respond to play materials. He could not tie his shoelaces or handle a fork or spoon. He did not dress himself; he still soiled; he shoveled his food; he was scapegoated and used as a homosexual victim by the other boys at the home. It was a new therapeutic service, and I was a new psychiatrist assigned to the worst case, and a great deal was expected of the new psychiatric service.

I squirmed through a number of sessions while Saul stared into space. I had my notebook at hand and my pencil sharpened, but he did not respond to questions. Before my psychiatric training, I had known how to engage small children. I was a favorite uncle to a number of them. One secret of my success was that I knew a few magic tricks and some sleight of hand I had learned from a roommate in the army who had been a vaudevillian. Bored, I surreptitiously began doing magic tricks, pretending that I was just whiling away the time while he pretended not to notice what I was doing. I was relieved years later when I learned that Anna Freud (1946) had written something that indicated she would have approved. But note that the psychiatrist is doing the playing and the child the observing. I suggest this can be a useful paradigm for all psychotherapeutic activities and for patients of all ages. The foregoing is but a variation on Harry Stack Sullivan's (1954) warning that the patient is as actively, and perhaps as accurately, evaluating the therapist as the latter is evaluating the patient.

Some six months passed, with these results. Saul had learned a pencil trick and was working on a posture trick. Somehow, on his own, he had, at the same time, learned to eat with a knife and fork, to dress himself, and to tie his shoelaces; he was no longer a homosexual victim, but was beginning to play baseball; he was learning at school. Perhaps more important to *him* was the fact that he knew I had come to enjoy his company; we even talked occasionally. And sometimes he smiled. There was little verbal communication for a long time and much of that was in the form of play.

Word play begins very early. I once asked a very little girl what she did when someone gave her a present.

Girl: I wait.

Therapist: What do you wait for?

Girl: I wait until Mommy says, "Say thank you," then I say, "Thank you."

An adolescent patient was ranting about his father:

> I can't stand the bastard. He makes me sick just to look at him. I can't stand him. And he expects me to write to him. Well, you know I did, last month. All I could write was, "Thanks for the check, Charlie." I couldn't write another word. But nobody can stand him. Nobody. What does he expect. *You* saw him once. I'll bet you couldn't stand him. He's nobody's cup of tea. Nobody's! Well, could *you* stand him?

The therapist thought for a moment and replied, "Well,

a psychiatrist has to try to make a cup of tea out of *anything* that comes his way."

The patient, a bright youngster, lapsed into roaring laughter that lasted a good five minutes. He emerged in a thoughtful mood, expressing a realization that he himself was no cup of tea, that he and his father were alike in too many ways, that there was more work for him to do, and that there *would* be an eventual reconciliation with his father, although he could not bring himself to do it at this time.

These examples may serve to illustrate some of the propositions offered. They fit the notion that humor offers a perspective broader than the immediate circumstances. For the adolescent patient the intervention pointed to an unexpected congruity in the matter at hand, in which the *manifest* common denominator or congruity seemed to have been a cup of tea. In fact, the common denominator was the therapist's experiences with both father and son, neither being a cup of tea. Laughter in response to a humorous remark has been ascribed to an immediate conscious linkage of unacceptable ideas, thus circumventing the repressive forces of the censor and permitting the latent to become manifest. The *direct* expression by the therapist of what the patient came up with by himself could have been threatening to him and resulted in defensiveness and a negative transference reaction.

A number of similar examples were reported by Schimel (1980):

A very competitive, prowess-oriented adolescent who was both a great athlete and intelligent, started the hour in a gloomy mood and recited a number of personal defeats.

First patient: And not only that, but I'm feeling lousy. I had to go to the doctor.

Therapist: What's wrong?

Patient: I have Victor's disease.

Therapist: Congratulations. What did you win this time?

Patient: I didn't win anything. I have sore gums, ulcers, the doctor said. He was surprised. He said only poor people, who are malnourished, get it.

Therapist: Oh, that's Vincent's disease.

Patient: I can't believe it. You've been telling me I'm
                        too busy with who's on top. Victor's disease!
                        So that's my problem.

A second patient began his session in a rage:

Second patient: The whole world stinks. And what do you do?
                        You just sit there. She hung up on me. There
                        was no reason for her to hang up on me. And
                        there's no reason to come here and hang out
                        this shit for you. I'm quitting. I didn't want
                        to come in the first place. Boy, if there was
                        ever a waste of time and money, this is it. This
                        is it! This is my last visit. I don't even like you.
                        I'm in this mess and you don't even say any-
                        thing. What the hell am I doing here? Say
                        something!
Therapist: (laughs): You're in a bad mood today.
Patient: Doc, you're unbelievable. . . . But, you're
                        right. I'm in the worst mood since the world
                        began. But, aren't you supposed to tell me
                        that it will all turn out all right? Aren't you
                        supposed to ask me more questions so you
                        can find out what I did wrong? Maybe I got
                        her mixed up with my mother or something.
                        I lash out at everybody when I'm unhappy.
                        And I'm unhappy a lot. Maybe. I don't really
                        care. It's just that when anybody says "no" to
                        me, I go bananas.

I suggest that the examples fulfill the criteria suggested for
the *constructive* use of humor in psychotherapy: (1) it can be
utilized in the service of candor, i.e., telling it like it is; (2) in
such a way that anxiety may, in fact, be diminished rather than
augmented; (3) thus permitting reflection and introspection;
and (4) the continuance of a true dialogue between patient and
therapist.

Humor and tenderness are linked. They share a certain
fragility, a delicacy, a nicety, a sensibility to nuance and shades
of meaning. They require a light touch, or they turn into some-

thing else. A capacity for playfulness and an openness to its use are necessary to inform the constructive expression of humor in psychotherapy.

Much psychotherapy could go better and less painfully if there were a lighter touch, an occasional laugh, and a shared view of the comedy as well as the tragedy of human life. Lionel Blitzsten, a pioneering psychoanalyst in Chicago, reported that one of his first patients was a devout Catholic. Following one of Blitzsten's interpretations, the patient leaped from the couch and shouted, "Now I know who you are; you are the apostle of the obvious." I believe this to be the basic role of the therapist.

We all know that humor, good humor, has a leavening effect in human affairs, that we can be eased by it, solaced by it, cheered by it, encouraged by it, inspired by it, even healed by it.

References

Freud, A. (1946), *The Psychoanalytical Treatment of Children.* New York: International Universities Press.

Fromm-Reichmann, F. (1950), *Principles of Intensive Psychotherapy.* Chicago: University of Chicago Press.

Grotjahn, M. (1957), *Beyond Laughter.* New York: McGraw-Hill.

Jones, E. (1956), *Sigmund Freud: Four Centenary Lectures.* New York: Basic Books.

Kubie, L. S. (1971), The destructive potential of humor in psychotherapy. *Amer. J. Psychiat.,* 127:861–866.

Schimel, J. L. (1978), The function of wit and humor in psychoanalysis. *J. Amer. Acad. Psychoanal.,* 6:369–379.

——— (1980), Some thoughts on the uses of wit and humor in the treatment of adolescents. *New Dir. Mental Health Serv.,* 5:15–23.

Sullivan, H. S. (1954), *The Psychiatric Interview.* New York: Norton.

18

THE FACILITATING FUNCTION OF THE FAMILY IN THE ADOLESCENT INDIVIDUATION PROCESS

ROGER L. SHAPIRO, M.D.

Frieda Fromm-Reichmann was working actively at Chestnut Lodge when I joined the staff in 1954. One of my vivid memories of that year is of her curiosity and enthusiasm in discussions of treatment of difficult patients in a supervisory seminar for new fellows she conducted every Tuesday morning at her home. Discussion of our cases always included efforts to clarify in detail the family relations and developmental histories of the patients we were treating in intensive psychotherapy. In her work with us as well as her contributions to clinical staff conferences, an interest in the quality of patients' family relationships seemed to me to pervade Frieda's work. This interest was at the center of Freida's collaboration with Gregory Bateson at the Center for Advanced Studies in the Behavioral Sciences at Stanford in 1955-56. Soon after she returned to Chestnut Lodge, she invited Bateson there to speak to us about family relations and schizophrenia. Although Frieda did not herself treat families, her influence was important in my decision to include intensive study and treatment of the family in research on adolescent development I began at the National Institute of Mental Health in 1958.

The task of my research group at the NIMH was investi-

Earlier versions of this paper were presented at the Michael Reese Hospital Department of Psychiatry Conference on "The Creativity and Challenges of the Adult Experience: Work, Family, and Intimacy," Chicago, March 18, 1983; and at the Chestnut Lodge Symposium, Rockville, October 7, 1983.

gation of the nature and genesis of serious psychological disturbances during adolescence (R. Shapiro, 1967, 1979, 1986; R. Shapiro and Zinner, 1971; Zinner and R. Shapiro, 1972, 1974; Berkowitz et al., 1974; E. Shapiro et al., 1975). The centrality of the interplay between the generations for understanding adolescent development led us to expand our work to include study of the family. Our research, which began as an investigation of the individual disturbed adolescent, soon included a study of the parents and the adolescent in interaction, and our initial focus on the adolescent identity crisis was soon integrated with an effort to understand the crisis of the parents at mid-life.

In addition to our sample of disturbed adolescents and their families, we studied a comparison group of families where the adolescents were developing well and manifested no serious disturbance. In both groups of families we became interested in the dynamics of the parents' marriages and the functions the children and adolescents played in the parents' psychological equilibrium. Our assumptions about the psychosocial determinants of ego strength in what Erikson (1961, p. 151) has called the cogwheeling of the generations, resulted in a detailed consideration of adulthood as well as adolescence as psychosocial phases.

In this chapter I want to discuss some of the findings in our investigation of families of disturbed adolescents, and contrast these findings to our observations of families where the adolescents are developing well. I want to focus in particular on the personality functioning of the parents in each type of family during childhood and adolescent development which require of the parents that they manage the acute anxieties of changing relationships and circumstances within the family. Their capacities to function without severe regression under conditions of change and loss have important consequences for the adolescent development of their children as well as the parents' own development at mid-life. Inability of the parents to manage these anxieties gives rise to characteristic patterns of regression in the family, confusion in adolescent identity formation, and increasing self-absorption in the parents in their middle years.

In the families we studied, the identity crises of the adolescent (Erikson, 1968), a consequence of their maturation and individuation as well as their actual separation from their parents, activated developmental crises in their parents. However, there were important differences between the behaviors of parents where the adolescents manifested pathology as contrasted with parents where the adolescents were functioning well. In families of disturbed adolescents, we observed episodes of family regression, manifested in an impaired capacity to mourn, a defensive organization of denial, splitting, and projection, and a general regression in ego functioning in the parents as well as the adolescents themselves. In families of adolescents who were functioning well, evidence of developmental crisis in the family was not accompanied by significant family regression. In these families, parents and adolescents managed the anxieties of change and loss with evidence of mourning but without severe ego regression, and manifested capacities for progressive individuation which supported separation and growth.

Study of processes of separation-individuation in individuals and families is facilitated by an object-relations-centered conceptualization of development, tracing the emergence of the personality from an initial undifferentiated state in infancy to a state of progressively differentiated and internalized self and object images in later infancy and childhood (Jacobson, 1964; Kernberg, 1976). This development undergoes a new integration during adolescence following maturation in the ego and the id at puberty. Separation and individuation processes are initially powerfully determined by experiences within the mother-child dyad. They are elaborated by the internalizations of experiences within the entire family during development. Family experience may facilitate processes of separation-individuation; or it may interfere with their accomplishment because of disturbances of differentiation in family members and complicating states of anxiety. Through analytic study of the family, links may be established between characteristics of intrapsychic structure within the developing individual and actual characteristics of the individual's primary object relationships.

It is my thesis that family regression, if it is activated by adolescent separation-individuation, will interfere with the nor-

mative sequence of adolescent regression and subsequent progression (Blos, 1967, 1979), thus compromising the adolescent
individuation process. To elucidate this thesis, I want first to
discuss a framework for the study of regressed versus mature
behavior in the family of the adolescent. Then I shall illustrate
these findings by contrasting material from two families in our
study, one in which the adolescents manifest borderline and
narcissistic pathology, and another in which the adolescents are
functioning well. I shall contrast the parents' capacities in these
two families to contain and work with the separation and individuation of their adolescent offspring, and to manage their
concomitant feelings of loss.

An Analytic Theory of Family Functioning: Unconscious Assumptions and Family Regression

Our findings from family observations suggest links between
adolescent character pathology and the activation of defenses,
regression, and consequent distortions in behavior among family members, as the child and adolescent develops. To study
these links we assess the level of regression and characteristics
of defenses in family transactions, and the nature of unconscious fantasies that are the motives for defense. Observations
of repetitive behaviors in families that appear to militate against
change, development, and individuation of the adolescent are
the evidence for inferences about the dynamics of unconscious
assumptions in family members that motivate and organize
these behaviors. These assumptions appear to derive from the
internalized developmental experience of both of the parents
in their families of origin. An organization of motives and defenses evolve in the marriage, conceptualized as the unconscious assumptions of the family. These are operative throughout
the development of the child and adolescent.

The constructs of unconscious assumptions of the family
and family regression originate in clinical observation. They
derive from the small group theory of Bion (1961), a conceptualization of both the conscious functions and tasks that define
groups, and the unconscious motives or assumptions (basic assumptions) in group members that may dominate group be-

havior and give rise to group regression. Our effort to conceptualize family behavior has been facilitated by using a similar framework, that of conscious family functions and tasks in contrast to a variety of unconscious assumptions which may dominate family behavior and lead to family regression.

When the family is in a situation of anxiety mobilized by unconscious assumptions, we find conflicting motivations and behavior that appear to be determined more by fantasy than by reality. Confused, distorted thinking emerges; understanding and adequate communication fail; and the ability of the family to work cooperatively or creatively on a task, to maintain a meaningful and progressive discussion, or to respond realistically to the problems under discussion breaks down. In short, when unconscious assumptions are mobilized, anxiety and defensive behaviors arise, activating disturbance in the family's reality functioning and family regression. In contrast, when unconscious assumptions are not mobilized, the family does not manifest anxiety and prominent defensive behavior. It remains clearly reality-oriented, is functioning on a mature level, and is functioning well in relation to tasks that facilitate development of children and adolescents.

In order to focus family observations on particular characteristics of the parents' relationship to the adolescent and the adolescent's relationship to the parents, we use the concept of delineation (R. Shapiro, 1967; Shapiro and Zinner, 1971). Delineations are inferred from behaviors through which one family member communicates explicitly or implicitly his perceptions and attitudes—his mental representation of another family member—to that other person. They may communicate a view of the other person that seems to be predominantly determined by his reality characteristics, or a view that appears to be determined by the mobilization of dynamic conflict and defense in the delineator. We call the latter category defensive delineations.

The concept of projective identification provides a highly useful means of conceptualizing one category of defensive delineations (Zinner and Shapiro, 1972). In episodes of family regression there is a rapid reduction in usual ego discriminations. This results in impairment in self-object differentiation, with increased splitting and projection and increased confusion over the ownership of personal characteristics which are easily projected onto other family members. The projecting individual then attempts to control this projected characteristic in the other person. When an individual assumes a role compatible with the projections of others in the family at the regressed level, these projections tend to fix him in that role. Family members project an aspect of their own personal characteristics onto him and unconsciously identify with him. The power of these projections with their accompanying unconscious identifications may push the individual into more extreme role behavior, and constrain other potentialities of development.

An Example of Regressed Family Functioning: Families of Borderline Adolescents

Evidence of family regression and ego regression in the parents is found in families of adolescents in our study who were in the borderline spectrum of personality disorders (Shapiro and Zinner, 1971; E. Shapiro et al., 1975; Berkowitz et al., 1974). The adolescents were hospitalized at the National Institute of Mental Health, where their program of treatment included individual psychotherapy on an average of three sessions per week, one hour per week of conjoint family therapy, and one hour of marital therapy per week for the parents. The individual therapist of the adolescent and the parents' marital therapist were co-therapists of the family therapy.

We find that families of borderline adolescents, including those who manifest pathological narcissism, reveal similar vulnerabilities and characteristics of family regression. In these families we find evidence of unconscious assumptions in family members which equate separation-individuation with loss and abandonment. These assumptions activate family regression in which differentiation between family members is compromised and defenses of splitting, denial, and projective identification are seen. Split self and object representations within family members are distributed among family members by projective identification. A situation of pathological mourning is evidenced in which the individuating and separating adolescent is no longer experienced and mourned as an integrated whole object. Instead, the threat of loss activates ego regression to a level of primitive splitting in the parents and projection of "badness" or "devaluation" into the individuating and separating adolescent.

The Grant Family

In the following case report, I will present findings in a family where the older son manifests combined narcissistic and borderline pathology, while the younger son manifests only borderline pathology. Excerpts from family therapy are selected to illustrate the parents' response to behavior of either adolescent signaling separation-individuation.

The Grant family consists of Mr. Grant, age fifty-three; Mrs. Grant, age forty-eight; son Michael, age eighteen; and son Paul, age sixteen. The father's work in the Foreign Service required frequent travel and the family lived overseas for several different periods. These tours of duty overseas interfered with Mrs. Grant's work as a public service lawyer, and were much resented by her. Michael began to have major difficulties during the last period abroad between fourteen and sixteen years. He refused to go to school, fought with his parents, and spent days wandering in the foreign city in which they lived. On several occasions he ran away from home, and delinquent activities got him into trouble with the local authorities.

Past history relevant to separation and loss includes the fact that each parent lost a mother during childhood; the father when he was six and the mother when she was ten. The father's father remarried after several years, but the new marriage was stormy and lasted only a few years. The father described a difficult and distant relationship to his own father. The mother's father did not remarry and she was cared for by her older sister.

Michael continued to have serious difficulties after the family's return to this country, when he was sixteen. He returned to school for serveral months, but then was expelled for drinking and smoking marijuana. Fighting with his parents escalated and he left home. He wandered around the country and worked sporadically for several months. Finally, he returned home, refused to work or go to school, and generally isolated himself from the family and from high school friends, except for his girlfriend, Kate. He became involved in Yoga and ate a vegetarian diet. He was frequently grandiose in his thinking, behaving contemptuously to his parents, and was hostile toward his brother, Paul. At other times, he expressed anxiety and hopelessness about the future and complained of depression, lack of confidence in himself, and loss of interest in anything. After much fighting and persuasion and with much hesitation, he finally saw a psychiatrist at his parents' insistence and was referred to NIMH and to our project.

Although Michael was the focus of his parents' concern, it was clear that Paul was also troubled. He was quiet and withdrawn throughout this period, had no friends, and was extremely irritable toward his parents. However, his performance at school was good, and the parents did not seem particularly concerned about him. We later learned that his isolation was necessary, if he was not to experience paranoid anxiety over his own (projected) anger and sexual feelings.

Excerpt 1: The first excerpt of family therapy is from the assessment interview prior to Michael's admission to the adolescent unit. The interaction, early in the session, demonstrates an initial sharp difference in the parents' delineations of Michael. The father expects him to be explicit about what his problems are. He clearly puts him into the role of being the family problem. The mother speaks for Michael and requires very little of him. She has difficulty distinguishing his anxiety from her own anxiety. She does not listen to him. We take this to be initial evidence of the mother's narcissistic relationship to Michael. She does not psychologically distinguish herself from him, and treats him as a sensitive and fragile aspect of herself, and as if he is having the same responses in the interview situation that she does. Michael's behavior early in the session is grandiose. He ignores his father's efforts to put him in the patient role and devalues the doctors. He attempts to dissociate himself from his mother's feelings of helplessness and sameness with him.

Father: Isn't it true that some basic dissatisfaction with

	things as they are brings you here or forces you here in some sense?
Michael:	Yeah, but look—everybody, you know has dissatisfactions—with things as they are, you know; I mean, I just went to the shrink and the shrink said, "Why did you want to come see me?" and I said, "Not particularly," and he said, "I think then, you know, you ought to do an inpatient thing"; so that was the way he saw things. I mean there were a lot of things he could have said—he could have said, "Why don't you hitchhike to San Francisco or something like that." I don't know.
Mother:	Michael, I'm—you know, I have something going on in my gut—I'm sympathizing with you because I—could tell from what you were saying before that you were kind of—probably terrified by this thing—starting and then you said something about your defenses and . . .
Michael (interrupting):	I'm not—I'm not terrified. It's like when I came in and talked with the doctor, he said, "Well, why don't you talk to me, I'm a doctor?" You know, well I don't care if you're God, you know, that doesn't mean I should talk to you. Well—if you were God, it might be different, you know, but I don't see *this* that way. But, just because you're a doctor doesn't mean I'm supposed to say, you know, it doesn't mean that it's all right that I should talk with him.
Therapist (to mother):	What were you starting to say? You were starting to say something about your response to Michael?
Mother:	Well, you know, I just think it's . . .
Therapist:	Something about your own gut.
Mother:	Yeah—I think it's frightening—he's not used to coming into a room with a lot of people—and strangers, so I think it's natural for Michael to be—anxious right now and he doesn't know what to say—particularly—and so I feel like I understand that—what he's struggling with—ah, so when

I say what's going on in my gut, I am sympathizing and, ah, realizing that I have some anxieties too, and ah, ah, I think that probably we all have. You know, when we're searching and—we don't know the answers and we're here; we're trusting you, you know, strangers to help us out.

Michael: I haven't! I haven't tried trusting him—I'm not—I mean, you probably are, you've figured that one out. . . .

Excerpt 2: The next excerpt is from a family therapy session two months after Michael was admitted to the hospital. The parents are complaining about how abusive Michael has been to his mother over the weekend. Both adolescents complain about their parents' overprotection and overconcern. It is clear that the parents are hurt and angry when their wishes for closeness and control in relation to their sons are rebuffed. There is evidence in this excerpt for a shared assumption in the family that autonomous functioning of a family member is experienced as abandonment.

In particular, the mother is sad and bereft at separation from Michael and wants contact with him even though she is rebuffed. She projects her own feelings of being a deserted, angry, empty creature onto him. She sees him as a scarecrow as he is leaving home to return to the hospital. When it is interpreted, she is able to see that much of the sadness really is her own response to the loss of a valued and exciting part of herself.

Mother: Well, you know, as he went out of the door he said—I put my arms on him like this and said, "Have a good week—or something like that," and obviously he didn't want this. Now I rarely . . .

Father: You put your arms around him, I think, is what we heard a minute ago.

Mother: I scarcely touch him in any way—because I feel that, you know, he doesn't want me to have anything to do with him—and he doesn't want to touch me or have me touch him or have me mother him or do anything. So most of the time I try to be very careful about this—perhaps I don't know, I had a simple surge of motherly something or other and just as I would to anybody—my husband going out the door—or anybody—of my children—of my family. I don't touch people usually—I'm not demonstrative usually—I think that occasionally I feel badly about Michael, I guess, and so I react to this and . . .

Father: But you see this is more of the same.

Michael: So you think if you hug me that's going to make everything really good?

Mother: No, I don't think any such thing.

Father: Michael is upset about it.

Therapist: I'm still wondering about the simplicity of the act. I don't think anyone in the family is all that simple.

Mother: Well, I think I was responding—I guess—to the sadness, you know, in Michael. He looks like a . . .

Michael (interrupting): Obviously I didn't want you to hug me—why did you do it anyway?

Mother (interrupting): Scarecrow often—most of the time—pardon?

Michael: Obviously I didn't want you to hug me. Why did you do it anyway? Every time when I leave and go out somewhere you always start talking, and, and, like it's really ridiculous—like I'm supposed to sit there and listen to whatever you have to say—you know, because I'm leaving, so you should put all this rap on me—I don't know—it's pretty far out—it's not very simple at all.

Therapist: It's even hard to locate the sadness, Mrs. Grant, because you say you see so much sadness in Michael and he says he sees so much sadness in you. I think there's a great effort in the family to put the sadness someplace else instead of people thinking about their own.

Mother: Well, I feel sad.

Therapist: I think you feel sad when he leaves and you start seeing him like a scarecrow—but I think it may be your sadness at that moment.

Mother: Okay, it's my sadness, it was my impulsive need

perhaps to get close to him or reassure myself—or something—I don't know. It was in that sense that I meant simple—it wasn't anything that one wouldn't do naturally with one's own family—it wasn't anything strange.

Excerpt 3: The next excerpt, taken from a family therapy session three months after Michael's admission to the hospital, provides a further view of Michael's relationship to his father. Father and son have been mutually antagonistic for years. The family has understood this as a consequence of the mother's special relationship to Michael. She felt Michael understood her better than her husband did.

The previous weekend the father found marijuana in Michael's room and flushed it down the toilet without talking to Michael about it at all. There was a fight later on, Michael saying he was furious at not being talked to. In the family session these events have been told. Father and son are both hurt by the distance between them. Each projects onto the other split-off, painful, and disappointing experiences with a father, with the consequence of increasing alienation.

Father: Michael did say he's very angry—but then he got over it, so he's plowed it under or something—you can't call it up now?

Michael: Call what up?

Father: Your angry feelings.

Michael: I'm angry all the time.

Father: What are you angry about—can you talk about it—as long as you can't talk about it, as long as you can't express it—particularly the part that relates to me—in some sense you are going to be tied to me—you're going to be hung up on it and you're never going to get rid of me.

Therapist: Maybe he thinks *you* want to get rid of *him*.

Father: Maybe he does. *Do* you?

Michael: I don't know—you seem to have gotten rid of yourself, you know.

Father: How did I get rid of myself?

Michael: Pardon me?

Father: How did I get rid of myself?

Michael: Well, you hid it away, I guess.
Father: You mean you don't see it.
Michael: No, I don't think I've ever seen it, actually.
[Brief omission.]
Mother: Michael, I couldn't hear what you said or I couldn't
              understand. You said he must have hid it
              away—what is it you felt he hid away?
Michael: Myself.
Mother: Is that what you were saying?
Michael: Um hum, he [therapist] said he [father] wanted to
              get rid of me—I said he [father] already got rid of
              himself—so he is trying to get rid of me now.
Mother (to father): What do you think of this?
Father: Well, it bespeaks an alienation which is all too plain,
              but I feel his distance—I've felt it for some
              time—but I haven't known how to budge it. . . . I
              know that something at least comparable hap-
              pened between my father and myself—I just
              crossed him off my list, so to speak. Maybe that's
              what Michael did to me. But it seems we ought to
              be able to talk about it in a way which would be
              wholesome.
Michael: Well . . .
Father: I'm not asking you to like me—it's not my right
              to—that's up to him.

Discussion of Excerpts: These excerpts contain examples of
a family functioning at a regressed level, dominated by unconscious assumptions equating individuation and separation with
catastrophic loss. Family regression militates against any realistic
experiences of phase-appropriate separation and suffuses individuation with anxiety. This is true for the parents as well as
the adolescents. Problems in the parents' individuation in their
own adolescent development are reactivated at the time of separation-individuation of their adolescent offspring.

The excerpts contain evidence of a narcissistic relationship
between Mrs. Grant and Michael, in which she has difficulty
differentiating herself from him and projects idealized aspects
of herself into him. The idealized relationship is stabilized only
by enlisting Michael as a self-object onto whom she projects the

characteristics of the idealized maternal image. She responds to Michael's separation-individuation from her as a narcissistic injury. In her narcissistic rage and depression, she projects onto Michael split-off, helpless, and devalued aspects of herself in relation to a dying mother who left her.

Mrs. Grant is unable to invest her husband or Paul with the idealized qualities she projects onto Michael. Both Mr. Grant and Paul are perceived by her as unempathic, remote, and critical. She relates to them as she did to her distant and critical father, and ignores and repudiates them as she felt he ignored and repudiated her.

Mr. Grant is an isolated, depressed, highly controlled, and intellectualizing man, who is pessimistic about the possibility of a good relationship with either of his sons. He responds to their rejection of him with intellectualizations and split-off hopelessness and angry repudiation, projecting onto them his own angry behavior with his own father. His rivalry with Michael for Mrs. Grant's interest is intense and overt. Mr. Grant's relationship with his wife is built upon his internal relationship with his own mother. His mother's death when he was six was experienced by him as a traumatic desertion, and he projects this split-off bad experience with a dying mother onto his wife when she withdraws from him, with ensuing rage and repudiation of her.

Michael manifests predominantly narcissistic pathology. He participates with his mother in a relationship in which his narcissistic equilibrium depends upon his involvement with her as a self-object. With separation-individuation, loss of this relationship with his mother has resulted in his grandiose feelings giving way to feelings of inferiority and worthlessness, with rage and efforts to project devaluation onto his mother. He attempts to regain narcissistic equilibrium through a relationship with Katie which is sexual and highly dependent, and modeled on the narcissism of his relationship with his mother. However, his fragile self-esteem cannot withstand the real challenges of school or work. He is very threatened by competition with men or peers, and fears of their malevolence have their origin in his relationship with his father.

Paul manifests overt borderline pathology. He is greatly impaired in personal relationships, experiencing paranoid anxiety with projection of destructiveness into any relationship in which he attempts to initiate satisfying activity with another person and exert independent control. He does not feel safe in the expression of either autonomous behavior or in the expression of emotional needs for nurture and satisfaction. He experiences himself as controlled by the other person, then feels enraged and projects that rage onto the other person.

An Example of Mature Family Functioning

A differentiation of mature in contrast to regressed family functioning can be made through comparing our findings in families of healthy adolescents with findings in families of adolescents who have borderline pathology. Our sample of adolescents who are functioning well came from a local private high school. Our study included individual interviewing and psychological testing of a group of adolescents who were selected because of good academic performance, and because they were student leaders in one area or another within the school. Over the period of a semester we conducted a weekly group meeting with these students, focusing on the theme of identity, and we saw the families in four weekly family study group meetings.

We studied eight families of adolescents from our school group. These adolescents showed no evident impairment in ego functioning and individuation, and no manifest disturbance either in research interviews or in psychological tests. Although the families were different in many respects, in the family group meetings there was positive evidence of intact self-object differentiation between members in all of the families, inferred from the following findings: (1) In parental delineations of the adolescent, there was clear differentiation of the adolescent from the parents. (2) Differentiation was preserved in those delineations by the parent determined by identification with the adolescent, and manifested in empathy. (3) Parents' delineations of the adolescent were not determined by evident dissociation and projection of aspects of the parents' personality characteristics. (4) Parents' delineations did not convey defensive remoteness, denial, and attributions to the adolescent of qualities disowned in the parents' own self. These characteristics of delineations are in sharp contrast to delineations of adolescents in families of borderline adolescents.

Furthermore, characteristics of the family as a group differed from those we found in our borderline sample. When the adolescent was functioning well, parents were frequently conscious of working explicitly to manage their feelings in such a way as to support adolescent individuation and separation. It was our impression that this support was maintained without obvious reaction formation or manifest denial. These parents did not give evidence of the mixed messages, confusion, and regression regularly activated in parents of borderline adolescents by issues of separation-individuation. Above all, these parents maintained the capacity to manage without regression the experience of mourning an integrated ambivalent whole object during separation. In brief, the families of healthy adolescents were able to maintain mature family functioning when contending with the developmental task of adolescent individuation and separation to a far greater degree than were the families of borderline adolescents.

The Ross Family

The family consists of Mr. Ross, age forty-eight; Mrs. Ross, age forty-five; son Walter, age seventeen, and a senior in high school; son Kent, age fifteen, and a sophomore in high school. Mr. Ross is a prominent lawyer and teacher. Mrs. Ross is trained as a teacher but has not been working regularly for a number of years. Walter is the family member in the school group we have been studying.

Excerpt 1

Father: You mean, why I was happy? Well, I think my two kids are unbelievably great. And you know, I have the feeling unless they almost artificially screw things up, they'll do *fine*. You know—I was pleased at their thoughts and the way they expressed them. I'm glad they're thinking about taking even their parents' advice not for granted. In other words the parents' advice must be good advice for them to follow it; they don't necessarily follow it just because it's a parent now; they're thinking things through. I'm not worried that they won't usually take my advice. I don't push my advice on them. I only say something when I really think I know, and often say, "You do what you think; your judgment is probably good on this; I don't quite agree with the way you're doing it, but I think you're doing a reasonable thing." I don't know if I give this impression to the children, but this is what I *think* I'm giving the impression.

Dr. S: You say you're not worried if they take your advice or not.

Walter: It's that you'll offer the advice, but you think that we'll generally make good decisions anyway. Even if it's not your advice.

Father: Yeah, I think so. If I were able to say, "Look, would you please *do* this, and let's not—discuss this—I think this is very important!" I have no DOUBT they would do it. I do it very, very rarely. You know, in an emergency. I say, "Look, would you discuss this later but do it now anyhow, just trust me," you know I have the feeling they would trust me, period. I—I don't know, I hope I have not often misused this—type of authority.

Mother: I'd rather say I think they're terrific because of the thing that you said, that we trust their overall judgment. The ability to make decisions. It isn't just school or wrestling or driving or any of this, but over and over again when there has been some choice to be made or some kind of decision, they have done what we felt was intelligent; and more than intelligent, they go out of their way for things.

Father: My wife's right. Obviously.

Excerpt 2

Mother: You know, they HAVE to be affected by the way we live and relate to what goes on around us. My husband has a thing that he carves out on pieces of wood or something; it says "WORK." This is his motto. It's almost as though it doesn't matter as to what the work is for as long as you're doing it. I would kinda like to *know!*

Dr. S: You probably recognize that in your own background, too, Mrs. Ross. Maybe a different way.

Mother: I don't think it's good to have that much pressure. That was too much.

Father: What *you* had.

Mother: What *I* had was too much. It was a conflict between a white-collar background, and no money. They never considered the fact that I can stop and earn the money and then go back. I *had* to go to college, even though there wasn't quite enough money to do it with. I would now advise anyone in the same situation: "For heaven's sake, stop at some point, get some money, and then do it where you don't have to have all the pressure and uncertainty and all the rest of it."

Dr. S: You made a contrast between what you experienced and the way you were trying to influence your kids. I'm not clear about the contrast. I feel there is one. I mean, you don't want to reproduce some of the things that happened in your own life.

Mother: Definitely. I'll give you an example I used once before. I told someone that in the family I was brought up in, the parents got for breakfast a grapefruit and the children got an orange. And I married into a family where the children get the grapefruit and if the parents can have a grapefruit too, that's fine, but if not, they're going to get the orange; and I just wasn't sure where in my life I got the grapefruit. Now, then, obviously I didn't like the idea of getting the orange. Therefore, I can't very well give oranges to my kids. Because this isn't right. Fortunately, I can have grapefruit with them, most of the time. But if there's any choice, the kids are going to get the grapefruit because I didn't like getting the orange.

Dr. S: But you don't like getting the orange now either.

Mother: Well; but I like the way they turn out with the grapefruit. *This* is a tremendous satisfaction.

Father: There has to come a time when you have to stop making the same mistake.

Mother: I have another quick example. I told his mother and she enjoyed it, so I remember it. I did not have to write a thesis for my master's at Teacher's College, it just so happened. So I said, well, Walter's my thesis. Because it was in guidance, you see. "Now, I'll see how this turns out, how's my thesis?" Well, my thesis is doing great! I'm not complaining; the second edition's coming along quite well, too. They are my, you know, as the ladies say, my jewels; and this is just fine. I'm having a real tough time, this year, because—what I have to do I know quite well. I have to say an easy good-bye. But it is killing me—it is pain like I have felt only several times [weeping; several seconds' silence].

Dr. S: You mean saying good-bye.

Mother: I went around picking violets the other day where I used to wait for you in middle school. The violets are still there. But I wouldn't want you to be like that. You were little boys, you were unsure. You're beautifully sure now, and if you're not, you know at least how to look for answers. So I'll just talk to myself some more [weeping].

Dr. S: I wonder what your mother's tears mean to you both?

Walter: Well, tears are sort of funny things around here. A lot of people get—an image, when somebody's crying—"Don't—don't touch it," and all this kind of stuff. And—you don't—with us. You just don't take it in the negative, scary fashion that a lot of people do. We've talked about—my grandfather, you know I felt very close to crying, but it's not—it isn't a sad thing. It sure sort of beats talking sometimes.

Kent: Sadness can be coped with. I mean, happiness should be—you know, savored.

Dr. S: You know, Walter, I think you're dodging the issue

	of saying good-bye, too.
Walter:	I'll tell you. I've been in the process now of saying good-bye for about two or three years now. And you know, by the time it actually comes around, it isn't going to be that much of a jump.
Dr. S:	But you have been in the process.
Kent:	I think I'm—starting. have you noticed?
Walter:	How?
Father:	You gotta—man, you gotta—that's just it! And sure it's a mixed thing, sadness and happiness. And we're not ashamed about tears. I cry. Kent, and I probably cry very easily. You know, I don't give a damn.
Dr. S:	I didn't get the feeling of shame. I had the feeling that Mrs. Ross was concerned because she was able to say so clearly that it is a hard thing for her to let the boys go; that it might be a problem for them, and wanted to hear whether it seemed to be.

Father (interrupting): To them it's not a problem.

Mother:	To them. To them. So I would say I'm doing all right. But this *is* what I was listening for.
Father:	This has been her whole life—for—seventeen years, and sure it's a tremendous problem for her. Intellectually she knows it and she knows that it's a right time. And every time, you know, Walt takes the car and drives someplace, it worries her; and the fact that they come and go and Walter drives Kent and they're independent, her usefulness in her own mind seems questioned. But she intellectually knows that this is correct. Now emotionally this is very difficult sometimes. Sometimes more, sometimes less. But you know, it's not always easy just because you know intellectually it's correct.
Mother:	You can see I have talked to him some about this already.
Dr. S:	I'm sure you have. I was wondering, Kent, you say you thought you were beginning, but do you have some more reaction to your mother's—feelings?

	Your father says you cry easily. I'm not sure what you feel.
Father:	No, he and *I* cry easily, I said.
Mother:	I've never seen Kent cry so much.
Father:	I didn't say so much. I said easily.
Kent:	I don't know. I—was thinking about not crying, myself, at the moment.
Mother:	Oh—thank you.
Kent:	I mean one cries when one is filled up with an idea. At the moment I was concentrating, on not quite concentrating on it. Uh, that's right.

Discussion of Excerpts: In the Ross family we find evidence of mature family functioning in the area of separation-individuation, although it is clear that the work of separation is difficult for each of the family members. Mrs. Ross, in particular, manifests conscious mourning. In her mourning, however, she maintains an internal relationship to an integrated whole object and gives no evidence of regression to splitting and impaired self-object differentiation. She is supported in her effort to separate and to mourn by Mr. Ross. He seems more to attempt to counter his wife's sadness than to attend to his own.

In this family unconscious and conscious assumptions appear to support adolescent individuation and separation. The parents appear to be well differentiated from the adolescents. The mother gets active encouragement and support from the father. The parents are alert to the problem of molding the adolescents to suit the parents' own needs. This may happen more than is apparent in the research interviews. The adolescents are certainly compliant to the family values. They give evidence of well-integrated functioning, good capacity to mourn, and if emotional difficulties were present, they are in the area of neurotic rather than borderline structure. The parents are well related to the adolescents but clearly differentiated from them. The mother, for example, is very clear about who gets the grapefruit and who gets the orange; the father is clear that both he and Kent cry, not much, but easily. We take this as evidence of good self-object differentiation and management of phase-appropriate mourning without ego regression.

Discussion

In this paper I attempt to define aspects of family functioning which support or interfere with capacities for individuation and separation in parents as well as adolescents. The family setting is a situation of dependency where specific anxieties over separation-individuation may be activated by unconscious family assumptions leading to family regression and to ego regression in individual family members.

In families where we observe severe regression in the parents, we find evidences of breakdown of the affectional and supportive functions of the marriage, with the child and adolescent then enlisted to perform these functions for the parents. These parents have frequently had severe disturbances over individuation in their own families of origin and adolescent developments and have initially been able to utilize marriage and the raising of children as a means of managing a narcissistic organization of affectional and dependency needs. Such parents experience the individuation of the adolescent as a traumatic loss. The parents must confront their own vulnerability to separation and narcissistic regression again in their middle years, and manifest regression and self-absorption rather than continuing individuation in the crisis of mid-life.

A conception of renewed individuation in adulthood is contained in Erikson's (1968) discussion of the developmental crisis of adulthood in which he articulates the polarities of generativity versus self-absorption and stagnation. Individuation is implicit in generativity which assumes the expansion of ego interests and of increased libidinal investment in parenting, teaching, and a range of adult activities. In contrast, Erikson describes self-absorption and stagnation, states of adult regression manifested in obsessive needs for pseudointimacy, interpersonal improverishment, self-concern, and often physical and psychological invalidism. He finds the clearest pathology of generativity in pathology of parental functioning that then results in the estrangements and disturbances of childhood and youth.

My effort in this paper has been to explicate a level of mature family functioning which promotes expanding generativity and renewed individuation in parents and separating adolescents. I have contrasted mature family functioning to regressed functioning in families of borderline and narcissistic adolescents. In the latter families, anxiety over separation and change has activated family regression, with states of identity confusion in the adolescent, and the emergence in parents of increasing narcissistic regression and self-absorption. The method of analysis of family observations I have described thus gives a body of data that fits well with Erikson's framework of the developmental crises of adolescence and adulthood.

In his paper "The Roots of Virtue" (1961, p. 164), Erikson says: "the individual ego can be strong only through a mutual guarantee of strength, given to and received by all whose life-cycles intertwine; and it can transcend itself only where it has learned to engage and to disengage itself responsibly from others." The work I have presented attempts to clarify the conditions of responsible engagement and disengagement within the family that allow continued ego growth in the adolescent and in the parents at mid-life.

References

Berkowitz, D., Shapiro, R. L., Zinner, J., & Shapiro, E. (1974), Family contributions to narcissistic disturbances in adolescence. *Int. Rev. Psychoanal.*, 1:353–362.

Bion, W. (1961), *Experiences in Groups*. London: Tavistock.

Blos, P. (1967), The second individuation process of adolescence. *The Psychoanalitic Study of the Child*, 22:162–86. New York: International Universities Press.

——— (1979), *The Adolescent Passage*. New York: International Universities Press.

Erikson, E. H. (1961), The roots of virtue. In: *The Humanist Frame*, ed. J. Huxley. New York: Harper, pp. 145–165.

——— (1968), *Identity*. New York: Norton.

Jacobson, E. (1964), *The Self and Object World*. New York: International Universities Press.

Kernberg, O. F. (1976), *Object Relations Theory and Clinical Psychoanalysis*. New York: Aronson.

Mahler, M., Pine, F., & Bergman, A. (1975), *The Psychological Birth of the Human Infant*. New York: Basic Books.

Shapiro, E., Zinner, J., Shapiro, R., & Berkowitz, D. (1975), The influence of family experience on borderline personality development. *Int. Rev. Psychoanal.*, 2:399–411.

Shapiro, R. L. (1967), The origin of adolescent disturbances in the family.

In: *Family Therapy and Disturbed Families*, ed. G. Zuk & I. Boszormenyi-Nagy. Palo Alto, CA: Science & Behavior Books, pp. 221–238.

———— (1979), Family dynamics and object-relations theory. In: *Adolescent Psychiatry*, ed. S. Feinstein & P. Giovacchini. Chicago: University of Chicago Press, pp. 118–135.

———— (1986), Family determinants of borderline conditions and pathological narcissism. In: *New Concepts in Psychoanalytic Psychotherapy*, ed. J. M. Russ & W. A. Myers. Washington, DC: American Psychiatric Press, 1988.

———— Zinner, J. (1971), Family organization and adolescent development. In: *Task and Organization*, ed. E. Miller. London: J. Wiley, 1976, pp. 289–308.

Zinner, J., & Shapiro, R. L. (1972), Projective identification as a mode of perception and behavior in families of adolescents. *Internat. J. Psycho–Anal.*, 52:523–530.

———— ———— (1974), The family group as a single psychic entity. *Internat. Rev. Psychoanal.*, 1:179–186.

PART IV
APPLICATIONS IN HISTORY
AND LITERATURE

19

TERROR, THE STARTLE RESPONSE, AND DISSOCIATION

LAWRENCE C. KOLB, M.D.

My gratitude to and respect for Frieda Fromm-Reichmann remain unbounded. I was one of her analysands. This mutually shared experience personally freed me in innumerable ways, which have affected my life from the termination of the analysis in 1950 until the present. In addition, I came to know what transference meant, to acquire a model for psychoanalytic work, and a zest for learning more of Frieda's thinking through her writings and those of her colleagues.

Only later did I come to know more of Frieda's earlier works—her admiration for the work of George Groddeck and her own insightful and penetrating writing in psychosomatic medicine, particularly as related to migraine. As with others I was impressed with Frieda's courageously pursuing her interest in the dynamics of schizophrenia. Her areas of study and her willingness to explore and modify analytic technology opened up new pathways.

The following observations are taken from patients suffering chronic posttraumatic stress disorders (PTSD) induced by long-continued exposure to combat in Vietnam. That is, in the older vernacular, war neuroses. The work initially represented an effort in applied psychoanalysis; the work is off the traditional track, as was much of Frieda's. I believe that my findings have direct bearing on the initiating factors for all dissociative states: namely, the flashbacks of the war neurotic, amnesias, fugues, hysterical psychoses, the "three-day schizophrenics," and multiple personalities. The findings related directly to theory of the stimulus barrier.

397

It is almost seventy years since the monograph *Psychoanalyses and the War Neuroses* (Freud, 1919) was published. Freud's introduction to that monograph makes clear his perception of the challenge to the libido theory which emanated from the phenomenology of the war neurosis. So too the nighttime phenomenology of the repetitive frightening dreams of combat questioned his theoretical position as regards dream theory.

These challenges to Freud's original theories may have been responsible for the ongoing interest of psychoanalysts in the posttraumatic states (Grinker and Spiegel, 1945; Kardiner, 1941; Krystal, 1975). Certainly as a group the psychoanalysts have made the most significant contributions to the understanding of these states.

It was Simmel's (Freud, 1919) successful therapeutic work using hypnosis during World War I, which undercut the idea that the war neuroses were due to "shell shock." Freud defined the condition as one due to overwhelming ego conflict.

Kardiner's work (1941) on the chronic cases from World War I remains a classic; his extraordinarily perceptive clinical observations, his definition of the constant symptoms, their possible coexistence with other personality disorders, and his suggestion that this neurotic process differed from the social neurosis (it was, in fact, for him a *physioneurosis*) are nuclear to the work reported here. Kardiner emphasized the importance of the continuing startle reaction as the potential source of the chronic irritability, hyperalertness, and explosiveness of these patients. These symptoms with the repetitive nightmares of combat and intrusive daytime thinking of the same he labeled as "constant."

My work with the chronic cases of PTSD endured by combat states was initiated eight years ago (Kolb and Mutalipassi, 1982). My patients suffered severe, persistent, socially maladaptive outcomes as the result of long-continued and high-level combat exposure.

To make comprehensible the evolution of my thinking about PTSD I think it best to commence at the beginning; that is, the observations made during my early attempts to provide treatment to men with PTSD. This added experience consists of personal examination of over 200 Vietnam veterans with chronic and delayed PTSD. About half of those with PTSD have been treated by me (Kolb, 1983, 1986) in individual or group therapy, hypnosis, narcotherapy as well as with appropriate drugs. I (1987) also have examined ten prisoners of war of World War II and a sizable number of missed chronic and delayed PTSD's from the Korean and World War II conflicts as well as many noncombatant-era veterans.

Among the earlier and more severely disturbed cases seen by me were a number of men with socially impairing, dissociative states (flashbacks) or panic attacks. My dynamic interpretation of these symptoms was that they represented evidence of persistence of intensely held repression of emotion unalleviated by previously administered treatment. Many indicated the persistence of "startle" with associated physiological arousal on exposure to sharp sounds produced by helicopters or other explosive noises. These men provided sketchy accounts without associated affect when pushed to describe their combat experience.

A decision was made to initiate treatment in eighteen such cases, using a modified form of narcosynthesis directed at verifying the existence of repressed emotion, providing emotional derepression, and through an audiovisual recording of behavior during the treatment to confront the patient with a continuing, more definitively dynamic psychotherapy. The narcosynthetic technique was modified as well to test the existence of startle. This was carried out by exposure of each patient to a brief train of combat sounds as the initiating stimulus for abreaction rather than by verbal suggestion, as was commonly practiced in treatment of severely disturbed, acute cases during World War II.

Fourteen of the eighteen men exposed to a moderate intensity combat sound stimulus of thirty seconds while in arousable pentobarbital anesthesia immediately responded with time regression and reenacted a Vietnam combat experience, with intense emotional abreaction of affects of fear, rage, indignation, sadness, and guilt. No responses were elicited by musical stimuli or by silence. Two noncombat veterans exposed to the sound train also failed to abreact.

The characteristics of this group of men have been described in some detail (Kolb and Mutalipassi, 1982). Behavioral reenactment of combat scenes from experiences of a decade or more in the past were as dramatic as any seen by me when I treated the acute cases of World War II. The emotionality was so evident that an effort was made to monitor electroencephalogram, cardiac and respiratory rate during later trials. Nothing of significance was recorded here, aside from barbiturate waves in the electroencephalogram. The assumption was made that the intravenous drugs had obscured related organ responses during the emotional storm.

To examine the hypothesis that autonomic arousal indeed did occur following startle by a meaningful sound stimulus reminiscent of combat, a collaborative study was begun with E. Blanchard of the Stress Laboratory of the State University of New York at Albany (1983). Two years ago Pallmeyer et al. (1986) of that laboratory exposed in a fully conscious state combat veterans, who meet the operational criteria for PTSD according to DSM-III, to a train of combat sounds of varying intensity and given at variable time sequences, interspersed with periods of music and silence, while monitoring by polygraph diastolic and systolic blood pressure, heart rate, electromyogram, fingertip skin temperature, and galvanic skin reflex. In addition to the physiological responses to the combat sounds, they were also exposed to an intellectual stress test and a variety of standardized psychological tests.

Their responses to these instruments were compared with the responses initially to those of a same-aged control group of healthy university students who had never served in the military. Later the following control groups were tested in precisely the same manner: ten veterans with and four without psychiatric disorders; and four civilians with other anxiety disorders. Exposure to the meaningful combat noise discriminated the PTSD combat veterans physiologically from all other groups, at statistically significant levels on both blood pressure indices, pulse rate, and muscle tension. The arousal of many men was so distressing personally that they terminated the experiment at low levels of sound intensity. This group also discriminated on all psychological tests. Since then an additional thirty-two patients with PTSD and seventeen controls have been assessed.

This work is confirmed by two other groups of researchers (Dobbs and Wilson, 1960; Malloy et al., 1983), so that there now exist three entirely independent and unrelated studies which demonstrate that American combat veterans from two wars, with the clinical symptomatology of PTSD, when exposed to meaningful stimuli reminiscent of combat exhibit abnormal behavioral and physiological arousal, as compared with 56 controls for a variety of groups.

These findings confirm Kardiner's hypothesis that the startle response is due to conditioning. They define a subgroup of combat veterans with chronic or delayed forms of PTSD who have a persisting, conditioned, emotional response to external stimuli reminiscent of battle sounds. Their histories indicate that they also respond to visual and olfactory stimuli, when those too are meaningful in tterms of combat stress. As such, they remain (1) at high risk for cognitive dissociation in drug-altered states of consciousness on exposure to such stimuli; and (2) respond with immediate and excess physiological arousal in cardiovascular and neuromuscular systems. We may postulate that in such men there exists an ongoing perceptual abnormality, defined as regressive impairment of ability to discriminate specific sensory inputs associated with the traumatic events. We postulate further that there exists excessive autonomic arousal of central adrenergic origin.

As to the latter, two other reports support this conclusion (Mason et al., 1985; Wenger, 1948) as well as the exploratory therapeutic work carried on at the Albany VAMC in prescription of adrenergic blocking agents (Kolb et al., 1984).

Pertinent here are some other clinical observations. Of seven men instructed by me to use a tape of combat sounds for desensitization (initially to be played at subliminal intensities), none was able to do so without arousing somatic responses. One, angered at his failures, played the tape at high intensity of his sound system, dissociated cognitively, and in a violent rage tore apart his workroom.

The other observation of pragmatic significance is related to surgical practice. Three men reported that following surgical procedures and while recovering in the intensive care unit, they were told they became confused and "acted crazy," tearing out the life-support tubings. Beyond that, the long-term follow-up of patients in continuing treatment had demonstrated time and again the recrudescence of the constant symptoms of the condition, as defined by Kardiner (1941), in the face of either a current stressful life event involving loss and arousing once again emotions of terror, sadness, or anger; or by threats to the individual's own body by acute illness or accidents. Here I will refer as well to Helen Hooven Santmeyer's description of the death experiences of three major male figures, all Civil War combat veterans, in her recent bestseller *And Ladies of the Club* (1985). She describes feeling their reexperiencing of combat scenes in terminal deliria and terminal dreams.

To illustrate the psychopathology of the startle response I have videotaped and will present two patient interviews where the patients describe the devastating effects of the salient, but little recognized, bit of psychopathology.

Case 1: This thirty-eight-year-old patient is a combat marine veteran of Vietnam, the sole survivor of an eighty-four-man platoon ambushed and wiped out at Khe Sanh by a North Vietnamese rocket attack. Subsequently, he remained at the Khe Sanh base camp during the rocket and artillery siege there. The unit was relieved in April 1968 and during withdrawal came under attack. His behavior then was uncontrolled in that he manned a machine gun and fired at any moving object. Then the patient was relieved from duty, treated for "combat fatigue," and on return to the United States was released to the custody of his father. The patient's strange behavior at home led to his parents building a small annex to the house for him in order to isolate him and save them embarrassment. Extraneous noises induced in him flight behavior in which he fearfully sought protective cover at the same time yelling to others to do the same. He was disoriented at such times, believing he was in Vietnam under attack. Following the death of his father he moved away from the family and has lived an isolated life. In recent years he only left his apartment briefly early in the day. At one time he went out to mass and a gymnasium. Later he discontinued these activities as following exposure to a fire siren near his church he dissociated, rushed about the church to seek cover, and finally ended hiding in the priest's cloak room. These behaviors, especially the many times he shouted combatlike noises, led his fellow renters to complain to his landlord and eventually brought him to the attention of mental health authorities.

On examination he appeared catatenoid but had none of the associated features of the catatonic state. Physically the only abnormality was a persistent tachycardia that was not associated with other diseases. He presented the classical symptoms of a chronic PTSD with repetitive nightmares, constant intrusive thinking of his war experiences, frequent startle reactions induced not only by auditory stimuli but also by visual, olfactory, and kinesthetic stimuli reminding him of his combat exposures. Associated with these symptoms were preoccupations about his bodily symptoms (palpitations, tensions), depression, survival guilt, and guilt associated with his combat experiences, shame and exquisite concern over humiliating others with his behavior.

Prior to entering the marines by enlistment, the patient was brought up in a warm family. He completed high school as an average student but showed musical talent both in composing and in playing percussion instruments. His relations were gratifying with both boys and girls in his classes. There is no history of personal or family mental illness. His physical health was good prior to enlistment.

I: Jim, can you tell me how you happened to come to the hospital?
P: I was recommended here from the Department of Mental Health.
I: How did the Department of Mental Health come to know you?
P: Through the police and flashbacks in the street and my landlord notifying them that I don't go out of the house.
I: How long have you been with this landlord?
P: I moved since then.
I: Prior to that move?
P: Prior to that almost ten years.
I: Almost ten years with him. You didn't go out of the house at all?
P: Very seldom.
I: When did you go out and for what reason?

P: I would go out early in the morning to get a newspaper or go to church.

I: What did you do about your meals?

P: The landlord used to buy them for me.

I: You arranged that?

P: Yes, sir.

I: Now you said the flashbacks in the street—what happened exactly?

P: Well, fire engine sirens or sudden noise do something to me. Things make me run and hide.

I: Did the police pick you up after you ran and hid? And how did that happen?

P: I was running and I fell into a ditch and I broke my wrist and other times I would hide in a basement or cellar and they would call the police.

I: How many times did they call the police?

P: I don't know how many.

I: So the police eventually took you to mental health.

P: Yes, sir.

I: Before you moved up here, where were you?

P: Long Island.

I: Who were you living with there?

P: I was living with my family.

I: Can you tell me what it was like when you came back to your family following your coming out of Vietnam?

P: It wasn't very pleasant. The family noticed my unusual behavior. Mostly from flashbacks. Isolation and different things.

I: How did you isolate yourself there?

P: My father had a partition built on the house. That's where I stayed.

I: Did you ask to have him do that? How did that happen?

P: No, sir. He told me it was for my benefit. I guess so that I wouldn't embarrass the family.

I: Did he tell you how you were embarrassing the family?

P: Yes, sir.

I: What did he say?

P: That my family entertained a lot and several times I would go into a flashback or fall asleep in a nightmare and I guess this was sort of embarrassing.

I: What did you do on such occasions? Do you remember any of them? Do you know anything about any of them?

P: No sir, just what they told me. I would run through the house screaming to everyone to keep their helmets on and get in a hole 'cause we're getting hit.

I: Now tell me, how do you feel at the present time?

P: Not well.

I: I notice you sit very rigidly and very constrained. Is there a reason for that?

P: I don't now.

I: What is your feeling inside?

P: Scared.

I: Are you scared all the time?

P: Yes, sir.

I: What do you think is going to happen?

P: That I'm going into a flashback and embarrass myself or someone or that someone is going to hurt me.

I: What do you think people might do to you?

P: Put me in the battlefield.

I: Oh? Where?

P: Vietnam.

I: Any particular field?

P: Khe Sanh, leading the platoon.

I: You have told me about that. Do you want to talk about that now or not?

P: I'll try.

I: Good. Go ahead.

P: Well, we were on a mission in the northern part of Vietnam and it involved two whole battalions of marines. And my platoon was the point of the battalion and we walked into a trap and got rocketed and I was the only one that made it. And I feel guilty over that.

I: How did you get out?

P: I was in the bomb crater and I waited until after the firefight and stayed there all night, and the next day I walked back to my company.

I: Do you want to say anything about that walk?

P: All my buddies were dead.
I: You saw them all?
P: Yes, sir.
I: And when you found your company, what happened then?
P: I went back to pick up.
I: You did that, too?
P: I wanted to.
I: Did you?
P: Yes.
I: How many men were there?
P: Eighty-three.
I: Eighty-three and you were the NCO?
P: I was the NCO of my squad.
I: Has there been any change in your condition since you have been coming to the hospital?
P: I would like to believe so.
I: How much do you believe it?
P: I'm still alive.
I: Yes.
P: I have a lot of hope that I'm going to get better.
I: Do you feel any easier being with people since you have been coming here and meeting the fellows from Vietnam?
P: No, sir.
I: Are you able to talk to any of them?
P: They try.
I: How do you feel when they talk to you?
P: I feel a little confused, I guess. I don't want to build up a relationship and go through what I went through in Vietnam all over.
I: What are you afraid of in a relationship?
P: I don't want to get close to anyone. And then have to lose them.
I: You don't want to lose them?
P: No, sir.
I: How was it when you lost your father?
P: I missed him.
I: Did you have as much pain and anger then as when you were in Vietnam?
P: No, sir.

I: It wasn't as bad?

P: No, sir.

I: Even though you were very close to him?

P: Yes, I was close to him.

I: You've told me that. All right; thank you very much.

P: You are welcome.

Case 2: The patient is a sixty-eight-year-old, married, World War II veteran who served with a tank unit. During the Battle of the Bulge his tank was struck by German artillery. He managed to clamber out in a dazed state, was picked up, and transferred through a series of military psychiatric units with the diagnosis of "combat fatigue." Released from service on return to the United States, he has been a continuing outpatient at several Veterans Administration hospitals. When exposed to loud noises he jumps and yells. On some occasions this behavior has led others to rush to help him. He has responded as though he were being attacked and struck out against his would-be helpers. This led to a number of brief admissions to psychiatric units of the VA hospital.

Except for emphysema, the patient is physically well. Developmental history failed to disclose evidence of physical or psychiatric disturbance prior to his military service.

The patient states that ever since he came home he has noticed he has been very irritable, tense, and exceptionally startled. The startle response is so great that it has very much upset his social life. He feels very conspicuous due to the fact that it occurs almost anywhere when he is exposed to a sharp sound.

I: Do you want to tell us a little bit about that? How you noticed this over the years?

P: Well, when I come out, the doctor there, I was in line to be discharged, I didn't know anything about what happened to me. The doctor there noticed me. He said you can go back to the hospital for a while, so I was there for over a year. I got discharged and my doctor sent me back to Framingham. I was real shaky and very tense all the time. I went to the GE to get a job and the doctor touched me and I jumped. He said we can't take a chance on you. It's better if you work outside, so I went down to a small plant in Pittsfield, Massachusetts, and they had an opening for a mail clerk, so I took that and in the meanwhile I was in outpatient from the time I got out of the hospital. So I tried to fight it. I tried to go see the movies, but anything anybody does do with some noise or anything lately I don't have any control over the nerves at all. Even the telephone sometimes rings, I jump; or if a dish should drop on the floor, I jump. I don't know. Something I don't believe my-self—so jumpy I am. I'm all right. I don't drive too much. My eyes are getting bad after all. I am sixty-eight and my eyes are not too good at night. I come over by bus. I feel I want to be independent. I don't want my wife or anybody.

I: You stay pretty much at home now?

P: I go in the morning and get my paper and I read and I lie down about 10:00. I relax. I don't go nowhere. Once in a while I know just where to go.

I: How do you sleep?

P: On my belly, I think.

I: No, I mean do you sleep through the whole night?

P: Yep, I sleep all night. Now.

I: Now?

P: Now. Before I used to wake up.

I: That's before you were put on the medication.

P: Yes. Before the medication.

I: What woke you up at night?

P: Well, a lot of time different things that happened in the war.

I: Did you dream about the war?

P: Yeah, I used to dream about it. People dying. Because I seen a lot of people dying. On the street. On the hill. We used to fire. We had orders to fire at will. We used to fire at anything. We went through a town after they were dead. We just took a shot at them. I don't know, maybe we were a little off.

I: Just rest a minute.

P (screams): I don't know. I don't know why the hell I should be like this. I don't know. I know I never could work near machinery. In other words, I'm not dead, but I am three-quarters dead. I'd be better off dead than alive instead of getting hit. I should have gotten hit in the brain. I'd be better off.

[Secretary in the background signaled to commence typing. Patient jumps.]

I: Even that upsets you?

P: No, I don't think so.

I: You are more used to that.

P: Yeah, I'm used to that.

I: What happens when people get near to you?

P: I don't go anywheres. I do go to meetings of the Veterans of Foreign Wars.

I: Let's say when someone comes up behind you.

P: Well, most of the time people don't touch you. If they do and I got something in my hand, I'm going to throw it up. That's why I don't go many places.

[Interviewer touches patient. Patient yells and quickly pulls away.]

I: That really upsets you?

P: I don't know what it is. I can't.

I: It has always been that way?

P: As I said, I don't know what it is. I don't know whether it is—I don't know. Like a magnet or something. You touch magnets—just like my nerves. They seem to. I don't like the sound of fireworks. I never go to fireworks. I went a couple of times and then I came out.

I: You have a bad time on the 4th of July, do you?

P: I stay away. I don't go for that.

I: Now we are going to play some music and other sounds for you and see how that goes. That doesn't upset you?

[Classical musical sounds are projected from a tape recorder.]

P: No. One thing that does help me. I do like musicals. Not that kind they have now. Those rock and roll. Music from the '40s. When I was young. I don't go to movies. The junk that it is today. As I said, I'm living day to day and some days I wish I was dead because I can't do what I want. I can't walk. I walk and I have to walk just so far. Hell, I got false teeth. Bad eyes. What the hell. [Combat sounds are projected from the tape recorder. He yells.] You don't have to do that.

I: Does that sound real to you?

P: Well, yeah. [Starts to cry and wipes face with back of hand.] An old man like me crying. That's nuts.

I: Now I'm going to try one more tape. [Sounds resembling machine guns are projected from the tape recorder.] Does that sound like the noises you heard in World War II?

P: Yeah, it sounds like it. [Breathing very heavily.] Don't let me do anything I don't want to do. That's fire. Somebody shooting. That's not a machine gun. That sounds like a rifle.

I: You've had enough.

P: I've had enough my whole life, never mind that. I wish you could put me to bed and put me to sleep forever and the hell with all this nonsense. Try to save me for what—I don't know. I am very disturbed and disgusted with everything.

We have then a clinical condition induced by either a single, massive, psychological assault or by recurrent or continued exposure to experiences associated with violent death, destruction, and/or mutilation of others. These experiences of high-intensity emotional stimulation induce the emotions of terror and fear. They are followed by a number of constant yet repetitive behavioral, cognitive, and physiological processes. In many, withdrawal from exposure, nonrecurrence of exposure, and avoidance of memory-arousing experiences similar to the terror-arousing exposure lead to extinction of these phenomena. Yet others go on to suffer delayed, recurrent, or persistent display of the consequences of the overwhelming emotional assault. I emphasize emotional and not psychological. Emotion implies stimulus facilitation and intensity; cognition may be facilitated or destroyed depending upon the intensity of the stimulation. Among those who fail to recover from the initial assault is the group with conditioned emotional response. This latter condition must exist as a consequence of a change in central nervous system functioning—a shift in threshold of response or exposure to either external or internal events which arouse the emotions of terror, fear, or anger.

The unconditional stimulus and response are contained in

the innate startle response of infancy. Startle response to loud sounds has been recognized as a behavioral manifestation of fear since the earliest studies of infant behaviors. That this innate reflex may be conditioned to associated percepts has been known for many years (Kolb, 1984). The central issue of delayed or chronic PTSD is the failure in cognitive processing to bring about the extinction of the startle reaction. Its persistence with episodic and recurrent arousal of fear and terror interrupts cognition, places the sufferers at high risk for dissociation, and permanently disturbs somatic homeostasis upon which stable self-image perceptions rest.

Much has been learned about conditioned fear from animal experimentation that is relevant to these considerations (Anderson and Parmenter, 1941). Animals with chronic neurosis induced by painful stimulation have startlingly similar behaviors to those of men with chronic PTSD. Solomon and Wynne (1954), on the basis of their studies of fear conditioning and recognition of nonextinction of responses to conditioned stimuli, suggested that there occurred a permanent shift in thresholds as well as in neuronal functioning. Certainly the clinical phenomenology in those with chronic PTSD-CER indicated a shift in threshold reaction time from point of perception of danger.

What is striking in the literature on PTSD is the paucity of thought given to potential neural change as causative of persistence of symptomatology. When Freud (1920) conceived of the *stimulus barrier* as the protective screen against excessive stimulation, he described in fact three barriers—the skin, the contact sensory barrier, and the cortical barrier. Ego functioning was postulated to rest upon the cortical neuronal barrier.

If we are to devise a comprehensive theory of the evolution of the stress disorders, we must go beyond ego (psychological) functions and reflect upon the consequences of high-intensity stimulation upon the structural framework on which it depends—that is, the cortical neuronal network.

Elsewhere, I have proposed a neuropsychological hypothesis (1987), which provides explanations for the varieties of PTSD, the reason for delay in some, intensification of symptoms, an exposure to meaningful stimuli, and classification of systems into those related to domestic dysfunctions and secondary personality dysfunction.

Briefly, the hypothesis runs as follows: we know from clinical observations that high-intensity auditory and visual stimulation of certain duration will cause deafness and blindness. We know that such loss of function is related to structural change in the peripheral sensory systems. If excessive, the changes proceed to exhaustion of neuronal enzymes and glycogen stores, diminished oxygen tension, decreased energy output, and irreversible anatomical change and permanent deafness. We know that clinically such loss of function may occur acutely, may be temporary or permanent—these outcomes relate to both intensity and duration of the sound stimulation. I shall not outline the data that support the summary statement (Hepler et al., 1984; Miller, 1974; Schuknecht, 1974).

The various forms of PTSD, as well as the course of the illness over time, suggest many analogies to the variety of hearing defects consequent to high-intensity sound stimulation. Such excessive stimulation may be conceived to lead to neurophysiological fatigue and structural change in the neuronal systems concerned particularly with cortical control of inhibition of the agnostic system, in this instance, the temperoanygaloid complex. The neuronal structures stressed may recover, be temporarily impaired, or suffer permanent damage.

Following traditional neurological theory lower brain centers are released (ventral medial nucleus of the hypothalamus and the locus coeruleus) after impairment of the cortical central system through excessive threatening and sensitizing stimulation. These lower brain centers contain high concentration of the neurotransmitter norepinephrine (Redmond, 1977). Physiologically the hypothalamic nucleus is known to be concerned with behavioral expression or rage and irritability, while the locus coeruleus is concerned with dreaming and sleep. If one accepts release of functioning of such centers as tending to certain behavioral expressions, the constant symptoms of PTSD become explainable in physiological terms. The proclivity of explosive rages, irritability, and hyperalertness may be assumed to follow lessened inhibition of the ventromedial nuclei, while the propensity to fear-laden dreaming and intensive thinking of trauma to overactivity of the locus coeruleus—both fields backing to cortex-induced actions and imagery.

Beyond the constant symptoms due to impaired cortical-released lower brainstem functions induce secondary reactive affective and avoidance symptoms in the suffering brain as well as the mobilization of all the neurotic and coping defenses in the attempt at restitution of personality.

To return to personality functioning, those sufferers of the persisting consequences of intense and prolonged fear-inducing experiences are left with variable defects in their capacity cognitively to inhibit the primitive action responses of flight, fright, or freeze. In those with conditioned emotional response there exists a high risk for dissociative responses expressed in defensive explosive rages with their recurrent reenactments of the past terror. Both dissociated states particularly may occur when cortical functioning is impaired through sleep, drowsiness, use of mind-altering drugs or during severe illnesses. Terror takes over—leading to dissociation! Dissociation appears clinically as a brief psychotic explosion.

The implications of these findings for treatment are many. Far from being a "simple neurosis," as Freud stated (1919), these forms of the condition are extraordinarily complex. The theory is to recognize both symptoms of "defect" and "conflict"; treat both and accept the limitation imposed by the existence of neural change and primitively fixed psychobiologically conditioning to fear and terror. Elsewhere (1986) I have written of the psychoanalytic theory and goal modification of the treatment parameters needed to apply a dynamic model in the treatment of the secondarily induced affective and neurotic symptoms.

My experience suggests that the initial therapeutic dilemmas are fewer with the chronic posttraumatic stress disorders of war, as compared with postconcentration-camp syndrome.

Much may be accomplished through the dynamic analytic processes, particularly in alleviation of depressive guilt, shame, and control of aggressivity, thus enhancing interpersonal skills and social adaptation.

References

Anderson, O. D., & Parmenter, R. (1941), A long-term study of the experimental neuroses in the sheep and dog. *Psychosom. Med. Mono.*, 11.

Blanchard, E. B., Kolb, L. C., Pallmeyer, T. P., & Gerardi, R. J. (1983), A psychophysiologic study of post-traumatic stress disorder in Vietnam veterans. *Psychiat. Quart.,* 54:220–228.

Dobbs, D., & Wilson, W. H. (1960), Observations of persistence of war neurosis. *Dis. Nerv. Syst.,* 21:40–46.

Freud, S. (1919), Introduction to *Psychoanalysis and the War Neurosis. Standard Edition,* 17:205–215. London: Hogarth Press, 1955.

———— (1920), Beyond the pleasure principle. *Standard Edition,* 18:3–64. London: Hogarth Press, 1955.

Grinker, R. R., & Spiegel, J. J. (1945), *Men Under Stress.* New York: McGraw-Hill.

Hepler, E. L., Moal, M. J., & Gerhardt, K. J. (1984), Susceptibility to noise-induced hearing loss. *Milit. Med.,* 149:154–158.

Horvath, T. (1980), Arousal and anxiety. In: *Handbook of Studies on Anxiety,* ed. S. Burrows & B. Davies. Amsterdam: Elsevier, pp. 89–116.

Kardiner, A. (1941), *The Traumatic Neuroses of War.* Washington, DC: National Research Council.

Kolb, L. (1983), Return of the repressed. *J. Amer. Acad. Psychoanal.,* 11:531–545.

———— (1984), The post-traumatic stress disorders of combat. *Milit. Med.,* 149:237–243.

———— (1986), Treatment of chronic post traumatic states. In: *Current Psychiatric Therapies,* ed. J. Masserman. New York: Grune & Stratton, pp. 119–125.

———— (1987), A neuropsychological hypothesis explaining post traumatic stress. *Amer. Psychiat.,* 144:989–995.

———— Burris, B. C., & Griffiths, S. (1984), Propranolol and clonidine in treatment of post-traumatic stress disorders. In: *Post-Traumatic Stress Disorder,* ed. B. A. Van der Kolk. Washington, DC: American Psychiatric Press, pp. 97–107.

———— Mutalipassi, L. R. (1982), The conditioned emotional response. *Psychiat. Ann.,* 12:979–987.

Krystal, H. (1975), Affect tolerance. *Ann. Psychoanal.,* 3:179–219.

Malloy, P. E., Fairbank, J. A., & Keane, T. M. (1983), Validation of a multimethod assessment of post traumatic stress disorder in Vietnam veterans. *Psychiat. Quart.,* 54:220–228.

Mason, J., Giller, E. L., Kosten, T. R., et al. (1985), Elevated norepinephrine/cortisol ratio in PTSD. *New Research Program and Abstracts,* p. 94.

Miller, J. D. (1974), Effects of noise of people. *J. Acoust. Soc. Amer.,* 56:729–740.

Pallmeyer, T. P., Blanchard, E. G., & Kolb, L. C. (1986), The psychophysiology of combat induced post traumatic stress disorder Vietnam veteran. *Behav. Res. Ther.,* 24:645–652.

Redmond, D. E. (1977), Alterations in the function of the nucleus locus coeruleus. In: *Animal Models in Psychiatry and Neurology,* ed. I. Hanin & E. Usdin. Oxford: Pergamon, pp. 293–305.

Santmeyer, H. H. (1985), *And Ladies of the Club.* New York: Berkeley Book.

Schuknecht, H. (1974), *Pathology of the Ear.* Cambridge, MA: Harvard University Press, pp. 302–303.

Solomon, R. L., & Wynne, L. C. (1954), Traumatic avoidance learning. *Psychol. Rev.,* 61:353–385.

Wenger, M. H. (1948), Studies in autonomic balance in army-air forces personnel. *Comp. Psychol. Monogr.* Berkeley & Los Angeles: University of California Press.

20

STRINDBERG'S ALCHEMY:
A PATHWAY TO RECOVERY

Donald L. Burnham, M.D.

Frieda Fromm-Reichmann was an inspiration to all who knew her. She embodied and imparted certain tenaciously held convictions about the mentally ill. Cardinal among these were deep respect for her patients and unfailing devotion to their personal dignity. She was convinced that she had fully as much to learn from them as they from her.

Like Sullivan, Adolf Meyer, and others of her era, she emphasized the restitutional, integrative, and creative aspects of schizophrenia. She looked always for the purpose and meaning of symptoms, especially their expressive and communicative meanings. She sought always to speak to the healthy core of the person, regardless of how hidden, battered, and withdrawn from the surface that core might be. Furthermore, she possessed an extraordinary capacity to reach, engage, and form an alliance with the intact health-striving sectors of the person.

It was my great good fortune to have known Frieda as a teacher and colleague at Chestnut Lodge from 1950 until her death in 1957. I learned enormously from her supervision of cases; I met with her both separately and in groups of two or three supervisees. With remarkable generosity of spirit she gave her unfailing interest to her supervisees and to the patients being discussed.

A measure of the value of her friendly wisdom was that one was likely to seek her counsel whenever a special crisis arose

A preliminary version of this paper was presented at the sixteenth annual Chestnut Lodge symposium held October 1970.

417

with any of one's patients. Somehow she would manage to be quickly available, perhaps in what would have been a coffee or tea break or en route to the train station or airport.

Frieda did not pull her punches when she had criticisms to make. However, as Gregory Bateson (1958, p. 99) once observed, she simultaneously would "lend the strength to receive the comment" as well as the encouragement to put it to constructive use.

Along with Drs. Marvin A. Adland, Harold F. Searles, and Alberta B. Szalita, I participated with Frieda in a study of intuitive processes in the treatment of schizophrenia. Papers arising from the study were published in 1955 in the *Journal of the American Psychoanalytic Association.* That same year inaugurated the annual Chestnut Lodge Symposium, of which Frieda was a prime mover.

It is in the hope of providing an illustration and possibly a small addendum to Fromm-Reichmann's teachings that I essay a study of August Strindberg's ventures into the realm of alchemy. I believe that they provide an example of how symptoms constitute not only a means of retreat from intolerable aspects of reality and conflicts but also a means of confronting and coming to terms with the intolerable.

For nearly three years, from 1894 to 1897, August Strindberg, titan progenitor of our modern theater, virtually abandoned creative writing, and poured his energies into scientific and pseudoscientific endeavors, including desperate efforts to make gold. That his shift of interest was drastic and earnest was confirmed by his reaction when two of his plays were performed in Paris where he was living at the time. Though this was an honor of which he had dreamed, one never before accorded a Swedish playwright, he told the newspaper writers who came to interview him that he was no longer interested in literature, that he was now a chemist.

This was a period of major psychological crisis for him. Subsequently he referred to it as his Inferno and wrote a book by that title. My goal in this paper will be to elucidate the part that alchemy played in this crisis and its eventual resolution.

How close his Inferno took Strindberg toward schizophrenic disorganization has been much debated. It is extremely difficult to know what in his retrospective account is factual autobiography and what is fictional elaboration or deliberate distortion. For instance, we don't know whether he truly believed that he had discovered how to make gold and thereby could overturn the basic laws of supply and demand and disrupt the economy of the entire world. Nor do we know how convinced he was that Anders Eliasson, a physician friend to whose home in southern Sweden he twice fled for brief period of rest and treatment, was trying to steal his gold-making secrets. At least for a time during his Inferno, he seems to have believed that his scientific labors would prove his intellectual power and his sanity. Many other persons felt that they proved just the opposite. However, aside from the question of his sanity and the difficulties off disentangling fact from fiction, certain aspects of the Inferno are beyond question. For one, his account of this life crisis is a magnificently rich psychological document; for another, he made a remarkable recovery which ushered in a period of astonishing literary productivity.

To turn more directly to the meaning alchemy had for him, I first assume that it represented an attempted solution of conflicts and a defense against intolerable feelings. I assume further that alchemy took on this significance for him at a time in his life when other attempted solutions and defenses were in danger of collapsing.

A synopsis of his pre-alchemy life situation reveals much in support of these assumptions. In the years 1889 to 1893 he suffered a shattering series of defeats. Following a public trial for blasphemy he was in great disfavor with publishers and producers. His attempts to found an experimental theater of his own, first in Copenhagen, then in Sweden, both failed. When the literary school of naturalism, of which he was an acknowledged leader, came under critical attack, he feared that he would become obsolete. Most painful of all, his first marriage collapsed and ended in divorce and loss of a bitter fight for custody of his three children. His finances became increasingly desperate. Often behind in alimony payments, he was forced to pawn or sell his most precious possessions, including his personal library. He felt ruined as a writer and became unable

to put pen to paper. He felt utterly unwanted and unappreciated in his mother country, Sweden.

When friends raised money and urged him to use it to join
them in Berlin, he again became an exile, as he had been for
several years in the 1880s. In Berlin he joined a bohemian
group of artists who gathered in a particular tavern and among
whom heavy drinking and complicated sexual entanglements
were rife. Another member of the group was Edvard Munch,
the Norwegian artist, who later moved to Paris, where he figured significantly in Strindberg's Inferno.

While in Berlin, Strindberg also met Frida Uhl, a twenty-
year-old Austrian with literary ambitions. They were soon married, but his hope that she would bring him a measure of peace
and inspiration to resume creative writing was quickly disappointed. Instead he turned increasingly toward science and alchemy. When Frida became pregnant, his absorption in alchemy
became nearly all-consuming.

But his turn toward alchemy had in fact begun before his
move to Berlin and his marriage to Frida. During 1890 and
1891 he had spent long stretches of time in remote island fishing
villages off the coast of Sweden, hoping that solitude and close
contact with nature and the sea would have restorative effects.
During these retreats he engaged in various nature studies
ranging over astronomy, zoology, and botany. One suspects
that he was particularly fond of plants because they were gentle
and, in contrast to animals, did not devour one another.

Nor was this his first romance with science. Years before,
he had been a premedical student until he flunked a chemistry
exam, a defeat which perhaps had something to do with his
later turn to alchemy.

Even earlier, in his boyhood, science had become an all-
absorbing interest at a time of enormous emotional crisis, precipitated by his mother's death when he was twelve. He was
guilty for thinking when she died that he would now possess
the gold ring she had promised him. His grief and efforts at
reparation had led him into solitary preoccupation with botany,
chemistry, and striving to invent a perpetual-motion machine.
Doubtless his unconscious urge was to defy the laws of nature

which dictate that energy decline and death are inevitable. Later he was to dream of inventing a one-man flying machine.

Thus we see that his turn to science in his mid-life crisis had its prototype in boyhood, with even a specific clue to his fascination with gold. By the time he arrived in Berlin in 1892 he was seriously seeking to transmute metals.

The idea of making gold appealed to him on many counts. To succeed would eliminate all poverty, debt, and dependency, not least his own. To make gold also would prove that he was productive and good, whereas his divorce and the unenthusiastic reception of his writings had made him doubt his worth and his sanity. He would prove himself a benefactor, not a malefactor; a creator, not a destroyer; and a provider, not a vampire and a thief.

The defeats that had led to his writing block had left him generally doubtful of his goodness and generative capacity. Moreover, he had come to view writing as vengeful and destructive, whereas earlier he had viewed it as constructive and reparative. Now its use as a vehicle for hate frightened and disgusted him. Witness this outcry:

> What an occupation! To sit and flay your fellow men and then offer their skins for sale and expect them to buy them. To be like a hunter, who in his need chops off his dog's tail, and after eating the flesh himself, offers the dog the bones, his own bones. To spy out people's secrets, betray your best friend's birthmark, use your wife as an experimental rabbit, behave like a Croat, chop down, defile, and burn, and sell. Fie, for shame! [A. Strindberg, 1969, p. 118; see also A. Strindberg, 1914, p. 185; and F. Strindberg, 1937, p. 75.]

In a letter to his wife he wrote, "Pen and ink disgust me. I feel landed in a blind alley, with no way out" (F. Strindberg, 1937, p. 193). In the next sentence he spoke of finishing a paper on sulfur and sending it to Berlin. In another letter he claimed to be writing lectures for the Humboldt Academy in Berlin and said, "Adieu, Literature . . . welcome Science!" (p. 195). His turn toward science seems to have been determined partly by a wish to go back to the primary real world of nature, having becoming disillusioned with the factitious, secondary worlds created by writers (Dahlström, 1958, p. 42).

Science also promised a new beginning. Again to Frida, he wrote, "We shall see whether this will alter my destiny and give me a new interest in life, now that every other is dead" (1937, p. 416).

These letters were written at times when he was apart from Frida and struggling to assert his independence. This struggle was central to his obsession with alchemy, for if he unlocked the secrets of the universe, he would no longer need support from others, be it from women, religion, or the approval of his fellowmen. In his quest for self-sufficiency he identified with such figures as Prometheus, Orpheus, Faust, Goethe, and Sir Francis Bacon. Common to these identifications was a wish for absolute power over life and death. Like Prometheus and Drs. Faust and Frankenstein, he wanted to create life himself, to make a homunculus, without the help of woman in the procreative process. He studied how to make synthetic food (Strindberg, 1897), the ultimate in self-sufficiency, and dreamed of finding a magic elixir that would circumvent death. Strindberg (1968) avowed that he had found the riddle of the Sphinx and would rival Orpheus in bringing back to life an inanimate nature that traditional scientists had killed (p. 185).

These alchemical ambitions consumed his interest to the exclusion of other persons and activities. His wife referred to sulfur as a hated rival. When their daughter was born, he kept to his part of the house which he had made into a chemical laboratory, and where he hung a copy of Rembrandt's *Man in the Golden Helmet* (F. Strindberg, 1937, p. 248), while mother and child kept to their part of the house.

His wife's pregnancy and delivery, during which he suffered couvade, had aroused intense envy and rivalry in him; he was obsessed with determining whether he or his wife was the more truly creative, and whether a child or a scientific discovery was the best guarantee of immortality. Apparently he took the attitude that his chemical apparatus was equal to her generative organs. Years later he referred to his third wife's uterus as her little "athanor," the name of a furnace used by alchemists (1965a, p. 135).

Envy and rivalry also pervaded his attitude toward his infant daughter, and revived earlier guilt over the deaths of several of his infant siblings and of his first wife's first two children. This in turn made him all the more frenzied to prove his good power to create and sustain life rather than to destroy it.

The height of his scientific ambitions matched the depth of his self-doubt. More than once, when his hubris was overtaken by despair, he was tempted to concoct not an elixir of life but a poison with which to end his life.

Although he proclaimed himself a modern Prometheus above the opinion of mere mortals, his reality testing still was sufficiently intact that he desperately wanted confirmation by recognized scientific authorities. He and a friend submitted samples of his supposed gold to two German professors who declined to agree that Strindberg had accomplished the miracle of transmutation (F. Strindberg, 1937, pp. 282–283). This left him only slightly daunted. He wrote to several famous scientists of the day, including Berthelot, the chemist; Flammarion, French astronomer and writer; and Haeckel, German biologist (McGill, 1965, p. 348). At most their responses gave him only slight and temporary respite from his doubts, although he is said to have cherished Haeckel's noncommittal reply as proof of his sanity. In the meantime he arranged to have his scientific ideas privately printed.[1] His own appraisal of these works was grossly inflated by his frantic wish to prove his goodness and to deny destructiveness. Referring to one of his "scientific" pamphlets, *Sylva Sylvarum*, he said, "Proudly aware of my clairvoyant powers, I there penetrated to the very heart of the secret of creation" (1968, p. 144). Another statement which reveals both the strength of his reparative wishes and his disparagement of his earlier creative writing was, "for the first time in my life I was sure of having said something new, great, and beautiful" (1968, p. 147).

---

[1] The titles of these pamphlets are fascinating. *Antibarbarus* (1894) appears to have been borrowed from the title of a German-published dictionary intended to preserve the purity of the Latin language, functioning thus as guardian of the mother tongue. *Sylva Sylvarum* (1896) appears to have been borrowed from Sir Francis Bacon's work of the same title. *Hortus Merlini* was evidently an allusion to Merlin's magical herb garden (Editorial, 1898; see also editor's notes in Strindberg, 1966, p. 252).

But most reviewers of his "science" writings did not share his enthusiasm and were sharply critical. Strindberg felt misunderstood, even persecuted, and treated like a charlatan or fool, for his prophetic genius. However, he found a more favorable reception in French journals devoted to alchemy and occult topics, which were an important current in the intellectual climate of the times. He became a frequent contributor to these journals and was elected an honorary members of the Alchemical Association of France (Mercier, 1969).

That the printing of Strindberg's pseudoscientific ideas was largely out of pocket to him, or rather, to certain of his friends, is evidence that his alchemy had the opposite of its intended effect. As with many defense mechanisms, it generated more of the very problems it had been designed to avert. Strindberg had hoped that his scientific labors would enrich him, provide well for his two families, and banish the specters of poverty, debt, dependency, and guilt. His wife had deep misgivings when he forsook creative writing for pseudoscience, and declared, "You can't keep a family on sulphur and chemistry!" (Collis, 1963). Nonetheless, she came partly to share his belief that he was on the brink of some of the greatest scientific discoveries of all time. It was almost a folie à deux. The result, however, was that his poverty increased, and this proud man, who dreaded dependency and any form of debt, was reduced to writing begging letters to friends.

Strindberg consciously intended his alchemy as a reparative, guilt-relieving gift to his family and to mankind at large. Here too, the effects often were the reverse of those intended: destructive and guilt-incurring. Sometimes he realized this with remorse, as when he purchased a sheet of palladium for an experiment and then thought this a theft from his wife and children, only quickly to rationalize it as "a theft that he must commit, as it would enable him to solve such an important problem" (1969, pp. 122–123).[2] On other occasions he argued that his alchemy would benefit his family greatly. In a letter to Frida he wrote, "And the little one! I often see her in my dreams.

---

[2] The theme of theft and wanting to possess that which one did not rightly own bore deep personal significance for Strindberg and recurs frequently in his writings.

Tell her that after cruel suffering, her father stands on the threshold of a door opening on to a beautiful future for his child" (1937, p. 435).

In other, more subtle ways, too, his tortured journey into alchemy and occult realms produced effects contrary to those he intended. Consider, for instance, his goal of autonomy, self-sufficiency, and full control of his own destiny. He arrived instead at a point where he felt at the mercy of mysterious external powers that exerted their control by supernatural means or by a fiendish influencing machine that directed his thoughts and caused him terrifying body sensations. His alchemy verged over into black magic and pervasive superstition. He looked everywhere for omens and signs by which to guide his actions. He virtually abdicated an autonomous position by projecting ego and superego controls onto outside agents. At the extremity of his crisis his superstitiousness defined a bird's flight north as a personal message that he should return to Sweden, and he tried to summon a conciliatory letter from Frida by a black magic ritual designed to make their daughter ill. His fondness for the expression, "Omen accipio!" revealed his passive receptivity toward outer controls.

Underlying his superstitiousness and his feeling controlled from the outside was a deep yearning for an omniscient and omnipotent protective presence. During his Inferno his view of the mysterious outer "Powers" shifted. He saw them less as persecutory and more as benevolent and he called himself a "providentialist." These changes occurred as he gradually became more accepting of his dependency wishes.

Even from the beginning of his Inferno, his scientific ideas expressed more than one side of his dependence conflict. While his quest for absolute separateness and self-sufficiency was designed to deny dependency, he was concurrently fascinated by ideas of fusion and union, particularly as represented in the concepts of hylozoism and monism. Hylozoism is the doctrine that all matter is alive; in other words, that matter and life are inseparable. Monism is the doctrine that there is only one fundamental substance or ultimate reality, which is an organic whole, with no independent parts. These concepts, a virtual credo for Strindberg, are part of the traditional philosophy of the alchemists to the effect that the ultimate constitutent of all matter is an undifferentiated "prima materia" (Lewis, 1963, p. 212). These ideas appealed greatly to Strindberg. They denied separateness, differentiation, and boundaries among living organisms, and even between the living and the nonliving. This touched his longing for a state of fusion, in which all distinctions and boundaries would be dissolved, particularly those between man and woman and between mother and child. Thus his "scientific" delvings were impelled by wishes for both separateness and fusion. His struggle to achieve a reconcilitation of these wishes permeated and shaped his entire Inferno crisis. He sought to discover "an infinite coherence" within the "grand disorder" which confronted him (1966, p. 60; see also Adamov, 1947, p. xiv).

Wishes for fusion underlay his obsession to prove that chemical elements—sulfur, for one—are not separate and distinct, but are various combinations of one basic substance and could be transmuted into one another. Adopting the motto, "All is in all," he said, "I know very well that psychologists have invented a nasty Greek name to define the tendency to see analogies everywhere, but that doesn't bother me at all, because I know that there are semblances everywhere, considering that everything is in everything, everywhere" (1966, pp. 61–62).

Strindberg's ambivalence about fusion is given eloquent expression in his play *To Damascus*, a dramatic synthesis and reworking of many of his Inferno experiences. There he has the Stranger, a representation of himself, speak of the effects of drink: "The wine frees my soul from my body—I fly into the ether—I see what no one ever divined—hear what no one ever heard." The following day, however, the Stranger feels "the beautiful pangs of conscience . . . the saving sensation of guilt and remorse . . . the sufferings of my body while my soul hovers like mist around my brow. . . . It is as if swaying betwixt life and death—when the spirit feels its wings lifted in flight and can soar into space at will." Then the Stranger turns from these thoughts of mystical union to lament that he is "a doomed soul, who will never again be one of the fold—no more than I could become a child again." Asked if he really has such thoughts, the Stranger replies, "That is how far gone I am! And

I almost feel as if I were lying carved up in Medea's caldron, simmering and seething, boiling eternally. If I don't turn into soap, I shall rise up rejuvenated out of my own brine. It all depends on Medea's skill" (1965b, p. 148).

This masterly condensed symbol makes the stages of a mental crisis analogous to the stages of an alchemical operation. It was a symbol Strindberg had employed earlier to portray a previous episode of great mental turmoil:

> He hardly thought any more, for all the activities of his soul lay as in a mortar stirred to a mush. Thoughts attempted to crystallize, but dissolved and floated away, memories, hopes, malice, tender feelings and a single great hate against all wrong, which through an unprobed natural force had come to govern the world, melted together in his mind as if an inner fire had suddenly raised the temperature and forced all solid particles to assume a liquid form [from Strindberg's short story "Pangs of Conscience," quoted in Brett, 1921, p. 60].

Elsewhere Strindberg employed the image of melting to describe the dedifferentiation of self in a love relationship when he wrote to Frida, "We hated each other because we love each other and fear the big melting-pot of love in which personality dissolves" (1937, p. 138).

In his allusion to Medea's witchcraft his imagery suggests more than one phase. The phase of melting down, dedifferentiation, and fusion is followed by a phase of reconstitution with the possibility of a new form emerging—in effect, a regeneration or rebirth in a purified, redeemed state.

The idea of a parallel between the operations of alchemy and the processes of personality reorganization and spiritual regeneration is by no means new. In ancient China, alchemists sought purity, immortality, and perhaps even literally golden bodies, by ingesting metals in place of ordinary food. Subsequently the Taoists modified this severe regimen to prescribed meditative exercises for the preparation of an "interior elixir" with which to give birth to a new, finer self (Welch, 1957, pp. 130–131; Duyvendak, 1954, p. 11).

Martin Luther expressed a liking for "the good art of al-

chemy" particularly "because of her allegorical and secret meanings which are very beautiful, signifying the resurrection of the
dead on the Day of Judgment" (as quoted in Wittkower and
Wittkower, 1969, p. 85).

In the United States in 1857 a remarkable book on alchemy
was published by Ethan Allen Hitchcock, grandson of Ethan
Allen of Revolutionary War fame. In addition to a distinguished
career as an army general and an unusually farsighted Indian
agent, Hitchcock devoted many years to an exhaustive study of
the writings of alchemists. The result of his studies was a book
which contended that the true purpose of many alchemists was
the improvement, transformation, and perfection of Man, and
that talk of transmuting metals was an allegorical means of
referring to processes of psychic and spiritual transformation
(Cohen, 1951).

In the 1880s Marcellin Berthelot, famous French chemist
and historian of science, published several important works on
medieval chemistry and alchemy. He pointed to a link between
alchemy and Gnosticism, a doctrine which contended that the
soul could be purified and joined to the Redeemer by emancipation from matter (London *Times Literary Supplement,* 1969;
p. 784).[3]

Early psychoanalysts, particularly Silberer and Jung, offered psychological interpretations of alchemy. Silberer pointed
out that the alchemists had sought to unravel the mystery of
the origin of life and to find new and better means of creating
life than those used by their parents. They attempted by magical
and artificial means to produce a homunculus. Silberer suggested, however, that the primary concern of the true initiates
of alchemy was the spiritual regeneration of Man (White, 1919;
Brink, 1919; Silberer, 1971).

Jung's deep interest in alchemy and other occult sciences
is well known. A chapter of his book *The Integration of the Personality* is titled "The Idea of Redemption in Alchemy." Here
Jung contended that the alchemists strove "to produce a quin-
tessence whose action can be compared with Christ's action

---

[3] Strindberg was greatly interested in Berthelot's ideas, and once wrote to him in
hope of enlisting Berthelot as a witness who would testify to the worth of Strindberg's
notions about the composition and possible transmutation of matter.

upon mankind" (1940, p. 267). He further observed that "the alchemist projected what I call the process of individuation upon the process of chemical transformation" (p. 276). Jung maintained that in trying to understand much of the work of the alchemists, "we are called upon to deal, not with chemical experimentations as such, but with something resembling psychic processes expressed in pseudo-chemical language" (p. 210). It was along these lines that Jung interpreted the alchemists' quest for a precious substance, whether an elixir or a wondrous stone, which would provide miraculous sustenance, renewal of strength, rebirth, and immortality. This life-remedy would purify and ennoble, sublimate the base, and perfect the imperfect. Today we find this parallel between operations of alchemy and processes of personality change condensed in the concept sublimation, which psychoanalysts borrowed from alchemists, whether consciously or unconsciously.

We cannot know whether Strindberg would have consciously agreed with these psychological interpretations of his delvings into science, alchemy, and the occult. In certain stages of his Inferno his interest appears to have been literal rather than metaphorical. Nonetheless, knowing his exquisite sensitivity to analogies, correspondences, and multiple levels of symbolization, we can surmise that ideas of personal transformation, purification, and conversion may not have been entirely unconscious. In the later phases of his Inferno, as he moved toward greater acceptance of his dependency wishes, his interests shifted from science to religion, with mysticism and occultism forming the bridge between. For a time his avowed mentor and redeemer was Emanual Swedenborg, who himself shifted from science to religion. Another influence was Sâr Péladan, leader of the Rosicrucians in Paris at that time. In Péladan's book *Comment on devient mage*, Strindberg read that the word "magie" meant "the art of the sublimation of man" (Valency, 1966, p. 291). He credited Péladan with ushering him back toward religion (1968, pp. 279–280). Then when he reworked his Inferno experiences in drama form, he emphasized the theme of religious conversion in the title *To Damascus*.

Religious overtones also are clear in his trying to understand his Inferno experiences as a guilt-punishment-repentance

sequence. He came to believe that his attempts to unlock the
secrets of the universe and to unveil the mysteries of life and
death were acts of presumptuous hubris for which he deserved
to be punished and purged by deep suffering. Here is his description of what was apparently a last fling at Faustian, god-
defying alchemy, followed by a turn to religion:

> ... with a supreme and final effort, I concentrated all my
> will on one goal. I *would* make gold—by the dry process,
> heating the constituents in a crucible. ... After remelting
> the material in the crucible three times over the fire, I
> stopped to examine it. The borax had run into the shape
> of death's head with two glowing eyes that pierced my soul
> with a glance of supernatural irony.
>
> Still not a trace of metal! And I gave up the idea of any
> further experiments [1968, p. 193].

Then he turned to his Bible for guidance, and, as was his
custom in his later years whenever beset by indecision and
doubt, picked a passage at random. If we can accept his account,
chance served up verses from Isaiah which bespoke God's anger
at those who presume to make and to worship false gods and
to usurp creative functions:

> Thus saith the Lord, thy redeemer, and he that maketh all
> things; that stretcheth forth the heavens alone; that spread-
> eth abroad the earth by myself; *that frustrated the tokens of the
> liars, and maketh diviners mad; that turneth wise men backward,
> and maketh their knowledge foolish.*

This caused Strindberg to think, "For the first time, I began
to have doubts about my scientific researches. Suppose they
were mere folly! I had sacrificed all the happiness of my life,
as well as that of my wife and my children, for an illusion!"
(1968, p. 194).

Later in his account Strindberg several times voices respect
for God, the Creator, and criticism for scientists who would
presume to question or tamper with His grand design, as in this
passage:

> The Creator, that great artist who extends his own being as

he creates. . . . All, without doubt, is the work of his hand . . . then along comes science and declares that there are gaps, missing links [1968, p. 197].

He quotes his friend Dr. Eliasson, at whose home he was twice briefly a guest-patient: "Above all: beware of occultism. That's an abuse of knowledge. It is forbidden to spy upon the creator's secrets, and woe to those who unravel them!" (1968, p. 211).

Whether Dr. Eliasson actually said this is problematical, but we can be quite certain that Strindberg's superego said it repeatedly. Strindberg claims that Eliasson also recommended Victor Rydberg's book *Germanic Mythology* as a better soporific than sulfonal. But instead of something soothing Strindberg found the legend of Bhrigu, who, "having been taught by his father, grew big with pride and imagined himself surpassing his master"; for this offense he was sent to hell (1968, p. 211). Strindberg took this as a personal message that *he* was in hell, being punished for "pride, presumption, and *hybris*" (1968, p. 211). In another spasm of repentance he wrote, "I had sinned through pride, through *hubris,* the sole vice that the Gods will not forgive. Encouraged by the friendship of Doctor Papus,[4] who had given his approval to my scientific research, I had imagined myself to have found the answer to the riddle of the Sphinx. I was the rival of Orpheus and it was my role to bring back to life an inanimate nature that had been killed by the scientists" (1968, p. 185).

In a letter to Marcel Réja, a friend who assisted in preparing the original French edition of *Inferno* Strindberg said: "If one approaches occult questions out of scientific or other curiosity, one will be broken like Maupassant, or pushed on the road of the Cross like Péladan, Huysmans, perhaps even Papus who ended as a Martinist, that is to say a monk" (Réja, 1966, p. 14).[5]

---

[4] Doctor Papus was the name taken by Dr. Gérard Encausse, a leader of the occult movement in France during the 1890s.

[5] Strindberg had been considerably shaken by the news of Guy de Maupassant's having become insane at approximately the same time as Nietzsche in 1889. He had identified strongly with each of these geniuses, and had even wondered whether his correspondence with Nietzsche might have precipitated Nietzsche's breakdown. It has been suggested that Maupassant's story *Monsieur Parent*, with its theme of uncertainty of paternity, may have been a model for Strindberg's play *The Father.* There is evidence that during his Inferno Strindberg saw himself and his wife reflected in several of Maupassant's stories.

Strindberg now seemed to feel toward science the same distaste, even disgust, that he had previously felt toward literature, and for many of the same reasons. More specifically, the "scientific" activities he had intended as instruments of reparation and proof of his goodness now threatened to become weapons of destruction.

A striking instance of this was his black magic attempt to cause his daughter to become ill, with the idea that a shared misfortune such as a sick child might reunite him and his wife and forestall their imminent divorce (1968, p. 145). In view of his envy of the child and his earlier efforts to force his wife to choose between him and the child, his black magic probably was unconsciously designed to get rid of the child so he could enjoy exclusive possession of the mother.[6]

Some time later he learned that the children of his first marriage had become seriously sick at about the time of his venture into black magic, even though they had not been his intended target. News of their illness caused him to be "filled with horror at myself. Frivolously I had called hidden forces into play, and the evil wish had gone out into the world only to return, guided by an invisible hand, and bury itself in my own heart" (1968, p. 160).

Another instance of his fear of the destructive potential of his "scientific" endeavors occurred when the director of the Paris Observatory died a few days after an occult journal had published a Strindberg article criticizing the astronomical system of the day. To this juxtaposition of events Strindberg associated another: Louis Pasteur had died the day after the publication of Strindberg's *Sylva Sylvarum* (1968, p. 250).

There is room for doubt as to whether these coincidental events, to which he attributed causal connections, were even as closely linked in time as he claimed; nonetheless the links were close in his mind and doubtless gave further impetus to his turn from science toward religion. Concurrently, the identifications

---

6. Eric Bentley (1945, pp. 551–552) has pointed out that in Strindberg's writings the theme of guilt associated with crimes of tyrannous possession is prevalent, and often is expressed in the metaphoric figures of vampire and creditor.

comprising his ego ideal changed from the likes of Prometheus and Faust to Job, Jeremiah, and Jesus. His sufferings seemed to him to mirror theirs, and the role of sacrificial victim was not without appeal for him. In a series of letters to his two-year-old daughter Kerstin, he addressed her as "Beatrice," thus also linking himself to Dante, whereas at her birth he had wanted to name her "Gretchen" after Faust's beloved (F. Strindberg, 1937, p. 299). That his view of her as Beatrice was more than a fleeting whim is affirmed by his making "Beatrice" the title of a chapter in *Inferno.*

His daughter was one of several feminine figures whom he cast in the role of protective mother-substitute as he retreated from his quest for total self-sufficiency and became more accepting of his dependency wishes. Another was Madame Charlotte, proprietress of a crémerie in the Montparnasse section of Paris frequented by Strindberg, Paul Gauguin, Mucha, and other artist friends (Sprinchorn, 1968, pp. 58–59). Another was a nursing nun in the Hôpital Saint-Louis where Strindberg was briefly hospitalized early in 1895 for treatment of psoriasis of his hands. He feared that it might be leprosy or syphilis, but he found the hospital nun a comfort. He called her "mother" and she called him "my child." She also encouraged him to be interested in religion, even telling him he had the makings of a clergyman.

Still another mother-substitute was his mother-in-law, at whose home in Austria he spent several months toward the end of his Inferno. This gave him the chance to become reacquainted with his two-and-a-half-year-old daughter, whom he had not seen since she was an infant. By then he was permanently separated from Frida, whom he never saw again. His mother-in-law, like the hospital matron, encouraged him toward religion; her Catholicism was strongly tinged with Swedenborgianism, and she credited Swedenborg with having helped her to recover from an emotional crisis. Since Strindberg had already been greatly attracted to Swedenborg's doctrines, partly through reading Balzac's *Séraphita* a few months before,[7] he

---

[7] By chance, while browsing in a Paris bookstall, Strindberg had come across a copy of this exposition of Swedenborgian ideas on a day which was both Palm Sunday and the anniversay of Swedenborg's death. Strindberg believed that it had been specially sent for his personal guidance (1968, pp. 161–164).

was receptive when his mother-in-law gave him a Swedenborg book to read.

With none of these three mother-substitutes, nor with any particular religion, for that matter, was Strindberg's acceptance of dependency complete. His continuing ambivalence toward women was particularly evident regarding oral supplies. Sometimes this was expressed on an extremely literal level: Would they provide life-sustaining nourishment or death-dealing poison?

This doubt assailed him in relationship with each of the mother-substitutes he found during his Inferno. Madame Charlotte arrived at her restaurant early one morning to find her kitchen pots heaped on the floor with Strindberg, in his underwear, dancing around them to exorcise the evil spirits that might poison the food (Sprinchorn, 1968, p. 59).

The hospital nun he ironically pictures as dispensing draughts of poison at a "banquet table of criminals and condemned men." He recalls that he and a fellow patient, "a death's head," toasted each other's health, one with strychnine, the other with arsenic. His comment on this scene was, "How dismal, yet one had to be grateful, which made me furious. Being grateful for something so wretched and so unpleasant!" (1968, p. 125).

This passage conveys in magnificently condensed form his lifelong struggle with intense oral dependency wishes. He was unable successfully to suppress or deny them. On the other hand, to have them gratified would place him in debt to his benefactor, and the very thought of this aroused his dread and fury. Wishes to steal or take by force the needed supplies aroused enormous guilt. One attempted solution was to strive to become his own supplier and thus totally self-sufficient. Another was to deny the goodness or worth of the supplies given him by others. To be convinced that women dispensed only bad food or poison would relieve him of any necessity to feel dependent, indebted, or grateful, and at the same time would justify his hate. This redefinition of the relationship between himself and the woman is similar to Freud's classic formulation in the Schreber case: "I don't love him; I hate him; he hates me," except, of course, Freud was talking of the denial of homosexual love and Strindberg was concerned with denying dependency on women. These two motives are, of course, not unrelated (Freud, 1911, p. 63).

The threat of poisoning by Madame Charlotte and by the hospital nun seems clearly derived from Strindberg's struggle with his dependency wishes toward them. We don't hear of poison in connection with his mother-in-law, but he did recount a vivid incident in which her serving him distasteful food seemed to deny or at least lessen his wish for oral supplies from her. He had been staying at her summer home, but the approach of autumn required a change of living arrangements. Strindberg rented a small house nearby, intending to stay there alone. The first night, however, he was seized by panic and felt as if suffocated by poisoned air. Before dawn he fled to his mother-in-law's apartment, and begged to be allowed to stay with her. She granted his plea, but soon he seemed driven to find something repellent about her. He seized upon her serving him calf's brains cooked in butter, a dish he loathed, as evidence that she was against him. Even then his ambivalence was such that he partly excused her by telling himself: "She is innocent of malicious intent; this really is the work of the devil" (1968, p. 238).[8]

The theme of receiving bad food from women recurs frequently in Strindberg's writings in allusions to witches' kitchens and witches' brews. He also spoke bitterly of the "bad blood" and inherited weaknesses that had been his mother's only gifts to him, as if to deny any reason to be grateful to her. His play *To Damascus* contains a remarkable symbolic allusion to his ambivalence about oral supplies from women. The Stranger—that is, Strindberg—says, "the Christmas rose you carry at your breast is a mandragora. According to symbolism it is the flower of malice and calumny—but in medicine it was once used as a cure for insanity. Won't you give it to me?" (1965b, p. 147). In another scene another character says, "This thing called love—it affects you like henbane" (1965b, p. 252). And in his book *A*

---

[8] Interestingly, in the next chapter of *Inferno*, Strindberg mentions that for a time his mother-in-law and her twin sister identified him with Robert le Diable, a legendary figure whose mother was said to have sold him to the devil. "Robert le Diable" was Strindberg's working title for *To Damascus* (1968, p. 242).

Madman's Defense, which depicts his first marriage, he complained bitterly that his wife provided better food for her pet dog than for him (1967, p. 199).

Strindberg's use of the imagery of good and bad food to express his ambivalence toward women found almost its exact counterpart in his alchemy. Would he produce an elixir of life or a deadly poison? He was similarly uncertain whether his literary products be reparative or destructive.[9] In these doubts he ambivalently identified with the archtypal image of woman as both giver and destroyer of life. As noted earlier, his striving for absolute self-sufficiency chiefly served his wish to eliminate any need to depend upon any woman for anything. This, however, was a wish he was unable to realize, for repeatedly he turned toward woman as his supplier, rescuer, and redeemer. Even in the last year of his life, at the age of sixty-two, he seriously considered a fourth marriage, this time to an actress who was forty years his junior, and whose mother prepared meals for Strindberg.

We have seen that alchemy gave symbolic expression to both sides of Strindberg's dependency conflict: his striving for separateness and his yearning for fusion. Especially in the later stages of his Inferno, alchemy also symbolized his striving toward redemption, restitution, and rebirth, along the lines of psychological interpretation offered by Hitchcock, Jung, Silberer, and others. The idea that his suffering might be a means of purification and redemption deeply preoccupied Strindberg, and he pondered the possibility of rebirth following death. In his *Damascus* play he speaks of emerging from torture "as pure as gold from the fire" (1965b, p. 215). In a novel *Black Banners* written several years later, Strindberg referred to a character as "resurrected from the dead after having steeled himself in the Bessemer ovens of Inferno" (as quoted in Johanneson, 1968, p. 235). Earlier he had written, "Morally I was bankrupt, and ready to pack myself off, I gathered up the tatters of my soul, I forged a suit of iron over my fire-hardened clay, and in the oven of pain and chagrin I burned the image of myself

---

[9] During his Inferno one of his most important "patron-saints" was Mateo Orfila, 1787–1853, a famous scientist of France whose magnum opus was a treatise on toxicology.

until it was hard as stone" (from Strindberg's "Vivisections II," as quoted in Vowles, 1962–1963, p. 262).

Rebirth was a prominent theme in his alchemical writings themselves; Strindberg (1897) spoke of revival operations and was intrigued by the possibility of transforming inert to live substances, thereby making the miraculous leap from inorganic to organic. His associations about gold extended beyond alchemical gold-making to thoughts about golden ages and a possible return to lost paradises and the innocence of childhood.

Strindberg read the *Metamorphoses* of Ovid and termed him the "most advanced of the transformists" (1966, p. 72). He particularly mentioned Ovid's version of the Greek legend of a flower's springing from the ground where the blood of Ajax fell when he killed himself. And he quoted Ovid's lines about the Golden Age:

> . . . there were rivers
> Of milk, and rivers of honey, and golden nectar
> Dripped from the dark-green oak-trees [1964, p. 6].

Strindberg coupled this quote with the suggestion that it may be wrong to feed babies milk, honey, and golden fruits which remind them of the golden age they lost upon entering the cruel, depriving world (1968, p. 114).

The idea of rebirth also led to his fascination with the chrysalis of the butterfly. He was well aware that "chrysalis" derives from the Greek word for gold, *chrysos*. But doubtless the greatest significance of chrysalis for him was that it so beautifully symbolized the miracle of transformation and rebirth. It contains, as Strindberg wrote, "A living corpse, which will surely come back to life!" (1968, p. 115).

In the meantime Strindberg achieved a variant of this miracle in his own life when he emerged from his Inferno to enter a period of renewed productivity in which he created some of the world's greatest dramatic literature. He did not succeed in making gold, but he did succeed in effecting a most remarkable self-cure. Moreover, his writings have had curative, purifying, and redemptive value for countless others.

Perhaps surprisingly, if one has never considered the idea

before, the theater and alchemy bear strong similarities to each other. Both entail symbolic representations of reality; and, in certain senses, both are concerned with the work of purification, cure, and redemption. In his *Poetics* Aristotle described how tragic drama arouses pity and fear and thereby provides emotional catharsis (in Oates and Murphy, 1944, p. 645). Ibsen (as quoted in Gilman, 1969, p. 184) once wrote, "In every new play I have aimed at my own spiritual emancipation and purification." Perhaps the person who has most explicitly linked the theater and alchemy was the sometimes mad French actor-director-playwright Antonin Artaud (1958; see also Brustein, 1964). In essays entitled "The Alchemical Theater" and "The Theater and the Plague," Artaud contends that the theater mobilizes intense conflicts which may, in turn, lead to sequences of redistillation, purification, and reconstitution analogous to the operations of alchemy. He points to the ancient Greek Mysteries as a prototype of theater which served the principal purpose of mental purgation and cure.

In discerning parallels between the plague and the theater, Artaud further emphasizes the mobilization of conflict and its eventual resolution through a scourging experience. Consider, for instance, these pungent statements:

> In the true theater a play disturbs the senses' repose, frees the repressed unconscious, incites a kind of revolt. . . . Like the plague, the theatre is a formidable call to the forces that impel the mind to the source of its conflicts. . . . The theatre like the plague is a crisis which is resolved by death or cure [Artaud, 1958, pp. 28–31].

The last statement could well be applied to Strindberg's Inferno crisis. Certainly this was much the view he took of it. His choice of the word "Inferno" gave metaphoric expression to his wish for expiation through suffering and to his craving for the purity and unity which punishing fire might bring to his divided personality.[10] The idea of rebirth from fire was put into eloquent imagery by Strindberg in what many consider his

---

[10] It also has been suggested that hell is a metaphor for "that state of tension and depression which precedes creation" (Milton, 1962, p. 311).

masterwork, *A Dream Play*,[11] when he has the castle forming the backdrop burst into flame, whereupon the flower-bud-shaped roof opens into a gigantic chrysanthemum[12] (1965c, p. 404).

It would be inaccurate to leave the impression that Strindberg's alchemy provided him with a total cure or something resembling Nirvana. The fact is that he remained a divided person who never approached complete resolution of his conflicts. Yet he did emerge from his Inferno substantially more integrated and capable of enjoying numerous pleasures and deserved satisfaction from his prodigious literary work. In the process of his remarkable recovery alchemy served him not just as a regressive sidetrip but as a major avenue to restitution. The gold he extracted from his sufferings was of rare quality indeed.

References

Adamov, A. (1947), Preface to *Inferno*, by August Strindberg. Paris: Griffon d'Or.

Artaud, A. (1958), *The Theatre and Its Double*. Trans. M. C. Richards. New York: Grove Press.

Bateson, G. (1958), Language and psychotherapy. *Psychiatry*, 21:96–100.

Bentley, E. R. (1945), August Strindberg. *Kenyon Rev.*, 7:540–560.

Bolton, H. C. (1898), The revival of alchemy. In: *Annual Report of the Smithsonian Institution for 1897*, pp. 207–217.

Brett, A. (1921), Psychological abnormalities in August Strindberg. *J. Eng. German. Philol.*, 20:47–98.

Brink, L. (1919), Abstract of "The Homunculus," by Herbert Silberer. *Psychoanal. Rev.*, 6:201–208.

Brustein, R. (1964), *The Theatre of Revolt*. Boston: Little, Brown.

Carter, J., & Muir, P. H., eds. (1967), *Printing and the Mind of Man*. New York: Holt, Rinehart & Winston.

Cohen, I. B. (1951), Ethan Allen Hitchcock. *Proc. Amer. Antiq. Soc.*, 61:29–115.

Collis, J. S. (1963), *Marriage and Genius: Strindberg and Tolstoy*. London: Cassell.

Dahlström, C. E. W. L. (1958), An approach to tragedy, I. *Modern Drama*, 1:35–49.

Duyvendak, J. J. L. (1954), *The Book of the Way and Its Virtue*. London: John Murray.

Editorial (1898), *L'Hyperchimie*, trans. B. Wollack, May, pp. 1–2.

Freud, S. (1911), Psychoanalytic notes upon an autobiographical account of a case of paranoia (dementia paranoides). *Standard Edition*, 12:9–82. London: Hogarth Press, 1958.

---

[11] In 1928 Artaud presented in Paris what was described as a bizarre and controversial production of this play under the title *Le Songe*. It closed after only two performances.

[12] Still another word-link to gold.

Gilman, R. (1969), *The Confusion of Realms.* New York: Random House.

Johanneson, E. O. (1968), *The Novels of August Strindberg: A Study in Theme and Structure.* Berkeley and Los Angeles: University of California Press.

Jung, C. G. (1940), *The Integration of the Personality.* London: Kegan Paul.

Lewis, L. J. (1963), Alchemy and the Orient in Strindberg's "Dream Play." *Scand. Stud.,* 35:208–222.

McGill, V. J. (1965), *August Strindberg: The Bedeviled Viking.* New York: Russell & Russell.

Mercier, A. (1969), Auguste Strindberg et les alchimistes français. *Revue de Littérature comparée,* 43:23–46.

Milton, J. (1962), A restless pilgrim: Strindberg in "The Inferno." *Mod. Drama,* 5:306–313.

Oates, W. J., & Murphy, C. T. (1944), *Greek Literature in Translation.* New York: Longmans, Green.

Ovid (1964), *Metamorphoses,* Trans. R. Humphries. Bloomington: Indiana University Press.

Réja, M. (1966), Preface to *Inferno,* by August Strindberg. Paris: Mercure de France.

Silberer, H. (1971), *Hidden Symbolism of Alchemy and the Occult Arts.* New York: Dover.

Sprinchorn, E. (1968), Introduction to *Inferno, Alone and Other Writings,* by August Strindberg. New York: Anchor Books.

Strindberg, A. (1894), *Antibarbarus.* Privately published.

———— (1896), *Sylva Sylvarum.* Privately published.

———— (1897), Le pain de L'avenir. *L'Hyperchimie,* No. 4, pp. 3–5.

———— (1914), *Fair Haven and Foul Strand.* New York: McBride, Nast.

———— (1965a), *From an Occult Diary: Marriage with Harriet Bosse,* ed. T. Eklund, trans. M. Sandbach. New York: Hill and Wang.

———— (1965b), *To Damascus.* In: *Eight Expressionist Plays,* by August Strindberg, trans. A. Paulson. New York: Bantam Books.

———— (1965c), *A Dream Play.* In: *Eight Expressionist Plays,* by August Strindberg, trans. A. Paulson. New York: Bantam Books.

———— (1966), *Inferno,* C. G. Bjurström; quoted passages trans. James H. Burnham. Paris: Mercure de France.

———— (1967), *A Madman's Defense,* trans. E. Sprinchorn. Garden City, N.Y.: Anchor Books.

———— (1968). *Inferno,* trans. D. Coltman & E. Sprinchorn. In: *Inferno, Alone and Other Writings;* ed. E. Sprinchorn. Garden City, N.Y.: Anchor Books.

———— (1969), *The Cloister,* ed. C. G. Bjurström, trans. M. Sandbach. London: Secker & Warburg.

Strindberg, Freda (1937), *Marriage with Genius,* ed. F. Whyte. London: Jonathan Cape.

Times Literary Supplement (London) (1969), *Review of Alchemy and the Occult. A Catalogue of Books and Manuscripts from the Paul and Mary Mellon Collection,* ed. I. MacPhail. Volume 1: 1472–1623; Volume 2: 1624–1790. New Haven: Yale University Library.

Valency, M. (1966), *The Flower and the Castle: An Introduction to Modern Drama.* New York: Grosset & Dunlap.

Vowles, R. B. (1962–1963), A cook's tour of Strindberg scholarship. *Mod. Drama,* 5:256–268.

Welch, H. (1957), *The Parting of the Way*. Boston: Beacon Press.
White, W. A. (1919), Review of "Problems of Mysticism and Its Symbolism," by H. Silberer, trans. S. E. Jelliffe. *Psychoanal. Rev.*, 6:227.
Wittkower, R. & Wittkower, M. (1969), *Born Under Saturn*. New York: Norton.

21

JOSEPH: A PSYCHOANALYTIC EXEGESIS

THEODORE LIDZ, M.D.

When I received the first Frieda Fromm-Reichmann Award, I attempted to say how meaningful it was for me thus to be linked to the memory of a beloved person who was a friend and mentor as well as a teacher. I vividly recall my first meeting with her in 1938 that took place under circumstances that were somewhat trying for me. No, I was not seeking admission to the psychoanalytic institute nor trying to convince her to be my analyst. When my wife, Ruth, and I had virtually decided to marry, she took me to visit Frieda–not exactly for Frieda to approve of me or sanction the marriage. Ruth seemed assured Frieda would approve of me for she was in love, but I was not so certain. Ruth had but recently arrived in the United States and Frieda, who had also lived in Heidelberg, was her oldest acquaintance in the United States. Perhaps more important, my father-in-law, Professor Karl Wilmanns, though a follower of Kraepelin who had little regard for psychoanalysis and analysts, shared a consuming interest in schizophrenic patients with Frieda and held her in high esteem. My wife-to-be wished her parents in Germany to receive an evaluation of their future son-in-law from a respected and reliable source.

We were invited to the opening of a show of the paintings by Gertrude Jacob in Frieda's home at Chestnut Lodge. Jacob,

I read Thomas Mann's series of books on the Joseph saga very many years ago. I have not reread them in preparation of this paper, both because of the limits of time and also because I wished to be free of Mann's influence. However, I would readily acknowledge an indebtedness for any overlapping concepts should there be such. I wish to express my thanks to Prof. Paul Schwaber for reading a first draft of the paper and for his very cogent suggestions, and Prof. Victor M. Lidz for tracking down information concerning grain storage in Egypt prior to the presumed time of Joseph's influence.

443

a fine painter and a psychiatrist and Frieda's very close friend, had died a year or so earlier. After I was introduced to Frieda, we looked at Jacob's paintings with great care and admiration. I then turned to Frieda and asked when (you will note: not "if") Jacob had studied with Lovis Corinth. There are times when one should take a chance. Frieda was clearly taken aback, somewhat astonished that I knew of Lovis Corinth, a German painter virtually unknown in the United States at that time, and that I could tell that her friend had been his student. Well, I had studied in Munich where Corinth was greatly admired and had acquired from my American artist friends who were also studying in Munich something of an eye for various artists' styles of painting. The fortunate happenstance gained Frieda's respect and regard that blossomed. However, one's luck does not always hold. The next time we visited, I, with the vast knowledge of a psychiatric resident, mentioned that certain groups of persons were likely to be sociopaths. I don't recall my list, but it included motorcyclists, particularly those with black jackets; soda jerks—they were not a type of jerk but it was the appelation given the young men who made ice-cream sodas and sundaes at the soda counters who liked to show off and flirt with female customers; people with bright colored convertibles, and so forth. Frieda said nothing but when we left she walked us to our car—a staid green Plymouth—and as we passed her garage, asked with a twinkle, "Would you like to see my new car?" and there it was—a shiny, bright blue convertible.

Later, following World War II, Frieda supervised my first control case, which she did with amazing tolerance but considerable strictness concerning proper psychoanalytic technique. I mention it because she would come to Baltimore for a day each week and supervise in her hotel room. The supervision was disrupted for a week or two when the hotel management refused to permit her to stay there because a different young man would come to her room every hour. Ruth Lidz and I continue to be reminded of Frieda every day and I think of her at least for a passing moment because, knowing my fondness of the painting by Jacob of the hills outside of Jerusalem that hung in her study, she bequeathed it to us, and it now hangs in our study.

One of the last times I had the opportunity to have a long talk with Frieda was a year or two before her death, and our conversation is the reason I have belatedly written this paper for the symposium commemorating the fiftieth anniversary of her arrival at Chestnut Lodge. We were attending a meeting in Atlantic City, then a resort devoid of gambling casinos but a favored spot for conventions, and we set off for a long stroll on the boardwalk. To my surprise, Frieda, who seemed a bit depressed, spoke of her recent appreciation of the importance of loneliness as a psychiatric problem because of a pervasive sense of loneliness that had come over her. I wondered why a person, beloved and sought after for help and who had helped so many patients thought to be beyond help, would be lonely. Was it Edith Jacobson who said, "To feel lonely is not to be number one for anyone"? I suppose that although Frieda was loved and needed, she was not number one for anyone except for patients for whom she sought not to be, or at least not remain, number one. Frieda's thoughts had turned to her native land and the relatives and friends who had been annihilated.

On the occasion when I last talked with Frieda, she spoke of writing a paper about Joseph, he who had been sold into slavery and achieved greatness in Egypt. I, too, had been considering writing a paper about Joseph, and we enthusiastically exchanged ideas.

Of course, it was not strange for two psychoanalysts and particularly two Jewish analysts to be interested in Joseph. As others, we had pondered the potential influence that temporally remote biblical figure had on Sigmund Freud. Joseph had probably been the most powerful Jew who ever lived for he had been granted complete power to govern Egypt by Pharaoh because of his interpretations of Pharaoh's dreams. Because of the Old Testament, the source of much Jewish tradition, Joseph, despite the 4,000 or so years since he lived, could not have been remote from Freud. Moreover, Freud, like Joseph, was the oldest child of a father Jacob's second marriage, in a sense also a child of his father's old age. How consciously or unconsciously had the extremely ambitious Freud sought to follow in the footsteps of his great progenitor?

However, the analogy with Freud was not what had attracted our attention to Joseph. Each of us had been drawn to a different aspect of the biblical story, but there was a relationship between our ideas. Frieda was wondering if she would have attained prestige and honor, or if she would have been able to achieve so much in fostering the analytic psychotherapy of schizophrenic patients had she not been forced to emigrate. "A prophet is not without honor save in his own country," and she, like Joseph, came into her own in a foreign land. Frieda had brought the knowledge and skills she had gained in pursuing her determined interest in the psychoanalysis of schizophrenic patients from a country in which her interest and skills set off little resonance—indeed, where her efforts were virtually ignored; she came to a locality where her specific abilities were sought after. The Baltimore-Washington area was almost the only place where, because of the influence of Adolf Meyer, William Alanson White, Harry Stack Sullivan, and Lewis Hill, the belief existed that schizophrenic disorders might well be distortions of the personality rather than a disorder of the structure or physiology of the brain, and that psychotherapy could change such patients' lives and even permit them to function normally. In Germany, Frieda may not have even attained the assurance and confidence to publish her papers and her book that have influenced so many psychiatrists for there academic psychiatrists were convinced that the only hope for schizophrenic patients lay in some future discovery of the biological cause of the illness; and psychoanalysts, following the teachings of Freud, had excluded schizophrenic patients from the sphere of their analytic efforts. It was good fortune, or the wisdom of Dexter Bullard, that had brought Frieda Fromm-Reichmann to the Baltimore-Washington area, and even more specifically to Chestnut Lodge. But the question of why recognition and greatness come to a person after being transferred to a new land, into a different culture, extends beyond Frieda, and we wished to learn what we could from the story of Joseph.

My own initial thoughts on Joseph derived from an interest in the difference in the relationships of a youngest or younger son to his father, particularly a son of his father's old age, from that of an oldest son. An oldest son is frequently caught up in an oedipal rivalry with his father that can inhibit his achievements lest he surpass his father and suffer from the essence of hubris that relates to fantasies of taking his mother away from his father. A youngest son, in contrast, is less likely to be treated as a rival for the mother by an aging father and often identifies with his father so that he considers his achievements to be extensions of his father's. Further, the biblical tale of Joseph and his forebears draws attention to the importance of sibling relationships, notably the rivalries of brothers and sisters, on a person's development, and how a younger offspring is likely to be impeded by the jealous animosities of older siblings. Then, too, we find in these tales how greatly the interrelationships between the parents, and the parents' rivalries with their own siblings, carry over into the next generation and influence the children's relationships with one another. My interest in the story of Joseph reflects my position as a youngest child of a father named Israel as well as my studies of the family influences on personality development and psychopathology.

One relationship between Joseph's attainment of greatness in a foreign land and his identification with Jacob may be that in Egypt Joseph was free from inhibitions about arousing his older brothers' jealousies and through his experience with them had learned to be diplomatic in displaying his genius. As far as his family was concerned, he had died; as far as his actual life was concerned, he had been reborn, free to use the capabilities derived from his identification with his patriarchal father and with the traditions of his people.

Let us first review the story of Joseph from a psychoanalytically oriented perspective, recognizing that, in a sense, the story of Joseph epitomizes much of the history of the Jews as a people. It is a story of success provoking jealousy, expulsion, or death; a rebirth in a new land; the achievement of prosperity and fame; and the spread of cultural concepts that raises doubts in the native inhabitants about their own culture with ensuing anti-Semitism and expulsion, so that the cycle starts anew.

Joseph, the eleventh son of Jacob, was the first son of Rachel, Jacob's beloved wife. Jacob's older sons were those of Rachel's older sister Leah whom he had been forced to marry before he could gain Rachel, and whom he never loved despite the six sons and at least one daughter she bore him; and the

sons of Zilpah and Bilhah, the handmaidens of his primary
wives Leah and Rachel. Rachel died in giving birth to Benjamin
when Joseph was still a child. Jacob transferred his love for
Rachel to her sons and became particularly loving and protective of them. Joseph was not caught up in a rivalry with his
father for Rachel as she had died and Jacob considered Rachel's
sons to be his true successors. Joseph remained close to his
father, identified with him, and as a child with much older
siblings could learn from them how to manage families, households, and properties, as well as how to avoid their errors that
created difficulties with their father. Indeed, Jacob's three oldest sons had provoked his wrath. Reuben, the oldest, had slept
with Bilhah, the mother of several of his brothers, and thus
committed a sin close to that of sleeping with his own mother,
and so lost his father's major blessing, the due of an oldest son.
The next two sons in the line of succession, Simeon and Levi,
had angered Jacob by the terrible vengeance they took on the
seducer of their sister, Dinah, and on his entire family and their
retainers even though the man's intentions were honorable and
he sought to marry Dinah—an uncalled-for vengeance that
forced Jacob and all of his dependents to migrate because of
fear of the wrath of the local inhabitants.

     In considering Joseph's position in his family, let us recall
that a beloved wife's favoritism of a son had in two prior generations led the father to confer his primary blessing on the
younger son and to serious hostility between brothers. Abraham's wife Sarah, barren into old age, had given her hand-
maiden Hagar to Abraham to produce a son, Ishmael, for him.
Sarah became hostile to Hagar who, though her maid, assumed
superiority over Sarah because she had produced Abraham's
successor. Later, when Sarah witnessed Ishmael "sporting," that
is, engaging in some sort of sexual behavior, she insisted that
Abraham banish Hagar and Ishmael as she thought Ishmael
would be a bad influence on her son Isaac.[1] As Hagar belonged

---

[1] Abraham's readiness to sacrifice Isaac, his son, to his God has provoked many
commentaries. I regard it as a reflection of a father's efforts to placate the ghost of his
own father—in whose image he creates his God, and at the same time eliminate the
danger that his son might kill him. It reflects a father's ambivalence toward a son who
preempts his wife's time and affection. In Greek mythology, Uranos and Kronos killed
their sons, and Tantalus fed his son to the gods. Isaac's rescue by God may be considered

to Sarah, she had the right to send her into the wilderness. Though after Sarah died Abraham took another wife who bore him six sons, he bequeathed all of his possessions to Isaac.

Isaac, married to Rebekah, Abraham's grandniece, had twin sons, Esau and Jacob. During Rebekah's pregnancy, the Lord told her, "Two nations are in why womb . . . and the elder shall serve the younger." Strange, the younger surpassing the elder in the tales of the Jewish patriarchs despite the tradition that the eldest receive the father's blessing and become his successor. Esau, the hunter with the more masculine character, was Isaac's favorite. However, Rebekah favored Jacob, her quieter and more domestic younger son, and connived to have him receive the blessing of his blind and dying father by disguising Jacob as Esau. The blessing included: "Be lord over thy brethren, and let thy mother's sons bow down to thee. Cursed be everyone that curseth thee, and blessed be everyone who blesseth thee." When he learned of his error, Isaac could not undo the blessing he had given Jacob, and thus a bitter animosity started between Esau and Jacob that led Rebekah to urge Jacob to flee to her brother Laban. There he immediately fell in love with Rachel, Laban's younger daughter, but to gain her he had to work seven years and marry her older sister Leah and then work another seven years as a brideprice for Rachel. Rachel was envious of Leah, of course, a feeling heightened by Leah's fecundity while she remained barren; and Leah was jealous of Jacob's love for her sister. Rachel, in contrast to Sarah and Rebekah, did not arrange for her sons to receive their father's primary blessing. She had died; but Jacob favored them because of her.[2]

Joseph, then, was favored by his father and could identify with him and feel free to become a great man without being

the essence of the covenant between Jehovah and Abraham—as it symbolized an end of the sacrifice of the firstborn son that must have alienated a wife from her husband and disrupted the unity of the family that is critical to any civilization. The sacrifice of Isaac is, in a sense, a variant of Laius's attempt to kill the infant Oedipus; and the Joseph saga is a variant of the Oedipus saga—but with the slaying of the child transposed to the jealous brothers. Both Oedipus and Joseph survived to become mighty rulers.

[2] Esau married Ishmael's daughter to gain his father's favor and thus Ishmael and Esau became the progenitors of the Arabs. The animosity of the rejected sons of Abraham and Isaac toward the sons who received their father's blessings would seem to have been transmitted across the thousands of years unto the present generation when the Arabs, the descendents of Esau and Ishmael, fled the land of their fathers.

rivalrous with Jacob. We may also consider that like many younger sons, he did not have an older son's responsibility of helping his father manage his possessions but was free to follow a path of his own choosing, and to dream and, as his parents' beloved child, to dream of greatness. Whatever Joseph learned by being the younger brother, he had failed to learn a lesson of paramount importance; namely, the need to allay the jealousy of his older siblings. Joseph's dreams required no accomplished interpreter of the unconscious. Even though dreams were considered prophetic rather than wish fulfillments, his narration of his dream of the sheaves of wheat antagonized his brothers, and Jacob scolded him for his presumption when he told his dream that the sun, moon, and eleven stars had bowed down to him. Then, too, Joseph considered himself as someone apart from the sons of Jacob's other wives, and brought home reports of his brothers' misbehaviors. When sent by Jacob to see his brothers who were tending their father's flocks, he wore the famous coat of many colors given him by his father as a mark of his special favor—perhaps the last straw that led his brothers to decide to kill him.

Whereas a younger son favored by his motther and father may not be impeded by concerns of surpassing his father or of displaying the essence of hubris that Joseph manifested in telling his dream that signified that his father and mother as well as his brothers would bow down to him, a younger brother can have serious qualms about appearing to surpass his older brothers. Joseph should have been very much aware of the problem because of his father's difficultieis with Esau whose birthright he had bought when Esau was starving and whose blessing he had stolen. A younger brother is likely to learn ways of hiding his ambitions and abilities or else find means of having his older siblings assume a parenting role and take pride in his achievements. If he does not, the older siblings not only can seek to block his progress, but their dislike can greatly affect all of his interpersonal relationships. Joseph apparently was so secure in his adolescent grandiosity, or perhaps so sure of his father's backing and blessing, that he did not take notice of the homicidal rage he was arousing in his older brothers.

The brothers would have killed Joseph had not Reuben,

their father's surrogate, dissuaded his brothers and had them place Joseph in a dry pit to die, and Judah then persuaded them to sell him into slavery instead of letting him die.[3] Taken to Egypt, Joseph was reborn into a new life in a foreign land, where even though a slave he could use his unusual abilities to move toward greatness, whereas at home they only provoked jealousy and anger. Joseph's brilliance and capacities that led Potiphar, the captain of the Pharaoh's guard, to place Joseph, the slave, in charge of his household also unwittingly made him too attractive to Potiphar's wife so that he was again cast into a pit—that is, a dungeon, but this time because of the wrath of a woman scorned.

However, aside from his own intellect, self-confidence, and the knowledge gained in his father's household, Joseph brought to ancient Egypt, with its ways that had become congealed over the millenia of its existence, the traditions and beliefs of another ancient culture with different ethical principles—for the ethics of the Jews were, even before being codified by Moses, probably related to the code of Hammurabi. Terah, Abraham's father, had dwelt in Ur of the Chaldees and took his sons to migrate to the land of Canaan. Ur already had a high culture, but one that differed greatly from that of Egypt. The Bible provides no reason why they left, but according to legend they were anti-traditionalists who refused to conform to the idolatry of the Chaldeans. Perhaps Terah. and Abraham already came from a people who refused to worship rulers, ancestors or idols—something we cannot know—but in leaving Ur, the Hebrews became a people who for much of their long history were rooted in their tradition and ethical code rather than in a homeland. For much of their history, the Jews have been culture carriers—the carriers of the culture of the people who expelled them as well as their own culture to which many adhered even when they became, or tried to become, loyal members of the community in which they dwelt.

Joseph had the confidence of being the blessed son of a

---

[3] The analogy with Jesus is noteworthy. He was killed and arose from His grave. Judah, rather than Judas, sold Joseph for pieces of silver and Reuben, who had not known he had been taken from the pit, returned to rescue Joseph only to find the pit empty.

father who had been directly blessed by God, and whose name God had changed to Israel—which means "he contended with God," because he had wrestled all night with a man, an angel or God, and was neither defeated nor would let go until the "man" blessed him. Joseph's grandiose dreams had indirectly landed him in an Egyptian prison where he soon became a warder even though a prisoner, and then his understanding of dreams brought him to the attention of a Pharaoh who was troubled by his dreams.

Joseph interpreted dreams prophetically. However, his interpretations of the dreams of the Pharaoh's butler and baker might also be taken as a conscious or unconscious awareness that the content of the two men's dreams reflected their respective innocence and guilt of the crimes of which they had been accused. The Pharaoh's dreams of the seven lean kine swallowing the seven fat kine, and of the seven blasted ears of grain consuming the seven full ears of grain might today be thought to reflect his anxieties that his country's prosperity would not endure; and Joseph's interpretation that seven years of prosperity would be followed by seven years of famine was possible because of his commonsense wisdom that during prosperous years food must be accumulated and stored for the lean years that inevitably would follow. Joseph may have become aware of the cyclic recurrence of famine by his family history, for Abraham and Sarah had left Canaan to dwell in Egypt to escape a great famine; and Isaac had been ordered by God to live through a famine in Canaan and not go to Egypt. In any case, Joseph urged a great increase in the storing of grain against future crop failure in a land that depended on the annual flooding of farm lands by the Nile to assure bountiful harvests. Joseph's wisdom extended beyond soothsaying for according to the Bible he governed for the Pharaoh for many years, becoming, as he told his brothers, "a father unto Pharaoh." During the years of plenty he built local and national storehouses for grain, and at a very young age ruled the country. Then, during the last years of the famine, he saved the people from starvation and at the same time greatly increased the wealth and power of the pharaohs. When the people had already used all their possessions to purchase grain and were starving, he told them that if they gave their land to Pharaoh, he would give them food—but he wisely excepted the priests. The people were grateful as they were permitted to remain on their land, but thereafter a rent of a fifth of every harvest had to be paid to Pharaoh.

The family aspect of the story of Joseph rounds out when his brothers come to Egypt from Canaan to purchase food for the family. Jacob, fearful of losing Rachel's remaining son, does not let Benjamin accompany his brothers. Joseph, hiding his identity and his understanding of his brothers' language, accuses them of being spies to force them to bring his beloved brother Benjamin to Egypt, and in the process learns of their remorse for selling him. Then, when Benjamin is finally before him, he witnesses their concerns for Jacob and their willingness to sacrifice themselves to protect both Jacob and Benjamin, and he knows they have suffered for their crime against him and are changed men. Joseph then reveals his identity to his brothers. He settles his father and his entire clan in the fertile land of Goshen. Despite the way his brothers have treated him, Joseph is benevolent toward them, very much affected by family bonds. Joseph explained his lack of hostility toward his older brothers because he believed, or made himself believe, that it had been God's way of assuring the family's survival. Had his brothers not sold him into slavery, he would not have, with God's help in interpreting the dreams, become the virtual ruler of Egypt and been able to provide his family with a secure home. Rivalry, envy, and jealousy are inherent in sibling relationships, but, as we see in the story of Joseph, sharing and love based on a common identification with parents can be equally prominent. The common heritage that binds people into tribes and nations is obviously most pronounced in siblings brought up in the same household. The importance of the ties between siblings and family loyalty is illustrated by the interruption of the narration of the story of Joseph by the tale of the terrible vengeance taken by the brothers against the seducer of their sister Dinah. Their excuse to Jacob, angered by the excess, was: "Are we going to let our sister be treated as a harlot?" which scarcely covered the situation, but rage incensed by jealousy and family pride banished reason.

The blessing of the younger son by Abraham and Isaac is more explicit in Jacob's blessing of Joseph's sons. When Jacob is dying, Joseph brings his sons Manasseh and Ephraim for his father's blessing. Though Joseph specifically seeks to have Manesseh, the elder, receive the blessing from Jacob's right hand, Jacob insists on blessing Ephraim with his right hand. Again the patriarch predicts, or confers the blessing, that the younger son will become greater than the elder. Jacob, as the younger son, may well have favored Joseph's younger son; but the repetition of the theme seems to indicate the importance of the younger son in the early history of the Jews.

Joseph was greatly honored in Egypt and Jacob's funeral was mourned throughout the land and all the elders of Egypt accompanied the funeral procession to Canaan. Jacob's descendents prospered and over several hundred years grew into a mighty nation within Egypt, so mighty that they were enslaved until under the leadership of Moses they were expelled and fled across the Red Sea. However, Joseph's position of being a Jew who was only second to an emperor was not unique in the annals of the Jews. In the reign of Xerxes, Mordecai, with the help of his niece Esther, who had become the queen, saved himself and all the Jews in the vast empire that stretched from India to Ethiopia from being slaughtered, and then became a chief advisor to Xerxes (Book of Esther). Daniel, according to the strange book of the Bible named after him, like Joseph, rose to power because of his ability to interpret dreams prophetically despite the ominous nature of his interpretations. Indeed, if the story can be, or rather could be, believed, he was a dream interpreter beyond compare for he was able to tell Nebuchadnezzar what he had dreamed and then interpret it. Daniel became one of the three presidents who ruled over 120 satraps and was so capable that when Darius was about to make him ruler of the entire empire, the other presidents and the satraps became jealous and had him condemned to death because of his religion; but, as everyone knows, Daniel survived the lion's den and gained even greater prominence under Darius and Cyrus. In modern times, Disraeli, whose Jewish heritage is apparent from his name, was Prime Minister when the British empire was at its zenith under Queen Victoria; and Blum was

Prime Minister of France just prior to World War II. At a different level, but pertinent to my thesis, the Jews who entered Spain with the Arabs were welcomed and found a safe haven for hundreds of years and came to constitute about a third of the bourgeoisie prior to their expulsion by the Inquisition because of their religion. Some Jews who fled Spain were invited into Poland and Russia to manage the estates of the nobility and flourished numerically, though not politically, and eventually were isolated, persecuted, and finally annihilated.

The story of Joseph and the Jews in Egypt is symbolic of how persons from a different culture achieve greatness in the land into which they migrate and of the recurrent theme of Jews expelled from one country migrating into another where they prosper but eventually fall prey to anti-Semitism and expulsion or annihilation. It directs attention to the importance of cultural relativity and how greatly people's cultures direct their ways of thinking, perceiving, and conceptualizing, and how the entry of a carrier of a different culture into a country not only can bring new perspectives to cope with crises but stimulate creativity. A truly creative individual is usually one who understands the world and categorizes experiences in ways that are somewhat aberrant from the conventional ways of the society. The oft-pondered relationship between genius and insanity—as, for example, in Isaac Newton and August Strindberg—concerns the ability to perceive and categorize experiences deviantly, albeit in the case of these two men with new constructive insights that altered the understanding of the world for those who followed them.

The human species differs from all other living organisms because its evolution depended largely on the selecting out of those genetic mutations that increased the capacities for using tools and particularly that tool of all tools, the word. Because of the capacity to utilize language, humans became capable of abstract thought, of conceptualizing a future, and being motivated by future goals rather than primarily through drives and conditioning. Equally important, language not only increased the capacity to cooperate with others, but also the capacity to transmit what persons learned across generations so that knowledge became cumulative. People extended the limits of the environments in which they could maintain their essential physiological homeostasis by modifying environments to meet these physiological limitations. The human capacity to adapt to very diverse environments depended little on genetic change, but primarily on learning and transmitting techniques of adapting to the environment. Thus, humans spread out over the globe capable of living anywhere provided their forebears had developed instrumentalities for coping with the environment and living together in it.

The adaptive techniques different peoples utilize to live in different environments, including the language they use, the techniques of acquiring food, the rules for propagating their group, and for gaining supernatural aid, are not part of the human biological endowment. They must be learned, and learned primarily from those who raise them; and so much is learned as part of their development as they are nutured in a family that much of it has often been mistaken as an inherent part of their biological endowment. Everywhere people living in different places developed different cultures; differing ways of thinking, speaking, and adapting to their environment, and for living cooperatively and interdependently in it. The human species can be defined in various meaningful ways, but quintessentially the human is the organism that cannot survive and develop into a person without assimilating a culture.

The culture's ways are inculcated from earliest childhood and become the way of understanding the world, the only way people in isolated societies know. The way of life in each culture has developed in response to environmental conditions and to essential human needs that are much the same everywhere, but also as a consequence of that specific culture's developmental history. Much in every culture is relativistic, but to the member of the society little seems arbitrary but the proper and essential way of life. The need to live in a society with a different set of meanings and values from one's own culture leaves people feeling anomic and lost. To the ancient Greeks, exile was the ultimate punishment.

The importance of culturally shared ways extends beyond requisites for living and the development of sustaining social structures. All peoples have required ways of attempting to cope with matters beyond their control: the contingencies of weather, famine, illness, loss of essential persons, death, as well as to explain what seems inexplicable. Whereas specific individuals may not need to believe in supernatural beings, it is an essential aspect of human existence that peoples require belief in some supernatural power to enable them to face exigencies of life beyond their control. An important, if not a major, aspect of such beliefs has to do with efforts to deny the finality of death; but perhaps still more important is the continuation into adult life of the child's dependency on parents, who the small child believes are omniscient or omnipotent. When adolescents come to realize that the security parents can provide is limited and uncertain, they find comfort in the belief that dead ancestors, and various deities conceived in the image of parental figures, will fill the omniscient parental role, and can be influenced to mediate between nature and themselves. Each culture tends to develop a common system of beliefs on how ancestor spirits or deities can be influenced to provide security for the group as well as individuals. These are beliefs that can never be proven and often run contrary to common observation—as the Holocaust recently challenged the powerful belief that Jehovah had a covenant with the Jews that went "I will curse all who curse you and bless those who bless you"; or more commonly by the misfortunes that befall good and pious persons. Beliefs that are unprovable and often run contrary to experience must be defended strongly, even with fierce intensity, for a people cannot survive without some means of attempting to ward off catastrophe or without beliefs that provide meaning to existence and direction to their lives. Paradoxically, the more an autocratic king or dictator persecutes people because of their religious beliefs, the more they need their beliefs to sustain their faith in a rescuing power or the meaningfulness of life despite their own fates.

Then, too, peoples, particularly prior to the blending of cultures in recent times through ease of communication and also the disruptions of belief systems by science, felt secure in knowing—that is, in feeling certain—that their way of behaving and understanding the world was the proper way of life. They lived correctly and all others were barbarians. Even societies that civilized people considered primitive and barbaric as the neolithic tribal societies in Papua New Guinea (Poole, 1983) and along the Amazon (Gregor, 1985; Murphy and Murphy, 1974) have considered other groups in their area with somewhat different cultures to be unregenerate savages. Persons have, in general, only felt secure and comfortable among those who shared their orientation to life and their ways of understanding existence. People who live in a society in which the culture's ways are believed to be the only proper way are spared much conflict and insecurity, for they know the path to follow even if they stray from it. We are currently witnessing a revolt by fundamentalist Christians in the United States against rationality and scientific evidence to preserve their sense of security in a world that has become purposeless anad increasingly precarious with the development of science.

The people of each society share a way of coping with problems of living; and a way of explaining what is beyond their understanding that they consider the only proper way. Joseph settled his father and brothers in the land of Goshen because their way of life as shepherds and herders was an abomination to the Egyptians. Ethnocentricity not only delimits people's understanding but also their capabilities. Persons who enter the society from a different culture are not bound by the natives' ethnocentricities, and their thinking is not constricted by its traditional ways of categorizing, and thus they have a potentiality for being truly creative through blending the two cultures or rearranging one of them. When Frieda Fromm-Reichmann brought a psychoanalytic orientation that derived from the treatment and study of psychotic patients rather than of neurotic patients, it enabled some psychoanalysts and psychiatrists to gain a new vision of the core problem of psychiatry, particularly because it was met by the concepts of Harry Stack Sullivan who was sufficiently deviant himself, in part because of his Hibernian ancestry, to have unusual insight into the psychotically deviant, as well as because of the influence of Adolf Meyer who not only introduced a Swiss orientation to the care of the mentally ill in the United States, but came from a family that was somewhat atypical in Switzerland because they were followers of the pragmatic folk philosopher Jacob Gujer (Bleuler, 1962), which prepared him to grasp the pragmatic and instrumental concepts of American philosophy and sociology and introduce them into American psychiatry (Lidz, 1966).

When Joseph was sold into Egypt he brought with him more than the knowledge garnered by a young and favored son concerning the management of a clan, and the freedom to emulate his elderly father. He brought a tradition of a specific family line who were accustomed to speak directly with their God and receive His reassurance of their blessedness and His protection; a belief in the predictive value of dreams gained from his father Jacob who was also a dreamer of significant prophetic dreams; a tradition of his forebears, the Jewish patriarchs who had utilized a variety of means and schemes to preserve themselves and their descendents (Schwaber, 1982); but also a way of regarding life that differed greatly from the rigidly held and congealed belief system of the Egyptians with their polytheism, deification of the pharaohs, and rather concrete ways of conceptualizing. Joseph brought with him knowledge of the ways of the Canaanites and even more clearly the traditions of the Hebrews that originated in Ur nurtured by the Tigris and Euphrates rather than the cyclically overflowing Nile. He was aware of the dangers of recurrent famine, and had a future orientation, and convinced the Pharaoh greatly to increase the storage of grain during a period of prosperous harvests for future contingencies.

Joseph's wisdom was welcome as it forestalled a disaster; but as it also encompassed a belief system that differed greatly from that of the Egyptians it contained the seeds of future disaster for his family and their descendents.

Peoples are discomforted by challenges to their way of life—and feel endangered by challenges to their belief system, particularly when they are beginning to have doubts about it and need to bolster it. They will defend the core beliefs of their culture with their lives, for without their culture they feel rootless and lost. Many wars have been fought to eradicate conflicting beliefs. Of course, wars have been waged to gain new territory for an expanding population; to gain the wealth of the conquered; to enslave other peoples; to expand commerce and so forth; but some of the most devastating wars have been to annihilate a people with divergent beliefs or to enforce their conversion. The task of the hero is to clear a space in chaos in which a culture can exist (Cowan, 1980; Lidz, 1981), but many heroes have been occupied with seeking to preserve a belief system that wards off the intrusion of chaos. And, perhaps the most remoreseless inquisitors and ardent missionaries have been persons who seek to vanquish inner doubts. Currently, Moslems in Lebanon who share many cultural characteristics are remorsely slaughtering one another over differences within Islam that seem minor to an outsider.

All persons can think, but few are willing or able to puzzle about fundamentals. They live according to a given way; a way given by their predecessors who they believe knew the proper way of assuring survival and for living together as a community. Even today, it is essential in the United States to preserve the Constitution written by the founding fathers, and to live in accord with the ethics propounded by Moses and Jesus.

Each culture developed different ways of influencing its ancestors or deities to preserve the people from harm, to mediate with nature in their favor. Some placate by sharing food with dead ancestors, firming bonds by a commensal meal which indicates the essence of unity and trust between people. Some sacrifice or seek to control through the performance of ritual. Some pray, beseeching a deity as they would a parent. Many people come to believe that nature can be controlled by ethical behavior. Jane Harrison (1912) puzzled over how it came about that people believe that "Dike," Natural Order, could be influenced by "Themis," Social Order.[4] Of course, what is considered ethical behavior is what is thought essential to the social order and varies greatly from culture to culture—in one society it was not only proper but essential constantly to sacrifice human hearts; in another to eat dead relatives as among the Fore people in Papua New Guinea; in others "to do unto others as you would have them do unto you." However, whatever the ethic, it rarely suffices unless reinforced by ritual.

---

[4] Dike and Themis "are not the same . . . they stand at the two poles and are even alien. Natural Law is from . . . the first pulse of life, nay even before . . . it rules over what we call the inorganic. Social order, morality, 'goodness' is not in nature at its outset; it only appears with man, her last work" (Harrison, 1912).

When the descendents of Jacob dwelt in Egypt, they brought with them an alien culture, a different way of living, a different perception of life, and, most important, a belief system that was very different from that of the Egyptians. Thus, they brought an inner threat to the Egyptians' sense of security and assurance that their ways of dealing with supernatural forces were the proper ways. Isis, Osiris, Horus, and Amman Re, and the divinity of the Pharaoh were not accepted by the Hebrews who nevertheless flourished under the protection of their own God. The Hebrews' prosperity despite their beliefs challenged the security the Egyptians felt that rested on the certainty that their ways of life and religion were correct.

The story of the welcome of the Jews into Egypt and their eventual expulsion has been repeated in many lands over the millenia. For most of the 4,000 or more years of their history, the Jews have been a people without a country, but nevertheless a people with a distinctive culture. They have, in general, defended a culture based on their Bible rather than a country. They have usually, though not always, assimilated the culture of the country in which they lived but without being totally assimilated, and some have maintained a distinct identity, culture, and religion. This has transpired, in part, because from their earliest days, they have had a reverence for learning. "The book," primarily the five books of Moses that recorded their history, laws, and their covenant with their God, Jehovah, rather than a megalith or a statue of a deity was their sacred object; and it led to a reverence for books and learning in general. Literacy and education became a fundamental characteristic of the culture. Of course, everywhere they dwelt some would lose their Jewish identity, but virtually everywhere, even in Ethiopia where they were separated from their co-religionists for thousands of years and did not know that other Jews existed, a core group adhered to the tenets and ways they believed assured a unity with their God. Because of their adherence to their culture, even after thousands of years, they remained "Falasha," that is, "strangers."

One might almost say that the Jews have worshiped their history and their laws, for the Torah—the book of Moses—is sacred; and each sabbath, as the core of the religious service, a portion of it is read from a scroll that is untouchable because of its holiness. No matter where the Jews lived, each boy was to be taught to read and was supposed to study the history and laws of the people that bound them together. Thus, the Jews have always had a dual, and sometimes a triple, orientation: that of the land in which they lived, that of their own culture, and often that of the land which they had left because of persecution. Still they, as other peoples, have believed that their own security, or at least the continuity of the Jews as a people, rested on the observance of the teachings of their religion that assured the protection of their God who was powerful enough to bless those who blessed them and curse those who cursed them. Although the reward for fidelity was often far from apparent—as in Poland and Russia in modern times—they could note that empires that had cursed them had fallen: Egypt, Assyria, Babylon, Rome, Spain, Czarist Russia, Poland, the Third Reich. They continued to exist.

The support of their God depended to a greater extent than in most cultures on the adherence to abstract ethics, and true Judaism (as opposed to the Hasidic sects of eastern Europe) was relatively devoid of mysticism and other worldliness. There is no heaven and no afterlife in the Mosaic code. What does the Lord require of thee? Micah answered, "Only to act justly and to love mercy, and walk humbly with thy God." They were indeed a stubborn people in regard to their religion, and persecution only augmented their stubbornness. Moreover, they were monotheists who believed in an abstract, ineffable God, and prayed for the day when all people would worship one God, and the name of God would be one. However, they were forbidden to proselytize, and even made it difficult for others to convert to Judaism.

There have been various causes for the anti-Semitism to which Jews have been subjected from biblical times. It has been their relative prosperity; their setting themselves apart as a unified group within a host country; their learning that brought advancement to a disproportionately large number, which sometimes included political power and often financial power; because "they killed our Christ"—though obviously God must have deemed it essential to sacrifice His only son. And, because

they had the audacity to consider themselves God's chosen people, the people with whom He had made His covenant and
upon whom He bestowed His blessing—thus they were subject
to the jealousy of others toward the favored child.[5] However,
beyond all such reasons for anti-Semitism has been the threat
to the security of the people posed by the presence of a people
with a different set of beliefs that raised doubts in the host
people about their own way of life and the security provided
by their religious beliefs. Raising any doubt about the belief
system and way of life that had been handed down to a people
by their forebears as the proper way of life opens the way for
the overthrow of the entire system of beliefs—for, as has been
noted, such beliefs are taken on faith and can be neither proven
nor disproven. Disbelief leaves a people naked in an aleatory
world, prone to anomie for they no longer have a way of life
in which meaning exists. Moreover, the religion of the Jews has
tended to discomfort for it relates the security provided by a
deity to ethical behavior and proper deeds more than to ritual;
and it has tended to emphasize benefits that would come in this
world rather than a promise of an eternal life of blessedness
(or damnation). A person did not gain a place in Heaven—during
those times in which Jews believed in Heaven—by dying in
battle to preserve the faith, by killing or converting infidels, or
by partaking in communion to assure resurrection along with
Jesus.

Of course, the Jews did not always adhere to the essence
of their religion, and relied on ritual and prayer that praised
God to gain His benevolence. In the days of Jeremiah, the Jews
in Egypt worshiped the Queen of Heaven—a forerunner of
Catholicism—as essential to their prosperity and well-being. In
modern times, most notably in Poland where Jews lived in constant danger of pogroms and were isolated from the encompassing intolerant Catholic communities, they became ingrown,

---

[5] The concept that the Jews are the chosen people of Jehovah is a misunderstand-
ing. Originally Jehovah was the God of the Hebrews in contrast to Isis, Re, Baal, Ishtar,
Cybele, Jove who were gods of other peoples. It came about that the Christians and
Muslims both accepted Jehovah—at least the God of the Old Testament as their god
as well—though in a modified form with the Christians adding deities and assimilating
certain near-Eastern rituals, and the Muslims emphasizing Paradise and conquest in
the name of Allah, etc.

narrowly ethnocentric, and the quest for knowledge became primarily a search for new interpretations of the Bible and the teachings of the rabbis, often together with a mysticism and belief in the curative powers of holy teachers—practices that are basically alien to Judaism.

In general, though, the Jews have been a disconcerting people who have shown that a way of life that differs from that of the people among whom they lived was not only feasible but could lead to prosperity and greatness. They denied the deification of kings; considered the polytheism of the Greeks and Romans as a superstition; sought by various means to eradicate the worship of idols and megaliths (unwrought stones) in which ancestor spirits were enshrined; insisted that Jesus was a Jewish teacher and a son of God only in the sense that all men were sons of God; and refused to accept Mary as the Mother of God who was the Son of God. Moreover, they have tended to remind others, as they did themselves, that they were faltering or failing in maintaining ethical principles—which created a sense of guilt that has often been managed most readily by projecting the ethical failures on the Jews who simply by their presence seemed to be their accusers. Inner danger creates anxiety that is difficult to tolerate and even more difficult to combat and is more readily managed when it can be transformed into an outer danger that can be eliminated by extermination.

The world, particularly the Western world, has changed profoundly and with accelerating rapidity since the beginning of the scientific era and the opening of the New World. Scientific discoveries and vast migrations have challenged and often disrupted traditional systems of belief, and the world grown small has brought awareness of the relativity of cultures. Neither the Jews nor any other migrating people are major culture carriers any longer for knowledge of diverse and divergent ways of living are conveyed into the home by television. Nevertheless, Jews have occupied central positions in shaping contemporary culture. Marx, Einstein, and Freud were major shapers of twentieth-century thought: Marx, though not Jewish, emerged from a Jewish heritage; and Einstein and Freud came from the Germanic-Jewish culture. Is it happenstance that the originators of the three concepts that made the modern world but also have threatened its security were Jews? Or is it that an understanding of the relativity of firmly held concepts was inherent in them because of the dual cultures they had assimilated. In a sense, they, like Joseph, carried new concepts that transformed an old world.

Perhaps science has changed the world, and the Jews welcomed as a creative influence will not ultimately be repudiated and expelled. The United States, and to a somewhat lesser extent Canada and Australia, are pluralistic societies that embrace a remarkable admixture of cultures and seek to permit divergent belief systems. Perhaps the dangers of bigotry and exclusion have passed, at least in the democratic, pluralistic societies, but it is apparent that some fundamentalist religious groups seek to protect their faltering systems of belief very militantly and threatened, seek to turn the United States into a land governed by biblical tenets. Thus far, the founding fathers' insistence on freedom of religion and expression remain the cornerstone of the national ethos. In contrast, nations that maintain autocratic or religious political systems are likely to seek to eliminate Jews or other discordant religious groups. The Soviet Union seeks to eliminate Judaism in its effort to eliminate a Jewish culture, perhaps because its rulers fear the dissidence inherent in a distinct culture within its borders, and the persistent desires of some Jews to negate the efficacy and legitimacy of Soviet communism by seeking to emigrate.

Contemporary Iran which chose to restore racial self-esteem rather than accept the modern scientific world that was threatening their way of life has few Jews, but it seeks to eliminate adherents of the B'hai religion for similar reasons: their presence with a strongly humanistic religion can become a serious challenge to the rigidly orthodox Shiite Moslem regime that insists on observances many Moslems resent. Why the Third Reich in Germany turned against the Jews who constituted only about one percent of the population is a complex issue that includes finding a scapegoat for economic crises and an effort to regain a purity of race (in a sense, a confusion with purity of culture) to restore self-esteem after a drastic defeat that left the nation with a hopeless economic situation and a grave loss of self-confidence.

We have considered the story of Joseph by means of what may be termed a psychoanalytic exegesis. It has provided not only some understanding of why persons displaced from one country to another can as culture carriers become creative and honored in the new land, but also why a younger child, because he is less likely to become caught in an oedipal rivalry with his father but rather tends to identify with him, may feel free to complete his father's life by achievement. He, like Joseph, runs the risk instead of provoking the jealous rage of older siblings, and may only surpass them when removed from them geographically or when pursuing a very different career. We have gone further and taken the story of Joseph as an epitome of the history of the Jewish people, the Israelites (the descendents of Jacob, renamed Israel because "he wrestled with God," and who seem to continue to be contentious) who as culture carriers have found a welcome in many lands but eventually as their host country weakens are considered dangerous as they challenge the country's prevailing ethos, and are expelled to carry their own culture and that of the expelling nation with them to their new refuge where the cycle starts anew.

References

Bleuler, M. (1962), Early Swiss sources of Adolf Meyer's concepts. *Amer. J. Psychiat.*, 119:193–196.

Cowan, B. (1980), Serpent's coils. *Southern Rev.*, 16:281–298.

Gregor, T. (1985), *Anxious Pleasures*. Chicago: University of Chicago Press.

Harrison, J. (1912), *Themis*. Cambridge, UK: Cambridge University Press. Reprinted: *A Mendiari Book*. New York: World Publishing, 1969.

Lidz, T. (1966), Adolf Meyer and the development of American psychiatry. *Amer. J. Psychiat.*, 123:320–332.

——— (1981), To carve a space out of chaos. *Triquarterly*, 52:7–20.

Murphy, T., & Murphy, R. (1974), *Women of the Forest*. New York: Columbia University Press.

Poole, F. (1983), Cannibals, tricksters and witches. In: *The Ethnography of Cannibalism*, ed. P. Brown & D. Tuzin. Washington, DC: Society for Psychological Anthropology.

Schwaber, P. (1982), The patriarchal tradition. In: *Father and Child*, ed. S. H. Cath, A. R. Gurwitt, & J. M. Ross. Boston: Little, Brown, pp. 383–398.

PART V

FROMM-REICHMANN'S DEVELOPMENT AS A THERAPIST

22

REMINISCENCES OF EUROPE

FRIEDA FROMM-REICHMANN, M.D.

At Chestnut Lodge, Fromm-Reichmann was rarely loquacious. In staff conferences or group supervision, she stated her observations and then let the other person continue talking. She never held forth with spontaneous lectures, as did others on the staff. Her papers and lectures similarly reflect her unembellished and modest style, built on a foundation of extraordinary firmness and self-confidence. Others sought her out, counting on her to listen actively and to respond with full honesty. She respected the other person's strength in hearing her undiluted opinion. But as a very private person, she was not usually forthcoming with accounts of her past. She left orders in her will to have all documents in her house burned. This was done.

In 1956, when Fromm-Reichmann was sixty-six years old and already troubled by deepening familial deafness, she left Chestnut Lodge for a year at Stanford University's Center for Advanced Studies in the Behavioral Sciences. There, she participated in the research project which came to be called "The Natural History of an Interview." She resided in the guest house of Dr. Irwin Kasle and Edna Cailie Sott, and over the course of the year spent much time with them and their children.

Over several evenings toward the end of that year, they and their mutual friend, Jane Weinberg, recorded informal interviews with Fromm-Reichmann. The recordings were not made professionally, and it seems that some of the material was inadvertently erased, as subsequent interviews were recorded over earlier material. Sometimes Fromm-Reichmann retold the same story during a later recording session. The transcript itself was difficult to read, with some sections inaudible, some made challenging by Germanic locution, and others by the feature of the rambling inherent in free association. It forms the basis for this chapter. Fromm-Reichmann's warmth and verve shine through, as she recounts her favorite anecdotes. For a fuller biographic account, the reader is referred to S. Hoff (1982).

A.-L. Silver

"I was born to be a psychiatrist because beginning at three, I knew all the secrets in the family and I took care not to disappoint my parents. Once, my mother had surprised my father by having a friend of hers do a portrait of me. Quite cute. I still see it in my inner eye. It's gone now; you weren't permitted to take these things out of Germany. So, here was a great surprise for my father. Father comes home from business and, poor fellow had a migraine attack, and so he doesn't see the picture. And my mother was miserable and later on, he noticed that he had disappointed her. He thought she came right behind the Lord, so, he was miserable; and I explained them to each other. I explained to her that he was sick, and what could he do? And I explained to him that she would understand, and couldn't he enjoy it now? And when he came home, he would put on a housecoat with some kind of buttons. When I see these buttons on somebody, leather-covered, I always think about this story."

The oldest of three girls, Fromm-Reichmann said, "these two sisters of mine suffered terribly because I worked out to the dot exactly the way Mother had dreamed. But I began to outshine her. That was not in the program." Her mother had been trained as a teacher, but was never employed; impressively, she and Frieda's three aunts all had memorized Goethe's *Faust* in its entirety. She had wanted Frieda to become a teacher.

"When I was nine, my mother got deaf after the birth of my youngest sister, and I heard her talk with my father about it in the next room. She worried that she would not be able to bring us up right, and now she had to stop having children. She wanted six more and she wanted a boy. And I was crazy about my mother and miserable—oh, to die! But for five years, she kept in pretty good contact with people and nobody knew that I knew. She could hear somewhat better than I can without a machine, so she got along. I knew when she went to the otologist, and I knew where she had her useless medicine, and finally, when I was fourteen, she was standing behind me as she did my long, long, long braids and she couldn't hear me. I always think about that now when I can't hear somebody behind me.

"My father brought up the question of my studying medicine. He said it would show that I really had college and university education, whereas you can be a teacher in languages without that. But I believed later—I worked that out in my analysis—that my mother didn't, of course, want me to go to medical school because then I would really know more than she did. She'd kill me if she heard me say that, but such it was. But he, I think, had some kind of feeling that I would do well at this.

"We always thought Father was treated as though he were a little dumbbell, which he wasn't. He was terribly in love with my mother and terribly impressed by her. She was always right and no one could say no when she said yes. She made it the most harmonious marriage you ever have seen because mother did everything right and so it was the most lucky family you could think of. If my mama went with her forehead toward a wall, the wall would give in [laughing]. But you know, I'm a little that way myself, only I handle it better because I realize it's not so charming.

"My father had a very definite feeling of what was what, and as I went into analysis, I gradually discovered that I saw him with my mother's eyes. He was short, with a very good-looking head, but the head was sitting on a wrong kind of torso. My father was among the leading people of the Jewish community. The uncle who had asked him to come to the city was 'it' and so he belonged, too. He was very religious, but all that stuff was a little boring. So he would not do this or that if one couldn't see it. He and the Lord had a very good relationship, whereas Mother and the Lord hadn't such a good relationship.

"He died in an elevator accident. As a result for a long time I had a very hard time to ride on self-service elevators. We all had. He was very deaf. He was sixty-five and so they wanted to retire him from his position at the bank. Since he didn't know anything about money, they had made him chief of personnel and he couldn't understand the employees finally. He had telephones and reinforcing telephones and extra enunciators on his desk, so his desk looked like a machine house. It didn't help. They did not yet have good machines; also, my sisters and I were still all unmarried and he thought that if he wore machines, we wouldn't get husbands. That was not such a wrong idea in these circles: two deaf parents and a deaf aunt.

"Well, anyway, he had to be retired and he was terribly hurt and terribly miserable. He had no reason really. He was the kind of person whom everybody loved. My father's birthday was last Sunday, February 19; and don't you believe that they ever pass us without our thinking of it. In the old days, I usually had something happen, a headache or one of my fantasies. These last years, I have succeeded to spend the day without it, but I would think of it. He's been dead thirty years exactly.

"I was just seventeen when I was ready for medical school. Everybody else was eighteen to twenty, so they decided I should stay home for half a year, and during that half year, I should decide. I must say, they decided. I decided later. My mother said, 'Why don't you first learn all the things I have done for you which made possible your studying for your Abitur?' And so I stayed home that term and learned to sew, how to mend, and how to cook, and how to do all female virtues. I remember I was forced to stay in the kitchen until I could prepare the meal for the whole family and some guests without the maid.

"At medical school, beginning with anatomy, there was a professor who felt women had no business studying medicine. He was already seventy, and he was told to teach it or to resign. He began to lecture, then put his finger in the jar in which pieces of the corpse were kept in formaldehyde. He shook his finger at me and I made a move. He said, 'No, I didn't tell you to come here with that bare neck of yours.' At that time, many of the women still wore the high necks, and I remember very well, I had a very light wool and it had a square neckline the way you wear it so much now. 'And I don't know why you came here anyway. The others, well, maybe they think they still can catch someone. But my God, you are so young and so pretty. You don't have to come to get yourself one.'

"He said if he had to teach us, that was one thing. But he would not let us do dissecting together with the boys. Now, they did that in the winter, and for obvious reasons they had to do it in one of the cellars. And then he said he didn't want us to come with white uniforms. They looked too much like night-gowns, and that wouldn't be good for the morale of the boys. And so, we were supposed to get ourselves colored things to wear.

"Well, my mother was right, after all. Anyhow, the anatomy class was in a very, very old building. Mind you, air conditioning didn't exist then in Königsberg. It was horrible to do it in sum-mer, but we survived. But the man, as we came to see him to ask his permission, the second in charge, said, 'Say, do you know how to cook?' I said, 'Yes.' And he said, 'Oh, that's good. I think every doctor should know something about diet and cooking and dietary science. And a woman therefore—I wouldn't admit any girl who would come here and say she doesn't know how to cook.'

"I adored obstetrics. I might have done it if it hadn't been that that's really one thing I couldn't do for physical reasons because I was too short. When my turn came, I had the time of my life. I delivered forty-four babies. You had to stay one month in the clinic, and whenever you could go, I went. I made the nurses mad in the delivery room because I wanted to take care of the babies afterward, and that was another's affair. The medical students did the delivery and off they went. And I never did. That was my great conflict with them. Anyway, that I would have liked to do. I still have pictures of that time with a baby on each arm where you can see how I enjoyed it.

"And then there was psychiatry. Here's what happened which made it definite for me that I would go into psychiatry. I was very shy. Oh, the whole atmosphere was quite suitable for being shy. One of the first psychiatric lectures I heard, in comes a manic-depressive. He looks at me and says, 'Bertchen, Bertchen, did I at last find you again?' All shyness was gone, and it said out of me—not *I* said *it*—*it* said, 'Yes, that's fine. I'm very glad, too. But you know, now the professor wants to talk to you. I'll come and see you later.' Nobody was more surprised than I was. All the students were, and everybody kind of gasped. And the professor was surprised. And then I went to see him afterward, much to the surprise of everybody. Whoever would say something to a crazy man and do it? I can still see what the man looked like, with my inner eye.

"Well, the story made a tremendous hullabaloo. The professor told it to the clinical director, and the wife of the clinical director was a friend of my mother. One day, I came home and my mother said, 'Why didn't you tell me about that big stunt you made there?' Well, I didn't know that I made a big stunt except that I knew at that point, ah, *this* I can do—like with your fingers.

"And the other such story happened even earlier. My seventh semester, we call it, I spent in Munich. And there was the great Kraepelin who said you can't treat schizophrenics because you can't understand the meaning of what they say. And I had no business going to psychiatric classes, but I thought I would go and listen to the great Kraepelin. And there I was even more shy. He presented an epileptic, and I still can tell you what he looked like. I left the class and thought, '*This* I could do better.' I was outraged about the way he did his talk in the presence of the patient about his epileptic seizures, about the epileptic character.

"Now here again, I must say I was brought up to believe in authorities and a great teacher was a great teacher. Who was I as compared with a great teacher? But I remember the most amazing thing which went so little with my conscious psychology I can't tell you how. I left that class and thought: Phooey! What an invasion of the dignity of the man, the way he presented him! And I could have done better, I thought.

"When I was an intern at the psychiatric hospital of the medical school of the University in Königsberg, nobody knew yet what psychotherapy was. But I knew it could be done. What I did was sit with the psychotics. Day and night, and night and day, and listen to them and just say a few kind things so that they went on.

"I got furious when they were mistreated. For instance, one day we made rounds, first the big boss and then all the associates. There was a man who didn't take off his cap as the great professor came in. One of the attendants or the head nurse asked him, 'Why don't you take off your cap?' And he said, 'But I can't. These birds which I have there underneath my cap will fly.' And everybody laughed no end. I was so mad I could have killed them, because I knew it meant something. But you must know at that time, one didn't yet know that it meant something. God, what a time I spent there, with the result that when I left there as an intern, a prima donna couldn't leave with more gifts, more flowers, more something. I still have one cut glass bowl from that time. That was again because I was so diligent spending so much time there.

"So, I took my boards in 1913. Graduating from medical school in Germany, you take your internship and write a doctoral thesis and a year later you get your M.D. My family all came to congratulate me, big Jewish family. The great uncle who played the great role in the family (he had the money and the reputation) said to my father, 'That's all fine. But you would permit her to become an insane doctor?' Well, I was shaking with fear about what he said to my poor father, because my father didn't stand up to that uncle. That was one of my miseries. But, by golly he said, 'George, I should have thought about that earlier. If I agreed with her studying medicine, I gave up the right to decide for her what specialty to choose.' The uncle, I shouldn't have judged him. In fact, later he gave me $10,000 to open my psychoanalytic kosher-Jewish hospital.

"Then came the war, and so, of course I went into psychiatry and neurology. At least I got a thorough neurological training. Now, I have forgotten all about it. My boss told me to take over the clinic. If I didn't handle three quarters of the clinic of that hospital, I don't know what. The Oberartz, Kurt Goldstein, the one next to the superintendent was there. I made it my job to do his job.

"I've had a life where I always had to be the muse, because I thought what they will do will be of greater significance. And what I could do was just to take off their jobs so that they could do their special work. So, this man was one of them. I used to call these 'my victims.' Somebody said the other day that it was me against myself, but obviously I got satisfaction because I did it time and again. Also, I got my compensation because since he then had time to do his scientific stuff, he took me along and taught me lots of things which otherwise I wouldn't have learned at that time. We published together and so it was a pretty good time.

"The Oberartz left, and I thought I might work some more with him, and told the boss I was considering leaving. He said, 'Well, would you stay if I put you in charge of a hospital for brain-injured soldiers?' The treatment of brain injury was new in World War I because of the trench fighting. For the first time, we saw brain lesions in otherwise healthy people. Now, I knew as much about brain injuries as the man in the moon. But thought I, 'Why not? It will be very interesting. I'll learn it." I said, 'Okay, if you send me to see the two existing hospitals, I'll do it.'

"It wasn't permitted for women to work in the Prussian army, so I worked as an associate of the university hospital and had a facsimile rubber stamp, and my name didn't appear. We began, I think, with twenty beds in that school. There were two school rooms, and the rest was internal medicine and surgery. Pretty soon, I had them all out of that school and had a 100-bed hospital. I had a clinic for them, became the consultant for the First and Seventeenth Army Corps, and had to run around and see the brain injuries. We decided who should be operated on and who should not, and when to operate, and to help to localize them and so on. And yet, officially I wasn't there.

"There was a great medical and military inspection. I called the boss and said, 'For heaven's sake, don't come today.' He didn't know the patients. It's so funny because of the anti-Semitism in the Prussian army and because they expected that a young medical officer would greet them and click his heels. And who greets them? Poor little me, still with my braids over the ears and my tortoise shell comb. And I said, 'The professor has asked me to apologize for him. He had to go to the front. He asked me, as his associate, to take you around.' Well, one of the hospital staff was a painter in his civilian life, and I had him do murals on my office walls, showing what happens in different lesions and what we do to get it in order. I showed them briefly what we were doing, and when I had talked long enough so that they were sure that they didn't know a thing about it, then I said, 'Well, if you wish, we can make rounds now.'

"Before rounds, I had said, 'Boys, we have inspection today. You know it's a little problematical that I as a woman am working here for the Prussian army. It's up to you whether you want me or not. If you want me, then this hospital has to look as though you had the greatest disciplinarian here. If you don't, well, you know what they'll say: 'See, a woman can't do it.'

"Now, you must know what discipline meant in the Prussian hospital. The beds had to be straight with a ruler. They wore hospital uniforms. The buttons had to be placed exactly, and they had to wear this and that kind of shoes, and their bedroom slippers had to be just there. And they had blackboards at the end of the bed. I don't think you have seen in the whole of Prussia a hospital which looked so reeking of good discipline as that one. It really was wonderful.

"As far as the clinic went, I said 'no' to office hours on Saturday. I was strictly orthodox then. So we had no office hours in a Prussian hospital. Everybody knew why. I ran the hospital for two years, but still it wasn't me. You can go over the excellent records of two years and you will not find my name anywhere.

"We were near the border. Once there was an order that all women had to leave since the Russians might besiege it and there wouldn't be enough food. My father said, 'Well, you girls, mother, you all leave.' And I got furious! I said, 'What?! To think I'm in charge of a brain-injured soldiers' hospital and suddenly I remember that I am a poor female. No, that can't be done.' Well, he could see that. He thought that was very horrible, but he could see that's how it was, and nobody went. They all stayed home.

"Then, a good friend of mine at the hospital got sick, and I did her service as well. She was a morphine addict and we tried at first to hide it. From seven o'clock to nine, I did her service and then I drank strong coffee and wrote papers. Sometimes I wrote through the night, then a shower and strong coffee and then to the hospital. And so it went. So, I think I did my wrinkles honorably.

"After two years I went to Frankfurt where Kurt Goldstein had gone and worked two more years with him there. Then, I decided to go into what I wanted to do, namely, psychiatry and psychotherapy. In my home town, the best Jewish psycho- therapist had died in the war. It was kind of a good idea to go and establish myself there. And I had to make money because at that time I had the child of this morphine-addicted friend with me, whom I brought up for three or four years, when she was a young teen-ager. Mother found me a nice home and office and a maid and a place where I could live with this girl in a nice part of the city where I liked to work. But I thought it was wiser first to get a little refreshed in psychotherapy.

"There was a man, maybe the only man at that time who really seriously did psychotherapy as such in Germany. That was J. H. Schultz. He was a professor in Jena, which is one of the small good universities in Germany, and I wanted to go there for two or three months and then go into practice. Schultz had just left Jena, and had taken over a sanatorium, 'Weisser Hirsch,' 'White Stag' near Dresden in the mountains. It was expensive. If there were 200 people, 150 came to reduce, thirty to get rid of diabetes, and the rest to have a good time.

"Schultz took over, and tried to make them aware of need- ing psychotherapy. The whole thing belonged to Lohmann of Lohmann underwear. He was a natural healer and believed in massage and baths and cutting wood and that kind of thing. So, that went on there, too. Also, it was a kind of place where the patients would invite you to come along to the opera, and there would be dances where the doctors would appear on the scene. It was a God-awful atmosphere, but here was Schultz, and he began to develop a psychotherapeutic department.

"After I had been there maybe three or four weeks, he asked wouldn't I want to stay. I said I couldn't because I had this little girl to take care of, and she couldn't very well stay there with me. Schultz said, 'Why not?' Then I couldn't stay because I ate kosher. And Schultz said, 'Why not? You tell them in the kitchen what you want.' I didn't want to go to their teas and to the opera with the patients, but I didn't want to shirk responsibilities. Every doctor had to take part in weekly speeches to the patients. So I did the speeches as long as I didn't have to do the other stuff. I stayed there for four years.

"I had gotten analyzed during the last two years I was in 'Weisser Hirsch.' I had discovered very early that there was something funny with a relationship between patient and doctor, that the patients got in such a funny way tied up with the doctor. There was something not right about that, but I didn't know what to do about it. And there, I read Freud about transference. And you must know at that time, nobody talked about it. And I find Freud—oh, what an experience this was—here was a psychiatrist who knew it and talked about it! It was really tremendous in that he said you can only fully understand it if you get analyzed, and so it was settled. I had to get analyzed to fully understand that, because it had bothered me as long as I had been a psychiatrist.

"My first analyst was Wittenberg, somebody in Munich whom nobody knows. A very decent fellow. Later, Erich went to him. We had decided when we both would be through, we wanted to take him out for champagne and he should teach us how to eat oysters. But, unfortunately, he died of cancer before that. An awfully nice fellow.

"I was a Zionist at that time, and other Zionists, usually in their early twenties and very poor, who needed therapy came to see me there. So, I worked eight hours at the sanatorium and eight hours with them. They couldn't pay then, but paid much later. I used the tips from the wealthy patients and from my relatives to make a sanatorium for them. They helped each other. For instance, one gave Hebrew lessons and the others would, let's say, mend his stockings for that. It was a perfect community and with very good therapeutic results.

"After a while, I found it was a little too much. And Erich Fromm was in the picture at that time, and he found it was a little too much. We decided to simply have our own sanatorium. We had maybe ten or fifteen patients in the house and lots of people who could live on the outside but would come for meals and for their therapy. We thought we would first analyze the people, and second, make them aware of their tradition and live in this tradition, not because the Lord has said so, but because that meant becoming aware of our past in big style.

Then we would do something not only for the individuals but also for the Jewish people.

"So, we had an old Russian-Jewish scholar who taught there, and Erich and I analyzed them, and we got more. Then I got one associate, Klages. The religious teacher was in love with me and talked with me about 'little Erich.' Erich was ten-and-a-half years younger than I am, and the religious teacher was maybe ten years my senior. Perhaps it would have been much better. You see, I began to analyze Erich. And then we fell in love and so we stopped. That much sense we had! Erich and I married when I was thirty-six, and we married in the middle of the sanatorium experience. Marriage in my mother's house, minion and mikvah. I went to the mikvah and I got tonsillitis—pretty near couldn't get married.

"We analyzed people for letting them work. I analyzed the housekeeper, and the cook, and you may imagine what happened if they were in a phase of resistance! It was a wild affair, and later we decided to cut it out. It was an interesting experiment, except that the people from Frankfurt came because we had kosher food and not because they wanted to be analyzed. The rabbis came because they could eat kosher food. They didn't want to be analyzed.

"We both went for training analyses. I went to Hanns Sachs, who was *the* training analyst of the German Psychoanalytic Institute. After four years, we decided we couldn't keep the sanatorium any longer because our conscience and hearts were no longer in it. So, Passover, Erich and I went into the park in Heidelberg and ate bread, not matzo. We couldn't do it at home because there were these people who, after all, relied on us, and the punishment for that is *korvat*! That means no children usually. If you can't have any, that is, if you both can't have any, then that family disappears from the universe. So that's the punishment you would get. But not that I believed that. Anyway, we did it and we were a little surprised that nothing happened actually, and then we began to eat food that was not kosher. The first thing I tried was ham and eggs. Now I especially like forbidden food—seafood, lobster, oysters. I like all the things I haven't eaten for thirty-six years of my life.

"My lord, what a day. We closed the hospital and then off

we went to get analyzed. And there I was with my husband. We sold the house in 1928. I stayed on one of the floors and opened a private practice, and in the meantime Erich was through with his training, but he had developed tuberculosis, so he went to Davos. In our hospital, he, an only son, helped with words; he helped marvelous with ideas. I learned lots from him along those lines, but not with action. But since I was a very active and very energetic female myself, that was all right. I got what I wanted: a very intelligent, very warm, very well-educated man who knew lots of things in another field from mine. Later on, he learned to do. When I visited with him in Davos, he had learned it already; there, he did the cooking.

"There was a German analytic journal for applied psycho-analysis called *Imago*. There was a special issue, maybe for Freud's birthday, and there I published a paper about the analysis of the Jewish food rituals, and Erich wrote a paper on analysis of the Sabbath or Yom Kippur, or both. And that's how we announced we were through. If you don't think that's in big style! And they were good papers at that."

Asked about her first impressions of America and its differences from Europe, Fromm-Reichmann said, "I feel so very strongly that the Americans are different from Europeans in that there is no tragedy and no fate. You *are* a success and you *are* a failure, and it's your fault if you are a failure, and if you try hard, you can be a success, including being the President of the United States. And there isn't such a thing as fate or energies outside yourself. Therefore, Americans say, 'I *am* a success' and 'I *am* a failure.' There are two British men whom I asked, and they said no, the British would also not say, 'I am a success.' They may say, 'I am successful,' but they wouldn't say, 'I am a success.' This, from the very beginning, when I came to this country, I experienced as the greatest difference."

She closed the interviews with a remark she made rather often, "So, if you want to know something for my epitaph, then I think we could say I wasn't lazy and I had lots of fun, but of another type as compared with many other people. It was a special type of fun."

Reference

Hoff, S. (1982), VI. Frieda Fromm-Reichmann: The early years. *Psychiatry*, 45:115–121.

23

THE EARLY FRIEDA, AND TRACES OF HER IN HER LATER WRITINGS

Jarl E. Dyrud

As Edith Weigert describes so beautifully in her introduction to Frieda's collected papers, there was an early Frieda, before psychoanalysis and before her becoming a physician, who had some fairly well-defined characteristics. She was much loved but not spoiled, a diminutive princess with a definite sense of responsibility for her younger siblings. How she came to be this way is a matter for conjecture, but that she was and remained so had been abundantly documented.

Eckhard Hess, whose work on pupillary reflexes is related to Frieda's very first paper, "Changes in Pupillary Reactions in Dementia Praecox" (1914), told me about their year together at the Stanford Center for Advanced Study in the Behavioral Sciences, where they were two of an interdisciplinary group studying nonverbal aspects of communication. "Frieda felt a very special responsibility for helping make anybody's party or project go well." This caretaking aspect of her personality may well have been a significant determinant in her choice of medicine as a career and of schizophrenia as a major interest.

I don't suppose anyone who has spent a significant part of his or her professional life at Chestnut Lodge would want to leave it all behind. We go on thinking about the intense experiences we had with our patients and colleagues—some gratifying, some devastating, few completely settled in our minds, but all shaping what we are today as therapists and teachers. For those of us who were there in the 1940s and 1950s, Frieda Fromm-Reichmann was the central figure around whom our training revolved.

I left in 1968 to teach at the University of Chicago. This may seem like a radical departure from the concentrated, inward-looking culture of the Lodge, but it was in the tradition. In my time there Alfred Stanton had left for Harvard, David Rioch for the Walter Reed Army Institute for Research, and Robert Cohen to the National Institute for Mental Health. Otto Will had spent a sabbatical year here at the University some years before I came and had created high expectations of what someone from the Lodge might bring to the teaching program.

Students wanted to know what influences had shaped the therapeutic orientation of the Lodge. On reflection, it seemed to me that although the Lodge had been a good psychoanalytic hospital before, Frieda had given it her own character. This led me to wonder what influences had shaped her.

In the winter of 1974 I set about reading in German some of Fromm-Reichmann's early and previously untranslated works. How those articles got into my hands was a matter of sheer good luck. The year before our biomedical librarian at the University of Chicago, Walter Necker, had asked me if there was anything I wanted him to find for me in the German medical libraries during his sabbatical year there. I asked him to bring me any of Fromm-Reichmann's papers which had not been previously translated into English. He delivered nineteen, far more than I had imagined existed. Her German bibliography actually lists thirty-five titles. She had been a prolific writer and researcher.

The neurological titles of the first dozen were not exactly inviting, but when I began reading them I realized that her early style of interacting with patients was clearly the beginning of the strong nonverbal strand of her therapeutic work which many of us saw as being most characteristic of her.

Fromm-Reichmann graduated from the Königsberg Medical School in 1914 at the beginning of World War I. Her doctoral thesis was on variations in pupillary reflexes in dementia praecox; so her interest in psychiatry was demonstrated early. This paper is of some current interest because she challenged much of the literature on neurological markers for dementia praecox, pointing out that variability was all that one actually found, except for a significant number of fixed pupils in catatonia. Work by Philip Holzman (1975) here at the University testifies to the importance of the problem she chose to address in her doctoral thesis. Parenthetically, I had always thought that Jews were totally assimilated in Germany in the early twentieth century. I was surprised to read in her introduction to her thesis the following: "I, Frieda Reichmann, a Jew, from Silesia." Could this have been her own asserton or was it a requirement?

After graduation she was assigned to work in a military rehabilitation hospital, very likely selected by Kurt Goldstein with whom she published a paper on bodily symptoms in dementia praecox, also in 1914. They worked together for six years, from 1914 to 1920. Her neurological training was intensively focused on her work with brain-injured soldiers. Here, as in schizophrenia, the etiology could be set aside as a treatment concern, but for a different reason: the etiology was no mystery—they had all been shot in the head.

Her papers in this period are filled with descriptions of techniques for retraining patients in behaviors disrupted by injury. The use of visual and tactile cuing to reestablish speech in aphasics, for instance, is a fascinating concept still being explored today. In their paper, "The Practical Application of Medical and Social Care to the Brain-Injured" (1917), she and Goldstein emphasize reeducation by means of "exercise treatment." I will paraphrase their findings:

> The treatment for local defects (aphasia, agnosia, apraxia) is set up in a way that the reestablishing of the lost elements of comprehension and speech is newly learned and memorized by exercise according to the same principles by which these elements are learned and taught in childhood. In addition to the exercise program, there are specialized workshops for the psychological and somatic rehabilitation of the brain-injured. Based on the exact medical examination, the basic principle is the close cooperation of the teachers in the special schools, the special instructors in the workshops, and the nurse on the ward, in order to diagnose and optimally influence the psychological defects of the patients.

While this series of papers on brain injury is neurologically precise, it is also pervaded by Fromm-Reichmann's concern with

the subjective sphere. She described her patients as each experienced the deficit in his own way. She saw the person not
as identical with his illness, but as someone who needs practical
help to overcome it.

The concept of the therapeutic team, the importance of its
close coordination over the patient's entire day, is explicitly
emphasized. The special teacher, the physical rehabilitation
worker, the nurse, are not described, as so often happens today,
as separately practicing their specialties in an eclectic bundle of
good intentions; they are seen instead to supply important and
specifiable segments of the treatment program. Her serious
commitment to this point of view is documented in her articles
that appeared in nursing journals, "The Nursing Staff and the
Care of the Brain-injured" (1919) and "The Nurse and the Care
of Mental Patients" (1922).

As I read the papers from this period of 1914–1920, what
stood out was Frieda's strong intention to have patients improve. There is an almost purely physical quality to her optimism in the face of catastrophic reactions in patients whose
ability to communicate or even empathize had almost vanished.
At times it seemed more like the loan of conviction to a person
who had lost it. This is very different from analytic neutrality.

Her will was certainly prominent, but it was, I believe, will
in Leslie Farber's (1976) first sense, "a will that is implicit, unself-
conscious, wedded to perception and integrated with motor
capability. Here action moves in a direction but not toward a
particular goal; it is open to possibility, freedom, and potentiality." Had it been will in Farber's second sense, i.e., the conscious selection of goals, I doubt if she would have endured this
period of her work. It seems paradoxical to speak of her work
as a trainer and reeducator with definite programs and sequences and at the same time to imply that her goals were
unspecified. I may relieve this tension to some extent by suggesting that she was content to provide the patient with an
opportunity to move in the desired direction with the end point
being determined in retrospect. In this way, movement and
direction became critical and can be reduced to smaller iden-
tifiable units, so that occasions for satisfaction can become al-

most a daily occurrence rather than tied to the distant ultimate goal of the treatment.

I speak of this early work which is not well known because it makes many points that we need to be reminded of today. Frieda did not confine herself even then to one treatment modality as some do, as if borrowing techniques from other sources would weaken one's theoretical position. She had a catholic taste for programs that worked, as her extensive list of sources indicates, and she judged them on the basis of how they contributed to her overall management of her patients.

When I knew her, her supervision never confined itself to the verbal, but emphasized expressive behavior in its broader ranges. She said that one had to be something of a lion-tamer to work with schizophrenics. You have to mean it. When I was baffled by a mute, immobile patient, she suggested trying to assume the same physical position the patient was in to glimpse how he felt. The subject matter of her early papers, that is, brain-injured soldiers and her neurological training, may have contributed to this sense of being a healer and educator more than a conceptualizer. Be that as it may, this physical dimension persisted in her attitudes and style of handling patients and is now very relevant to rehabilitative approaches to chronic schizophrenics which, as in behavioral training or in dance therapy, emphasize the role of reestablishing sequences of behavior.

It is no coincidence that Marian Chace's pioneering work in dance therapy started at Saint Elizabeths hospital, was developed further and for the rest of her life at Chestnut Lodge. She had come to the Lodge at the invitation of Fromm-Reichmann, the director of psychotherapy.

After the war, Frieda moved to J. H. Schultz's psychiatric clinic near Dresden. They wrote a paper together in 1921, "On the Rapid Cure of Peacetime Neuroses," a delightful transition piece. They reported three cases treated on the assumption that peactime neuroses might represent flight into illness from an unbearable conflict, just as wartime neuroses did.

The cases consisted of a hysterical woman with a richly neurotic history who had not spoken for a week after a quarrel with her husband, a woman who had a sudden and severe development of phobias, and a man who developed severe anxiety attacks following an appendectomy. All recovered within a few weeks of treatment which might best be described as psychoanalytically oriented hypnotherapy. They used a form of hypnagogic imagery and suggestion not too dissimilar from what Breuer and Freud reported using with Anna O. in 1895, but without Breuer's reluctance to focus on sexual symbolism when it appeared. This active use of psychoanalytic theory for rapid symptom removal has continued to have its adherents to this day. Hanscarl Leuner, for one, in his paper "Guided Affective Imagery" (1969), reports on following what appears to be a similar technique with equally dramatic results.

In their discussion, it is of course impossible to know what was Frieda and what was Schultz, but some of the lines sound so typically hers that I am inclined to assume that they were. For instance:

> The peacetime neuroses with their apparently different conflicts and symptoms react promptly to such a simple psychotherapeutic approach if we have the courage to act and are not restrained by pedantry.
>
> The rapid results of this form of psychotherapy lead us to a positive criticism of the principles and results of pure psychoanalytic work. We do not underestimate the extraordinary accomplishments of psychoanalytic investigations and practice for the knowledge and treatment of mental illness, we use it ourselves in many cases. On the basis of these investigations, however, we must consider the limits of its area of usefulness. Many psychotherapists under the influence of psychoanalytic thought, who often come to us for help, have this complicated approach and none other for the uncovering and treatment of psychopathological mechanisms. They therefore come to a correspondingly circumstantial and lengthy investigation of what lies behind each psychoneurosis. But the psychopathological structure of many neuroses, as shown in the foregoing observations, is so simple that in our opinion it is not scientifically valid to set the entire armamentarium of psychoanalytic method against them.

It has been said that if Freud had been a good hypnotist, psychoanalysis would never have been invented. Frieda apparently was a good hypnotist, but she moved rapidly and enthusiastically into psychoanalytic training. The next eight papers which follow in her bibliography reflect her enthusiasm for psychoanalysis. With two exceptions they may appear disappointing at first glance in that the focus is didactic rather than clinical, and the empathic quality, which was most evident in her earlier work with Goldstein and remained clearly in evidence in her papers with Schultz, lies submerged in these first psychoanalytic papers. For good reason, four of them were pedagogical in style and substance. She was writing for teachers in the *Journal of Psychoanalytic Pedagogy,* reaching out to teachers as she had to nurses earlier. She wrote on the pedagogical implications of psychoanalytic instinct theory, the history and development of social inferiority feelings, and intestinal disturbances caused by improper training.

The most engaging pedagogical paper is, "On the History of the Development of Social Inferiority Feelings" (1931). The crux of the analysis was her oedipal attachment concealed behind her apparent embarrassment over her father's profession. The animal doctor was unconsciously related to the unacceptable animal side of the patient's nature.

On the surface we find very little evidence in these papers of Frieda's involvement in the revolutionary *Zeitgeist,* but in Germany at that time, the most elementary exposition of psychoanalysis was revolutionary. Erich Fromm, her student and later her husband, was a Marxist, not a bloody revolutionary but an intellectual Marxist. The moral laxity of the Weimar Republic is indirectly addressed in a paper published in 1924, "The Sociology of the Neuroses." Here she pointed out how, in a social environment that condoned every excess, the neurotic and the potential pervert were poorly supported in strengthening their weak reality principle against strong inner urges. The contemporary emphasis on exclusively male social groups and the glorification of male activities were powerful negative influences on callow youths, serving as an affirmation of homosexuality.

Her 1927 *Imago* paper on the Jewish food ritual also was quietly revolutionary in its direct tackling of Jewish orthodoxy. She used two case vignettes to support her argument that the ritual was valuable in binding incestuous drives and very likely was developed for that purpose.

Another evidence of her courage was that rather than becoming an outpatient practitioner of psychoanalysis, she established her own sanatorium, more in the independent spirit of Georg Groddeck. We can only speculate on the social interactions that shaped her career choices, but we can understand how the product of these influences led Dexter Bullard to recruit her to Chestnut Lodge.

It was clearly a happy decision for both. As one reads her *Principles of Intensive Psychotherapy*, written at Chestnut Lodge, her early style is merged with psychoanalytic theory even as her debt to Sullivan is also evident in the interpersonal view she takes.

Her work has struck many people as being unique within the psychoanalytic framework. In contrast to the analysts she criticized in 1921, her art was not subjugated to method; her experience was not entirely accounted for by theory. She was far from the role of the analyst apart. She was interested in the patient's total care. Members of the treatment team, administrators, nurses, and anyone else involved in patient care found that she tried very hard to share her understanding. Her enthusiasm, persuasiveness, and practicality certainly stayed with her from their early beginnings. I remember her often saying to us, "I am telling you this so that we will not be working at cross-purposes." I suspect that she may have said the same thing to her treatment team in World War I.

Publications of Frieda Fromm-Reichmann
1914

Über Pupillenstörungen bei Dementia Praecox [Changes in Pupillary Reactions in Dementia Praecox]. *Arch. Psychiat. Nervenkrankh.*, 53:302–321.
Über die körperlichen Störungen bei der Dementia Praecox [Bodily Symptoms in Dementia Praecox] (with Kurt Goldstein). *Neurol. Centralbl.*, 33:343–350.

1915

Klinische Beobachtungen an Schussverletzungen peripherischer Nerven [Clinical Observations on Gunshot Peripheral Nerves]. *Arch. Psychiat. Nervenkrankh.*, 56:290–327.

Über Schussverletzungen peripherischer Nerven [Observations on Gunshot Peripheral Nerves]. *Deutsche Med. Wochenschr.*, 41:668–671.

Über nervöse Folgezustände nach Granat-Explosionen [On Nervous Sequelae of Shell Shock] (with Ernst Meyer). *Arch. Psychiat. Nervenkrankh.*, 56:914–952.

1916

Beiträge zur Kasuistik und Symptomatologie der Kleinhirnerkrankungen [Cases and Symptomatology of Cerebellar Injuries] (with Kurt Goldstein). *Arch. Psychiat. Nervenkrankh.*, 56:466–521.

Über nervöse Störungen nach Hirnverletzungen [On nervous disturbances after brain injuries]. *Arch. Psychiat. Nervenkrankh.*, 57:914–952.

1917

Zur neurologischen Kasuistik der Kleinhirnverletzungen [Neurological symptoms from injuries to the cerebellum]. *Arch. Psychiat. Nervenkrankh.*, 57:61–72.

Zur Berufsberatung hirnverletzer Kriegsbeschädigter [Vocational counseling with brain-injured soldiers]. *Seitschr. Kriegsbeschädigtenfürsorge in Ostpreussen*, 2:362–363.

Zur praktischen Durchführung der ärztlichen und sozialen Fürsorgemassnahmen bei Hirnschussverletzten [Medical and social care of gunshot brain injuries]. *Arch. Psychiat. Nervenkrankh.*, 58:114–140.

Knochendefektdeckungen bei Hirnverletzen [Bone transplantations on skull defects after brain injuries]. *Med. Klin.*, 13:226 & 820.

Fürsorge für Kopfschussverletzte [Social care of the brain injured]. *Med. Klin.*, 13:591.

Über die diagnostische Bedeutung der Tuberkulinreaktion unter besonderer Berücksichtigung des cytologischen Befundes [The diagnostic meaning of the tuberculin reaction under special consideration of the cytological findings]. *Med. Klin.*, 13:591.

Diskussion zu: Nervöse Folgeerscheinungen nach Hirnverletzungen [Discussion of nervous symptoms from brain injuries, at the Meeting on Brain Injuries, Würzburg, 1917]. *Zeitschr. ges. Neurol. Psychiat.*, 51:10.

Beitrag zur differentialdiagnostischen Bedeutung der Baranyschen Zeigerversuche [Barany's fingerpointing test] (with Arthur Blohmke). *Arch. Ohren-Nasen- u. Kehlkopfheilk.*, 101:80–107.

1918

Kasuistischer Beitrag zur Frage des Vorbeizeigens bei Stirnhirntlesionen [The fingerpointing test in injuries of the frontal lobe] (with Arthur Blohmke). *Int. Zentralbl. Ohrenheilk. u. Rhino-Laryngol.*, 16:42–50.

Zur Übungsbehandlung der Aphasien [On reeducation after aphasia] (with Eduard Reichau). *Arch. Psychiat. Nervenkrankh.*, 60:8–42.

1919

Die Aufgaben des Pflegspersonals bei der Versorgung Hirnverletzter [The task of the nursing staff in the care of the brain injured.] *Die Irrenpflege,* 23:21–29.

Über corticale Sensibilitätsstörungen, besonders am Kopf [On cortical disturbances of sensation, especially of the head] (with Kurt Goldstein). *Ergebn. ges. Neurol. Psychiat.,* 53:49–79.

1920

Über praktische und theoretische Ergebnisse aus den Erfahrungen an Hirnschussverletzten [Practical and theoretical results of experiences with brain-injured soldiers] (with Kurt Goldstein). *Zeitschr. innere Med. u. Kinderkrankh.,* 18:405–530.

1921

Über Schnellheilung von Friedensneurosen [On rapid cure of peacetime neuroses]. *Med. Klin.,* 17:380–384.

Über Trivalinismus [On Trivalin addiction]. *Deutsche Med. Wochenschr.,* 47:858–859.

1922

Zur Einteilung der Psychopathien [A classification of the psychopathies]. *Arch. Psychiat. Nervenkrankh.,* 63.

Aufgaben der Schwester bei der Pflege Nervenkranker [Tasks of the nurse and the care of mental patients]. *Die Schwester,* 5:162–166.

Zur Psychopathologie des Asthma bronchiales [The psychopathology of bronchial asthma]. *Med. Klin.,* 18:1090–1092.

1923

Zur Psychologie entopischer Phänomene [The psychology of entopic phenomena]. *Zeitschr. ges Neurol. Psychiat.*

Zur Schilddrüsenbehandlung der Dercumschen Krankheit [The treatment of the thyroid in Dercum's disease]. *Deutsche. Med. Wochenschr.,* 49:1018–1019.

1924

Über Psychoanalyse [On psychoanalysis]. *Deutsche. Med. Wochenschr.,* 50:758–761.

Zur Sociologie der Neurosen [Social factors in neuroses]. *Zeitschr. ges. Neurol. Psychiat.,* 89:60–67.

1927

Das jüdische Speiseritual [The Jewish food ritual]. *Imago*, 13:235–246.

1929

Zur psychoanalytischen Trieblehre [The psychoanalytic instinct theory]. *Zeitschr. Psychoanal. Pädagogik*, 3:266–268.

1930

Pädagogische Diskussionsbemerkungen zur psychoanalytischen Trieblehre [Pedagogical Implications of Psychoanalytic Drive Theory]. *Zeitschr. Psychoanal. Pädagogik*, 4:38–44.
Zur Entstehungs-Geschichte sozialer Minder Wyertigkeitsgefühle [On the History and Development of Social Inferiority Feelings]. *Zeitschr. Psychoanal. Pädagogik*, 5:19–29.

1931

Zur Bedeutung der Angehörigen Aussagen in der Psychotherapie [Evaluation of the Statements of Relatives in Psychotherapy]. *Der Nervenartz*, 4:257–268.
Darmstörungen als Folge von Fehlerziehung [Intestinal Disturbances Caused by Improper Training]. *Zeitschr. Psychoanal. Pädagogik*, 5:460–465.

References

Farber, (1976), *Lying, Despair, Jealousy, Envy, Sex, Suicide, Drugs, and the Good Life*. New York: Raven Press, pp. 217–228.
Holzman, P. S. (1975), Smooth-pursuit eye movements in schizophrenia: Recent findings. In: *The Biology of the Major Psychoses: A Comparative Analysis*. ed. D. X. Freedman. New York: Raven Press, pp. 217–228.
Leuner, H. (1969), Guided affective imagery: A method of intensive psychotherapy. *Amer. J. Psychother.*, 23:4–21.

24

CHESTNUT LODGE—THE EARLY YEARS: KRISHNAMURTI AND BUBER

Benjamin I. Weininger, M.D.

When I became a resident at Chestnut Lodge, there were four other psychoanalytically trained psychiatrists, Dexter Bullard, Sr., Marjorie Jarvis, Edna Dyar, and Frieda Fromm-Reichmann. It was a small staff, including psychiatric nurses and nurses' aides. The clinical conferences were informal, and there was a sense of a community, a sense of family.

In the early days we were not as conscious of the fact that the hospital environment itself can be a factor in keeping the psychotic person chronically ill. In our work, the main emphasis was on the relationship between therapist and patient. We discussed our concerns about the patients with the nurses and aides, but it was not given enough of a central importance, as it is now. The physical surroundings and the psychological environment are now enhanced by more extensive discussions with nurses, aides, and with administrators. Dexter and Frieda were the main supervisors. In addition, each of us had other supervisors as well. I commuted to New York City every other week to work with Harry Stack Sullivan and later with Karen Horney.

During the clinical conferences and shared supervision, the main emphasis was placed on countertransference reactions that were interfering with the patients' improvement. We lived with an assumption that every person in the hospital, no matter how many years he had been ill, had a chance to improve. Adequate medication was not available in the early years.

Sullivan taught that if it were not for a drive toward mental health, we psychiatrists would be out of business. This natural drive in most of us is blocked in varying degrees by a combination of different cultural influences in the childhood years, transmitted through members of the family and later by social and political factors in the society. In his relationships with others, a psychotic person has been hurt many times, and more intensely hurt than most of us. He or she feels rejected not only by a person but also by the social community. He feels exiled. The sense of being exiled is a catastrophic happening to any person. Socrates chose death rather than exile.

In another context Sullivan said, "We are more simply human than otherwise." Loneliness is at the core of all of us, and we escape from this daily by the many distractions available to us—telephone, the mail, the newspaper, compulsive eating, drinking alcohol, and many, many others. In a person who experiences psychosis, the loneliness and feeling of isolation reach a point of being endurable, but at such a deep level that it is not conveyable to any other person. Harry Stack Sullivan, who was my teacher and friend for eighteen years, once told me that, although his theory of personality revolved around anxiety and the avoidance of anxiety at its center, one could as well place loneliness at the center of the theory of interpersonal psychiatry.

When I finished my residency at Sheppard Pratt and went to Chestnut Lodge as a member of the staff, I was the first staff member who came to Chestnut Lodge since Frieda Fromm-Reichmann arrived. The first patient given to me was a young woman with wild-looking, disheveled hair. She was on the disturbed ward, walking here and there, occasionally shouting or talking incoherently. She had lived in this condition on the disturbed ward for the last two years.

I had planned to see her one hour every day. She was constantly moving about. I had myself locked up in the room with her alone, where neither of us could escape until the hour was over. I did not use a watch since this kept me from being fully present. At the end of each hour the nurses aide opened the door. I stood at one end of the wall. She stood at the opposite end near the window, shouting and talking as if she were addressing someone outside of the window. We were on the fourth floor of the building. Occasionally she turned and waved her hand, indicating that I should leave. Sometimes she spat in my direction.

I was sensitive and open to the slightest indication of contact with me. At first these contacts were momentary, followed by a withdrawal. She needed the contact, but she could not cope with the devastating effects of a possible rejection. I emphasize the importance of paying attention to the slightest evidence of contact because any move toward contact *is the drive toward mental health* and, in my experience, this is more important than being overly concerned with the patient's pathology.

I was prepared to see her almost daily for years if necessary. After intermittently trying to drive me away for six months, she turned around and looked at me, eye to eye, as if seeing me for the first time. She moved toward me and, halfway, I moved toward her and asked her to talk to me. We stood near each other, and she talked slowly for two hours. This continued for several days. Then I asked her to come meet me in my office on the first floor. She reviewed her history and, several months later, she left the hospital. I continued to see her. Within a couple of years she married a divorced man who had three children. I kept in touch with her from time to time for the next ten years, and she did not have a recurrence during that time. This was fifty years ago.

It is important to say here that I was a catalyst. Often a person sick for many years has a spontaneous remission. It has been my experience that, if a therapist does not reach a psychotic person in some meaningful contact while the person is still sick, and there is a spontaneous clinical recovery without contact, such recoveries tend to relapse into psychotic states more frequently. They seal themselves off and do not reveal themselves again, unless, of course, they break down again, and at that time a contact is again a possibility.

Another patient, a man of about thirty-five, came to the hospital because in his last suicide attempt he cut his throat and almost bled to death. He was hospitalized before, but when he left the hospital he made another suicide attempt. This last one was almost fatal. He talked repetitiously of his discouragement with life, of not being a worthwhile person. He felt that people thought of him as a homosexual and that no one would want to be associated with him. He did not see any point to living. The trouble for him began when he left college. He never got past the rah-rah days of fraternity life and he was preoccupied with people thinking of him as a homosexual. I supervised this person with Sullivan and at the end of one year he seemed to be getting more depressed. His minister came to see him and we both were very concerned. He could not see any point in living and reemphasized his unworthiness as a person, hardly fit for human companionship.

While I was at Sheppard Pratt Hospital my clinical director said to me, "Bennie, you would do anything to cure a patient." This trait in me often helped in a critical situation but caused me recurrent problems. In recent years I arrived at a balance and am selective regarding which patients I accept or what I am willing to do. With this person, I knew that I had to try something different. I asked the nurse to pack his things; I was going to take him on a vacation with me for the weekend. No questions were asked and we left on Saturday morning and returned Sunday evening. It was an uncomplicated overnight stay; we took walks, went sightseeing, and talked. There was no sexual involvement. When I met him Monday morning, he was cheerful and had no complaints. He was clinically well. I saw him daily for the next several months, and he continued feeling well after he left the hospital. He came to see me from time to time to tell me how well things were going for him. He did not make another suicide attempt. Sullivan thought that he recovered because there was no sexual involvement. I also thought that his self-esteem was boosted by a doctor taking the time off to spend the weekend with this person who felt so unworthy of human association.

After I completed my formal psychiatric training, I was inclined to be experimental in approach with both my patients and my life. There was a difference in my relationship with my patients and friends, in actual fact. Subjectively, I did not feel any difference.

It is also important to note that sometimes psychoanalytic therapy over a period of many years by itself does not help the patient recover. I will give one such example. A young man, age eighteen, had been showing evidence of slowly withdrawing into himself. He was a painter of pictures, huge landscapes. I saw him five times a week sometimes for two hours each time. I was supervising him with Sullivan. His usual gestures with his hands were to wave me away. He was not communicative, except on one occasion where he talked to me for two hours. We were standing in the ward. He had one hand over his head in readiness to hit me. His hand over my head indicated that he experienced my being that close to him as a threat. I asked him to put it into words. He continued to talk slowly and hesitatingly, and I was surprised to find that as we spoke, he held his hand up the entire two hours.

Sullivan told me I had a cured schizophrenic. The man never talked to me again and Sullivan's curiosity was aroused. He came to see this patient in the ward when I was there. Sullivan entered and raised his hand high in a gesture of acknowledgment and said something like, "Hi." The patient's interest was heightened and he could not take his eyes away from Sullivan, although he did not talk. I was impressed how easily Sullivan was able to establish contact instantly on a nonverbal level with a schizophrenic male patient. After seeing him for two years with no significant further contact being established, Frieda Fromm-Reichmann began to see him as her patient. She saw him almost daily in one- or two-hour sessions for the next two years, but she also seemingly did not succeed. Next, Dexter Bullard, Sr., tried for another two years with a similar outcome.

The patient's brother was a Menninger-trained analyst and after six years decided to transfer him to a state hospital near New York City, where the brother lived. After he had been there for a year or so, they decided to give him electroconvulsive therapy. He apparently improved greatly and his brother asked me to visit him in the state hospital to see if I thought he was well enough to leave the hospital and live with an attendant. When I visited him, I was in for a real surprise. He was clinically well. He spoke easily with me, although slowly, and he was clear about everything. He remembered his experiences at Chestnut Lodge, and he remembered me very well.

I recommended that he leave the hospital with an attendant. He continued to be well. Here it is worth mentioning that a slow onset schizophrenic episode usually has a poor prognosis. It is my opinion that if he had not had all that previous therapy for six years, the shock treatment by itself would not have induced such a radical change. He was not blocked off from communicating at a feeling level.

I have also learned from treating patients with a sudden acute psychotic episode that sometimes a few contacts, whether in a hospital or not, can effect not only a clinical recovery but a recovery with subsequent insight, when and if the psychiatrist is able to establish an instantaneous nonverbal contact with the person.

In my early years in private practice I seldom hospitalized a psychotic patient. With all the experience and supervision at Sheppard Pratt Hospital and at Chestnut Lodge, I felt comfortable with psychotic patients who were outside of a mental hospital. I could not do that now. It requires being available at all times, and I now leave that to my younger colleagues, most of whom are not willing to do this because of the complexities in modern medical practice. Most such patients are hospitalized.

However, I would feel remiss if I said nothing more about the fact that, in an acute psychotic episode, even one contact can start the process of recovery. Here are two examples: one in a hospital setting and another outside of a hospital setting.

While at Sheppard Pratt, Lewis B. Hill, my third analyst, referred Anton Boison to me. He was the founder of pastoral counseling. His psychotic episodes were public information, since he wrote about his experiences. He had two previous hospitalizations before seeing me. During his first stay he was hospitalized for about one year, and the second time one-and-a-half years. The length of stay in a hospital, short or long, does not determine the kind of recovery. When I saw him for the first time, he was lying in bed. After introducing myself, I asked him why he was here. He told me that he felt a messianic mission to help the world. He also acknowledged that he was confused. From my own background and experience I was familiar with the sense of mission, and I acknowledged his sense of mission. I believe he felt that I understood something of what he had said. The next day he was out of bed, and out of his state of confusion. I subsequently saw him every day; he was back at work in three weeks at Elgin, Illinois State Hospital, where he was the chief of hospital chaplains. He told others that his quick recovery was due to the fact that I did not do a conventional psychiatric examination.

I visited him six months later at the Elgin State Hospital. Although he was very pleased to see me, I recognized a certain detachment in his personality—a clinical recovery without the basic change in openness, which I had previously observed in the young artist who had six years of therapy plus shock treatments. From Boisen's writings I first learned that psychotic patients with a religious content had a better prognosis than persons with a paranoid content. I later made this observation myself.

The last example is of a seventeen-year-old French girl whom I saw two years ago. At the time she was living in San Francisco and going to a special school to improve her English. The school had two-and-a-half more weeks to go before she would finish. That was when I first met her. In San Francisco she was a boarder at a private home. She became confused and belligerent. She sometimes hit people and stayed out until two A.M., sorting through garbage pails. The family could no longer take it. The father returned from Paris, and she lived for a few days with a relative. Here too, she was belligerent and hostile.

I was asked to see her for the purpose of recommending a hospital; I agreed to see her one time. The father came into my office as scheduled. She remained in the car, spending fifteen minutes pinning a rose in her hair. We could see through the window a girl walking backward toward the door. I said, "Is that your daughter?" and he said, "Yes." Father and daughter sat on the same couch, each at one end. My attention was on the daughter, as if the father was not in the room. I did not even see him with my peripheral vision.

She said that she was very angry, that people were trying to control her life. She described some of the events, and she was quite confused. After the hour I suggested that I would need to see her one more time, the next morning, before making a recommendation.

The next morning the father appeared first and said a miracle had happened. "My daughter is well." I talked with the daughter alone this time. She said that she was confused, that since the age of twelve she had many crises in her life. We reviewed each crisis and the sequence of events that led up to it. The last crisis was that her mother committed suicide.

We had one more visit and she seemed clear and had some new awareness. I recommended she complete her two weeks of school in San Francisco, which is about 300 miles from Santa Barbara, where I live. She went back to Paris to finish her last year of high school and wrote me, thanking me for the "comprehensive help" I had given her. I answered her letter. I received another letter six months later. Her father's woman friend committed suicide, another devastating shock, and she had difficulty in studying and developed some conflict with one of the students. One year later I heard that she was in a hospital in Paris with another breakdown. Her father thought of bringing her back to me, but it did not happen. Her family problems and her personal life experiences were too much for a young troubled person.

The editor, Ann-Louise Silver, asked me to write something about Buddhism and Krishnamurti. I will include Martin Buber since these two had a series of conferences on different occasions with leading analysts in the Washington area and both had a significant influence on my life and my work.

My interest in the mystical and in the religious mind is understandable in terms of my background. We lived on the west side of old Chicago in an orthodox Jewish neighborhood. Some of the Hasidic rebbes who came from Eastern Europe stayed in our home until they found an appropriate synagogue. Although it was more than sixty years ago, I still vividly remember a young Hasid who had sideburns, a small beard, and was an ascetic-looking saintly man. The fringes of a white prayer shawl could always be seen hanging from under his shirt. His daily life was centered around prayer, and one could hear him praying frequently throughout the day. There was a prayer and blessing for every occasion, upon rising, before meals, washing before eating, at sunset, and bedtime. The Sabbath eve was a special day of celebrating with joy and dance. There were usually visitors and guests at the Friday evening meal.

The Hasidic movement arose following the intense persecution of the Jews during the eighteenth century. It followed upon a period of decadence in the Jewish religion, when the scholars had separated themselves from the people. The rabbis were caught up in pride about their learning. The renaissance among the new rabbis was a flowering of a sense of community. These new rabbis were humble, sharing a sense of equality and social solidarity. They had very little, but they celebrated with song and dance together every Sabbath. In a society where individuality is of central concern, humility is hard to come by. The leaders of the Hasidic community were Zaddiks, saintly mystics.

My interest in psychoanalysis began with reading Alfred Adler. Adler stressed that mental health depends on having a social sense, a sense of community, *Gemeinschaftsgefühl*. This strong social feeling was present in the Hasidic community.

Between my first and second year of medical school I suffered from duodenal ulcer pains and went with my mother to live in the country for the summer. My father worked during the week and came to visit during the weekends. I slept on the porch and stayed in bed all day drinking milk, cream, and powders. A young farmer, Harry Kinchen, who was our neighbor, came to visit me every day. Harry, too, was an orthodox Jew. He talked of me about Leo Tolstoy's philosophy, about Jesus, about the Sermon on the Mount, and about Krishnamurti. He talked much about love. His strong presence and new ideas reached me at a deep level. My anxieties suddenly subsided. I felt well and happy. I became a vegetarian—stopped the milk, cream, powders. I had what William James called a "religious experience." It has been described as "seeing the light," like walking out of a dark movie into the light.

Only about ten years later did I realize that what happened nonverbally between Harry and myself was the trigger that allowed the anxiety to subside. After being in this new state of consciousness for about three months, I returned to medical school in the second year. The conflicts that were with me before the summer returned—the sense of inadequacy with women, conflict about sex, some rebelliousness with my mother. My ulcer also returned, along with the milk, cream, and pow-

ders. However, I never completely lost the message that "Men
Live by Love." Although I lost my way many times and lived
and acted negatively toward others and myself, when the storms
passed, the "Men Live by Love" message returned, like a com-
pass to the North Pole. I never had to look for a basic direction
in life.

I now have some understanding of the function of a religious experience of this kind. Williams James called it the religion of the troubled soul. This happening helped me to
become aware of what my potential as a human being might
be. The event was also an unconscious attempt to help me catch
up in areas of my life where there was arrested development.
In my situation I was an indulged only child, and I needed to
catch up with "all men and brothers."

The drawback of a mystical experience is that one is easily
led astray by a belief that one has already arrived someplace.
However, it required the next sixty years to work through the
many self-centered conditional reactions that I learned in the
first twenty-one years. If a person with a very low self-esteem
whose earlier years were more traumatic than mine is confronted with rejection, a mystical experience can be part of a
psychotic break with confusion. A sense of divine mission may
follow, rapidly alternating with a sense of being among the
damned and self-blame and rage for causing all the misery.

My interest in Buddhism was aroused first through the
teaching of the self-taught philosopher Krishnamurti. Later,
Martin Buber reawakened my early contact with Hasidism; co-
incidentally his philosophy in some respects was similar to Zen
Buddhism. These two mystic philosophers, Krishnamurti and
Buber, both had discussion groups and seminars with the leading psychoanalysts in the Washington area mostly associated
with Chestnut Lodge and the Washington School of Psychiatry.

I was living in Santa Barbara, California, at the time Buber
was here and I was invited to come to Washington by my lifelong
friend, Margaret Rioch, during the last week of the Buber seminars. I had the privilege of being seated next to Buber at
dinner. I had not yet read anything of Buber, and awkwardly
asked him, "What is the significance of a teacher or therapist
touching his pupil?" I do not clearly remember his response,

although I know now he would have said that touching a pupil can be of help in learning for teacher and pupil alike. The problem arises when the touching has a sexual intent.

About five years later I became close friends with two rabbis, Herschel Lyman and Henry Rabin. My interest in Hasidism was reawakened and I spent the next two years studying Buber's Hasidism. Suddenly one morning the vivid memory of the dinner meeting with Buber, seven years ago, came to me; I also remembered that the following morning when the seminar opened, the first thing he brought up was: "What is the significance of a teacher or therapist touching his pupil?" I realize now that he demonstrated to me one of the essences of his teaching at that time. He acknowledged me by taking the question seriously, thought about it, and brought it up for discussion the next morning. Affirmation of the other person is one of the key elements in his teaching.

Martin Buber was a universal genius who was very learned. He questioned everything about being human, everything about society, politics, religion, and anthropology. He was engaged in writing books and having conferences for over sixty years. His translater and biographer, Maurice Friedman, with whom I have become close friends, completed a three-volume biography of Buber that covered both his life and teachings. I read the biography with great delight.

At one point in his life, Buber was a mystic absorbed with God. Because of the unforeseen consequences of this perspective he realized that it was of greater significance to pay full attention to whatever concrete reality one is confronted with in daily life. Although Buber devalued the mystical, when I read Buber, on almost every page, I experienced an ecstasy similar to the kind I had during the religious experience at twenty-one. I therefore am inclined to believe his mystical sense never left him but was incorporated into a larger view of the human and of the world.

In Hasidism and in Zen Buddhism, telling stories to point the way is very important. In more recent years the pioneer humanistic psychologist, Abraham Maslow, predicted that psychotherapists will increasingly tell these kinds of stories to their patients. I cannot in this chapter indulge myself as I would like by telling many stories. I will be brief with a few:

A Hasid asked the rebbe, "What is the most important thing we need to be doing?" The rebbe answered, "Whatever you are doing at the moment." Buber's God was known as a "Moment God."

A student came to the rebbe and said, "I did not come to hear your teaching, I came to see how you tie your shoelaces."

There are also many Zen stories:

A man saw a tiger and to escape the tiger he clung to a branch below the surface of a cliff. As he was clinging to it, a black and white mouse was nibbling at the branch, and as he looked below there was another tiger waiting there. He glanced to one side and saw a ripe strawberry, and with one hand he took the strawberry and tasted it and said, "How sweet."

One final story common to Sufism, Hasidism, and Zen Buddhism. A man came to visit his friend Aaron and knocked on the door. Aaron said, "Who is it?" and the man said, "It is I." The door did not open. He came back several days later and knocked again and the same thing happened and the door did not open. On the third visit when Aaron asked, "Who is it?" the man answered, "It is Thou" and the door opened.

Buber attributed much of human problems to a lack of a basic existential trust. For those who are not familiar with Buber's unique contribution to psychology and sociology, there is the Fourth William Alanson White Memorial Lectures series (1957), in which he discussed "Distance and Relation," "Element of the Interhuman," and "Guilt and Guilt Feelings." While in Washington he also discussed "The Unconscious" with the analysts in the area. There is a chapter on this in Buber's book, *A Believing Humanism* (1967).

In 1950, Sullivan wrote "The Illusion of Personal Individuality." In this article one sees the similarity between Krishnamurti's teaching and the interpersonal theory of psychiatry. Frieda Fromm-Reichmann was very much "taken" by Krishnamurti. She asked me how I knew that the analysts would be receptive to Krishnamurti. He also on several occasions mentioned to me how much he liked Frieda. They had several private sessions. Krishnamurti had a very charismatic personality.

I must confess that when a number of analysts showed interest in Krishnamurti's teaching, I felt affirmed and my compulsive interest in Krishnamurti began to fade.

In a period of over sixty years, about forty of Krishnamurti's books were publilshed, many of them by Harper and Row. I can only sketch most inadequately a few of his teachings as I understand them. He traveled around the world every year teaching in different cultures for almost sixty years. He questioned everything in our culture and in every culture; every expert, whether political, socioeconomic, religious, or psychological. Reliance on the authority of another perpetuates our conflicts and suffering in our relationships and in the world. "Be a light unto yourself."

The crisis in the world is a crisis in consciousness. What goes on in consciousness in the content of our thoughts goes on in the world. Political and social systems may change, but no radical change toward a humane, compassionate world would be possible unless there is a transformation of consciousness. In one of my discussions with Krishnamurti in 1945, he told me that he did not realize how much Buddhism he had absorbed from his culture, until he read Rhys Davies's book (1932) on Buddhism.

Recently, the late David Rioch, one of my very dear friends, brought the living Harry Stack Sullivan back to us in the May 1985 issue of *Psychiatry*. One of the things that David discussed was Sullivan's "Spider Dream," something he often referred to in his teachings:

> Sullivan was an industrial surgeon in Chicago and he wanted to be a psychiatrist but wasn't sure he could be one. He applied to the St. Elizabeths Hospital in Washington, D.C. Dr. William Alanson White was the director. On the evening before he was to meet Dr. White, being anxious about the forthcoming meeting, he dreamt that he was a boy running in a grassy field and then stopped to look at the funnel-shaped, sheer white web of a field spider. He saw the little black spider come up the funnel but then it got bigger as it came out and rapidly grew in size virtually filling the field.

He was terrified but he thought quickly—"If I look carefully and see exactly what this thing is it will go away." He acted accordingly examining various parts precisely. At once the apparition shrunk in size and backed down into the funnel, an ordinary field spider. "Then I knew I could be a psychiatrist" [p. 142].

Sullivan's genius was his capacity to pay attention. When he was with me, most of the time he was fully present, more so than most persons I know. When we feel that we need to maintain a certain image of ourselves, then our attention is not free, but becomes selective. The attention is restricted by overconcern with maintaining one's illusory psychological security of the self. Attention was the healing factor of the spider dream, as it is the healing factor in psychotherapy. If the therapist or teacher does not feel threatened by the need to maintain an image, then he is fully present with the other person, and that free attention reduces anxiety and allows "healing through meeting."

Along similiar lines Krishnamurti describes this process in more detail in *The Flame of Attention* (1984). Attention acts like a flame that burns through past conditioning. Krishnamurti had a very charismatic personality that aroused one's attention. His emphasis was on self-knowledge in the mirror of relationships. He taught the importance of paying attention not only to the content of thought, but also to the structure of thought. His views in thought at first glance seem paradoxical. The content of our thoughts is based on memory, and this includes accumulated knowledge from the past. We need this for survival. Also, thoughts are the cause of our personal conflicts and conflicts in the world. These thoughts refer to conditioned memories, conscious and unconscious, in our relationships with others. The content of our thoughts contains our beliefs, images of self and others, and prejudices. Separate nationalism, separate religious beliefs create the conflicts and violence in the world. The structures of thought differ further in that, no matter what the contents are, the thoughts are themselves involved in clock time—in a movement from the past projected into the future, and from the painful present to the past or to the future. For example, I feel violent and greedy now and am uncomfortable with this. I wish to improve and become less so, but this takes time. I will be less violent later, tomorrow. Krishnamurti says, "There is no psychological tomorrow."

Acknowledgment, awareness, attention, full attention to the violent feelings are now required, but the movement of thought enters and takes us away from the violence now, toward nonviolence later. This takes time and creates the inner conflict between the way we are and the way we would like to be. The problem is caused by the content and process of conditioned thought which is based on memory. Conditioned thought is always involved in clock time away from the experiential immediacy of the now, as is also Buber's "Moment God." "In the absence of thought," Krishnamurti (1985) says, "there is silence and infinite space in the mind, and in this silent space there is intelligence and compassion."

In my own experience there are moments when my mind falls silent, and in this silent space I feel no separation between myself and a tree, a stone, a bird, or another person.

Finally, in conclusion the teaching of Gautama Buddha. I am an interested student and not a scholar of Buddhism. I have attended many Buddhist retreats, Burmese and Tibetan, and have had a special interest in Zen Buddhism. I attended a ten-day workshop at Erich Fromm's in Mexico with D. T. Suzuki, who first introduced Zen Buddhism in this country, and later I became friends with Alan Watts, who made Zen Buddhism popular in this country. At my home in Santa Barbara there is a Tibetan Buddhist center maintained by my wife, Janice Chase, for meetings held by Tibetan Buddhists who now live in Nepal, India, and some parts of the United States.

I will give a brief sketch of Buddhist teachings from Huston Smith's *The Religions of Man* (1958); this sketch is not only brief but minimal, as I understand it. It is good to remember that the Buddha gave these teachings 2,500 years ago. Buddha's incentive for pursuing a journey of search was his extreme sensitivity to the suffering that he saw in the world. He was trying to find out if there was meaning to his suffering. He tried everything from overindulgence to extreme asceticism. He was reduced to skin and bones. He talked to many teachers.

He found no answers. One day he sat under a Bodhi tree and decided to sit there until he understood the cause of human suffering.

"To understand Buddhism it is of utmost importance to gain some sense of the impact of Buddha's life and those who came under its orbit. It is impossible to read the accounts of Buddha's life without emerging with the impression that one has been in touch with one of the greatest personalities of all time. The veneration felt by all who knew him is contagious" (Smith, 1958, p. 86).

I will mention only the aspects of Buddhist teaching that I was able to experiment with. The Buddha discovered that "Thana" was the root cause of human suffering. Translated that means "thirst," "craving," "desire," "attachment." Because of the common usage of these terms, Western people see this as negative philosophy, a denial of life, relinquishing all desire and attachment. I understand "Thana" and attachment to mean self-centered desire. To the extent that these cravings are lessened, the living force becomes positive rather than negative.

Buddhism is known as being the middle way, often misunderstood as meaning moderation. Abandoning all self-centered attachment is extreme rather than moderate. The middle way implies holding to your own ground, not being swayed by your surroundings, being pulled this way and that. I have often been pulled this way and that by my environment. Moderation is not a direction but a byproduct of the middle way. One of the Buddha's most impressive teachings was rejecting all authority. "Do not accept something because it is in a book or because your teacher says it." He rejected what is handed down by tradition and ritual. He rejected all speculation about where we came from or where we go after we die. He felt that profitless speculation is seeking for easy solutions and avoiding the difficult task of self-advance.

The principle that all of us, from the earliest years, rely on the authority of others is a necessary fact for survival in a given culture. For the last fifty years I have realized the negative consequences of relying on the authority of others in the adult years. Although I have not been able to apply this principle, it has always been in the back of my mind. As the years passed by, this questioning of every authority began to take effect with unceasing intensity and has been one of the most important parts of my life. The process of getting weaned from one's parents directly or indirectly is a difficult and lifelong affair.

The last teaching of the Buddha is known as the eight-fold path and is a psychological guide, for Buddhists, right views, right resolve, right speech, right action, right attention, right effort, right livelihood, right meditation. Recently, right speech reminded me of the importance of what I say about people and to people.

In my opinion, Buddhism and psychoanalysis supplement each other. A number of scientists have become interested in Oriental philosophy with an attempt to integrate the philosophy and psychology of East and West.

Any verbal discussion of life itself is a concept, not experiential, and the Buddha was silent in this matter, and this also is the principle in Zen Buddhism. The Buddha with unwavering perseverance and with compassion encouraged his listeners (in modern psychological language) to grow up.

In my opinion, psychoanalysis and Buddhism supplement each other very well. A number of scientists have become interested in Oriental philosophy and in Buddhism—David Boehm, Fritz Capra, Jonas Salk, Rupert Sheldrake, Ken Wilber, Jean Houston, and many others. Buddha summarized his teaching to his "disciple" Ananda, "Therefore, Ananda. Be ye lamps unto yourselves. Betake yourselves to no external refuge. Hold fast to the Truth as a lamp. Hold fast as refuge to the Truth. . . . Work out your own salvation with diligence" (Smith, 1958, p. 97).

No authority can help us "be a light into yourself."

References

Boisen, A. (1960), *Out of the Depths: An Autobiographical Study of Mental Disorder and Religious Experience*. New York: Harper & Row.

Buber, M. (1957), Distance and relation: Elements of the interhuman; guilt and guilt feelings. *Psychiatry*, 20:97–129.

——— (1967), *A Believing Humanism: My Testament, 1902–1965*. New York: Simon & Schuster.

——— (1970), *I and Thou*. New York: Scribner's.

Davids, R. (1932), *A Manual of Buddhism*. London: Sheldon Press.

Fine, R. (1985), *The Meaning of Love in Human Experience.* New York: Wiley.
——— (1986), *Narcissism: The Self and Society.* New York: Columbia University Press.
Friedman, M. (1985), *The Healing Dialogue in Psychotherapy.* New York: Aronson.
——— (1986), *Martin Buber and the Eternal.* New York: Human Sciences Press.
Houston, J. (1982), *Lifeforce: The Psycho-Historical Recovery of Self.* New York: Dell.
James, W. (1929), *The Varieties of Religious Experience. A Study in Human Nature; Being the Gifford Lectures on Natural Religion Delivered at Edinburgh in 1901–1902.* London: Longmans, Green.
Krishnamurti, J. (1983), *The Network of Thought.* New York: Harper & Row.
——— (1984), *The Flame of Attention.* New York: Harper & Row.
Maslow, A. (1971), *The Farther Reaches of Human Nature.* New York: Viking.
Rahula, W. (1974), *What the Buddha Taught.* New York: Grove Press.
Rioch, D. (1985), Recollections of Harry Stack Sullivan and of the development of his interpersonal psychiatry. *Psychiatry,* 48:141–158.
Smith, H. (1958), *The Religions of Man.* New York: Harper & Row.
Sullivan, H. S. (1950), The illusion of personal individuality. *Psychiatry,* 13:317–332.

25

INTERVIEW WITH JOANNE GREENBERG: WITH THREE POEMS BY JOANNE GREENBERG

Laurice L. McAfee, M.D.

Joanne Greenberg, author of *I Never Promised You a Rose Garden* and former patient of Frieda Fromm-Reichmann, was invited to speak about her treatment at the 1985 Chestnut Lodge symposium commemorating the fiftieth anniversary of Fromm-Reichmann's arrival at the hospital. Greenberg was unable to attend the symposium but agreed enthusiastically to a series of interviews with this staff psychiatrist who read a paper based on them at the symposium. In revising that talk for this article, I have tried to retain *much* of Joanne's colorful conversational style.

In June 1985 I traveled to Joanne's home outside Denver, a lovely house resembling a small ski lodge on a foothill of the Rockies. It lay off an unpaved road up a small slope. My first sight was of a wooded area with a jeep parked next to a 1940 Dodge. I was startled at seeing an old car so familiar to me from my childhood and so prettily restored. I was to learn later that Joanne's husband of more than thirty years renovated these old cars as one of his many hobbies.

Joanne greeted me at the door wearing jeans, a plaid shirt, and her welcoming grin soon to become very familiar to me. She wore her dark gray hair close-cropped and seemed surprisingly tall. We sat in her living room overlooking the snow-

An earlier version of this paper was presented at the October 4, 1985, Chestnut Lodge Symposium, commemorating the fiftieth anniversary of the arrival of Frieda Fromm-Reichmann.

capped Rockies and without much preamble began to talk of
her treatment with Fromm-Reichmann, whom she referred to
fondly as Frieda. We were subsequently to talk that day for
about seven hours and two days later for another four hours.

Joanne is the author of thirteen books; her first novel, *The
King's Persons,* was published in 1963. Her second book *(Rose
Garden)* was published under an assumed name—Hannah
Green. It was a semibiographical account of her treatment ex-
perience at Chestnut Lodge as a sixteen- to nineteen-year-old
schizophrenic.

Joanne is a fifty-two-year-old married mother of two sons,
living as she has for the past thirty years outside Denver. Her
husband, Albert, told me that she is considered a native Colorado author and is often asked as such to participate in state
cultural activities. She teaches a sixth-grade enrichment program part-time as she has for the past twenty-eight years; she
is also a professor of anthropology at the nearby Colorado
School of Mines where she has developed courses for the school
in cultural anthropology (her college major) and in fiction writing. She spends each morning writing until eleven A.M. Her
sons, now twenty-nine and twenty-seven, are living on their
own, one in Boston, the other in Denver. The older is an acoust-
ical engineer for rock bands; the younger works for a bank and
is considering law school.

Joanne was a patient at the Lodge from 1948 through 1952.
For the first two years she lived at Little Lodge, a small cottage
with a homelike ambience and open doors. At more difficult
times she was placed on Main IV, then as now a locked unit for
more severely disturbed patients. When she entered Chestnut
Lodge, she was sixteen—the youngest age for admission at that
time.

As a child growing up in New York, Joanne said about
herself: "I was bonkers. I knew it, all the kids knew it, but we
never talked about it. I did my best to hide it." She was given
a Rorschach as part of a school project when she was nine and
her parents were told that it revealed some problems. They
took her to a child psychiatrist whom she saw for five sessions,
but when she seemed to be getting worse, they discontinued
treatment. By ten, she was so preoccupied with her inner world

that she began to have severe difficulties with perceptions, especially of time and space. She could not take athletics because she lost a sense of depth perception. She recalled that from early childhood she could not be certain about the existence of doorways and would hide this difficulty by following other children in and out. By this time, she was having visual hallucinations; auditory hallucinations developed later.

At thirteen, she had some episodes of transient blindness which an ophthalmologist identified to her parents as inconsistent with an organic cause. Her mother took her for evaluation to a New York analyst, Richard Frank. After seeing her for three months, Frank said to Joanne, "You know you are awfully sick and should be in a hospital." She experienced this with a great sense of relief. Frank wanted her to come to Chestnut Lodge and, since the age of admission was sixteen, asked her if she could "hang on" for the next two years. She saw him once a week over that time but had great difficulty, giving up school entirely at age fifteen. New York became a nightmare for her. She had some self-destructive episodes which she now feels were not suicidal, but signs of distress, and she was to tell Fromm-Reichmann later in her treatment that she experienced herself as committing several murders during that time. In referring to that period, Joanne mentioned that she was never on phenothiazines and thought that she might have done better if they had been available in the sense that she might not have been so symptomatic, but she did not convey any doubts about the subsequent role of psychotherapy in her ultimate outcome.

As we began to talk about Joanne's therapy with Fromm-Reichmann, I asked her what she felt was the most meaningful aspect of it. Joanne replied that in her life metaphors have always been tremendously important and the metaphor that Frieda introduced to her was that they were colleagues in a vital work; this, of course, stood against a medical model that Fromm-Reichmann consciously espoused all the time—that there was a doctor; it was always vertical in her conversation, in her metaphor. But it was always horizontal in the way she acted, in the way she actually did it. I said, "You mean in the way she related to you?" Joanne answered, "All the time. Frieda kept saying, 'Take me along. If you don't take me along, how

can I know where you are going? Where are you now?' It happened a lot. Frieda would say, 'I don't know what it's like to be
mentally ill. I don't have a clue. That's your job to tell me. It's
your job to share with me. Do your job! How can I know where
you are unless you take me and do your job? You're the expert."

I commented, "Fromm-Reichmann obviously was well
known by the time you came. What was it like in the beginning?"

Joanne said, "People had told me how famous she was."
Unit staff seemed to her to be saying, "This is a great doctor
and don't you blow it." "I think," Joanne reflected, "that I was
in a bind with Frieda—she couldn't be much good in my mind
or what was she doing messing with me? If she were any good,
she'd be treating someone worth messing with." So Joanne
thought the whole thing was a scam and decided in her mind
that this was one Fromm-Reichmann wasn't going to take.

In a sense, Frieda started with a strike against her because
she did have these credentials on her wall—all that stuff. While
the place wasn't littered with awards, there were enough there
to make people know that she was in fact who she said she was.
Frieda had to get over that and Joanne thought she did it rather
easily. She told Joanne, "Yes, you know, all true, there it is";
and in a sense she conveyed, "What are we going to make of
that? How are we going to get around that to the real work we
have to do?"

Joanne went on to describe the difference in Fromm-Reichmann's bearing, manner, and view of the role of a doctor in
hospital life. Joanne laughed here and said, "Her view of the
doctor as the authority was so Germanic. You should have seen
her on the wards. It was a howl. She would walk in there and
people moved back as if she were parting the Red Sea—and she
acted that way. She was very short and wide and she would go
through like a ballbearing. She expected people to respond in
a very regal way."

And yet when it came to relations with the people around
the Lodge in Rockville, then a sleepy small town, Frieda was
out of it, consciously, permanently, out of it as though she were
a Martian. Joanne recalled a day when another patient turned
in a false alarm and a volunteer fire department truck came
clanging through, the firemen shouting, "Where's the fire?"

These were the people that had to leave their drugstore, their this and that, in the middle of the day and go out to fight a fire. Joanne obviously empathized here with the firemen, relating it to her experience for ten years as a fire-and-rescue volunteer for her Hill community outside Denver, a job she gave up only recently. Frieda just airily said to the firefighters, "Oh, no, it's all right, you can go home now." They were furious and it seemed like they wanted to tear her head off; but she implied, "No, no, my man," with a wave of her hand.

Joanne added, "But, in therapy, as soon as Frieda got in, that vertical business gave way to the horizontal business. As soon as she got down to therapy, she changed, almost visibly."

At this point, I said that it sounded to me as if when Frieda were listening to Joanne report on her inner experiences, she knew where the boundary was to shut off that doctor-knows-it-all manner. That came across in *Rose Garden* and in Fromm-Reichmann's published work. Joanne replied, "I think so. Part of that was linguistic which I alluded to but didn't use in the dialogue of *Rose Garden*. Frieda had a very metaphoric colloquial English which she could use. She chose when she wanted to use it. Frieda had a full complement of foul language which in the late 1940s and early 1950s you didn't use, but she used it."

Joanne described writing a paper once on Fromm-Reichmann's language and reporting on the origins of many of her American colloquialisms. Frieda was on a ship coming to the United States and an American psychiatrist told her that she would find a lot of new words coming up in her dealings with her patients. She was amused with the enthusiasm he had for teaching her all these terrific words. Every day he would find a couple of new ones for her to think about, and Joanne and she laughed about that later in treatment.

Joanne went on to say, "Frieda had a lot on her plate at first. I think, for one thing, when I got to Chestnut Lodge, I had never been anything but sick for years and years, so I had to do a lot of adolescent stuff, and there was a mess with the creativity and how my secret world would fit in with that. Frieda seemed to know enough not to get overly enthusiastic and not to confuse what I wrote with what I was. That would have been very dangerous, I think, and she skirted it very well. I feared that when I would not be sick, that if I gave that up, since madness and creativity were equated in my mind at the time, I would have to give the latter away and then not have anything. And Frieda had to say bullshit without saying it. The first time we met, she said, 'Look, we're not at war, you don't have to give up, you're not going to have to give up one thing that you don't want to give up', and I had thought, 'hah, hah, hah, so's your old man', and sensing that, Frieda had said, 'We'll see.'

"Instead of opposing me directly, she would play for time. She would usually say, 'Well, let's see, I don't think so.' Frieda was also pretty good at looking things up. She would say, for example, 'I think Schubert was a good musician in spite of, not because of, his problems, and Schumann also because he noticed that he did work in pretty healthy times for him and when he was sickest of all, he did little. If your theory were true, he was most creative when he was sickest.' "

Joanne continued, "And I knew that that wasn't true for me: when I was my sickest, I didn't work at all. So I gave Frieda high marks for that even though it didn't get worked out completely until a lot of other stuff was working itself out."

Joanne went on, "But the thing that she said, almost every day, 'You're never going to have to give up anything unless you want to. You can keep your darling sense of—and Frieda had a very, she could have a very 'smarmy' voice—'You can keep your darling, darling symptoms, and your darling scratching, and your darling burning, and you can keep your darling Gods and so forth.' "

I interrupted Joanne here to ask if Fromm-Reichmann said that to her sarcastically. Joanne replied, "Yeah, oh yeah, but not angrily. I don't know how she got to do that." "You could feel the difference?" I asked. "Apparently," she replied.

I asked Joanne, "You didn't feel that as hostile?" She replied, "It was worse than hostile, but Frieda was angry at them—the Gods—not at me. She hated them. She told me that. She didn't want anything to do with them. She said, 'I don't like them, tell them I don't believe in them, tell them I think they're keeping you from everything that's good and valuable, tell them we are at war. Make no apology for that. I'm not on their side. I'm on your side.' "

Another thing Joanne confided about the early phase of treatment was that she had been extremely generous in criticizing Fromm-Reichmann's age. She elaborated, "Because I was afraid she would give out on me and I really didn't want that to happen, I was careful with the hostility I felt was in me. I wanted to be careful of it. 'Don't blow it now,' I said to myself. I accused her of being too old. I told her she was going to croak on me and then she gave me the statistics on her family. She said her sister was sixty, her cousin was seventy-five. It turned out she was not as right as she thought. I recall saying something to her like, 'So we are a long-lived family, so da da da da. You're going to croak on me.' And Frieda said, 'I don't plan to.'"

When it came to issues in treatment involving the family, Joanne recalled that Frieda was most helpful in reality testing. Joanne said, "My mother had a weight problem and was always compulsively dieting, not eating, you know, and yet she used to bake the most scrumptious cakes and candies and pastries for everybody and then almost aggressively not eat them herself. Frieda was the first person who put this together with my weight problem and said, 'What is this? She is making cakes and these pastries. My God, I got a Christmas present from your mother you would not believe.' I said, 'Oh, she never eats them herself.' Frieda replied, 'Well, what the hell. What were you supposed to do in that? Where did you fit in?' I said, 'Well, I guess I was really not supposed to eat them either.'

"Most of the things that happened in the family were things I never put together—ambivalence and so forth on a daily basis regarding family habits. I don't think Frieda did this to attack my parents. She told me that my mother was sane. She said, 'Your mother does not have mental illness and I don't think you can get away with blaming her or dumping on her.' She didn't say it exactly like that, rather, 'Your mother has made her adjustment the best she can.' When other things I told Frieda didn't fit, she would do this. I mean she would play the reality thing. For example, I told her I had killed quite a few people in New York when I was thirteen to sixteen. I killed a man in a brown suit. But Frieda asked, 'Where was it?' 'Oh, it was in the train station,' I replied, 'I shoved him in front of a train.' When Frieda asked me how close the next person was standing, I said right next to me. She said, 'You would have been seen.' I was unable to avoid that reality."

Joanne went on to add, "I used to X people out a lot. I felt if you've seen one, you've seen them all. I even X-ed Frieda out when she went on vacations, but she was always real, right from day one. If annoyed, annoyed; if angry, angry. She didn't get angry much. She did get annoyed and she got impatient and she would look. She wouldn't say she was impatient. She'd give you a look. And, I think, when you're reality testing, you need that. Another thing Frieda used to do a lot, and sometimes annoyingly so, was to sum up at the end of the hour. Today we talked about ghosts, we talked about the car, etc. She would always make sure I couldn't fix it after the hour, couldn't confuse it or X it out."

Joanne commented that a lot of what she had talked about so far was the early stuff in treatment when she was establishing the ground rules. One of her most valuable memories of the treatment, which came later, was Frieda's trust in Joanne's sense of humor and in Joanne's capacity to understand other people's metaphors, including Frieda's own.

Joanne experienced this in the treatment with the telling of all kinds of jokes to each other. "A lot of Jewish jokes but also homey things," she recalled. Frieda didn't often indulge in personal remarks, but on one occasion she presented something which surprised Joanne and stuck with her graphically. In speaking about her family in Germany, Frieda said, "Oh, yes, we all played something. My sister played the flute. In fact, she's now a musicologist, and my other sister was interested in music. We were a very musical family." The expression Frieda gave to that remark was infinitely funny because it spoke of a whole social hierarchy, of a crushing culture where at four o'clock one does this and in the musical evening one plays not what one likes, but what is supposed to be played. "It was a joke," Joanne added, "and Frieda knew that I was hearing the joke and it put a lot of trust in me."

Joanne described other meaningful experiences at the Lodge. One occurring after a year at the Lodge was her first cold wet sheet pack. She said, "I was on Main IV, having a very tough time. A doctor, whom I don't remember—since I subscribed to the theory that if you've seen one person, you've seen them all—said, 'I think you need to be in one of these.' So he put me in one. I think it would be a bad idea for anyone who was claustrophobic to be in a cold pack, but for me it was the first time that I was ever able to look down into my mind, to get clear, to be clear. Once that happened to someone who had never had that, I think he would do anything on earth to get it again. That kind of stillness had clarity, all of that yelling that went on all of the time inside me, wasn't there and I was at the end of it. You're not going anywhere. You are not going to hurt you or it or anything. That's all, that is it. You can fight and fight and fight. I knew that the ability to stop dead and look inside myself was what well people have. And I knew that that high feeling in the pack was coming from me, not a drug. I learned for the first time that there's a difference between inside and outside and that inside then became available to me. Once I saw that, once I learned that, I would do anything to promote it."

Joanne continued, "I also experienced some of the staff as helpful. It was after World War II and we had some returning servicemen who had been in combat and had seen it all and were both kind and bright. I was starving to death intellectually, but didn't realize it. One older navy career officer meant a great deal to me. When I could talk, he and I would talk about anything and everything."

Joanne went on to ask if student nurses still rotated through the Lodge as they did then and said, "In the early part of my treatment, my experience with them was awful. They were all the wonderful, strong young people I was not." At that time, Joanne saw them as a living jibe to herself and would hear, "this is what you will never be." However, she recalled that by the time she was an outpatient, she used the student nurses for role modeling and questioned them about how one talked to a boy, how one got a date.

At this point, the discussion returned to the subject of her therapy. I asked whether she experienced Fromm-Reichmann as having erred in any aspect of the treatment. Joanne replied that the two of them had disagreed many times over the years about whether therapy was strictly a scientific manner. Frieda seemed convinced that it was and that any other doctor with the right training and techniques could do what she was doing with Joanne. "It's scientific and because it's scientific, it's quantifiable and it's interchangeable," said Frieda; but Joanne still feels that Frieda was wrong.

This attitude of Fromm-Reichmann was to lead to what Joanne thought was a mistake by Frieda which created a turmoil in Joanne during one summer when Frieda was away for a vacation. Joanne acted out a great deal during that time, burning and cutting herself. Frieda, on her return, took the approach that Joanne had done badly with the interim doctors because she was trying to show Frieda that she was able to be spoiled and to throw tantrums because she had not wanted Frieda to go away. From Joanne's perspective, when Frieda left, Joanne X-ed her out and tried to relate to the interim doctors and found them to be literalists. She admitted that there probably were several levels not available to her for working with these other doctors at the time, but what got to her was their literal interest in the secret world and in her special language and she felt that she had already worked out in therapy that the symptoms, the language, and the secret world were a metaphor, not the illness itself.

Joanne said, "Remember in *Arsenic and Old Lace* when one of the characters thought he was Teddy Roosevelt and somebody asked if he had been told that he really wasn't Teddy Roosevelt? The sister said, 'Yes, we tried once, and he went upstairs and went under the bed and would not be anybody.' Well, crazy is better than nobody, so in a sense you need to be reassured that you are crazy and you are so scared that the reassurance isn't going to be right for you that rather than saying it, you have to do it. And that's the burning and that's the hallucinating and that's the metaphors of the hideous loneliness and terror—that mixture, that bouquet. That's not the illness, it's a metaphor. I'm putting this into words now because I'm free to do it. I couldn't then and the only thing I could do then was either freeze up or get crazier and I did both simultaneously."

Frieda had to leave for her vacation, but Joanne felt that Frieda's belief that other doctors could continue the work as well as she did kept her from giving Joanne an understanding that what she would be getting was a kind of holding, something or somebody to hold onto which would be different from therapy. Joanne came to feel over the years that Frieda's scientific approach, emphasizing as it did the doctor's technique and training, was also wrong because it seemed to alter Frieda's "we are colleagues" approach to the work so vital to Joanne. She felt that Frieda never saw that.

Hilde Bruch, with whom Joanne later became friends, told her once that Joanne was lucky because Frieda said one thing but did another. They decided that if Frieda had lived longer, she might have modified her view. From Joanne's perspective, the personalities have to fit in therapy and if the symptoms are metaphors, the therapist has to be someone who understands those metaphors or at least is amenable to learning them so that when they appear in the therapeutic dialogue, the right amount of weight is given to them.

Joanne gave an example from later in her therapy of the way in which Fromm-Reichmann worked with Joanne's symptoms as metaphor. Earlier in the treatment, Frieda had approached Joanne's fears of her aggressivity—for example, her idea that she had committed murders in New York—with reality testing. Although Joanne had been able to hear Frieda, she still perceived herself as a very aggressive person in that she was still X-ing people out, freezing them out and making them all faceless.

Fromm-Reichmann presented Joanne with a new metaphor, saying, "Let's assume that there's an island, let's assume that every symptom you have is the prime cultural directive on that island, and go to that island and tell me what's going to happen." Joanne said to Frieda, "Well, what island features reclusive, seclusive, terrified, angry people?" Frieda replied, "Well, there's an island in which the most seclusive, most reclusive, angriest, most aggressive, most whatnot, hallucinating person is a queen. Now what?" Joanne replied, "Well, I'd better just get another island. I'll have to find another island because this isn't going to work at all. I mean, if aggression is seen as positive, I'll have to get a whole bunch of new symptoms." And Frieda and Joanne both laughed and Frieda said, "Well, you know, there goes your big chance." Joanne added, "This was important to me because I think I began to see that I was using my symptoms as the metaphor that they were—they were not the illness. If you perceive the symptoms as the illness, it seems to lower down on you, pushed on you from some outside force. Frieda was telling me through metaphor that the illness is inside you and because it isn't outside, because it's inside, it's fixable, it's surmountable."

This discussion of how much weight to give to symptoms was to come up again when Joanne spoke about getting out of the Lodge. She was an inpatient for a little over two years and then she gradually moved out, continuing to see Fromm-Reich-mann over the next three years as she got her degree from American University in cultural anthropology.

In speaking about that period, Joanne said, "I got out of the Lodge. I went to remedial school. I went to college. Nobody in college knew anything about my illness. When you got out the first thing you learned to do was lie and do it well. I never did it well . . . I didn't do it well for years but I did it. And I made up a biography to explain my absences to the people outside when they needed to know something but not too much.

"I hit it very, very lucky. I went out and found a rooming house where nobody bothered you and they didn't have any other hospital people at all and that was good. Still, moving out was a pretty grim deal. There was the separation and for some-body that had had so little else, it was tough to make that break. For one thing, you have to fight against all of the real good, honest people that you can talk to—they are in the mental hospital and you're trying to get out and you are out there with a whole lot of people you can't talk to. It's really tough.

"I had two returns to the hospital while I was at school. Excuse me for saying so, but I think those were partly something you people don't pay enough attention to. If you are as sick as I was for as long as I was, there are a whole lot of issues about figuring out the difference between problems and symptoms and the convalescent process takes a long time. For doctors it seems if you are well now, ready for discharge, you should be able to do anything. I just disappointed those people so much when I came back—both times. I mean, you could see faces fall."

"Frieda or unit staff?" I asked Joanne. "Everybody else," she said, "but Frieda knew what was going on." The two of them sometimes laughed about it. Fromm-Reichmann would say, "You know they are all upset here, you have them asking these questions, but most of the time she seemed to understand when I would tell her, for example, that this seems more psychotic than that but it isn't. This is not crazy, this is better."

As Joanne moved toward termination, there were new issues in her life which brought new aspects in her relatedness to Frieda. I asked Joanne if Fromm-Reichmann's limited personal experiences of certain things ever came up in the treatment—home life, children. Joanne said, "I only remember one time when I was getting over—I want to call it a love affair—and I was having a wonderful time. I cried, I moaned, I walked the floor. At that time, I was getting well and I really knew the difference and I was glad for the suffering because it was so instructive. I was beginning to know the difference between problems and symptoms and I felt so good being a regular person. I think Frieda faced it fairly honestly. She said, 'I don't know what this is like. I never had a child. I don't know what your mother is feeling for you now. It's different with me.' I told her, 'What do you mean? You're as much my mother as anybody.' Frieda replied, 'Not so. We are limited together in a lot of things we do and I don't have, lucky for you, the investment in the whole psychic health and happiness that your mother has.' "

As Joanne established herself at American University and had an apartment of her own, she gradually began to invite people in. Fairly late in treatment, Frieda said, "You never invite me to your apartment." Joanne felt afraid that where Frieda was concerned, she, Joanne, would somehow blow it as a hostess, she would not know how to act. Frieda did not visit.

When Frieda and Joanne began to speak of her finishing treatment, Joanne always had the feeling that she could come back if she needed to. It was at Frieda's suggestion that sessions were diminished to once a week, once every two weeks, once a month during that last year. When Joanne asked, "What's going to be finishing?" Frieda said, "You're going to become too bored here. You're going to become too busy in your outside life and that's when you'll be finished, when you are tired of it."

At this point, I asked if Joanne ever got a feeling from Frieda that Frieda had a personal investment in Joanne doing well. Joanne laughed and said she tried to make Frieda's life a living hell over that. She said, "I used it whenever I could, telling her that I was a monograph and that she would publish." Fromm-Reichmann would let her go on for awhile and then say quietly, "Well, you know maybe there are other things I can study." That was experienced by Joanne with great relief because, as she put it, "My family does have a whole lot of freight, a lot of stuff wound up in what you're doing and how you turn out and all the rest of it."

Frieda was telling me no, I wasn't so special for her. I asked Joanne if that meant that Fromm-Reichmann was totally neutral in the relationship; Joanne replied, "No, I always felt she liked me. When I would threaten to kill myself, Frieda would say, 'Well, I would think that that would be a hell of a waste after being together all these years, a hell of a waste.' But it came across that while she might feel sad, she was telling me, 'You do what you have to do, Joanne, and I will too.' But something in Frieda looked beyond my illness into where I was and she liked me and that meant a lot because nobody did at all. The big thing is she liked me for the health that was in me, not the sickness in me. She liked the part of me that could joke and the part that rope danced. She liked my writing. She didn't like my whining. She didn't like my complaining. She didn't like my hiding behind stuff. One of the issues had to do with special. I had been diagnosed, IQ-ed, as someone brilliant. That isn't so; as a matter of fact, what I have is a high verbal score. All the rest of it leaves a great deal to be desired. My spatial sense is not the best, my math is not the best. I tried very hard to impress her. She wasn't buying, yet she still liked me. And I found that that was really exceptional. "I'm metaphoric, my speech is highly colored. Frieda knew that and it was perfectly all right with her and she knew that highly colored speech isn't crazy, which was a great blessing in my opinion."

After Joanne stopped treatment, was finishing up at American University, was engaged to Albert, her present husband, and was going to move to Colorado, Frieda wrote her from Santa Fe and said to drop in. The understanding was not drop in as a patient, not a granddaughter, but maybe a great niece—that way. That's what Joanne wanted. She said, "I wanted Frieda as an older person in my life. She was so valuable in my life, although I didn't want to be her patient anymore." Frieda did attend Joanne's wedding after being reassured that Frieda would not cause Joanne to be self-conscious about therapy. Joanne has a picture of Frieda at the wedding, in which Frieda looks "luminescent."

I asked Joanne if after therapy she ever thought of Fromm-Reichmann as a person with qualities she didn't like. Joanne replied, "I think she might have been somebody I liked, but she was a very take-charge person. As a therapist, I think she sat on a lot of her take-charge impulses and made herself not do that, but as a friend, I felt she would know what was right and what you should do and I think that would have been tough for me to handle because my respect for her was extremely great. I would have wanted to have kept her good view of me, but I think that would have made things difficult. She seemed to me very much the cosmopolitan, but then she was, she had very advanced musical and cultural tastes and all the rest of it, so I didn't see her as limited at all. Yet, I didn't see her as a role model particularly. I don't know what that was."

I asked Joanne how she felt about the ongoing controversy in psychiatry today about the value of regressive experience when we have medications and other means of trying to prevent prolonged periods of regression. She replied, "That question is a hummer because I think you can tear yourself up horrifically when you do it—when you regress. That was a climate in the 1950s and 1960s where to get in touch with insanity was to be creative. Maybe the strongest thing I'd like to say ever to anybody is that creativity and mental illness are *opposites*, not complements. It's a confusion of mental illness with creativity. Imagination is, includes, goes *out*, opens out, learns from experience. Craziness is the opposite: it is a fort that's a prison. It doesn't open out on anything. It's a gun that you aim at your own throat. I don't understand how people can confuse the two.

"Some of the people at the Lodge were people who were too soft on mental illness in that they thought it was creative and lovely or at least until they had seen enough of it. People would tell you what perceptive things a patient had said. The thing is I want to choose my perceptions. I don't want them to come out of some kind of unconscious soup. I want it to be something I choose to say, not something that says me." Joanne added that being understood in that state felt horrifically dangerous, "I don't know how Frieda got around that. I remember the danger. I used to call her 'Fire Touch' because I had to watch out for that stuff. It's bigger than you are. It's more powerful. It can kill. She asked if I were familiar with the pointing of the bone ritual in anthropology; you know, the point controls a hundred-mile swath of stuff—people, houses, whew!" Joanne laughed, "What a pity we're not as powerful as that."

It was to be ten years after her therapy at Chestnut Lodge that Joanne Greenberg would write *I Never Promised You a Rose Garden.* Joanne had written a summary of her treatment with Fromm-Reichmann at Frieda's suggestion while still a student at American University; Frieda had liked it and suggested that she write a complementary part of the treatment, but Frieda then had gone to Stanford to participate at the Center for Advanced Study in the Behavioral Sciences and had died shortly thereafter. Joanne did not feel that this stirred the creation of *Rose Garden.*

She felt she had two other colleagues in the book's inception. One was Ken Kesey who wrote *One Flew Over the Cuckoo's Nest,* which seemed to her to represent the kind of confusion of creativity and insanity she detested; the other was Bruno Bettelheim who wrote an article entitled "The Forgotten Lesson of Anne Frank" at a time when Eichmann had been extradited to Israel for trial for war crimes. Bettelheim wrote that the Jews had had a death wish and had gone to the death camps for this reason. Troubled and confused by this idea, Joanne consulted one of her long-standing Hill friends who had survived the Holocaust and he said that one did one of two things with an experience such as the Holocaust (which one cannot fit with ordinary life): you forget it or you change. He felt that Bettel-heim may have done the latter.

That statement was very meaningful to Joanne in terms of her own experience with mental illness. She was a published author, she was a mother, she was Hill—a part of her community outside Denver—she belonged there, but it seemed that she needed to write this book because she hadn't forgotten the experience, but before she changed it too much. Yet her feelings were mixed. She had missed out on an awful lot of living. She had a whole personality to construct. She said, "I didn't want to deal with such people, I didn't want to be thought sick. I wanted to be okay. I wanted to be average. I certainly didn't want to write this damn thing."

Joanne decided to write the book under the assumed name Hannah Green to protect her sons and her husband, who had colleagues and clients in the mental hygiene system in Colorado. Holt, her publisher, was very protective of her privacy. After the book was in print by Hannah Green, however, she started to have dreams about it. One she recalled was that she had been in an accident and was dying and someone asked her if there was anything they should know and she said to them, "I've got a lost child." This dream made her realize that writing the book under another person's name had been emotionally costly.

Joanne recounted that there have been some funny incidents for her in secretly being Hannah Green. People who didn't know Joanne's identity as the author of *Rose Garden* have told her of Hannah Green's suicide, her many hospitalizations. Joanne even heard on the "Phil Donahue Show" that Hannah Green was never schizophrenic at all.

Joanne Greenberg feels strongly that what she experienced was not unique, not special, but what happens to many people who make the giant leap from sick to well. She does not see psychotic illness and health as being on ends of a continuum, but as being totally separate experiences with a line between them.

Some very well-meaning people have tried, according to Joanne, to humanize the experience of craziness by saying, "we all have our moments, we all get angry, we all get frightened." Here, Joanne said, "Kiddo, you're swimming, I'm drowning.

Don't swim up to me and tell me we are all drowning; I don't know if I can make it through the next wave. It's a lie to tell me we all have our moments, even though we do. I have never had a moment like the moments I had when I was sick."

When asked to elaborate on the level of stress experienced, Joanne said, "I know what it's like to be frightened, but I have *never* been as terrified as when I've been mentally ill. After treatment, I was once in a fire all alone, fire burning all over my head. I was a volunteer fireman. And I had a breathing apparatus and couldn't see, couldn't hear—smoke does funny things to your hearing—it was a smoky, fire-filled house and my partner was who-in-the-hell-knows where. And I was terrified. But take those few real moments and multiply the terror level by fifty and keep punching those buttons all the time—that's the terror I had when I was sick."

Joanne said that people who are sick have a difficult time giving up the illness in part because the line is all they have to steer by. Reexperiencing the line was what she perceived herself to have been doing when she returned twice to the hospital after getting out. She recalled that Fromm-Reichmann used to say that the leap from sick to well was an act of faith. Joanne remembered that Frieda once said to her, "I'm asking you to dive 250 feet into a wet wash rag. I'm telling you that there is water in the pool."

Joanne asked me, "Would you jump out of an airplane without a parachute because somebody tells you, well, 'we changed gravity, we repealed that so it's okay to jump now'?" Not waiting for my answer, she went on to add, "And, it's not only one jump. For me in the early days it was a daily jump until I got used to gravity. Somewhere along the line I had a couple of hours of good ole hard-core sane! Once I had that I knew I'd never settle for less—it's too good—even when it's bad, it's good." Joanne added that she had had some real-life difficulties over the years and that now when she felt bad going through them, she had alternatives. She said, "I call up my friends, I talk to my husband, I go skiing, I sing. None of those were available to me when I was sick. I built stuff out of my own life and my own self so that I could have places to go besides crazy."

Joanne called *I Never Promised You a Rose Garden* a work of fiction on her part. After interviewing her, I felt that that was a statement of the distance between that ill teen-ager whose focus was on the world of metaphor and inner preoccupation and the mature woman who could recall and recount in such graphic detail her experience of the real interactions she had had in treatment with Fromm-Reichmann. I came away from that experience with no doubts as a clinician that Joanne Greenberg had been schizophrenic, that she no longer was schizophrenic, and that she had in fact made the leap from sick to well and not only had survived but conquered.

[Joanne Greenberg, author of many novels and short stories, has contributed the following poems. She noted to me, "I think it is something that Frieda would have liked because it was the kind of work I was doing when I saw her, and that is poetry."—Ed.]

FOUR EYES

In wonder I move, unsteadily,
From the blur, day-color to the darker office blur
To peer at the realities, now at one more remove,
Through my magnificent spectacles.
How beautiful are all clean edges
That are mine to contemplate at leisure
Through the changed spaces.
Years ago in some moment's inattention
The edges have slipped away
Leaving only a little light there to deceive me.
Now, through the sweat I sweat or my tears,
Or the mists of my face that print
An image of me in the inside lens
(The Queen, Her Jubilee in
In the bottom of a soup-bowl.)
I can see again.
It is dependence, a weakness,
One of a growing number, common as eyebrow-scale—
And in spite of looking at all of them

Through the shining lenses, cleaned for the occasion,
They stay recalcitrant, blurred, outside my discipline
And without an edge.

LOVE POEM

The moon is gone; it must be after four.
Cars are not frequent; now and then
They pass and give assurance of the world.
One benediction streetlight. No one walks
From grace beneath our window through the dark
Then blessed and blessed again to the next corner.
Beside me he breathes softly in and out:
Two different tones in antiphon, asleep.
I am awake, remembering with awe
How many years I lay in narrow beds
Blinking away the quiet tears of doubt.
Love that has come too soon
For celebration in the solitudes
Beyond the curve of his embracing arm
Is not my poverty.
When dawn subdues the streetlights I may sleep,
Then rising into ordinary day,
Hold my secret like blessed bread.

THE RUNNING POEM

In the day—race up to high pasture;
My poem is running in the fast herd—
Not the first, (not) the wild, sweat-sided stallion
Out-racing by a century, convention;
Not the second or the third. Here she comes,
That steady-paced cinnamon mare,
A dependable mare with good lines.
I will have to cut quick when she passes;
I am making my move, leaning low,
Handing the rope to obedient loops,
Getting close, closing in, I see nothing else
But her eyes and her motion.

Then I throw and rock back, laying
Line in the air; it goes wide, but she's caught.
She breaks from the herd. It beats past us,
We are stopped. Neither breathes. We stare
The rope down. I run up and vault her. I cling, knees, legs, thighs,
She breaks, breaks alive, she plunges and screams
And tears away wall-eyed.
I'll ride this rope
To the end of her rush; I'll cling or be thrown,
Snap my skull, break my ribs, and it's worth it
Because for this moment of thundering motion,
For the sob-out-of-breath and the hitch-in of breathing,
The three-footed beat, the spread to touch ground,
The time before judgment, comes measuring, measuring—
She's perfect.
Blown mane and deep chest,
Nothing lame in this moment, wind-broken or spavined or frightened or wanting,
We are running together at a clean, hard run
And the wind is behind us.

PART VI
A HISTORY OF THE WASHINGTON PSYCHOANALYTIC INSTITUTE AND SOCIETY

26

A HISTORY OF THE WASHINGTON PSYCHOANALYTIC INSTITUTE AND SOCIETY

Douglas Noble, M.D.
and
Donald L. Burnham, M.D.

Section I. 1914–1929

A. General Background; Beginnings of Psychoanalysis in America

In his autobiography, *Free Associations,* Ernest Jones (1959) stated that there was a psychological moment in all countries when interest in psychoanalysis became acute. In the United States this moment occurred just before World War I when Abraham Brill, Ernest Jones, and a small group of interested friends led in founding the New York Psychoanalytic Society and, for those few psychoanalysts outside New York City, the American Psychoanalytic Association.

The first meeting of the American Psychoanalytic Association was held in Baltimore on May 9, 1911. James J. Putnam was elected president, and Ernest Jones, secretary. The other charter members were Trigant Burrow, Ralph C. Hamill, John T. MacCurdy, Adolf Meyer, G. Lane Taneyhill, and G. Alexander Young. William Alanson White joined the group later, and served as its president from 1916 to 1919 and again in 1928.

White had helped to gain acceptance for Freud's ideas when he provided an eloquent defense of the principles of psychoanalysis at the 1913 meeting of the American Medico-Psychological Association (Overholser, 1956).

White's book, *Mental Mechanisms* (1911) is considered by some to be the first book by an American about psychoanalysis (Burnham, 1967). In 1912, in defense of basic psychoanalytic principles, he wrote an article, "The Fundamentals of the Freudian Psychology" (1912; Burnham, 1967, p. 34). At St. Elizabeths Hospital, where he was superintendent from 1903 until his death in 1937, White encouraged his staff in psychoanalytic studies and investigations. However, he was apparently ambivalent about certain aspects of psychoanalysis; to wit, his statement at the 1919 meeting of the American Psychoanalytic Association in Atlantic City: "the time has come to free American psychiatry from the domination of the Pope at Vienna" (Oberndorf, 1953, pp. 135–136).

Another prominent psychiatrist who assisted the acceptance of psychoanalysis in the United States was Adolf Meyer. In 1910 he came to Johns Hopkins, where in 1904 Lewellyn F. Barker had already inaugurated a program of psychotherapy (Burnham, 1967, p. 76). Among Meyer's staff at Hopkins were several who were highly knowledgeable in psychoanalysis, including Trigant Burrow, who, with Meyer's encouragement, had studied with Jung in Zurich in 1909. Another was C. Macfie Campbell. Still another was G. Lane Taneyhill, a charter member of the American Psychoanalytic Association, and its president from 1921 to 1922. Oberndorf (1953, p. 125) credits his contribution thus: Taneyhill "for seven consecutive years from 1917 to 1925 . . . gave elective courses in psychoanalysis to third and fourth year medical students. They are the first regularly catalogued courses in any medical school for which students received the usual credits toward a degree." Oberndorf also credits Taneyhill as one of the first analysts to use the couch in this country: "At that time in America, psychoanalytic treatment in private practice and in the outpatient clinics was generally conducted face to face; none of us had placed the patient in the recumbent position which has since become so characteristic of psychoanalytic procedure. Dr. G. Lane Taneyhill of Baltimore was one of the first psychoanalysts in this country to use the couch."

B. Beginnings of the First Washington Psychoanalytic Society

On July 6, 1914, the Washington Psychoanalytic Society was organized at St. Elizabeths Hospital in Washington, D.C. This first meeting marked the beginning not only of the Society, but of a close and continuous association between St. Elizabeths Hospital and psychoanalysis in Washington.

In 1913, White and Smith Ely Jelliffe had initiated publication of the *Psychoanalytic Review,* the first psychoanalytic journal to be published in English. Prior to publication in 1937 of the *Bulletin of the American Psychoanalytic Association,* notes on the meetings of the American were published in the *Psychoanalytic Review.*

The first meeting of the Washington Psychoanalytic Society was attended by Bernard S. Glueck, James C. Hassall, Percy Hickling, John E. Lind, Mary O'Malley, and William A. White. White was appointed President *pro tem* and an abstract of Alfred Adler's (1912) *The Neurotic Constitution* was presented by Glueck, who was, with Lind, then engaged in translating it. After discussing Adler's work, White gave a diagrammatic presentation of "The Libido and Its Development."

Glueck, brother of noted criminologist Nelson Glueck, had joined the staff of St. Elizabeths Hospital in 1908. There he found the atmosphere charged with psychoanalytic enthusiasm. In the summer of 1911 he went to Europe, where he worked with Kraepelin and Alzheimer in Munich, and with Ziehen in Berlin. He had wanted to go on to Vienna to meet Freud, but was prevented from doing so for lack of funds. At one point he was analyzed by Edward Glover. Besides the Adler work, he also translated Schilder's (1928) *Introduction to a Psychoanalytic Psychiatry,* and, with Bertram D. Lewin, Franz Alexander's (1930) *Psychoanalysis of the Total Personality* (Glueck, 1956).

The charter members of the first Washington Psychoanalytic Society were A. B. Evarts, Bernard S. Glueck, James C. Hassall, Percy Hickling, John E. Lind, J. J. Madigan, J. P. H. Murphy, Mary O'Malley, Thomas A. Poole, Robert Sheehan, F. M. Shockley, William A. White, and Tom Williams (Hadley, 1928).

The second meeting of the Society was held at St. Elizabeths

Hospital on October 10, 1914, when White (1915) read his paper "The Unconscious," and was formally elected president.

On November 14, 1914, Glueck (1915) read his paper "The God-Man or Jehovah Complex." A policy was inaugurated that meetings be held at the homes of members on the second Saturday of each month. The wives of members were invited to the scientific sessions and to the social gatherings afterwards when refreshments would be served.

It was also decided that anyone who had attended a meeting should be considered a member unless there was specific opposition to his acceptance; future applicants would have to have their names presented to the Society by a member. An assessment of 25¢ per member was made to defray expenses of mailing, etc. Glueck suggested that at each meeting, before the presentation of the formal scientific paper, a half-hour be devoted to discussion of interesting clinical material encountered in daily practice. It can be readily envisaged that with fresh awareness of the phenomena elicited by the psychoanalytic method, members came to these meetings eager to compare experiences.

During the first year of the Society's existence, attendance at the meetings slowly increased, and at the fourth meeting, on December 12, 1914, when Hassall (1915) read his paper, "The Role of the Sexual Complex in Dementia Praecox," eleven persons were present. At the end of the first year, however, D. D. V. Stuart of Baltimore apparently felt that things were moving too fast; hence, at the ninth meeting, on May 8, 1915, the paper he presented was "A Plea for the More Conservative Use of Psychoanalysis."

At about this time, Edward J. Kempf joined the staff of St. Elizabeths Hospital and plunged into active participation in the organizational affairs and the scientific program of the Society. He was its second president. He presented five papers in 1915–1917. Earlier, at the Central Indiana Hospital for the Insane, Kempf had conducted psychoanalytically oriented psychotherapy of the psychoses, work he continued at St. Elizabeths Hospital (Burnham, 1967, p. 155). He was one of the first, if not the first, full-time clinical psychiatrists on the staff of a public mental hospital to be free from ward duties in order to devote all his time to psychoanalytically oriented psychotherapy (Lewis, 1926).

Other papers presented during 1915–1916 were by White, Trigant Burrow, and C. Macfie Campbell. Campbell was at this time Associate Professor of Psychiatry at Johns Hopkins Medical School. He had written papers in 1910 and 1912 on the application of psychoanalysis to the treatment of the psychoses and an even earlier paper, "Psychological Mechanisms with Special Reference to Wish-Fulfillment" (1908). He also published one of the first translations in this country of a psychoanalytic paper by Ferenczi (1908), "On Habit-Neuroses and Psycho-Neuroses in the Light of Freud's Investigations and Psycho-Analysis" (Burnham, 1967, p. 28). Subsequently, Campbell moved to Harvard as professor of psychiatry. There he helped some of his graduate students to obtain fellowships for psychoanalytic training.

The fourteenth meeting of the Society, on November 11, 1916, was the first held at St. Elizabeths Hospital after the hospital had legally acquired that name. Previously it had been designated "The Government Hospital for the Insane." At this meeting several new members were introduced, including Ross McClure Chapman, later the fourth president of the Society and also director of Sheppard and Enoch Pratt Hospital; Lucile Dooley; Walter Freeman; and Dallas Sutton, who became the first psychiatrist in the Naval Medical Corps to reach the rank of Admiral. Dooley (1920) read a paper on Charlotte Bonté.

Throughout the 1916–1917 year, when Dr. Hickling, alienist for the District of Columbia, was the third president of the Society, the titles of the papers read indicated a wide scope of interest and a great depth of scholarship. In addition to Dooley's paper on Charlotte Brontë, Taneyhill and Hickling presented well-documented case reports, as did T. V. Moore, a priest and psychiatrist.

In 1917 there was a remarkable predilection for papers bearing animal titles, for which no explanation—analytic or other—was offered. Smith Ely Jelliffe and L. Brink (1917) presented a paper on "The Role of Animals in the Unconscious," Hassall (1919) on "The Serpent as a Symbol," and Moore (1918) on "The Hound of Heaven."

During 1917, when the United States entered the World War, many of the large number of medical officers stationed at St. Elizabeths Hospital attended the meetings of the Society, among them a Captain Searles (not related to Harold Searles of the present Society). The next year, however, when several leaders of the Society left for military duty, it became necessary to discontinue the meetings.

The twenty-sixth meeting of the Society, on April 13, 1918, was its last until it was reorganized in 1925.

C. The Society Reconvenes

On June 13, 1925, the Washington Psychoanalytic Society was reactivated. The seven-year hiatus was attributed by Samuel Silk, for many years assistant superintendent of St. Elizabeths Hospital, to the existence of two other professional societies whose membership partly overlapped that of the Psychoanalytic Society. These were the Washington Society for Nervous and Mental Diseases, founded in 1907, and the Washington Psychoanalytic Association, organized in 1924.[1]

The first meeting of the Washington Psychoanalytic Society after the lengthy recess was convened through the efforts of Percy Hickling and Mary O'Malley. They issued invitations to the meeting to all the earlier members, as well as to others they thought would be interested. After reporting a balance of $3.93 in the treasury, O'Malley moved that everyone present—former members, newly invited physicians, and others—be elected to membership. The motion was carried without dissent. Hickling was elected for the second time to the presidency of the Society, to serve until the next regular election of officers, when Nolan D. C. Lewis was elected the Society's fifth president.

At this reactivating meeting Ernest E. Hadley made his first appearance at the Society. Having been declared a member, he was appointed by Hickling to be secretary-treasurer *pro tem.*

An active scientific program was instituted almost immediately. At the next meeting Harry Stack Sullivan (1926b), then at Sheppard and Enoch Pratt Hospital, read a paper on ero-

---

[1] The various organizations and their founding dates are listed in the Appendix.

genous maturation. During the following year papers were pre-sented by Nolan D. C. Lewis (1926) on "A Psychoanalytic Approach to Children Under Twelve"; Trigant Burrow (1927) on "The Group Method of Analysis"; Ernest Hadley (1926) on "Comments on Pedophilia"; and E. Hiram Reede on "The Soul Image as Defined by Jung," a penetrating study on the life and work of Charles Dickens.

At about this time, Count Korzybski came to St. Elizabeths Hospital. There White gave him the opportunity to pursue his research in semantics which led to the publication of his well-known book, *Science and Sanity* (Korzybski, 1933). For several years, until he moved to New York, Korzybski took an active part in the scientific work of the Society. At the meeting on March 29, 1926, he read a paper on "The Scientific Method in Psychopathology."

D. Change of Society's Name

At the March 1926 meeting it was proposed that the Society be renamed "The Washington Psychopathological Society," with the justification that the new name would permit a broader range of scientific pursuits and the Society would thus better serve the needs of the many psychiatric and nonmedical members whose interests were not primarily in psychoanalysis.

At this time there was a growing number of out-of-town speakers. While the scientific programs followed psychoanalytic lines, the discussions seem at times to have gone rather far afield. Nolan Lewis's paper, "Alcoholism and Paranoia," read at the December 1926 meeting, elicited an especially lively dis-cussion, mostly of members' personal reminiscenses of their own experiences with alcohol. (This was during the prohibition era, when such exchanges were a prominent feature of many social and professional gatherings.) White contrasted the effects of pre- and post-Volsteadian products. Sullivan suggested that control experiments be carried out on the psychopathology of teetotalers. Hickling related that he had once been given a bottle of liquor allegedly brought over on the Mayflower; he could not remember its effects. The lady members of the Society were invited to report their experiences, but they demurred, calling attention to the lateness of the hour. The meeting was then adjourned in an orderly manner.

In 1927 and 1928 a series of distinguished visitors came to Washington to conduct seminars and address both the Washington Psychoanalytic Association and the Washington Psychopathological Society. Among others, these included Jung's pupil Beatrice Hinkel, Joseph Jastrow, Sandor Ferenczi, Fritz Wittels, A. A. Brill, B. Lewin, C. Oberndorf, and Paul Schilder.

In 1928, sixty persons—a record attendance for the Society at that time—greeted Karl Buehler, Professor of Psychology at the University of Vienna, who read his paper, "A Criticism of Psychoanalysis from the Standpoint of Child Psychology." Another distinguished visitor was Dorian Feigenbaum (later one of the founders of the *Psychoanalytic Quarterly*), who read a paper on "The Contribution of Psychoanalysis to the Problem of Paranoia."

The Washington Psychoanalytic Association had been founded in 1924 with Ben Karpman as one of its leaders. Some of its membership overlapped with The Washington Psychoanalytic Society (later The Washington Psychopathological Society). At the same time there was rivalry as to which organization would officially represent psychoanalysis in Washington. As events unfolded, a new society, The Washington-Baltimore Psychoanalytic Society, was founded in 1930 and the activities of The Washington Psychoanalytic Association waned, though some of the core members continued meetings until Karpman's death in 1962 (Prager, 1969).

Section II. 1929–1957[2]

A. Founding of the Washington-Baltimore Psychoanalytic Society

In 1928 and 1929, Hadley several times approached Dr. A. A. Brill, president of the American Psychoanalytic Association from 1929 to 1935, to discuss the desirability of establishing a psychoanalytic society and institute in the Baltimore-Washing-

---

[2] The material in this section is taken from information supplied by Frieda Fromm-Reichmann, Ernest E. Hadley, William Silverberg, Edith Weigert, and the personal recollections of Douglas Noble.

ton area which would be approved by both the American and the International Associations. Heartily in agreement with the idea generally, Brill inquired about developments in the Washington Psychoanalytic Association, but did not specifically pursue the subject of Hadley's overtures. Later, events in the meantime permitting, Hadley again approached Brill.

"How," asked Brill, "would you present the matter to the International Psychoanalytic Association?" "Suppose," proposed Hadley, "the present members of the American Psychoanalytic Association in this area (Hadley had become a member of the American in 1927) were to organize and apply through you. Wouldn't the International consider it favorably?" Brill replied, "Naturally I can't answer that question, but why don't you send me a confidential report on everybody down there and I'll think it over."

On May 16, 1930, Hadley sent Brill a confidential report listing the potential members in the Washington area and their known qualifications, and asked Clara Thompson to do the same for potential members in the Baltimore area.

In his prompt reply to Hadley on May 17, 1930, Brill wrote, "You gave me a very good report and I believe that in the light of what you say I will recommend the matter to the International Association." Some discussion followed about a name for the proposed psychoanalytic society. "I don't see," observed Brill, "why you should call it the Middle Atlantic Society. Why not call it the Washington Society?" Since the group comprised members from both Baltimore and Washington, however, the name "Washington-Baltimore Psychoanalytic Society" was finally decided upon.

It appears that Sullivan worked with Hadley in these preliminary negotiations with Brill. This is borne out by Silverberg's recollection that when he was asked to serve as Secretary *pro tem* of the organizing group, Sullivan instructed him as to those to be invited to the organizing meeting and had his secretary provide Silverberg with their addresses. Among the prospective members of the proposed Society were Lucile Dooley, Benjamin Karpman, G. Lane Taneyhill, and Clara Thompson, who, according to Silverberg, had agreed not to join any new society unless all four were included. Everyone on the list replied except Karpman, but it was several months after the Society had been formed before Silverberg learned that Karpman had never received his invitation. It appeared that Silverberg had been given, wittingly or unwittingly, an outdated address for Karpman. Another verson of how Karpman came to be left out has been attributed to Dooley; it was her impression that Brill had informally sent word that the group would receive his approval only if Karpman were excluded.

In any event, subsequent to the correspondence with Brill, an organizing meeting was held at Hadley's office at 1835 I Street, N.W., Washington, D.C., on May 31, 1930. Present were Anna C. Dannemann Colomb, Lucile Dooley, Ernest E. Hadley, Nolan D. C. Lewis, Edward Hiram Reede, William V. Silverberg, Harry Stack Sullivan, and Clara Thompson. Though he did not attend that meeting, William Alanson White had indicated his willingness to be a charter member of the new Society. Later, Ross McClure Chapman, Philip S. Graven, Loren B. T. Johnson, Adolf Meyer, and G. Lane Taneyhill also became charter members. These fourteen physicians, all members of the American and International Psychoanalytic Associations, constituted the Society's charter membership. Harry Stack Sullivan, then Vice-President of the American Psychoanalytic Association, presided, and Ernest E. Hadley was Secretary *pro tem.* After adoption of a constitution, the following officers were elected:

President:	Clara Thompson, M.D.
Vice-President:	Edward Hiram Reede, M.D.
Secretary-Treasurer:	William V. Silverberg, M.D.
Councilors:	Ernest E. Hadley, M.D.
	Nolan D.C. Lewis, M.D.
	Lucile Dooley, M.D.

Thompson served as president for the first two years of the Society's existence. It is not known whether any arrangements were made for a substitute for her when she went to Budapest in 1931 for analysis with Ferenczi.

In 1932, when the American Psychoanalytical Association reorganized to become a Federation of Branch Societies, its three Constituent Societies were the New York, Chicago, and

Washington-Baltimore Societies. The Boston Society became affiliated in 1933.

At the Twelfth International Psycho-Analytical Congress held in Wiesbaden in September 1932, the Washington-Baltimore Psychoanalytic Society was formally admitted to the International Psycho-Analytical Association.

In the fall of 1930 regular monthly meetings of the Washington-Baltimore Society had been inaugurated and held in the homes of various members. At the first meeting, on October 18, 1930, Silverberg (1932) had read a paper, "Notes on the Mechanism of Reaction Formation."

A nucleus of deeply interested, active members—Dooley, Hadley, Lewis Hill, Silverberg, and Thompson—participated regularly in the scientific and organizational activities of the Society. Others, among them Ross Chapman and Adolf Meyer, maintained their membership and some interest in psychoanalysis, but took little part in the Society's program.

A considerable number of the papers presented at the early meetings of the Society were published in the *Psychoanalytic Review,* of which Smith Ely Jelliffe and William A. White were co-editors.

In 1934, Frieda Fromm-Reichmann, a training analyst and pupil of Georg Groddeck and Kurt Goldstein, came from Germany, and for the rest of her life was an active participant in the educational and scientific work of the Society.

In 1938, the Society was further strengthened by the arrival of Edith Weigert, another training analyst from Germany, who played a cardinal role in the development of the Society and Institute.

Before coming to Washington, both Fromm-Reichmann and Weigert had written Dooley, asking how favorable the professional climate would be for them here. Dooley encouraged them to come (Prager, 1969).

B. Beginnings of Training Program and Institute

It was hoped that an institute could be established soon after the Society was organized. Background for this was the growing interest within the American Psychoanalytic Association toward establishing more formal training programs and standards. Several specific steps in that direction had been taken.

In his Presidential Address to the American on December 27, 1927, William A. White (1928) had sketched his vision of the shape that a psychoanalytic institute might take.

At the meeting of the American on May 8, 1930, changes in the constitution were approved, among them more rigid requirements for the analytic training of future members. (*Psychoanal. Rev.,* 17:495, 1930)

The New York Psychoanalytic Institute opened in 1931, and the Boston and Chicago Institutes, the following year. The Washington-Baltimore Society also saw the beginning of formal training in 1932. Thus it was the fourth psychoanalytic training program to be established in the United States.

Hadley, Hill, and Silverberg led in establishing the Washington-Baltimore Society's training program. Reminiscing years later, Silverberg said that originally the Society's major purpose had been to provide meetings for a scientific group, with educational functions secondary.

The proposed Washington-Baltimore Institute was to be modeled after the New York Psychoanalytic Institute. In making plans, Silverberg gathered together a small group in Baltimore known as the "Miracle Club," while a similar group was formed in Washington.[3]

---

[3] After reading a preliminary draft of this history, Dr. Ralph M. Crowley offered a different description of the Miracle Club. Crowley (1968) commented, "I can find no evidence that the 'Miracle Club' had anything to do with plans for a Washington-Baltimore Institute. I often heard Clara Thompson speak of the 'Miracle Club.' According to her, it was a club which met regularly to discuss the members' cases, sort of group supervision or case seminar type of thing, because there was nothing like it in the area. I never heard of the existence of two miracle clubs, one in Washington and one in Baltimore. I thought and understood there was only one that met in Baltimore at Clara's apartment and included people from both Washington and Baltimore. The Washington people were, of course, Jarvis and Saunders."

Crowley refers also to Green's description of the Miracle Club meetings of early Washington-Baltimore Society members at Clara Thompson's apartment in Baltimore: "Every Sunday in the winter of 1930–31, a group of them met at her apartment to discuss their difficult patients. These discussions turned out to have such a good influence on their treatment of these patients that the group was dubbed the 'Miracle Club.' Both these meetings were terminated in June of 1931 with her departure for Budapest, where she spent the next two years in psychoanalysis with Sandor Ferenczi. . . . The members of the club were Lewis B. Hill, Eleanora B. Saunders, Marjorie Jarvis, Bernard S. Robbins, and William V. Silverberg. Sullivan did not participate in these discussions as he had left Baltimore at this time to work in New York and to teach at Yale with his friend Edward Sapir, the renowned anthropologist" (Thompson, 1964, p. 355).

Beginning in January 1933, Silverberg, the chairman of the Society's Training Committee, conducted the Washington-Baltimore Society's first course—fifteen seminars on Freud's Five Case Histories. It was attended by a gathering of interested people, lay persons as well as physicians and analysts. This constituted the beginning of the education program of the Society, though it was some years before the Institute was formally founded and accredited.

In the scholastic year 1933–1934, the following program was initiated:

Autumn

The General Theory of Neuroses	Lewis B. Hill
Three Contributions to the Theory of Sex	Ernest E. Hadley
Technical Seminar:	
Section A	Lucile Dooley
Section B	Lewis B. Hill
Genetic Psychology (elective)	Nolan D. C. Lewis

Winter

The Special Theory of the Neuroses	Lucile Dooley
The Technique of Psychoanalysis	Lucile Dooley
Technical Seminar:	
Section A	Lucile Dooley
Section B	Lewis B. Hill

Spring

The Theory of the Instincts	Lewis B. Hill
The Technique of Dream Interpretation	Ernest E. Hadley
Technical Seminar:	
Section A	Lucile Dooley
Section B	Lewis B. Hill
Medical Psychology (elective)	Nolan D. C. Lewis

Further investigation reveals that in 1932 a comparable case discussion group began to meet in Washington. This group included Lucile Dooley, Philip Graven, Ernest Hadley, E. Hiram Reede, and William Silverberg. Whether they also called themselves a "Miracle Club" is not known.

Apparent in the teachings of Dooley, Silverberg, and Thompson were the influences of their varied backgrounds.

Dooley's early training was in psychology. She obtained her Ph.D. degree from Clark University in 1916, and her M.D. degree from Johns Hopkins in 1922. She received personal analysis from L. Pierce Clark and Nolan D. C. Lewis. In 1931–1932, while studying at the Vienna Psychoanalytic Institute, she was analyzed by Ruth Mack-Brunswick. During her stay in Vienna she also had, in English, tutorial work with Robert Waelder (Prager, 1969).

Silverberg was a medical school graduate from Columbia in 1921. He received part of his psychiatric training at Manhattan State Hospital, an important locus of some of the beginnings of psychoanalysis in the United States. From 1928 to 1930 he studied at the Berlin Psychoanalytic Institute, where he was analyzed by Franz Alexander. Upon his return to the United States, he was for two years director of research at Sheppard Pratt Hospital. There he took over Sullivan's special ward for schizophrenic patients after Sullivan moved to enter private practice in New York City.

Thompson had personal analysis with Ferenczi in Budapest during the summers of 1928 and 1929, and for two years continuously from 1931 until Ferenczi's death in 1933. In an unpublished paper, Thompson (1955) attributed to Sullivan her decision to seek analysis from Ferenczi, "I would not have gone to Ferenczi, because who would have the nerve to go to Budapest all alone, if Sullivan hadn't insisted that this was the only analyst in Europe he had any confidence in, and therefore, if I was going to Europe and get analyzed, I had just better go there. So, I went."

Society activities, including the training program, developed rapidly both in Baltimore and Washington. Silverberg was the first director of the Society's training program, but in 1933 he and Clara Thompson, after her return from Budapest, moved to New York City. Both, however, continued their teaching affiliation in Washington, as well as their participation in the Society's affairs. In fact, Silverberg conducted regular seminars in Washington and later weekly supervisory sessions with a group of candidates.

Lewis Hill was director of the Society's training program from the time Silverberg moved to New York until 1940, when the institute was established with Hill as its first director. In 1949 Hadley succeeded Hill in that office.

Establishment of the Institute had been recommended by a Society committee consisting of Dexter M. Bullard, Dooley, and Hill. Their recommendation was approved at a meeting of the Society in December 1939.

At the May 1940 meeting of the American Psychoanalytic Association in Cincinnati, the Washington-Baltimorte Psychoanalytic Society was authorized to organize a Washington-Baltimore Psychoanalytic Institute.

C. Role of Women in the Psychoanalytic Movement

Women have played a prominent role in the development of the psychoanalytic movement in the Washington area. Throughout its history, they have been represented in a larger proportion than that found among the medical professional generally.

Mary O'Malley, then clinical director of St. Elizabeths Hospital, was the only woman in the group of six who met in 1914 to organize the Washington Psychoanalytic Society, and the only woman among its thirteen charter members. In 1930, when the Society was newly organized, three of the fourteen charter members were women: Anna C. Dannemann Colomb, Lucile Dooley, and Clara Thompson. By 1938 their representation had increased; of the twenty-seven members, two of whom were honorary, nine were women, all vigorous participants in the scientific and organizational activities of the Society. There were Anna Colomb, Lucile Dooley, Frieda Fromm-Reichmann, Agnes Bruce Greig, Gertrude Jacob, Marjorie Jarvis, Amanda L. Stoughton, Edith Weigert, and Winifred G. Whitman.

Anna C. Dannemann Colomb was on the medical staff of St. Elizabeths Hospital. She was active in local psychoanalytic affairs from the 1920s to the 1940s, when she transferred her practice to New Orleans, where she was influential in establishing a training center.

Lucile Dooley became a member of the Society in 1916, and was its president from 1933 to 1935 and from 1938 to 1939. During World War I, when many of the male staff members of St. Elizabeths left for military service, the seven women on the medical staff met for twenty minutes every morning before rounds. At these meetings Dooley, at that time a medical student at Johns Hopkins, presented a series of informal talks on psychoanalysis. These information presentations were the forerunner of regular lectures on psychoanalysis for interns and residents at St. Elizabeths. William A. White, then superintendent of the hospital, was so encouraged by the women's interest that he published the outlines of Dooley's (1919) lectures in the *Psychoanalytic Review* and, as soon after the war as possible, installed a psychoanalytic staff of five—three physicians and two psychologists with some analytic training. This was perhaps the first formally organized psychoanalytic work in this region. Dooley undertook heavy teaching responsibilities in the early education program of the Society, and afterwards, until her retirement in 1954, in the Institute. She also devoted much of her time to training analysis and supervision. Her special psychoanalytic interests were the mind of genius (Dooley, 1916, 1920, 1930a) and the manic-depressive psychoses (Dooley, 1918, 1921, 1930b).

Clara Thompson was from 1930 to 1932 the first elected president of the newly formed Society. Despite her move to New York in 1933, she continued to teach in the Society's training program until about 1950, when, under new leadership, the William Alanson White Institute in New York took a separate course from that of the Washington-Baltimore Psychoanalytic Institute. As her writings indicate, her psychoanalytic interests ranged widely, but with some considerable focus on the psychology of women (Thompson, 1964). She died in 1958.

Frieda Fromm-Reichmann trained in Germany and came to this country in the 1930s. She was a training and supervising analyst and contributed richly to the scientific and organizational affairs of the Society and Institute until her death in 1957. Her primary interest was in the psychoanalytic psychotherapy of schizophrenia, about which she wrote extensively (Fromm-Reichmann, 1950, 1959). She was president of the Society from 1939 to 1941.

Edith Weigert also trained in Germany and came to the United States in the 1930s. In addition to her service as a training and supervising analyst, she provided prodigious talents for calming troubled organizational waters at times of conflict. Weigert was president of the Society from 1944 to 1946. Among her extensive writings have been numerous essays on areas of mutual concern between psychoanalysis and religion.

Sarah S. Tower was an outstanding teacher and organizational leader in psychoanalysis in the Baltimore section of the Society and Institute. Upon her arrival in the Washington area from Vienna via Cambridge, Massachusetts, Jenny Waelder-Hall assumed a position of strong leadership, especially among those in the Society and Institute who were considered to be in the more orthodox band of the psychoanalytic spectrum. Both Tower and Waelder-Hall have played significant parts in leading the Baltimore Institute since the division of the Washington-Baltimore Institute.

Edna G. Dyar came to the Society in the late forties and participated in its educational activities. Under her direction the Society's Community Psychoanalytic Service was launched in 1949.

Marjorie Jarvis trained at St. Elizabeths Hospital and later was on the staff at Chestnut Lodge. She became a member of the joint society in 1935 and was for many years an active training and supervising analyst.

Agnes Bruce Greig, who became a member of the Society in 1938, received her medical training in Toronto. She was the first child psychiatrist and child analyst in Washington. For many years Greig gave generously of her time and energies to the School Guidance Center, a facility for gifted children which was established in 1941. After her death in 1959, the School was renamed in her honor "The Agnes Bruce Greig School." Among her publications were "The Problem of the Parent in Child Analysis" (1940) and "A Child Analysis" (1941).

*D. Relationship of the Society and Institute with the William
Alanson White Psychiatric Foundation and the Washington School
of Psychiatry*

From the mid-thirties until 1949, the history of the training
programs conducted by the Washington-Baltimore Psychoanalytic Society from 1932 to 1940, and by the Washington-Baltimore Psychoanalytic Institute after 1940, was in various
respects intertwined with the histories of the William Alanson
White Psychiatric Foundation and the Washington School of
Psychiatry, although the Society and Institute were separate
organizations from the Foundation and the School throughout
the period.

Part of the impetus for establishing the William Alanson
White Psychiatric Foundation arose from Hadley's quest for
funds to endow a psychoanalytic training program. Among the
possible donors, one appeared who promised the desired endowment, but with the stipulation that a foundation first be
legally incorporated to receive the promised funds. The prospective donor wished to remain anonymous. Hadley conferred
with Dooley, and then with Sullivan and others. The name
proposed was "The William Alanson White Psychoanalytic
Foundation." White responded with pleasure, but expressed
his preference for the title "The William Alanson White Psychiatric Foundation," in reflection of his wish that general psychiatric studies be included as well as psychoanalytic studies and
training. Accordingly, this title was adopted. The change of title
resulted in Brill's resignation as a trustee of the Foundation,
since he felt that his name no longer had the same value to the
organization. In the meantime, Hadley learned that the prospective financial benefactor had died suddenly a few days after
they had met to discuss plans for the Foundation. Nonetheless,
the Foundation was established in 1933.

In 1936 the Foundation inaugurated the Washington
School of Psychiatry with Sullivan as head of the Division of
Psychiatry, Edward Sapir as head of the Division of Social Sci-
ences, and Hadley as head of the Division of Biological Sciences.
Hadley's title was professor of human biology and director of
the biological sciences.

A further provisional faculty list included:

Lucile Dooley, Professor of Psychoanalysis

A. A Brill, Lecturer with Professorial Rank in Psychoanalytic Training

Karen Horney, Lecturer with Professorial Rank in Psychoanalysis

N. Lionel Blitzsten, Assistant Professor of Psychiatry

Lewis B. Hill, Assistant Professor of Psychiatry

Karl Menninger, Research Associate in Psychiatry

Clara Thompson, Research Associate in Psychopathology

An arrangement was made between the Washington School of Psychiatry and the Washington-Baltimore Psychoanalytic Society for students in the Society's training program to take didactic courses given under the auspices of the School.

As the Washington School of Psychiatry developed, Sullivan assumed an increasingly predominant position. White's death in 1938 perhaps left the situation more open to the serious disagreements that arose between Sullivan and various others who had joined him in establishing the Foundation and the School. Dooley, who had been appointed professor and head of the Department of Psychoanalysis in the School, resigned from the School and the Foundation in 1941, and Lewis Hill resigned in 1944.

Hadley remained with the White Foundation for some time longer, especially in connection with the journal *Psychiatry*, published by the Foundation. He was a member of the three-man publications committee of the Foundation from 1938 through 1945 and was chairman for the last three of those years. After a series of disagreements with Sullivan over the management of *Psychiatry*, Hadley resigned from the Foundation in 1945.

In the meantime Sullivan was a strong presence in the Washington-Baltimore Psychoanalytic Society and Institute, though he never headed either and for a time was not on the Education Committee.

Early in his career Sullivan was strongly Freudian in his orientation and in the concepts and terminology he employed, as his early papers amply attest. Later Sullivan began to develop his own theory of psychopathology and took special pains to distinguish the concepts and semantics of his theory from those of Freudian libido theory, while still acknowledging indebtedness to Freud. These efforts, in addition to personality clashes, led to serious controversy within the Society. They were also viewed with strong disapproval by the American Psychoanalytic Association. Sullivan and the Washington group came to be viewed as synonymous, especially after the Washington-Baltimore Society divided into separate societies in 1946. Actually there was a wide spectrum of views throughout this period, and Sullivan by no means spoke for the entire group. Nonetheless, some in the American came to hold in disrepute the Washington group as a whole. They were regarded as a deviant group engaged in diluting psychoanalysis—if they were teaching it at all. It must be said that Sullivan and some of his followers were less than tactful in dealing with their critics in the American, and opportunities for mutual understanding were frequently missed.

It also seems probable that the somewhat complicated, and not always clearly defined, relationship between the Washington School of Psychiatry and the Psychoanalytic Institute provided some basis for criticism from the American. It also led, as mentioned before, to factionalism within the Society and the Institute.

Among the leading training analysts, Bullard, Fromm-Reichmann, and Weigert had associated themselves closely with Sullivan and with teaching his interpersonal theory of psychiatry. Dooley and Hadley, while not discounting the values in interpersonal theory, had tended to maintain a distinctly more orthodox psychoanalytic position. They were at pains to clarify and preserve the distinctions between Sullivan's ideas and mainstream psychoanalytic principles and theory.

Probably most sympathetic to Sullivan's views were those candidates and members (Fromm-Reichmann, for example) whose major interest was in the psychotherapy of the psychoses, which involved some modification of psychoanalytic technique and theory. Sullivan had for many years worked almost exclusively with schizophrenic and obsessional states and was never greatly interested in the transference neuroses proper or in the manic-depressive psychoses.

Sullivan's relationship with organized psychoanalysis underwent certain shifts. Early in his career he was very active and much respected within the American. He was elected to membership at the meeting of the American in Atlantic City on June 3, 1924. At that meeting he presented a paper "The Oral Complex" (1925a). For the next few years he presented a paper at nearly every meeting of the American. For several years he was an elected member of the Executive Council of the American. In 1932 he headed the committee which drafted the new constitution whereby the American was reorganized into a Federation. He, Brill, and Oberndorf were instrumental in the formation in 1933 of a Section on Psychoanalysis within the American Psychiatric Association.

During the 1930s other members of the Washington-Baltimore Society also were active in the American, particularly Hadley, who was Secretary of the American from 1931 through 1936, and Lewis Hill, who was secretary of the American in 1937 and president in 1940.

E. Leaders During the 1940s

During the 1940s, other leaders besides Sullivan were Frieda Fromm-Reichmann, Edith Weigert, Lucile Dooley, Lewis Hill, and Ernest Hadley.

Upon her arrival at Chestnut Lodge, *Frieda Fromm-Reichmann* pursued her well-known research in the psychopathology and treatment of schizophrenia. She had a broad background in neurology, psychiatry, and psychoanalysis, and invariably contributed cogently to a scientific discussion or to the resolution of a clinical problem. Generous of her time to the teaching and administrative work of the Society and Institute, she conducted many training analyses and supervisory sessions. Although she was primarily interested in schizophrenia, the range of patients she treated, both in training analyses and in her private practice, was probably broader than Sullivan's. Moreover, she had a thorough grasp of psychoanalytic theory and the treatment of the neuroses. She was president of the Washington-Baltimore Psychoanalytic Society from 1939 to 1941 and actively participated in its affairs and those of the Institute until her death in 1957.

Edith Weigert, trained in Berlin, had, before coming to Washington, treated schizophrenic patients at Sheppard Pratt

Hospital and elsewhere. She was elected to membership in the Society in June 1938, and in 1939 became a training analyst and member of the Educational Committee. In her long and productive career, though maintaining an interest in the psychoses, she devoted the greater part of her prodigious energies to training psychoanalytic candidates through training analysis, supervision, and seminars. She was president of the Society from 1944 to 1946 and has served both as chairman of the education committee and as director of the Institute. In these capacities she made notable efforts to hold the group together at times of serious friction.

Lucile Dooley, a gentle, scholarly woman, made her earliest contact with psychoanalysis through L. Pierce Clark of New York, whom she met at his summer home in Newtown, Connecticut, and who loaned her several of Brill's translations of Freud's works. Reading the papers given at the 1909 Conference on Psychoanalysis at Clark University inspired her to enroll there to study under Professor G. Stanley Hall; she obtained her Ph.D. degree in psychology from Clark University in 1916. She had her first personal analysis with Clark and later observed that it had consisted largely of reporting her own dreams until he told her that she was to interpret them herself. Later she was also analyzed by Nolan D. C. Lewis (Prager, 1969).

From Clark University she came to St. Elizabeths Hospital to work as a lay analyst under the direction of Edward J. Kempf, one of the first persons in the United States to apply psychoanalysis to the treatment of psychotic patients. On the advice of William A. White, Dooley went to Johns Hopkins to obtain medical training. There she met Clara Thompson and was instrumental in arousing her interest in psychoanalysis. She also persuaded Thompson to join her in working summers at St. Elizabeths Hospital.

In her early work at St. Elizabeths, Dooley was interested in the application of psychoanalysis to the treatment of manic-depressive psychoses. In 1925 she left St. Elizabeths to enter private practice.

As mentioned earlier, Dooley spent 1931 to 1932 in pursuit of further psychoanalytic study at the Vienna Psychoanalytic Institute. Upon her arrival in Vienna, she first consulted Freud.

He had no time in his schedule to analyze her, however, but referred her to Ruth Mack-Brunswick. While in Vienna, she also met three times a week with Robert Waelder, who gave her, in English, private quasi-tutorial instruction in psychoanalysis theory and technique (Praeger, 1969).

Upon her return from Vienna, psychoanalytic training, activities, including training analyses, supervision, and seminar teaching, absorbed the bulk of her efforts. When differences developed with the Baltimore group, Dooley leaned sympathetically toward them because their ideas were more strictly Freudian.

For over twenty-five years *Lewis B. Hill* was in the forefront of the Washington-Baltimore psychoanalytic movement. In 1929 he came to this area from Massachusetts, where he had been assistant superintendent of the Worcester State Hospital, an important wellspring in American psychology and psychiatry.

Soon after Hill's arrival at Worcester, David Shakow introduced him to Ray Willoughby, a staff psychologist who had had some analytic training. Hill became interested in psychoanalysis, began his personal analysis with Willoughby in 1925, and decided to shift the direction of his career (Shakow, 1968). Teaching was Hill's greatest love, and it remained his primary interest throughout his career.

On moving to the Baltimore area, he became clinical director of Sheppard Pratt Hospital, a post he held from 1929 through 1931. During this time he completed psychoanalytic training with members of the Washington-Baltimore Psychoanalytic Society, including analysis with Clara Thompson.

In 1933 Hill journeyed to Budapest for supervision with Ferenczi. It seems likely that Ferenczi's death that same year shortened Hill's stay in Europe.

Upon his return later in 1933, after a brief interval in which Hadley served as interim chairman, Hill was appointed to succeed Silverberg as director of the training program of the Washington-Baltimore Society. He occupied that post until 1940, when he became director of the newly organized Institute; he served in that capacity until 1949. He was also president of the Washington-Baltimore Society during 1935–1938, and president of the American Psychoanalytic Association during 1940–1941.

His book *Psychotherapeutic Intervention in Schizophrenia* (1955) is a classic contribution to the scientific literature on schizophrenia.

Ernest E. Hadley played a memorable role in the development of the Washington Society and Institute. A graduate of the University of Kansas Medical School, he came to Washington in 1920 to intern at Walter Reed Army Hospital. In 1921 he joined the staff of St. Elizabeths Hospital. While there he obtained psychoanalytic training, including analysis with Philip Graven, and engaged in the investigation of the psychoses. In 1929, at a time when it was considered hazardous to do so, he became one of the first psychoanalysts to enter private practice in Washington. He actively associated himself with the founders of the Washington Psychoanalytic Society and worked faithfully and continuously with the Society and Institute. He was three times elected president of the Society, and held various offices in the Institute, of which he was director at the time of his death in 1954.

Hadley was chairman of the Committee on Standards of the American from 1934 to 1952, secretary of the American from 1931 through 1936, and chairman of the Committee on New Constitution whose work culminated in the reorganization of the American in 1946. The new by-laws adopted at that time wrought a fundamental change in the structure of the American from a federation of constitutent societies to a national association of individual members.

In 1940 Hadley was asked to accept nomination for the presidency of the American. He declined, however, in favor of Lewis Hill, who was elected. In 1952 when he accepted the nomination, he lost to Ives Hendrick after a tie count and a second ballot.

Hadley's course in dreams and the demonstration of the free association process in the analysis of dreams was for years a mainstay in the curriculum of the Institute.

Hadley was devoted to student training, and even in the early 1950s when his health was failing, he continued his work with them both in Washington and in New Orleans, where he was a major contributor to the development of a psychoanalytic training center. So keen was his interest in training that during the last years of his life he reduced his private practice to only one patient, devoting the remainder of his time to training analyses and supervision of candidates at the low standardized fee set by the Institute, a considerable financial sacrifice for him.

F. The Postwar Period

Immediately after World War II, the surge of applicants for psychoanalytic training placed a strain upon the educational capacities of the Institute. Partly in an effort to accommodate the greater number of candidates, Fromm-Reichmann and some of the other training analysts experimented with conducting training analyses at a three-hours-per-week frequency, and with supervision of pairs of candidates who alternated in presenting their case material. It was the opinion of Fromm-Reichmann and others that these changes helped to meet the increased demand for training without entailing any essential departure from the psychoanalytic method. When the supply of training and supervising analysts and the demand for training became more equal, these methods were discontinued.

Another immediate postwar phenomenon was that some of the classes conducted in conjunction with the Washington School of Psychiatry became inordinately large and of mixed composition. A few lectures were given to groups of as many as 150 students, comprising not only psychoanalytic candidates but psychiatric residents and trainees in such fields as social work and education.

After Sullivan's death in 1949, the Institute ceased all joint teaching activities with the Washington School of Psychiatry. The School has continued to teach broad psychiatric disciplines, while the Institute has been concerned exclusively with teaching psychoanalytic theory and techniques.

G. Washington-Baltimore Separation

Still another contemporaneous development was the increased divergence between various components of both the Society and the Institute. In part the line of cleavage was geographical, and the difficulties of travel between Baltimore and Washington during World War II were a factor. However, there were other, probably more cogent factors, including ideological differences and personality clashes, which produced lines of potential split within the Baltimore and Washington groups.

In 1946 the Washington-Baltimore Society applied to the American Psychoanalytic Association for approval of separation into two societies. Approval was granted in 1947.

At that time it was discussed whether to divide the Washington-Baltimore Institute into two separate institutes. Lewis Hill, then director of the Washington-Baltimore Institute, felt that such a division was not yet feasible because of a shortage of training analysts in Baltimore. Therefore the Institute continued for several more years as a joint operation, although it was conducted in each of the two cities by a separate Education Subcommittee.

Meanwhile, certain of the ideological and personality clashes intensified. Jenny Waelder-Hall was a central figure in many of them. Though a member of the Washington Society after the Washington-Baltimore Society divided, she was critical of much of the training in the Washington Division of the Institute and refused to participate in it, preferring rather to work with the Baltimore Division, which she felt offered a greater emphasis on "classical analysis" more in tune with her training in Vienna. Several of the Washington group, particularly Dooley and Amanda Stoughton, shared some of Waelder-Hall's opinions concerning the supposed unorthodoxy of the Washington training program. Ultimely, in 1952, Stoughton and Waelder-Hall joined the Baltimore Society.

Waelder-Hall's sharpest clash was with Sullivan. With the aim of welcoming Waelder-Hall to the Washington psychoanalytic community soon after her arrival to the area, Weigert had invited her to a seminar led by Sullivan. It was quickly apparent that Waelder-Hall and Sullivan were in sharp disagreement. Thereafter Sullivan was a principal target, almost a *bête noire*, for Waelder-Hall's criticisms of the Washington group—criticisms that persisted, however, even after his death.

Waelder-Hall resisted efforts by Hadley, Fromm-Reich-

mann, Weigert, and others to encourage her greater participation in the program of the Washington Division of the
Institute.

In the meantime plans for amicable division of the Institute
were being made by Hadley, the director, and by Hill and Weigert, chairman, respectively, of the Baltimore and Washington
Education subcommittees. By 1950 Baltimore had enough
training analysts to make separation feasible.

For a time Waelder-Hall and eight like-minded colleagues
planned to form a third society to be named the Maryland–District
of Columbia Psychoanalytic Society. However, after deferral of
their application for recognition by the American Psychoanalytic Association, the Waelder-Hall faction decided instead to
join the Baltimore Society.

Then, at the December 1952 meeting of the American,
approval was given for the division of the Washington-Baltimore Institute into two. After provisional approval, three years
of full institute status was granted to both institutes in May
1955.

Eloquent testimony that the years of fruitful joint endeavor
were not entirely forgotten at the instant of separation were the
elections of Hill to honorary membership in the Washington
Society and Institute, and of Hadley to similar status in the
Baltimore Society and Institute.

H. Clara Thompson and Training in New York

Some years earlier, in the 1940s, there had been important
developments in New York involving Clara Thompson and
William Silverberg, both charter members of the Washington-
Baltimore Society. Upon her return from Budapest in the sum-
mer of 1933, Thompson moved from Baltimore to New York
City. There she renewed her friendship with Silverberg and
Sullivan, and formed a new friendship with Karen Horney, who
moved from Chicago to New York in 1934. Upon coming to
New York, Erich Fromm also became friendly with this group.

In 1941 Thompson, Silverberg, and Karen Horney resigned from the New York Psychoanalytic Society to form the
Association for the Advancement of Psychoanalysis and its

teaching arm, the American Institute for Psychoanalysis. Among the charter members of this new Association were Ernest Hadley, Benjamin Weininger, and Marjorie Jarvis from Washington, and Lionel Blitzsten from Chicago. Subsequently Ralph Crowley joined, and Sullivan was made an honorary member.

The American Psychoanalytic Association, however, took the position that membership in both the American and the Association for the Advancement of Psychoanalysis would be inconsistent with the spirit of the constitution of the American. Thereupon, in 1942, the Washingtonians—Crowley, Hadley, Jarvis, Sullivan, and Weininger—along with Blitzsten, resigned from Horney's Association for the Advancement of Psychoanalysis.

The following year, 1943, Thompson resigned from the Horney group in protest over Erich Fromm's being banned from training analyst status in the Horney Institute. Later that year Thompson joined with Sullivan, Erich Fromm, Frieda Fromm-Reichmann, and Janet and David Rioch, to form the New York Division of the Washington School of Psychiatry, which subsequently became the William Alanson White Institute. For several years in the 1940s this group in New York also had a working arrangement with the Washington-Baltimore Psychoanalytic Institute. In 1942 Thompson rejoined the Washington-Baltimore Society, from which she had resigned in 1936. She, Janet Rioch, and Ralph Crowley were training and supervising analysts in the Washington-Baltimore Institute. Their New York training analysands were enrolled as candidates in the Institute. In addition, Fromm-Reichmann and Sullivan traveled regularly to the New York Division of the Washington School to present seminars and conduct supervisory sessions, and candidates from the New York Division traveled regularly to Washington for supervision with them. There were problems in administering this arrangement. Among them were difficulties in coordinating the records kept in New York and in Washington.

In 1949 the connection between the William Alanson White Institute in New York and The Washington-Baltimore Institute was dissolved. Probably Sullivan's death in 1949 contributed to this dissolution since he had been one of the strongest links between the two groups.

Several of Thompson's group in New York retained their membership in the Washington Psychoanalytic Society and in the American Psychoanalytic Association. A few members of the Washington Society who moved to New York joined the Columbia Society rather than the William Alanson White group. Others, like Crowley, became members in both the Columbia and White Societies.

I. Hadley's Death; New Leaders

In the midst of these developments, Ernest Hadley, whose sound judgment and leadership had been invaluable to the growth of the Institute, died in 1954 of a coronary thrombosis after an elective hernia operation. At the time of his death, he was director of the Washington Institute. Edith Weigert succeeded him in that post, and Robert A. Cohen became chairman of the Education Committee, an office he held from 1954 to 1959. Weigert and Cohen worked together most successfully at a time when it was imperative that friction within the group be kept to a minimum and that skill and tact be exercised in dealing with the American regarding the Institute's accreditation, which was finally obtained in 1955. In the face of considerable prejudice in the parent organization against the Washington group, the restraint, wisdom, and lack of defensiveness of these two served the Institute well.

During the 1950s, a new group of analysts was assuming positions of leadership in the Society and Institute. Robert Cohen was one. Rex E. Buxton was very active in the Washington Institute and undertook heavy responsibility for training analyses and teaching. He worked for some years with Hadley and Hill toward the establishment and growth of the Training Center in New Orleans, which had been inaugurated in 1948 under sponsorship of the Washington-Baltimore Institute. These three made frequent visits to New Orleans, where Samuel Barkoff and Anna C. Dannemann Colomb, members of the Washington Society, had transferred their practices and had taken initial steps toward establishing a psychoanalytic training center. The three visiting analysts taught regular courses in psychoanalytic theory and technique, and conducted supervision and some training analyses as well. Several of the New Orleans candidates made trips to Washington as often as twice a week for their training analyses. Of outstanding value, and still a subject of legend, were the seminars Hadley and Hill conducted jointly in which they exchanged their views and aired their differences before the students. After Hadley's death, Buxton assumed responsibility for the New Orleans affiliation and sponsorship. The establishment there of a psychoanalytic institute took longer than had been anticipated, mostly because it was some years before the requisite number of training analysts became available. Not until the graduates of the New Orleans group had achieved the necessary experience to become training analysts themselves was creation of the Institute possible. Several members of the Washington and Chicago institutes assisted Buxton in his efforts, and eventually a strong faculty was organized, led by Carl P. Adatto, Henry H. W. Miles, Norman H. Rucker, and William C. Thompson. Accreditation was received from the American in 1948 as a Study Group, in 1953 as a Training Center, in 1955 as a Constitutent Society, and finally in 1961 as an Independent Institute.

In 1958, under Buxton's leadership, the Washington Institute undertook sponsorship of a training center in North Carolina staffed by faculty members of Duke University and the University of North Carolina. George C. Ham had gone there from Chicago; Milton L. Miller, from Los Angeles; John M. Rhoads, from Philadelphia; and David A. Young, from Boston. With Sidney Berman's assistance, Lucie Jessner, formerly of the Harvard Medical School, inaugurated a program of training in child analysis at the University of North Carolina. Other members of the Washington Education Committee who made regular visits to the North Carolina Training Center to teach and do organizational work were Alexander Halperin, Stanley L. Olinick, and Marion B. Richmond.

In 1965, the Duke-University of North Carolina Institute was accredited as a Provisional Institute. Sponsorship by the Washington group then ceased, though some of its faculty members continue to be invited to North Carolina as visiting lecturers.

Frieda Fromm-Reichmann, Edith Weigert, Mabel Blake Cohen, and other faculty members of the Institute continued their affiliation with the Washington School of Psychiatry after the Institute had separated from it. In addition, upon Sullivan's death in 1949, Mabel Cohen succeeded him as editor of *Psychiatry*.

Fromm-Reichmann spent 1955–1956 as a fellow of the Center for Advanced Study in the Behavioral Sciences at Palo Alto, California, where she engaged in scientific conferences with colleagues in other disciplines. Afterwards she returned to Washington to resume active teaching and clinical work.

J. Community Psychoanalytic Service

In 1949 a notable development took place in the Washington Institute. Under the direction of Edna G. Dyar, the Community Psychoanalytic Service was inaugurated. In organizing the Service, Dyar consulted with Ralph Crowley, who had the previous year organized the Low-Cost Psychoanalytic Service of the White Institute in New York. Inasmuch as Chicago, Topeka, and Columbia had previously set up low-fee services, the Washington program was the fifth of its kind (Crowley, 1958). The Service provided psychoanalytic treatment for a limited number of patients who could not afford the regular fee; instead, they contributed a nominal amount to the Institute according to their financial ability. Their treatment was conducted by candidates in training, each of whom was required to analyze one patient without fee for a minimum of two years. Also without fee was the supervising analysts' weekly supervision of a minimum of one, and later two, Institute cases each. The patients were selected by a Clinic Committee, and consideration was given not only to the potential educational value to the candidate, but to the benefits that might be expected to accrue from the analysis to the patient and to others. Thus, mothers and school teachers were given preference.

K. Developments in the 1950s

In 1953 the Society and Institute acquired its first Institute building at 1720 M Street, N.W., Washington, D.C. The building was an old, run-down residence, fortunately situated next to the headquarters of the D.C. Medical Society, which graciously offered its auditorium to the Institute for large meetings. The building was restored and remodeled to provide a meeting room for a maximum of forty persons, executive offices, seminar rooms, and a library. After Hadley's death, the library was greatly augmented by the legacy of his books on psychiatry and psychoanalysis, and was renamed the Ernest E. Hadley Memorial Library. This name has been retained, although when acquisitions were received from the libraries of Dyar, Fromm-Reichmann, and others, they were placed in specially designated sections.

The 1950s, especially after the Institute was accredited, saw steady growth in the Washington Psychoanalytic Society and Institute. The new research centers at the National Institute of Mental Health, where Robert Cohen served as Director of the Division of Clinical and Behavioral Research, Walter Reed Hospital, St. Elizabeths Hospital, the Naval Medical Center, Chestnut Lodge, and the George Washington University and Georgetown University Medical Schools, provided a constant flow of applicants for psychoanalytic training. Although many of them were well-grounded, serious, and promising students of psychoanalysis, the Institute could accept only a limited number for training.

As the number of applicants came to exceed the ability of the Institute to accommodate them, two schools of thought developed. One was that a large number of students should be accepted, despite recognition that some would not complete their training and that large classes might be undesirable. The other was that a limited number of students should be accepted, with careful selection procedures and intensely individualized training. Those who advocated accepting a large number of students emphasized community need and felt that the Institute should strain its facilities to the utmost to meet this need. Others, however, maintained that this approach would dilute the intensive personal training necessary for psychoanalysis. These debates have continued, not only in our own Institute but in institutes throughout the country.

In the 1950s, subcommittees were created to handle the increased load of the Education Committee: the Admissions Committee, to screen applications; the Candidate Progress Committee, to counsel and appraise the candidates' progress; and the Curriculum Committee. In addition, various *ad hoc* committees were appointed to conduct graduation examinations and to handle whatever student and faculty problems might arise. The system of subcommittees was inaugurated while Robert Cohen was chairman of the Education Committee. Its principal purpose was to achieve broad distribution of administrative involvement and responsibility; its goal was directly to involve as many members of the Education Committee as possible in the operations and decisions of the Institute. Toward this end, a system was devised to rotate the membership and chairmanship of each of the subcommittee. Such a broad distribution of administrative responsibility was unusual, perhaps unique, among psychoanalytic institutes.

In the early years of the Institute, both the faculty and student body were small, and usually each member of the Education Committee had considerable first-hand knowledge of the capabilities of each candidate. Readiness of a candidate for graduation was judged by the Education Committee as a whole. The candidate was invited to prepare a paper for presentation to a scientific meeting of the Society. If his paper was approved, the candidate was considered a graduate and his election to Society membership followed automatically.

As the Institute grew, it was no longer possible for all members of the Education Committee to have first-hand knowledge of each candidate. Hadley therefore introduced a new graduation procedure. Upon the recommendation of the Candidate Progress Committee, the Education Committee invited the candidate to prepare a paper demonstrating his competence in the theory and practice of psychoanalysis. After studying his paper, the Examining Committee, composed of three members of the Education Committee, conducted a formal examination of the candidate and made its recommendation for or against his graduation. Upon the required ratification of a favorable recommendation by the Education Committee, the candidate was graduated.

In the late 1950s, members of the Society came to feel a need for a program of postgraduate education. This culminated in the establishment in 1961 of the Postgraduate Development Committee. The Committee encouraged the formation of study groups and arranged, in addition to the regularly scheduled scientific meetings of the Society, to have special lecturers from time to time. Even before this program was formally established, David Rapaport gave a memorable series of seminars on ego psychology.

With the growth of the Institute, the problem of selecting faculty for the positions of instructors, teaching analysts, and training analysts became increasingly difficult, and attempts were made to study methods of selection. In the 1950s, because of the desperate need, most of the Society members participated in the teaching program of the Institute. As the size of the Society increased, there were more members available to accommodate the Institute's teaching needs. On the other hand, however, it became necessary to select from the membership those best suited for teaching, supervision, or the conduct of personal analyses. This is a continuous process.

By 1957 the Institute and Society were firmly consolidated and entering a period of steady growth and harmony. An indication of the development of the Society and Institute is afforded by the following table:

	Members (Society)	Candidates (Institute)	Faculty
1941–1942	25	20	7
1945–1946	27	25	10
1954–1955	45-50	65	25

APPENDIX

Organizations in the Development of Psychoanalysis in the Washington-Baltimore Area

Washington Society for Nervous and Mental Disorders, founded   1907

Washington Psychoanalytic Society, founded   1914
Washington Psychoanalytic Association, founded   1924
Washington Psychoanalytic Society, reactivated   1925
Washington Psychopathological Society (change in name of
    the Washington Psychoanalytic Society)   1926
Washington-Baltimore Psychoanalytic Society, founded 1930
    Accredited as a Constituent Society by the
    American Psychoanalytic Association   1932
Washington-Baltimore Psychoanalytic Society, approved by
    the American Psychoanalytic Association for division
    into the Washington Psychoanalytic Society and the
    Baltimore Psychoanalytic Society   1947
Washington Psychoanalytic Institute and Baltimore
    Psychoanalytic Institute each given full institute
    status by the American Psychoanalytic Association 1955

References

Adler, A. (1912), *The Neurotic Constitution. Outlines of a Comparative Individualistic Psychology and Psychotherapy,* trans. B. S. Glueck & J. E. Lind. New York: Moffat, Yard, 1917.
Alexander, F. (1930), *Psychoanalysis of the Total Personality,* trans. B. S. Glueck and B. D. Lewin. New York: Nervous & Mental Disease Monograph Publishing Co.
Burnham, J. C. (1967), Psychoanalysis and American medicine, 1894–1918: Medicine, science, and culture. *Psychological Issues Monograph* 20. New York: International Universities Press.
Burrow, T. (1927), The group method of analysis. *Psychoanal. Rev.,* 14:268–280.
Campbell, C. M. (1908), Psychological mechanisms with special reference to wish-fulfillment. *N.Y. State Hosp. Bull.,* 2:12–26.
——— (1910), The form and content of the psychosis: The role of psychoanalysis in psychiatry. *N.Y. State Hosp. Bull.,* 3:3–21.
——— (1912), The application of psychoanalysis to insanity. *N.Y. Med. J.,* 95:1079–1081.
Dooley, L. (1916), Psychoanalytic studies of genius. *Amer. J. Psychol.,* 27:363–417.
——— (1918), Analysis of a case of manic-depressive psychosis showing well-marked regressive stages. *Psychoanal. Rev.,* 5:1–46.
——— (1919), Outline of a series of talks on psychoanalysis. *Psychoanal. Rev.,* 6:214–225.
——— (1920), Psychoanalysis of Charlotte Brontë, as a type of the woman of genius. *Amer. J. Psychol.,* 31:221–272.
——— (1921), A psychoanalytic study of manic-depressive psychoses. *Psychoanal. Rev.,* 8:38–72, 144–167.
——— (1930a), Psychoanalysis of the character and genius of Emily Brontë. *Psychoanal. Rev.,* 17:208–239.

—— (1930b), Psychoneuroses that resemble manic-depressive psychosis. *Proc. Assoc. Res. Nerv. Dis.*

Emch, M. (1953), Reflections on the Life of N. Lionel Blitzsten, 1893–1952. *Psychiatry*, 16:87–91.

Ferenczi, S. (1908), On habit-neuroses and psycho-neuroses in the light of Freud's investigations and psycho-analysis, trans. C. M. Campbell. *N.Y. State Hosp. Bull.*, 2:849–868, 1909.

Fromm-Reichmann, F. (1950), *Principles of Intensive Psychotherapy*. Chicago: University of Chicago Press.

—— (1959), *Psychoanalysis and Psychotherapy: Selected Papers*, ed. D. M. Bullard. Chicago: University of Chicago Press.

Glueck, B. (1915), The God-man or Jehovah complex. *N.Y. Med. J.*, 102:496–499.

—— (1956), Reflections and comments. In: *Centennial Papers, Saint Elizabeths Hospital, 1855–1955*. Baltimore: Waverly Press.

Greig, A. B. (1940), The problem of the parent in child analysis. *Psychiatry*, 3:539–545.

—— (1941), A child analysis. *Psychoanal. Quart.*, 10:395–430.

Hadley, E. E. (1926), Comments on pedophilia. *N.Y. Med. J.*, 124:157–162.

—— (1928), Presidential address. *Psychoanal. Rev.*, 15:384–392.

Hassall, J. C. (1915), The role of the sexual complex in dementia praecox. *Psychoanal. Rev.*, 2:260–276.

—— (1919), The serpent as a symbol. *Psychoanal. Rev.*, 6:296–305.

Hill, L. B. (1955), *Psychotherapeutic Intervention in Schizophrenia*. Chicago: University of Chicago Press.

Jelliffe, S. E., & Brink, L. (1917), The role of animals in the unconscious with some remarks on theriomorphic symbolism as seen in Ovid. *Psychoanal. Rev.*, 4:253–271.

Jones, E. (1959), *Free Associations. Memories of a Psycho-Analyst*. London: Hogarth Press.

Korzybski, A. (1933), *Science and Sanity*. Lancaster, PA: Science Press.

Lebensohn, Z. M. (1956), Contributions of Saint Elizabeths Hospital to a century of medico-legal progress. In: *Centennial Papers, Saint Elizabeths Hospital, 1855–1955*. Baltimore: Waverly Press.

Lewis, N. D. C. (1926), The psychoanalytic approach to the problems of children under twelve years of age. *Psychoanal. Rev.*, 13:424–443.

Lorand, S. (1966), Sandor Ferenczi, pioneer of pioneers. In: *Psychoanalytic Pioneers*, ed. F. Alexander, S. Eisenstein, & M. Grotjahn. New York: Basic Books.

Millet, J. A. P. (1966), Psychoanalysis in the United States. In: *Psychoanalytic Pioneers*, ed. F. Alexander, S. Eisenstein, & M. Grotjahn. New York: Basic Books.

Moore, T. V. (1918), The hound of heaven. *Psychoanal. Rev.*, 5:345–363.

Oberndorf, C. P. (1953), *A History of Psychoanalysis in America*. New York: Grune & Stratton.

O'Malley, M. (1914), Psychoses in the colored race. *Amer. J. Insan.*, 71:309–339.

—— (1923), Transference and some of its problems in psychoses. *Psychoanal. Rev.*, 10:1–25.

—— (1929), Significance of narcissism in the psychoses. *Psychoanal. Rev.*, 16:241–271.

Overholser, W. (1956), An historical sketch of Saint Elizabeths Hospital. In:

Centennial Papers, Saint Elizabeths Hospital, 1855–1955. Baltimore: Waverly Press.

Perry, H. S. (1964), Introduction. *The Fusion of Psychiatry and Social Sciences,* ed. H. S. Sullivan. New York: Norton.

Schilder, P. (1928), *Introduction to a Psychoanalytic Psychiatry.* New York: Nerv. and Mental Disease Publishing Co.

Silverberg, W. V. (1932), Notes on the mechanism of reaction formation. *Psychoanal. Rev.,* 19:56–63.

Sullivan, H. S. (1925a), The oral complex. *Psychoanal. Rev.,* 12:31–38.

—— (1925b), Varieties of regression. *Psychoanal. Rev.,* 12:333.

—— (1926a), Regression. *State Hosp. Quart.,* 11:208–217; 387–394; 651–668.

—— (1926b), Erogenous maturation. *Psychoanal. Rev.,* 13:1–15.

—— (1934), Psychiatric training as a prerequisite to psychoanalytic practice. In: *Schizophrenia as a Human Process,* ed. H. S. Perry. New York: Norton, 1962.

Taneyhill, G. L. (1916), Notes on psychoanalytic technique. *Psychoanal. Rev.,* 3:461.

Thompson, C. M. (1955), Unpublished "History of the William Alanson White Institute," presented before the Harry Stack Sullivan Society on March 15, 1955.

—— (1964), *Interpersonal Psychoanalysis. The Selected Papers of Clara M. Thompson,* ed. M. R. Green. New York: Basic Books.

White, W. A. (1911), *Mental Mechanisms.* New York: Nervous & Mental Disease Monograph Publishing.

—— (1912), The fundamentals of the Freudian psychology. *N.Y. Med. J.,* 95:969–970.

—— (1915), The unconscious. *Psychoanal. Rev.,* 2:12–28.

—— (1928), Presidential address. *Psychoanal. Rev.,* 15:121–131.

—— (1935), *Outlines of Psychiatry,* 14th ed. New York: Nervous & Mental Disease Monograph Publishing.

INDEX

Tension, 82, 84–85
Termination
in treatment, 59, 155, 341, 525
Test. *See also* Rorschach, Wechsler-
Bellevue
diagnostic, 85
psychological, 55–56, 60–61,
70–72, 76
Therapist. *See* Analyst
Therapist-administrative split, xviii,
3–4
Therapy. *See also* Working alliance
impasse, 349, 351–352, 356
setting, 148
Thompson, S., 5, 11, 272
Thought, 173, 508–509
Tower, S. S., 553
Trager, G. L., 108
Transference, 10, 41–42, 72, 79–81,
83–85, 88, 132–133, 152,
154, 159, 165, 166, 174–175,
176, 252, 322–324, 345, 351,
356, 479
based on simile, 181
borderline patients, 146, 292,
295, 297, 303, 305,
308–314
countertransference, 150, 166,
333
definition, 79
dyadic conflicts in, 149
negativism, 65, 367
neurosis, 165, 200, 322
psychosis, 80, 155
in regressed patients, 149–150
in schizophrenic patients, 200,
203
Transitional object, 326–327
Trauma, 245
Trust, 76, 139
Tyler, R., 96

Uhl, F., 420

Vacation
of therapist, 33

Vengeance, 340, 349
Visual imagery, 162, 164
Von Domarus, E., 95

Waelder-Hall, J., 553, 562–563
Washington-Baltimore Psychoanalytic Institute, 547–551,
554–567
Washington-Baltimore Psychoanalytic Society, 544–563
Washington Psychoanalytic Association, 542, 544
Washington Psychoanalytic Society
and Institute, 539–544,
565–571
Washington Psychopathological Society, 543–544
Washington School of Psychiatry, 24,
91, 360, 554–556, 561, 564,
567
Wechsler-Bellevue Intelligence Scale,
55
Weigert, E., 92, 94, 251, 319, 483,
547, 551, 552, 556, 557, 565,
567
Weinberg, J., 469
Weininger, B., 495–496, 498,
502–505, 564
White, W. A., 261, 446, 537–538,
539–540, 541, 543, 546, 547,
552
Psychiatric Foundation,
554–555
Institute, 6, 359–360, 564
Will, O., xix, 1, 5, 6, 11, 89, 100,
131–132, 184, 484
and women, 137–138, 253
as analysand of Fromm-Reichmann, 132–134
as therapist, 137, 139–142
Wilmanns, K., 443
Winnicott, D. W., 151, 153, 159, 166,
306, 326
Winstead, E., and H. Sullivan, 185,
191
Wit, in psychotherapy, 362–363